STALIN

A BIOGRAPHY

ROBERT SERVICE

STALIN

A BIOGRAPHY

WITHDRAWN

The Belknap Press of
Harvard University Press
Cambridge, Massachusetts

Copyright © 2004 Robert Service

Printed in the United States of America

First published in the United Kingdom by Macmillan,
an imprint of Macmillan Publishers Ltd

Library of Congress Cataloging-in-Publication Data

Service, Robert.
Stalin : a biography / Robert Service.
p. cm.
Includes bibliographical references and index.
ISBN 0-674-01697-1 (alk. paper)
1. Heads of state—Soviet Union—Biography. 2. Soviet Union—
History—1925–1953. [1. Stalin, Joseph, 1879–1953.] I. Title.

DK268.S8S4237 2005
947.084'1'092—dc22
[B]   2004061115

CONTENTS

FOUR: WARLORD

CONTENTS

FIVE: THE IMPERATOR

Preface

Francesco Benvenuti, Adele Biagi, Geoffrey Hosking and Arfon Rees read the draft and, as so many times in the past, offered invaluable suggestions. Katya Andreyev (on the Second World War), Jörg Baberowski (on the 'national question'), Yoram Gorlizki (on the years after 1945), Mark Harrison (on Soviet economics), George Hewitt (on Georgian language and culture), Stephen Jones (on Georgian Marxism and culture), John Klier (on Jews) and David Priestland (on the 1930s) read several chapters. I also appreciate advice on particular matters from Bob Allen, Rosamund Bartlett, Vladimir Buldakov, Bob Davies, Norman Davies, Simon Dixon, Richard Evans, Israel Getzler, Ali Granmayeh, Riitta Heino, Ronald Hingley, Vladimir Kakalia, Oleg Khlevnyuk, Vladimir Kozlov, Slava Lakoba, Melvyn Leffler, Hugh Lunghi, Rosalind Marsh, Claire Mouradiane, Zakro Megreshvili, Simon Sebag Montefiore, Silvio Pons, Al Rieber, David Saunders, Harry Shukman, Peter Stickland, Martin Stugart, Ron Suny, Steve Wheatcroft, Jerry White, Faith Wigzell and Jackie Willcox. I am grateful to Matthew Hingley for creating a CD of my 78 rpm discs of Stalin's speeches and to Vladimir Kakalia for making a present of some of these discs. Georgina Morley, Kate Harvey and Peter James, on the editorial side, have been invariably helpful with their their suggestions for improvements.

The book benefited from discussions in the Institute of Russian History in the Academy of Sciences, the Institute of World History and the Russian State Archive for Socio-Political History, and more recently it was helpful to discuss the Stalin question at the International Summer University near Gagra in Abkhazia and at the National Library in Tbilisi. (Stalin as a student at the nearby Spiritual Seminary in the late 1890s was banned from using that library.)

St Antony's College's Russian and Eurasian Studies Centre has been an incomparable environment for the research. My colleagues Archie Brown, Alex Pravda and Jackie Willcox have supplied constant counsel and encouragement. I have also benefited from the Monday seminars run by our Centre, where several of my papers touching the Stalin question have been discussed. Oxford librarians Jackie Willcox and Angelina Gibson have looked out for material being published in Russia. Simon Sebag Montefiore generously shared with me his notes on the unpublished memoirs of Kandide Charkviani. Heinz-Dietrich Löwe and Shaun Morcom obtained other material for me. Liana Khvarchelia and Manana Gurgulia, organisers of the Abkhazian Summer University with Rachel Clogg and Jonathan Cohen of Conciliation Resources, secured access for me to Stalin's dacha at Kholodnaya Rechka, Rachel Polonsky to Molotov's apartment in central Moscow: my thanks to all of them them. Zakro Megreshvili assisted me in obtaining and translating Georgian political memoirs; Elin Hellum rendered a Swedish newspaper article into English.

The line of influential interpretations of Stalin and his career has remarkable homogeneity in several basic features overdue for challenge. This book is aimed at showing that Stalin was a more dynamic and diverse figure than has conventionally been supposed. Stalin was a bureaucrat and a killer; he was also a leader, a writer and editor, a theorist (of sorts), a bit of a poet (when young), a follower of the arts, a family man and even a charmer. The other pressing reason for writing this biography is that the doors of Russian archives have been prised ajar since the late 1980s. Difficulties of access remain, but many dusty corners of Stalin's life and career can now be examined. Documentary collections have also appeared which have not yet entered a comprehensive biography. Historians and archivists of the Russian Federation in particular have been doing significant work which has yet to be widely discussed.

Stalin's life calls up questions of historical approach. Most accounts have fallen into one of two categories. Some have been focused on his personality and motives and the effect of these on politics and society; others illuminate the general history of the USSR and elsewhere and take for granted that we already know most of what we need about him as an individual. Neither category is adequate by itself and I offer a synthesis in the following chapters. Thus while it is vital to examine Stalin's peculiar personality, it is equally necessary to analyse the environment in which he grew up and the political and other pressures under which he operated. Accounts are also divided between those which highlight the specificity of a given period and those which pick out the more durable factors in his career and his party's history. This book is intended to bridge that artificial dichotomy. Thus, while detailed investigations of the Great Terror are essential, so too is a consideration of the whole set of circumstances produced by the October Revolution (and indeed by earlier situations). The aim is to bring together what are usually called intentionalism and structuralism as well as to combine what may be termed synchronic and diachronic approaches.

Several sections of the book have involved examination of records from archival files and recent documentary collections: on Stalin's childhood in Gori; on his education; on his 1904 'Credo'; on his armed robbery campaign; on his time in Siberia; on his activity in 1917, in the Civil War and in the Soviet–Polish War; on the politics of 1922–3; on his marriages; on his motives in the Great Terror; on his leadership in the Second World War; and on his speeches and manoeuvres in 1952–3. Significant factual data have been unearthed in this process. The chapters also reinterpret certain important aspects of his life: the Georgian national background; his cultural development; the political authority of Stalin before, during and soon after the October Revolution; the rupture with Lenin in 1922–3; the origins and consequences of the Great Terror; the oddly impersonal 'cult'; the style of rulership and the constraints on his despotic power; and the multidimensionality of his political career. A final point is that the book is intended as a general depiction and analysis. From his birth in 1878 to his death in 1953 Stalin was a human earthquake. Each episode in his lifetime of impact requires careful attention. But sense also has to be made of the interconnectedness of him and his times across a long – altogether too long – existence.

One personal experience in the course of the research stands out from the others. In December 1998 I interviewed Kira Allilueva, Stalin's niece, in her flat in north Moscow for a radio programme I was making with Sheila Dillon of the BBC. Kira Allilueva's refusal to be embittered by her uncle's imprisonment of her – and her zest for life and fun – is a vivid memory. On that occasion she presented me with a copy of her uncle's poetry. (The early chapters show why Stalin's verses are important to an understanding of him.) It was the first time I had met someone who had known Stalin intimately. (An attempt in 1974 to interview Lazar Kaganovich, whom I spotted in Moscow's Lenin Library, met with a curt refusal. Still, it was worth a try.) Kira Allilueva's insistence that all the many sides of Stalin need to be understood before he can be comprehended is a principle that informs this book.

Oxford, June 2004

A Note on Renderings

Stalin changed his name many times before the Great War and only started consistently calling himself Stalin in 1912. In the interests of clarity I have called him Dzhughashvili until 1912 and Stalin thereafter even though many acquaintances knew him by nicknames (Soso, Soselo and Koba) and by pseudonyms (including Ivanovich and several others) both before and after that year. And although he was christened Yoseb Dzhughashvili, I have mainly used the more familiar Joseph Dzhughashvili. The names of other Georgians are given by a conventional transliteration into English but without the diacritic signs. The territory to the south of the Caucasus mountain range presents a nomenclatural difficulty. In order to emphasise its intrinsic significance, especially in part one of the book, I refer to it as the south Caucasus rather than – as in Russian geographical and administrative parlance – the Transcaucasus; the exceptions to this are official Soviet designations such as the Transcaucasian Federation. As for transliteration from Russian, I have used a simplified version of the Library of Congress system with the qualification that endnotes are given in line with the full system. Dates are given according to the calendar in official use at the time in Russia. The authorities employed the Julian calendar until 1918, when they switched to the Gregorian one.

Maps

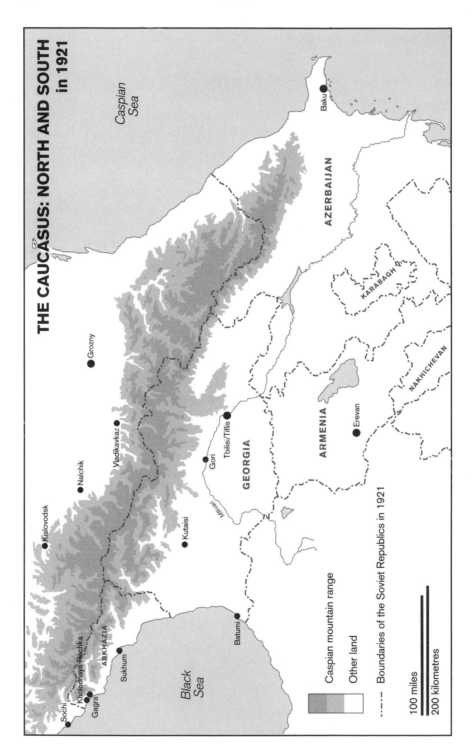

THE CAUCASUS: NORTH AND SOUTH in 1921

Caspian Sea

Black Sea

Baku

AZERBAIJAN

KARABAGH

NAKHICHEVAN

ARMENIA

Erevan

Grozny

Vladikavkaz

Nalchik

Kislovodsk

Kutaisi

Gori

Tbilisi/Tiflis

GEORGIA

Mtkvari

Batumi

ABKHAZIA

Sukhum

Gagra

Kholodnaya Rechka

Sochi

Caspian mountain range

Other land

Boundaries of the Soviet Republics in 1921

100 miles

200 kilometres

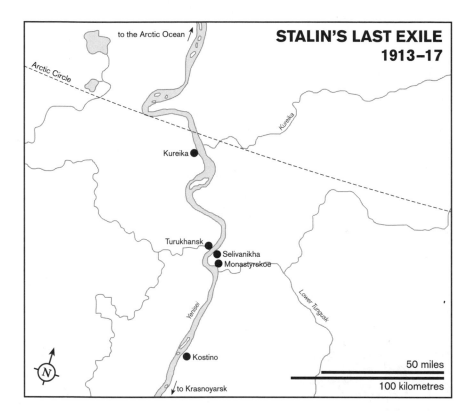

to the Arctic Ocean

Arctic Circle

STALIN'S LAST EXILE
1913–17

Kureika

Kureika

Turukhansk
Selivanikha
Monastyrekoe

Yenisei

Lower Tungusk

Kostino

to Krasnoyarsk

N

50 miles

100 kilometres

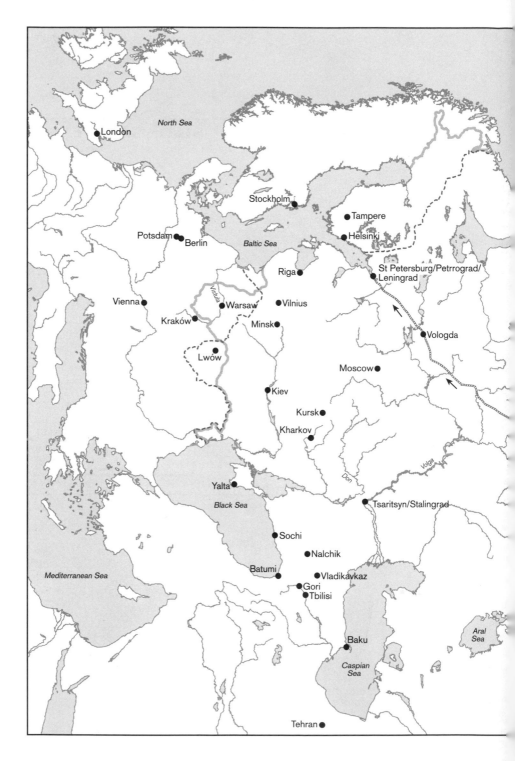

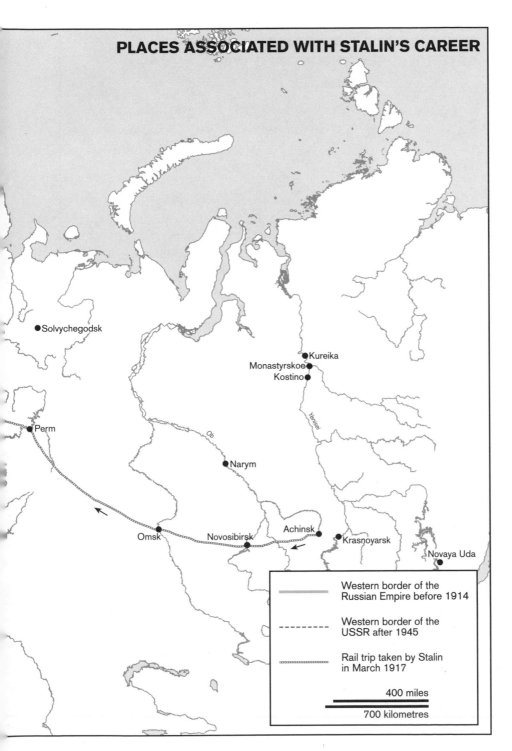

PLACES ASSOCIATED WITH STALIN'S CAREER

● Solvychegodsk

● Kureika
Monastyrskoe ●
Kostino ●

● Perm

Ob

Yenisei

● Narym

Achinsk
Omsk   Novosibirsk ●   ● Krasnoyarsk
                                                      ● Novaya Uda

	Western border of the Russian Empire before 1914
- - - - -	Western border of the USSR after 1945
▒▒▒▒▒▒	Rail trip taken by Stalin in March 1917

400 miles

700 kilometres

THE USSR AND EASTERN EUROPE
AFTER THE SECOND WORLD WAR

Leningrad

Stockholm

Tallinn

ESTONIA

RUSSIAN SOVIET
FEDERAL SOCIALIST
REPUBLIC (RSFSR)

SWEDEN

Riga

LATVIA

DENMARK

Copenhagen

KALININGRAD
PROVINCE
(RSFSR)

LITHUANIA

Vilnius

Kaliningrad

Minsk

BELORUSSIA

Berlin

GERMAN
DEMOCRATIC
REPUBLIC

Warsaw

POLAND

Kiev

Prague

UKRAINE

CZECHOSLOVAKIA

Vienna

MOLDAVIA

AUSTRIA

Budapest

Kishinëv

HUNGARY

ROMANIA

Belgrade

Bucharest

YUGOSLAVIA

ITALY

Sofia

Rome

BULGARIA

Tirana

Istanbul

ALBANIA

GREECE

TURKEY

The USSR

Countries which acquired
communist governments

300 miles

400 kilometres

Athens

N

PART ONE

THE REVOLUTIONARY

1. STALIN AS WE HAVE KNOWN HIM

Joseph Stalin is one of the most notorious figures in history. He ordered the systematic killing of people on a massive scale. In his years of power and pomp, from the late 1920s until his death in 1953, he personified the Soviet communist order. The October Revolution of 1917 in Russia had given rise to a one-party, one-ideology dictatorship serving as a model for the transformation of societies across a third of the globe's surface after the Second World War. Although Lenin had founded the USSR, it was Stalin who decisively strengthened and stabilised the structure. Without Stalin, the Soviet Union might have collapsed decades before it was dismantled in 1991.

After Lenin died in 1924, most people were surprised when Stalin emerged the victor from the ensuing conflict among the party's leaders. By the end of the decade he had rejected the compromises the party had reluctantly accepted in order to survive in power after the Civil War in the former Russian Empire. Stalin marched the Soviet Union in the direction of industrialisation. Millions of peasants died while agriculture was collectivised. The network of labour camps was expanded and Stalin reinforced his despotism through the Great Terror of the late 1930s. Hitler's Operation Barbarossa against the USSR in 1941 caught Stalin disastrously off guard. But the Red Army fought back and, with Stalin as supreme commander, defeated the Wehrmacht. After the Second World War the USSR asserted its dominion across the eastern half of Europe. Stalin's reputation, for good or evil, rose to its climax. When he died in 1953, he was mourned by millions of fellow citizens who had abundant reason to detest him and his policies. He left the Soviet Union as a world power and an industrial colossus with a literate society. He bequeathed institutions of terror and indoctrination with few rivals in their scope. The history of the USSR after his death was largely a series of attempts to conserve, modify or liquidate his legacy.

Stalin left no memoirs. Before the late 1920s no one troubled to write more than a brief sketch of him. Those who did put words into print scorned him. The unsurpassed chronicler of Russia in the year 1917, Nikolai Sukhanov, dismissed him as 'a grey, dull blank'.[1] Trotski and his sympathisers such as Boris Souvarine and Isaac Deutscher ridiculed Stalin as a bureaucrat without an opinion or even personality of his own; this had also been the line taken by leaders of other revolutionary parties – Mensheviks and Socialist-Revolutionaries – who had been forced into foreign exile.[2] Despite the diversity of their political orientations, all such writers agreed when characterising Lenin's successor. Stalin's lack of talent appeared to them as axiomatic. His defects were thought obvious. Stalin had not lived as an émigré before the fall of the Imperial monarchy in the February Revolution! He was neither a polyglot nor a decent orator! He was a mere administrator! Such features were offered as proof that he deserved second-rate status among the party's leaders. Even friendly comrades in the decade after the October Revolution thought that his only strong suit was administration and that the important decisions of state should be left to them and not to Stalin.[3]

Ambitious and resentful, Stalin set about embellishing his reputation. In 1920 he stressed that Lenin, at their first meeting in 1905, had struck him as an unobtrusive figure. The aim was clear. Stalin was indicating that this was the kind of man who had founded the communist party and whom he sought to emulate: he was offering a self-portrait. But showiness was not for him. Stalin's aide Ivan Tovstukha produced a biographical sketch in 1924, mentioning his postings in the October Revolution and Civil War;[4] but this was hardly a coloratura piece of writing. Always Stalin and his associates stressed his eagerness to fit into a political collective. The self-preening political protagonists in the Soviet Union – Lev Trotski, Grigori Zinoviev, Lev Kamenev and Nikolai Bukharin – were contrasted with the modest Party General Secretary.

Resuming his ascent to the political summit, Stalin arranged for weightier claims to be made on his behalf. Approved biographies appeared, each more hagiographical than the previous one. In 1938 a grandiose account was published, written by Party Central Committee stooges and anonymously edited by Stalin.[5] The chapters represented him as the contemporary genius of world communism; and the growing tendency was to depict him as the equal of Lenin as party leader, exponent of Marxist theory and global statesman. This image was picked up in the West by commentators impressed by the industrial and educational progress made in the USSR in the 1930s. From 1941, when the USSR entered the struggle against Nazi Germany, the praise for Stalin was unstinted. *Time* magazine fêted him as its Man of the Year, who alone had the tenacity to lead his country to military triumph. After the Second World War, when the Cold War broke out and the Western Allies turned him from hero into villain, the number of Stalin's admirers fell drastically away. Yet among his critics there were few who still thought him a mediocrity. Revered or detested, he was recognised as one of the twentieth century's outstanding politicians.

Some saw him as Lenin's authentic successor who drove the automobile of Revolution along a road mapped out by Lenin. Others regarded him as Leninism's great betrayer. Playing up Russian national interests, he was painted as little different from the emperors of old. Supposedly Stalin wanted to achieve chiefly the objectives that had eluded the greatest of the Romanovs.[6] Such a desire was reflected in Stalin's foreign policy of westward expansion. In the USSR this took the form of privileging the ethnic Russians in postings, education and status. Stalin was depicted as an exponent of traditional Russian imperialism.

Another image of Stalin had him mainly as a power-hungry killer. Once having gained supreme authority, supposedly, the latent psychotic urges were released and the carnage of the 1930s began. Some contended that this could not have happened unless the doctrines and practices of the Soviet one-party state had already been put in place; but they also insisted that the mayhem would not have occurred in 1937–8 unless an unhinged dictator had controlled the party and the political police.[7] Stalin did not just incarcerate and murder. In applying physical and mental torment to his victims, he degraded them in the most humiliating fashion. He derived deep satisfaction from this. Although he himself did not beat those whom the police held in the Lubyanka prison, he encouraged the most brutal measures. He delighted in keeping even his closest associates in unrelieved fear. Definitions of insanity are controversial, but undeniably Stalin's personality was a dangerously damaged one and this personality supplied the high-octane fuel for the journey to the Great Terror.

Or was he just a bureaucratic mediocrity protecting the interests of the administrative cadres of the one-party state? According to this interpretation, the administrators in party, police and economic commissariats aspired to expand their authority and privileges. Already in the 1920s they had abandoned their revolutionary commitment. Thus Stalin understood what they wanted and used his position in the Central Committee Secretariat to fulfil their desires. As the USSR's supreme bureaucrat he too was bound to benefit from such an outcome. That the administrative cadres should have come to wield this power was attributed to deep tensions in Soviet state and society. The October 1917 Revolution had been made in the name of the working class and the poorest sections of the peasantry. But these groups failed to confirm themselves in power. The resultant tensions made for a situation that gave opportunities to the 'bureaucracy'. Unscrupulous and well disciplined, the functionaries of party and state steadily formed themselves into a caste separate from the rest of society, and Stalin's grey eminence was their leading incarnation.[8]

Hardly a year has passed since Stalin's death in 1953 without the publication of yet another biography. For three decades the material was common to all: the memoirs, old and new, together with the files excavated from the archives at the command of Nikita Khrushchëv – Stalin's successor in the Kremlin – as he shoved Stalin off the pedestal of communist esteem from the mid-1950s. Then in 1985 Mikhail Gorbachëv became Party General Secretary. Gorbachëv resumed the campaign against Stalin and all his works and a flood of documentary data was released. But it took the rise to power of Boris Yeltsin in 1991 for most scholars to gain access to the archives. It was a heady period in which to carry out research. The inconceivable had become reality: the Central Party Archive on Pushkin Street in Moscow was opened to independent scholarship and a vast number of holdings were declassified.[9] This is a process with a long road yet to travel, and there has been occasional regression. But any comparison with earlier years is salutary. It is now possible to explore the political, ideological, cultural and private life of Joseph Stalin to a degree of intimacy that was previously impossible.

Writers in Russia have taken their opportunity. Their forerunner was the Soviet communist dissenter Roy Medvedev, who wrote a denunciation of Stalin in the mid-1960s.[10] The book was refused publication in the USSR and was circulated there only in illicit copies. Its basic analysis was not novel: Medvedev argued that Stalin was a cynic and a bureaucrat with a maladjusted personality who suffocated the revolutionary ideals of Lenin. Under Gorbachëv there were further attempts to analyse Stalin. Dmitri Volkogonov, while showing that Stalin was a murderous dictator, called for his virtues as an industrialiser and a military leader also to be acknowledged.[11] Later biographers in Russia objected to such equivocation, and Edvard Radzinski produced a popular account that focused attention on the psychotic peculiarities of his subject.[12] While adding new factual details, Volkogonov and Radzinski offered nothing in their analyses not already available in the West.

Western historians themselves largely ceased to reconsider the basic conventional wisdom developed between the 1920s and 1950s. The differences between accounts centred on particular aspects of his personality, attitudes or policies. The disputes have been highly charged. There has even been controversy about whether Stalin was responsible for the lunges towards the Great Terror. American scholar J. Arch Getty proposed that the state's terrorist measures sprang not from Stalin's initiative but from pressures applied by a group of Politburo members aiming always to raise the rate of industrial expansion and resenting the passive resistance of the lower echelons of the party and governmental officialdom.[13] It was alleged that Stalin was merely a power broker among the Kremlin's politicians. Supposedly he only instigated the mass killings in order to comply with the strong opinions expressed in the supreme ruling group. This was an extraordinary claim. Even the long line of writers who denied that the Gulag victims were truly to be numbered in the millions had assigned decisive responsibility to Stalin.

Nowadays virtually all writers accept that he initiated the Great Terror. The exceptions, however, do not lack support. Among them are those Russian nationalists who feel nostalgic about the Soviet victory in the Second World War and regret the collapse of the USSR. Many Georgians, too, resent any attack on their most famous compatriot even if they recognise that he committed appalling abuses against Soviet society. Yet among the rest of us there remains much controversy. There are several ways in which I hope to illuminate the murky corners of Joseph Stalin's life. One involves looking closely at his upbringing, family life, wives, children and other relatives. This was difficult until recently: Stalin had taken care to excise references to his private life from published material. He also executed or imprisoned many who knew him well. Even his sister-in-law Anna Allilueva, who carefully submitted her draft memoir for his comments, was thrown into the Lubyanka. Stalin's personality was mysterious in his lifetime, as he meant it to be; and many of the best-known sources on him, especially the memoirs by Trotski and Khrushchëv, offered accounts pervaded by political hostility.

Since the late 1980s it is has been possible to make a closer analysis. Stalin's private life and entourage have been investigated by Simon Sebag Montefiore and Miklós Kun.[14] His preferences in food and leisure were not drastically abnormal, at least until he achieved despotic power. Many in his entourage felt that his enemies had exaggerated his defects of personality. Such information provides an avenue towards understanding his public career. I make no apology for intensifying the examination of him at school, in the seminary, in early party groups and in the intimacy of his family. His medical condition and psychological profile also deserve attention. Such material contributes to an assessment of his motives and comportment in his public career.

Another theme of the book is the degree of Stalin's influence before Lenin's death. No biography fails to depreciate his already developed skills as a politician. This book benefits from the political and psychological insights of Robert Tucker, Adam Ulam, Robert McNeal and Ronald Hingley.[15] Yet even these works assumed that Stalin did not count for much among Bolsheviks before 1917. Tucker contended that Stalin's attitude to Lenin amounted to mere hero-worship through to the 1930s.[16] Lenin's unchallenged dominance is also the key theme of the study by Robert Slusser, who characterised Stalin in 1917 as 'the man who missed the Revolution'.[17] Purportedly Stalin was Lenin's errand boy before and during 1917. The same approach has been maintained with reference to the years after the October Revolution as biographers have insisted that Stalin was a dour bureaucrat in the backrooms of Bolshevism. At most, he has been depicted as Lenin's trouble-shooter – the man who was sent into emergency situations with a specific brief from the Kremlin. But credence is rarely given to the possibility that Stalin's membership of the supreme bodies of the Bolshevik party and the Soviet government shows that he was already an established member of the communist ruling group. The following chapters question this long-established historical opinion.

And the biographers, while rightly stressing that Stalin came to wield enormous power from the 1930s, have usually omitted to note that he was not omnipotent. He had to operate the machinery of the system of power he inherited. He could modify it, but he was unable to transform it without shattering the basis of 'Soviet power'. In the Great Terror of 1937–8 he strove to eliminate tendencies in politics that restricted the impact of central commands: clientelism, localism and administrative passive resistance. He also tried to liquidate the obstructive trends pervading Soviet society which counteracted the Kremlin's policies. Not only administrators but also workers and collective-farm labourers found ways to defend themselves against Moscow and its requirements. Stalin's introduction of fresh policies from the late 1920s was accompanied by adjustments to the communist order. But these adjustments induced a syndrome of interests which obstructed further basic change. It is conventional to depict Stalin as an unimpeded despot. Without doubt he could introduce internal and external policies without contradiction in the Politburo. But I shall show that his personal rule depended upon his willingness to conserve the administrative system he had inherited. He also had to assimilate himself in many ways to the mental outlook of the people of the Soviet Union if he wanted to go on ruling them without provoking revolt.

Stalin, custodian-in-chief of the Soviet order, was also its detainee. In order to rule despotically through the communist dictatorship, he had to restrict his impulse to eliminate practices which inhibited the imposition of a perfect system of vertical command. Powerful though he was, his powers were not limitless. This consideration is not a fine scholarly point but helps towards an understanding of the vicissitudes of his career. To the end of his life he sought to keep the Soviet order in a condition of controlled agitation. Aiming to conserve personal despotism and party dictatorship, he strove to disrupt trends towards a stabilisation which might conflict with his larger purposes. But constraints of power existed even for Stalin.

The purposes of Stalin at any rate sprang not only from his psychological drives and practical calculations but also from his world view. Marxism was a guiding philosophy throughout his adult life. But it was not the only ingredient in his thinking. His Georgian origin, his cultural interests and his ecclesiastical training left their mark. Russian national traditions also had a growing importance, especially from the 1930s. He was not an original scholar. Far from it: his few innovations in ideology were crude, dubious developments of Marxism. Sometimes the innovations arose from political self-interest more than intellectual sincerity. But about the genuineness of Stalin's fascination with ideas there can be no doubt. He read voraciously and actively. His insertion of nationalist themes into official Soviet ideology ought to be seen for what it was. Stalin deployed the nationalism he found congenial. This was not the nationalism of Church, peasant and village. It was not even the nationalism of the tsars; for although he extolled Ivan the Terrible and Peter the Great, he excoriated most other past rulers. Stalin's was a Russian nationalism of the state, of technology and intolerance, of atheism, of cities, of military power. It was so idiosyncratic a compilation as to be virtually his own invention – and it overlapped substantially with Soviet Marxism as it had been developed since the death of Lenin.

Yet he continued to be pragmatic, and his ability to decide large international questions with the leaders of the world's great powers led some historians to conclude that Stalin was a statesman in the tradition of the tsars. There was something in this. Stalin was eager to be taken seriously by American and European leaders and to secure concessions to Soviet interests at the conference table. He also strained to understand the complexities of the problems of the USSR itself in administration, economy and society. He was a ruler of great assiduity and intervened in the minutiae of policy whenever he could.

The question, however, has remained about his sanity. Stalin's obsession with personal control was so extreme and brutal that many have pondered whether he was psychotic. Roy Medvedev, the Soviet historian–dissenter, denied that Stalin was insane.[18] Robert Tucker too maintained a cautious stance and argued that Stalin, while not being clinically mad, had a personality damaged by his experiences as a child. Robert Conquest agreed but stressed the unhealthy appetite Stalin had for vengeance and murder. All this brings up the matter of the nature of the 'enemies' whom Stalin sought to eliminate. Were they phantoms of his imagination without existence in objective reality? Medvedev, Tucker and Conquest agree that his was a deeply maladjusted personality. Quite how peculiarly he behaved in his intimate circle has become ever clearer since the doors of the archives have opened. The atmosphere in his family in the 1920s was highly charged and the fact that his wife Nadezhda was mentally unstable made things worse. In politics he was exceptionally suspicious, vengeful and sadistic. Stalin had a gross personality disorder.

But was his behaviour merely the reflection of a Georgian upbringing? Ideas of personal dignity and revenge were widespread in his native land, especially in the rural areas. Practically every biographer has assumed that this had an influence on his subsequent career. But Georgia's culture was neither uniform nor unchanging. Stalin imbibed ideas in Gori and Tbilisi which were rejected by others, and an exclusive ascription of his personal and political comportment to his national origins is inappropriate. The dysfunctionality of the Dzhughashvili family was remarked upon by his friends. His own odd character was worsened by his later experience of being underappreciated by his comrades in the revolutionary movement; and the tenets and practices of communism confirmed his harsher tendencies. (All leading Bolsheviks condoned the Red Terror in 1918: this was yet another reason why they tended to ignore Stalin's extremism until the late 1920s.) He was also influenced by the books he read about previous Russian rulers, especially Ivan the Terrible; and he annotated Machiavelli's *The Prince*. There were many interacting factors which contributed to Stalin's extraordinary ferocity.

Yet although he exaggerated the strength and intent of the opposition to him, such opposition was not insignificant in its potential. There was method in Stalin's alleged madness. Conquest and Medvedev have pointed to the existence of groupings of internal party critics.[19] Getty has indicated that Stalin was unhappy with passive resistance to his policies among the party's officials in the provinces.[20] Khlevnyuk has indicated his persistent concern about past and current members of the communist central leadership.[21]

This book is intended to show that Stalin's worries went wider and deeper than his concern about internal party critics. He really did have a multitude of enemies. None of them had much chance against him. His defeated opponents gossiped against him, and some subordinates in the party formed little groups to conspire against him. There were plenty of delegates to Party Congresses who felt that his power had become overmagnified after the First Five-Year Plan of 1928–32. More broadly, outside the party, multitudes of people had reason to bear him a grudge: Bolsheviks expelled from the party; priests, mullahs and rabbis; Mensheviks and Socialist-Revolutionaries; nationalists among the non-Russians – and indeed among the Russians; peasants; even workers and soldiers. His unpopularity was as great as his power at its peak, and the fact that he fostered a cult of the individual for himself meant that no one in the country could fail to identify him as being personally responsible for the policies that had brought suffering to the country. This was a situation that was unlikely to improve in the near future. At the very moment of his political victory Stalin had much cause to be worried.

The following chapters offer a comprehensive portrait of Stalin in his time. They investigate not only what he did but also why he did it and how he was allowed to do it. He is examined simultaneously as leader, administrator, theorist, writer, comrade, husband and father. His social background, schooling, nationality and ways of work and leisure are analysed. Stalin as a psychological type also needs to be considered – and his habits of daily life as well as the large scale of his political manoeuvres and statesmanship enter the account.

The charge has been laid that such an approach runs the risk of 'humanising' the communist leaders. I plead guilty. Stalin carried out campaigns of carnage which have been described with words outside the lexicon of our species: monstrous, fiendish, reptilian; but the lesson to be learned from studying several of the twentieth century's most murderous politicians is that it is wrong to depict them as beings wholly incomparable to ourselves. Not only is it wrong: it is also dangerous. If the likes of Stalin, Hitler, Mao Tse-tung and Pol Pot are represented as having been 'animals', 'monsters' or 'killing machines', we shall never be able to discern their successors. Stalin in many ways behaved as a 'normal human being'. In fact he was very far from being 'normal'. He had a vast desire to dominate, punish and butcher. Often he also comported himself with oafish menace in private. But he could also be charming; he could attract passion and admiration both from close comrades and from an immense public audience. On occasion he could be modest. He was hard-working. He was capable of kindliness to relatives. He thought a lot about the good of the communist cause. Before he started killing them, most communists in the USSR and in the Comintern judged him to be functioning within the acceptable bounds of political conduct.

Of course, they overlooked the other side of Stalin. It was a side that had been plentifully evident after the October Revolution. He had killed innumerable innocents in the Civil War. He had gone on to cause hundreds of thousands of deaths in the First and Second Five-Year Plans. He was a state murderer long before instigating the Great Terror. The neglect of his propensities appears inexplicable unless account is taken of the complex man and politician behind the 'grey blur' he presented to a multitude of observers. Stalin was a killer. He was also an intellectual, an administrator, a statesman and a party leader; he was a writer, editor and statesman. Privately he was, in his own way, a dedicated as well as bad-tempered husband and father. But he was unhealthy in mind and body. He had many talents, and used his intelligence to act out the roles he thought suited to his interests at any given time. He baffled, appalled, enraged, attracted and entranced his contemporaries. Most men and women of his lifetime, however, underestimated Stalin. It is the task of the historian to examine his complexities and suggest how better to understand his life and times.

2. THE FAMILY DZHUGHASHVILI

Stalin's official biography appeared in 1938. His early life was described in the five opening sentences:[1]

> Stalin (Dzhughashvili), Joseph Vissarionovich was born on 21 December 1879 in the town of Gori in Tiflis Province. His father Vissarion Ivanovich, a Georgian by nationality, was descended from peasants of Didi-Lilo village, Tiflis province and was a cobbler by trade who later became a worker at the Adelkhanov Shoe Factory. His mother Yekaterina Georgievna came from the Geladze family of bound peasants in Gambareuli village.
>
> In autumn 1888 Stalin entered the Gori spiritual school. In 1894 Stalin finished school and entered the Orthodox spiritual seminary in Tiflis.

The Soviet media at the time of the book's publication deluged citizens of the USSR with extravagant claims on his behalf; but the years of boyhood and adolescence attracted meagre attention.

Communists of Stalin's vintage discouraged accounts which dwelt on the personal aspects of their lives. For them, politics mattered above all else. But Stalin had a fastidiousness which was extreme even by the standards of his party, and he summoned the authors of his biography to the Kremlin to discuss their draft.[2] It was evidently at his insistence that just two short paragraphs covered his early years. The last thing he wanted, as a Georgian ruling over Russians, was to shine a bright light on his national origins. There were other reasons why his childhood embarrassed him. As a man from an unhappy family he did not intend the world to know about the damage it had done to him – and he was very far from being proud of his father. As a revolutionary and militant atheist he disdained to acknowledge the contribution made by the Imperial regime and the Orthodox Church to his personal development. Frugality with facts served a further purpose. By wrapping himself in mystery in the eyes of Soviet citizens, Stalin hoped to enhance popular admiration for himself as a ruler. From his studies of Russian history he knew that the most effective tsars had restricted knowledge about their private lives and opinions. By limiting what his biographers could write, he aspired to rise in the esteem of Soviet citizens.

Falsification came easily to him. The first sentence of that official biography was a lie because Joseph Dzhughashvili entered this life not on 21 December 1879 but on 6 December 1878. The truth has been ascertained by searches in the parochial records in Gori.[3] It is uncertain why he practised this deceit. But it was not a mistake: Stalin was always careful about such details. We can only speculate at this distance in time. Apparently he started to fib about his birthday after leaving the Spiritual Seminary in Tbilisi, and it may be that his motive was to avoid military conscription: certainly many Georgians in those years tampered with the records for this purpose. Another possibility is that he was simply trying to confuse the police as to when he entered the revolutionary movement.[4]

About some things he told the truth. His father Besarion (or Vissarion in Russian) was indeed a cobbler married to Ketevan (or Yekaterina in Russian) and they lived in Gori. The Dzhughashvilis were subjects of the Russian tsars. The completed conquest of the Caucasus region had occurred only recently when, in 1859, the Islamist rebel Shamil from Dagestan had been captured by Imperial forces. Parts of Georgia had not altogether lost their autonomous status until the second half of the nineteenth century. It had been the east Georgian ruler Irakli II who in 1783 had requested that his kingdom should become a Russian protectorate. Further territorial adhesions followed from the territory of the Georgians. Steadily the tsars repealed the agreements to grant exemptions from the pattern of rule in the rest of their empire. Garrisons were established. The Georgian Orthodox Church's autocephaly was abolished in 1811. Russian peasants were given land in Georgia. The teaching of the Georgian language was restricted in schools and seminaries. The Georgian press was cramped. Georgians were robbed of their national dignity by the Russian administrators and commanders sent to the south Caucasus.

The little town of Gori in central Georgia lies by the fast-flowing River Mtkvari (or Kura, as the Russians call it). It is surrounded by hills. On the highest of them, to the north, there perches a large medieval fort – Goristikhe – which in the nineteenth century was almost as big as the town it overlooked: its crenellated walls and towers stretch like a huge octopus down the slopes. The valley is wide at Gori and the nearby hills are wooded with hazel, walnut, fir and chestnut trees. On clear days the mountains of the Caucasus are visible in the distance. When Joseph was a boy, the population tipped a little over twenty thousand. Most churches in the town belonged to the Georgian Orthodox Church; but many Armenians, a few hundred Russians and some Jews also lived there – and there was even a religious colony of Dukhobors.[5] The best local education, available only to boys, was offered at the Spiritual School. Most employment in Gori was connected to trade with peasants who came to the town with sacks of grapes, potatoes, tomatoes, nuts, pomegranates and wheat as well as their cattle, pigs and sheep. The town is over fifty miles by road from the Georgian capital Tbilisi, which it took two days to reach on foot. There was much poverty in Gori. This had been the norm for peasants for centuries; but most nobles too in the late nineteenth century had fallen on hard times.

Gori had no large enterprises; its economy was dominated by handicrafts and trade. Onions, garlic, cucumbers, sweet peppers, cabbages, radishes, potatoes and aubergines grew in a perfect climate, and the Atenuri wine produced from the Ateni grape was highly appreciated. The sheep and cattle kept on the little hillside farms were famous for their succulence. In Gori itself there was a flourishing commerce in leather and wool, and craftsmen made shoes, coats and carpets. Shops and stalls were everywhere. Most of the owners were tailors, cobblers and carpenters. Professional employment was mainly confined to the priests and teachers. Policemen kept order. There were several taverns where men took solace in the bottle. It was a scene that had changed little since the Russians had entered Georgia at the request of its various rulers from the late eighteenth century. Yet even Gori was changing. In 1871 it acquired a railway station down by the River Mtkvari. The trains enabled passengers to get to Tbilisi in two or three hours. Commercial and industrial penetration of the area was just a matter of time.

Georgians like the Dzhughashvilis dressed plainly. Women wore long black skirts and, when they were in church, they donned head-scarves. The priests had black cassocks. The other men were no more colourful. Black jackets, shirts and trousers were customary and there was no pressure on working-class males to look smart. Men expected to rule their households with their wives' complete obedience – and Besarion was notorious for his bad temper and violence. Women carried out all the domestic chores, including the cooking. This was one of the glories of old Georgia, whose cuisine was a stunning combination of the tastes of the eastern Mediterranean and the Caucasus. Outstanding dishes included sturgeon in pomegranate sauce, spicy pork kebabs and aubergines with walnut paste. The basic salads were also excellent. The Kutaisi combination of tomatoes, onions, coriander and ground walnuts was a meal in itself. But poor families, even if they retained links with the countryside, would rarely have the opportunity to eat such a diet in full. In fact people like the Dzhughashvilis would subsist mainly on beans and bread. Life for most inhabitants of Gori was hard and there was little prospect of betterment.

Besarion married nineteen-year-old Ketevan Geladze on 17 May 1874. Her father had died when she was young and she and her mother had had to get by as best they could in the little village of Gambareuli.[6] Ketevan – known to family and acquaintances as Keke – quickly became pregnant. In fact she had two sons before Joseph's arrival. The first was Mikhail, who died when only one year old. Then came Giorgi, but he too died young. Joseph alone survived early childhood. Taken to church on 17 December 1878, he was baptised by archpriest Khakhanov and catechist Kvinikadze.[7]

Christened Joseph, he was known to everyone by the diminutive Soso. Little else – in fact nothing at all – is known about the very earliest years of his life. It might have been expected that Joseph's mother and father, having suffered the loss of two sons in infancy, would have treated their third with special care and affection. This would also have been in keeping with the Georgian tradition to dote on a new baby in the family. The Georgians are more like the Italians and Greeks than the peoples of northern Europe in child rearing. Besarion Dzhughashvili was an exception because he never showed his son any kindliness. Keke tried to make up for this. Though a strict and demanding mother, she made him feel special and dressed him as well as her finances allowed. Besarion resented this. Keke set her heart on Joseph becoming educated and entering the priesthood whereas Besarion wanted him to be a cobbler like himself. Almost from the beginning the Dzhughashvilis had an unhappy relationship; and far from alleviating the situation, Joseph's arrival exacerbated the tension between them.

Besarion had a temperament that often flared up into angry violence against his wife. His commercial ambitions did not meet with success. His cobbler's shop failed to move with the times by producing the European-style shoes – rather than traditional Georgian footwear – which were becoming the popular norm.[8] Whatever he tried always ended in failure, and his lack of success as an independent artisan and his loss of local esteem probably aggravated his tendency to volcanic outbursts. His drinking got out of control. He spent more time guzzling wine at Yakob Egnatashvili's tavern than tending to his family obligations.[9]

Keke according to most accounts was a devout woman. She attended church, consulted priests and was eager for her son to become one of them. But there were rumours which placed her in a different light. Sergo Beria, son of Stalin's police chief from 1938, wrote that his grandmother – who befriended Keke in old age – told of a loose-living woman with a line in smutty talk: 'When I was young I cleaned house for people and when I came upon a good-looking boy I didn't waste the opportunity.' When Besarion could not supply money for the family's needs, Keke allegedly went out and sold her body.[10] A less extreme version was that, although she was not serially promiscuous, she had an affair with one of Gori's prominent personalities. The usual candidates were tavern keeper Yakob Egnatashvili and local police chief Damian Davrishevi.[11] As is not unusual in such a situation, proof is lacking; but circumstantial evidence filled the gap for the gossip-mongers. When Stalin attained supreme power, he promoted the sons of Egnatashvili to high rank and this is sometimes taken as a sign of special kinship with them.[12]

Soso's paternity was also sometimes ascribed to Damian Davrishevi. Damian's son Joseph, a childhood friend of Joseph Dzhughashvili, could not help noticing their physical likeness; and in later life Joseph Davrishevi did not exclude the possibility that they were half-brothers.[13] Enquiries were made in the late 1950s in order to gather damning evidence on Stalin; and the authorities were not averse to discovering whether the image of Keke as a God-fearing, simple peasant woman was a myth. If mud could be thrown at his mother, some of it would land on him. But nothing of the kind was found.

Yet if rumours of this kind were rife during Stalin's childhood, they can hardly have calmed Besarion's troubled mind. They may well have been the fundamental motive behind his descent into drunkenness, hooliganism and domestic violence. Known as Mad Beso, he got into scrapes as his business went into decline. He was going to the bad, and Keke took what solace she could in the local church. She also eked out a living by working as a cleaner and seamstress: she was determined that the family should not be dragged down by her bad-tempered, incompetent husband. Beso himself saw that there was no commercial future for him in Gori. Like other artisans, he sought work in the growing industrial sector in Tbilisi. There he became employed as a labourer in

Emile Adelkhanov's large shoe factory in 1884. The hours were long, the pay low. Beso continued to drink heavily and there is no sign that he remitted much money home to Keke. His visits to Gori brought wife and son no solace: drunkenness and violence were all they could expect from the wastrel. The more he degenerated, the more Keke took emotional and spiritual refuge within the walls of the parish church.

Other versions exist of Joseph's ancestry. The most bizarre suggests that one of the most famous ethnographers and explorers of the day, the noble Nikolai Przewalski, had an illicit liaison with Keke Dzhughashvili and that Joseph was the product. This is not only unlikely: it is physically impossible. Przewalski was not even present in Georgia at the time when Joseph Dzhughashvili was conceived.[14] None of this is very surprising. As rulers from obscure backgrounds become famous it is conventional for legends to grow up about them, and often the rumour starts that in reality their parentage was more illustrious than it seemed.

A variant of this is that the leader was not of the nationality that was claimed. In Stalin's case the word was that he was not Georgian at all but an Ossetian. This would trace the ancestry of the Dzhughashvili family (but not the Geladze) to the mountains beyond Georgia's northern frontier. The name itself could well have a non-Georgian root of precisely this kind. The peoples of the Caucasus had moved around the region for centuries and even the sleepy town of Gori had its interlopers long before the Russians imposed themselves. Behind the story of Ossetian descent, though, lies the innuendo that this explains the wildness of Stalin's later tyranny since the mountain peoples are widely regarded as less civilised than the town dwellers of the valleys. For some Georgians, moreover, such a genealogy expunges their shame in being associated with so notorious a despot. None of his school friends mentions any of this in his memoirs, but attention was almost certainly drawn to it in his childhood.[15] Although Joseph Dzhughashvili grew up proud of belonging by birth and culture to the Georgian people, he may have disguised an early sense of being different from most other boys in the town.

The stories told by Stalin to friends and relatives from the 1930s onwards are one of the main sources for what happened in his childhood. Yet it hardly needs to be emphasised that he was an inveterate liar – and even when not lying directly, he often exaggerated or distorted the truth. His usual tale of childhood was filled with outbursts of drunken violence by Besarion, but all his stories have to be treated with caution. When in 1931 Stalin was asked about his childhood by the writer Emile

Ludwig, he strenuously rebuffed suggestions of mistreatment: 'No,' he asserted, 'my parents were uneducated people but they didn't handle me at all badly.'[16] This was out of line with his other recollections. He told his daughter Svetlana about how he stood up to his father and threw a knife at him when Keke was taking yet another beating. The knife missed its aim. Besarion hurled himself at young Joseph but was too slow to catch him. Joseph ran off and was hidden by neighbours until his father's rage had spent itself.[17]

The memoirs of his friends without exception affirm that Beso was a brute to his son. Keke too was reportedly not averse to giving him a thrashing.[18] If this was true, the Dzhughashvili household was filled with violence, and little Joseph must have grown up assuming that this was in the natural order of things. Perhaps he contradicted this when being interviewed by Ludwig because he sensed that he was being probed for a psychological origin of his political severity. No psychoanalytical sophistication is required. Like many who have been bullied in childhood, Joseph grew up looking for others whom he could bully. Not everyone beaten by parents acquires a murderous personality. Yet some do, and it would seem that more do than is true for general society. What made things worse for Joseph's subsequent development was that his father's violence was neither merited nor predictable. It is scarcely astounding that he grew up with a strong tendency towards resentment and retaliation.

Keke Dzhughashvili was strict with him but also smothered him with attention and affection. In an unguarded moment with Soviet army commander Georgi Zhukov in the Second World War he said that she never let him out of her sight till he was six years old. He also said that he had been a sickly infant.[19] This was putting it mildly. Around the age of six he fell victim to smallpox. His mother was frantic. Smallpox was often a fatal disease and for a time it looked as if she would lose him. Poor families like the Dzhughashvilis could not afford doctors' visits and their medicines. Most people in Gori in any case retained faith in the rural ways of dealing with disease. A female healer – Stalin was later to call her a *znakharka* when speaking in Russian – was summoned to treat Joseph. Against the odds, he recovered. The after-effects were limited to facial pockmarks. Joseph Dzhughashvili had had a narrow escape. This was to be a pattern in years to come. Although Joseph was prone to illnesses, his physical resilience saw him through.[20]

It would not be a surprise if the crisis strengthened maternal protectiveness. Keke's disappointment in her husband was sublimated into high expectations of her Joseph – and the fact that he was her only surviving child intensified her preoccupation with him. Keke was a typical Georgian woman of the period. There was no realistic opportunity for her to break out of the vicious circle of poverty. The best she could do was to earn a little from cleaning and sewing for better-off families. This would alleviate the poverty. But basic improvement would have to wait until the next generation. Joseph was her sole hope.

Yet she could not keep him in the house for ever. Joseph had a mind of his own and wanted to be accepted by the other boys. Once Joseph started to go out on to the streets, however, he had to cope with another challenge. The boys in Gori formed gangs in each little district. There was a lot of rough-and-tumble. There was much mixing of the various national groups. Respect accrued to those lads who could look after themselves in wrestling contests organised out of sight of the adults. Fist fights were common. Joseph, who had been tied to his mother's apron strings, took time to assert himself. His contemporary Kote Charkviani wrote: 'Before he was enrolled at school, not a day passed without someone thumping him, and he would either go back home in tears or else he himself would rough someone up.'[21] But as Charkviani noted, Joseph was determined to prevail. No matter how many times he was knocked down, he got back up and fought on. He broke the rules if it helped him to win. Joseph was sly. He was also ambitious: he wanted to lead the gang and was resentful when he did not get his way.

But his mother continued to adore him and point him in the direction of an ecclesiastical career; and he was obliged to conform whenever she was near him. Regular church attendance was obligatory. Soon he caught the attention of influential figures in the town. Joseph was God-fearing and bright. He was exactly the sort of boy whom the priests wanted to admit to the Gori Spiritual School, especially in the light of his mother's wish for him to enter the clergy. Joseph was given a place in summer 1888 in his tenth year. His studies would start in September.

Poor though the Dzhughashvili family was, Joseph was being given a chance only a few dozen boys got in the town: he was going to be educated. He would receive a small stipend of three rubles a month.[22] A portrait of him as he commenced his studies comes from a memoir by Vano Ketskhoveli:[23]

> I . . . saw that among the pupils was standing a boy I didn't know,
> dressed in a long *akhalukhi* [a plain, cloth body-garment] which

went down to his knees, in new boots with high tops. He had a thick leather belt tightly drawn around his waist. On his head was a black cloth peak-cap with a varnished peak which shone in the sun.

No one else wore either an *akhalukhi* or such boots, and the other pupils pressed around him out of curiosity. Obviously his mother was very eager to dress her son as well as possible; she had coddled him since birth. She herself had never been to school, and probably she did not understand that by dressing him up differently, she did him no favours with his fellow pupils.

Gradually he began to stand up to her. When out of her sight, he pulled off his white collar and mixed with the other boys on the streets.[24] He adopted the same routines at school. All first-hand accounts recorded his pugnacity towards rivals. But he was also devout, hard-working and determined to succeed, and the path on which he was stepping offered the chance for him to move out of the poverty he endured at home.

His intelligence and diligence had been recognised. His peculiarities were noted by acquaintances: he was volatile, sly and resentful. But nobody yet felt that these features existed to an abnormal degree. He had had a rougher upbringing than most other boys in the town and much was forgiven him. It was only in retrospect that the cocktail of permanent harm to his personality became detectable. He was mistreated by his father, and detested him. At the same time his mother handled him as a very special person; much was expected of him. Being an only child, he was spoiled. This can only have increased his resentment at the way his father behaved towards him. The fuss made of him by Keke protected him for a while against the rough games of the local boys. But the will to prove himself had not been cosseted out of him, and his father's recurrent violence gave him a competing model of the kind of man he wanted to be. Although he desired to become a priest, he also wished to prove his toughness. He had known no fairness from his father; he would show none to those contemporaries who got in his way. He was not the strongest fighter on his streets but compensated by using methods that others avoided. His constant wish was to get on top and stay there: this was one of the few attitudes shared by his father and mother, albeit in their different ways.

The upbringing of young Dzhughashvili did not predetermine the career of Joseph Stalin. There were too many contradictions in his personality and parental treatment for a single possible result to be predictable. A lot more had to happen before psychological settlement occurred, and this included his particular experiences as well as events in the wider world. Yet without the childhood experienced by Joseph there would have been no Stalin. For the tree to grow there had to be a seed.

3. THE SCHOOLING OF A PRIEST

Joseph took time to benefit fully from his educational opportunity. Not having spoken Russian at home, he stayed in the preparatory classes for two years. But he proved a quick learner and already knew enough of the language to leap over the beginners' class. He started the full course in September 1890.[1] Beso Dzhughashvili had never liked the idea of his boy becoming a scholar. At some early stage of Joseph's course at the Gori Spiritual School,[2] there was a terrible row between Beso and Keke. The angry Beso triumphed and took Joseph back to Tbilisi with him to work at the Adelkhanov Shoe Factory. Joseph was to become an apprentice and drop Keke's plan for him to enter the priesthood.[3] Beso was a drunk and a failed artisan; but his attitude was not unusual. He insisted that what was good enough for him in employment was equally appropriate for his offspring.

The authorities categorised the Adelkhanov Shoe Factory as among the most decent in Georgia towards its eighty workers since, unlike rival factories, it had its own medical facilities. Yet most people thought Emile Adelkhanov, who had opened his enterprise in 1875, a harsh exploiter of his workforce. Wages were low and the conditions were especially harsh for young boys – indeed the same authorities worried about the large number of youngsters employed by Adelkhanov and about the effects on their health and upbringing in the grim, rectangular building.[4] Adelkhanov was no philanthropist. When the terms of trade turned against him at the end of the century, he instantly cut wages. The result was a bitterly fought strike.[5] For Beso Dzhughashvili, however, Adelkhanov's cost-cutting recruitment of minors was a definite attraction. The extra money, however small initially, would come in useful: Joseph could start to pay his own way. He would not see much of the centre of Tbilisi with its palaces, cathedrals and grand shops. They lodged in a cheap room in the Avlabari district on the left bank of the River Mtkvari and each day walked down past the Metekhi Prison and over the bridge into the winding, cobbled streets of the Ortachaala district where the factory stood. Joseph's first encounter with capitalism was raw, harsh and dispiriting.

Yet he cannot have failed to note how different Tbilisi was from Gori. A mixture of cultures existed around the Adelkhanov Shoe Factory. Apart from the rival Mantashëv Shoe Factory there were synagogues for the Tbilisi Jews, several Armenian churches and half a dozen Georgian churches. Near by there were the sulphur baths used by the great Russian poet Alexander Pushkin earlier in the century. The entire area, including the gently bubbling stretch of the River Mtkvari, lay across hot springs valued for their medicinal properties. During his time in the factory, Joseph Dzhughashvili was being shown that a wider world of experience existed than he could possibly have imagined as a schoolboy in Gori.

If Beso had continued to prevail, there would have been no Stalin – and world history would have been different. To rise to the peak of the Russian Communist Party in the 1920s it was to be essential to have a fluent and plausible pen; and much as he resented the priests who taught him, Joseph owed them a lasting debt for his education. He was also beholden to his mother's refusal to accept defeat. Doting on her departed son, she went to the priests in Gori and got them to help her to constrain Beso to release Joseph from factory work. Beso relented, and after a few months Joseph returned to his desk at the Spiritual School. Unsurprisingly he had not become a proficient cobbler in that brief period. His tasks had been limited to fetching and carrying for the adults in the factory. But he had seen enough of contemporary manufacturing to avoid a repetition of the experience. It proved to be his only opportunity to know industrial work directly, but not once did he refer to it in print. Although he was to write in later years about 'the working class' and 'the factory system', he was mostly drawing on conversations he had with workers of the sort he never became.

Beso Dzhughashvili began to fade from the lives of Keke and Joseph. It is not known how many times, if any, he returned to Gori. What is sure is that he never lived there for any lengthy time again. His drinking seems to have taken him over as he moved from job to job. There is a legend that Joseph murdered Beso. Not a scrap of evidence has been found for this and the truth was probably much more prosaic. Beso, having made a mess of his life, coped on his own. He worked in factories, drank in taverns and eventually lost all control of his life. According to some accounts, he died before the turn of the century; but the likelihood is that Beso, alone and destitute, died of cirrhosis of the liver in 1909.[6]

In Beso's absence, Joseph reverted to the exclusive care of his mother. Quite how Joseph dealt with the breakdown in his parents' marriage and his father's departure is unclear. But clues survive. When he published poems in 1895–6, 'Besoshvili' was among his pseudonyms. This was clearly not an accidental choice. Nor was the reference in one of his early articles to how the capitalist economy put independent craftsmen under huge commercial pressure and forced most of them to give up their workshops and enter factory employment. The conclusion is irresistible. Joseph did not share his father's ambition for him. He did not like being beaten. He had erupted in fury at Beso's ill-tempered demands and behaviour. But Joseph was a thoughtful as well as sensitive child. When he started to think as a Marxist, he came to see Beso as a victim of history.[7] This would surely not have happened if, at the back of his mind, Joseph had not retained a feeling of affection and understanding for his father. This may appear paradoxical. Stalin, Beso's victim, kept fond thoughts of the man who had maltreated him. This is not an unusual reaction. The fact that Beso had passed out of his life probably helped Joseph to sanitise his recollections.

Back in Gori, Joseph resumed the life of church, school and the streets. It was an eventful period. While standing outside church one day, Joseph was knocked down by a phaeton. This was a horse-drawn trap, typically with two or three seats for its occupants, primitive suspension-hoops and a simple set of shafts. Open to the air, it was one of the cheapest forms of carriage. The driver that day in Gori lost control of his horse. The phaeton careered towards the crowd by the church wall and young Joseph Dzhughashvili did not move out of the way in time. It could have been a fatal accident.[8]

Although the boy's left arm and his legs were badly damaged, he quickly recovered.[9] Soon he was attending school again. The physical harm, however, was permanent. Joseph's arm was left shortened and lacking in flexibility. It was to be the reason why he was not called up into the Imperial Army in 1916–17. Thus an unruly horse, by trampling the Gori youngster, was instrumental in saving him from potential annihilation in the Great War. The accident made him ungainly and apparently embarrassed about his appearance. Another point of psychological stress was added to the list. Nor did the injury enhance his prowess in the trials of strengths among the boys of the town. But he was determined to prove himself. Schoolmate Joseph Iremashvili recalled how young Dzhughashvili continued to use dirty methods to win his wrestling bouts.[10] Nothing satisfied him except the leading position. He could not abide his friend David Machavariani heading their street gang. Sometimes he went off and joined another gang rather than accept orders from Machavariani. It was this kind of behaviour that led him to become known for his 'bad character'.

When this got him nowhere, he accepted David Machavariani's leadership. Like everyone else, he had to pass a series of initiation tests in order to join the gang. Would-be members needed to prove their mettle by going for a long run, carrying out an act of theft and submitting to be beaten with a strap. Others in the gang were Peter Kapanadze and Joseph Davrishevi.[11] Young Dzhughashvili never forgot these days and was to keep in touch with Peter when they were old men.[12] These friends remembered Joseph as rather gawky. He never mastered Georgia's traditional dances. The *lekuri* (which was known in Russia as the *lezginka*) remained beyond his powers. There was competition among the town boys to perform it well. When another fellow did it better, Joseph moved over to his rival and deadlegged him.

His mother started working as a seamstress at the Davrishevis, and Joseph Dzhughashvili began to see a lot of Joseph Davrishevi. Some days they climbed up to the fortress above the town to see the birds living in the walls. But they did not always get on well. Joseph Dzhughashvili was not averse to stealing his friend's food. When a dispute broke out, Davrishevi's father came out and gave them another dish. Dzhughashvili justified his misdemeanour by telling his friend that it had ensured that they should receive double the normal amount.[13] Sometimes, though, he pushed his luck too hard. Keen to show how tough he was, he challenged stronger boys to fight. Downed ten times in a tussle with a lad from another gang, he was badly beaten up. His mother fetched him home and complained to police chief Davrishevi, but he replied: 'When an earthenware pot clashes with an iron pot, it's the earthenware pot which gets cracked and not the iron one.'[14]

Joseph's misdemeanours were not confined to his fights with other boys. The bright student at school was a scamp on the streets. Among his victims was a mentally deficient woman called Magdalena. His partner in crime was young Davrishevi. Magdalena possessed a Persian cat, and the two lads teased her by tying a pan to its tail. On her name day they crept into her kitchen while she was at church and stole an enormous cake.[15] The affair was resolved without undue fuss but Davrishevi, who could hardly claim innocence, concluded that it showed that Joseph Dzhughashvili was a queer and nasty piece of work from the beginning. Another boyhood memoirist, Joseph Iremashvili, came to the same opinion. Both Davrishevi and Iremashvili imputed primary responsibility to their friend. By the same token they asserted that Dzhughashvili had a leading role even if he never achieved his goal of gang leadership. Young Dzhughashvili was cantankerous, volatile and ambitious; he was also frustrated: he never supplanted David Machavariani in the gang. But apparently this was not a situation he accepted. He resented it. He had talent and wanted others to recognise it. He was reluctant to bide his time. Others ought to show him greater respect than he currently received.

There was also a wider aspect to his character's formation. He was brought up near the mountains of Georgia where traditions of blood feud persisted, and it has been suggested that his propensity for violence, conspiracy and revenge sprang from this culture. There is an obvious difficulty here. Most Georgians entering educational institutions in the late Imperial period tended to accommodate themselves to a less traditional worldview. If indeed the culture of the mountainside was an influence upon him, Joseph was peculiar in failing to evolve away from it. Not all Georgians were obsessively vengeful. The customary stress on compensation for injury did not have to involve the principle of an eye for an eye and a tooth for a tooth. Negotiations between the perpetrator and the victim of hurt – or their relatives – were another way of dealing with the problem. There was something quite extraordinary about Joseph's vindictiveness. As he grew up, he was notorious for this characteristic: he enjoyed crushing his rivals – it was never enough simply to defeat them. Georgian popular culture had a broad emphasis on honour. This involved loyalty to family, friends and clients. Joseph by contrast felt no lasting obligation to anybody. He was later to execute in-laws, veteran fellow leaders and whole groups of communists whose patron he had been. On the surface he was a good Georgian. He never ceased to revere the poetry he loved as a youth. He hosted lavish dinner parties after the Caucasian manner once he was in power. He liked to carouse; he dandled children on his knee. But his sense of traditional honour was non-existent. If he retained a number of attitudes and customs from his childhood, there were many which he abandoned. The history of the twentieth century would have been a lot less bloody if Joseph Dzhughashvili had been a better Georgian.

Not only popular culture but also Georgian literature had an influence on him. He loved the national classics, especially the thirteenth-century epic poetry of Shota Rustaveli (who was revered by Georgians as their Dante).[16] Another favourite was Alexander Qazbegi's story *The*

Patricide, which had been published to much acclaim in 1883: Joseph loved it. The main character was called Koba. The plot involved episodes from the history of the great resistance led by Shamil against Russian Imperial power in the 1840s. Koba was an *abrek*. The term implies not just a robber but a man of the mountains with fearless hostility to all authority. *Abrek*s live by their cunning as well as violence but do not prey upon ordinary people. Their code of honour allows and encourages them to be ruthless. What they punish is treachery. They do not expect life to be easy or God to rescue them from misfortune; and *The Patricide* suggested that betrayal by friends and acquaintances is something only to be expected. But revenge is sweet; the *abrek*s will always pursue to the death those who have wronged them. Koba declares: 'I'll make their mothers weep!'

The *abrek*s caused greater damage to civil society than Qazbegi allowed. As a Georgian urban story-teller he strove to suggest that the old ways of the Caucasus had a certain nobility. Russian writers such as Pushkin, Lermontov and Tolstoi also put Caucasian robbers into their works but seldom – until Tolstoi's *Hadji Murat* in 1912 – gave a convincing interior view of the mind of mountain outlaws. Qazbegi was not in their class as a literary figure, but his immediate popularity with Georgian readers was enormous. His treatment of the Shamil resistance ignored reference to its Islamist purpose. He provided Georgians with a sense of national worth. Qazbegi was offering an admiring portrait of the violent traditions of the mountains: blood feud, vengeance, personal honour and life beyond the law. This was a romantic view more extreme in its particular aspects than anything offered in Walter Scott, Lord Byron or Alexander Pushkin. Qazbegi implied that the dominant values in cities and towns in Georgia – Christianity, commerce, education, law and administration – were inferior to the savage beliefs and customs of the mountains.

Gori lies in a valley and its inhabitants were not the rough mountaineers who lived by thievery, kidnapping and murder. One of his school friends, however, recalled how impressed Joseph was by Qazbegi's work:[17]

> Koba was Soso's ideal and the image of his dreams. Koba became Soso's God, the meaning of his life. He wanted to be the second Koba, a fighter and hero – like him – covered with glory . . . From then onwards he called himself Koba, he absolutely didn't want us to call him by any other name.

Works of literature allow for diverse interpretations. Qazbegi's story is unusually straightforward, and Stalin's subsequent preoccupation with revenge and personal honour indicate that the basic message was successfully transmitted.

It is in this connection that one of the most gruesome events of Joseph's childhood should be interpreted. While he was a schoolboy, two 'bandits' were hanged on the gibbet in the centre of Gori.[18] The event left a deep imprint on the boy's mind, and many years later – when biographical details about him were published – he allowed an account of the hanging to be reproduced. His biographers have frequently adduced his remembrance of the events as evidence of his psychological peculiarity. That Joseph developed a gross personality disorder can hardly be denied. But he was not alone in witnessing or remembering the hanging. It was the most remarkable event in Gori of the last quarter of the nineteenth century. What happened was as follows. Two men of the mountains were being pursued by a policeman on horseback who tried to take possession of their cow. They resisted. In the ensuing altercation they shot him. Strife between brigands and the police was not unknown in Gori and the surrounding area. Shoot-outs occurred not infrequently. Urban inhabitants more often than not took the side opposed to the police. Hatred of the authorities was widespread. Defence of family, property and native village was thought justifiable regardless of Imperial legislation. So when the captured brigands were sentenced to death, the popular interest – and not just Joseph's – was intense.[19]

Police chief Davrishevi had anticipated the potential for unrest near the gibbet and forbade his own son to go outdoors. Joseph Dzhughashvili went accompanied by two other friends. What did they see? The popularity of the convicts led the authorities to order drummers to march to the square and to keep up a din. The sentence was announced in Russian. This too was scarcely well designed to quieten the mood of spectators. Someone tossed a stone from the crowd as the executioner, defended by soldiers, went about his business. A disturbance broke out. The police were on the point of panic as the brigands were strung up. Death was not swift in coming. The ropes had been tied inefficiently and the victims took an unbearably long time to expire.[20] The town's inhabitants did not think the punishment fitted the crime. The miscreants had not offended the local honour code: they were protecting what they thought was their own. They were local heroes. Young Davrishevi, himself the son of one of the town's highest officials, described them as 'holy martyrs'.[21] When Joseph and his mates attended the hanging, they partook of the general atmosphere.

This is not to deny that Joseph had an unusual attraction to violence in dealing with enemies. The Empire was meting out punishment to its recalcitrant subjects. The inhabitants of Gori resented this but could do nothing to stop the process. Neither Joseph nor his friends left a record of his impressions. But it would not be improbable that he concluded that state power was a crucial determining factor in the life of society and that, if any basic change was going to happen in society, force would be needed to countervail against the status quo. He may also have thought that the drastic punishment of delinquents helped to secure a regime. Certainly there was little in his early years that discouraged a viewpoint on human affairs without a place for purposive violence.

Joseph completed his course at the end of the summer term 1894 and the Board of the Gori Spiritual School recommended him for transfer to the Tiflis Spiritual Seminary, and the paperwork was put in hand.[22] His behaviour on the streets was not reproduced in the classroom, where he was a well-behaved boy as well as a quick learner who earned warm plaudits. He swiftly picked up Russian even if his accent remained heavily Georgian; he assimilated arithmetic and literature and the Bible. His schoolwork in Gori had been exemplary and he had a stupendous memory and agile intellect. He attended church regularly and had a decent singing voice, an asset for an aspiring priest as Orthodox Church services have always involved an emphasis upon choral chants. Sermons were rare and pastoral duties outside the liturgy were few. Joseph was dutiful. In Gori he was remembered as 'very devout'. One of his fellow students, when asked for his memories in 1939, said that Joseph had punctually attended all divine services and had led the church choir: 'I remember that he not only performed the religious rites but also always reminded us of their significance.'[23]

Despite the disruption caused by illness and factory employment, he had caught up with other pupils. The School Board was impressed. The scroll he received gave him the highest marks in every subject except arithmetic. (This was not a permanent defect: in later life he was in fact careful and effective at checking the statistical tables proffered to him by subordinates.)[24] The Board Chairman inscribed the scroll with 'excellent' against the behaviour category. For other subjects, too, he got top marks: Old Testament, New Testament, Orthodox catechism, liturgy, Russian with Church-Slavonic, Georgian, geography, handwriting and Russian and Georgian church music. He obtained a four instead of a five in ancient Greek.[25] But the blemishes were minor. Joseph Dzhughashvili had completed the course at the Gori Spiritual School with distinction. The Georgian ecclesiastical world lay at his feet. But he was a boy with a complex personality that made many acquaintances feel uncomfortable. Academically talented, he wanted to be admired as a tough lad on the streets. He loved his mother and accepted her ambitions for him and yet he was bright and had a mind of his own. Priests wrote highly of him. Yet his friends, when they came to write memoirs, recalled things about him which had echoes in his later career. They may have invented or exaggerated everything. But probably they were right that Joseph Dzhughashvili was demonstrably Stalin in the making.

4. POET AND REBEL

Joseph Dzhughashvili, aged fifteen, left for Tbilisi in September 1894. This time he went not to the Adelkhanov Shoe Factory but to the Tiflis Spiritual Seminary. Tiflis was the conventional foreign variant of the Georgian name Tbilisi; it was used not only in Russian but also in other European languages. Founded by the Russian Imperial authorities, the Tiflis Spiritual Seminary was at the top of Pushkin Street in the heart of the city. Although provided with board and lodging free of charge, Joseph Dzhughashvili had to pay for his tuition. This would have been a problem if he had not been able to earn a regular five rubles for singing in the Zion Cathedral down by the River Mtkvari.[1] He was not the only alumnus of the Gori Spiritual School who left for Tbilisi. Along with him at the Seminary were friends of his own age from Gori, including Peter Kapanadze, Joseph Iremashvili, Vano Ketskhoveli and M. Davitash-vili.[2] (Joseph Davrishevi, whose father earned a decent salary, could afford the fees at the First Classical Gimnazia in Tbilisi.) Loneliness was not going to be a problem for Joseph Dzhughashvili.

He was arriving in the capital of Russian Imperial power in the south Caucasus. Tbilisi at the end of the nineteenth century was the largest city in that region of the Russian Empire with 350,000 inhabitants – only Baku on the Caspian Sea with 220,000 came remotely near in size. The Viceroy lived there and governed the dozens of peoples of the region, from the northern slopes of the Caucasus range down to the Ottoman border, on behalf of Emperor Nicholas II. The east Georgian kings had chosen Tbilisi as their capital for good reason. Like Gori, it straddled the River Mtkvari, which ran north from the mountains of Turkey; still more important in earlier centuries had been the fact that it lay across one of the ancient caravan routes that had enabled trade between central Asia and Europe. Consolidating Georgia's permanent place in the Russian Empire, the St Petersburg government built the Georgian Military Road from Vladikavkaz to Tbilisi. This route went from north to south. (The railway linking the south Caucasus with

Russia went from Baku up the Caspian coast.) Two army corps were based in the garrison on Tbilisi's east bank. Having completed the conquest of the region in the first half of the nineteenth century, the Romanovs allocated the personnel, communications and force needed to retain it.

Tbilisi, unlike Gori, had a multinational population wherein the Georgians themselves were a minority. Along with them were Russians, Armenians, Tatars, Persians and Germans. Russians lived in the centre on the west bank. Armenian and Persian bazaars lay near by. Georgians had their district on the other side of the river. To the north of them lived German immigrants who had moved there, mainly from Württemberg, at Emperor Alexander I's invitation.

Joseph therefore faced a conflict of cultures much more intense than in Gori. The Russian quarter in the centre contained the City Hall, the Viceroy's Palace, the General Staff headquarters, the Orthodox Cathedral and other churches, the Imperial Bank, the Public Library and the Military Museum. The streets were straight, the buildings tall and recently built. The German quarter was distinguished by its cleanliness and social order. The Armenians and Persians, who were the city's great entrepreneurs, had noisy, bustling bazaars trading in silverware, carpets and spices. Georgian shopkeepers specialised in groceries, fish and footwear. On the south-eastern side of the town there were the factories and the prison which were familiar from his time working for Adelkhanov. There was also a large railway depot and repair works in the capital's Didube district. The city bustled with high-booted Russian soldiers, Tatar men in their green and white turbans (and their becowled wives) and Germans carefully attired in the mid-European style. These inhabitants themselves were outshone by the resplendence of the traders from the heights of the Caucasus in their traditional costumes: Ossetians, Kabardians, Chechens and Ingush.

Georgians had only a limited influence over the city's affairs. St Petersburg's appointees, usually Russians, ran the administration and led the armed forces. Banking was in Russian and Jewish hands and the largest commercial enterprises were owned by Armenians. The Russian hierarchy dominated the Georgian Orthodox Church since, in 1811, Emperor Alexander I had sanctioned its incorporation into the Russian Orthodox Church. The Tiflis Spiritual Seminary entered by Joseph was subject to the ecclesiastical authorities in St Petersburg.

The Seminary was a large building with a raised portico of Corinthian columns surmounted by a pediment. Built by the sugar millionaire

Zubalishvili, it had been bought from him in 1873 by the Russian Orthodox Church and converted to ecclesiastical use. The frontage was architecturally crude. There were no steps to the portico, which had been included for display rather than practical function. The peoples of the Caucasus were meant to be impressed with the grandeur of Imperial power, and the Seminary symbolised the suzerainty of the Romanovs over the spiritual as well as the temporal affairs of the region. The rest of the building was like a barracks.[3] There were four floors. Near the entrance were the cloak room and the refectory. The first floor contained a large hall which had been converted into a chapel. The second and third floors consisted of classrooms and the fourth was given over to dormitories. The décor was plain and there was no privacy for the seminarists. An open corridor connected the dormitories; personal belongings were on open view. Cassocks, textbooks and Bible were standard issue. Like their fellows halfway down Golovin Prospect at the First Classical Gimnazia, the seminarists were being trained to serve God, Tsar and Empire.

At the time of Dzhughashvili's arrival the Exarch of Georgia was Archbishop Vladimir. The Rector from 1898 was Germogen, a Russian. The Seminary Inspector was a Georgian called Abashidze. The Russian priesthood was not known for liberal political and social convictions. The appointees to the Georgian Exarchate were even more reactionary than the norm in Russia and several were to identify themselves publicly with the cause of Russian nationalism in later years. Many were virulent anti-semites propagating notions that can now be recognised as proto-fascist. While functioning in Georgia, they regarded it as their duty to stamp out signs of Georgian national assertiveness.[4] They carried this intolerance to an extreme. The Georgian language was severely restricted in the Tiflis Spiritual Seminary and students were required to speak and write Russian or else face punishment. Archpriest Ioann Vostorgov, who influenced ecclesiastical educational policy across the Russian Empire, gave the rationale for this. He argued that Tbilisi was highly multi-ethnic and that there was no sense in privileging Georgian over other languages.[5] Some priests less courteously referred to Georgian as 'a filthy language'.[6]

The rules were strict. Seminarists were allowed into the city for just an hour a day. Gestures of respect were demanded for the Rector and his staff. Discipline was administered from Inspector Abashidze's office to the left of the foyer. Miscreants were punishable by solitary confinement. The authorities recruited informers from among the seminarists to stamp out insubordination. Only approved books were allowed into the building. Regular inspections were made of the lockers. The food was plain, and only those who lived in lodgings got relief from a diet heavily reliant on beans and bread. Seminarists went to bed early in the evening and rose early in the morning. The shock to Joseph and his fellow newcomers can hardly be exaggerated. Always in Gori they could come and go as they pleased after school. Rector Germogen's regime prohibited all that. What made things worse for Joseph was his age. He was already in the second half of his adolescence when he left Gori. Often the Seminary took in boys in their thirteenth year. Being three years older than the normal first-year seminarists, Joseph was less easily malleable.

His biographers have tended to underrate the quality of the curriculum. The reason is the usual one: they have uncritically reproduced what Stalin's enemies in the revolutionary movement published on the topic. For them, he was an ignoramus with inadequate schooling. Stalin himself reinforced this impression. As a revolutionary he disliked drawing attention to the benefits he derived from the Imperial order. In fact only very bright boys were admitted to the Tiflis Spiritual Seminary and the schooling was pitched at a higher level than in less prestigious ecclesiastical institutions. There were two such seminaries in Tbilisi: one for Georgians, the other for Armenians; they attracted youths who lacked the finance to enter the First Classical Gimnazia. Indeed some parents entered their boys for the seminaries in the knowledge that the course could be used as a qualification to go on to secular higher education.

The curriculum helped to form the person who became Stalin. It was taken for granted that the Russian and Church-Slavonic languages had already been mastered.[7] Students at the Tiflis Spiritual Seminary, being the best recruits from the local Georgian schools, were expected to tackle a wide range of subjects. Christian vocational training was not predominant at first: not only Russian literature and history but also Greek and Latin were studied.[8] Of course, the pedagogy had a political orientation. Secular literature was chosen from works thought to support the Imperial government; and the course in history was based on the textbook by D. I. Ilovaiski, whose priority was to praise the tsars and their conquests.[9] The standard curriculum required pupils to master Xenophon's *Anabasis* and, by the fourth year, to come to terms with Plato's *Apology* and *Phaedo*.[10] Although the curriculum in secular subjects was not as expansive as in the gimnazias it gave pupils a fairly broad education by the European standards of the time.

Joseph started well. In his first-year exams he scored the highest marks in all but one subject:[11]

Holy Scripture	5
Russian literature	5
Secular history	5
Mathematics	5
Georgian language	5
Latin	—
Greek	4
Church-Slavonic singing	5
Georgian-Imeretian singing	5

His Gori schooling had left him weaker in Greek than in other subjects (and perhaps his late entrance to the Seminary precluded him from starting Latin).

The later years of the Seminary curriculum increased its emphasis on the Christian faith and on practical preparation for the priesthood. In the sixth year Joseph Dzhughashvili had only one weekly period of Greek and no Russian secular literature or history nor any science or mathematics. The gap was filled by ecclesiastical history, liturgy, homiletics, dogma, comparative theology, moral theology, practical pastoral work, didactics and, as before, Holy Scripture and church singing.[12] The curriculum irked the young seminarists. All the allowable works of Russian literature predated Alexander Pushkin. Other banned classics were the novels of Lev Tolstoi, Fëdor Dostoevski and Ivan Turgenev. Georgian poetry and prose were proscribed. Even Shota Rustaveli, the thirteenth-century poet, was prohibited.[13] National sensitivities and cultural aspirations were affronted by the curriculum and rules of the Tiflis Spiritual Seminary, and the Rector had no answer other than to reinforce his reliance on surveillance and punishment. As Joseph Dzhughashvili progressed from year to year, his sympathies moved towards those who kicked against the regulations. Intelligent and patriotic, he refused to accept the conditions. Secretly he talked to seminarists who felt the same. Whenever they could, they undermined the imposed regime.

Joseph's personal development had a long tradition. Within a few years of its foundation the Seminary had given trouble to the authorities. Rebelliousness was constant. Silva Dzhibladze, a future Marxist, was expelled in 1884 for physically assaulting the Rector. Two years later a certain Largiashvili, a seminarist from Gori, went a step further and stabbed the Rector to death.[14] During Lent in 1890, while Joseph

Dzhughashvili was still at the Gori Spiritual School, the Tbilisi seminarists went on strike. Bored by the endless meals of beans, they refused to attend lessons unless the diet was changed. Among the strike leaders were Noe Zhordania and Pilipe Makharadze.[15] Zhordania was to become the leader of Georgian Menshevism and Makharadze a leading Georgian Bolshevik. Their demands were expanded to include teaching in the Georgian language and courses in Georgian history and literature. The boycott of classes went on for a week and Zhordania and Makharadze produced a handwritten journal to agitate for sustained support.[16] Another food strike broke out in 1893 and led to the expulsion of Akaki Chkhenkeli, Vladimir Ketskhoveli and Severian Dzhugheli. They all became famous as Marxists. Mikha Tskhakaya and Isidore Ramishvili also entered the Marxist movement after leaving the Seminary.[17]

The Russian Orthodox Church had become the finest recruiting agency for the revolutionary organisations. Each year the specific complaints of the seminarists were the same: the restricted curriculum, the denigration of Georgian culture, the harsh discipline and the grim meals at Lententide. The antagonism of the priests to all things secular, national and modern was simply counter-productive. Rector Germogen and Inspector Abashidze did Karl Marx's work for him.

There was no strike in Joseph's time at the Seminary. But resistance to the rules was systematic and he was quick to join the rebels. Their minds thirsted for intellectual nourishment beyond the menu of the official curriculum. Out and about in the city they found what they wanted. Seminarists feared denunciation if they borrowed disapproved books from the nearby Public Library. Instead they sought out the *Iveria* and *Kvali* editorial offices and Zakaria Chichinadze's bookshop. There they could read and talk about things banned by the priests. *Iveria* was edited by the poet and commentator Ilya Chavchavadze. While calling for Georgian cultural freedom, Chavchavadze eschewed anything but the mildest demands for social and economic reform. Giorgi Tsereteli's *Kvali* was more radical. Coming out every Saturday, it attracted contributions from critical intellectuals across a wide range which included both agrarian socialists and Marxists (and in January 1898 Tsereteli handed over the editorship lock, stock and barrel to Noe Zhordania without any political conditions).[18] Zakaria Chichinadze was a socialist sympathiser. Chavchavadze, Tsereteli and Chichinadze had many disagreements while concurring on the need for some reform and for Georgians to struggle to that end. They understood that the key to success lay in their campaign to win the hearts and minds of youths like Joseph.

As editors and publishers they were very enterprising. The Imperial censorship was a patchy phenomenon. Tight and intrusive in St Petersburg, it was slacker in Georgia and Finland. The harsh control over ideas in the Seminary was not replicated outside its walls. Although overtly nationalist works were picked out for attention, pieces on social, economic and historical themes were permitted to appear. Before the turn of the century, moreover, the chief perceived danger to the Romanovs was thought to come from those intellectuals who called for armed struggle, regional autonomy or even secession from the Russian Empire. Chavchavadze offered no direct challenge to the monarchy or the social order. But the Marxists too were deemed to be not unduly menacing since they appeared to be preoccupied with social and economic grievances; none of them demanded Georgian territorial autonomy, far less independence. The chief censor in Tbilisi, Giorgi Zhiruli, cheerfully admitted to his ignorance of Marxism. In such an environment it was possible to have a lively public debate. Marxists in Russia had to content themselves with thick journals published in St Petersburg and with intermittently appearing émigré newspapers.[19] The debate for the soul of the Georgian nation was intense as conservatives, liberals and socialists contended with each other.

Joseph Dzhughashvili was more confident than most first-year seminarists. He had begun to write his own verses, and quickly after arriving in Tbilisi he set about trying to get them published. His themes were nature, land and patriotism. Ilya Chavchavadze appreciated his talent. Joseph's first printed poem, 'To the Moon', appeared in the magazine *Iveria* in June 1895. Giorgi Tsereteli's *Kvali* was no less enthusiastic about his work, and Joseph – writing under pseudonyms such 'I. Dzh-shvili' and 'Soselo' to avoid detection by the Rector and the Inspector – had six poems published in 1895–6.[20]

The poem 'Morning' was a touching work written in the romantic literary style then conventional in Georgian literary circles:[21]

> The pinkish bud has opened,
> Rushing to the pale-blue violet
> And, stirred by a light breeze,
> The lily of the valley has bent over the grass.
>
> The lark has sung in the dark blue,
> Flying higher than the clouds,
> And the sweet-sounding nightingale
> Has sung a song to children from the bushes

Flower, oh my Georgia!
Let peace reign in my native land!
And may you, friends, make renowned
Our Motherland by study!

Nobody would claim that this in translation is high art; but in the
Georgian original it has a linguistic purity recognised by all. The themes
of nature and nation commended themselves to readers. The educa-
tionist Yakob Gogebashvili, who had contacts with revolutionaries in
Tbilisi,[22] valued the poem so highly that he included it in the later
editions of his school textbook, *Mother Tongue* (*deda ena*).[23]

There was a nationalist edge to Joseph's poems even though he
restrained himself in order to avoid annoying the Tbilisi censor. His
images were those of many writers in the oppressed countries of Europe
and Asia of that time: mountain, sky, eagle, motherland, songs, dreams
and the solitary traveller. The closest he came to disclosing his political
orientation was in an untitled work dedicated to 'the poet and singer of
peasant labour, Count Rapael Eristavi'. For Joseph, Eristavi had identified
himself with the plight of the poor toilers of the Georgian countryside.[24]

Not for nothing have the people glorified you,
You will cross the threshold of the ages –
Oh that my country might rise.

Eristavi, born in 1824, was an ethnographer and folklorist as well as poet.
His focus on the need for social and economic reform made him an
unmistakable opponent of the status quo in the Russian Empire. According to one of Joseph's fellow seminarists, the poem dedicated to Eristavi
was interpreted as revolutionary in content.[25] This may be an exaggeration. But Joseph was undeniably offering a work intended to criticise the
status quo.

The legend of a rejected Georgian youth was a figment of Stalin's
imagination. He was welcomed by the Georgian cultural elite. As soon
as he left Gori, there was no going back except for holidays. Tbilisi
offered the promise of realised ambition. His friends, whether they had
come from rich or poor backgrounds, felt the same. They had an
eagerness to make a mark in the world outside the town of their birth.

Stalin later made out that he and his comrades crept into Chichinadze's shop and, short of funds, surreptitiously copied out the forbid-
den texts into their notebooks. Supposedly they did this in relays to
relieve the pain to their hands. A less likely situation is hard to imagine

in a well-ordered enterprise. (Not that this has stopped biographers from taking the story at its face value.) Chichinadze was on the side of those who opposed the Russian establishment in Tbilisi. When the seminarists came on to his premises, he surely greeted them warmly; and if copying took place, it must have been with his express or implicit permission.[26] The spread of ideas was more important to the metropolitan intellectual elite than mere profit. It was a battle the liberals could scarcely help winning. Chichinadze's shop was a treasure house of the sort of books the youngsters wanted. Joseph Dzhughashvili was fond of Victor Hugo's *The Year Ninety-Three*. He was punished for smuggling it into the Seminary; and when in November 1896 an inspection turned up Hugo's *Toilers of the Sea*, Rector Germogen meted out a 'lengthy stay' in the solitary cell.[27]

According to his friend Iremashvili, the group also got hold of texts by Marx, Darwin, Plekhanov and Lenin.[28] Stalin told of this in 1938, claiming that each member paid five kopeks to borrow the first volume of Marx's *Capital* for a fortnight.[29] Much as they liked Ilya Chavchavadze and Giorgi Tsereteli, they were not in intellectual thrall to them. Some works by Marx and his followers were legally published in the Russian Empire. Others were passed secretly from hand to hand. The Orthodox Church had lost the contest to retain the loyalty of its livelier seminarists in the Georgian capital. The true struggle was among the various political and cultural trends outside the Seminary. Chavchavadze, a conservative reformer, hoped for a revival of national culture; Tsereteli, a radical liberal, aimed at basic socio-economic reform. By the 1890s, though, they were having to compete with advocates of diverse strands of socialism. Marxism was on the rise in Georgia and Joseph Dzhughashvili was already becoming attracted to its tenets.

As his time in the Tiflis Spiritual Seminary drew to an end, Joseph had become thoroughly alienated from the authorities. He had ceased to study hard from his second year when he became involved in writing and publishing.[30] He was also drawing back from the world of literature. Despite the patronage of Ilya Chavchavadze and Giorgi Tsereteli, he no longer sought to be a poet. He tossed aside the opportunity to join the Georgian cultural elite. Instead he intensified his studies of socialism, politics and economics. Having hurtled like a small meteor across the Tbilisi literary scene in 1895–6, he just as suddenly disappeared. It would appear that he entirely stopped composing poetry. Few people apart from his publishers and his close friends at the Seminary had an inkling that he had ever published any. (When Yakob Gogebashvili reprinted

'Morning' in 1912, it was under the original pseudonym.)[31] Dzhughashvili searched for a different way of life from the kind offered either by the priesthood or Tbilisi literary circles. His alter ego as a rough-voiced militant from the depths of society was beginning to emerge; and as far as most people knew, this persona was the only Dzhughashvili who existed.

He detested the disciplinary regime at the Seminary. On 28 September 1898 he was the centre of a group found to be reading prohibited material. Joseph had even taken notes on it.[32] Inspector Abashidze, exasperated by infringements, reported:

> Dzhughashvili, Iosif (V.I.) in the course of a search of the pos-sessions of certain fifth-year pupils spoke out several times to the inspectors, giving voice in his comments to discontent about the searches conducted from time to time among the seminarists. In one of them he asserted that such searches were not made in a single other seminary. In general, pupil Dzhughashvili is rude and disrespectful towards persons in authority and systematically fails to bow to one of the teachers (A. A. Murakhovski), as the latter has frequently reported to the inspectors.
>
> Reprimanded. Confined to the cell for five hours by order of Father Rector.

Joseph's behaviour was almost asking for trouble and the Rector's reaction aggravated the tension in the young man. It was only a matter of time before Joseph threw up his priestly vocation.

He stuck it out almost to the end of the course. There were pragmatic reasons for this. A piece of paper attesting completion of the seminary training, even if he declined to enter the priesthood, would have given him the qualifications (if he had the necessary money) to become a student in one of the Russian Empire's universities. But Joseph had no private source of income and had no connection with any organisation which might support him. He would have to make his living for himself from scratch. Consequently his disappearance from the Tiflis Spiritual Seminary in May 1899, as the last examinations were about to be sat, was an act of existential choice. He left no explanation of his decision to the authorities. In later years he pretended that he had been expelled for carrying out 'Marxist propaganda';[33] but the reality was that he had left of his own accord. His was a wilful spirit. He had lost his religious faith and was beginning to discover a different way of interpreting the world in Marxism. He was also impulsive. Joseph Dzhughashvili had had enough: he left the priestly environment on his own terms. Always he wanted the world to function to his wishes. If he left a mess behind him, too bad. He had made his decision.

He abhorred the Imperial authorities. He had national pride. In Tbilisi he responded to the intellectual effervescence of Georgian public life at the end of the nineteenth century. He already considered himself a man of outstanding ability. He had already shown his ambition by getting his poems published.

The contours of Joseph's later personality were already disclosing themselves. He was dedicated to self-improvement through daily study. His capacity for hard work, whenever he thought such work was useful, was immense. The Imperial order had given him a usefully wide education, albeit an education underpinned by Christian liturgy and tsarist loyalism. He was literate and numerate; he had a pleasing style in poetry. In his spare time he had started to acquaint himself with broader ideas about society and to study Marxist texts. He also read Russian and European classic novels. He was obviously capable of going on to university and had an acute analytical mind. His problem was what to do with his life. Having abandoned Christianity, he had no career ahead of him; and his family lacked the resources and desire to enable him to enter an alternative profession. For the next few years he was to expend much energy trying to decide the fundamental question for rebels in the Russian Empire: what is to be done? Another question also exercised his mind: with whom to do it? Young Dzhughashvili, fresh out of the Tiflis Spiritual Seminary, had yet to formulate his answers.

5. MARXIST MILITANT

Leaving the Seminary, Joseph Dzhughashvili had to find paid employment without delay. Gori held no attraction. Only Tbilisi offered serious opportunities and Joseph anyway wanted to combine work with revolutionary activity. For a while he eked out a living by giving private lessons;[1] but on 28 December 1899 his friends helped to get him a job at the Physical Observatory in Mikhailovski Street. He worked there for three months. It was his only period of sustained employment until after the October Revolution. Joseph bought the Russian translation of Sir Norman Lockyer's *Astronomy*, first published in 1874, for reference.[2] His daily duties required him to record the temperature and weather four times. The only technical necessity was to read the magnetic tape, which he needed to sign each day before consigning it to the Observatory files.[3]

He had been sleeping at the Observatory off and on since October when Vano Ketskhoveli – his school friend in Gori – started work there. By the end of the year M. Davitashvili, yet another Gori school friend and former seminarist, had joined them in the same single room.[4] The cramped conditions were alleviated by the fact that Davitashvili often stayed with relatives in the city. Then in January 1900 Joseph and Vano were given a two-room flat on the ground floor overlooking the pleasant garden at the back of the building. Soon they had welcomed ex-seminarist V. Berdzenishvili as fellow tenant.[5] All were hostile to the Imperial order and wanted revolutionary change. The flat became a meeting place for other dissenters. Mikhailovski Street was the busiest left-bank thoroughfare in Tbilisi so that friends could come and go without attracting suspicion. Among those who made contact was Vano Ketskhoveli's elder brother Lado (who had been expelled from the Seminary in 1893).[6] Joseph and Lado hit it off despite the difference in years. Both were strong-willed and ambitious. They were practical organisers in the making. It was a matter of time before they would want to move beyond their discussions in the Physical Observatory.

Having repudiated the Seminary and its regulatory code, Joseph wanted to look the part of a tough, unsentimental revolutionary. His father had worked in a factory. So, too, had Joseph briefly: he needed no one to teach him the mores of the working class in the Russian Empire. Joseph refused to wear the typical three-piece suit of the Marxist theoretician:[7]

> [He] wore a plain black Russian shirt with a red cravat typical of all social-democrats. In winter he also put on a long brown overcoat. For headgear he wore only a Russian cap . . . One did not see him except in a rumpled shirt and unpolished shoes. Altogether he aimed to show that his mind was not a bourgeois one.

His slovenliness signalled a deliberate rejection of 'middle-class' values. Yet at the same time there was a complication. The cut of his shirt was Russian but the fact that it was black marked him out as a Georgian. The national ambiguity reflected a will to live on his own terms. He wanted to appear 'proletarian' while also being taken for an 'intellectual'. To workers he was a teacher and an organiser; to educated comrades he was an organiser and a potential pupil.

Groups of Marxists in Tbilisi scrabbled around to obtain the political texts they needed. Works by Marx, Engels, Lassalle and Dickstein as well as Georgi Plekhanov and Alexander Bogdanov were carefully studied in the 1890s.[8] Works on earlier generations of Russian revolutionaries, on the Paris Commune of 1871 and on the French Revolution were also examined.[9] Among the Marxist groups was one led by Lev Rozenfeld and Suren Spandaryan. Rozenfeld was to become better known under his pseudonym Kamenev. Kamenev and Spandaryan would later become comrades of Dzhughashvili. Kamenev had been a pupil at the First Classical Gimnazia. His father was a leading engineer and entrepreneur who helped to construct the oil pipeline from Baku to Batumi. Confidently he gave talks on Marxist theory. Dzhughashvili attended one of them at the suggestion of his Gori friend Davrishevi and was impressed.[10] It was a situation of historical irony: Kamenev, who played a part in attracting him to Marxism, was to be shot by Stalin's political police (known at that time as the NKVD) in 1936. At any rate these ex-students of the Seminary and the Classical Gimnazia felt there was a world to be explored. Workers were at its analytical core but were not yet a fulcrum of Marxist activity.

Although he was tied to the Observatory premises for long hours each day, Joseph's tasks were hardly onerous; he could read what he wanted while he was on duty. It was a welcome change from the

Seminary. He used his leisure productively. Among the recently published books he acquired was Alexander Bogdanov's *Short Course in
Economic Science*. Not all the works in his growing library were Marxist.
Joseph also bought *General Philosophy of the Soul* by the mid-nineteenth-
century exiled Russian aristocrat Alexander Herzen. Nor did he give up
his interest in Georgian, Russian and European literature. But Marxism
was at the centre of his plans for his future. He always did things with a
definite purpose. In this case the purpose was clear. Joseph planned to
revive his writing career with contributions to Marxist discussions in
Georgia.

The best among the possibilities for him at the turn of the century
was the newspaper *Kvali*, which had been handed over to a surprised
Noe Zhordania in 1898 (and which had published some of Dzhughashvili's poems before he abandoned literary ambition). *Kvali* made an
impact on the Georgian intelligentsia with its critical analysis of social
and economic conditions. The Caucasian office of the Imperial censorship took a gentle approach to *Kvali*, and Zhordania directly upbraided
the chief censor when he objected to a particular issue of the newspaper.[11] Yet it was Joseph Iremashvili, who like Dzhughashvili had
declined to complete his priest's training, who first offered an article to
Kvali. Dzhughashvili congratulated his friend on his piece on the agrarian
question.[12] Meanwhile Iremashvili noted how hard Dzhughashvili was
studying. On the table in the Observatory flat lay a pile of works by
Plekhanov and Lenin (whose real name was Vladimir Ilich Ulyanov) –
already Dzhughashvili was Lenin's admirer.[13] Dzhughashvili was not yet
ready with something to say. He had become cautious. Instead he threw
himself into propaganda activity among the workers of Tbilisi. This was
the norm for Marxist intellectuals. While educating themselves through
the works of Marx and Engels, they popularised Marxist ideas among
railwaymen, shoemakers and textile-factory labourers. Dzhughashvili was
given two workers' circles to lead.[14]

Joseph's progress was disturbed on the night of 21–22 March 1901.
The police raided several homes inhabited by Marxists, and the Observatory was on their list. Joseph had been under surveillance virtually
since starting work there.[15] Several of his friends across the city were
arrested but he was untouched. It was not the last time that he was lucky
(which later gave rise to the suspicion that he was an agent of the
Imperial political police, the Okhrana).[16] But obviously he could not
return to the Observatory without the risk of being detained. He opted
for an existence on the run. His mind was made up. He lived for

revolution and knew that this would bring frequent uncomfortable episodes along with it. Prison and exile were eventually inevitable. For the next few weeks he moved from house to house of political associates.

The Georgian Marxists took their nation's development seriously. But Georgia posed problems. Most Georgians did not think of themselves first and foremost as Georgians. They saw themselves as belonging to one or other of the large ethnic groups in Georgia and some of them, especially the Mingrelians, spoke their own different language. But Georgian Marxists believed that encouragement of a national consciousness would enhance political development and, ultimately, the dissemination of socialist ideas. Another difficulty was geopolitical. The Marxists could see that Georgia's independence would put the country at the mercy of the Ottoman Empire. Marxism in any case taught them to see salvation not by means of secession from Russia but through the advancement of the working classes in all countries. All of them wanted Marxism to become a united force regardless of national backgrounds across the entire Caucasus. Georgians, Armenians and Azeris should be encouraged to struggle together against the Romanov monarchy and its political and social order. The Marxists of the Caucasus should also adhere to the Russian Social-Democratic Workers' Party, founded in 1898, which covered the entire Russian Empire.

Marxism had been growing in influence among dissenting intellectuals and workers from the mid-1880s. They were inspired by ideas developed by the political émigré Georgi Plekhanov, who suggested that capitalism was developing fast across the empire and that the working class was the group in society best able to bring about an end to the Romanov monarchy and to initiate changes which eventually would lead to the achievement of socialism. Other socialists stuck to an earlier Russian tradition which Plekhanov had abandoned. These were revolutionaries who looked mainly to the peasantry to bring down the oppressive order of state and society. Such revolutionaries, guided by Viktor Chernov, were to form the Party of Socialist-Revolutionaries in 1901. Chernov shared ideas with Marxists but claimed that the social structure of the Russian Empire had not yet changed as much as Plekhanov asserted; he also saw the industrial workers as being little different, socially and culturally, from the peasantry. Also active in the Russian Empire were liberal political groups. Initially they were headed by Pëtr Struve, who had started public life as a Marxist. In 1905 they were to establish the Constitutional-Democratic Party. The

Constitutional-Democrats (or Kadets) advocated liberal democracy and capitalism as the solution to the problems of the country.

The Marxists, though, dominated public debate in Georgia. They triumphed over the liberals and conservatives who already existed there. Socialist-Revolutionaries acquired no following in the south Caucasus. The main rivals to Marxism were the Social-Federalists, who were Georgian socialists with a strongly nationalist orientation which demanded the transformation of the Russian Empire into a federal state with Georgia as one of its constituent subjects. But the Social-Federalists failed to win over the majority of dissenting opinion. Noe Zhordania's was the dominant voice among Georgia's Marxists. He had a strong personality, moral force and flair with the pen.[17] Marxism in Georgia was largely the product of his ideas and activity. Zhordania, too, understood that independence for the Georgians would expose them to invasion by the Ottoman Empire. He was not invulnerable to challenge to his authority. Pilipe Makharadze, Mikha Tskhakaya and other Marxists thought him too soft on Georgian liberals. But Zhordania saw Georgia's Marxists as the leaders of a national movement against the political and economic system of tsarism. To this end he co-operated with all trends of anti-Romanov opinion in Georgia. It was this that had induced the liberal Giorgi Tsereteli to transfer possession of *Kvali* to him.

Dzhughashvili's friend Lado Ketskhoveli agreed with Zhordania's critics and was keen to counteract the trend by practical action. Ketskhoveli argued for the establishment of a clandestine newspaper. Although *Kvali* had its uses, it could not propagate a full revolutionary message for fear of the Imperial censorship.[18] Ketskhoveli and Dzhughashvili generally advocated tighter forms of 'underground' organisation than Zhordania approved. Whereas Zhordania hoped to broaden the opportunity for ordinary workers to join the Marxists and contribute actively to party life, his younger critics thought it risky to let authority slip from the hands of experienced organisers such as themselves. This dispute affected the whole Russian Social-Democratic Workers' Party at the turn of the century. The beginnings of the split which occurred in 1903 between Bolsheviks and Mensheviks were already detectable. Agreement existed that the techniques of clandestine party activity had to be respected. Beyond this point there were the symptoms of a split which became a gaping wound in Georgian Marxism in the years ahead.

Lado Ketskhoveli shrugged off Zhordania's control by setting up an illegal Marxist newspaper, *Brdzola* ('Struggle'), in Baku on the Caspian coast. Zhordania had obstructed any such venture in Georgia for fear of jeopardising the publication of *Kvali*. For Ketskhoveli, Zhordania's reaction was a further indication that the Tbilisi Marxist leadership was making too many compromises. Baku's population included Russians, Armenians and Georgians as well as an Azeri majority. He quickly found a press in Baku[19] and by forging documents purporting to come from the governor of Yelizavetgrad he was able to get the owners to go ahead with the printing.[20] Cunning and strong-minded, he set up the kind of Georgian-language newspaper he wanted. Copies were sent to Marxist groups throughout the Caucasus. Later in life Dzhughashvili pretended that he had co-founded *Brdzola*. In reality it was exclusively Ketskhoveli's work. Dzhughashvili also overstated the degree of antagonism between the two of them and Zhordania. Tensions certainly existed and were increasing; but co-operation persisted, and Ketskhoveli eventually turned to Zhordania to write the editorial for one of *Brdzola*'s issues.[21]

Meanwhile Dzhughashvili was making a nuisance of himself in the Georgian capital. The Tiflis Committee of the Russian Social-Democratic Workers' Party was riddled with political and personal disputes. (Georgia's Marxists, never aspiring to secession from the Russian Empire, referred to their capital by the Russian name Tiflis.) But Dzhughashvili made everything worse. One memoir, without directly naming him, identifies a 'young, muddled comrade from the intelligentsia, "energetic" in all matters'. According to this account, the individual, 'invoking conspiratorial considerations as well as the unpreparedness and lack of [political] consciousness among workers, came out against admitting workers to the committee'.[22] The Marxists of Tbilisi took this to be an unpleasant opinion unpleasantly delivered – and the context makes it virtually certain that Dzhughashvili was the comrade in question. Another contemporary, Grigol Uratadze, wrote more directly that Dzhughashvili was arraigned before his comrades and found guilty as a 'slanderer'.[23]

In November 1901, after being withdrawn from propaganda work in Tbilisi by the City Committee, Dzhughashvili left for Batumi on the Black Sea coast seeking to spread his ideas in a more receptive milieu. But many Marxists in Batumi did not take to him. Dzhughashvili kept ranting about the sins of commission and omission of the Tiflis Committee. This was bad enough. But the comrades in Batumi could not stand his 'personal capriciousness and his tendency to despotic behaviour'.[24] What is notable here is that objections were made less to policy

than to attitude and comportment. Nastiness to acquaintances had been
his hallmark since he had been a youngster. Ambition too had been a
characteristic. But he wanted to rise to revolutionary eminence on his
own terms; and whenever others baulked him, he told them they were
wrong and stupid. He was a clever young man who thought he had the
answers to the difficulties experienced by Marxist propagandists in the
south Caucasus. Stressing the need for clandestine activity, illegal propaganda and control over the workers, Dzhughashvili was a Bolshevik in
waiting.

He was not ineffective in Batumi. He worked with fellow Marxists
and pipeline and port workers to stir up revolt against the employers.
Contact was made with likely recruits to the party. The Rothschild and
Mantashëv enterprises were his favourite spots. At the same time he kept
in contact with Ketskhoveli hundreds of miles east in Baku. Strikes broke
out in Batumi and Dzhughashvili and his group were involved. He
was doing what his ideology and policies induced him to do. He was
involved, too, in the organisation of a protest demonstration by workers
on 8 March 1902. They were demanding the release of strike leaders
imprisoned a few days earlier. The demonstration had fatal consequences. The town authorities panicked at the sight of six thousand
angry marching workers and troops fired on them. Fifteen demonstrators
were killed. A massive Okhrana investigation followed. There were
hundreds of arrests. Police spies had penetrated the Batumi Marxist
organisation and it was only a matter of time before Dzhughashvili's
whereabouts were discovered. He was taken into custody on 5 April and
detained in Batumi Prison.

One resident, Hashim Smyrba, regretted Dzhughashvili's departure.
Dzhughashvili had stayed for a while in hiding with him. Hashim, a
peasant who was probably an Abkhazian, took to him and expressed
regret that he wasn't a Moslem: 'Because if you adopted the Moslem
faith, I'd find you seven beautiful women to marry.'[25] The scene was
recounted to indicate that Dzhughashvili had always had the common
touch. But Smyrba was an elderly peasant outside the revolutionary
movement. The fact that few workers testified on Dzhughashvili's behalf
decades after his stay in Batumi was surely significant. He kept himself
to himself. He was self-sufficient and did not want to rely on others
when he did not need to. Already he was something of a loner.

Dzhughashvili in any case no longer depended on the goodwill of
comrades in Batumi or Tbilisi. He kept in close contact with his friend
Ketskhoveli in Baku. His article on 'The Russian Social-Democratic

Party and its Immediate Tasks', covering many political and organisational questions of the day, was the main item in the second issue of *Brdzola*.[26] Ketskhoveli did not mind. Although he remained chief editor he recognised that he was better at organising than at writing or editing. They made a dynamic pair. *Brdzola* became a publishing success in the clandestine Marxist movement across the south Caucasus. According to Stalin's own account, he became drawn to the writer's life and seriously contemplated abandoning clandestine political activity and entering university – and not just as a student but as a professor.[27] (He never explained who would have paid his way for him.) Another aspect of his early literary career continued to exercise him in old age. This was the 'peaceful' content of several of his writings. Even in *Brdzola*, unworried about the censor's office, he had avoided a direct summons to revolution.

Reportedly Ketskhoveli swore at him for being too moderate; but Dzhughashvili was to claim that until the shooting of workers in Batumi in March 1902 he had been justified in his measured tone. All then changed: 'The tone was altered.' Never again did Dzhughashvili hold back in contest with the opponents of Marxism in Georgia or the Russian Empire as a whole.[28] Ketskhoveli and Dzhughashvili were discovering for themselves that their basic inclinations were not peculiar to them or to Georgia. In December 1900 some Russian émigré Marxists, on the initiative of Lenin, had founded *Iskra* ('The Spark') in Munich. Its supporters advocated clandestine political activity as the key to future impact. One of *Iskra*'s contacts in the south Caucasus was Lev Galperin, who worked for *Brdzola*. Material started to arrive from Germany at Batumi in 1901–2.[29] *Iskra* was campaigning for control over the Russian Social-Democratic Workers' Party. Its ideas were more developed than those of Ketskhoveli. Lenin and his comrades wanted no compromise with the middle class. They urged the formation of militant, tightly organised groups. They stood for centralisation, discipline and doctrinal orthodoxy. *Brdzola*, however, was wrecked by the Okhrana even before Dzhughashvili's arrest: on 14 March 1902 the entire editorial and supporting group except for Abel Enukidze and Bogdan Knunyants were taken into custody in Baku.[30]

While the *Brdzola* group languished in the gaols of Batumi and Baku, Noe Zhordania continued to elaborate the strategy and tactics of Georgian Marxism. Both Zhordania and Lenin felt that the founding parents of Marxism in the Russian Empire – Georgi Plekhanov, Pavel Axelrod and Vera Zasulich – had failed to discern the advantages of appealing to the peasantry. Lenin was out to attract peasant sympathy by offering to restore the strips of land lost to the gentry landlords through the Emancipation Edict of 1861. Many Russian Marxists thought the proposal too indulgent to the peasantry; they preferred the orthodox emphasis on campaigning among the working class. But Zhordania criticised Lenin for insufficient audacity. Instead he urged that all agricultural lands should pass into the hands of peasants. Dynastic, ecclesiastical and noble estates should be expropriated. Most Georgian workers had ties with the countryside. Georgia was a predominantly agrarian society. Not only that: Zhordania urged Georgian Marxists to go out among the peasants and recruit them to the ranks of organised Marxism.[31] Very quickly his comrades answered his call. The campaign paid off. Nowhere else in the Russian Empire were peasants so ready to hearken to Marxists. Marxists could boast of their hegemony over the Georgian political opposition to the Romanov monarchy.

Dzhughashvili did not approve of Zhordania's strategy. He agreed that the peasants should be promised the transfer of all agricultural lands and that Lenin's proposal was too timid. But he disliked the idea of diverting so much propaganda and organisation to the peasants. He insisted on the need to operate among the 'workers'. He also made a point of the need for Marxists to report on and explain the vicissitudes of the labour movement outside the Russian Empire, especially in central and western Europe.[32]

About a further point of dissent with Zhordania, however, he was always to show extraordinary reticence. Dzhughashvili was still far from abandoning all his Georgian patriotism. He wished a distinct Marxist party to be formed in Georgia. Whereas Zhordania aimed for a regional organisation covering the entire Caucasus regardless of its ancient national and ethnic boundaries, Dzhughashvili demanded a Georgian territorial demarcation in the party.[33] The difference between Zhordania and Dzhughashvili was large; it was even larger between Dzhughashvili and those other comrades such as Mikha Tskhakaya who were to become Bolsheviks. Tskhakaya agreed that the books, pamphlets and newspapers had to be written in the Georgian language – otherwise no Georgian workers would get acquainted with Marxism – but like other radical Marxists, he felt that Zhordania's preoccupation with Georgia's national and cultural development gave off a whiff of nationalism. Dzhughashvili's idea for a territorially demarcated organisation in the south Caucasus seemed equally malodorous to radicals who espoused Marxism because it offered a path to modernity and away from nation-alist strife.

Such an idea in fact had echoes more widely in the Russian Social-Democratic Workers' Party. The Jewish Bund – the Marxist organisation based in the western borderlands of the Russian Empire and dedicated exclusively to work among Jews – was criticized by the *Iskra* group for demanding territorial autonomy inside the party despite the fact that other ethnic groups lived in the same region. (Marxists in the south Caucasus avoided such requests on behalf of a single national or ethnic group.) This request was discussed at the Second Party Congress in August 1903. When *Iskra*'s representatives opposed any such national-territorial principle for organisation, the Bundists walked out. Wilful and independently minded, Dzhughashvili was risking being classified as a Marxist who could not accept the Russian Social-Democratic Party's commitment to internationalism.

Dzhughashvili, though, was undeterred. He had begun to make a mark for himself. Having moved involuntarily from Tbilisi, he did not gain a reputation as a congenial comrade; but this did not prevent him from imposing himself. In Batumi he found a set of workers ripe for being influenced by his summons to revolutionary activity; and he helped to organise the strikes and demonstrations against the monarchy. From Batumi he kept in touch with Baku, and Dzhughashvili was developing his skills in Marxist propaganda. Detention in Batumi Prison cut short his literary career, but he went on discussing his controversial strategic inclinations and giving papers on them.[34] He was held there for a year before being transferred to Kutaisi. Transferred back to Batumi, he was finally – in autumn 1903 – dispatched to the southern part of mid-Siberia. The destination was Novaya Uda in Irkutsk Province, where he arrived on 27 November. He escaped in early 1904 and made for Tbilisi. (This required two attempts. On the first occasion he foolishly failed to kit himself out with warm clothing for the Siberian winter and he was recaptured with badly frozen ears and face.)[35] The second attempt succeeded. From Tbilisi he travelled the length and breadth of the south Caucasus.

Grigol Uratadze, fellow prisoner in Kutaisi Prison, left a helpful memoir of Dzhughashvili in these years. He wrote long after Dzhughashvili had become Stalin and dictator of the USSR; and the two men were long-standing political opponents. Nevertheless the memoir has some credibility since Uratadze made no pretence that Dzhughashvili already seemed a potential dictator. Uratadze started by saying: 'As an individual Stalin had no special distinguishing features.' But then he contradicted himself:[36]

He was a very dry person; one might even say that he was desiccated. For example, when we were let outside for exercise and all of us in our particular groups made for this or that corner of the prison yard, Stalin stayed by himself and walked backwards and forwards with his short paces, and if anyone tried speaking to him, he would open his mouth into that cold smile of his and perhaps say a few words. And this unsociability attracted general attention.

This was extraordinary behaviour for a prisoner with only a limited opportunity to talk to others. He had arrived in Kutaisi Prison as the sole 'intellectual' in the group of prisoners transferred from Batumi.[37] Yet he neither helped to keep up their morale nor sought out contact with intellectuals from his own party.[38]

Kutaisi Prison was nostalgically remembered as a 'university' for its inmates.[39] Marxist prisoners read books and discussed ideas. Dzhughash-vili, however, kept to himself. His strangeness impressed Uratadze:[40]

He was scruffy and his pockmarked face made him not particularly neat in appearance . . . In prison he wore a beard and had long hair brushed back. He had a creeping way of walking, taking short steps. He never opened his mouth to laugh but only at most to smile. And the size of the smile depended on the volume of emotion evoked in him by a specific event; but his smile never turned into a full-mouthed laugh. He was completely imperturbable. We lived together in Kutaisi Prison for more than half a year and not once did I see him get agitated, lose control, get angry, shout swear or – in short – reveal himself in any other aspect than complete calm-ness. And his voice exactly corresponded to the 'glacial character' which those who knew him well attributed to him.

If this were to be the only such testimony about him, it would be easily dismissed. But it fits with everything said about his personality before and after his period of confinement.

Escaping at last from Novaya Uda, he returned to his Bolshevik comrades in a mood to impose his vision.[41] In his absence there had been fundamental changes in the Russian Social-Democratic Workers' Party and Lenin, for a while, emerged the victor. At the Second Party Congress, which was held in Brussels and London from July to August 1903, Lenin's *Iskra* group had trounced the other trends. But at the moment of their triumph the Iskraists fell apart. Lenin's supporters advocated a particularly exigent set of conditions for party membership.

His erstwhile associate Yuli Martov, who had helped him to drive out the Bund, found himself in a minority. Martov agreed on the need for clandestinity, centralism, discipline and ideological unity. But, like Zhordania in Georgia, he frowned on policies designed to restrict the number of party members. It was Martov's belief that Lenin had gone over to an authoritarian and counter-productive organisational campaign. They and their supporters voted against each other. Lenin won and called his followers the Majoritarians (bol'sheviki or Bolsheviks), and Martov in a fit of self-abnegation allowed his men and women to be known as the Minoritarians (men'sheviki or Mensheviks).

Detailed news of the dénouement at the Second Party Congress took time to filter back to Georgia. The split between the Bolsheviks and Mensheviks among the exiles was not reproduced in Tbilisi. The same was true in most Russian cities. But two general trends nevertheless emerged across the Russian Empire, and Georgia was no exception. Misha Tskhakaya was among the first to declare himself a Bolshevik. Dzhughashvili too sided with Lenin. But having fled from Novaya Uda, he was not met warmly in Tbilisi. The reason was his oft-repeated call for an autonomous Georgian party. A vigorous rebuke was prepared for him and he faced the threat of being drummed out of the Bolshevik faction before it was properly formed. He was given a choice: if he wanted to stay with the Bolsheviks, he had to write out a statement of his beliefs to be vetted by leading comrades for orthodoxy.[42] This was a humiliating experience for a man as proud as Dzhughashvili. But he was realistic. He had to prove himself a disciplined, orthodox Bolshevik. If he wanted to regain acceptance, he had to recant, to engage in what later, when he ruled the USSR, became known as self-criticism. Seventy copies of his 'Credo' were produced and sent to other radical Marxists in Georgia. The 'Credo' definitively repudiated the campaign for Georgian Marxists to have their own autonomous party – and his recantation was a success: he survived the expected censure.

In the 1920s he was to send emissaries to the Caucasus to trace the copies made of the 'Credo' he had written in 1904.[43] Almost certainly he had them all destroyed. (In the preface to the first volume of his collected works, writing in 1946, the editors claimed that every single copy had been lost.)[44] But the unpublished memoirs of Sergei Kavtaradze, who was a Tbilisi Bolshevik and was associated with Stalin after the October Revolution, broadly indicate what had been in Dzhughashvili's 'Credo'.[45] After he had recanted, a cloud of suspicion still swirled around his head. Even his promise to avoid repeating his mistakes failed to quieten criticism. He was called a 'Georgian Bundist'[46] (which was a peculiar appellation for a person whom many subsequently branded as an anti-semite). Tskhakaya went the rounds of the radical Marxists and pleaded on Dzhughashvili's behalf.[47] He survived and went on to flourish in the Bolshevik faction. He was energetic, determined and ambitious. He was quirky: he did not accept ideas just on the say-so of others; he changed his policies only when extreme pressure was put upon him. He was cantankerous and conspiratorial. He retained a strong feeling that the national sensitivities of the Georgians and other peoples should be respected. He had started out in Lado Ketskhoveli's shadow but had begun to distinguish himself by his own opinions and activity. No one among Georgian Marxists doubted his talent.

Events in the Russian Empire were about to test his revolutionary mettle. Peasants since the turn of the century had been buffeted by adverse commercial conditions; they also continued to resent the amount of land held by the gentry. Workers demanded higher wages. Among the intelligentsia there was frustration about the refusal of the Emperor and his government to reform the political system. Several non-Russian nationalities – especially the Poles, Finns and Georgians – chafed against their treatment by St Petersburg. Rural unrest was growing. Industrial strikes rose in frequency and intensity. Clandestine political parties and trade unions were being formed. It was in this situation, in 1904, that Nicholas II decided to go to war with Japan. One of his calculations was that a short, victorious war would revive the prestige of the Romanov monarchy. It was a foolish mistake. All too quickly the Russian armed forces found that the Japanese, who had built up their military and industrial capacity in recent years, were more than a match for them.

6. THE PARTY AND THE CAUCASUS

The Imperial monarchy confronted an emergency situation by early 1905. On 9 January there had been a political demonstration in St Petersburg. Its purpose was to present the Emperor with a petition for the granting of general civic rights. The result was a massacre when the security forces were ordered to fire on the demonstrators. Scores of people were killed. Nicholas II was not to blame for the carnage, but across the country he was held responsible. Police and army stood by helplessly as protest meetings were held. Strikes broke out. Poland and Georgia were focal points of unrest. Peasants moved to assert themselves against the landed gentry. The monarch and his ministers, already discredited by the defeats in the unfinished war with Japan, suddenly looked vulnerable. Workers elected their own councils (or 'soviets'). The armed forces along the Trans-Siberian Railway were in mutinous mood. The efforts of the Okhrana were futile: political parties operated with decreasing fear of arrest, and although their contact with most people had been frail in previous years, they quickly attained popular confidence. This was a trial of strength with the Romanov regime unprecedented since the Pugachëv revolt of 1773–5.

For the Russian Social-Democratic Workers' Party the surprise was as great as it was for every other political group. Lenin in Switzerland was taken aback; so too were his followers in St Petersburg and the rest of the Russian Empire. Yet most émigrés were cautious about returning until after Nicholas II issued his October Manifesto promising reforms. In the meantime the revolutionary militants were left to their own devices. The Bolsheviks held a self-styled Third Party Congress in London in April 1905 and fixed their general strategy. They aimed at armed uprising and the formation of a provisional revolutionary dictatorship. They aspired to the total expropriation of land belonging to the monarchy, Church and gentry.

Dzhughashvili was not among the Georgian participants: he had not yet allayed the doubts about him among Bolsheviks. It was his friend and senior comrade Mikha Tskhakaya who headed the country's group, and Tskhakaya did not fail to criticise the growing cult of Lenin in the Bolshevik faction. There was a practical aspect to this. Many Congress delegates, objecting to Lenin's reluctance to shift the Central Committee's base to Russia, thought the émigrés had become too comfortable abroad; and they succeeded in getting a commitment to such a transfer. Dzhughashvili, back in Georgia, was among those who argued that, if revolution was to succeed, maximum resources had to be concentrated in the Russian Empire. He had been coming back into his own before the revolutionary outbreaks. He travelled to Baku and Kutaisi before basing himself in Tbilisi. He published articles in the recently founded *Proletarians Brdzola* ('Proletarian Struggle'), including one on the national question which stayed within official Bolshevik lines. He wrote to the Bolsheviks in emigration. When strikes and demonstrations were held after Bloody Sunday on 9 January 1905, he threw himself into a frenzy of writing and organising – and he was a leader of the Bolshevik Tiflis Committee whose policy of armed uprising separated them definitively from the city's Mensheviks. Sometimes this involved him in open disputations about the respective merits of Bolshevism and Menshevism; on other occasions he put the general Marxist case against the party's local rivals: the Anarchists, the Social-Federalists and the Socialist-Revolutionaries. Everywhere he went in the Georgian capital he was in the thick of things.

For many of his comrades, though, he was still excessively willing to make compromises on the 'national question'. When he refused to help them in their dispute in the party's Caucasian Union Committee in line with local Bolshevik policy, Sergei Kavtaradze accused him of being a 'traitor'. But Dzhughashvili was unmoved. For him, Kavtaradze and others failed to separate matters of primary and secondary importance. 'I don't intend to have a dispute with the Union Committee over this ... But you do as you like.' With that he lit up a cheap cigarette and stared unblinkingly at Kavtaradze; he wanted his critics to know that he would not be pushed around again. Kavtaradze understood the gesture and never forgot it.[1] Dzhughashvili was a fellow who would fight battles only when there was a decent chance of winning them. Ideological rectitude was all very well. But practical results were also important, and unnecessary squabbles should be avoided. His difficulty lay in his inability to gather a group of followers around him. In his eyes, the Georgian Bolsheviks were too rigid in their Leninism whereas the Georgian Mensheviks had the wrong policies.

When revolution had come to the south Caucasus, it took the regional authorities as much by surprise as it did elsewhere. I. I. Vorontsov-Dashkov was sent as viceroy and found himself in an invidious situation. Strikes and demonstrations affected nearly all towns and industrial settlements. Resistance to the Imperial forces was widespread. The strongest revolutionary impetus came from Noe Zhordania and the Georgian Mensheviks, who put themselves forward as both Marxists and national defenders against Russian power. The villages of Guria in western Georgia were especially responsive to the appeal of Menshevism. But everywhere in the Caucasus there were national and ethnic stirrings. On both sides of the mountain chain previously suppressed leaders emerged to challenge Nicholas II and his government. Not everywhere was the conflict characterised by tensions with St Petersburg. Inter-ethnic tensions, long contained by Russian armed forces and the straitjacket of the growing capitalist economy, snapped the patience of society. In the north Caucasus, religious traditionalism came to the fore and violence between Islamists and their rivals grew in intensity. Around the great oil city of Baku the mutual hatred of Armenians and Azeris burst into terrible violence as the Moslem Azeris massacred the Christian Armenians despite the precautions taken by Vorontsov-Dashkov.[2]

The Armenians in Baku, as in Tbilisi, were led by persons of the greatest wealth, whereas Azeris were typically the poorest section of the labour force. Vorontsov did not underestimate the difficulties and decided to minimise the use of violence to secure the restoration of Imperial order in the south Caucasus.[3] Elsewhere in the Russian Empire in the last quarter of 1905 the armed forces were intensively at work. The workers' soviets were being vigorously suppressed and the armed uprising of the Moscow Soviet was ruthlessly put down. Peasant rebels were being rounded up. The rebel cities in 'Russian' Poland were brought to heel. Mutineers in army and navy were arrested and shot. Georgia revolted. Zhordania and his Mensheviks, as well as Bolsheviks such as Dzhughashvili, exulted. Their organisations swelled with recruits. They ceased to hide their activities and the Viceroy moved steadily to a combination of force and consultation. Georgian Marxists dominated the political scene. They did not aim at secession any more than the Bolsheviks. Georgia's fate in their estimation was tied up with revolutionary developments in Russia.

But Dzhughashvili had made his choice: the Bolshevik strategy seemed the most commendable to him. What struck his acquaintances about him was his extraordinary polemical crudity. He had little in the way of wit. His speeches, such as he gave, were dry and aggressive. He aligned himself strongly with Bolshevism and deeply detested the Mensheviks he encountered. 'Against them,' he declared, 'any methods are good!'[4] He distinguished himself in his practical capacities; and, with the exception of Lev Trotski who led the Petersburg Soviet from autumn 1905, he had a much more influential role in the events of that turbulent year than any other member of the first Party Politburo formed after the October Revolution. Dzhughashvili debated frequently with the Georgian Mensheviks. He talked at workers' meetings. He was one of the most productive writers for *Proletarians Brdzola*. Always he urged Marxists to oppose outbreaks of inter-national violence. He vigorously promoted Bolshevik policies and called for the monarchy's overthrow by an uprising which would bring a provisional revolutionary government to power. Marxists should unite workers and peasants in a political alliance. Compromise with the middle class on the Menshevik model was to be rejected.

Yet the prospects for Bolshevism in the south Caucasus had never been bleaker. Dzhughashvili wrote dispiritedly to Lenin in May:[5]

> I'm overdue with my letter, comrade. There's been neither the time nor the will to write. For the whole period it's been necessary to travel around the Caucasus, speak in debates, encourage comrades, etc. Everywhere the Mensheviks have been on the offensive and we've needed to repulse them. We've hardly had any personnel (and now there are very few of them, two or three times fewer than the Mensheviks have), and so I've needed to do the work of three individuals . . . Our situation is as follows. Tiflis is almost completely in the hands of the Mensheviks. Half of Baku and Batumi is also with the Mensheviks . . . Guria is in the hands of the Conciliators, who have decided to go over to the Mensheviks.

Evidently he thought the comrade in Geneva ought to know the bitter truth about the factional balance among Marxists in the south Caucasus.

Throughout the year Menshevism under Zhordania's aegis thrust itself forward as the leading agency of Georgia's rebellion against the Imperial monarchy. Bolshevism was in a small minority among the Georgian revolutionaries. Thus Dzhughashvili had chosen a factional allegiance which seemed to doom him to obscurity. The peasantry across Georgia followed the Mensheviks; and although he continued to argue that their strategy diverted attention from propaganda and organisation among the working class, he was a voice crying in the wilderness. He must have blamed Bolshevism's weakness in Georgia to some extent on its failure – despite his advice in 1904 – to present the faction as a champion of national interests. He himself, however, was not infinitely flexible. He too wished to focus revolutionary activity on the towns, the workers and Marxist orthodoxy. Bolshevism did best in the south Caucasus where industry was well developed. This was the case in Baku. But Dzhughashvili did not despair: he had taken a deliberate decision that the basic strategy of the Bolsheviks was correct and that sooner or later it would triumph. For the rest of the year he predicted the imminence of the Romanov monarchy's overthrow. Like all Bolsheviks, he declared that violent uprising and a revolutionary dictatorship were essential for this end.

Nicholas II started to panic in October 1905. Workers had formed their own councils (or 'soviets') which began by organising strikes and came to supplant the official bodies of self-government. Peasants moved against the landed gentry by illegal pasturing of livestock and stealing wood from forests. In Poland and Georgia the authorities were coming close to losing control. On advice from Count Witte, Nicholas II issued his 'October Manifesto' promising reform. In subsequent weeks it became clear that this would involve an elected parliament to be known as the State Duma as well as a Basic Law which would establish the framework that would define and constrain the powers of the Emperor, the government and the Duma. These concessions bought time and support for the monarchy; and although the Bolsheviks proceeded to organise an insurrection in Moscow, the armed forces steadily reasserted authority across the empire.

Stalin's revolutionary impatience had not faded: he continued to argue for uncompromising adherence to the strategy of Bolshevism. Such was his growing success in Tbilisi that he was a natural choice as delegate to the factional conference held by the Bolsheviks in Tampere (Tammerfors) in Finland in mid-December 1905. It was there he met Lenin at last. According to his later account, he was taken aback by the unprepossessing appearance of the leader of Bolshevism. Dzhughashvili had been expecting a tall, self-regarding person. Instead he saw a man no bigger than himself and without the hauteur of the prominent émigré figures.[6] The Tampere Conference proved awkward for Lenin. Most Bolsheviks, including Dzhughashvili, rejected his preference for the faction to take part in the elections to the State Duma. They aimed at armed insurrection and the establishment of a 'revolutionary democratic dictatorship of the proletariat and the peasantry', and they saw no point in wasting energy on elections called on Nicholas II's terms. Lenin's demand for tactical finesse left them cold. Having become Bolsheviks because they liked Leninist radicalism, they were disappointed that their leader was already compromising with the institutions of the Imperial order. Lenin himself backed down rather than lose his following at the Conference.[7]

Dzhughashvili was infused with the current factional mood. He was still developing as a politician. His difficulties with fellow Georgian Bolsheviks in 1904 showed that he was not lacking in strategic flexibility (and he continued to suggest compromises in policy in the years ahead). But in 1905 he lived and breathed ideas of armed insurrection and revolutionary dictatorship. He genuinely thought that the Imperial monarchy could be replaced. He therefore refused to countenance a policy of settling for a political order prescribed by Nicholas II. In fact a growing number of Bolsheviks came to recognise their mistake in not following Lenin's advice. Lenin himself decided to put further pressure on his faction by agreeing to reunification with the Mensheviks at a Party Congress – he could not stand so many Bolsheviks purporting to be more 'Leninist' than himself. Such a move was also precipitated by the fact that the two factions, despite maintaining a separate existence in emigration, often co-operated in the Russian Empire.

The venue chosen for this Fourth Party Congress was Stockholm. Dzhughashvili was the only Bolshevik among sixteen delegates selected to represent Georgia. They made their way secretly via Moscow and St Petersburg to Helsinki. From there, disguised as teachers on an excursion, they took a steamer to the port of Åbo. At that point they split into smaller groups.[8] Dzhughashvili caught the steamship *Wellamo* and sailed to the Swedish capital. Arrangements had been made for him to stay at the Hotel Bristol with fellow Bolshevik Kliment Voroshilov. Bolshevik 'conspiratorial' schemes had been rumbled by the Stockholm police. Scores of alien-looking newcomers without obvious commercial or professional purposes were bound to attract attention. Dzhughashvili was apprehended and interrogated by Commissioner Mogren, a constable and an interpreter called Alexei. He gave his name as Ivan Ivanovich Vissarionovich and claimed he was a political refugee and a national democrat. He reassured the police that he was not being funded by Finns (which was a worry for the Swedish security agencies in those years). He also promised to report regularly to them during his stay. He indicated that he intended to go to Berlin before returning home. Dzhughashvili, like others, was released as a harmless visitor.[9]

He then enjoyed himself with the rest of the Bolshevik factional delegation. His modest expenses were covered by the party. This was the first period he spent outside the Russian Empire. The party had fraternal relations with the Swedish social-democrats and with their help had obtained the use of the People's House for the Congress proceedings. Little attempt was made to prevent the Okhrana from knowing about the event – and anyway the Okhrana had plenty of informers and received detailed reports on proceedings at the apex of the Russian Social-Democratic Workers' Party regardless of precautions taken by the revolutionaries. Each faction discussed its internal affairs. There were also negotiations among the factions. The atmosphere was convivial even though there was no time for delegates to see much of the city beyond their hotels and the People's House. For Dzhughashvili, though, this did not matter. He had read articles by the luminaries of the Russian Social-Democratic Workers' Party – Plekhanov, Axelrod, Lenin, Martov, Bogdanov and Maslov – over many years. (Alexander Bogdanov, a philosopher and organiser, had become almost as influential among Bolsheviks as Lenin himself.) Now Dzhughashvili saw them gathered together in a single large hall. The agreed task was to sort out the problems between the Bolsheviks and the Mensheviks as well as to settle a common set of policies, and Dzhughashvili was able to play his part.

While advocating reunification, Lenin did not disarm himself politically. He maintained a Bolshevik Centre separate from any party body involving the Mensheviks. He also continued to sanction armed robberies by Bolsheviks as a means of raising cash for political purposes. The Fourth Congress prohibited both these things. Lenin and his associates acceded in public while ignoring the ban in reality – and Dzhughashvili, as the main organiser of the Bolshevik campaign of robbery and extortion in Georgia, was an integral figure in this systematic deceit.

It was at the Fourth Congress that Dzhughashvili – using Ivanovich as his pseudonym – advanced his claim to be taken seriously by the ascendant party leaders. He was elected to the commission which checked the mandates of delegates. He also challenged the reliability of Georgian Menshevik reports on the situation in Georgia. This stirred controversy. His own speech, though, was questioned by Mensheviks and he was asked to justify himself. He shouted back: 'I'll give you my answer in my own time!'[10] He declared: 'It's no secret to anyone that two paths have been marked out in the development of Russia's socio-political life: the path of quasi-reforms and the path of revolution.' For Dzhughashvili, the Mensheviks had foolishly adopted ideas diverting them from a Marxist strategy:[11]

On the contrary, if the class interests of the proletariat lead to its hegemony and if the proletariat must go not at the tail but at the head of the current revolution, it is self-evident that the proletariat cannot hold back either from active participation in the organisation of armed insurrection or from a seizure of power. Such is the 'scheme' of the Bolsheviks.

With a zealot's confidence he freely attacked veterans of the Russian Marxist movement, including Plekhanov and Axelrod.[12]

He also participated robustly in the debate on the 'agrarian question', and his contributions were mentioned by other contributors.[13] The Menshevik specialist Pëtr Maslov had proposed campaigning for the 'municipalisation' of the land as a means of appealing to the peasantry. Such a scheme would transfer arable soil to the property of district councils. Lenin by contrast had expanded his ideas by suggesting land nationalisation; he wanted the central government to own the land. Both Maslov and Lenin desired to expropriate the landed gentry without compensation and to put all fields cheaply at the disposal of the peasantry. They aimed to stipulate the terms of this tenure. But most Bolsheviks, following a certain S. A. Suvorov, regarded Lenin's proposal as being as impractical as Maslov's. Among them was Dzhughashvili. Stepping up to the platform, he made a case for simply letting the peasants take over the land without restrictions. This would enable the alliance of working class and peasantry to become a reality, and Marxists would succeed in competing with the Socialist-Revolutionaries for rural popular support.[14] Suvorov and Dzhughashvili wanted the land to be declared 'the common property of the entire people'. The internal Bolshevik dispute, however, did not get out of hand because the Mensheviks held a majority at the Congress and land municipalisation became official party policy.

Yet again Dzhughashvili had spoken confidently for Bolshevism without automatically consenting to everything advocated by Lenin. He acknowledged him as his faction's leader. But his obedience was not blind: Dzhughashvili thought his direct daily experience of the Russian Empire kept him in closer touch with revolutionary possibilities than the émigrés.

There was anyway a reason outside politics for Dzhughashvili to feel cheery: he had found a woman he wanted to marry. He was in his late twenties and most of his friends were already in wedlock. The woman who caught his eye was Ketevan Svanidze. This was a sister of Alexander, a friend from the Spiritual Seminary. Alexander Svanidze, like Dzhug-hashvili, was a Bolshevik; Dzhughashvili would therefore be able to rely on her understanding of the demands of the life of a revolutionary. The courtship was a rapid one. Ketevan worked as a seamstress for the French dressmaker Mme Hervieu in Tbilisi's Sololaki district. Wanted by the police, Dzhughashvili needed to be careful about his assignations with her; but luckily for him Ketevan's employer was a kindly soul and let him meet his love in the back room of the shop. On one occasion, though, Mme Hervieu nearly regretted her indulgence when Lieutenant Pëtr Stroev strode into sight accompanied by two snarling German dogs bred for manhunts. She raced to warn him, and he escaped in the nick of time by the back entrance.[15] Ketevan had a fine figure and was a sympathetic and kindly woman; and she was content with a life of hearth and home: she had no ambition to become active in the revolutionary movement. What she saw in him is not known. No one in the Svanidze family, which became prominent in Soviet public life in the 1930s, mentioned the subject. Perhaps she thought him very dashing after the derring-do in the couturier's. At any rate he was physically slim and mentally intense and, as he showed in the years after her death, his appearance and personality had appeal for many women.

Ketevan and Joseph complied with religious propriety and on 16 July 1906 they took their marriage vows in a full Georgian Orthodox ceremony at the Zion Cathedral on the north bank of the Mtkvari. If the priest knew that several witnesses in the congregation were militant atheists (and failed seminarists), he kept quiet about it. After the wedding there was the conventional Georgian reception. Food and wine were plentiful, and the *tamada* (toastmaster) was the oldest Bolshevik in Georgia, Mikha Tskhakaya.[16] Dzhughashvili's expectations were conventional: Ketevan's function was to cook for him, clean and sweep their rooms and supply him with offspring – and it would seem that Ketevan was entirely content with the arrangement. This was in character for Dzhughashvili. It was never to his liking that relatives or friends might have an intellectual edge over him. A son was duly born to the couple on 18 March 1907. They named him Yakob.[17]

The role of husband did not tie him down and he remained busy writing and organising in Tbilisi. Among his written pieces was a lengthy series of articles on 'Anarchism or Socialism'.[18] Among the results of his organisational activity were the proceeds of crime, as Dzhughashvili, using Semën Ter-Petrosyan as Bolshevik robber-in-chief, presided over a series of armed thefts.[19] At the beginning of 1907, still based in the

Georgian capital, he helped to found the newspaper *Mnatobi* ('The Torch'). Like Lenin, he welcomed German Marxist theoretician Karl Kautsky's pamphlet on *The Driving Forces and Prospects of the Russian Revolution*, which inadvertently lent support to the Bolshevik case for a revolutionary alliance of workers and peasants; and Dzhughashvili wrote a preface for the Georgian edition. By then Dzhughashvili was Georgia's leading Bolshevik. Doubts about his doctrinal orthodoxy were a thing of the past. Both in Georgia and Finland, where the Bolshevik Centre continued to function, his merits were acknowledged by fellow members of the faction. However, the political fortunes of Bolshevism in his homeland were dispiriting; and when he heard that the Fifth Party Congress was to be held in April 1907 in London, he knew the Menshevik participants would challenge his right to represent Tbilisi Marxist groups. He had worked intensively for little practical reward except a rise in esteem among Bolsheviks.

Expecting a wrangle over his mandate as a delegate, Dzhughashvili travelled to London on the papers of 'Mr Ivanovich'. Since he was not yet a prominent party figure outside Georgia, the Congress organisers had no reason to lodge him near the leaders – Plekhanov, Axelrod, Lenin and Martov – in middle-class Bloomsbury. Instead he joined the mass of delegates in the East End. Jewish immigrant families from the Russian Empire lived there in their thousands at the turn of the century (and, like the Irish, were a substantial minority).[20] This was the best spot for delegates to avoid attention from the Special Branch. They could also get cheap lodgings and it would not much matter if they could speak no English.

He never spoke of his London impressions. Perhaps his visit was too fleeting and busy for him to form much of an opinion. He had been allocated a room at 77 Jubilee Street in Stepney. The Congress was held at the Brotherhood Church three miles to the north on the corner of Southgate Road and Balmes Road.[21] Thus the militant atheists in the Russian Empire debated the overthrow of the Romanovs in a place of Christian worship whose usual congregation consisted of pacifists and followers of the artist, writer and moderate socialist William Morris.[22] Returning to his room each night, he occupied himself with writing and planning. His landlord was a Russian-speaking cobbler, probably Jewish, who had fled the Russian Empire. A witness of his brief stay has left us his account. This was a lad called Arthur Bacon, who earned halfpennies in the district for running errands and carrying out little tasks. He often came to the cobbler's home to rake out the grate and fill it with coal and kindling, and Dzhughashvili used him to take messages to the various Bolshevik delegates staying in the vicinity. The cobbler's wife addressed the envelopes since Dzhughashvili's English did not stretch to writing out names.

Although young Bacon voted Conservative on growing up, he remembered Mr Ivanovich with affection. Dzhughashvili liked the toffees the boy brought with him. The boy had financial reason for gratitude: instead of the usual halfpenny, he received a two-bob piece for conveying a message to a comrade.[23] Since this was 4,700 per cent above the going rate, Dzhughashvili's financial acumen was not all it might have been.

Whereas he had made his mark at the Stockholm Congress by harrying the Menshevik leaders and distancing himself from Lenin's agrarian policy, he did little to distinguish himself in London. As expected, a dispute broke out over his mandate. In the end he was allowed to attend the Congress without a vote.[24] There were further procedural disputes. Three days were spent in arguing about the agenda. The situation was complicated by the inclusion of various organisations from the 'national' borderlands – the Poles, the Latvians, the Armenians and the Bundist Jews – in the proceedings. Consequently neither the Bolsheviks nor the Mensheviks held a firm majority and there was much discussion behind the scenes to secure agreement. Lenin offered Zhordania and the Georgian Mensheviks a deal whereby they could run party business in Georgia without interference in return for their not taking sides against the Bolsheviks in the Russian Social-Democratic Workers' Party as a whole. Zhordania refused.[25] If Dzhughashvili had heard of the proposal, he would scarcely have been pleased. Lenin's collusion with Zhordania would have ruined everything Dzhughashvili had fought for in the south Caucasus since becoming a Bolshevik. It would also have taught him that the region was not hugely important to Bolshevism's leadership. A clash between Lenin and Dzhughashvili would have been inevitable.

The Bolsheviks at the Congress anyway came under fire for maintaining their separate Centre, for carrying out armed robberies and for failing to share party funds with the Mensheviks. The Bolsheviks, though, were equally aggressive. Although they now thought it desirable to participate in Duma elections, they rejected the idea of co-operating with liberals in the chamber; they accused Mensheviks of selling out the revolutionary cause. The proceedings were intensely controversial. A Central Committee of fifteen members was formed. Five were Bolsheviks and there were four Mensheviks. The balance of power was held by the 'national' organisations in the party. A joint central newspaper, *Sotsial-demokrat*, was to be revived. But this fooled no one. The Russian Social-Democratic Workers' Party was a house divided against itself.

7. ON THE RUN

Joseph Dzhughashvili returned from the London Congress to a revolution which was on the retreat. His career over the next few years reflected the situation. He fixed Baku as his base and for several months organised, wrote and edited on the faction's behalf among the oilfield workers. It had become the opinion of leading Bolsheviks of the south Caucasus that Tbilisi, while being the administrative and cultural centre of the Caucasus, was inferior in the opportunities it offered for propaganda and organisation of the kind likely to advance the Bolshevik cause. He went there with Stepan Shaumyan.[1] He mocked the Mensheviks of Georgia for their preoccupation with the more backward inhabitants and economy of his homeland: his own political development was continuing.[2] But the Okhrana caught up with him. On 25 March 1908 he was arrested while operating under the alias of Gaioz Nizheradze and locked up in Bailov Prison on the outskirts of Baku.

Years of imprisonment, exile, escape and rearrest followed. On 9 November he was escorted to Vologda in the Russian north. This was a small provincial capital, famous only for its lacemaking, 370 miles to the east of St Petersburg. On arrival he was ordered to move over four hundred miles east to Solvychegodsk, an old town fifteen miles from the nearest railway on the River Vychegda. Arriving on 27 February 1909, he immediately plotted an escape. On 24 June he succeeded and, after staying for a few days in St Petersburg, returned to the south Caucasus and worked again as a clandestine Bolshevik organiser in Baku and Tbilisi. But he was not long at liberty. On 23 March 1910 he was seized by the police and confined in Bailov Prison. This time his pseudonym was Zakhar Melikhyants. It took six months before the authorities decided on his sentence (and in the meantime he managed to write a 'Letter from the Caucasus' which he got published in the party's central organ *Sotsial-demokrat* in Paris).[3] On 23 September he was sent back to Solvychegodsk. On 27 June 1911 he was allowed to move to Vologda.[4] On 6 September he made yet another escape disguised as a certain P. A.

Chizhikov. He arrived in St Petersburg, where he contacted his old friend from Tbilisi, Sergei Alliluev.[5] The Okhrana, however, had been informed. He was arrested on 9 September and, on 25 December, redispatched under guard to Vologda.

The Imperial authorities were crushing the revolutionary movement. Peasant rebels were subjected to courts martial and executed. Industrial strikes were suppressed. Mutinies in the Imperial Army and Navy were savagely put down. Where provinces remained restless, emergency powers were granted to governors and military commanders. Revolutionary agitation was ruthlessly quelled, and the main leaders of the socialist parties – the Russian Social-Democratic Workers' Party and the Party of Socialist-Revolutionaries – returned to Switzerland and other European countries to regroup their forces until the next great political crisis.

Nicholas II did not revoke the Basic Law he had sanctioned in early 1906. But he regretted allowing an electoral system which returned a large socialist contingent in both the First and Second State Dumas. On 3 June 1907 Pëtr Stolypin, his Prime Minister, redrafted the system so as to produce a conservative majority in the Third State Duma which would convene in November. Stolypin, however, also saw that agrarian reform was essential. Having worked as a governor in Saratov Province, he saw the village land commune as a source of chronic social instability; he introduced legislation to allow peasants to set up by themselves as independent farmers. He financed schemes to encourage migration to virgin lands in Siberia. Stolypin with the Emperor's consent strove for a working relationship with the Third State Duma, especially with the Octobrist party led by Alexander Guchkov. He also permitted the continued existence of local trade unions and a press which was no longer as hobbled as before 1905. Out-and-out revolutionary propaganda and organisation, however, continued to be quashed. Stolypin's rule was a forceful, intelligent attempt to conserve the Imperial order. He was detested not only by the revolutionaries but also by those at court who suspected that his collaboration with the Duma derogated from the powers of the Emperor. But Stolypin survived. The Russian Social-Democratic Workers' Party, which had 150,000 members in spring 1907, was quickly reduced to a handful of thousands as the state resumed control.[6]

Dzhughashvili's was an existence populated by comrades, spies, policemen, girlfriends and peasant landlords. Everything was done on the assumption that an unwary word might result in arrest. Friendly acquaintances might turn out to be police informers. The Okhrana, despite being a small organisation, husbanded its resources well and infiltrated all the revolutionary parties. Dzhughashvili could trust only his oldest friends and his immediate family.

He had got used to fending for himself; and although he had a wife and baby son, his party duties continued to keep him away from home after his return from the Fifth Party Congress. Such domestic peace as he had was abruptly brought to an end on 22 November 1907 when Ketevan, after weeks of suffering, died. The probable cause was tuberculosis. Joseph and Ketevan had been married for less than two years. Her death shattered his poise. His schoolmate Joseph Iremashvili accompanied him at the church funeral, and recorded the scene in Tbilisi when the widower took him firmly by the arm: 'Soso, this being softened my heart of stone; she's passed away and with her have gone my last warm feelings for people!' Then Dzhughashvili laid his right hand across his chest and declared: 'In here everything is so empty, so unutterably hollow!'[7] Iremashvili concluded:[8]

> I expressed my condolences to Koba. It was as honestly and sincerely offered as I could do it, but I knew that thereafter Koba was bereft of any moral restraint and that he would from then onwards surrender himself entirely to his fantastic plans, which were dictated solely by ambition and vengeance.

Bereavement, according to Iremashvili, had the profound consequence of hardening his attitudes to the rest of humanity.[9]

Iremashvili wrote his memoir years after fleeing from Soviet Georgia; he can hardly have remembered Joseph's exact words in the churchyard. He had also become Stalin's personal and political enemy and wanted to sell as many copies of his book as he could. Did he perhaps embroider the truth? In other memoirs about the period before 1917 a different Joseph Dzhughashvili is depicted: introverted, secretive, taciturn and unemotional.[10] Yet even if Iremashvili exaggerated or invented a little, he should not be dismissed. He had known Dzhughashvili since early childhood and knew all about the emotional side of his personality. They had been seminarists together when Dzhughashvili was writing poems in a romantic vein. Moreover, they were Georgians attending an Orthodox funeral and Joseph Dzhughashvili acted conventionally in showing family and friends how deeply he mourned his wife.

Dzhughashvili's reported comment is anyway a clichéd one which indicates a widower more concerned with himself than with Ketevan or his son. He had not even bothered to live with her throughout the last months of her illness. That Joseph was shaken by her death, though, is beyond dispute. What is less plausible is that this single event was the decisive one in turning him into a man seeking murderous revenge on humanity in general. There were many such events in his long life. His friends and associates noted how each event made him harsher in his dealings with the world. Iremashvili stated that even before Ketevan's death it was obvious that Joseph acted with contempt towards everyone except his mother, wife and son.[11] Her passing left him with his young son Yakob. Yet he did not let bereavement get in the way of political activity. Having chosen the life of a full-time revolutionary, he was not going to let parenthood burden him. Total personal freedom was required for this, and he asked his in-laws, the Svanidzes, to take Yakob off his hands. Ketevan had three sisters and a brother. To Joseph's relief, these relatives were happy to foster the lad. They also stood by Joseph when he ran out of money.[12]

He must have compared himself ruefully with émigré Bolsheviks in their little colonies in Switzerland and France. Most leading emigrants could live off private incomes. They could visit libraries, write letters to each other and go on holidays without worrying whether the Okhrana was tailing them. (The police agents in their midst did not much alter the daily habits of the émigrés even though everyone knew they existed.) They had time to write and opportunities to publish. They could meet foreign revolutionaries. They did not need to grub out a life while being constantly on the run. They were not threatened by prison or Siberian exile.

Apart from his comrades, Dzhughashvili was alone in the world. He saw nothing of his mother who was still in Gori. His father had long passed out of contact. Not that this stopped Joseph thinking about him. In one of his early articles he offered the following account:[13]

> Let's take a simple example. Just imagine a cobbler who had a tiny workshop but could not survive the competition with larger bosses and closed his workshop and perhaps went off to work in the shoe factory belonging to Adelkhanov in Tiflis. He entered employment with Adelkhanov not to become a permanent hired labourer but rather in order to save some money, put aside a little capital and reopen his workshop. As you see, that cobbler *already* has a proletarian condition but his consciousness is *not yet* proletarian: it is thoroughly petit-bourgeois.

These details are so near to the pattern of his father's life that Joseph must surely have been describing him. Beso's fate was an unhappy one. After splitting from Keke and Joseph he had gone on working and drinking in Tbilisi, and Joseph later claimed that he was stabbed to death in a tavern brawl in 1909.[14]

If Joseph mourned him, he left no sign of it; indeed it is not even known how quickly he learned of Beso's death. Dzhughashvili's focus in this period was on evading arrest. He was adept at the techniques. But his recurrent success at foiling the police again led to the rumour that he had a dubious association with the Imperial authorities. Was he an employee of the Okhrana? The Menshevik Isidore Ramishvili in 1905 had accused him of being 'a government agent, spy and provocateur'.[15] Such unsubstantiated tales were repeated down the years. There has even been an allegation that the Okhrana file on him was passed around the party in the 1920s and that Stalin instigated the Great Terror in the late 1930s mainly in order to eliminate those who had been initiated into knowledge of his employment.[16] In fact the most exigent analysis of the evidence gives no serious grounds for thinking that Dzhughashvili was a police agent. This does not mean that he failed to exploit whatever links he had with the Okhrana. He was arrested and interrogated many times. It is easily credible that he let drop information which would incriminate the enemies of his faction or even his rivals inside the faction. There were recurrent queries in particular about Stepan Shaumyan's arrest and apparently some fellow Bolsheviks sought to call Dzhughashvili before a party tribunal. Arrest and exile spared Dzhughashvili this fate.[17] Shaumyan was the other towering figure of Bolshevism in the south Caucasus; it would have been in character for the ambitious Dzhughashvili to get him out of the way.

Yet the Okhrana preferred to keep its main informers out of prison; and Dzhughashvili, although he sometimes received light sentences, was incarcerated or exiled too frequently and lengthily to have been a police employee. He was to spend the Great War through to the February 1917 Revolution in Siberia even though the state authorities could have used him productively if he really had been working for them.

Clandestine political activity was complex and demanding, and Dzhughashvili's leading position required that he kept a wide range of acquaintances and sources of information. Comrades were among these; they were indispensable if a solid revolutionary core was going to be maintained. But he also had to seek information on a wider plain. Inhabiting working-class areas where informers were many and where imprisonment was a constant danger, a revolutionary leader had to live on his wits – and Dzhughashvili was remarkable for his number of contacts. The Georgian Menshevik Artëm Gio left an account of the rounding up of Marxist militants in Tbilisi. Bursting into a friend's flat, Dzhughashvili was astonished to find Gio waiting for him there. 'I just wasn't expecting it,' he exclaimed: 'How has it happened? Haven't you been arrested?'[18] Gio was explaining how he had evaded the fate of others, when in walked a stranger. Dzhughashvili reassured Gio: 'You can talk freely and boldly ... He's a comrade of mine.' The newcomer turned out to be a Georgian who worked as a police interpreter. He had rushed over to tell Dzhughashvili the latest news: several close comrades (including Dzhughashvili's future father-in-law Sergei Alliluev) had been taken into custody. In fact a detachment had already been assigned to arrest Dzhughashvili in the evening. The interpreter, however, was disconcerted by Gio's presence and, once he had passed on his information, he ran off.[19]

This was an obscure but significant episode in Dzhughashvili's career. It showed that he got up to pretty unorthodox business; for his interpreter was not a Marxist militant but – in Dzhughashvili's words – 'a great nationalist'.[20] The interpreter so hated Russian Imperial rule that he willingly helped other opponents of tsarism: he deliberately mistranslated words so as to save Georgian militants from trouble. Gio's memoir was an unusual one. Bolsheviks were conventionally depicted as having nothing to do with the police, and it cannot be discounted that his book was published in 1925 in Leningrad only because Stalin's factional adversary Zinoviev controlled the press in that city and wanted to besmirch his reputation. Yet the making of revolution in the Russian Empire required multifarious talents and a flexible moral code. Dzhughashvili possessed the qualifications.

It was nevertheless a dangerous game. Another of Dzhughashvili's contacts was a certain Kornev. Dzhughashvili gave the code words to be used by Gio when meeting Kornev. Yet Kornev seemed shifty to Gio, who thought to himself: 'Either he's an Okhrana agent or a great coward!'[21] Although he was working in a tailor's workshop, Kornev obviously had no experience of cutting and sewing. Everything about him was suspicious. From this it was a small step to conclude that 'in his hands was the thread by which he [thought] to infiltrate our organisations'.[22] Gio made his excuses and went into hiding; his instincts told him that Dzhughashvili's trusted contact was a police spy and that Dzhughashvili himself had been fooled. This may have been the case.

Another possibility is that Dzhughashvili was more willing than most revolutionaries to take risks with the lives of his comrades. Egotistical and calculating, he judged situations in terms of his self-interest. People mattered to him only in so far as he could use them for the good of the cause or for his own political advancement and private comfort and pleasure. His recklessness in clandestine revolutionary work was of a piece with the other manifestations of his personality.

If Dzhughashvili's relationship with the police retains some mystery, there need no longer be any doubt about another murky aspect of his activities. Before the Great War the accusation was made that he was involved in organising armed robberies and that he continued this activity even after the Fifth Party Congress banned it. The evidence for this remained shaky for a long time. Dzhughashvili, though, never expressly denied having participated in this criminal activity. For years he simply discouraged public interest in the matter; and when he mounted to supreme power, he suppressed all mention of it.

His duties in Georgia on behalf of Bolshevism stretched far beyond purely political activity. He was also involved in the organisation of 'exes'. This was the party abbreviation for expropriations or, more directly, robberies. During the 1905–6 Revolution there were many Marxist groups across the Russian Empire involved in attempts to fund the party by thefts from banks. The Bolsheviks were among them, and Georgia was a centre for their efforts. There were good reasons for this. Banditry was common in the mountains and popular opinion was very far from regarding it as contemptible. The tradition of the *abrek*, who stole and murdered while cocking a snook at official authority and distributing some of his ill-gotten gains to the local poor, remained strong. (This was at the core of the novel by Alexander Qazbegi, *The Patricide*, which the young Joseph Dzhughashvili had so much admired.) Bolsheviks in Georgia saw themselves as canalising such customs towards a similarly altruistic purpose: the seizure of the profits of capitalism for the benefit of a party dedicated to the cause of the people. The recent Party Congress had firmly banned the organisation of exes. But the Bolshevik Centre continued to demand that they should be undertaken. Lenin and his comrades needed the money.

Dzhughashvili was the man in charge of the Georgian Bolshevik operations and the practitioner was the Armenian Semën Ter-Petrosyan who masqueraded under the pseudonym Kamo.[23] Dzhughashvili and his friend from school Joseph Davrishevi led rival groups of political robbers from houses on Mount David in Tbilisi. The police knew what was happening. One of the protégés of Joseph Davrishevi's father Gori gendarme chief Damian Davrishevi, a certain Davydov, was in charge of policing the area. Wanting a peaceful life, Davydov asked Joseph Davrishevi to avoid making trouble on his pitch – and Davrishevi assumed that a similar approach had been made to Dzhughashvili. Davrishevi was able and daring and, although he belonged to the Social-Federalists (who were socialists but also anti-Marxists and overt nationalists), Dzhughashvili tried to get him to cross over to the Bolsheviks. Davrishevi refused. (Georgia's Bolsheviks of course had suspected Dzhughashvili of being attracted to Georgian nationalism. Was his appeal to Davrishevi yet another piece of evidence for them?) Dzhughashvili and his fellow Bolsheviks at any rate took no notice of Davydov's request. Incidents recurred on Mount David. The two groups went on raising their respective party finance by persuasion, fraud, extortion and armed robbery. Owners of businesses were easily intimidated. Even the entre- preneurial family of the Zubalovs, who had constructed the building that later became the Spiritual Seminary, made financial subventions to Davrishevi.[24] Dzhughashvili kept quiet about the names of his providers. Yet it is not unlikely that the Zubalovs, one of whose dachas in the Moscow countryside he was to occupy with his second wife from 1919, yielded to Bolshevik demands in the period of revolutionary upsurge.

They pulled off their greatest coup on Erevan Square almost within sight of the Spiritual Seminary in Tbilisi on 12 June 1907. Kamo arrived in the disguise of an Imperial general in a comfortable horse-drawn carriage. They knew that a large quantity of banknotes was about to be delivered by stagecoach. Bombs were thrown at the guards. Kamo and his accomplices picked up linen bags with a quarter of a million rubles inside, and Kamo himself drove his coach away at full speed, taking advantage of the chaotic, bloody scene. He brought the proceeds of the robbery to the Bolshevik Centre base in Kuokkala in Finland. Lenin was delighted.

Dzhughashvili had taken a brief trip to Berlin shortly beforehand[25] – probably this involved some consultation with the Bolshevik leader- ship abroad. Afterwards Lenin, Dzhughashvili and Kamo wished to keep everything about the robbery strictly secret. Dzhughashvili and Kamo felt especially vulnerable since several Marxists in Tbilisi knew who had been organising the robberies. The Mensheviks, still outweighing the Bolsheviks in Georgia, set about their enquiries in November 1907. Silva Dzhibladze was put in charge of the commission set up to try the suspected participants. Dzhibladze himself had a less than saintly past;

he had been expelled from the Tiflis Spiritual Seminary for a physical assault on the Rector.[26] But he drew the line at breaking party policy. Dzhughashvili was identified beyond all reasonable doubt as the *éminence grise* behind the Erevan Square affair.[27] By then, though, Dzhughashvili was nowhere to be found. Worried about being sought by the police or being asked to account for himself to the Mensheviks, he had fled into hiding in Baku.[28] Mensheviks were to claim that he was expelled from the party.[29] What is clear is that the Bolsheviks, having made so much money from the robberies, ceased this criminal activity and that Dzhughashvili became ever more prominent in the politics of Bolshevism in the south Caucasus. He and Kamo remained friends and saw each other often during and after 1917. They justifiably felt they had carried out Lenin's instructions with great diligence.

Dzhughashvili made it his task to harry Menshevism in the south Caucasus. This factional strife mattered as much to him as the organising of revolutionary activity among the Baku workers and the oversight of the expropriations. His zeal and intelligence had brought him to the forefront of Bolshevism in the region. In Georgia he was 'famous as the second Lenin'.[30] He regularly derided the pride taken by Mensheviks in their successes with the Georgian peasantry in 1905–6. Thus he declared that class struggle was better organised in Baku on the Caspian coast with its great concentration of working-class inhabitants. While Zhordania and the Mensheviks directed their energy at activity among Georgians in Georgia, Dzhughashvili moved among Russians, Armenians and Azeris as well as people of his own nationality. He had genuine chutzpah, even claiming that the Mensheviks in Tbilisi were reluctant to take on the Bolsheviks in debate. This was unfair: Zhordania was always willing to accept any such challenge. But Dzhughashvili was not trying to be fair. He wanted to discredit Menshevism and would use any material that lay to hand. Generally he accused Zhordania of an obsession with legal activity which was tantamount to a policy of closing down the clandestine party network.[31]

Zhordania retorted that the Mensheviks had overlooked neither Baku nor the working class but were actually stronger than the Bolsheviks there.[32] The truth lay somewhere between Zhordania and Dzhughashvili. The Mensheviks regarded Georgia as their citadel. Yet they also worked in other places, including Baku, and at times were more effective than the Bolsheviks. But the differences in strategy held the factions apart. Whereas Bolsheviks operated almost exclusively among the workers, the Mensheviks took other classes such as the peasantry very seriously. The Mensheviks were much more willing than the Bolsheviks to use the State Duma as an instrument of political organisation and propaganda. The Bolsheviks, despite the failure of revolution in 1905–6, kept alive the dream of organising an armed uprising against the Imperial monarchy.

Dzhughashvili was a frontline attacker of Menshevism in one of the regions most important for the revolutionary cause in the Russian Empire. His intransigence was just what Lenin wanted in a follower. Dzhughashvili himself had acquired a broader perspective on politics since attending great party gatherings in Tampere, Stockholm and London, and his preference for working in Baku rather than in Tbilisi was a significant one. He no longer saw himself as primarily a Georgian Marxist; his role had become one of a Marxist who could work anywhere in the south Caucasus or in the empire as a whole. When reporting on the Fifth Party Congress, he commented:[33]

> The national composition of the Congress was very interesting. According to the statistics, Jews constitute the majority in the Menshevik faction, followed by Georgians and Russians. In the Bolshevik faction, however, Russians are in the majority ... followed by Jews, Georgians, etc. One of the Bolshevik delegates (I think it was comrade Alexinski) jokingly remarked that the Mensheviks are Jewish whereas the Bolsheviks are an authentic Russian faction; thus it would do no harm if we, the Bolsheviks, carried out a small pogrom in the party.

This is one of the first signs that Dzhughashvili recognised the importance of revolutionary propaganda, recruitment and organisation among the largest national group in the empire, the Russians.

Dzhughashvili's comments were later used against him as proof of anti-semitism. They were certainly crude and insensitive. But they scarcely betokened hatred of all Jews – or indeed of all Georgians. He, a Georgian, was repeating something that a Russian Bolshevik had said about Russians and Jews. For many years into the future he would be the friend, associate or leader of countless individual Jews. What counted for Dzhughashvili was the march of history; he recognised that, if the Imperial monarchy was going to be overthrown, Russians as well as Jews and Georgians had to be encouraged to play an active part. What is more, he was publishing his comment three decades before Hitler's extermination of eastern Europe's Jews. Dzhughashvili before the Great War may not have had a special fondness for Jews as Jews, but he did not object to them either. Indeed this was his attitude to all humanity. He neither liked nor hated particular peoples; his guiding principle was to judge how they could be encouraged or compelled to abet the achievement of the kind of state and society he approved. Despite these reservations, the comment had an insensitive undertone. A pogrom was a pogrom. It signified popular mass violence against Jews. Dzhughashvili at the very least had made an unpleasant political jest. He was also implicitly suggesting that the Jewish influence in the Russian Social-Democratic Workers' Party should be counteracted. His internationalism was not an unambiguous commitment.

Nevertheless his own national assertiveness was on the decline and he began to write not in Georgian but in Russian. His first such article appeared, after his return from London, in the Baku Bolshevik newspaper *Bakinski rabochi*.[34] From then onwards he confined his Georgian writings to letters to comrades and relatives. He largely ceased to write in his native tongue for the political public. It was a familiar step for Georgian Bolsheviks to take. To belong to the ranks of Bolshevism involved a commitment to internationalism and to the medium of Russian in the framework of organised Marxism across the empire. For a while he taught himself Esperanto. For Dzhughashvili and many young revolutionaries this language, invented by the Polish Jewish scholar Ludwig Zamenhoff, would provide one of the cultural underpinnings for the socialist order which they wanted to create around the world.[35]

At any rate it was not suspicion of Dzhughashvili's anti-semitism which most disturbed his acquaintances at the time. Semën Vereshchak knew him in Bailov Prison outside Baku and was struck by his personal nastiness. Dzhughashvili kept putting one prisoner against another. On two occasions this involved violence:[36]

A young Georgian was being beaten up in the corridor of the political block [of the prison]. Everyone who could joined in the beating with whatever came to hand. The word went round the block: provocateur! . . . Everyone thought it his duty to deliver the blows. Finally the soldiers came and halted the beating. The bloodied body was carried on a stretcher to the prison hospital. The administration locked up the corridors and cells. The assistant prosecutor arrived and an investigation was started. No one was found responsible. The corridor walls were covered in blood. When everything had calmed down, we began to ask each other who it was we had beaten. Who knows that he's a provocateur? If he's a provocateur,

why hadn't he been killed? . . . Nobody knew or understood anything. And only a long time afterwards did it become clear that the
rumour had started with Dzhughashvili.

On another occasion a criminal known as Mitka Grek stabbed to death
a young worker. Allegedly Dzhughashvili had told Grek that the man
was a spy.[37]

Revolutionaries had no compunction about eliminating those who
were informing on them or disrupting their activity. The point about
Dzhughashvili, however, was that he did this sort of thing on the quiet.
The customary examination of the accused was not made. Dzhughashvili
simply made up his mind and instigated action.[38] He put his fellow
conspirators in the path of danger while keeping clear of the deed. He
was decisive, ruthless and supremely confident. Yet he was also brave.
This is usually overlooked by those who seek to ascribe every possible
defect to him. Even his detractor Semën Vereshchak conceded that
Dzhughashvili carried himself with courage and dignity in the face of
the authorities. On Easter Day in 1909 a unit of soldiers burst into the
political block to beat up all the inmates. Dzhughashvili showed no fear.
He resolved to show the soldiers that their violence would never break
him. Clutching a book in his hand, he held his head high as they laid
into him.[39]

Such behaviour was extraordinary enough for Vereshchak to remember with awe. Other usual aspects of Dzhughashvili's comportment were
less endearing. He got over his wife's death with unseemly haste and,
whenever he was out of prison, chased skirt with enthusiasm. Slim, silent
and confident, he had always been attractive to women. He acquired a
girlfriend, Tatiana Sukhova, in Solvychegodsk in 1909. He had arrived
there with southern clothing unsuitable for the bleak winter of the
Russian north. Sukhova helped him out; she even gave him money and
helped him to escape.[40] On another of his stays in Solvychegodsk he
went out with local schoolgirl Pelageya Onufrieva. She was only seven-
teen years old at the time. This was not the last of his sexual conquests
of adolescents[41] and not all his comrades approved then or later. Still
less desirable was his handling of Maria Kuzakova. She owned one of
the large wooden houses in Solvychegodsk where he found lodgings.
Kuzakova was a young peasant widow. In due time she produced a baby
whom she christened Konstantin. There was little doubt on the question
of paternity. Those who saw Konstantin as an adult recorded how like
Stalin he was in appearance and even in physical movement.[42]

Dzhugashvili did not intend to stand by mother and child. He regarded women as a resource for sexual gratification and domestic comfort. He liked to relax with them socially only if they had the characteristics he found congenial. His partners had to be supportive and unchallenging. His requirement of a woman was that she should be devoted to him alone, and Kuzakova suited him for a while. Yet his liaison broke a code. Like other revolutionaries, Bolsheviks believed they had a mission to build a better world on principles of collective good. Dzhughashvili had selfishly used Kuzakova to gratify his lust, and neither then nor later did he think his attitude objectionable. This was the way he whiled away his sentence by the River Vychegda until 27 June 1911 when he was allowed to move to Vologda. He travelled to Kotlas and took the new railway westward. He never saw Solvychegodsk again.

8. AT THE CENTRE OF THE PARTY

Émigré leaders of the Russian Social-Democratic Workers' Party had been slow to recognise Joseph Dzhughashvili as a leader of any talent. The elite's composition was not fixed in stone, but without patronage from one of its members it was difficult for anyone to join it. Dzhughashvili did not help himself by staying in the south Caucasus and Russia. At gatherings in Tampere and Stockholm he had been forthright in his opinions. On each occasion he had made objection to Lenin,[1] who was the only leader who was ever likely to suggest including him in the Central Committee. Lenin's focus remained on Russia; he was even willing to leave Georgia to the local Mensheviks if only they agreed to keep their noses out of Russian Marxist affairs.[2] Dzhughashvili dissented. For him, the industrial and commercial expansion in Baku, Tbilisi and Batumi gave the region an importance equal to the regions of central and northern Russia; and he did not change this attitude until the Bolshevik faction gave him jobs elsewhere. What was already clear was his willingness to stand up for his opinions at party gatherings outside the region. He had not joined the Marxist movement to bury his mind under the bushel of official policy.

Promotion, when it came, proceeded from the hands of Lenin. After years of uneasy and patchy co-operation with the Mensheviks Lenin had had enough. By 1911 the disadvantages of sharing a party with them as well as with the various non-Russian regional organisations outweighed the advantages. Essentially he was planning to turn the Bolshevik faction – or rather those Bolsheviks who stayed loyal to him – into the Russian Social-Democratic Workers' Party and to treat all other factions as if they had placed themselves outside the party's ranks.

The Mensheviks had denounced Lenin's sanctioning of bank robberies as a means of financing Bolshevism. They also wanted their share of the money owed to the party as a whole from the legacies inherited from two sisters called Schmidt. But Lenin aimed to hold all the funds in Bolshevik hands. This was not the only problem. The non-Russian

Marxist parties – the Poles, Latvians and Lithuanians and the Jewish Bund – were causing trouble by criticising his policies. Even inside the Bolshevik faction there was dissent. Lenin had expelled Alexander Bogdanov from its midst only to find that many Bolsheviks continued to regard such schismatism as unnecessary and counter-productive. Never having been short of confidence and cunning, Lenin convoked a gathering in Prague. Despite ensuring that all but a couple of participants would be Leninist loyalists, he called it a Party Conference. Essentially he was abandoning even the semblance of collaboration within the same party as the Mensheviks. Proceedings started in January 1912. Lenin's divisive tactics disconcerted delegates and some did not shirk from condemning his obsessive émigré polemics. But he got his way. A Party Central Committee was elected and Lenin set about acting as if the Mensheviks did not exist.

Dzhughashvili was stranded at the time in Vologda; but the town was on a direct rail route to St Petersburg and Lenin was far from having forgotten him. A 'party school' had been held by Lenin in 1911 at Longjumeau outside Paris, and Dzhughashvili was one of the individuals he had wanted to have with him. 'People like him', he said to the Georgian Menshevik Giorgi Uratadze, 'are exactly what I need.'³ Longjumeau was a quiet village where Lenin had devised a programme of lectures and recruited several Marxist lecturers, in addition to himself, to train younger Bolsheviks in the niceties of party doctrines and history. The objective was to inculcate an unflinching loyalty to Bolshevism among the students; and Dzhughashvili, who had yet to make his mark as a Bolshevik writer at the faction's higher levels, was a natural choice. Another Georgian Bolshevik in Lenin's sights was Dzhughashvili's future associate Sergo Ordzhonikidze, who studied at Longjumeau and impressed him. Somehow or other, though, Dzhughashvili did not receive an invitation. Perhaps Lenin simply failed to get anyone to go with the message to Vologda. Ordzhonikidze at any rate impressed Lenin in Longjumeau to such an extent that he entrusted him with the practical arrangements of convoking the Prague Conference.⁴

Had Dzhughashvili attended the Longjumeau course, he would perhaps have been given this task. He would almost certainly have gone to Prague and might even have been elected to the Central Committee. He had a broader range of skills, especially as a writer and editor, than his friend Ordzhonikidze. Yet such an election would not have done him a favour. The new Central Committee included a certain Roman Malinovski, who was a paid agent of the Okhrana. All those Central

Committee members who returned to the Russian Empire, except for Malinovski, had been arrested within weeks. It was also in 1912 that Malinovski, a leading trade-unionist among the metalworkers of St Petersburg, stood as Bolshevik candidate for the Fourth State Duma and won a handsome victory. The Okhrana was able to stay informed about the most influential bodies of Bolshevism – the Central Committee and the Duma faction – and to influence their discussions.

The arrest of most returning members of the Central Committee, however, turned the fortunes of Joseph Stalin. Having missed the chance to attend the Longjumeau party school or the Prague Conference, he was available for activity at the highest level of the Bolshevik faction. Lenin saw him as a man who could act for him in several capacities. Dzhughashvili was an organiser of good repute. He never complained about assignments: already his capacity for hard work was well known. Although he had had disagreements with Lenin on policy, he was not unusual in this, and anyway they concurred in 1911–12 on most practical matters affecting the Bolsheviks. He had a basic understanding of Marxist theory. He was a fluent writer and an able editor. He had a forthright manner whenever someone had to pull an individual or committee into compliance with the faction's official line. Lenin and Grigori Zinoviev, who were temporarily in Paris before moving the Central Committee's foreign base to Kraków in the Polish lands of the Habsburg Monarchy, decided to co-opt Dzhughashvili (or Ivanovich, as they currently referred to him) to the Central Committee. Sergo Ordzhonikidze was sent in February 1912 to Vologda to tell him the news in person.[5]

Communication with the emigration was slow and Lenin fretted: 'There's no word of Ivanovich. What's happened to him? Where is he now? How is he?'[6] By then Dzhughashvili was classified as one of the rare useful comrades. But Lenin need not have worried. Ordzhonikidze easily found the co-opted comrade in Vologda and informed him that the Central Committee wanted him to flee the town and work as one of its main leaders in the Russian Empire. At last he had joined the elite of the Bolshevik faction.

Dzhughashvili left Vologda with false papers on 29 February 1912. His first stay was in the Caucasus. There he wrote material justifying the formation of the new Central Committee despite the fact that the Mensheviks and other factions of the Russian Social-Democratic Workers' Party had been illegitimately excluded from membership. He concentrated his efforts in Baku and Tbilisi. But his fresh duties meant that he was no longer to confine himself to one region of the Russian Empire.

On 1 April he left by arrangement with Lenin for Moscow, where he met up with Ordzhonikidze. Then he went on to St Petersburg. His duties were onerous and important. He wrote for and helped to edit the Bolshevik newspaper *Zvezda* ('The Star'); his literary fluency was much appreciated by the hard-pressed metropolitan Bolsheviks. At the same time he liaised with Bolshevik deputies to the Third State Duma seeking to found a more popular daily, *Pravda* ('The Truth'). Dzhughashvili became its editor. There were three working rooms at the newspaper's headquarters and the printing press had two rooms elsewhere.[7] He can hardly be said to have kept out of sight of the Okhrana. He had to hope that the police, for reasons of their own, would not want to arrest him.

Pravda appeared for the first time on 22 April 1912, and Dzhughashvili had contributed an article, 'Our Aims', to the issue. He had done as he was told from Kraków and inserted himself into the core of the St Petersburg Bolshevik leadership. *Pravda* was the faction's legal daily newspaper. Its objective was to gather support among industrial workers for Bolshevism at a time of rising popular discontent with the Tsar and employers. Miners on strike in the Lena goldfields in Siberia had been shot by the authorities on 4 April. A wave of protest demonstrations swept across the empire. St Petersburg was in tumult. The long period of quiescence in the labour movement since 1906 was at an end. Bolshevik militants started to outmatch the Mensheviks in political appeals. Consequently the Bolsheviks ceased to be of use to the Okhrana as a divisive force in the Russian Social-Democratic Workers' Party. It may have been no coincidence that orders were put out for Dzhughashvili's arrest as soon as *Pravda* started to be sold. The truth has not yet been unearthed from the files of the Ministry of Internal Affairs. Dzhughashvili was arrested on 22 April and confined in the House of Preliminary Detention in the capital. On 2 July he was sent under escort to Narym District near Tomsk in western Siberia, where he was sentenced to remain for three years. After the long journey by 'arrest wagon' on the Trans-Siberian Railway to Tomsk he was put on board the *Kolpashevets* steamer and taken down the great River Ob towards Narym.

Until his confinement Dzhughashvili had been writing more intensively than in any previous period of his life. It was also in this period that some of his adolescent verses were reprinted in the latest edition of Yakob Gogebashvili's Georgian literary anthology *Mother Tongue*.[8] But he told no one about this. (It is not even certain that he himself knew about the publication.) Just a few flashes of his poetic side still occurred. In a proclamation he wrote for May Day 1912 he declared:[9] 'Nature is waking from its winter's sleep. The forests and mountains are turning green. Flowers adorn the meadows and pastures. The sun shines more warmly. We feel in the air new life, and the world is beginning to dance for joy.' This was the last romantic outburst he made in print. For the rest of his life he never repeated such gushing verbosity. Indeed it had been a long time since he had indulged himself in this way.[10]

The same proclamation referred to none of the regions of the Russian Empire except Russia. It was aimed exclusively at Russian workers and called on them to 'raise the banner of the Russian [*russkoi*] revolution'. Too much weight of interpretation cannot be placed on this. (Not that this has stopped some biographers from trying.) Dzhughashvili was working in the Russian capital, writing in Russian and appealing to Russian industrial workers. Naturally Russia was at the core of his message, as would not have been the case if he had still been in Tbilisi. Nevertheless there was a detectable shift in his political persona around this time. His main pseudonym from 1912 was Stalin. This was an unmistakably Russian name derived from the word for steel (*stal*). Although it was not the first time he had turned to the Russian tongue for a false identity, he had usually reverted to Georgian ones. Now, though, he was building up his image in the Russian Social-Democratic Workers' Party and no longer wanted to be known merely as a man from the Caucasus. He was laying ever greater emphasis on the need for a general solution to the problems of the Russian Empire; and he wanted to play an integrated part in that solution.

Stalin in person, of course, was not credible as a Russian. He knew he looked, sounded and behaved in a 'southern' manner. He revered Georgian literary classics. He would never be Russian. And, contrary to what is widely suggested, he did not really try.[11] If he had really desired to de-Georgianise his political profile among Bolsheviks he would have ceased to write on the 'national question'. Jews like Zinoviev and Kamenev wanted to be known as internationalists and hardly ever drew attention to their ethnic ancestry. Stalin too wished to be regarded as an internationalist; he also aimed to be taken seriously in Russian socialist politics. But he continued to urge the party to promote the interests of the non-Russians under a future socialist administration. His 1913 booklet *The National Question and Social-Democracy* was to do much to raise his reputation in the party; it also solidified his relationship with Lenin, who described him in a letter to the writer Maxim Gorki as 'the wonderful Georgian'.[12] What is clear is that Stalin had long ceased to make a special case for the Georgians in his statements on the national question. When he wrote or said anything, he treated them no better or worse than other non-Russian peoples. He offered his co-nationals no prospect of preferment, while himself remaining a Georgian in appearance, accent, demeanour and residual culture.

This meant little to Stalin as he made his way under guard to Narym. He stayed for a few days in Kolpashevo, a village where several leading Bolsheviks were living in exile. They included Mikhail Lashevich and Ivan Smirnov. Stalin also came across his Bolshevik friend Semën Surin as well as his Bailov Prison acquaintance Semën Vereshchak: he had supper with them, recuperated and then set out north-east along the River Ob to his assigned destination in Narym.[13] It was not quite the worst place of exile in the Russian Empire. Narym, unlike towns at a more northerly latitude, lay just within the zone of agriculture. But conditions could have been better. The winter was bleak. Economic life largely revolved around hunting and fishing. Contact with St Petersburg was infrequent and subject to police surveillance.

Fellow Central Committee member Yakov Sverdlov greeted Stalin in Narym and offered him a room. They did not get on well. Even the agreement on housework broke down. Whereas Sverdlov aimed at a modicum of order, Stalin was slovenly and selfish. They had agreed to fetch the post, and whoever stayed behind was expected to tidy the house. Years later they compared memories about how Stalin got out of this arrangement:[14]

> *Stalin:* I liked to creep out for the post on [Sverdlov's day to do
> it]. Sverdlov had to look after the house whether he liked it
> or not – keep the stove alight and do the cleaning . . . How
> many times I tried to trick you and get out of the housework.
> I [also] used to wake up when it was my turn and lie still as if
> asleep.
> *Sverdlov:* And do you think I didn't notice? I noticed only too
> well.

Although Sverdlov laughed good-naturedly, he had not thought it pleasant at the time. Stalin's behaviour was doubly selfish. Whoever walked to the post office would meet up with other comrades and gain a respite from the dreariness of exile. Everyone found the conditions depressing and Stalin's egocentricity was widely resented.

The two of them planned to flee from Narym to resume clandestine political activity. They were encouraged in this by the Central Committee in Kraków. Two escape 'bureaux' existed, one in Kolpashevo, the other in Narym. Sverdlov made the first attempt but was caught near Tomsk. Then Lashevich made a dash, followed by Stalin and Sverdlov on 1 September.[15] It was an eventful trip. They had devised a clever scheme requiring the diminutive Sverdlov to hide in a laundry basket. Stalin was accosted by a gendarme who made a move to examine the basket by pushing his bayonet into it. Stalin got him to desist by bribing him. This story, told by Stalin three decades later, cannot be verified.[16] But it is not implausible. Fugitive revolutionaries regularly exploited inefficiency and venality among the Imperial agencies of law and order.

Stalin and Sverdlov stayed with the Alliluev family in St Petersburg.[17] Quickly they restored links with party organisations in the empire and with the 'foreign' part of the Central Committee in Kraków. All this time they had to keep at least one step in front of the Okhrana. The electoral campaign for the Fourth State Duma was in full cry and Stalin stayed in the capital to help and direct Bolshevik activities. He also began writing again for *Pravda*. On 19 October he contributed the leading article on 'The Will of the Voters' Delegates'; and Lenin printed his piece 'The Mandate of the St Petersburg Workers' in the émigré newspaper *Sotsial-demokrat*. On election day, 25 October, the Bolsheviks did well by securing six seats. The need for co-ordination was paramount and Stalin made a last-minute trip to Bolsheviks in Moscow to confer with Roman Malinovski and other newly elected individuals. With the ending of the electoral campaign it was equally urgent to strengthen contact with Kraków. Stalin, after briefly returning to St Petersburg and assuring himself that arrangements for the Duma were in place, bought train tickets for Poland in early November. He was going to consult Lenin. For the first time they would meet as fellow members of the Central Committee.

The trip was memorable for Stalin. As the train approached the border with Austrian Poland, he found himself in a carriage with a passenger reading aloud from a Russian nationalist newspaper. He could not stop himself from shouting across at him: 'Why are you reading that rubbish? You should read other newspapers!'[18] Alighting from the train, he had to get help in crossing the border to Kraków. He wandered around the market till he bumped into a friendly cobbler. Stalin used his charm: 'My father was also a cobbler, back in my homeland, Georgia.' The cobbler, refusing any recompense, took Stalin to his home, fed him and at dusk escorted him by a winding route across the hills into Austrian Poland.[19]

He arrived in time for a meeting between the Central Committee members and three Bolshevik Duma deputies. Stalin did not enjoy the experience. In November there had been a Bolshevik plan to organise a one-day political strike and demonstration outside the Tauride Palace in St Petersburg. When the Mensheviks opposed this as being dangerous and unproductive, the Bolshevik faction had backed down. Lenin heard about this in Kraków and drafted an angry article.[20] His ill temper had not spent itself before the three Duma deputies arrived in Poland. Stalin agreed that the Bolshevik faction had made a mistake, but he doubted that the best way to bring them into line was to browbeat them:[21]

> Ilich recommends 'a hard policy' for the group of six [Bolshevik Duma deputies] inside the faction, a policy of threatening the majority of the faction, a policy of appealing to the rank and file *against* the faction's majority; but Ilich will give way since it is self-evident that the [Bolshevik] six are not yet well enough developed for such a hard policy, that they are not prepared and that it's necessary to *start* by strengthening the six and then use them to thrash the majority of the faction as Ilya [Muromets] used a Tatar to thrash the Tatars.

Stalin believed that the Bolsheviks could win over the Mensheviks in the Duma faction. He had attended a faction meeting and could testify that this was feasible. Persuasion really could work. Stalin thought Lenin inept and ill informed to insist on tactical intransigence.[22]

On much friendlier terms with Stalin was Lev Kamenev, an acquaintance from their Tbilisi days as well as a Central Committee member. Feeling lonely in Kraków, Stalin wrote him what can only be called a billet-doux:[23] 'I give you an Eskimo kiss on the nose. The Devil take me! I miss you – I swear to it like a dog. There's no one, absolutely no one, to have a heart-to-heart conversation with, damn you. Can't you somehow or other make it over here to Kraków?' Still strengthening his position in the Russian Social-Democratic Workers' Party leadership, he was reaching out to potential friends who could help him.

Having returned briefly to St Petersburg, Stalin worked with the six Bolshevik Duma deputies before travelling again to Kraków at the end of December for a further meeting of the Central Committee with the Bolshevik Duma group. He stayed abroad for the longest time in his life and got on to more amicable terms with Lenin. Yet despite being invited to eat with Lenin and his wife Nadezhda Krupskaya, he insisted on finding a restaurant. Puzzled by this reaction, Lenin went in search of him. He found him eating with a bottle of beer on the table. From then onwards Lenin ensured that alcohol was provided at his home and they resumed their political conversations in a social setting. Meanwhile Stalin's behaviour became material for local ribaldry. Ordering a meal in Russian at a train station on the line between Kraków and Zakopane, he noticed that other customers entered the restaurant and got served while he was kept waiting. He received his soup after an inordinate wait. Offended, he turned the bowl upside down and walked out. Lenin had to explain to him, supposedly the party expert on the national question, that Poles disliked having to speak Russian.[24]

Lenin had the knack of putting Bolsheviks at their social ease, and Stalin steadily settled down. The two of them conversed endlessly. Stalin fitted Lenin's bill as a quintessential Bolshevik. He was tough and uncomplaining. (As yet Stalin had not displayed his self-pitying, ranting side.) He appeared to conform to a working-class stereotype. He was also a committed revolutionary and a Bolshevik factional loyalist. Stalin was obviously bright and Lenin, who was engaged in controversy with Zhordania and other Mensheviks on the national question, encouraged Stalin to take time out from his duties to write up a lengthy piece on the subject. Already in 1910 Lenin had cited Stalin (under the pseudonym K.S.) as a more authoritative commentator on the Caucasus than the more famous Zhordania.[25] Now he encouraged him to deepen his researches and publish the result.

With this in mind Stalin in the second half of January 1913 travelled on to Vienna, where he could use libraries with fuller holdings in Marxist literature than were available in Kraków. He stayed for a few weeks with fellow Bolsheviks on the southern edge of the city, not far from the palace of Schönbrunn, in a first-floor flat on the Schönbrunnerschlossstrasse. Stalin's comrades had got lots of books ready for him. He was given a desk and a divan.[26] (Stalin never objected to sleeping on the simplest frames.)[27] For several weeks he read in Viennese libraries and wrote up his work in the flat. He frequently consulted local comrades about the German-language texts of Bauer, Kautsky and the Marxist journal *Die Neue Zeit*.[28] Stalin was a man on a mission. He lived the national question and expatiated about it even on social occasions. Six-year-old Galina, the daughter of his Bolshevik hosts, got thoroughly bored on their walks in Vienna's well-kept parks: 'You're not talking about the nation again!'[29] Stalin, cut off from his son Yakob in Georgia, took to Galina as he did to other lively children. She was his match: she did not believe him when, with his heavy accent, he teasingly promised to bring her some 'green chocolate' from the Caucasus.[30]

He took extensive notes and wrote up most of the text of his booklet before returning to Russia. Initially he published 'The National Question and Social-Democracy' in the St Petersburg Marxist journal *Prosveshchenie* ('Enlightenment').[31] Back in the capital in mid-February 1913, Stalin resumed his part in the complex game played between the revolutionary parties and the Okhrana. The police had long ago accepted that a policy of total suppression of the revolutionary movement would not work, and indeed they had acted on this awareness since the 1880s. (The problem was that the Okhrana could change the rules of the game at will, and the result could be prison or exile for individual revolutionaries.) Stalin had to take the usual risks. This time he stayed not in the less savoury districts of the capital but in the centre, at 44 Shpalernaya Street, in the rented apartment of the Bolshevik Duma deputies F. Samoilov and Alexander Badaev.[32] The Okhrana was aware that Stalin was carrying out instructions of the émigré leadership in Kraków – or at least that he was doing so to the degree that he wished. Stalin realised that the Okhrana knew who he was and what he was up to. The Okhrana hoped to get clues about wider circles of Bolshevik activity; Stalin aimed to give no clues while continuing to guide the Duma faction towards the desired end.

Evidently his presence in St Petersburg was no secret. At any time he could be arrested. With Lenin's blessing, he was directing the faction's activity in the capital. He could hardly, however, strut about. He had to be wary. The fact of his voluntary obscurity in 1912–13 led many to go on supposing that he was a nonentity among Bolsheviks before the Great War. Such an idea was seriously awry. He had risen to the summit of the Central Committee and saw his talents as lying in the work he could do in the Russian Empire.

The inevitable happened on 23 February 1913. Stalin went to a ball for International Women's Day at the Kalashnikov Exchange. It was a big occasion and many militants were heading for the same destination. The Okhrana, however, had decided that the time had come to arrest him. Apparently Malinovski had tipped off his controllers about Stalin's whereabouts that day, and he was grabbed and handcuffed on arrival. He had finished his lengthy article on 'The National Question and Social-Democracy' (which was later republished as *Marxism and the National Question*) and delivered it to the offices of *Prosveshchenie* in the capital.[33] This was a legally published Marxist journal that carried items of doctrinal theory and contemporary analysis. The fact that its editors welcomed his article was a signal of his rising importance among

Marxists of the Russian Empire. The piece was thought sufficiently impressive to be turned out as a booklet. Stalin had also left behind an article, much briefer, for *Pravda*.[34] This was a report on 'The Situation in the Social-Democratic Group in the Duma'. Its contents justified the harsh line taken by the Bolsheviks in comparison with the Mensheviks. Stalin himself was out of action in the capital's House of Preliminary Detention.

He was not to know that he would not taste freedom's delights again for exactly four years; for it was to be precisely on International Women's Day in 1917 that female textile workers went on strike in the capital and forged the first link in a chain that pulled down the Imperial monarchy some days later. No further works by Stalin were printed between his arrest and Nicholas II's abdication. Scarcely had he penetrated the central precincts of the Bolshevik faction when he was cast to the winds of tsarist justice. He had known the risks. Recurrent arrest and exile were the norm for the revolutionaries who did not emigrate. He must have hoped that he would be sent again to somewhere like Solvychegodsk or Narym and that the Central Committee would enable him to escape and resume his important political functions. He would not be put on trial. His immediate future depended on the police. Stalin awaited the decision with his customary fortitude.

9. KOBA AND BOLSHEVISM

Dzhughashvili was by no means an outstanding thinker. This would not raise an eyebrow if his followers had not gone on to laud him as a figure of universal intellectual significance. He always had plenty of detractors. Most of the early ones were persons who – at least by implication – suggested that they themselves were thinkers of distinction. They deluded themselves. Scarcely any leading figure in the Russian Social-Democratic Workers' Party made an original intellectual contribution. Plekhanov, Lenin and Trotski were brilliant synthesisers of the ideas of others – and not all of those others were Marxists. Each took his personal synthesis to an idiosyncratic extreme. This was also true of Bukharin, who tried his hardest to effect a deepening of the Marxist perspective in the light of contemporary philosophy, sociology and economics. Only Bogdanov can be categorised as an original thinker. Bogdanov's amalgam of Marx and Engels with the epistemology of Ernst Mach led him to reject economic determinism in favour of a dynamic interplay of objective and subjective factors in social 'science'. He made a serious contribution through his work on the importance of ideas for the control of societies by their elites across the course of human history. Bogdanov's *Empiriomonism* was a *tour de force*.[1]

Yet the other leading figures succeeded in persuading their comrades that they too were of exceptional cultural significance. Stalin before the Great War made no such claim for himself. Nor in subsequent years did he suggest that he had made an original contribution. He always claimed to have been merely a loyal Leninist.[2] He called himself a *praktik*, meaning that he was more a practical revolutionary than a theoretician. When he published 'Anarchism or Socialism' in 1906–7, many readers thought he could hardly have been the authentic author. His school friend Davrishevi assumed that another Bolshevik, perhaps Dzhughashvili's comrade Suren Spandaryan, had written it. But Spandaryan put Davrishevi right. It really was Stalin's article.[3] 'Anarchism or Socialism' was not a coruscating work. Stalin privately admitted this after the

Second World War (when his comment was treated as extraordinarily modest).[4] It was nevertheless a work of practical importance at the time of publication. This has been overlooked by his biographers, who have ignored the fact that anarchists were active in Tbilisi after the turn of the century. Georgia was recognised as a place where a fundamental challenge to the Imperial monarchy would take place. Émigré anarchist leaders had sent propagandists on missions to Tbilisi. Stalin flung himself on the available literature on Marxism before writing his urgent reply.[5]

In fact he kept to Bolshevism's general line before the Great War. He endorsed the precepts of strict party discipline as formulated in Lenin's *What Is To Be Done?*; he also shared the Leninist viewpoint on revolutionary stages, dictatorship and class alliances in 1905. Rival versions of Marxism in the Russian Empire, he declared, were betrayals of the faith. He accentuated the need for leadership and a revolutionary vanguard and for the avoidance of 'tailism'. The vanguard should organise insurrection and seize power. He was also unafraid to oppose projects put forward by Lenin himself and to do this in open debate. On most matters, though, he agreed with Lenin; and Lenin for his own part badly needed Dzhughashvili's contributions on the national question. Whereas the Mensheviks had several theorists who wrote about the nationalities in the empire, the Bolsheviks had only Dzhughashvili (or Stalin, as he was invariably known in public from this period onwards). No wonder Lenin warmed to him.

Although several aspects of his thought surfaced only in his years of power, it is unlikely that they did not already exist. Stalin had grown up when imperial countries around the world were applying naked military force. Force based upon technological and organisational superiority ruled supreme. The British Empire covered a fifth of the world's land surface. The age of blood and steel had arrived. Capitalism was triumphant. Marxists believed that socialism would achieve a further victory and that capitalism itself was destined for defeat. A new stage in the history of humankind was believed imminent. Radical Marxists anticipated civil war between the middle classes and the working classes on a global scale. From such conflict there would come good for following generations. Marxism justified the sacrifice of millions of human beings in the pursuit of revolution.

The perfect society was anticipated once the military conflict was ended. The poor would inherit the earth. This would be achieved through 'proletarian dictatorship'. The need for repressive methods would persist until the resistance of the old propertied classes had been crushed. Although the dictatorship would be ruthless, Stalin and other Bolsheviks expected little trouble. The numerical and organisational weight of the proletariat, they believed, would soon crush all opposition. The old society would be eliminated and class privileges would be eradicated. The state would embed 'modernity' in all sectors of life, and it would be a modernity superior to the existing capitalist variants.[6] Universal free schooling would be established. Material production would be standardised; the wastefulness of capitalism would be surmounted. Every citizen would enjoy access to work, food, shelter, healthcare and education. This militant set of ideas suited Stalin. He lived for conflict. He constantly wanted to dominate those around him. He had also found an ideology that suited this inclination. Everything about Bolshevism fitted his purposes: struggle, repression, proletarian hegemony, internal party rivalry, leadership and modernity; and already he saw himself as a true leader within a party which itself sought to lead the 'proletarian masses' into the brave new world.

Yet Stalin was not a blindly obedient Leninist. On several important questions he thought Lenin to be misguided and said so. At the Bolshevik Conference in the Finnish industrial city of Tampere in December 1905 he had objected to Lenin's plan for the party to put up candidates in the forthcoming elections to the First State Duma. Like most delegates, Stalin thought it a waste of time for the Bolshevik faction to participate in the electoral campaign – only later, like many Bolsheviks, did he come over to Lenin's idea.[7] He did not change his mind, however, on the 'agrarian question'. Lenin advocated that the 'revolutionary-democratic dictatorship of the proletariat and the peasantry', after the monarchy's overthrow, should turn all agricultural land into state property. Stalin continued to reckon this naïve and unrealisable. He proposed instead that the dictatorship should let the peasants grab the land and do with it whatever they wanted.[8] He also believed that Lenin's demand for a radical break with Mensheviks in the State Duma would simply confuse and annoy the Duma's Bolsheviks. Both Lenin and Stalin were zealots and pragmatists. In important instances they disagreed about where zeal should end and pragmatism begin. Their mutual dissent touched on matters of operational judgement, not on revolutionary principles. Yet such matters were intensely debated within Bolshevism. Lenin hated his followers interpreting Leninism without his guidance. Stalin was one of those leading Bolsheviks who was unafraid to stand up for his opinions without walking out of the faction.

He also had reservations about Lenin's intellectual priorities in philosophy. In 1908 Lenin published a work of epistemology, *Materialism and Empiriocriticism*. At its core was a ferocious attack on his close collaborator Alexander Bogdanov. He objected to Bogdanov's apparent philosophical relativism. For Lenin it was axiomatic that the 'external world' existed independently of its cognition by the individual human mind. 'Reality' was therefore an objective, discernible phenomenon. Lenin contended that Marxism constituted an irrefutable corpus of knowledge about society. He insisted that the mind functioned like a photographic apparatus accurately registering and relaying data of absolute truth. Any derogation from such premises, he asserted, implied a movement away from Marxist materialism and opened the intellectual gates to philosophical idealism and even to religion. Bogdanov, whose commitment to each and every statement of Marx and Engels was far from absolute, was castigated as an enemy of Marxism.

Stalin thought Lenin was wasting his time on topics of marginal importance for the Revolution. In a letter to Vladimir Bobrovski from Solvychegodsk in January 1911 he declared the epistemological controversy 'a storm in a tea-cup'. Generally he ridiculed the émigrés.[9] Stalin thought that Bogdanov had done a convincing philosophical job and that 'some particular mistakes of Ilich [were] correctly noted'.[10] He wanted all Bolsheviks to concentrate on the large practical topics, and there were plenty of these needing to be discussed before appropriate policies could be formulated. Stalin was willing to criticise 'the organisational policy of the editorial board' of *Proletari*.[11] This board at Lenin's behest had expelled Bogdanov from its membership. Stalin was indicating his dissent not only from Lenin's epistemology but also from his enthusiasm for splitting the faction into ever tinier bits. He advised a moderation of polemics. Stalin counselled the leaders of the two sides in the factional controversy – Lenin and Bogdanov – to agree that 'joint work is both permissible and necessary'.[12] Such an idea motivated Stalin in the next few years. Indeed he maintained it throughout 1917; for when Lenin was to demand severe disciplinary measures against Kamenev and Zinoviev, it was Stalin who led the opposition to him.

So at that time he was what was known as a Conciliator inside Bolshevism. He despised the émigré shenanigans and wanted the Bolsheviks, wherever they lived, to stick together. It was a question of priorities. Philosophy was not as important as the making of revolution. For this purpose it was essential to keep Bolsheviks together, and Lenin must not be allowed to endanger such an objective.

Yet Lenin tolerated Stalin, and much of his positive attitude is

attributable to Stalin's booklet *Marxism and the National Question*.
Stalin's later enemies unceremoniously dismissed the work. It was said
that Stalin either did not really write it or wrote it only with decisive
help from others. Supposedly his ghost writer was Lenin. That Lenin and
others assisted with their suggestions about the draft is undeniable. This
is a quite normal procedure for sensible writers: it is better to have
necessary criticism before than after publication. Another hypothesis was
that Stalin's inability to read foreign languages, except for a few phrases
with the help of a German–Russian dictionary, meant that he could not
have read the works by Austrian Marxists appearing in his footnotes.
Anyone who has read *Marxism and the National Question*, however, will
know that most of the references to books by Otto Bauer, Karl Renner
and others are made to the widely available Russian translations. The
other point is that Lenin was a proud author. If he had really written the
book, he would have published it under one of his own pseudonyms.

Lenin liked *Marxism and the National Question* because Stalin agreed
with him about the basic solution. An additional advantage was that
Stalin was not a Russian but a Georgian. After the turn of the century
the Marxists of the Habsburg Monarchy – especially Bauer and Renner
– argued that the empire was a patchwork quilt of nationalities and that
nation-states could not neatly be cut out of it. Their answer was to offer
every nation a representative body of its own at the centre of the empire
with the mission to enhance national interests. The Mensheviks, with
encouragement from the Jewish Bund as well as from Noe Zhordania,
adopted Bauer's plan as the future basis of state structure in the Russian
Empire once the Romanovs had been overthrown. Stalin, however,
adhered to the official Bolshevik position that administrative autonomy
should be given to non-Russians in areas where they lived in concentration. The Finns in Finland and the Ukrainians in Ukraine were the
usual examples. Thus the Bolsheviks hoped to maintain a centralised
state while acceding to national and ethnic aspirations.

Stalin was not simply parroting Lenin's earlier writings. There is a
passage in *Marxism and the National Question* which merits close
attention since it deals with Georgia. It deserves to be quoted in full:[13]

> Let us take the Georgians. The Georgians of the years before the
> Great Reforms [of the 1860s] lived in a common territory and spoke
> a common language but strictly speaking they did not constitute a
> nation since, being split into a whole range of principalities cut off
> from each other, they could not live a common economic life and

they waged wars among themselves for centuries and devastated each other, fomenting trouble between the Persians and the Turks. The ephemeral and accidental unification of the principalities which a successful tsar was occasionally able to carry out at best covered only the surface of the administrative sphere – and it was quickly wrecked on the caprices of the dukes and the indifference of the peasants.

So much for the idea that Georgians were a primordial nation, fully developed before their incorporation in the Russian Empire.

Stalin's argument continued as follows:[14]

Georgia as a nation made its appearance only in the second half of the nineteenth century when the collapse of feudal law and the rise of the country's economic life, the development of the means of communication and the birth of capitalism established a division of labour among Georgia's regions, finally shattered the economic isolation of the principalities and bound them together as a single whole.

This is crude materialist history, but it has a cogency within the analytical frame constructed by Stalin for the examination of nationhood. In order to be considered a nation the Georgians had to share not only their 'psychic' background and territory but also their economic life.

This was not an original point among Georgian Marxists. Zhordania, too, had always stressed that sharp contrasts separated the many regions of tiny Georgia.[15] There was a difference in emphasis, however, between Zhordania and Stalin. Whereas Zhordania wanted most inhabitants of Georgia to assimilate themselves to a Georgian identity, Stalin continued to acknowledge that Georgianisation was nowhere near fulfilment. Both Zhordania and Stalin were socialist internationalists. Yet Stalin was not off the mark when highlighting the nationalist ingredients in the outlook – however unconsciously held – of his Menshevik adversaries. Stalin questioned in particular whether the Mingrelians and Adzharians, who lived in western Georgia, should be regarded as Georgians.[16] What are we to make of this? The first lesson is surely that Stalin was a more sensitive analyst of his native Georgia and the surrounding region than is usually thought. (Not that we should feel too sorry for him: in later years he turned into the most brutal ruler the Caucasus had known since Tamurlane – and this of course is why his earlier sophistication has been overlooked.) In any case he rejected Menshevik policy as offering simplistic solutions based on inaccurate demographic data.

Stalin stressed that nationhood was a contingent phenomenon. It could come with capitalism. But under changing conditions it could also fade. Some national groups might assimilate to a more powerful nation, others might not. Stalin was firm on the point:[17]

> There can be no disputing that 'national character' is not some permanent given fact but changes according to the conditions of life ... And so it is readily understandable that the nation like any historical phenomenon has its own history, its beginning and its end.

It would consequently be senseless for Marxists of any nation to identify themselves permanently with that particular nation. History was on the march. The future lay with socialism, with multinational states and eventually with a global human community.

In writing about Marxists, Stalin was saying much about himself and his developing opinions. The young poet who had called on fellow Georgians to 'make renowned our Motherland by study' had vanished.[18] In his place there was an internationalist struggling for the cause of the proletariat of all nations. The Stalin of *Marxism and the National Question* did not regard the Russians as a problem. Describing contemporary Georgia, he asserted:[19]

> If campaigns of repression [by the government] touch 'land' interests, as has happened in Ireland, the broad peasant masses will soon gather under the banner of the national movement.
>   If, on the other hand, there is no truly serious *anti-Russian* nationalism in Georgia, this is above all because no Russian landlords or Russian big bourgeoisie exist there who might feed such nationalism among the [Georgian] masses. What exists in Georgia is *anti-Armenian* nationalism but this is because there is an Armenian big bourgeoisie which, by crushing the small and as yet weak Georgian bourgeoisie, thrusts the latter towards anti-Armenian nationalism.

Stalin's analysis pointed to the complexity of the national question in the Russian Empire. It anticipated the bringing together of Russians and Georgians in harmony within the same multinational state.

Evidently he assumed that the Russian Empire, when revolution at last overthrew the Romanovs, should not be broken up into separate states. Even Russian Poland, which Marx and Engels had wanted to gain independence along with other Polish-inhabited lands, should in Stalin's opinion stay with Russia.[20] His rule of thumb was that 'the right of secession' should be offered but that no nation should be encouraged to realise it.

What motivated Stalin was the aim to move 'the backward nations and nationalities into the general channel of a higher culture'. He italicised this phrase in his booklet. The Menshevik proposal for 'national-cultural autonomy' would permit the most reactionary religious and social forces to increase their influence and the socialist project would be set back by years:[21]

> Where does ['national-cultural autonomy'] lead and what are its results? Let's take as an example the Transcaucasian Tatars with their minimal percentage of literacy, their schools headed by omnipotent mullahs and with their culture pervaded by the religious spirit ... It is not difficult to understand that organising them into a cultural-national union means to put their mullahs in charge of them, to proffer them up to be devoured by reactionary mullahs and to create a new bastion for the reactionary stultification [*zakabalenie*] of the Tatar masses by their very worst enemy.

Stalin's point was not without plausibility.

He then posed some pertinent questions:[22]

> What about the Mingrelians, Abkhazians, Adzharians, Svans, Lezgins and others speaking different languages but not having their own literature? How to relate to such nations? Is it possible to organise them into national unions? But around which 'cultural matters' can they be 'organised'?
>
> What about the Ossetians, of whom the Transcaucasian Ossetians are assimilating (but as yet are far from having assimilated entirely) as Georgians while the Ossetians of the North Caucasus are partly assimilating as Russians and partly developing further by creating their own literature? How can they be 'organised' into a single national union?
>
> To which national union should the Adzharians be ascribed who speak Georgian but live by Turkish culture and profess Islam? Shouldn't they be 'organised' separately from the Georgians *on the basis of religious matters* and together with the Georgians *on the basis of other cultural matters*? And what about the Kobuletsy? The Ingush? The Ingiloitsy?

Zhordania had no answer to such questions.

Stalin's counter-proposal was for regional self-rule, as Lenin had counselled since 1903. This would be undertaken in such a fashion as to give each ethnic group, however small, the right to use its own language, have its own schools, read its own press and practise its own faith.[23] The response to Stalin and Lenin was acerbic, and it was led by Stalin's Georgian antagonist Zhordania. For Zhordania the important point was that capitalist economic development had scattered nations over vast areas. It was therefore impractical to protect national and ethnic rights on a purely territorial basis. Leninism was therefore a doctrine from 'the old world'.[24] Another claim by Zhordania was that 'the Russian part of the party', by which he meant the Bolsheviks, was insensitive to the acuteness of national oppression in the Russian Empire.[25] In truth Bolsheviks and Mensheviks were better at criticising each other than at providing a solution which would not lead somehow to oppressive results. If the Ukrainians were offered Bolshevik-style regional self-rule, Jews and Poles in Ukraine would have reason for concern. If Ukrainians acquired the right to Menshevik-style cross-territorial self-organisation, the prospects for central supranational government would become chaotic. Stalin and Zhordania were wrestling with a question with no definitive theoretical solution.

By and large, though, the dispute was conducted with intellectual rigour even though the language on both sides was intemperate. Stalin's commentary on the Caucasus was taken seriously even by those who disagreed with him. He had said nothing offensive except to the ears of the most extreme nationalists. Indeed little attention was later drawn to his booklet when his enemies were searching for dirt on him.

The exception was the passages in *Marxism and the National Question* on the Jews. According to his categories, the Jews could not be considered as a nation because they did not live in a discrete territory. They had a language – Yiddish – and a religion of their own; and they were conscious of their Jewishness. But the matter of territory was crucial for Stalin and he took Bolshevik ideas on nationhood to their logical conclusion. his attack on the Jewish Bund was direct:[26]

> But [national-cultural autonomy] becomes even more dangerous when it is imposed on a 'nation' whose existence and future is subject to doubt. In such circumstances the supporters of national autonomy need to guard and conserve all the peculiarities of 'the nation' including not only useful ones but also those which are

harmful so long as 'the nation might be saved' from assimilation and 'might be protected'.

The Bund inevitably was obliged to start down this dangerous road. And down that road it actually has gone.

Stalin noted that whereas other Marxist parties had called for the general right of nations to speak their own language, have their own schools and follow their own customs, the Bund mentioned only the Jews. It had therefore, in his opinion, become a nationalist organisation.[27]

He excoriated the Bund's preoccupation with Yiddish and with the Jewish Sabbath. He noted that some Bundists even wanted separate hospitals for Jews. All this flew in the face of the wish of Marxists to bring national and ethnic groups of workers together in a single political organisation. For Stalin it was going altogether too far to suggest that all Jewish workers should be allowed to take off the hours of work from twilight on Friday to twilight on Saturday.[28]

All this threw petrol on to the flames of controversy: Mensheviks and Bundists were infuriated by his analysis. But Stalin stood his ground and published an explanatory self-defence in the same journal.[29] Most of the Menshevik leaders happened to be Jews. Lenin's attacks on them had invited the accusation that the Bolsheviks were anti-semitic.[30] This overlooked the fact that several Bolshevik leaders too were Jews – Lenin himself had a Jewish grandfather.[31] But appearances in politics mattered as much as reality, and Stalin's repudiation of Jewish demands for recognition of nationhood and of entitlement to self-rule seemed another case of Bolshevik hostility to Jews. Stories also surfaced that Stalin made anti-semitic remarks in private. Against this is the incontrovertible fact that Jews were among Stalin's friends and associates before and after the Great War. However, the Jewish Bund was on the other side from the Bolsheviks in most disputes in the Russian Social-Democratic Workers' Party before the Great War. Stalin and Lenin were eager to attack the Bundists and their aspirations. Factional considerations as well as ideology were involved in the Bolshevik–Menshevik controversy. It would be difficult to find Stalin guilty of anti-semitism simply for what he wrote in his Meisterwerk on the national question.

10. OSIP OF SIBERIA

The months of waiting ended when the St Petersburg police sentenced Joseph Stalin to four years of exile. Marched from prison on 2 July 1913, he was taken to an arrest wagon bound for Siberia. Convicts were usually accompanied by friends and relatives who shouted support from the platform through the barred slits in the sides of the wagon. Nobody in the capital, however, was willing to bid Stalin farewell. His wife Ketevan was dead and his mother far away in Gori; and the Alliluev family, known to be active Bolshevik supporters, would have been ill advised to come to the station. No sooner had he risen to the crest of the Bolshevik faction than his fortunes fell to the ground. From having been leader of Bolshevism in St Petersburg with responsibility for both the Duma faction's activities and the editorial line of *Pravda* he was reduced to being one arrested revolutionary among hundreds. Stalin was put in manacles. He slept on a hard wooden bunk. He and his comrades were fed and watered like cattle as the train made its way eastwards across the Eurasian plain. They peered through the barred slits as the train pulled out. Within minutes of departure they lost sight of the last feature of the Russian capital, the cupola on St Isaac's Cathedral. The tundra and taiga of Siberia awaited them.[1]

The government was watching with concern as the slogans of Bolshevism attracted discontented factory workers, and Bolsheviks like Stalin were a threat to the Imperial order as the industrial strike movement expanded. Stalin's convict record was also noted. The Minister of Internal Affairs had no reason to show indulgence to this leading revolutionary who had escaped several times from previous places of exile. He and his comrades were sent to Turukhansk District in Yenisei Province in Siberia's far north-east. Turukhansk's reputation was a dreadful one. It was the place of detention for those revolutionaries in previous decades who had broken their terms of punishment. Stalin's periods in exile in Novaya Uda, Solvychegodsk, Vologda and Narym were going to seem pleasant in comparison. No place under Imperial administration was bleaker than Turukhansk.[2]

At nearly six hundred thousand square miles, Yenisei Province was larger than Britain, France and Germany combined. It stretched from the town of Yeniseisk north down the River Yenisei to the Arctic Ocean. Population was sparse in Turukhansk District. Before the First World War there were fewer than fifteen thousand inhabitants and most of these belonged to tribes which had lived there for centuries. Monastyr-skoe, the district capital, had fewer than fifty houses (although the New York and Montreal fur company Revillion had a branch there and graphite mining took place further north).[3] The climate was harsh. Winter with its frequent snowstorms lasted nine months; the tempera-ture sometimes fell to sixty degrees below zero and the daylight was of short duration. Summer brought its own discomforts because the sun hardly set and the mosquitoes bit through clothing. Agriculture was impossible since the ground remained frozen regardless of season. Flour and vegetables were imported from Russia's gentler climes and livestock husbandry was unknown. The people of Turukhansk District hunted and fished for subsistence.[4]

Escape from the far-flung villages was exceptionally difficult. The telegraph line, ending at Monastyrskoe, facilitated police surveillance.[5] The tundra was so heavy that flight west to the River Ob or east to the River Lena was not a realistic option. Those trying to flee by river faced hazards of a different nature. The route to the north was arduous, especially in the vast stretch above the Arctic Circle. Authorities checked the identities of all passengers, boats were few and the water melted for only a few weeks annually. The southward alternative was little better. The steamship was under constant watch; and when anyone took a boat or dog-sleigh from village to village, peasants were under orders to report this to the police.[6] It was over six hundred miles from Monastyrskoe to Yeniseisk and 170 miles from Yeniseisk to Krasnoyarsk. The chances of getting unnoticed all the way upriver to Krasnoyarsk were small. As a place of detention, Monastyrskoe was almost as effective as Devil's Island or Alcatraz.[7] Stalin and his fellow prisoners had plenty of time to ponder this on the journey along the Trans-Siberian Railway until they reached Krasnoyarsk.

From there they travelled downriver by steamship. Stalin had been preceded to Monastyrskoe by Yakov Sverdlov, fellow member of the Russian Bureau of the Central Committee and an acquaintance from an earlier period of exile. Both were assigned by administrative order to villages around Monastyrskoe: Stalin went to Kostino, Sverdlov to Selivanikha.[8] Kostino was ten miles and Selivanikha three miles from Monastyrskoe.

A large colony of revolutionaries lived in the neighbouring villages. Most had recently arrived. Until the 1905 Revolution the Ministry of Internal Affairs had sent such convicts to Tobolsk, Narym or Yakutia. Such places had proved easy to flee from. Ill-paid policemen and impoverished peasants were seldom difficult to suborn with a small bribe. Turukhansk District had been used fitfully in the 1890s – the future Menshevik leader Yuli Martov had served his sentence there. By the time Stalin arrived, the revolutionary colony had grown. Resident exiles belonged mainly to those parties regarded as the greatest threat to political and civil order; these included not only Bolsheviks and Mensheviks but also Anarchists and Socialist-Revolutionaries. Monastyrskoe was consequently a hive of ideological variety. Dispute usually took place without undue polemics. Exiles had made up their mind about party allegiance. Each party maintained shared books and facilities among its members. Messages from Russia were passed on; pleas were made on behalf of individuals who were in poor health or who ran out of money. The revolutionaries kept intellectually alert in anticipation of eventual return to political work upon release.

Although the conditions of detention were bad under the Romanovs, they were nowhere near as oppressive as Stalin made out in the 1930s. The revolutionaries could keep up their spirits through social gatherings. Someone even composed a 'Turukhansk March'. Its words were more stirring than poetic and the refrain went as follows:[9]

> Boldly, brothers, boldly
> Let's meet the evil storm
> With our laughter
> And a song that's brave!

The 'evil storm' referred less to the local weather than to the oppressive tsarist regime. Every exiled militant, while yearning to leave Siberia and overthrow the Romanovs, easily found rooms to rent. Each had a stipend of fifteen rubles a month. This was enough to cover rent, which cost about two rubles, and basic food requirements.[10] But game was plentiful and the revolutionaries bought the equipment to fish and trap. They could also work for local peasants.[11] Many exiles had family members in Russia who sent money; others – one of whom was Stalin – relied predominantly on being subsidised by their party. Turukhansk did not have the harshest penal regime, but it was not an easy one either.

Central Committee member Sverdlov welcomed Stalin. They knew and disliked each other from their shared exile in Narym District in 1912. Stalin was as self-absorbed as before and shut himself away from everyone. He ignored the custom of giving a detailed report on general politics and the prospects of revolution on the basis of recent direct experience in Russia. The other exiled Bolsheviks were deprived of up-to-date information which only he could supply.

Within months of Stalin's arrival, both Stalin and Sverdlov were ordered further north. The new governor of Yenisei Province in mid-March 1914 transferred his two Bolsheviks to a still more distant place. He had been alerted to their plans to escape.[12] Stalin had tried to allay suspicion by writing to Malinovski on 10 April 1914:[13]

> Apparently someone or other is spreading the rumour that I won't stay in exile till the end of my sentence. Rubbish! I inform you and swear like a dog that I'll remain in exile till the end of the sentence (till 1917). Sometimes I've thought of leaving but now I've rejected the idea, rejected it definitively. There are many reasons and, if you like, I'll write about them in detail some time.

In the same letter he offered to supply articles to *Pravda* on 'The Foundations of Marxism' and 'The Organisational Side of the National Question'.[14] But the Okhrana was not fooled. Lenin wanted Stalin and Sverdlov to be helped to leave Siberia, and quantities of money had been arriving for them at Monastyrskoe from party comrades in Russia.[15]

Stalin and Sverdlov would have been better served if the Central Committee had sent money not directly to them but to intermediaries. In any case the Central Committee was penetrated by spies. Okhrana agent Malinovski, with whom Stalin corresponded, told the Department of Police in St Petersburg in November 1913 about the intention to organise an escape. Stalin and Sverdlov were important detainees. By administrative order they were to be moved to the bleak hamlet of Kureika.[16] There they would be the sole convicts and most of the residents would be Ostyaks.

Both were depressed. Whatever chance they had of making it up-river to Krasnoyarsk would all but disappear in Kureika. Sverdlov had particular cause to feel downcast as he explained in a letter to his sister Sarra:[17]

> Joseph Dzhughashvili and I are being transferred a hundred kilo-
> metres to the north, eighty kilometres within the Arctic Circle.
> There will be only the two of us at the spot, and we'll have two
> guards. They have reinforced the surveillance and cut us off from
> the post. The post comes once a month with a courier who is often
> late. In practice there are no more than eight or nine deliveries a
> year.

Their geographical knowledge was faulty. There were two places called
Kureika north of Monastyrskoe. The one which Sverdlov had in mind
was by the river of the same name far beyond the Arctic Circle. The
governor had specified another Kureika, which stood on the western
bank of the River Yenisei just below the line. Even so, it was seventy-five
miles downriver from Monastyrskoe, and that was quite far enough to
lower their spirits.[18]

Although the location was not as bad as they had feared, it was quite
bad enough. Stalin made his own contribution to the unpleasantness. In
Monastyrskoe he had taken possession of books bequeathed to resident
Bolsheviks by fellow exile Innokenti Dubrovinski. When Stalin moved
on to Kureika, he simply took the books off with him. Another
Bolshevik, Filip Zakharov, went out to remonstrate with him and was
treated 'more or less as a tsarist general would receive a rank-and-file
soldier who had dared to appear before him with a demand'.[19]

Stalin and Sverdlov disliked the noisiness of the Kureika family they
lodged with. They had no kerosene and had to use candles if they
wanted to read during the long winter.[20] But the worst thing was the
relationship between them. Sverdlov wrote:[21] 'One thing is that I don't
have a room to myself. There are two of us. I've got the Georgian
Dzhughashvili with me, an old acquaintance whom I met in a previous
exile. He's a fine fellow but too big an individualist in daily life.'
'Individualist' was a damning word among Marxists, who required the
subordination of personal inclinations to collective needs. Driven to
distraction, Sverdlov decided to move house; he wrote to a friend in May
1914:[22]

> I have a comrade with me. But we know each other only too well.
> What is more, and this is the saddest thing, a person is stripped
> bare in front of you in conditions of exile and imprisonment and
> becomes exposed in every little detail. Worst of all, he is visible
> solely from the viewpoint of 'the details of daily life'. There's no
> room for the large features of character to reveal themselves. Now I

live in a separate apartment from the com[rade], and we rarely see each other.

Sverdlov got himself transferred back to Selivanikha at the end of September on grounds of ill health.[23]

Stalin meanwhile got on with life in his own egocentric fashion. He had always had an eye for adolescent girls but when he moved in as a lodger with the Pereprygin family, he behaved quite scandalously by seducing the fourteen-year-old daughter. Not only that: he made her pregnant. Even in that lightly administered area it was impossible to keep things quiet. The police became involved. Stalin was interviewed, and had to agree in due course to marry the unfortunate girl. This saved him from prosecution in the courts.[24] He subsequently abrogated the accord. For Stalin, the relationship was no more than a way of relieving the sexual frustrations of exile. He lived like a feudal knight among the impoverished Pereprygin family and took what he fancied whenever he liked. He acted as if he had rights without obligations. He had contempt for all human conduct but his own.

His political activity was weakened by the fact that his postal contact with the world outside Kureika was intermittent.[25] This was intensely irritating because war had broken out in Europe. The assassination of Archduke Franz Ferdinand of Austria by a Serbian nationalist in July 1914 had provoked a general diplomatic crisis. The Austrian government had delivered a humiliating ultimatum to Serbia. Russia, which had stepped back from the brink in previous emergencies in the Balkans, decided to take the Serbian side. Austria's expansion into the region was to be resisted at last. The complication was that Germany had opted to stand by Austria in the event of a Balkan crisis. The Russian Imperial Army mobilised and Nicholas II refused to stand it down when the Germans delivered an ultimatum to St Petersburg. Russian forces poured through East Prussia towards Berlin. Austria occupied Serbia. France and the United Kingdom honoured their treaty obligations and declared war on Russia's side against Germany and Austria–Hungary. The German Imperial Army defended itself in the east and, violating the neutrality of Belgium, thrust across into northern France. Without anyone having intended it, a European war had broken out.

This was happening while Stalin and his fellow exiles could have no part in the campaign waged by Lenin and his supporters against Russian participation in the war against the Central Powers. Indeed Lenin from the safety of Switzerland urged all Marxists to work for the defeat of Nicholas II's forces. Strikes were organised in factories, especially in the capital (which was renamed Petrograd because St Petersburg was thought to sound too Germanic). Bolsheviks sent anti-war propaganda to Russian POWs in German and Austrian camps. The leading Bolshevik writers debated the political and economic motivations of the belligerents in the Petrograd press. The Okhrana was active in retaliation, and the local Bolshevik groups were repeatedly broken up; and although Lenin was indefatigable, he lost many supporters to demoralisation as well as to the prison system.

Stalin, however, did not worry about such dangers; he wanted to get back into action in Russia and was intensely frustrated by his continued exile. He wrote to Malinovski appealing for help from the party:[26]

> Greetings, friend!
>
> I feel a bit uncomfortable writing, but needs must. I don't think I've ever experienced so terrible a situation. All my money's gone, I've got some sinister cough along with the worsening freezes (37 degree below), a general rundown in health; and I've no store of bread, sugar, meat, kerosene: all my money has gone on running expenses and clothing and footwear. Without such a store everything here is so dear: rye bread costs 4½ kopeks a pound, kerosene 15 kopeks, meat 18 kopeks, sugar 25 kopeks. I need milk, I need firewood, but ... money, I haven't got money, friend. I don't know how I'll get through the winter in such a condition ...
> I don't have wealthy relatives or acquaintances and have absolutely no one to turn to, so I'm appealing to you, and not only to you but also to Petrovski and to Badaev.

He requested that these Bolshevik Duma deputies – Malinovski, Petrovski and Badaev – should send money from the 'fund of the repressed' which they and the Menshevik deputies maintained. Perhaps they could send him sixty rubles?

Stalin expressed his hope that Nikolai Chkheidze – leader of the Menshevik Duma deputies – might look kindly on him as a fellow Georgian.[27] This was a message of despair: no one was more hated by the Georgian Mensheviks than Stalin. Meanwhile he was sorting out his thoughts in Siberia. He read voraciously; there was no time to feel sad about his fate.[28] Co-opted to the Central Committee in 1912, he continued to receive financial assistance by bank transfers from Petrograd. Despite the Okhrana's persecuting attentiveness, the Bolshevik faction did not cease to tend to Stalin, Sverdlov and others.[29] The local police oversaw such transactions. The regularity of the transfers, being no secret to the Ministry of Internal Affairs, naturally gave rise to the suspicion that Stalin was secretly planning an escape. He would need to bribe policemen and pay for rail tickets if this was to be successful.

If ever he made it back to Petrograd, he knew he could count on help from Sergei and Olga Alliluev (whose youngest daughter Nadya was to become his second wife after the October Revolution). He wrote affectionately to Olga on 25 November 1915:[30]

> I'm so very grateful to you, deeply respected Olga Yevgenevna, for your good and pure feelings towards me. I shall never forget your caring attitude to me! I look forward to the moment when I'm liberated from exile and can come to Petersburg [as the Bolsheviks continued to call the capital] and personally thank you and Sergei for everything. I've only got two years at most left.
>
> I received the parcel. Thank you. I only ask one thing: don't waste any more on me; you yourselves need the money. I'll be happy if from time to time you send postcards with scenes of nature and the like. Nature in this accursed district is appallingly barren – the river in the summer and snow in winter are all nature provides here, and I'm driven mad with longing for scenes of nature even if they are only on paper.

Stalin did not often behave gracefully, but he could when he wanted.

He was not entirely removed from active politics. The trial of the Bolshevik Duma faction and its adviser Lev Kamenev in early 1915 in Petrograd had brought disruption to Bolshevism. The charges related to both politics and revolutionary etiquette. Instead of just denouncing the Imperial government, Kamenev had distanced himself from Lenin's policy that the best result in the war for the European Marxist movement would be the defeat of the Russian armed forces by the Germans. Even so, Kamenev could not escape a sentence of Siberian exile. On arrival in Turukhansk District he was again put on 'party trial'. The proceedings took place in Monastyrskoe, and Sverdlov and Stalin were present, as were the members of the Bolshevik Duma fraction. Most participants chose to support Lenin's policy.[31] Stalin was friends with Kamenev; they remained on these terms throughout their Siberian exile and for several years subsequently. Stalin, though, jibbed at Kamenev's failure in open court in Petrograd to show solidarity with the faction's official policy. Probably Stalin had reservations about Lenin's calls for 'European Civil War' as a realistic policy both militarily and politically;

but Kamenev needed to be pulled back into line. Discipline was discipline. Kamenev had committed an infringement and had to be punished.

Stalin started to enjoy life in Kureika. He took up fishing: this brought an enhancement of his diet as well as genuine pleasure. He had had lessons from the Ostyak men and soon, according to his own account, got better at it than the Ostyaks themselves. Supposedly they asked him what his secret was.[32] In any case, he was locally accepted and became known as Osip (or, less pleasantly, as Pockmarked Oska).[33]

Fishing in Siberian exile could be dangerous, as he later recalled:[34] 'It happened that the tempest caught me on the river. At one time it seemed that I was done for. But I made it to the bank. I didn't believe I'd get there: the river was in great tumult.' On another occasion a snowstorm blew up. He had had a good day by the water along with Ostyaks from his village and had a large haul of sturgeon and sea-salmon.[35] Foolishly he went off home before the others. The storm – known in Siberia as a *purga* – blew up suddenly. It was too late to turn back and it was a long way in nearly blinding conditions to Kureika. If he had been sensible, he would have abandoned the fish. But the fish were his food for the month; and anyway Stalin was stubborn. He trudged through the heavy snow, head down into the bitter wind. By the light of a new moon he thought he glimpsed shadowy figures near by; he called out to them, relying on the local tradition of helping strangers in a mess. But the figures moved on. They were in fact the villagers with their dogs whom he had left earlier; and when they saw the snow-covered, gesticulating form, they credulously assumed it was a water demon. Stalin himself was not sure that the figures had been human beings and did not try to catch up with them.[36]

He trudged on by himself. There was a distinct possibility he would not be able to find the village even if he survived the cold. But he got there. Unfortunately he was still an apparition in white, from his bearded face down to his boots. Dragging himself to the nearest hut, he was a bizarre sight. 'Osip,' one of the villagers cried, pressing himself against the wall in fright, 'is that you?' Stalin replied: 'Of course it's me. And it's not a wood spirit!'[37] For millions of peasants in the Russian Empire retained the ancient pagan superstitions even if they belonged to the Orthodox Church or some other Christian denomination. Belief in spirits, devils and witches was widespread, and in eastern Siberia the Church had made little impact upon popular notions. Stalin had yet again been reminded that he lived in a society where the ideas of the Enlightenment were as yet thinly spread. He thawed out; he ate and drank. Then he took to his bed and slept for eighteen hours.[38]

He told another of his stories many years later. At a 1935 Kremlin reception he narrated how he was sitting on the river bank as men of the village went off fishing at the start of the spring floods on the River Yenisei. When they returned, they were one man short. They did not draw attention to this; but Stalin questioned them and was told the missing man had drowned. What struck Stalin, he said, was how little they thought about the death. If he had not mentioned the subject, they would have gone back to their huts without comment. Stalin pondered the event. He felt sure that if a cow had been sick, they would have gone out and tried to save it. But the loss of a man for them was a 'triviality'. The point was, he said, that it was easy to make a man whereas animals were a more complex task.[39] This was nonsense. Perhaps Stalin thought so too; but the fact that he repeated it about two decades later meant that he either believed it or had invented it and decided it suited his current political interest: in the mid-1930s he wished to stress the importance of conserving Bolshevik cadres.[40]

Stalin remembered his time in exile with fondness. Despite what he claimed in his begging letters to party comrades, he was generally healthy. He was treated as a respected visiting member of a community. For the first time he was living closely for a lengthy period with non-Georgians and non-intellectuals. Most were Ostyaks, but a number were Russians. This experience would serve him well when, years later, he became their political overlord. For the rest of his life he talked about his days in Siberia, the fishing, the climate, the conversations and the people. These experiences, even though he was there against his will, uplifted him. He enjoyed the wonder and admiration shown him by the Kureika villagers. They knew he was a 'southerner', but had no idea where Georgia was. They saw he loved books: in a culture of oral tradition this in itself marked him off as a man apart. Even his pipe was an object of awe. Sitting in the hut in the evening, he would pass it round for others to take a puff. Visitors to the villagers popped round specifically to try out this locally unusual mode of smoking. Having chatted with the renowned revolutionary in their midst, they departed happy.[41]

Obviously contact with the central leadership of the Bolshevik faction grew ever trickier in the Great War. In 1915 Stalin and Suren Spandaryan, a fellow Central Committee member, wrote to Lenin. Stalin's part of the letter went as follows:[42]

> My greetings to you, dear Vladimir Ilich, the very warmest greetings! Greetings to Zinoviev, greetings to Nadezhda Konstantinovna! How are things, how is your health? I live as previously, I munch my bread and am getting through half the sentence. It's boring but what can be done about it? And how are things with you? You must be having a gayer time ... I recently read Kropotkin's articles – the old scoundrel has gone completely off his head. I've also read a little article by Plekhanov in *Rech* – what an incorrigible, blabbing old woman! Eh! ... And the Liquidators with their [Duma] deputy-agents of the Free Economic Society? There's no one to give them a beating, the Devil knows! Surely they won't remain unpunished like this?! Cheer us up and inform us that soon there'll be an organ to give them a right good thrashing straight in their gobs – and without respite.

This was the rant of a man wanting to show off his militant style to his leader. The references to beating were repetitious. The frustrations of exile leaped off the page. Stalin hoped to impress on Lenin that, when his term of exile ended, he could be a useful right-hand man for him in the Russian political underground; but he did not miss the opportunity to remind Lenin how different their circumstances were.

Exile had its bright moments for Stalin, but generally it brought the worst out of him. He was an emotionally needy person: people around him were also liable to be subjected to the lash of his tongue or simply to daily insensitivity and egotism. He belonged to a revolutionary party which made a virtue of placing individual satisfaction below the needs of the collective good. It was a party which also cherished comradely good humour. Stalin was not really unsociable. He had friends. He liked a joke and was an amusing mimic. But his friends had to acknowledge his primacy. Stalin had a deep need to dominate. This was why his fellow exiles found him exasperating. At close quarters he was painful to deal with; the Siberian sojourn concentrated everyone's attention on the uncongenial sides of his character which in other circumstances they overlooked because of the perceived benefits he brought to the cause of Revolution.

11. RETURN TO PETROGRAD

The kaleidoscope of Stalin's life was given two abrupt twists in the winter of 1916–17. The first was an unpleasant experience, the second brought delight. In December, as the Imperial Army replenished itself with fresh levies, the government threw the net of conscription wider. Ministers decided to use even political convicts. This was a difficult step. Such people had been exempted from call-up in the war on the ground that they would conduct hostile propaganda among the troops. Compulsory enlistment had always been problematic. In 1915 the conscription of Moslems had touched off an uprising in Russian central Asia. Meanwhile the fighting against the Central Powers had settled down to a fairly static contest and the losses were enormous on both sides of the trenches. Yet morale in the Imperial Army remained robust. The early bottlenecks in military production, transport and supply had been unblocked. The Supreme Command was planning to innovate in a bid to organise a successful offensive, and General Brusilov was being given his chance to prove himself. There was no shortage of food or equipment at the front. But more men were needed. Stalin was among those revolutionaries ordered to submit himself for a medical check with a view to his inclusion in the army of Nicholas II.

They had to travel to Achinsk. This was a town lying a mile north of the Trans-Siberian Railway and a hundred miles to the west of Krasnoyarsk. Stalin, Kamenev and other Bolsheviks – as well as scores of Mensheviks, Socialist-Revolutionaries and Anarchists in exile in Turukhansk District – had to make the arduous journey up the Yenisei to Krasnoyarsk in north Siberia's coldest months. It would take weeks. None of the selected men supported the Imperial government's military objectives (although many Mensheviks and Socialist-Revolutionaries would have readily supported a democratic post-Romanov government in defending the country).[1]

Stalin said his goodbyes in Kureika and set off for Monastyrskoe. There is no sign that he gave any thought to the emotional wreckage he left behind in the Pereprygin family. In Monastyrskoe he joined a group of fellow potential conscripts. The police chief lined them up on the street, and they were cheered by comrades who knew they might never see them again. Steamships could not operate in the winter and the trip up the Yenisei would be made by dog-drawn sleighs from village to village. Before the departure someone ran over to them. This was the deputy accountant in the Revillion company office who had fetched a mandolin and a guitar which the Bolsheviks had forgotten to take.[2] Stalin loved to sing. The trip was not going to be without recreation. Yet the temperature was always several degrees below zero and the wind cut into the faces of the travellers. The long journey from Kureika to Achinsk was one of the most exhausting that Stalin ever made. On reaching Achinsk, he was leaner than for many years; and the long nights of the deep north in winter had given his complexion a distinct pallor.[3] But he had enjoyed himself. The party had stopped at many small hamlets. Stalin had sung to his heart's content and, despite the rules, delivered political speeches at open meetings.[4]

His mood sank on his arrival in Krasnoyarsk as he faced the possibility of conscription. He had just one option left. This was to ask permission from his guard Kravchenko to spend a week there before moving on to the enlistment headquarters.[5] The request was granted. (Did he bribe Kravchenko?) Yet he worried in vain. Army doctors rejected him for military service because of his damaged right arm. He never carried a rifle for Tsar and Motherland.

Since his term of exile was due to end in mid-1917 he was allowed to stay in Achinsk with other revolutionaries rejected for military service. These included his friend Lev Kamenev. Stalin went frequently to Kamenev's rented house. The Bolshevik Anatoli Baikalov later gave an unappealing picture of the scene. Stalin had his pipe perpetually on the go. He stuffed it with *makhorka*, the pungent tobacco favoured by workers and peasants. The smoke and smell annoyed Kamenev's wife Olga. According to Baikalov, 'she sneezed, coughed, groaned, implored' Stalin to put out his pipe, but he ignored her. This was typical behaviour. He turned curmudgeonly conduct into an art form when women made unwelcome demands. He expected admiration and compliance from them – and then he could be charming. But no one in a skirt, not even pretty Olga, was going to order him around.[6] It may not have helped that Olga was intelligent and articulate and that she was the sister of Trotski, sworn enemy of the Bolsheviks. The end of his isolation in Kureika had not improved his mood or his manners; his uncouthness increased in direct proportion to the lowering of the appreciative respect he craved.

His acquaintances found little to appreciate. Stalin was taciturn and morose. Although he listened intently, he barely contributed to discussions on the war and international relations. Instead Baikalov was attracted to Kamenev's lively presence and grasp of the arguments;[7] and writing over two decades later, Baikalov recalled that Kamenev dismissed Stalin's rare comments 'with brief, almost contemptuous remarks'.[8]

The Kamenevs and Baikalov had prejudices that disabled them from appreciating that Stalin was no ignoramus. They were fluent conversationalists. They came from well-to-do families in which such exchanges were normal: Kamenev's father was an engineer and businessman, Baikalov's the owner of a gold mine. Both Kamenev and Baikalov had been educated in gimnazias.[9] They were culturally confident in public whereas Stalin still spoke haltingly in Russian,[10] and four years among the Ostyaks had done nothing to enhance his linguistic facility. Baikalov deplored Stalin's failure to be witty. (Intellectuals were meant to be scintillating conversationalists.) Kamenev and Baikalov also underestimated the virtues of silence. When listening to Kamenev, Stalin felt he was learning. All his life he devoted himself to accumulating knowledge. His attentiveness, memory and analytical skill were razor-sharp even if he did not brag about this to others; and although his Marxism lacked the range of other Bolshevik leaders, he was working to extend himself. At any rate when Stalin was among individuals who encouraged him to relax, he was a delightful purveyor of jokes and mimicry. He also understood Russian perfectly on the page and was an excellent editor of Russian-language manuscripts.[11] He was undervalued, and quietly he resented the fact.[12]

This would not have mattered in the annals of Russian and global history if a second event had not spun him around in the winter of 1916–17. The cause was political tumult in Petrograd. Nicholas II spent an unhappy Christmas. The one bright spot was Brusilov's December 1916 offensive, which pushed the Germans back several miles. It was a long-overdue Russian military success. But the rest of the news was grim. Leaders of the conservative and liberal parties in the Fourth State Duma murmured ever more openly about the need for a change of regime if the armed forces were ever to defeat the Central Powers. One of them, Alexander Guchkov, sounded out the generals for a *coup d'état*. The dynasty's reputation was in tatters. Rasputin, the 'holy man' who had helped to alleviate the effects of the haemophilia of the heir to the throne

Alexei, had been assassinated in December but the stories about him – his gambling, philandering, blaspheming and political venality – continued to cling to Nicholas and Empress Alexandra. In fact it is doubtful that the liberals or conservatives could have done much better. The prolongation of the war put immense and inevitable strain on transport and administration; it also made unavoidable the printing of money to finance the war effort, and this was bound to cause inflation. Nicholas II dispersed the Duma on 26 February 1917. He was determined to keep hold of the situation.

This might have worked if popular opinion had not been so hostile to the Romanovs. Peasants were complaining about fixed grain prices and about the deficit in industrial goods as the result of the priority given to the production of armaments and military equipment. Garrison soldiers disliked the possibility that they might be mobilised to the front. Workers were angry about the deterioration of living and working conditions. Even if they had gained higher wages, the effect was ruined by the devalued currency. Factory strikes occurred in December 1916 and were put down with severity. Yet the grievances remained.

Unbeknown to the revolutionaries in Achinsk, industrial conflict recurred in Petrograd in the last week of February 1917. Trouble erupted among female textile workers on International Women's Day and quickly spread to the workforces in the Putilov armaments plant. The dispatch of garrison troops to control the crowds was counterproductive because soldiers took the side of the strikers and either joined them or handed over their weapons. Order collapsed in the capital. Police fled, generals panicked. The politicians in the dispersed Fourth State Duma sensed that an opportunity to settle accounts with the Romanov monarchy had at last arrived, but lacked the nerve to take action. Even the revolutionary parties were in a quandary. The suppression of the December strikes made them pause for thought. The clandestine networks of Mensheviks, Bolsheviks and Socialist-Revolutionaries had not yet been repaired and morale was still at a low ebb. But the fervour of the strikers was unquenchable, and soon there were demands for the formation of a Petrograd Soviet.

Nicholas II was late in comprehending the scale of the opposition. Hurrying back from Mogilëv towards Petrograd, he was told the game was already up. He took the advice of the Supreme Command; he consulted the speaker of the dispersed State Duma, Mikhail Rodzyanko. At first he wanted to preserve the dynasty by transferring the throne to his haemophiliac son Alexei. No one at court thought this sensible. Then he approached his brother Grand Duke Mikhail, but Mikhail refused the offer. Nicholas II succumbed and on 2 March abdicated to public delight across the empire. Euphoric crowds took to the streets of every town and city.

News travelled to Siberia along the telegraph lines faster than newspapers could be carried by rail. The Bolshevik group in Achinsk was jubilant. Nicholas the Bloody had been overthrown. The dynasty was at an end. The revolutionaries in the town gathered together regardless of party affiliation just after Grand Duke Mikhail's refusal was made known. A spirited discussion followed. Feeling the need to contribute actively to the political outcome, many exiles signed a telegram congratulating the Grand Duke on his civic gesture. Stalin later claimed that his friend Kamenev appended his signature. Kamenev vehemently rejected the accusation; and even Stalin admitted that Kamenev had immediately regretted his action. In March 1917, in any case, Kamenev and Stalin agreed on their strategic objectives. A Provisional Government was formed on 3 March with the sanction of the Menshevik-led Petrograd Soviet. The Prime Minister would be the liberal Prince Georgi Lvov and liberals, especially the Constitutional-Democrats (or Kadets), dominated the cabinet. Only one socialist, the Socialist-Revolutionary Alexander Kerenski, became a minister. The original Bolshevik scheme for the establishment of a 'revolutionary democratic dictatorship' had been thwarted, and Kamenev and Stalin were willing – like most Mensheviks, most Socialist-Revolutionaries and many Bolsheviks – to give the Provisional Government their support conditional on ministers promulgating the basic civil freedoms and limiting themselves to a defensive war against the Central Powers.

As quickly as they could get tickets, the Bolsheviks in Achinsk made their way from Krasnoyarsk along the Trans-Siberian Railway to Moscow and then onwards to Petrograd. Chief among them were Kamenev, Stalin and former Duma deputy Matvei Muranov. The experience was very different from the earlier trip each had made towards their place of exile. They travelled as normal passengers rather than in the arrest wagon. Because of their recent detention near the main line they were going to reach Petrograd before most other leading exiles, not to mention the émigrés. Kamenev and Stalin in particular were committed allies; they agreed on policy, and Stalin was not keen to resurrect the old business of Kamenev's behaviour at the 1915 trial. Their intention was to seize control of the Bolshevik Central Committee in the capital. They aimed to make up for years lost in Siberian detention.

On 12 March 1917 the three of them stepped off the train at the Nicholas Station in east-central Petrograd. Light snow was falling, but Stalin and his companions hardly noticed. Kureika had accustomed them to a lot worse. They were back in Petrograd at last! In his hands Stalin carried a wicker suitcase of medium size; his personal possessions were few and he had no savings to his name. He was wearing the same suit he had worn on his departure in July 1913.[13] The one sartorial difference was that he had *valenki* on his feet. These were the long padded boots worn by Russians in the winter.[14] He was pinched-looking after the long train trip and had visibly aged over the four years in exile. Having gone away a young revolutionary, he was coming back a middle-aged political veteran. Stalin had written to alert his old friend Sergei Alliluev of their arrival.[15] He expected him to be at the station and, perhaps, to have passed on the message to the Russian Bureau of the Central Committee. Fellow passengers and railway personnel had been fêting Stalin, Kamenev and Muranov as heroic fighters against the fallen regime. An honorific reception in Petrograd was anticipated.

In fact no one turned up at the Nicholas Station. There were no bands, no speeches, and no ceremonial escort to party headquarters at the house of the Emperor's former mistress Matilda Kseshinskaya.[16] They had to fend for themselves. When they had left the capital for Siberia, they had been Central Committee members and they expected to be treated with due decorum. They had a rude surprise.

The fact that Shlyapnikov and Molotov, who led the Bureau, had not greeted them was not an accident. Kamenev, Muranov and Stalin expected to be given seats on the Bureau alongside the existing members who had much lower standing in Bolshevism; but the Bureau had other thoughts. If Stalin was willing to overlook Kamenev's breach of revolutionary etiquette, the Bureau was not so indulgent. He had sinned; he had shown no repentance. It would also seem that Stalin's reputation for uncomradely behaviour had preceded him. A struggle for leadership in the Russian Bureau was unavoidable. There was also a political angle to this. The Russian Bureau under Shlyapnikov and Molotov had objected to any support, however conditional, for the Provisional Government. They advocated outright opposition. They also knew that there were many Bolshevik militants not only in the districts of the capital but also in the provinces who felt the same. They edited the new factional newspaper *Pravda* on this basis and strove to win all Bolsheviks to their side. They were already not best pleased by Kamenev's arrival, and when they discovered which side he – together with Stalin and Muranov – was taking in the current political debate they were determined to avoid having rank pulled on them.

The position was clarified on 12 March when the Bureau decided to include only those new members 'whom it considers useful according to its political credo'.[17] Muranov fell easily into this category and was given a place. Then Stalin's case came up for consideration:[18]

> About Stalin it was reported that he was an agent of the Central Committee in 1912 and therefore would be desirable in the membership of the Bureau of the Central Committee, but in the light of certain personal features which are basic to him the Bureau of the Central Committee reached its decision to invite him [to join] with an advisory place.

Stalin had been snubbed. Even his career had been misrepresented; for he had not been a mere 'agent' of the Central Committee but a co-opted full member since 1912. Exactly which 'features' had riled the Bureau was not specified. His underhandedness in political and personal dealings had probably done for him. Kamenev, though, was entirely rejected for membership: he was allowed to contribute to *Pravda* only on condition that he did this anonymously; he was also required to give a satisfactory explanation of his past behaviour.[19]

Stalin made his way to the Alliluev apartment after the Bureau meeting. He had written to Olga Allilueva in 1915 saying that he would visit them as soon as his exile was over.[20] When he paid his call, only daughter Anna was at home. Her parents and brother Pavel were out at work and the younger daughter Nadya was having a piano lesson elsewhere. Her brother Fëdor (or Fedya) too was out.[21] By the end of the day the whole Alliluev family had returned. They talked with their visitor late into the night. A bed was offered to him in the sitting room, where Sergei also slept; and Olga and the girls went off to the bedroom. Joseph made a positive impression on everybody. Anna and Nadya were very taken with him. Sixteen-year-old Nadya especially enjoyed his jollity. The noise from the bedroom disturbed Sergei, who had to work next day at the electricity station. But Joseph intervened on the girls' behalf: 'Leave them alone, Sergei! They're only youngsters . . . Let them have a laugh!' Next day, before he left for the Russian Bureau, he asked if he could lodge with them. The apartment was not big enough for all of them but he was held in such affection that the family decided to look for a larger one. Anna and Nadya were given the task. Joseph was equally keen: 'Do please make sure you keep a room for me in the new apartment.'[22]

Stalin's priority was to sort out his position in the Russian Bureau. After leaving the Alliluevs, he hurried to headquarters and raised a fuss. This time he was more successful. The result was an agreement to find work for Kamenev on the ground that Bolshevik émigrés, presumably including Lenin, continued to value him highly. Stalin was added to the *Pravda* editorial board. Kamenev joined him on 15 March and Stalin was appointed to the Presidium of the Bureau on the same day.[23] Persistence and experience were paying off. Molotov was pushed out of the Bureau.[24] Evidently there had been a fierce dispute and Shlyapnikov and Molotov had lost. *Pravda* began to toe a line approved by Stalin and Kamenev, and the Russian Bureau ceased to demand the Provisional Government's removal.

The position of Stalin and Kamenev was soon to be a matter of shame for them, and Stalin apologised for his failure to take a more radical view; but he had not been as moderate as his later enemies, especially Trotski, liked to suggest. It is true that he refused to attack the Mensheviks in public. Equally undeniable is Stalin's espousal of a policy of mere 'pressure' upon the Provisional Government.[25] Yet he consistently denounced those Mensheviks who advocated straightforward defence of the country. Stalin demanded more; he proposed that Bolsheviks should co-operate only with Mensheviks who accepted the line of the Zimmerwald and Kienthal Conferences and actively campaigned for an end to the Great War. He did not want unity at any cost.[26] Moreover, he wanted the Petrograd Soviet to go on intimidating the Provisional Government. The Soviet, he declared, should work to bind 'metropolitan and provincial democracy' together and 'turn itself at the necessary moment into an organ of revolutionary *power* mobilising all the healthy forces of the people against counter-revolution. The immediate objective was to ensure that the Provisional Government did not go over to the side of the counter-revolution. The speedy convocation of a constitutional assembly was essential.[27]

Nor did Stalin fail to introduce a theme untouched by *Pravda* before he returned: the national question. He demanded linguistic equality for the non-Russian nations. He called for regional self-rule. More than any other Bolshevik in Petrograd in March 1917 he understood that Bolshevism had to appeal to the peoples of the borderlands. Deliberately he opposed talk of federalism.[28] Orthodox Bolsheviks aimed at forming a unitary state and Stalin agreed with this; but 'self-determination' was possible within the framework of the policy he and Lenin had proposed before the war. 'National oppression' had to be eradicated, and the

Provisional Government as a cabinet pursuing the interests of capitalism had not shown the necessary sympathy.[29]

Kamenev and Stalin continued with their combative programme at the unofficial gathering of Bolsheviks and Mensheviks from across the country which was held at the end of March 1917. The Russian Bureau selected him to speak to the joint debate on the Provisional Government. His criticism of the post-Romanov regime was a damning one:[30]

> The elites – our bourgeoisie and the West European one – got together for a change in the décor, for the substitution of one tsar for another. They wanted an easy revolution like the Turkish one and a little freedom for the waging of war – a small revolution for a large victory. Yet the lower strata – workers and soldiers – deepened the revolution, destroying the foundations of the old order. Thus there were two currents in motion – from below and from above – which put forward two governments, two different forces: 1) the Provisional Government supported by Anglo-French capital, and 2) the Soviet of Workers' and Soldiers' Deputies. Power was divided between these two organs and neither of them has the fullness of power. Tensions and conflict between them exists and cannot but exist.

Stalin finished by saying that political rupture with the 'bourgeoisie' was desirable and that 'the sole organ capable of taking power is the Soviet of Workers' and Soldiers' Deputies on an All-Russia scale'.[31]

A separate session of Bolsheviks took place. It was here that Kamenev denounced the warmth of official Menshevik support for the Provisional Government and urged the need to back the Petrograd Soviet.[32] The Bolsheviks and Mensheviks, after all their organisational divisions since 1903, belonged to the same party once again. They were the largest two factions in the Russian Social-Democratic Workers' Party. At the central level they maintained separate bodies, but across the country – especially outside Petrograd – they worked together. This was an unsustainable situation. The right wing of Menshevism advocated vigorous national defence whereas all Bolsheviks wanted a robust campaign for a multilateral peace. Kamenev and Stalin planned to resolve matters by calling upon the anti-defencist Mensheviks to split themselves off from their faction's right wing.

Among Bolsheviks, Kamenev was frank about his calculations:[33]

> It's wrong to run ahead of things and pre-empt disagreements. There's no party life without disagreements. Within the party we'll

survive petty disagreements. But there is one question where it's impossible to unify the non-unifiable. We have a single party together with those who come together on the basis of Zimmerwald and Kienthal, i.e. those who are against revolutionary defencism.

We need to announce to the Mensheviks that this wish is only the wish of the group of people gathered here and is not obligatory for all Bolsheviks. We must go to the meeting and avoid presenting particular platforms. [We should do this] within the framework of a wish to call a conference on the basis of anti-defencism.

Such a statement, made three days before Lenin's arrival in Petrograd, indicates that Kamenev and Stalin were very far from having a gentle attitude to Menshevism. Implicitly they aimed at schism on the basis of a policy on war and peace which was bound to bring the party into direct conflict with the Provisional Government.

This was a plausible strategy, and it is only because the Bolsheviks within weeks had started to go it alone and then, months later, made their October Revolution that the audacity of the Kamenev–Stalin strategy became forgotten. Both Kamenev and Stalin after 1917 had to forswear their strategy as the more radical policy of seizing power without Menshevik assistance was turned into one of the sacred items of Bolshevik history. The episode is anyway important for the light it sheds on Stalin's career. He and Kamenev, despite the Russian Bureau's hostility, had barged their way into the leadership of the faction and elaborated a strategy which, if it had been continued, could have produced a party of radical opposition to the Provisional Government. Factional allegiances were extremely fluid in March and April. The clever idea of tempting left-wing Mensheviks into a Bolshevik embrace had solid political potential. Kamenev and Stalin had been both nimble and determined. They had seen much more of Russia in the twentieth century than Lenin; they had experienced the atmosphere of revolutionary politics in Petrograd since the February Revolution. Their plan for a campaign for radical policies on peace, bread, land and government had the potential for huge popularity.

Lenin violently disagreed. Based in Switzerland, he wrote his 'Letters from Afar' which demanded the overthrow of the Provisional Government. The original strategy of Bolshevism, enunciated since 1905, had been for the workers to overthrow the monarchy and establish a temporary revolutionary dictatorship, uniting all socialist parties, which would implement all imaginable civic freedoms and establish a capitalist economy. Leninist strategy had been made obsolete by the formation of the liberal-led Provisional Government and its promulgation of civic freedoms. Lenin never properly explained why he suddenly thought Russia to be ready for the second great projected stage in its revolutionary development – namely the 'transition to socialism'. But he insisted that this was the only true policy for Bolshevism. He got his chance to fight for his ideas when, at the end of March, the German government allowed him and a group of anti-war Russian Marxists to travel across Germany to Scandinavia before making their way to Petrograd.

Telegrams preceded him, and the Russian Bureau prepared a suitable greeting. Kamenev together with other leading Bolsheviks from Petrograd travelled out to meet him at Beloostrov as the train stopped briefly at the Finnish–Russian administrative frontier on 3 April. Lenin did not mince his words. He picked on Kamenev as the originator of the Russian Bureau's conditional support for the Provisional Government and cursed him heartily.[34] (Stalin avoided such a tirade only because he had not gone to Beloostrov with the welcoming group.)[35] Lenin's mood had not lightened when the train arrived after midnight at the Finland Station in Petrograd. He angrily denounced the Lvov cabinet yet again, and was brusque towards Menshevik leader Nikolai Chkheidze, who headed the Petrograd Soviet delegation deputed to greet him as a renowned returning revolutionary. Then he went off to the Tauride Palace, where he addressed a Bolshevik factional gathering and called for a transformation of strategy. Lenin was heard with incredulity. But he would not be thwarted; again at a joint session of Bolsheviks and Mensheviks he declared that all compromise with the Provisional Government was intolerable. Lenin was on the rampage all through 4 April and Kamenev and Stalin watched impotently. From being dominant leaders they had become spectators.

To the Russian Bureau members who had been pushed aside by Kamenev and Stalin this brought delight. At last they had someone of sufficient standing among Bolsheviks to demand ultra-radicalism. They were enraptured by Lenin and his ideas, which he reduced to a few hundred words and published as his *April Theses*. There were plenty of others in the faction elsewhere in the country who were equally annoyed with the policy of conditional support for the Provisional Government. Bolshevism had always stood for revolutionary extremism. For those Bolsheviks, in Petrograd and across the country, who approved of giving conditional support to the Provisional Government, the arrival of Lenin was akin to a bull crashing into a china shop. Every Bolshevik, on both sides of the debate, was transfixed by the sight of a returning leader full of bile and confidence; and already it was clear that party members had to choose definitively between the rival strategies of Kamenev and Lenin.

Stalin, like many others, went over straightaway to Lenin's standpoint. He never bothered to justify the decision. Hurtling from meeting to meeting in those early days after his arrival in Petrograd, Lenin rallied the ultra-radicals and cajoled the doubters. It was a political *tour de force*. Yet at the same time there was less difficulty for Lenin than appeared at the time. Bolshevism had always cleaved to an extremist agenda. Until 1917, indeed, the faction had anticipated forming a 'provisional revolutionary democratic dictatorship of the proletariat and the peasantry' in the event of the Imperial monarchy's overthrow. A government of Kadets had always been a hateful possibility in the mind of Bolsheviks. Kamenev and Stalin, the advocates of a deal with elements in the Menshevik faction, had always had an ulterior motive. Stalin shifted his ground on 4 April, but not to the extent that he abruptly turned from a 'moderate' into an 'extremist'. And in bending to the Leninist wind, he did not accept Lenin's proposals in their entirety. He continued to believe that Lenin had much to learn about revolutionary Russia (and even about non-revolutionary Europe!).

Yet he could not fail to see the difference between Kamenev and Lenin. Kamenev had been Stalin's senior Bolshevik, his friend and his ally. But Lenin was a real leader. From April 1917 until Lenin's medical incapacitation in 1922 Stalin gave him allegiance. It was often a troubled relationship. They had disputes every year through to Lenin's death. But they got on well between February and October; and Lenin took Stalin under his patronage and promoted his career in Bolshevism.

PART TWO

LEADER FOR THE PARTY

12. THE YEAR 1917

The months between the February and October Revolutions were momentous for Russia. Politics became free and visible. Petrograd was festooned with red flags and devoid of police. Its festivals were those of the socialist leadership of the capital's Workers' and Soldiers' Soviet. The 'Internationale' was sung on ceremonial occasions. There was bravado everywhere and socialism was at a peak of popularity. The Provisional Government under the liberal Georgi Lvov ruled only by leave of the Petrograd Soviet. The political far right vanished after the fall of the monarchy. Order on the streets was maintained by 'mass organisations' such as the Red Guard. Military officers learned to consult their troops. Public life was dedicated to the service of the people. Camaraderie was demanded on all official occasions. If decisions had to be taken, the assumption was that they would be preceded by debate and that workers, peasants and soldiers should have influence over what was resolved. Soviets sprang up in towns across the country. Elected by the lower social orders, they intervened in public affairs whenever their leaders – the Mensheviks and the Social-Revolutionaries – felt that the bodies of central or local government contravened the agreement with the Provisional Government on universal civil freedom and defensive war.

Stalin worked with Lenin to prepare a conference of Bolsheviks later in April. He was one of many leading Bolsheviks in Petrograd and the provinces shifting their opinions under the impact of the debate started by Lenin. They were joining those other Bolsheviks who had always resented giving the slightest support to the Provisional Government. Several Mensheviks even converted to Bolshevism in disdain for their official leadership's policy, and the entire Inter-District Organisation, which had previously been anti-Bolshevik, joined the Bolsheviks in May.[1] The gap between Bolsheviks and Mensheviks had always been wide but the original émigré split in 1903 had been followed by several attempts at reunification; and although the Prague Conference of 1912 had divided the Russian Social-Democratic Workers' Party yet again, Bolsheviks and

Mensheviks in many Russian cities continued to co-operate with each other for many weeks after the February Revolution. But steadily the radical difference in policies counted and the Bolshevik and Menshevik factions definitively became entirely separate parties.

Stalin, even after accepting Lenin's *April Theses*, did not adopt all the leader's policies. Lenin demanded state ownership of the land. Stalin continued to argue that it would alienate the peasants who wished to have total control over the countryside.[2] The land, he insisted, should be transferred to the peasantry without conditions,[3] and perhaps he thought that once Lenin gained direct experience of Russian conditions he would see the point. Stalin also shunned the more provocative of Lenin's slogans on the war. Like Kamenev, Stalin omitted to call on soldiers and workers to turn the existing 'imperialist war' into a 'European civil war' between Europe's proletariats and its bourgeoisies.[4] Kamenev and Stalin understood that if the Bolsheviks were to increase their popularity, they had to stress that they were the only party in Russia which could bring about peace. Equally noteworthy was Stalin's avoidance of terms such as 'the dictatorship of the proletariat'.[5] He had his ears open to attitudes in society. Workers and soldiers saw the downfall of the monarchy as inaugurating an order of freedom and democracy. Ideas of dictatorship were regarded as characteristic of the monarchy overthrown in February 1917. Stalin defended his ideas – and it was not he but Lenin who eventually had to amend his position.[6]

Meanwhile the Provisional Government plunged into difficulties. The war dragged on and Russia's armies appeared increasingly inferior to their German enemy. The dislocation of the economy worsened. Food supplies fell. Factories faced closures as metal, oil and other raw materials failed to be delivered. Banks ceased to bail out industrial enterprises. The civilian administrative system, which was already creaking under wartime strains, started to collapse. Transport and communication became unreliable. At the same time the demands of popular opinion intensified. Workers called for higher pay and secure employment. Soldiers in the garrisons supported a peace policy: they were horrified by the possibility of being transferred to the front line. Peasants wanted higher prices for their harvest; they also insisted on possession of all agricultural land and an end to the war. Shopkeepers and artisans demanded protection against the interests of big business. Ukrainians, Finns and Georgians wanted proof that the authorities in Petrograd were not putting them at a disadvantage. The Provisional Government made concessions. It introduced arbitration tribunals to industrial disputes. It increased prices paid for grain. It overlooked the insubordination of the garrisons. It granted massive autonomy to local organs of self-rule. It promised to hold elections to a constituent assembly at the earliest opportunity.

Ministers refused to sanction further reforms until after the defeat of the Central Powers. The problem manifest since the February Revolution was that the Provisional Government lacked the capacity to restrain those groups in society which demanded that reforms be introduced immediately. The Petrograd Soviet's permission had been crucial in the establishment of the first cabinet, and the soviets, factory–workshop committees, army committees and village land communes proceeded to restrict the capacity of ministers to govern. The armed forces were disabled from enforcing the Provisional Government's will by the insistence of garrison soldiers on ignoring orders they disliked. The police had always been useless at confronting civil disobedience – and anyway they had virtually disbanded themselves on the Imperial monarchy's overthrow.

If Stalin had any doubts about following Lenin, they were dispelled by events in Petrograd. Minister of External Affairs Pavel Milyukov had sent a diplomatic note to London and Paris affirming that Russian war aims remained what they had been under Nicholas II. Since these aims included territorial expansion at the expense of the Ottoman Empire there was much popular revulsion among the workers and soldiers of the capital. The Provisional Government had come to power with the Petrograd Soviet's support on the clear understanding that the war would be fought defensively and that expansionism had been disavowed. On 20–21 April a political demonstration against the cabinet was held by the Menshevik and Socialist-Revolutionary leadership of the Petrograd Soviet. Similar demonstrations occurred in cities across the country. Some Bolsheviks in Petrograd called for armed uprising against the Provisional Government, and Lenin had to disown them as his party's representatives. All the same the whole Milyukov affair played into Lenin's hands. To many as yet unpersuaded Bolsheviks as well as to a rising number of workers and soldiers it appeared that he had been proved right and that the Mensheviks and Socialist-Revolutionaries were to blame for having trusted the Provisional Government.

Opinion in Bolshevism turned definitively in Lenin's favour as he gathered support from those who had been pushed aside by Kamenev and Stalin in March. Lenin achieved this by imposing his status and personality on listeners and readers, and he had the advantage that many veteran Bolsheviks, although they had not developed exactly his ideas on strategy, felt uneasy about offering even conditional support to the liberal-led Provisional Government.[7] Kamenev too aligned himself with him. Lenin for his part abandoned some of his more outrageous slogans. He no longer demanded the transformation of 'the imperialist war into a European civil war'. He temporarily ceased in public to urge 'dictatorship' and 'revolutionary war'.[8] Although Lenin had not yet made all the adjustments required by the Russian political environment, Kamenev believed that he was not the revolutionary fanatic he had seemed at the Finland Station. Stalin formed the same opinion. Putting aside his previous conciliatory attitude to the Provisional Government, he became an unequivocal advocate of Leninism. Milyukov completed the job for Lenin; and when the Bolshevik Party Conference started on 24 April, he knew that victory would be his.

There was a coming together of Lenin and Kamenev at the Conference to advocate unconditional opposition to the Provisional Government. They also demanded drastic measures to end the Great War. Lenin continued to promote his policy of land nationalisation and the Conference voted in his favour. Stalin, despite having put an opposing case in *Pravda*, held his tongue. He soon felt vindicated: Lenin became convinced in midsummer that the land should be handed over to the peasantry through 'land socialisation'.

Stalin and Lenin had been allies on the national question since before the Great War and it was Stalin who gave the report to the Conference. Both sought to make the Bolsheviks attractive to non-Russians in the former Russian Empire. The result, though, was the Conference's most contentious debate. The majority in the preparatory commission voted against Stalin and for Georgi Pyatakov. Most Bolsheviks did not like the commitment of Lenin and Stalin to national self-determination, including even the possibility of secession from the former Russian Empire. It seemed that official policy ignored internationalist principles and indulged nationalism; this appeared to neglect both global economic trends and the interests of the world's working classes. Bolshevik policy supposedly ought to give proletarian revolution precedence over national self-determination. According to Lenin, Pyatakov underestimated the hatred for Russia and Russians in the borderlands. Hostility would be dissipated only if the Ukrainians and Finns were told they had the right to independence. He predicted that such an offer would allay anti-Russian feelings and reconcile not only Ukraine and Finland but also other non-Russian territories to continued union with Russia.

Stalin picked up these themes and added another. Whatever policy was formulated for the former Russian Empire, he maintained, would have implications abroad. If the Bolsheviks were seen to treat their national minorities decently, they would encourage movements of national liberation around the world. The policy would act as a 'bridge between West and East'. Stalin's stirring contribution won the day.[9] He had needed support from Lenin and Zinoviev. Nevertheless he had acquitted himself well in the first report he had delivered to a party conference. He had not flinched when picked out for personal criticism. This had come from the veteran Georgian Bolshevik Pilipe Makharadze, who queried how Stalin would handle the 'separatist aspirations' of nations in the south Caucasus. Makharadze also wondered whether the establishment of local administrations on a national-territorial basis could solve the problem of the complex national intermingling in Georgia and elsewhere.[10] At the very moment Stalin was enjoying himself as the party's expert on the national question, another Georgian had got to his feet to challenge him. Stalin did not let his irritation show. He concentrated his fire on Pyatakov and Dzierżyński and ignored Makharadze's barbed questions. Pyatakov was a young Bolshevik theorist who had criticised Lenin's revolutionary strategy throughout the Great War; Dzierżyński had only recently joined the Bolsheviks from the Polish Marxist organisation and had never accepted Bolshevik official policy on the national question.

Without Lenin's support, however, Stalin might still not have been elected to the Central Committee. Most delegates hardly knew him; it had to be spelled out that one of his other pseudonyms was Koba: not everyone yet knew him as Stalin. But his basic problem was the possibility that someone might repeat the objections made about him in March. Lenin stepped in: 'We've known com[rade] Koba for very many years. We used to see him in Kraków where we had our Bureau. His activity in the Caucasus was important. He's a good official in all sorts of responsible work.' With this recommendation he could breathe again and did not have to face the opposition confronting lesser-known but still controversial candidates such as Teodorovich, Nogin, Bubnov and Glebov-Avilov. Nor did Lenin have to make quite the lengthy speech of defence he had to devote to Kamenev's candidature. Stalin had climbed to the party's summit: he came third after Lenin and Zinoviev in the votes for the Central Committee.[11]

The intensity of political work had been hectic from the moment Stalin had reached Petrograd. A typical day would involve meetings at the Central Committee's offices at the Kseshinskaya mansion. Often these would last into the night. Stalin was not one of the party's orators; according to one of his associates, 'he avoided making speeches at mass meetings'.[12] His failings were obvious. His voice did not carry without a microphone[13] and he spoke with a thick accent. He did not declaim or swagger like a natural actor. If a speaker from the Central Committee was required, the choice would usually fall upon Grigori Zinoviev (or Lev Trotski and Anatoli Lunacharski who joined the Bolsheviks in summer). Occasionally Lenin, too, turned out for an open meeting after conquering his own initial diffidence. Stalin steered clear of such functions unless specially requested by the Central Committee. Policy-making and organisation were his preferred activities. He also liked tasks associated with the editing of *Pravda*. Although his work was done behind the scenes, it was not limited to the internal administration of the party. That role fell to Yakov Sverdlov, who headed the Central Committee Secretariat. Stalin was rising in the party without the rest of the party yet noticing. But those who concluded that he was a 'grey blank' simply demonstrated their ignorance of central party life.[14]

He did not get round to moving in with the Alliluev family as agreed in March.[15] Yet they had kept the room free for him, and the Alliluev youngsters – especially Anna and Nadya – were eagerly looking forward to his coming. Like other Bolshevik leaders, he slept where and when he could. He was making new friends. He also took out women he fancied. It was a disorderly, exhausting existence, but it was not one without its social pleasures.

Meanwhile the Provisional Government failed to keep clear of trouble after April. Among its problems was conflict between its liberal and socialist members. The Mensheviks Irakli Tsereteli and Mikhail Skobelev and the Socialist-Revolutionary Viktor Chernov insisted that regional self-rule should be granted to Finland and Ukraine. The Kadets walked out on 2 July rather than accept cabinet responsibility. The Socialist-Revolutionary Minister of Military Affairs, Alexander Kerenski, had started an offensive against the Central Powers a few days earlier. Political crisis ensued. The Bolsheviks, having embarrassed the Provisional Government in spring, wanted to test the political waters again. They organised a massive protest demonstration on 4 July. Their slogan was 'All Power to the Soviets!' and they aimed to supplant the government. Kronstadt garrison sailors were invited to participate with their weapons in hand. The Provisional Government, supported by the Mensheviks and Socialist-Revolutionaries, banned the demonstration.

But such was the popular discontent that crowds went on gathering in Petrograd. At the last moment the Bolshevik Central Committee feared the use of superior force by the authorities and strove to call off the demonstration. Yet the Provisional Government had had enough. Lenin's financial connections with the German government were exposed and a warrant was issued for his arrest. Petrograd Bolsheviks went into hiding as leading figures such as Lev Trotski, Lev Kamenev and Alexandra Kollontai were taken into custody.

The Alliluevs put their vacant room at Lenin's disposal. On the run from the authorities in the 'July Days' he took refuge at first with the Bolshevik activist Nikolai Poletaev. But Poletaev as a former Duma deputy was well known, and Lenin was grateful to move in with the Alliluevs. He stayed there for a few days before arranging to flee north to the countryside at Razliv. Disguise was essential. He decided to get rid of his beard and moustache. Stalin, who arrived at the Alliluevs' to see him off, performed the task of the party's barber-in-chief.[16] (It would be some years before he became its master butcher.) When Lenin looked in the mirror he was pleased: 'It's very good now. I look just like a Finnish peasant, and there's hardly anyone who will recognise me.'[17] While Lenin stayed with the Alliluevs, Stalin moved in with fellow bachelors Vyacheslav Molotov and Pëtr Zalutski – as well as with Ivan Smilga and his wife – in a largish apartment on Petrograd Side.[18] Molotov and Stalin put their disputes behind them after Stalin admitted: 'You were the nearest of all to Lenin in the initial stage, in April.'[19] There were new strains, however, on their relationship. In old age Molotov recalled that when they shared a flat, Stalin poached a girlfriend – a certain Marusya – off him.[20]

A week or so after Lenin's departure Stalin, despite concern that his presence might endanger the family,[21] moved in with the Alliluevs. By then they had relocated to a more central district and were renting a bigger apartment at 17 Tenth Rozhdestvenskaya Street. There were three rooms, a kitchen and bathroom and the steps into the whole building were 'luxurious' and were manned by a uniformed concierge. There was a lift to the fifth floor where the Alliluevs lived. Stalin was given his own room.[22] A lot of the time he was alone, as Anna and Nadya had left Petrograd for the summer vacation and Fedya was working as hard as their parents Sergei and Olga.[23] He brought his few possessions – manuscripts, books and a few clothes – in a wicker suitcase. Olga fussed over Joseph (as she called him), insisting that he get a new suit. When Joseph pleaded lack of time, she and her sister Maria went out and bought him one. He asked them to put some thermal pads into the jacket. He also said his throat infection made it uncomfortable to wear a normal collar and tie. Olga and Maria were more than happy to indulge him, and Maria sewed two vertical velvet collars on to the suit. Although he looked no dandy, his appearance certainly became smarter.[24]

Nadya returned to Petrograd for the start of the school term at summer's end. She turned sixteen only in September but was already fed up with schooling and had to put up with a certain amount of teasing because of her family's Bolshevik sympathies.[25] Coming back to the flat on Tenth Rozhdestvenskaya, she developed a passion for housework. One day the noise of the tables and chairs being moved around brought Stalin out from his room: 'What's happening here? What's all the commotion? Oh, it's you! Now I can see that a real housewife has got down to work!' This flummoxed Nadya, who asked: 'What's up? Is that a bad thing?' Quickly Stalin reassured her: 'Definitely not! It's a good thing! Bring some order, go ahead . . . Just show the rest of them!'[26]

Stalin liked a woman who looked after the household. He also expected and needed to be admired, and was searching for an enclave in his very busy political life where he could relax. Perhaps he was beginning to take a fancy to Nadya. He might be more than twice her age, but this had not inhibited him with adolescent girls in Siberia. For the time being, however, he went on acting almost as a father to her in the evenings. He read Chekhov's 'Chameleon' and other short stories to the young Alliluevs and recited Pushkin. Maxim Gorki was another favourite. When friends of the youngsters turned up, he was fun with them too.[27] Before turning into bed, he resumed his work; and sometimes he was so tired that he dropped off to sleep with pipe still alight: he once singed the sheets and nearly set the flat ablaze.[28] But the blend of work and family atmosphere was congenial to him. It was a new experience (if we except the periods of exile). He was in his late thirties. He had seldom had a settled life among people who were fond of him. Among the Alliluevs he found a sanctuary at last. A gap in his feelings was being closed; it was scarcely a surprise that he soon took one of the family as his wife.

Still, though, he had to do much for himself. The Alliluev family was busy every day, and Stalin's movements were anyway unpredictable. He therefore bought his food on the way back from work. At the corner of Tenth Rozhdestvenskaya Street he would stop at a stall and buy a loaf of bread and some smoked fish or a sausage. This would constitute his dinner – or, if party business had been hectic, his missed lunch.[29]

Politics, though, was the greater object of his affections. He found his deepest urges satisfied in power and prestige. He had not given up his ambitions as a Marxist theorist. But his current inclinations were towards practical matters such as helping to lead the Central Committee, edit *Pravda* and plan the manoeuvres of the Bolsheviks in Petrograd. The unpleasantness of his reception by the Russian Bureau in March was far behind him; he was solidly established in the central party leadership. He worked madly. His jobs in the Central Committee and at *Pravda* involved so much writing with pen or pencil that calluses appeared on the fingers of his right hand.[30] With the work came authority. Lenin and Zinoviev were fugitives. Trotski, Kamenev and Kollontai were in prison. The party leadership fell into the hands of Stalin and Sverdlov since they were the only members of the inner core of the Central Committee who were still at liberty. Such a situation would have disconcerted many. But Stalin and Sverdlov overbrimmed with confidence as they sought to repair the damage caused to the party by the July Days – and Stalin relished the chance to show that he had political skills which few in the party had as yet detected in him.

By the start of the clandestine Sixth Party Congress in late July there was no doubt about Stalin's eminence among Bolsheviks. He was chosen by the Central Committee to give its official report as well as another 'on the political situation'. Frissons of past mutual hostility no longer bothered Stalin and Sverdlov. As Central Committee Secretary, Sverdlov did not represent a proper rival to Stalin. Indeed Sverdlov was an administrator *par excellence* and although could also be called upon to give rousing speeches in his booming bass voice, he had no aspirations to an independent political persona: he left it to others to think up policies. This was a partner after Stalin's own heart as he sought the limelight in the Bolshevik party.

The July Days in Petrograd had had a damaging impact on the party in the provinces, and delegates from the provinces grumbled that the Central Committee had mishandled affairs in the capital and overlooked the needs of the rest of the party. Stalin stood up undaunted. The criticism, he noted:

> comes down to the comments that the Central Committee kept no contact with the provinces and concentrated its activity in Petrograd. The charge of isolation from the provinces is not without foundation. But there was no chance of covering the entire provincial network. The charge that the Central Committee really turned

into a Petersburg Committee has partial validity. That's how it was. But it was here in Petrograd that Russia's politics were swirling.

Having dealt with the objections, he insisted that the Congress should focus on future strategy. At present the soviets remained under the control of the Mensheviks and Socialist-Revolutionaries, and Lenin – still hiding in Finland – wanted to drop the slogan of 'All Power to the Soviets!' Stalin quietly resisted this move. He understood that if the party was going to gain popularity it needed to project itself as the eager agent of the 'mass organisations'.

Stalin also made a notable contribution to the debate 'on the political situation'. Yevgeni Preobrazhenski, a promising young delegate (who was to join the Central Committee in 1919), wanted a greater emphasis on the need for revolutions elsewhere in Europe. Stalin disagreed:[31]

> The possibility is not excluded that Russia may prove to be the very country that paves the way to socialism. Until now not a single country enjoys such freedom as Russia and has tried to establish workers' control of production. Moreover, the base of our revolution is wider than in Western Europe where the proletariat directly confront the bourgeoisie in complete isolation. Here the workers are supported by the poorest strata of the peasantry. Finally, the apparatus of state power in Germany functions incomparably better than the imperfect apparatus of our bourgeoisie which is a dependency of European capital. We must reject the outmoded idea that only Europe can show us the way. There is dogmatic Marxism and there is creative Marxism. I stand on the ground of the latter.

This statement acquired significance several years later when Stalin, by then the Party General Secretary, demanded that the focus of party policies should be directed at constructing 'socialism in a single country'.[32]

Politics were changing fast outside the Bolshevik party. Alexander Kerenski, who became premier after the July Days, sought to restore political order. He held a State Conference to rally support from parties and other public organisations. Among those who were well received at the State Conference in right-wing political circles was Kerenski's Commander-in-Chief Lavr Kornilov. Kerenski and Kornilov hatched a plan to transfer frontline units to Petrograd (where the troops in the garrisons were notoriously unreliable). At the last moment, on 28 August, Kerenski unjustifiably suspected Kornilov of plotting a coup d'état. Kornilov was ordered to keep his forces at the front. This convinced Kornilov that

Kerenski was no longer fit to govern the country at war, and he decided to overthrow him. Panic ensued in Petrograd. Kerenski's military resources were weak and he relied on socialist agitators to meet the trains and dissuade the troops from obeying Kornilov. Among the much-needed agitators were Bolsheviks as well as Mensheviks and Socialist-Revolutionaries. Kornilov was arrested. Kerenski survived, but already his days looked numbered.

And Bolshevism grew again as an open political force. Yet it did not do this any longer under the dual leadership of Stalin and Sverdlov. On 30 August the Central Committee considered a confidential request from Zinoviev to return to work. There were risks in this. Not only might Zinoviev be arrested but also his restoration to the Central Committee might provoke a renewed attack on the party by the authorities. Zinoviev was told that the Central Committee was 'making every effort for him to be as close as possible to party and newspaper work'.[33] This did not put off Zinoviev, and he attended the meeting of the Central Committee the very next day.[34] The Central Committee recognised it needed a revolutionary leader of his talent. The same was true of Trotski even if many Bolsheviks continued to regard him with hostility. Released from prison, he was itching to have a public impact. On 6 September the Central Committee made fresh dispositions of personnel. The *Pravda* editorial board, previously led by Stalin, was expanded to include Trotski, Kamenev, Sokolnikov and a Petersburg Committee representative. Trotski was also assigned to help edit *Prosveshchenie* and to join the Central Executive Committee of the Congress of Soviets. Although Stalin too was assigned to the Central Executive Committee, his deficiencies as an orator meant that Trotski would be the party's leading figure on it.[35]

Stalin's weeks in the political sun were over. The next task for the Central Committee was to organise the Bolsheviks for the Democratic Conference convoked by Alexander Kerenski. This was set to occur in the Alexandrinski Theatre on 14 September and Kamenev was selected as the main Bolshevik speaker. Stalin joined Trotski, Kamenev, Milyutin and Rykov on the commission which drew up the party's declaration.[36] The Democratic State Conference brought together the socialist parties from across the former empire. Among Mensheviks and Socialist-Revolutionaries there was rising discontent about the Provisional Government's incapacity to alleviate social distress and refusal to intensify reform. Alexander Kerenski was becoming almost as much their *bête noire* as he already was for the Bolsheviks. The Central Committee's strategy was to persuade delegates to the Democratic State Conference that Kerenski needed to be replaced by a socialist government. The Mensheviks and the Socialist-Revolutionaries remained in charge of most soviets in urban Russia even though both the Petrograd Soviet and Moscow Soviet had fallen into the hands of the Bolsheviks. The declaration therefore called on all socialists, including Bolsheviks, to unite their forces in pursuit of common objectives. This was agreed on the assumption that it was in line with the strategic compromise accepted by Lenin in Finland.

The specific demands of the Bolsheviks were comprehensive, and these would inevitably lead to disputes with the Mensheviks and the Socialist-Revolutionaries. While aiming to set up an all-socialist administration, the Bolshevik Central Committee insisted that the policies should be radical. The landed gentry needed to be expropriated. Workers' control should be introduced and large-scale industry nationalised. A 'universal democratic peace' should be offered to the peoples of the world. National self-determination had to be proclaimed. A system of comprehensive social insurance should be established.[37]

What the Central Committee had not bargained for was that Lenin had ceased to believe – if ever he had believed – in the possibility of peaceful revolutionary development. On 15 September the Central Committee discussed a letter from him demanding the start of preparations for armed insurrection.[38] He said nothing about an all-socialist coalition. The thing for him was to overthrow Kerenski and set up a revolutionary administration. His frustrations in hiding were poured into writing. Articles flowed from his pen in Helsinki, each stipulating that the Bolshevik caucus should make no compromise at the Democratic State Conference: the time for talking had ended. In 'Marxism and Insurrection' he called for 'the immediate transfer of power to the *revolutionary democrats headed by the revolutionary proletariat*'.[39] His summons to uprising caused consternation among several Central Committee members. At the same Central Committee meeting there was heated discussion, and Stalin confirmed his support for Lenin by proposing that the letter be sent to the most important party organisations for discussion; but the Central Committee in the end decided to burn the letter and keep only one copy for the records. This was agreed by a vote of six to four.[40]

Bolshevik party policy on the central question of governmental power was in flux. Radical opinion was strengthened by Trotski's return to open activity. Throughout the country, moreover, there were many socialist leaders and activists who sought the Provisional Government's removal. More and more city soviets, trade unions and factory-workshop committees were acquiring Bolshevik majorities in late September and early October. Sooner or later the question had to be answered: were the Bolsheviks going to seize power? If so, when would they do it? And if they did it, would they act alone or in some kind of socialist alliance? Stalin, though, had made his choice. He no longer saw the point of compromise of any kind with the Mensheviks. (Trotski had made the same transition.) His future lay with the Bolsheviks and with them alone. His position in the Bolshevik Central Committee was firmly held but he had next to no political authority outside its framework. He was one of the most influential yet one of the most obscure of Bolsheviks. If he had died in September 1917, no one – surely – would have written his biography.

13. OCTOBER

Petrograd in October 1917 was more placid than at any time since the fall of the Romanovs. The schools and offices functioned without interruption. Shops opened normally. The post and tram systems operated smoothly. The weather was getting brisk; people were wrapping up well before going outdoors but as yet there was no snow. Calm prevailed in the Russian capital and heady mass meetings were a thing of the past. Leading Bolsheviks who plotted insurrection had reason to worry. What if Lenin was wrong and the popular mood had turned away from supporting a revolutionary change of regime?

Yet the subterranean strata of politics were shifting. Lenin, holed up in Helsinki since mid-July, was frustrated by the Bolshevik Central Committee's refusal to organise an uprising against the Provisional Government. Instinct told him the time for action had arrived, and he decided to take a chance and return secretly to Petrograd. Bolshevik leaders who met him secretly in the capital had to weather the anger of his demands for an insurrection. He was softening them up for a confrontation at the Central Committee on 10 October. Twelve members attended. Everyone knew there would be trouble. The minutes of the meeting were skimpily recorded – and this means that no trace survives of Stalin's contribution. At any rate the crucial statements appear to have been made by Sverdlov and Lenin. Sverdlov as Central Committee Secretary was keeper of information on the party's organisational condition and political appeal across the country. Convinced by Lenin's arguments in favour of an uprising, he put a positive gloss on his report by stressing the rise in party membership. This gave Lenin his chance: 'The majority of the population is now behind us. Politically the situation is entirely mature for a transfer of power.'[1]

Two Bolshevik Central Committee members opposed Lenin. One was Kamenev, who had never been a radical among Bolsheviks either in 1917 or earlier in the war. The other, surprisingly, was Zinoviev, who had been Lenin's adjutant in the emigration before the February

Revolution.[2] Kamenev and Zinoviev together carried the dispute to Lenin. They dismissed his extreme optimism and pointed out that many urban soviets had yet to be won by the Bolsheviks. They stressed that the party's electoral following was all but confined to the towns. They cast doubt on the assumption that the rest of Europe was on the brink of revolution. They feared the outbreak of civil war in Russia.[3]

Yet the vote went in favour of Lenin by ten votes to two. Stalin was among his supporters; he had left his association with Kamenev entirely behind him. He was convinced that the time had come to seize power. His mood can be gauged by the article he published in *Rabochi put* ('The Workers' Way' – this was the successor to *Pravda* and was under his editorial control). Stalin had high hopes:[4]

> The revolution is alive. Having broken up the Kornilov 'mutiny' and shaken up the front, it has flown over the towns and enlivened the factory districts – and now it is spreading into the countryside, brushing aside the hateful props of landlord power.

This was not an explicit call for insurrection. Stalin did not want to present Kerenski with a motive to close down the Bolshevik press again; but he warned that Kornilov's action had been the first attempt at counter-revolution and that more would follow. Collaborationism, by which he meant the assistance given to the Provisional Government by Mensheviks and Socialist-Revolutionaries, had been found politically bankrupt. The Kadets had been shown to be 'a nest of and a spreader of counter-revolution'. Soviets and army committees should prepare themselves to repel 'a second conspiracy of the *Kornilovshchina*'. Stalin was adamant that 'the full might of the great Revolution' was available for the struggle.[5]

The Central Committee met again on 16 October. Representatives of Bolshevik party bodies in Petrograd and the provinces were invited to attend. Lenin again made the case for insurrection. He claimed that the moment was ripe even though there were reports that workers were unenthusiastic about a seizure of power. Lenin argued that 'the mood of the masses' was always changeable and that the party should be guided by evidence that 'the entire European proletariat' was on its side. He added that the Russian working class had come over to the Bolsheviks since the Kornilov Affair. Ranged against him were Central Committee members inspired by Kamenev and Zinoviev. Lenin's critics denied that the Bolsheviks were strong enough to move against the Provisional

Government and that a revolutionary situation existed elsewhere in Europe. Even Petrograd was an insecure citadel for Bolshevism. Zinoviev maintained: 'We don't have the right to take the risk and gamble everything at once.'[6]

Stalin supported Lenin:[7]

> It could be said that it's necessary to wait for a [counter-revolution-ary] attack, but there must be understanding about what an attack is: the raising of bread prices, the sending of Cossacks into the Donets district and suchlike all constitute an attack. Until when are we to wait if no military attack occurs? What is proposed by Kamenev and Zinoviev objectively leads to the opportunity for the counter-revolution to get organised; we'll go on to an endless retreat and lose the entire revolution.

He called upon the Central Committee to have 'more faith': 'There are two lines here: one line holds a course for the victory of revolution and relies on Europe, the other doesn't believe in revolution and counts merely upon staying as an opposition.'[8] Sverdlov and other Central Committee members also came to Lenin's aid; and although Trotski was absent because of his duties in the Military-Revolutionary Committee of the Petrograd Soviet, Lenin won the debate after midnight. The voting again went ten to two in his favour.

Lenin went back into hiding and sent furious letters to comrades in the Smolny Institute. This was the former girls' secondary school in the centre of the capital where the Petrograd Soviet and the central bodies of the various parties – including the Bolsheviks – were based. Lenin was keeping up the pressure for armed action. Kerenski was considering his options and came to the conclusion that drastic action was required before the Bolsheviks moved against him. Tension rose on 18 October when Kamenev breached party discipline by stating the case against insurrection in the radical left-wing newspaper *Novaya zhizn* ('New Life').[9] While not revealing precisely what the Bolshevik Central Committee had decided, he dropped very heavy hints. Lenin wrote to the Smolny Institute demanding the expulsion of the 'strike-breakers' Kamenev and Zinoviev from the party.[10] On 19 October Zinoviev entered the proceedings with a letter to *Rabochi put*. Its contents were at variance with the position he had so recently espoused. Zinoviev claimed that Lenin had misrepresented his position and that Bolsheviks should 'close ranks and postpone our disputes until circumstances are more propitious'.[11] Quite what was intended by Zinoviev is unclear. Perhaps he

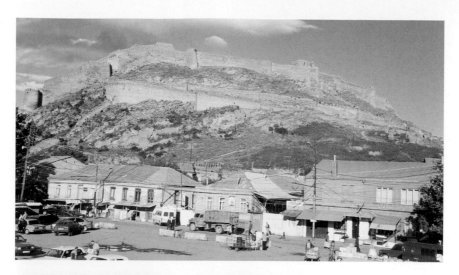

Above. View of Gori Fortress taken from the town.

Far left. Stalin's mother Ketevan.

Left. Stalin's first wife Ketevan Svanidze.

Below. The balcony of one of the houses Stalin grew up in – a shrine-complex was erected over it in the 1930s.

Above.
The Mantashëv Shoe Factory in Tbilisi.
Once a place of dirt and poverty, it is now
being turned into luxury flats.

Above left.
The front of the Tiflis Spiritual Seminary.
It is now a museum of Georgian
national culture.

Left.
The Physical Observatory
on Mikhailovski Street.

Opposite.
Stalin as a young man.
This photo has been heavily 'improved' by
Stalinist air-brushers.

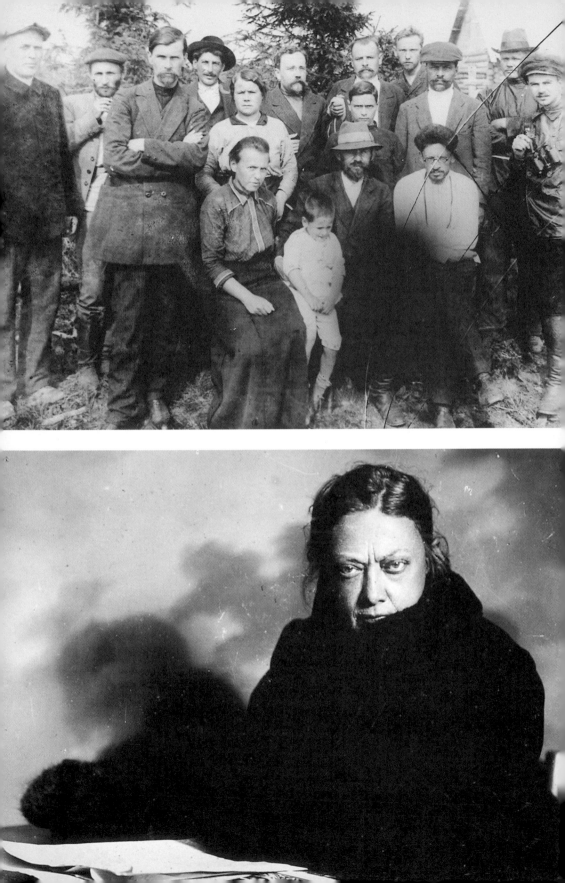

Vladimir Lenin. Taken in January 1918, this was his first official portrait after the October Revolution (and after he had regrown his beard).

Opposite top. Group photograph of Bolshevik exiles in Turukhansk District. Stalin, wearing a black hat, stands at the back next to his friend (at that time) Lev Kamenev. Yakov Sverdlov, sporting a bouffant hairstyle and spectacles, is seated to the right.

Opposite left. Nadezhda Krupskaya.

Lev Trotski.

Lev Kamenev.

Grigori Zinoviev.

Nikolai Bukharin.

General Secretary Stalin in 1924.
This was an official portrait by
M. S. Nappelbaum.

Stalin's second wife Nadezhda Allilueva – Nadya.

wanted to be able to go on arguing the case in the Central Committee (whereas Kamenev had undeniably breached confidentiality and jeopardised the party's security).

This spat fell into the lap of Stalin as chief editor of *Rabochi put*. He decided to accept Zinoviev's conciliatory move and print his letter.[12] But neither Zinoviev nor Stalin explained how Kamenev and Zinoviev as opponents of armed action could work with Lenin, Trotski and those committed to insurrection. On 20 October the Central Committee adjudicated. It was a fiery session and the first occasion when Stalin and Trotski seriously fell out with each other. Trotski was blunt. Stalin, he insisted, had been out of order in publishing Zinoviev's letter. Sokolnikov, Stalin's editor of *Rabochi put*, denied involvement in the editorial decision. Stalin stood exposed as the person responsible.[13] Kamenev resigned from the Central Committee in despair at the policy of insurrection. Stalin continued to support Lenin's policy, but the indignities of the debate induced him to present his resignation from the editorial board.[14]

He recovered his poise only when his request was rejected. This seemed the end of the matter; nobody knew how deeply he resented any shock to his self-esteem – and Trotski in 1940 was to pay the ultimate personal price. In terms of Bolshevik political strategy it remains unclear why Stalin was indulgent to Kamenev and Zinoviev. He never explained his thinking. But it would be in accord with his usual attitude to regard Kamenev and Zinoviev as allies in the struggle to reduce Trotski's influence to a minimum. Lenin's growing penchant for Trotski was a threat to the authority of Central Committee veterans. Another possibility is that Stalin sensed that the opponents of insurrection would ultimately stay with the party. Milyutin quickly moved back into line with official policy. Perhaps Stalin believed that a disunited party could not carry through the necessary armed manoeuvres against the Provisional Government. At any rate it was on his best form that he returned to the Central Committee on 21 October. Stalin, not Trotski, drew up the agenda for the forthcoming Second Congress of Soviets. His scheme marked down Lenin to speak on 'land, war and power', Milyutin on workers' control, Trotski on 'the current situation' and Stalin himself on the 'national question'.[15]

At the same Central Committee meeting Stalin was included in the list of ten members deputed to reinforce the Executive Committee of the Petrograd Soviet. He was at the centre of political operations.[16] Already he belonged to the Military-Revolutionary Committee. He also had a vibrant influence in the Party Central Committee and, despite the contretemps over Zinoviev, was among its most trusted leaders.

The Provisional Government was the first to act in the contest with the Bolsheviks. On the morning of 24 October, on Kerenski's orders, troops arrived at the premises of *Soldat* and *Rabochi put*, broke some machinery and seized equipment. Stalin was present. He watched as the edition which he had signed into print was seized and an armed guard stationed at the door. He can hardly have been surprised by Kerenski's measures. Stalin's anonymous editorial had stated:[17]

> The existing government of landlords and capitalists must be replaced by a new government, a government of workers and peasants.
>
> The existing pseudo-government which was not elected by the people and which is not accountable to the people must be replaced by a government recognised by the people, elected by representatives of the workers, soldiers and peasants and held accountable to their representatives.
>
> The Kishkin–Konovalov government should be replaced by a government of soviets of workers', soldiers' and peasants' deputies.

Kishkin was Minister of Internal Affairs, Konovalov the Minister of Industry. Stalin recommended readers to 'organise your meetings and elect your delegations', ending with the invocation: 'If all of you act solidly and staunchly, nobody will dare to resist the will of the people.'[18] The revolutionary intent was obvious even if Stalin pragmatically refrained from spelling it out.

Presumably it was his editorial duties that prevented him from attending the Central Committee on the same day. Trotski too was absent, but this did not inhibit him from denigrating Stalin as a man who avoided participation in the decisions and activities connected with the seizure of power.[19] The story got around – and has kept its currency – that Stalin was 'the man who missed the revolution'.[20] Proof was thought to lie in the assignments given by the Central Committee to its own members. Here is the list of assignments:[21]

> Bubnovv – railways
>
> Dzierżyński – post and telegraph
>
> Milyutin – food supplies
>
> Podvoiski (changed to Sverdlov – surveillance of Provisional Government after objection by Podvoiski)

Kamenev and Vinter   — negotiations with Left SRs
[who were on the radical extreme of the
Party of Socialist-Revolutionaries]

Lomov and Nogin   — information to Moscow

Trotski thought this demonstrated the marginality of Joseph Stalin to the historic occasion being planned.

Yet if inclusion on the list was crucial, why were Trotski and Lenin omitted? And if commitment to the insurrection was a criterion, why did the Central Committee involve Kamenev? The point was that Lenin had to remain in hiding and Trotski was busy in the Military-Revolutionary Committee. Stalin as newspaper editor also had tasks which preoccupied him, and these tasks were not unimportant. As soon as he had the time, he returned to the Smolny Institute and rejoined his leading comrades. There he was instantly given a job, being sent with Trotski to brief the Bolshevik delegates who had arrived in the building for the Second Congress of Soviets. Stalin spoke about information coming into the Central Committee offices. He emphasised the support available for the insurrection from the armed forces as well as the disarray in the Provisional Government. Stalin and Trotski performed their task well. There was recognition in the Central Committee of the need for tactical finesse. A premature rising was to be avoided; and in order to gain the acquiescence of the Left SRs it was sensible to act as if every measure was merely an attempt to defend the interests of the Revolution against its militant enemies.[22]

The Petrograd situation was dangerously fluid. Troops were on their way from outside the capital to help the Military-Revolutionary Committee, which already controlled the central post office. Stalin was confident that facilities could be established to restore *Rabochi put* despite the raid on the press earlier in the day.[23] Everything would depend on the balance of forces assembled next day by the Military-Revolutionary Committee and the Provisional Government. Kerenski faced a decisive trial of strength.

Stalin went back to the Alliluevs' apartment for the night. There was no time for jokes or story-telling. He was tired out. Yet he had carried out his duties more than satisfactorily. Anna Allilueva heard him saying: 'Yes, everything's ready. We take action tomorrow. We've got all the city districts in our hands. We shall seize power!'[24] He lay down for the last few hours of undisturbed rest he would have for several days. He did not sleep very long. An emergency Central Committee meeting was called before dawn on 25 October and Stalin had to be present. Even the 'strike-breakers' Kamenev and Zinoviev attended. The minutes have not survived the October Revolution, but the agenda must surely have been devoted to the practical side of seizing power. The military planning was finalised and discussion took place about the new revolutionary government, its personnel and its decrees. Lenin was charged with drafting decrees on land and peace. When the moment came, the Council of People's Commissars had to be able to make its purposes clear.[25]

The fact that Stalin was not asked to direct any armed activity has perpetuated a legend that he counted for nothing in the Central Committee. This is to ignore the broader scope of the meeting. The Military-Revolutionary Committee had already made its dispositions of the garrisons and Red Guards. Stalin's functions had previously precluded him from involvement in such activity and it would have been folly to insert him at the last moment. Yet the meeting also deliberated on what was to happen when the Provisional Government was declared overthrown later in the day. Stalin took part in the deliberations as light began to dawn. Already he knew he would have immense tasks to discharge when daylight came.[26] Expectancy intensified. He and his Central Committee comrades snatched food and drink as they talked. They went on consulting each other. They greeted messengers from all over Petrograd and sent others out on errands. Although their eyes were red with lack of sleep, their concentration was acute. This was the time of their lives. The Dictatorship of the Proletariat was about to be proclaimed and Revolution was going to spread across Russia and would soon break out in Europe.

The events of 25 October 1917 were historic by any standard. Acting through the Military-Revolutionary Committee of the Petrograd Soviet, Trotski and other Bolshevik leaders controlled the garrisons of the capital and directed troops loyal to them to seize post and telegraph offices, government buildings and the Winter Palace. In the night of the 24th–25th Lenin returned to the Smolny Institute to resume command of the Central Committee. It was he who coaxed and ordered Bolsheviks to stick to the agreed purpose. Power had to be seized without delay. Across the capital the Military-Revolutionary Committee secured important buildings of administration and communications. Meanwhile hundreds of delegates had gathered for the opening of the Second Congress of Soviets of Workers' and Soldiers' Deputies. At Lenin's insistence the overthrow of the Provisional Government was brought forward. He sensed there might be trouble at the Congress if the seizure of power were not a *fait accompli*, and he continued to cajole his Central Committee comrades into action. The Provisional Government was no more. Although the Bolsheviks were not an absolute majority at the Congress, they were easily the largest party – and the Mensheviks and Socialist-Revolutionaries were so annoyed by the night's events that they walked out. Power fell comfortably into the hand of the Bolshevik party.

Stalin had no role visible to the public eye. He did not speak at the Congress. He did not direct the Military-Revolutionary Committee. He did not move around Petrograd. Much as he had enjoyed the politics of revolution in earlier months, he was little to be seen on that historic night. Characteristically he got on with his assignments and did not poke his nose into the business of others. Here is the testimony of Fëdor Alliluev:[27]

> At the time of the October [seizure of power] comrade Stalin didn't sleep for five days. Crushed by tiredness, he finally fell asleep while sitting in a chair behind his table. The enraptured Lunacharski tiptoed up to him as he slept and planted a kiss on his forehead. Comrade Stalin woke up and jovially laughed at A. V. Lunacharski for a long time.

Such joviality seems odd only if the later myths about him are believed. When he came back from Siberia, acquaintances had warned of the unpleasant features in his character, and these had been discussed at the April Party Conference. But he had gained a better reputation in following months. Not once did he come to notice for bad temper, insensitivity or egocentricity. If anything was held against him, it was that he was too supportive towards Lenin on the national question.

He had done his jobs – important party jobs – with diligence and efficiency. With Sverdlov he had run the Central Committee in July and August. He had edited the central party newspaper through to the seizure of power in October. Since April he had helped to bring about the pragmatic adjustment of party policy to popular demands. He felt at home in the environment of revolutionary Russia; and when he came back to the Alliluev flat he was greeted by admirers. He wrote, edited, discussed and planned with eagerness.

The composition of the new revolutionary authority reflected this. The Council of People's Commissars – or Sovnarkom in its Russian acronymic form – was announced on 26 October. The title was a joint idea of Lenin and Trotski. Lenin was delighted: 'That's wonderful: it has the terrible smell of revolution!'[28] The Bolsheviks wanted to avoid associating themselves with 'capitalist' political culture with its cabinets, ministers and portfolios. There would not be a premier but a chairman. This would be Lenin. The People's Commissar for External Affairs would be Trotski. Rykov, Shlyapnikov, Lunacharski, Milyutin and Nogin were other original members. Stalin too was on the list. His post was newly invented and had no precedent under Nicholas II or Kerenski. Stalin was to be People's Commissar for Nationalities' Affairs. Although his functions and powers were yet to be defined, the basic objective was to set up an institution with a view towards winning over the non-Russians in the former empire to the side of Sovnarkom. When *Pravda* resumed publication, Stalin was relieved of the editorship. His energies had to be reserved for the Central Committee, Sovnarkom and his own People's Commissariat. Stalin's position at the centre of revolutionary politics was confirmed.

Initially it had been Lenin's hope to share posts with the Left Socialist-Revolutionaries, who were impressed by the determination of the Bolsheviks to impose immediate agrarian reform benefiting the peasantry. But negotiations quickly stalled. Lenin was less eager to have a coalition with the Mensheviks and the other Socialist-Revolutionaries. But many in the Bolshevik Central Committee felt otherwise; indeed most Bolsheviks in Petrograd as well as in the provinces assumed that the overthrow of the Provisional Government had been made in the cause of establishing a revolutionary government uniting all socialist parties. For several days the Bolshevik Central Committee engaged in talks with them. Lenin and Trotski wanted them to break down; and when this duly occurred, several People's Commissars indicated their disgust by resigning from Sovnarkom. These included Rykov, Milyutin and Nogin. All this occurred against a background of political and military emergency. The Menshevik-led railwaymen's union threatened to strike until such time as a broad coalition was formed. Kerenski, having escaped from the Winter Palace, rallied a force of Cossacks and moved on Petrograd. In the provincial cities there was armed conflict as Bolsheviks seeking to support Sovnarkom confronted their adversaries.

The railwaymen failed to show the required determination, and Kerenski was defeated on the Pulkovo Heights. The collapse of the coalition talks, however much he himself had been to blame, gave Lenin the pretext to consolidate a purely Bolshevik central government. In November the Left Socialist-Revolutionaries recognised the practical situation and agreed to join Sovnarkom as the junior partner in a two-party coalition. Lenin came to see Stalin in an ever brighter light. Stalin never wavered. Lenin asked him to explain the official party line to Bolsheviks who had come to Petrograd for the Second Congress of Soviets.[29] He also got him to co-sign Sovnarkom decrees confirming the closure of newspapers hostile to the revolutionary government.[30] Stalin had resisted the calls to walk out of Sovnarkom when the Bolsheviks attained a monopoly of power. Such individuals were not legion in the Bolshevik Central Committee. Lenin needed all the available talent; and being keen to dominate Sovnarkom, he did not find it disadvantageous to have Stalin and others as a counterweight to the charismatic Trotski.

14. PEOPLE'S COMMISSAR

The decree announcing his appointment as People's Commissar for Nationalities' Affairs gave his surname as Dzughashvili-Stalin. The publicity gratified a man as yet unknown to most citizens. Lenin and Trotski were the outstanding figures in Sovnarkom and the Bolshevik Central Committee; Zinoviev, Kamenev, Bukharin and Lunacharski were also famous. Despite his newly achieved prominence, however, Stalin continued to work in the shadow of the other leaders. Fëdor Alliluev, who was his first personal assistant, was to recall:[1]

> In those days comrade Stalin was genuinely known only to the small circle of people who had come across him in work in the political underground or had succeeded – after October [1917] – in distinguishing real work and real devotion to the cause from chatter, noise, meaningless babble and self-advertisement.

Stalin acknowledged that others had gained greater acclaim between the February and October Revolutions. He admitted he was not much of an orator. But he turned this into a scalpel to cut his rivals. In his estimation, he did not boast or show off but concentrated on practical deeds.[2] But Stalin liked to say such things about himself rather than hear them from other people, and Fëdor's writing was consigned to the archives unpublished.

Stalin needed his cunning. His institution not only lacked personnel: it did not even have finance or its own offices. Its staff had to work from rooms in the Smolny Institute for want of anything more spacious. Funds remained short because all the bank workers were on strike. Stalin sent his deputy Stanisław Pestkowski to plead for a subvention from Trotski, who had got hold of the banknotes from the main safe at the former Ministry of Foreign Affairs. When Stalin and Pestkowski at last sequestered a suitable building, they pinned a crude notice on the wall to claim it for the People's Commissariat of Nationalities' Affairs.[3]

Things were no better after the Soviet government transferred itself to Moscow in March 1918 in order to move out of the range of Germany's immediate military menace. Offices were assigned to the People's Commissariat in two separate buildings on different streets despite Stalin's protest. He resorted to the desperate measure of commandeering the Great Siberian Hotel on Zlatoustinskaya Street. But the Supreme Council of the People's Economy, headed by Nikolai Osinski, had beaten him to it. Stalin and Pestkowski did not take this lying down. They tore down Osinski's notice and put up their own. Lighting matches to find their way, they entered the building from the back. But Osinski complained to Sovnarkom and Stalin had to move out. 'This was one of the few cases,' Pestkowski recalled, 'when Stalin suffered defeat.'[4] It was even difficult to gather personnel. Most Bolshevik militants wanted nothing to do with a body whose brief involved concessions to national sensitivities – even Pestkowski disliked being attached to it.[5] Stalin relied increasingly on the Alliluev family and asked Fëdor's younger sister Nadya to work as his secretary.[6] One day she was a schoolgirl bored with lessons at the gimnazia,[7] the next she was an employee of the revolutionary government.

The vagueness of party policy remained troublesome. Although Bolshevik objectives had been declared, detailed measures had never been formulated. Stalin was left to sort out the detailed implementation of policy on the national question on his own. His great asset in this task was that he enjoyed Lenin's trust. When Lenin went off on vacation to Finland at the end of 1917, the government's dealings with the Ukrainian regional authority – the Rada – were tense in the extreme. General Kaledin was assembling and training a counter-revolutionary force in south Russia. The situation in the south Caucasus was boiling up. Revolutionary stirrings in Estonia needed attention. Some Bolshevik leaders rose to the level of the duties assigned to them in Sovnarkom; others could not cope or messed up their jobs. Stalin thrived on his responsibilities.

It was of course Lenin who headed the Bolshevik collective leadership. Even Trotski stood in his shadow. Stalin ungrudgingly acknowledged that Lenin was the hub of the Sovnarkom governmental machine, and on 27 December he sent an urgent request for him to come back from his holiday in Finland to help in Petrograd.[8] Lenin insisted on Stalin coping on his own; he continued his brief holiday with wife Nadezhda and sister Maria. Stalin went on reaffirming the objectives which he and Lenin had been espousing before the October Revolution. There was to be national self-determination for all the peoples of the former Russian

Empire. Confirmation should be given that no privileges would be accorded to the Russians. Each people would have the right and the resources to develop its own culture, set up schools in its own language and operate its own press. Freedom of religious belief and organisation would be guaranteed. (The exception would be that churches, mosques and synagogues would lose their extensive landed property.) For those national and ethnic groups living concentratedly in a particular area there would be regional self-administration. The Russians as a people were hardly mentioned. The era of empire was declared at an end.

Lenin and Stalin designed these extraordinary promises to allay suspicions among non-Russians that the Bolsheviks would discriminate against them. By offering the right of secession, Sovnarkom tried to reassure the non-Russians that the revolutionary state would treat each national and ethnic group equally. The consequence, it was firmly expected, would be that the other nations would decide that the Russians could be trusted. The huge multinational state was to be preserved in a new and revolutionary form.

There were exceptions to this pattern. Following the Provisional Government's precedent, Lenin and Stalin accepted the case for Polish independence. It would have been fatuous to act otherwise. All Poland was under German and Austrian rule. Sovnarkom was recognising a *fait accompli*; it was also trying to make the point that, whereas the Central Powers had subjugated the Poles, the revolutionary government in Petrograd sought their political and economic liberation. There was one domain of the Romanovs where practical proof could be given of such a commitment. This was Finland. Relations between Russian and Finnish Marxists had always been warm, and the Bolsheviks had benefited from safe-houses provided for them. The Bolshevik party had supported the steady movement of popular opinion in Finland towards a campaign for massive autonomy from the Russian government. Outright independence was not widely demanded. Yet Lenin and Stalin, to the world's amazement, encouraged the Finns to take up such a position. A delegation of Finnish ministers was invited to the Russian capital and a formal declaration of secession was signed on 23 November (or 6 December according to the Gregorian calendar adopted by Sovnarkom in early 1918). This was a policy without parallel in history. A former imperial power was insisting that one of its dependencies, whether it liked it or not, should break away from its control.

The motives of Lenin and Stalin were less indulgent than they seemed. Both felt that the Finnish Marxists would stand an excellent chance of achieving dominance in an independent Finland. This would enable the Bolsheviks and their comrades in Finland to resume close operational ties and, eventually, to re-include Finland in the multinational state governed from Petrograd. There was a further aspect to Sovnarkom's policy. This was the calculation that a single act of secession from the former Russian Empire would constitute wonderful propaganda in favour of socialist revolution elsewhere, especially in eastern and east-central Europe.

Lenin and Stalin also began to modify their ideas so as to increase the party's appeal to regions inhabited mainly by peoples who were not Russian. Dropping old Bolshevik arguments, they came to espouse the federalist cause. They held back from explaining what they meant by federalism. Their enemies pointed out that the new policy sat uneasily alongside Bolshevism's permanent commitment to centralism and dictatorship; but neither Lenin nor Stalin was troubled by the criticism: they had come to the conclusion that if the Bolsheviks were to expand their authority into the borderlands of the former Russian Empire, they had to espouse federalism. Stalin's old Gori friend Davrishevi, the Social-Federalist, had always wanted to turn the Russian Empire into a socialist federation. In fact Lenin and Stalin had not been converted to federalist principles. They had no intention of turning Ukraine, Georgia and other countries into equal members of a federal union. But they wished their propaganda to make an impact and were willing to change their terminology. Central control over the 'borderlands' remained an imperative. Essentially Lenin and Stalin hoped to charm them and bring them back under rule from the Russian capital. They stole slogans; but their own basic ideas and purposes remained intact.

As the area under Soviet control expanded, at least in the towns, the People's Commissariat for Nationalities' Affairs acquired additional importance. Stalin chaired the meetings when his other duties in government and party did not distract him, and he empowered Stanislaw Pestkowski and Ivan Tovstukha to handle business in his absence. Dozens of departments were founded in the People's Commissariat to take care of specific nationalities. Stalin's energetic leadership surmounted the teething problems and the provinces began to experience the results in the early months of 1918. He sent out funds for national and ethnic groups to set up presses in their languages. Schools were established on the same lines. This trend had begun under the Provisional Government; the Bolsheviks vigorously reinforced it and put it at the core of their propaganda. A central newspaper, *Zhizn natsionalnostei* ("Nationalities'

Life"), was created to spread the message to the parts of the country where the Bolshevik presence was weak. A plan was developed for local self-administration to be granted to nations which constituted a majority in any particular region, and Stalin hoped to found a Tatar–Bashkir Republic by the River Volga. He was going out of his way, on behalf of the Central Committee, to show that an authentically internationalist state was being constructed.[9]

Other Bolsheviks were introduced to represent the interests of the nations to which they belonged.[10] But membership was fluid and sessions were chaotic, and often the appointees were newcomers to the party. Departments often failed to co-operate with each other. It was soon recognised too that functionaries might use the People's Commissariat to push the case for their nations more assertively than Sovnarkom had envisaged.[11]

The danger existed that things might get out of hand. Stalin discovered this early on. A bright young Tatar called Sultan-Galiev joined the party in November 1917. A fluent writer and speaker, he was an obvious man to recruit to the People's Commissariat. Sultan-Galiev was eager to raise the banner of Revolution among Moslems in general. Unfortunately he proved difficult to regulate. As Commissar of Moslems' Affairs in Inner Russia he quickly annoyed other members of the People's Commissariat of Nationalities' Affairs by his initiatives, and his loyalty to Bolshevism was questioned.[12] Indeed his campaign to spread socialism among Moslem believers eventually led him to propose a pan-Turkic republic separate from Sovnarkom's control. (He was arrested in 1923 and executed in the Great Terror.) Although Sultan-Galiev was a notorious source of trouble for the Bolsheviks, he was not the only recruit to the party who was thought excessively tolerant of nationalism and religion. Stalin and Lenin had taken a risk in insisting on trying to attract the non-Russians to Bolshevism through various concessions. In 1917 they had earned criticism at the April Party Conference; and in 1918–19 the difficulties of realising the policy were already manifest. Work in the People's Commissariat was a bed of nails.

Stalin did not flinch. At the Third Congress of Soviets in January 1918 he took pride in the government's proclamation of 'the right of all peoples to self-determination through to complete secession from Russia'. He compared Sovnarkom favourably on the national question with the Provisional Government and its 'repressive measures'. According to Stalin, such conflicts as had broken out since the October Revolution arose from clashes about class and power rather than about nationhood.[13] Nevertheless his attitude was castigated by the Socialist-Revolutionaries for being 'infused with a centralist power'. He gave no ground: he said the country faced a simple choice between 'nationalist counter-revolution on one side and Soviet power on the other'.[14]

His capacity to stand up to leaders of other parties as well as his editorial experience and expertise on the national question made Stalin an obvious choice – along with Sverdlov – to chair sessions of the commission drafting the Constitution of the Russian Socialist Federal Soviet Republic (or RSFSR). There had been no thought about the details before the October Revolution. Even general principles had been left unclear: Lenin and Stalin had advocated federalism while skirting round what this would involve. Out of the hearing of the zealots in his People's Commissariat for Nationalities' Affairs, Stalin admitted that many non-Russian groups were making no demands at all for autonomy: Russia was not tormented by nationalist strife. Stalin admitted that even the Tatars and Bashkirs, to whom he wanted to grant an autonomous republic, were displaying 'complete indifference'. He therefore wished to avoid specifying the national aspects of the Constitution while this situation persisted.[15] But something of substance had to be inserted if the non-Russians were to be won over, and Sverdlov and Stalin insisted on this in the teeth of opposition from the Bolshevik left.[16] Bolsheviks had to be pragmatic in spreading the power and ideology of the Revolution. The national question offered an opportunity to win converts to socialism.

This did not save Stalin from personal attack. The Left Socialist-Revolutionaries had representatives on the commission, and they did not hold back from criticising him. A. Shreider objected that he had no principled commitment to national rights and used federalist rhetoric to disguise an imperialist purpose. Official Bolshevik policy was allegedly little different from the measures of Nicholas II:[17]

> Stalin's structures are a typical imperialist construction; he's a typical kulak [rich peasant] who without embarrassment declares he's not a kulak. Comrade Stalin has got so used to such a position that he's even assimilated imperialist jargon to perfection: 'They beg from us and we grant to them.' And of course – according to Stalin – if they don't make the request, then we don't give them anything!

This was calumny; for Stalin was offering autonomy even to national groups not demanding it. It is readily imaginable what happened to Shreider in later years. Stalin did not forget much in life. As the chief persecutor of the kulaks from the late 1920s he did not take kindly to being compared to a kulak or to any other 'enemy of the people'; and he never forgave a slight.

His sensitivity was exposed in March 1918. It was then that Menshevik leader Yuli Martov published an article on the past sins of the Bolsheviks, mentioning that Stalin had been expelled from his own party organisation before the Great War for organising armed bank robberies. Stalin arraigned Martov before the Moscow Revolutionary Tribunal for slander.[18] That Stalin should have expended so much energy in trying to refute Martov's allegation was a sign of his continuing feeling of insecurity at the apex of politics. He had a Georgian sense of personal honour; indeed he had it in an exaggerated form. Martov had besmirched his reputation. Stalin got his name cleared by a Bolshevik-run court. (It was noticeable that Stalin did not deny involvement in the organisation of the robberies: he did not chance his arm by risking the possibility that Martov might summon witnesses.)[19] The Moscow Revolutionary Tribunal found in Stalin's favour, but not before Martov dredged up other embarrassing episodes from Stalin's past. He mentioned that comrades in prison in Baku had tried Stalin for participation in the robbery campaign; and Isidore Ramishvili was called as a witness. Martov also brought up the story that Stalin had had a worker beaten to within an inch of his life.[20]

The libel case was the overreaction of a hypersensitive man. If Stalin had not made a fuss, hardly anyone would have noticed what Martov had written. Stalin's resentment did not end with the conclusion of the trial. When in 1922 Lenin asked him to transfer funds to Berlin for the medical care of the dying Martov, Stalin refused point-blank: 'What, start wasting money on an enemy of the working class? Find yourself another secretary for that!'[21]

This was not the only aspect of his inner life revealed in these months. Debating nations and administrative structures in the Constitution commission, he forcefully declared: 'The Jews are not a nation!' Stalin contended that a nation could not exist without a definable territory where its people composed the majority of inhabitants. This had always been his opinion,[22] and it ruled out the possibility of granting the Jews an 'autonomous regional republic' such as he was proposing for others.[23] Was this evidence of a hatred of Jews for being Jews? Stalin differed from Lenin inasmuch as he never – not even once – commented on the need to avoid anti-semitic impulses. Yet his People's Commissariat for Nationalities' Affairs had its own Jewish section and funded

Yiddish newspapers, clubs and folk-singing ensembles. Many Jews belonged to his entourage over the next two decades. To a considerable extent he was just sticking to a dogmatic version of Marxism. But there was probably more to it than that. Nothing can be proved, but probably he felt uneasy in dealing with Jews because they were unamenable to administrative control on a simple territorial basis – and he also had a growing rivalry with several leaders of Jewish origin in his party: Trotski, Kamenev and Zinoviev.

At any rate the commission's records scarcely refer to Lenin. Matters were debated on their merits within the frame of Bolshevik and Left Socialist-Revolutionary ideas. Stalin was his own man. Indeed it was the Left Socialist-Revolutionary M. A. Reisner who brought up Lenin's name. His objection was that Stalin's project reflected the 'anarchic' tendencies embodied in Lenin's recently published *The State and Revolution*. Stalin's response was a distinctly sniffy one:[24] 'Here there's been mention of comrade Lenin. I've decided to permit myself to note that Lenin as far as I know – and I know very well – said that [Reisner's own] project is no good!' The rest of the commission agreed and accepted Stalin's draft with its advocacy of national-territorial administrative units.[25] His colleague Sverdlov's phrasings were pushed back in favour of those proposed by Stalin.[26] Sverdlov had been the individual most responsible for embedding the general structures of administration in the Soviet republic after the October Revolution. This was yet another sign of Stalin's ever-rising importance among the Bolsheviks, and his expertise on the national question gave him a ladder to climb higher and higher.

If he was a rare Bolshevik moderate on the national question, though, he was constantly extreme in his advocacy of state violence and dictatorship. Stalin was convinced that severe measures should be applied against the enemies of Sovnarkom. He was in apocalyptic mood: 'We definitely must give the Kadets a thorough beating right now or else they'll give us a thorough beating since it's they who have opened fire on us.'[27] Violence, dictatorship and centralism slept lightly in the Russian political mind – and many conservatives, liberals and social-democrats were already beginning to think that they had been wrong to stick after the February Revolution to principles of universal civil rights, gradualism and democracy. Bolshevism had never carried such an inhibiting legacy. Those Bolsheviks who had yearned for a gentle revolution could usually be persuaded to accept the case for authoritarianism. There was no need to persuade Stalin.

Bolsheviks had always talked casually about terror and its uses for a revolutionary administration. Yet until power had come into their hands it was unclear how keenly they would resort to it. If there were any doubts about this, Lenin and Trotski quickly dispelled them in the weeks after they overthrew the Provisional Government. Lenin established an Extraordinary Commission for the Struggle with Counter-revolution and Sabotage (Cheka in its Russian acronym) – and he ensured that it would remain beyond regular supervision by Sovnarkom. In subsequent years he supported nearly all pleas by Felix Dzierżyński and other Cheka leaders for permission to expand the application of methods of state terror. Not every Bolshevik leader approved this development. Kamenev on the right and Bukharin on the left of the ascendant party leadership urged that violence should be deployed on a more predictable basis and should be reduced in scope. Stalin was never one of these. Terror attracted him like a bee to a perfumed flower. Not once had he offered an opinion on the matter before the October 1917 Revolution, yet his preference for arbitrary state violence was speedily evident. When Bolsheviks in Estonia telegraphed him about eradicating 'counter-revolutionaries and traitors', he replied with hot approval: 'The idea of a concentration camp is excellent.'[28]

State terrorism had already been installed as a permanent item in his mental furniture. It appealed to his coarse personality. But the attraction was not just psychological; it was also based on observation and ideology. Stalin and other Bolsheviks had grown up in an age when the world's great powers had used terror against the people they conquered; and even when terror was excluded as a method, these powers had had no scruples about waging wars at huge cost in human lives. By such means they had spread a superior economic system around the world. This system had been defended by the application of harsh authority. Colonial peoples had suffered. The working classes of the imperial powers themselves were exploited and oppressed. The Great War had impoverished the many while enriching the few. The point for Stalin was that violence was an effective weapon for capitalism and had to be adopted by the Soviet revolutionary state for its own purposes. Coming to power in Russia, the Bolsheviks had to be realistic. The Bolshevik leadership believed that the Paris Commune of 1871 had failed for want of ruthlessness. Bolsheviks would not repeat the mistake. Even if they had expected their revolution to be easier than it turned out to be, they had always been willing to meet fire with fire. Stalin needed no one to persuade him about this.

Yet it was in foreign policy that Lenin most appreciated Stalin.

Lenin and Trotski around the turn of the New Year understood that they lacked the armed forces to carry socialism into central Europe by 'revolutionary war'. Yet whereas Trotski wished to stick by the party's commitment to revolutionary war, Lenin concluded that policy ought to be changed. When Germany and Austria–Hungary delivered ultimatums to Sovnarkom, Lenin urged the Bolshevik Central Committee to sign a separate peace. Most Central Committee members – as well as the entire Left Socialist-Revolutionary Party – rejected his argument that the priority should be the preservation of the Soviet state. For them, a separate peace would involve the betrayal of internationalist ideals. Better to go down fighting for European socialist revolution than to collude with the robber-capitalist governments of the Central Powers.

Stalin had always been sceptical about the prognosis of imminent revolutions in the rest of Europe and the failure of the proletariats elsewhere in Europe to rise against their governments did not surprise him. The propensity for strategic and tactical compromise he had always shown in internal party affairs was now applied to the policy of the revolutionary state. If the Central Powers could not be overthrown by revolution or defeated in war, the sensible alternative was to sign a peace with them. This was in fact already the opinion of Lenin, whose reputation for compromise in the party's internal quarrels was slighter than Stalin's but who had always insisted on the need for flexibility of manoeuvre in the wider field of politics. Sverdlov, Kamenev, Zinoviev and a few others in the Central Committee stood shoulder to shoulder with Lenin. But the voting in the Central Committee was heavily against them at the preliminary discussion on 11 January 1918. Trotski won the day by arguing for a policy based on the following formula: 'We're stopping the war, we aren't concluding peace, we're demobilising the army.' This, he suggested, had the merit of avoiding an intolerable compromise with the forces of international imperialism.[29]

Lenin kept to his argument without personalising his critique. Stalin was less inhibited. Like most other leading Bolsheviks, he disliked and distrusted Trotski, and at the same meeting he let his feelings show:[30]

Comrade Trotski's position is not a position at all. There's no revolutionary movement in the West: the facts are non-existent and there's only potential – and we can't operate on the basis of mere potential. If the Germans start to attack, it will reinforce the counter-revolution here [in Russia]. Germany will be able to attack since it possesses its own Kornilovite armies, its guard. In October we were talking about our 'crusade' because we were told that mere mention of the word 'peace' would stir up revolution in the West. But this has proved unjustified.

This was the first blow in a political contest which ended only in August 1940 when Soviet agent Ramón Mercader drove an ice-pick into Trotski's cranium in Coyoacán in Mexico.

Even so, Stalin's supportive statement irked Lenin. He objected to the comment that 'a mass movement' did not exist in the West, and said that the Bolsheviks would be 'traitors to international socialism if [they] altered [their] tactics because of this'. Lenin wanted to reassure the advocates of revolutionary war that if ever it looked as if a rupture of peace talks would serve to stir up the German working class to revolution, then 'we have to sacrifice ourselves since the German revolution in force will be much higher in strength than ours'.[31] It was not so much that Stalin had said that revolutionary initiatives were impossible in the West. Nor had he claimed this in 1917.[32] Yet he was loath to gamble on 'European socialist revolution' – and for Lenin this was one compromise too many with the revolutionary strategy he had elaborated in the party before October 1917. These tensions did not much matter at the time. Lenin needed every supporter he could get. Again and again in ensuing days Stalin voted on Lenin's side.[33] Always his line was that Bolsheviks needed to be practical: they could not beat the Germans militarily and the newly born Soviet state would be crushed unless a separate peace was concluded with the Central Powers.

He was as frantic as Lenin. On 18 February 1918 he protested to the Central Committee: 'The formal question is superfluous. A statement must be made directly on the essence of the matter; the Germans are attacking, we don't have the forces; it's high time to say directly that negotiations have to be resumed!'[34] He vividly appreciated the armed might of the enemy: 'They only need to open their hurricane-like fire for five minutes and we shan't have a soldier left standing at the front. We must put an end to the nonsense.'[35] On 23 February he expostulated: 'The question stands like this: either the defeat of our revolution and the unravelling of the revolution in Europe or we obtain a breathing space and strengthen ourselves. This is not what's holding up the revolution in the West. If it's the case that we lack the means to halt a German attack by armed might, we must use other methods. If Petrograd has to be surrendered, it would not amount to a full surrender or to the rotting away of the Revolution. There's no way out: either we obtain a breathing space or else it's the death of the Revolution.'[36]

The Leninists did not gain a majority in the Central Committee until 23 February. By that time the German terms had hardened. The separate peace would require Sovnarkom to disclaim sovereignty over the western borderlands of the former Russian Empire. It was, in Lenin's phrase, an obscene peace. Ukraine, Lithuania, Latvia and Estonia were to be allowed to fall into the grasp of the Central Powers. Half the human, industrial and agricultural resources of the domains of Nicholas II were to be forsworn at the little frontal town of Brest-Litovsk if Sovnarkom wished to avoid being overthrown by the Germans. No other political party in Russia would accede to such terms. The Left Socialist-Revolutionary Party, already annoyed by the forcible local expropriations of peasant-produced grain, walked out of the Sovnarkom coalition and organised an unsuccessful *coup d'état* against the Bolsheviks in July 1918. Nevertheless Lenin and his followers pressed forward with their chosen strategy. The Treaty of Brest-Litovsk was signed on 3 March 1918. For Lenin, the peace offered a 'breathing space' for the Bolsheviks to strengthen and expand the Revolution at home and to prepare the revolutionary war in central Europe that had hitherto been impractical. A Red Army started to be formed; and Trotski, who had condemned the separate peace, agreed to become People's Commissar for Military Affairs. Other Bolshevik opponents of the treaty drifted back to the Central Committee and Sovnarkom.

Stalin's assignments in spring 1918 confirmed his high status in the ascendant party leadership. In internal and external affairs he had stuck by Lenin. He had not done this subserviently. In the Brest-Litovsk dispute he had taken an angle of argument different from Lenin's; and, contrary to the conventional stereotype of him, this continued to be true after the signature of the treaty. When the German armies overran the agreed demarcation line between Russia and Ukraine in May, he reconsidered the whole peace deal. Unlike Lenin, he suggested a resumption of armed hostilities. He put this case at the Central Committee and Sovnarkom.[37] But Lenin won the discussion without Stalin by his side, and the dissension between them faded. Lenin, in the light of future events, should have learned from the episode that his People's Commissar for Nationalities' Affairs was a politician who knew his own value and was determined to stand up for himself. Stalin fought his corner in the Central Committee and dominated his People's Commissariat. His competence and adaptability had been tested in the fire of an October Revolution which had yet to be secured. His advocacy of ruthless measures was as ferocious as anything put forward by Lenin, Trotski or Dzierżyński. He expected others to recognise what he could offer for the good of the cause.

15. TO THE FRONT!

On 31 May 1918 Stalin was given an important fresh assignment. Food supplies for Russia had reached a critically low point and Sovnarkom was close to panic. The decision was to send two of the party's most able organisers, Stalin and his previous Bolshevik opponent Alexander Shlyapnikov, to procure grain in the south of the Soviet republic. The Volga region and the north Caucasus were traditional areas of agricultural abundance, and Stalin and Shlyapnikov were given full powers to obtain food wherever it could be found. Stalin was to make for Tsaritsyn, Shlyapnikov for Astrakhan.

His Alliluev assistants in the People's Commissariat for Nationalities' Affairs would accompany him. Fëdor would come as his aide and Nadya as his secretary. They arrived with their luggage at the Kazan Station in Moscow two days later. Chaos awaited them and their Red Army guards. Beggars and pickpockets swarmed in the booking hall and on the platforms. There were also the many 'sack-men' who travelled to Moscow to sell flour, potatoes and vegetables on the black market. Sometimes passengers had to sit around for days before they could board a train. The atmosphere was frantic. When announcements of departure were made, a rush occurred to get a seat or a space in the corridor. Every compartment would be crammed with people and it was common for the disappointed ticket holders to clamber to the tops of carriages and ride unsheltered from summer heat or winter cold. Stalin had a sheaf of documents indicating his priority over other passengers. But the People's Commissar for Nationalities' Affairs had to lose his temper before the station officials granted a compartment to him and his party. He was being given yet another display of the extreme disorder of revolutionary Russia.[1]

The travellers from Moscow, after many halts on the way, reached their destination on 6 June.[2] Tsaritsyn, later called Stalingrad and now — ever since Khrushchëv's posthumous denunciation of Stalin – Volgograd, was one of the cities on the River Volga built in the late seventeenth century as Cossack outposts. In most ways it was an unremarkable place. It was not even a provincial capital but was subject to the administrative authorities in Saratov. Yet geographically and economically Tsaritsyn was of strategic importance. The city handled regional trade in grain, timber and livestock. It was also a vital entrepôt. Situated at the first great angle of the Volga for ships heading upriver towards central Russia from the Caspian Sea, Tsaritsyn had been a great staging post since its foundation. The construction of rail links increased its significance. A main line ran directly south from Moscow to Rostov-on-Don and a branch was built from Kozlov down to Tsaritsyn and on to Astrakhan on the Caspian coast. Tracks had also been laid from Tsaritsyn west to Rostov-on-Don and south-east to Tikhoretskaya junction and the mountains of the north Caucasus. Control over Tsaritsyn and its environs would enable Sovnarkom to gain food supplies over a vast area.

Sovnarkom's brief to Stalin was to improve the supply of grain. He had been preceded to Tsaritsyn by Andrei Snesarev, a former Imperial Army general who had enlisted with the Reds. The functions of Stalin and Snesarev were meant to complement each other. The combined application of political and military muscle was thought the best method of securing bread for Moscow and Petrograd.[3]

Sovnarkom had misjudged its People's Commissar. Stalin interpreted his duties in grain procurement, which relied on the use of the Red Army, as entitling him to impose himself over all the military commanders in the region. Rejection for service as a private in the Imperial Army had not made him diffident about taking charge of the North Caucasus Front. A month later he informed Lenin:[4]

> The food-supplies question is naturally entwined with the military question. For the good of the cause I need full military powers. I've already written about this and received no answer. Very well, then. In this case I myself without formalities will overthrow those commanders and commissars who are ruining the cause. That's how I'm being nudged by the interests of the cause and of course the absence of a scrap of paper from Trotski won't stop me.

Stalin was greedily seizing his opportunity. His renown in Moscow came nowhere near to matching that of his most eminent comrades in Sovnarkom and the Party Central Committee. This was a situation for him to prove his mettle militarily and politically. He was determined to rise to the challenge.

There were several threats to the Bolsheviks across the Soviet republic by the middle of 1918. A Russian 'Volunteer Army' was being trained in Novocherkassk. It was led by Generals Alexeev and Kornilov, who had escaped from Petrograd and planned to march on Moscow. The Volunteer Army was the first of the self-styled White armies which objected to socialism and internationalism and sought the restoration of the pre-1917 social order through the military destruction of the Reds. In September, another armed force under the Socialist-Revolutionaries had been forced out of Kazan – seven hundred miles to the north of Tsaritsyn – by the Red Army. Trotski's reorganised system of command and recruitment was already proving effective. Yet the regiments of the Socialist-Revolutionaries had not been crushed. Retreating to the Urals, they regrouped and were joined by officers of the type being gathered by Alexeev and Kornilov in the south. In November a coup took place in Omsk, and Admiral Kolchak got rid of the Socialist-Revolutionaries and reorganised the army on his own terms. These armies denounced Bolshevism as a betrayal of Mother Russia. Cossacks led by General Krasnov were attacking the Bolsheviks and their sympathisers in the area south of Tsaritsyn. They were well equipped and had high morale; they detested Lenin's Sovnarkom for its socialism, atheism and hostility to national traditions. Stalin's assignment had put him in personal danger – and he and his Alliluev companions were never unaware of the risks.[5]

Later enemies overlooked the nerve he showed in the Civil War. He was not a physical coward; he put Lenin, Kamenev, Zinoviev and Bukharin in the shade by refusing to shirk wartime jeopardy. Yet he was hardly a war hero, and his subsequent eulogists overdid their depiction of him as a commander of genius who saved the October Revolution from the banks of the Volga.

Stalin's assignment in the south was important. Without food the Soviet regime was doomed. The German occupation of Ukraine as well as the presence of Alexeev and Kornilov in Rostov-on-Don had perilously narrowed the Soviet state's agricultural base. Krasnov's raids by late July had disrupted communication with Tsaritsyn. South Russia and the north Caucasus were crucial areas of wheat production, and Lenin in Moscow was determined to clear the bottlenecks in procurement and shipment. White armies were not the only menace. Many local armed groups also interfered with trade and traffic; and although some of them were mere bandits, others had a political or religious motive. The nationalities of the area wanted autonomy from Moscow. The disintegration of the Russian state in 1917 had given them an opportunity to revert to self-rule as well as brigandage. Charged with restoring the passage of grain from this turbulent region, Stalin shouldered a weighty burden. But he never flinched; he carried his responsibilities with pride and imparted his determination to his fellow travellers.

Tsaritsyn's authorities had thought he would function as the baleful 'eye of Moscow'.[6] They were wrong. Stalin showed total disregard for instructions from the capital. Immediately upon arrival he set about purging the Red Army and the food-collection agencies of the middle-class 'specialists' he collectively detested. This was in blatant contravention of official policy. Stalin did not trouble himself with Lenin's potential objections: 'I drive everyone onwards and curse everyone I need to.' He referred to the specialists as 'cobblers'.[7] This was a significant metaphor for the cobbler's son who wanted to prove his prowess as an army commander; it was also a breach with the line approved by the Central Committee.

Despite having only the powers of a food-supplies commissar, Stalin imposed himself on all the military and civil authorities in the vicinity: Andrei Snesarev, commander of the North Caucasus Front; Sergei Minin, chair of the Tsaritsyn Soviet; and Kamil Yakubov, leader of the food-supplies missions in the region. If Stalin wanted to be known as a fighting man, he had to do something unusual. The Whites had cut the railway line between Tsaritsyn and Kotelnikovo. Stalin braved danger by going out to inspect the situation. This was not typical of him: during the rest of the Civil War and throughout the Second World War he avoided any such venture.[8] But from Tsaritsyn he took an armoured train down to Abganerovo-Zutovo where a railway-repair brigade was at work restoring the line. Putting his life at risk, he returned two days later with his reputation enhanced.[9] Back in Tsaritsyn Stalin called together the city functionaries and, parading his authority as a member of the Party Central Committee and Sovnarkom, announced a total reorganisation of the military command in Tsaritsyn. He was making his bid for supremacy on the North Caucasus Front.

Shrewdly he got fellow Bolsheviks on his side. Sergei Minin was one. Another was Kliment Voroshilov, who was itching to take command in the field despite his lack of military experience. Both were more than happy to join Stalin in forming their own Military Council to oversee operations in the region (which was renamed the Southern Front). On 18 July Stalin and his new associates sent a telegram to Lenin demanding the sacking of Snesarev and confirmation of their Military Council.[10]

The request was granted. Lenin and his comrades in Moscow accepted that tighter co-ordination of military and economic measures was vital in Tsaritsyn for the security of food supplies. Stalin was delighted. Setting himself up not in a hotel but in a sequestered railway carriage halted outside the city station, he looked a new man. On arriving in Tsaritsyn, he called for a cobbler to order a pair of black, knee-length boots to go with his black tunic. The cobbler arrived at the railway carriage and took the measurements. 'Well,' asked Stalin, 'when will they be ready?' 'In five days,' replied the cobbler. Stalin exclaimed: 'No, you can't mean that! Come on! My father could make two pairs of such boots a day!'[11] The anecdote shows how little Stalin had learned about shoemaking. Nevertheless from summer 1918 till the day he died, military-style clothing was normal for him. Stalin became known not only for his long boots but also for his light-coloured, collarless tunic. He abandoned suits, ordinary shirts and shoes for ever.[12] He started to comport himself with a soldierly bearing. He carried a gun. He adopted a brisk way of carrying himself as a commander. This was a deeply congenial development for him; Stalin enjoyed himself in Tsaritsyn despite the dangers.[13]

He also gained contentment in his personal life. Nadya Allilueva, who had accompanied him from Moscow, was no longer merely his secretary but had become his wife. According to their daughter's account many decades later, they had already been living as a married couple in Petrograd after the October Revolution.[14] Chronological exactitude is impossible. Bolsheviks in those days rejected weddings as bourgeois flummery. What is certain is that on his return from Siberia he did not intend to remain celibate. There were plenty of Bolshevik women to take his eye and he went out with a few in 1917.[15] But he wanted the settled home life which his nomadic existence had prevented. (His cohabitations in Siberia had been of the seigneurial variety.) In the flush of their passion they went off to serve the Revolution together on the North Caucasus and Southern Fronts.

Joseph was a communist party leader and Nadya's family were dedicated to the party's cause. He was amusing and still in his physical prime, and probably his talent for handling political business appealed to Nadya. The fact that Alliluev family life had been constantly disrupted by revolutionary commitments may also have drawn Nadya towards an older man who seemingly offered dependability. She may have seen him as the father she had seen little of when growing up.[16] Nadya had not discerned Joseph's curmudgeonly egotism. Joseph, though, had yet to witness the symptoms of Nadya's mental volatility.[17] So while he glowed in the warmth of her admiration of him, she enjoyed his attentions.

Without being a beauty, she had long dark hair parted down the middle and tied up in a bun; her lips were broad and her eyes friendly even if her teeth 'gappy'.[18] He liked women with a full figure like Nadya's. He did not worry that she was less than half his age. He had read more than her and seen more of life, and he surely thought he would always dominate the marriage. The Alliluevs had given him succour and all of them got on well with him. He was gaining not only a wife but also – at last – a stable and supportive wider family.[19]

There was only one thing about his situation in Tsaritsyn that annoyed Stalin. This was the interference in his activities from Moscow, and nobody irritated more than Trotski. Stalin had formed the Revolutionary Council of the Southern Front on 17 September. Immediately he received orders from Trotski, his military superior as Chairman of the Revolutionary-Military Council of the Republic, to cease challenging his decisions.[20] Stalin telegraphed to Lenin that Trotski was not on the spot and failed to understand conditions across the region:[21]

> The point is that Trotski, generally speaking, cannot get by without noisy gestures. At Brest[-Litovsk] he delivered a blow to the cause by his incredibly 'leftist' gesturing. On the question of the Czechoslovaks he similarly harmed the common cause by his gesturing with noisy diplomacy in the month of May. Now he delivers a further blow by his gesturing about discipline, and yet all this Trotskyist discipline amounts in reality to the most prominent leaders on the war front peering up the backside of military specialists from the camp of 'non-party' counter-revolutionaries . . .

Stalin reminded Lenin that Trotski had an anti-Bolshevik past; his resentment of the haughty political interloper was unmistakable. Trotski in his view was not to be trusted.

Stalin called for stern measures:

> ✓Therefore I ask you in due time, while it's still not too late, to remove Trotski and put him in a fixed frame since I'm afraid that Trotski's unhinged commands, if they are repeated . . . will create dissension between the army and the command staff and will totally destroy the front . . .
>
> I'm not a lover of clamour and scandal but feel that if we don't immediately produce the reins to put a constraint on Trotski, he'll ruin our whole army in favour of 'leftist' and 'Red' discipline which will sicken even the most disciplined comrades.

This analysis commended itself to leading Bolsheviks who knew the history of the French Revolution. A military leader, Napoleon Bonaparte, had seized power and rejected much of the social radicalism introduced by Maximilien Robespierre. Trotski seemed the likeliest military candidate for such a role in the drama of Russia's October Revolution. There was acute annoyance among party members about his insistence on employing former Imperial Army officers. Trotski was also reviled for shooting political commissars for disobedience or cowardice. An informal Military Opposition began to coalesce against him in late 1918.

Yet Trotski had grounds to be horrified by events in Tsaritsyn. Lenin began to take his side. Stalin was a law unto himself on the Southern Front. It was not always a law shared by the official party leadership. Lenin insisted that if the Civil War was to be won, the average Russian peasant (and not just the poorest of them) had to be won over to the side of the Reds. Persuasion rather than violence had to be the priority. Lenin's declarations were riddled with contradiction. He had set up the hugely unpopular 'committees of the rural poor' in order to introduce 'class struggle' to the countryside and had also conscripted peasants and expropriated grain by means of armed urban squads. But certainly at the same time he was minded to win support among the mass of the peasantry.

Stalin was less ambiguous than Lenin. Might, for him, was right, effective and economical of resources. He put villages to the torch to intimidate neighbouring ones to obey the demands of the Reds. Terror was undertaken against the very peasants who were being depicted in official propaganda as one of the twin pillars of the Soviet state. Stalin treated the Cossacks in particular as enemies. The term de-Cossackisation was in currency.[22] Stalin wrote in a letter to his old Bolshevik rival Stepan Shaumyan:[23]

> In relation to the Dagestani and other bands which obstruct the movements of trains from the North Caucasus, you must be absolutely merciless. A number of their villages should be set on fire and burned to the ground so as to teach them not to make raids on trains.

This was in the fiercest Imperial Army tradition under General Yermolov in the Caucasus in the early nineteenth century and General Alikhanov in Georgia in 1905.[24] Stalin was ordering Shaumyan to conduct a campaign of exemplary terror. When 'bands' operated against trains, the nearby villages were to be razed to the ground. The message was to go out that complete compliance alone would save localities from the Red Army's savagery. Wanting to conciliate the non-Russian national groups across the country, he nevertheless prescribed brutal measures against those among them who failed to restrain anti-Bolshevik outbursts.

He subjected his own Red Army conscripts – including Russians – to severe discipline. Bothering little with persuasion, he assumed they would never help the Reds unless force was used.[25] He threw armies into action with little caution. He acted as if sheer numerical superiority would bring victory. He did not care that a vastly greater proportion of Red than White soldiers died. Lenin commented on the reckless disregard for lives on the Southern Front; and although he did not mention Stalin by name, it was obvious whom he held responsible.[26] Lenin cleared Trotski of any blame for the running of the Red Army and confirmed the Central Committee's policy on the recruitment of Imperial officers.[27] Trotski sent his aide Alexei Okulov to find out what was happening in Tsaritsyn. His report was disturbing. Stalin, having sacked Imperial officers from their posts of command, had arrested dozens of them and held them on a barge on the River Volga. Among them was Snesarev, whom he accused of heading a conspiracy to sabotage the Red war effort and aid the Whites.[28] Stalin's apparent intention had been to sink the barge and drown all on board.[29] Snesarev on Moscow's orders was released and the Revolutionary-Military Council of the Republic transferred him to the command of the Western Front. Stalin, infuriated, continued with Voroshilov to demand sanctions against the allegedly counter-revolutionary officers. Voroshilov was to claim that, if he and Stalin had not acted as they did in Tsaritsyn, the Whites would have overrun all Ukraine.[30]

Stalin passionately believed that conspiracies were ubiquitous in Russia. He already had a tendency to suspect that plots existed even when no direct evidence was available. He was not alone in this. Lenin and Trotski too referred in a casual manner to the organised linkages among the enemies of the party; and Trotski had a notorious willingness to treat even Bolshevik party activists as traitors if they belonged to regiments in the Red Army which had failed to obey his orders. Stalin was more like Trotski than he pretended. When an adequate supply of munitions did not come through to Tsaritsyn in September 1918, he howled to Lenin: 'It's some kind of casualness or treachery in official uniform [*formennoe predatel'stvo*].'[31] To Stalin's way of thought there always had to be an agency of deliberate maleficence at work when things went wrong. Traitors therefore had to exist even in the leadership of the People's Commissariats in Moscow.

Stalin applied violence, including terror, on a greater scale than most other central communist leaders approved of. Only Trotski with his demands for political commissars to be shot alongside army officers if unsanctioned retreats occurred was remotely near to him in bloodthirstiness – and Trotski also introduced the Roman policy of decimating regiments which failed to carry out higher commands. Stalin and Trotski invariably ignored pleas to intervene on behalf of individuals arrested by the Cheka. Even Lenin, who resisted most attempts by Kamenev and Bukharin to impose control over the Cheka, sometimes helped in such cases.[32] Yet Stalin's enthusiasm for virtually indiscriminate violence made even Trotski seem a restrained individual. This was a feature that his comrades forgot at their peril in the 1930s.

A contrast also existed between Stalin and Trotski in their basic attitude to Bolshevism. Trotski, who had joined the Bolsheviks late in his career, paid little attention to the party. Stalin pondered much on the party's place in the Soviet state. He took a copy of the second edition of Lenin's *The State and Revolution* around with him in the Civil War. This book says nothing about the communist party in the transition to socialism. Stalin was aware of this lacuna. Making notes in the margins, he asked himself: 'Can the party seize power against the will of the proletariat? No, it cannot and must not.'[33] He added: 'The proletariat cannot attain its dictatorship without a vanguard, without a party as the only [party].'[34] Lenin had said no such thing in *The State and Revolution*. But Stalin, like Lenin, had modified and developed his ideas since October 1917. The party had become the supreme institution of state. Stalin was among the many Bolsheviks who sought to incorporate this into communist doctrine. The theory had been that the proletariat would run its own socialist state. Stalin's unease was reflected in his comment that 'the party cannot simply replace the dictatorship of the proletariat'.[35]

In the Civil War, however, he lacked the time to write pamphlets; and not one of his articles for *Pravda* had the range of those composed by Lenin, Trotski, Zinoviev and Bukharin. But he went on thinking about large subjects. Party policy on the national question was prominent among them. Another was the institutional framework of the Soviet state. The report he wrote in January 1919 with Dzierżyński on a military disaster at Perm was a disquisition on the chaotic relations within and among the armed forces, the party and the government. Their recommendations had an influence on the decisions taken to establish the party as the supreme agency of the state and to regularise the lines of command from the party to all public institutions.[36] Only the fact that Stalin's later propagandists made exaggerated claims for the report has induced historians to overlook its importance. In truth he was a reflective and decisive political operator and Lenin appreciated him for this.

This was the trip on which Stalin became friends with Dzierżyński's personal assistant Stanisław Redens. Nadya accompanied Stalin to Perm, and soon Redens had fallen in love with her elder sister Anna and married her. Redens became a leading figure in the Cheka.[37] Personal, political and military life was intertwined for Bolsheviks in the Civil War and Stalin was no exception. His recent marriage had no impact on his public activities; he spent the Civil War mainly on or near the fighting fronts. Recalled to Moscow in October 1918, he resumed his work in the Party Central Committee and Sovnarkom. But by December he was off again. The White Army of Admiral Kolchak had swept into the Urals city of Perm and destroyed the Red Army units there. Stalin and Dzierżyński were sent to conduct an enquiry into the reasons for the military disaster. They returned and made their report at the end of January 1919. Stalin stayed in Moscow again until being dispatched in May to Petrograd and the Western Front against the invasion by General Yudenich from Estonia. In July he moved on to a different sector of the same front at Smolensk. In September he was transferred to the Southern Front, where he stayed into 1920.[38]

Stalin was a law unto himself. When transferred to Petrograd on the Western Front in mid-1919, he showed macabre inventiveness in dealing with disorder and disobedience. The Red Army on the Western Front entirely failed to impress him. Almost as soon as he arrived, the Third Regiment went over to the Whites. Stalin was merciless. On 30 May he telegraphed Lenin from the Smolny Institute that he was rounding up the renegades and deserters, charging them collectively with state treason and making their execution by firing squads into a public spectacle. Now that everyone saw the consequences of betrayal, he argued, acts of treachery had been reduced.[39] Not everyone enthused about Stalin's intervention. Alexei Okulov, transferred to the Western Front after exposing Stalin's misdeeds in Tsaritsyn, put a spoke in his wheel yet again. Stalin telegraphed angrily on 4 June demanding that Lenin should choose between Okulov and himself. Existing conditions, he ranted, were 'senseless'; he threatened to leave Petrograd if his ultimatum was not complied with.[40]

His military activity was centred in the Revolutionary-Military Councils attached to the various fronts, and from 1919 he joined them as the Party Central Committee's appointee. His kind of fighting involved giving orders: he was never directly involved in physical violence. His inexperience was total and nobody has been able to find evidence that he looked at books on warfare[41] (whereas Lenin had studied Clausewitz, and Trotski had reported the Balkan wars before 1914 as a newspaper correspondent). But he was madly eager to prove himself as a commander. The Central Committee recognised his worth by its successive use of him on the Southern Front, the Western Front, again the Southern Front, the South-Western Front and the Caucasian Front. Qualities which earned him praise were his decisiveness, determination, energy and willingness to take responsibility for critical and unpredictable situations.

There was a price to pay. Stalin hated to operate in a team unless he was its leader. There was only one fellow communist to whom he would defer and that was Lenin. Even Lenin found him a handful. Stalin was vainglorious and extremely touchy. He detested Trotski. He hated the entire Imperial officer elite. He had an almost pathetic need to feel appreciated, and at the drop of his Red Army peaked cap he would announce his resignation. Such was his egotism that he was willing to disregard orders even if they came from the Central Committee or its inner subcommittees. He was capricious in the extreme. Once determined upon a course of action, he steered as he pleased. He wasted an inordinate amount of the Central Committee's time with his demands for commanders to be sacked and for strategy and tactics to be altered. His application of repressive measures to the social groups hostile to the Soviet state was excessive even by the standards of the communist leadership in wartime Russia; and, still more than Trotski, he had a tendency to regard anyone who failed to show him respect as an enemy of the people.

The conventional image of Stalin's ascent to supreme power does not convince. He did not really spend most of his time in offices in the Civil War period and consolidate his position as the pre-eminent bureaucrat of the Soviet state. Certainly he held membership of the Party Central Committee; he was also People's Commissar for Nationalities' Affairs. In neither role were his responsibilities restricted to mere administration. As the complications of public affairs increased, he was given further high postings. He chaired the commission drafting the RSFSR Constitution. He became the leading political commissar on a succession of military fronts in 1918–19. He was regularly involved in decisions on relations with Britain, Germany, Turkey and other powers; and he dealt with plans for the establishment of new Soviet republics in Estonia, Latvia and Lithuania. He conducted the enquiry into the Red Army's collapse at Perm. When the Party Central Committee set up its own inner subcommittees in 1919, he was chosen for both the Political Bureau (Politburo) and the Organisational Bureau (Orgburo). He was asked to head the Workers' and Peasants' Inspectorate at its creation in February 1920.

Far from fitting the bureaucratic stereotype, he was a dynamic leader who had a hand in nearly all the principal discussions on politics, military strategy, economics, security and international relations. Lenin phoned or telegraphed Politburo members whenever a controversial matter was in the air.[42] There were few corners of high public affairs where Stalin's influence was unknown; and the Politburo frequently turned to him when a sudden emergency arose. The other great leaders – Lenin, Trotski, Kamenev, Zinoviev, Sverdlov, Dzierżyński and Bukharin – had settled jobs that they held for the duration of the Civil War and beyond. In most cases these jobs involved making public appearances – and Trotski in the Red Army did this with relish and to huge acclaim. There was also prestige for the prominent leaders of the October 1917 seizure of power: Lenin, Trotski and Sverdlov were examples. Since the Bolsheviks were led by doctrinaires, prestige also accrued to those who wrote fluently and often. Lenin, Trotski, Kamenev, Zinoviev and Bukharin continued to publish books in the Civil War. Stalin could not compete in these arenas. He was always on the move. He was a poor orator in any formal sense and had little opportunity to write.

His merits tended to be overlooked even though he was an integral part of the ascendant political group. The trouble was that he had yet to realise his importance in the eyes of the group, the party or society at large. Just occasionally he allowed his resentment to show. In November 1919 he tried to resign his job as Chairman of the Revolutionary-Military Council of the Southern Front. Lenin, alarmed, rushed to get a Politburo decision to implore him to reconsider. Stalin was too useful to be discarded. Yet what was attractive to Lenin was horrific to the enemies of Bolshevism. Stalin in the Civil War was an early version of the despot who instigated the Great Terror of 1937–8. It was only because all the other communist leaders applied the politics of violence after the October Revolution that his maladjusted personality did not fully stand out. But this is no excuse. No one acquainted with Stalin in 1918–19 should have been surprised by his later 'development'.

16. THE POLISH CORRIDOR

The Civil War in Russia between the Reds and the Whites was over by the end of 1919. Once the Red Army had conquered the Russian lands it was a matter of time before the outlying regions of the former empire were overrun. Reds drove the last White army, under General Anton Denikin, into the Crimean peninsula. Denikin handed his command to Pëtr Wrangel, who instantly changed policies towards civilian society. Among these was a promise to the peasants that land would not be restored to the gentry after the Civil War. Realpolitik was overdue if the Whites were to improve their military prospects. Nevertheless the material and logistical position of the forces under Wrangel was hopeless unless the Red political and military command made a fundamental mistake. Wrangel's men were preparing for their escape abroad.

Victory in the Civil War encouraged communist leaders to seek opportunities to expand 'Soviet power' to the West. They itched to spread revolution. In March 1918 Lenin – with help from Stalin, Kamenev, Zinoviev and Sverdlov – had adjured the party to be patient at a time when most Bolsheviks had wanted a 'revolutionary war'. But even before the German military collapse in November 1918 Lenin had given orders to assemble massive supplies of conscripts and grain so that the Red Army might intervene in strength in Germany.[1] Expansionist ideas did not disappear with the Treaty of Brest-Litovsk. The Communist International (known as the Comintern) had been formed on Lenin's initiative in Petrograd in March 1919 to inaugurate, expand and co-ordinate the activities of communist parties in Europe and around the world. The Bolshevik party leadership in the Kremlin sent advisers and finance to the governments briefly established in Munich and Budapest, and the Red Army would have been made available if the fighting in the Civil War in Russia had permitted.[2] In summer 1920 Lenin wet his lips as he contemplated the situation in Czechoslovakia, Romania, Hungary and northern Italy. It seemed that the chain of Western capitalism in

Europe would at last be broken. A military campaign to 'sovietise' such countries was anticipated.[3]

Did Bolshevik leaders genuinely have the resources to instigate the creation of fraternal socialist states? Their answer should have been no: the former Russian Empire was in an economic and administrative mess. But triumph in the Civil War had bred overconfidence among Bolsheviks. They had seen off the Whites, and the British and French expeditionary forces had been withdrawn. Who could now resist them? There was also a second consideration in their minds. The Soviet state was isolated. The expansion of the October Revolution was not just an aim: it was a basic need deriving not only from ideology but also from a practical dilemma. The Politburo – and even the cautious Stalin agreed on this – recognised that the Revolution would remain imperilled until it acquired allied states in the West.

During the early campaigns of the Civil War the operational assumption was that foreign territory began at the borders of the former Russian Empire. For this reason the Politburo acted as if it expected the Red Army to reconquer the borderlands as soon as the fighting in Russia was brought to completion. Progress seemed very satisfactory in 1920. Azerbaijan and Armenia were brought to heel – and Stalin and his friend Sergo Ordzhonikidze were regularly involved in strategic and political discussions at the highest level.[4] But the Baltic region remained a problem. Attempts had been made to establish Soviet republics in Estonia, Latvia and Lithuania; but in each case there were counter-coups, and these countries regained their independence in 1918–19.[5] Estonia inaugurated full diplomatic relations with the RSFSR in February 1920. The international situation was unstable. The Bolsheviks did not perceive the western borderlands, any more than those to the south, as foreign places, and Stalin held to this viewpoint with noticeable tenacity.[6] But what happened to such countries would depend on what occurred in the broader framework of war and peace in Europe. Bolshevik leaders had to decide on a permanent policy.

Things were brought to a head by armed conflict between Poland and the RSFSR. Clashes had taken place while the Civil War was in spate, and the Polish commander-in-chief Josef Piłsudski had long aspired to form a federal union with Ukraine. In spring 1920 Piłsudski struck deep into Ukrainian territory. On 7 May his forces occupied Kiev, surprising Red Army officers as they waited at bus stops. Sovnarkom appealed for a patriotic war of defence. Sergei Kamenev took supreme military command and his main front commander was the twenty-five-year-old Mikhail Tukhachevski. Volunteers rallied to the Red Army's banners. Kiev was retaken on 10 June and, after an agreement with the Lithuanian government, a joint offensive seized Vilnius and transferred it to Lithuania. The advance of the Reds was practically unopposed. The British government warned the Soviet leadership to halt its troops, but the Party Central Committee on 16 July took the strategic decision to take the war on to Polish territory, and Lenin informed Stalin and others on the same day.[7] (Stalin, based in Kharkov in eastern Ukraine, had been unable to attend.)[8] The military command of the Western Front prepared to cross the River Bug and move on Warsaw. European socialist revolution beckoned, and on 23 July the Politburo set up a Provisional Polish Revolutionary Committee under Julian Marchlewski.[9]

The British government tried to prevent the spread of communism by calling for peace negotiations and suggesting a new border between the Soviet state and Poland. This was the Curzon Line, named after the British Foreign Secretary in 1920. The advance of the Red Army into central Europe had to be halted. The Politburo had taken such overtures more seriously earlier in the war when Piłsudski looked like winning. But the rapid march of the Reds across Ukraine changed Lenin's stance and he started to advocate an invasion of Poland.

Stalin was unenthusiastic. He had been warning all summer about the resurgence of White military capacity in the Crimea, and he questioned the wisdom of taking on the Poles while Wrangel remained a threat.[10] Even Trotski and Radek, who had opposed Lenin over Brest-Litovsk, were disconcerted by Lenin's position.[11] Stalin's objections were not confined to his chronic scepticism about European socialist revolution and his concern about Wrangel. He doubted that the Red Army was adequately co-ordinated and organised. He worried about the length and strength of the lines of supply.[12] From his base with Red forces in Ukraine he had reason to think he knew what he was writing about. The Soviet state was insecure from attack by the Whites. Plans for a military breakthrough to Poland and Germany were unrealistic. Stalin repeatedly mentioned the danger posed by Wrangel from the Crimea.[13] He also reminded Lenin not to underestimate the strength of nationalism among the Polish working class. Stalin was surprised that Lenin, usually his ally on the national question, failed to sense the danger awaiting the Red Army in this respect. He wanted the care used at Brest-Litovsk in 1918 to be applied to the decision on war or peace with Poland.

Lenin would not be thwarted. He had never envisaged revolutionary war as a crude war of conquest. It was rather his assumption that workers across Europe were expected to rise up in support of the Red Army. The leftist elements in the European socialist parties, he anticipated, would rally to the communist cause and the obstacles to the establishment of revolutionary governments would be removed. The Red Army had only thirty-five divisions. The Imperial Army had assembled nearly a hundred divisions against Germany and Austria–Hungary at the outbreak of the First World War. Lenin brushed this aside. Class conflict in Europe would more than make up for the inadequacies of the Red Army. The die was cast by the Politburo. Warsaw would be taken and the way cleared for an advance on Berlin where, as Lenin believed, the Reds would find political disarray they could exploit. The German communists should make an alliance with the German far right to sweep away the Treaty of Versailles of 1919 which had taken territory and colonies from Germany, imposed heavy reparations and restricted its military reconstruction. Then they should turn against their right-wing enemies, and a revolutionary state would be installed.[14]

Having lost the discussion at long distance from the Politburo, Stalin accepted the decision. Indeed he developed an eagerness to prove himself in the campaign. He had been spending much time in previous months on yet another dispute about his posting and its responsibilities. In November 1919 he had made a characteristic attempt to intimidate Lenin and the Politburo by threatening to resign.[15] His explanation was more colourful than usual: 'Without this, my work on the Southern Front will become pointless and unnecessary, which gives me the right or rather the duty to move away anywhere – to the Devil even – rather than stay on the Southern Front.'[16] The Politburo, already habituated to his tantrums, rejected his ultimatum.[17] In January 1920 the Southern Front was re-formed as the South-Western Front with the task of defending Ukraine against both the Poles and Wrangel's Crimean forces. But Stalin was transferred in February to the Caucasian Front. He did not like this;[18] he wanted to be active where the fortunes of the Revolution were crucially threatened: he resented being regarded as the man from the Caucasus whose expertise was limited to Caucasian affairs. On 26 May Stalin's tenacity was rewarded when he was assigned to the South-Western Front, where battles with the Poles were anticipated.

On 12 July Lenin sent a message to him in Kharkov:[19]

I request Stalin 1) to accelerate arrangements for a furious intensification of the offensive; 2) to communicate to me his (Stalin's) opinion. I personally think that [Curzon's proposal] is pure skul-duggery with the idea of annexing Crimea.

Previously sceptical about the Polish campaign, Stalin telegraphed his euphoric agreement:[20]

> The Polish armies are completely collapsing, the Poles have lost their communications and administration and Polish orders, instead of arriving at their address, are falling ever more frequently into our hands; in short, the Poles are experiencing a collapse from which they will not soon recover.

Stalin scoffed at Lord Curzon's proposal of a truce followed by peace talks in London:[21]

> I think that imperialism has never been so weak as now at a time of Poland's defeat and we have never been as strong as now. Therefore the more firmly we conduct ourselves, the better it will be both for us and for international revolution. Send on the Politburo's decision.

Lenin and Stalin, advocates of caution at Brest-Litovsk in 1918, had become the warmongers of the Bolshevik leadership.

In Stalin's opinion it was imperative 'to seize the maximum we can' before any cease-fire might occur. He aimed to take Lwów.[22] This was a personal preference: the fall of Lwów would not only benefit the Soviet cause but also bring him kudos as the city's conqueror. The trouble was that, as Stalin had warned, Wrangel's forces remained a serious threat. Stalin typically called for a policy of executing White officer POWs to a man.[23] Learning that things were not going well for the Red Army in the Crimea,[24] he put this failure down to the cowardice of the Soviet Commander-in-Chief Sergei Kamenev. His mind was focused on glory in Poland as he and his command staff moved westward.[25]

Stalin and Lenin also undertook preliminary planning for the kind of Europe they expected to organise when socialist seizures of power took place. Their grandiose visions take the breath away. Before the Second Comintern Congress, Lenin urged the need for a general federation including Germany, and he made clear that he wanted the economy of such a federation to be 'administered from a single organ'. Stalin rejected this as impractical:[26]

> If you think you'd ever get Germany to enter a federation with the same rights as Ukraine, you are mistaken. If you think that even

Poland, which has been constituted as a bourgeois state with all its attributes, would enter the Union with the same rights as Ukraine you are mistaken.

Lenin was angry. The implication of Stalin's comment was that considerations of national pride would impel Russia and Germany to remain separate states for the foreseeable future. Lenin sent him a 'threatening letter' which charged him with chauvinism.[27] It was Lenin's objective to set up a Union of Soviet Republics of Europe and Asia. His vision of 'European socialist revolution' was unchanged since 1917. But Stalin held his ground. The Politburo had to acknowledge the realities of nationhood if the spread of socialism in Europe was to be a success.

These discussions were hypothetical since the Red Army had not yet reached Poland, far less set up a revolutionary government in Warsaw. Stalin himself had caused one of the operational snags. This occurred when he ordered his military and political subordinates to regard Lwów as their priority. He failed to mention that such a command would disrupt the general strategic plan approved by Trotski and Tukhachevski on campaign and by Lenin in Moscow. Stalin was ignoring the precedence given by these others to the capture of Warsaw; instead he diverted the armed forces of the South-Western Front away from a line of convergence with those of the Western Front.

The battle for Warsaw took place across four sectors. Lasting from 12 to 25 August, it settled the outcome of the war.[28] Tukhachevski's original plan had been to attack even sooner, before the Poles had time to regroup for defence of their capital. His losses had been substantial. Supplies and reinforcements were unlikely to be forthcoming. The exhausted Red Army, harassed by the Polish inhabitants, had to win a very quick victory or else lose everything.[29] Piłsudski grabbed his chance. In successive sectors he repulsed the Red advance. Sergei Kamenev, the Supreme Commander, had planned to move forward on two fronts: the Western under Tukhachevski and Smilga and the South-Western under Yegorov and Stalin. Kamenev failed to co-ordinate them. The South-Western Front was still charged with protecting the Soviet state against Wrangel from the Crimea: it was therefore aimed in two different directions at once. On 22 July, furthermore, Yegorov had pointed his line of march towards Lublin and Lwów and daily increased the gap between himself and Tukhachevski. This was a recipe for confusion and dispute, and Stalin was never one to hold back from aggravating a difficult situation.

The Red Army had urgent need of a revised strategic plan. Such a plan could be devised only at the highest political level. On 2 August the Politburo resolved to split the South-Western Front into two and give half its forces to the Western Front and the other half to a reformed Southern Front tasked with defending Ukraine against Wrangel.[30] Yet no action followed until 14 August, when Sergei Kamenev ordered the transfer of forces from the South-Western Front with immediate effect.[31]

The impracticality of Kamenev's injunction infuriated Stalin. Yegorov and Stalin were already engaged in their attack on Lwów before the start of the battle of Warsaw. Although the distance between Warsaw and Lwów as the crow flies is two hundred miles, the geography of the region made quick movements of troops impossible. It was swampy and roadless. The Polish inhabitants were almost universally hostile to the Reds, who were regarded as yet another Russian invading force. Stalin, who was always quick to criticise the professional military men inherited from the Imperial Army, told Kamenev in no uncertain terms: 'Your order pointlessly frustrates the operations of the South-Western Front, which had already started its advance.'[32] When Yegorov dutifully complied with Kamenev's order, Stalin refused to counter-sign the latest dispositions and left the task to his deputy R. Berzins.[33] But the Cavalry Army of Stalin's associate Semën Budënny was heavily involved in fighting in the vicinity and it was not until 20 August that the attack on Lwów was abandoned. By then the battle of Warsaw was nearing its catastrophic conclusion for Tukhachevski and the Western Front.

That Stalin had been obstreperous when reacting to the change in strategy is indisputable. But he was soon accused of something more serious. It came to be said that an obsession with military glory had caused him to withhold forces from Tukhachevski. He therefore appeared to be the culprit for the defeat of the Reds. This is too strong a verdict. In fact he did not block the transfer of troops: he simply refused to give his personal counter-signature. Certainly he was not guiltless. On 12 August he had supported the deployment of the Cavalry Army against Lwów despite knowing about the Politburo's intention to divide the South-Western Front's forces between a Western Front and a Southern Front. Even so, it is hardly likely that the forces reassigned to the Western Front would have reached Warsaw in time for the battle even if Stalin had not approved the Lwów operation.[34] Yet without acting insubordinately, he undoubtedly did much – and must have done it knowingly – to make it next to impossible for Kamenev and Tukhachevski to carry out any further redeployments of the South-Western

Front's forces. To that extent he acted as he had done throughout the Civil War. He behaved as though he had a monopoly on military judgement and that those who opposed him were either fools or knaves.

By the time the siege of Lwów was lifted, Stalin was far away. Returning to Moscow for the Politburo meeting on 19 August, he was raging to justify himself. Both Lenin and Trotski were present. The fighting before Warsaw was continuing; Wrangel was moving north from the Crimea. At the same time there was an opening for the Red units on the Caucasian Front to push down through Azerbaijan into Persia. The entire military situation was in flux in three directions. Item number one, however, was the strategic confusion left behind at Lwów. Stalin decided that political attack was the best form of defence: he castigated the entire campaign. He stressed the neglect suffered by the armies facing Wrangel, and noted that the result could be a resumption of the Civil War in Russia. His blistering onslaught produced a result; for despite a counter-report from Trotski, the Politburo decided 'to recognise the Wrangel Front as the main one'.[35] In a week when the fate of the Polish campaign was in the balance, this was extraordinary phrasing. To outward appearances Stalin had trounced his enemy Trotski at the Politburo and secured the strategic reorientation he favoured.

Yet his triumph was not what it seemed. There was no acknowledgement in the Politburo that Stalin's plans and behaviour in the Soviet–Polish War had been appropriate. Lenin and Trotski continued to blame him. A clue to the intensity of the dispute was given by an item further down the agenda sheet, which related to Stalin's position. After some discussion he was formally awarded a fortnight's holiday.[36] Yet again he was claiming exhaustion and, no doubt, was feeling under-appreciated. This was the pattern of behaviour established in the Civil War whenever he failed to get his way.[37]

Stalin's anger went on simmering. He neither took his holiday[38] nor dropped his case against the Supreme Command and its patron Trotski. He felt humiliated, and when he went back to the Politburo on 1 September he demanded his own demission from 'military activity'. No one seriously expected him to serve in the Red Army after the end of armed hostilities in Poland; but the plea was granted and Stalin left the Revolutionary-Military Council of the Republic.[39] He had craved to be a member since its creation. But he would no longer serve on it if his counsel was going to be overridden. He refused to forget what he took to be the slights he had suffered. At the same Politburo session there had been hurried discussion about foreign policy, and Trotski had successfully proposed a 'policy of compromise peace with Poland'.[40] For Stalin, this was hard to bear. Trotski and the Supreme Command were in his eyes co-responsible for the war's mismanagement. Now Trotski apparently wanted to enjoy the plaudits of peacetime. Stalin had warned against the whole Polish campaign. He had sounded the alarm about Wrangel. He had been asked to deal with two military fronts as if they had been one and then been asked to cope with yet another front.

For some days he buried himself in those affairs for which he had been most respected before the Civil War. The Politburo at his instigation was planning to appeal to the indigenous peoples of the Caucasus at the expense of the Cossacks. The decision was taken in principle, and Stalin was asked to supervise implementation on Moscow's behalf.[41] He also took charge of the complex Bashkirian affair. The Bashkirian Revolutionary Committee had behaved disloyally to the Soviet state and several members had been arrested. Stalin proposed to transfer them to Moscow for interrogation.[42] This was important political work. Yet at the same time Stalin did not want to be known as a Georgian who specialised in the national question. He belonged to the Central Committee and Sovnarkom in his own right, and he wanted this recognised. He had opinions about general policy. He felt he knew as much as anyone about politics and society in the provinces. Resentment grew like rust on an iron nail. Like everyone in the Politburo, he was also feeling the physical and emotional impact of his exertions of the past few years. Unlike the others, he felt under-appreciated. Nothing indicated that his feelings were going to be spared as the Ninth Party Conference approached.

Lenin arrived at the Conference on 22 September and showed unwonted contrition. Reality had to be faced: it was 'a deep defeat, a catastrophic situation'. The secret project for the 'Sovietization of Poland' had been disastrous. The Red Army, instead of being greeted by Polish workers and peasants, had been repulsed by a 'patriotic upsurge'. So how had the miscalculation occurred? Lenin admitted that he had thought that Germany was on the boil and that Poland would be a mere bridgehead towards Berlin. He also admitted: 'I absolutely do not pretend in the slightest fashion to knowledge of military science.' The Red Army, he conceded, had been set an impossible task. Probably the Politburo should have accepted Curzon's proposal and parleyed for peace. The best option was to sue for a treaty and wait for a turn of events 'at the first convenient opportunity'.[43]

Stalin's latest resignation was one too many for the stressed Lenin.

Stalin's imperiousness and volatility appeared excessive; Trotski by contrast seemed at least dependable in a crisis. Trotski took his chance and bluntly criticised Stalin's record in the Soviet–Polish War and accused him of 'strategic mistakes'.[44] Information from returning political commissars confirmed this accusation and Lenin repeated it in the early sessions.[45] The Politburo was revealed as a nest of jealousies and criticisms. Several in the audience were aware that Lenin had been less than frank about his own part in the débâcle. The fundamental blunder had been to invade Poland at all and this was primarily Lenin's error. Indeed he had been warned of the likely consequences by Trotski and Stalin. Trotski had argued that the Red Army was already exhausted, Stalin that the Poles would rise up against the invasion.[46] Some Conference delegates indeed castigated Lenin directly and the session ended in an angry dispute. When proceedings were resumed next day, Stalin insisted on the right of reply. It was a brief speech. Having pointed out that he had expressed early doubts about the invasion, he made no defence of his behaviour on campaign, and the Conference moved on to other business.[47]

From Stalin's viewpoint, this was very unsatisfactory. He had had his chance to make his case and at the last moment he had thrown it away. And the lasting effect was to fix the primary responsibility for the disastrous campaign in Poland solely on himself. There had been searing controversies in the past. The October 1917 decision to seize power and the November 1917 rejection of a broad socialist coalition government had caused uproar in the Central Committee, and for some weeks a number of Central Committee members refused to sit in government with Lenin. The Brest-Litovsk dispute had been still more raucous: Bukharin and his supporters had seriously contemplated forming a government without Lenin. But the controversy over the Soviet–Polish War introduced a fresh element. Stalin, a leading member of the ruling group, was accused of insubordination, personal ambition and military incompetence. It was a remarkable list of faults.

Stalin's half-cocked reaction is difficult to explain. He was an extremely proud man. He was jealous too – jealous to an inordinate extent. He deeply resented criticism and was easily slighted. He was also very pugnacious. So why did he decide to mumble a few words about the prehistory of the invasion and then go back to his seat? If the boot had been on the other foot, neither Lenin nor Trotski would have failed to give a lengthy speech of self-justification.[48] Probably Stalin felt himself on weak ground and had suffered a last-minute collapse of confidence.

The evidence was incontrovertible that he had behaved badly, and in any case it was not the first time that his contumacy had been mentioned. At the Eighth Party Congress he had been reprimanded by Lenin for using tactics that led to far too many Red Army soldiers being killed.[49] The difference at the Ninth Party Conference was that nothing positive was said about him to balance the negative. He had been disgraced; none of his friends had taken the trouble to speak on his behalf. He saw no point in prolonging his misery by dragging out the discussion. He hated to be seen whingeing.[50] His constant need was to appear tough, determined and practical.

Yet he did not intend to forgive and forget. Trotski's accusation had added yet another grievance to the list of things for Stalin to brood about. The only wonder about this episode is that he did not cultivate a grudge against Lenin. Stalin continued through to the end of his days to express admiration for him. It has been mooted that Stalin regarded Lenin not just as a hero but also as a substitute father to be emulated.[51] This is going beyond the evidence. There were many occasions before and after October 1917 when Stalin clashed virulently with Lenin. But about his fundamental esteem for Lenin there is no serious doubt. There was no deference, still less servility; but Stalin exempted Lenin from the treatment he reserved for the rest of the human race – and he was biding his time to take his revenge on Trotski.

17. WITH LENIN

The contretemps between Lenin and Stalin vanished like snow in the sun. The reason was political. In November 1920 Trotski attacked the Soviet trade unions, and suddenly Lenin needed Stalin's assistance. Conventional trade unionism, according to Trotski, had no place in the revolutionary state; his case was that Sovnarkom safeguarded workers' interests and that trade unions should be constitutionally subordinated to its commands. This suggestion riled the Workers' Opposition, which was campaigning to enable the working class to control factories, mines and other enterprises. Lenin objected to the Workers' Opposition and in practice expected the trade unions to obey the party and government. Yet Trotski's demand for the formal imposition of this arrangement would affront workers unnecessarily. Lenin vainly tried to get Trotski to back down. Factions gathered around Trotski and Lenin as they wrote furious booklets and addressed noisy meetings. Although Bukharin formed a 'buffer group' between the two sides, this group too became a faction. Not only the Workers' Opposition but also the Democratic Centralists (who, since 1919, had campaigned for a restoration of democratic procedures in party life) entered the fray. The party was enveloped in a bitter conflict lasting the long winter of 1920–1.

Lenin enlisted Stalin to organise supporters in the provinces. Stalin was carrying out the function discharged by Sverdlov in the Brest-Litovsk dispute in 1918. A particular effort was made to discredit the other factions. Party rules were bent but not broken; Lenin knew that Stalin, whom he teased as a 'wild factionalist', would do whatever was necessary for victory.[1] The Central Committee Secretariat was led by Preobrazhenski, Krestinski and Serebryakov, who were sympathisers of Trotski and Bukharin. Stalin therefore sent trusted supporters of Lenin into the provinces to drum up a following for him and indicate how to organise the campaign against Trotski. While Stalin arranged things in Moscow, Zinoviev travelled the country giving speeches on Lenin's behalf. Trotski made a similar tour; but as the time of the Tenth Party Congress approached in March 1921, it was clear that victory would lie with the Leninists. Stalin co-ordinated the faction as its delegates assembled in Moscow. The Leninists drew up their own list of candidates for election to the Central Committee. This was gratifying for Stalin. Trotski, who had been in Lenin's good books in the Soviet–Polish War, had fallen into disfavour.

Factionalism had distracted the Bolsheviks from recognising a fundamental menace to their power. Garrisons of troops were mutinying. Factory workers in the main Russian industrial cities went on strike. And across the entire state there was trouble with the peasantry. Whole provinces in Ukraine, the Volga region and west Siberia rose against the Bolshevik party dictatorship. The demands of mutineers, strikers and village fighters were broadly the same. They wanted a multi-party democracy and an end to grain requisitioning. The revolt of the Tambov province peasantry at last brought the Politburo to its senses, and on 8 February 1921 its members decided on a momentous change in policy. Grain requisitioning would be replaced by a graduated tax in kind. Peasants would be left to trade the rest of their harvest on local markets. This New Economic Policy would take the sting out of rural discontent and allow the Red Army to mop up rebellions. There would be no political concessions: the objective was to save the Soviet state in its existing form from destruction. A commission was established to draft a full policy for consideration at the Tenth Party Congress. There was no dispute in the Politburo. Measures needed to be changed for disaster to be avoided.

The Party Congress, starting on 8 March, was surprisingly quiet. The New Economic Policy (or NEP) in its rudimentary form was approved almost on the nod and the Leninists won the debate on the trade unions without difficulty. Stalin organised the faction as supporters arrived in Moscow. Criticism from the Workers' Opposition was easily rebuffed; neither Alexander Shlyapnikov nor Alexandra Kollontai managed to stir the Congress with pleas for the working class to have greater direct influence on policy in the Kremlin and on conditions in the workplace. The reason for the easy victory of Lenin's faction had little to do with Lenin's eminence or Stalin's cunning.[2] On 28 February the Kronstadt naval garrison, thirty-five miles off the Petrograd coast, had started a mutiny. These sailors in 1917 had been among the party's most eager supporters. The mutiny shocked the Congress into recognising that the entire Soviet regime was under fundamental threat. Congress delegates volunteered to join the troops sent to suppress the Kronstadters. Trotski led the military offensive on Kronstadt. Unity was everything. Lenin was virtually unopposed when stating that the NEP – a retreat from the economic system of the Civil War years which was becoming known as 'War Communism' – should be accompanied by a political clampdown. No factional activity in the party would be permitted and all factions were required to dissolve themselves.

After the Congress, Lenin asked Stalin to secure the control of Lenin's group over the central party apparatus. Because of his other obligations – in the Politburo, the Orgburo, the People's Commissariat for Nationalities' Affairs and the Workers' and Peasants' Inspectorate – this was not going to be his prime task but would add substantially to his heavy workload. It was with some reluctance that he agreed to supervise the Department of Agitation and Propaganda in the Central Committee Secretariat.[3]

This aspect of political activity, though, was vital for a ruling party in a state dedicated to imposing a single ideology. Among the problems was the large number of institutions involved. The most influential was the People's Commissariat of Enlightenment, whose deputy leader was Lenin's wife Nadezhda Krupskaya. Resenting Stalin's attempt to assert the party's authority, she appealed to Lenin. Stalin wrote bluntly to Lenin:[4]

> What we are dealing with here is either a misunderstanding or a casual approach . . . I have interpreted today's note from you to my name (to the Politburo) as you posing the question of my departure from the Agitprop Department. You will recall that this job in agitation and propaganda was *imposed* on me (I was not looking for it). It follows that I ought not be objecting to my own departure. But if you pose the question *precisely now*, in connection with the misunderstandings sketched above, you'll put both yourself and me in an awkward position – Trotski and others will think that you're doing this 'for Krupskaya's sake' and that you're demanding a 'victim', that I'm willing to be a 'victim', etc. – which is undesirable.

Stalin's patience had snapped. This was obvious in his simultaneous request to step down from the People's Commissariat for Nationalities' Affairs.[5] He wanted and needed to be appreciated. Asking to resign was his usual way of signalling this. Lenin understood the code and backed down. Stalin was too important a member of his team to be allowed to leave.

Lenin distrusted Trotski after the trade union dispute. What also worried him was that Trotski wished to raise the influence of state economic planning in the NEP. Trotski was not the only problem for Lenin; the entire central leadership made life difficult for him. When even the head of the Soviet trade union movement Mikhail Tomski refused to toe the party line, Lenin called for his expulsion from the Central Committee.[6] The leading group had not been so fissiparous since 1918. When Lenin's request was turned down, he was at his wits' end and did not mind saying so. The ill health of several of his comrades, as the immense physical strain of recent years took its toll, aggravated the situation. Zinoviev had two heart attacks. Kamenev had a chronic cardiac condition. Bukharin had been very poorly and Stalin had suffered from appendicitis. In the absence of these strong supporters of the NEP, Lenin alone had had to implement the measures decided by the Politburo.[7] He was eager to have Stalin back at his side. Having recruited him to the Leninist cause in the trade union dispute, Lenin supported a proposal to make him General Secretary of the Russian Communist Party.

Molotov's year in charge of the Secretariat had not been a success;[8] indeed no one since Sverdlov's death in March 1919 had got on top of the job.[9] Lenin was disappointed. He and Molotov had regularly conspired at Central Committee meetings. Passing a message to Molotov, he ordered: 'You're going to make a speech – well, speak out as sharply as possible against Trotski!' He added: 'Rip up this note!' A furious row followed between Molotov and Trotski, who knew that Molotov had been put up to it.[10] Lenin's own health gave him trouble in 1921. He doubted Molotov's ability to rein back Trotski in his absence. Lenin concluded that a firmer grip should be applied in the Party Orgburo and Secretariat.

It was in this atmosphere that Stalin's candidature as Party General Secretary with Vyacheslav Molotov and Valeryan Kuibyshev as his Assistant Secretaries was informally canvassed at the Eleventh Party Congress in March–April 1922. Yevgeni Preobrazhenski, one of Trotski's allies, saw what was coming. Taking the platform, he took exception to Stalin's multiplicity of posts.[11] Preobrazhenski was complaining about the way that Stalin was accumulating excessive central power; but above all he was arguing that someone with so many posts could not carry out all his functions effectively. At any rate there was no formal decision at the Congress about the General Secretaryship; and when the matter was discussed at the next Central Committee plenum, on 3 April, the complaint was made that Lenin and his close associates had pre-empted debate by agreeing to pick Stalin for the job. Apparently Lenin had written 'General Secretary' next to Stalin's name in the list of candidates he put forward for election to the Central Committee.[12] But Kamenev smoothed things over and Stalin's appointment was confirmed on condition that he delegated much more to his deputies in the Workers' and Peasants' Inspectorate (or Rabkrin) and the Nationalities' Affairs Commissariat. The party had to come first.[13]

Conventionally it has been supposed that Stalin was put in office because he was an experienced bureaucrat with an unusual capacity for not being bored by administrative work. The facts do not bear this out. He was an editor of *Pravda* in 1917 and a policy-making intimate of Lenin immediately after the October Revolution. He had spent most of the Civil War as a political commissar. He went on military campaign in Ukraine and Poland in 1920; and although he had posts in Moscow in the Party Orgburo, the People's Commissariat for Nationalities' Affairs and Rabkrin, he had never had much time to devote to them. What is more, Stalin was known for his restlessness when administrative meetings in the capital were dragged out. But of course he had to sit through a lot of them, as did Lenin, Kamenev, Zinoviev, Trotski and the other leaders. They headed a state that had yet to be consolidated. Unless they saw to implementation and supervision of administrative decisions as much as to the making of policy, the state would fall apart before it was made. The reason why Lenin chose Stalin was less administrative than political. He wanted one of his allies in a post crucial to the maintenance of his policies.

Lenin stressed that the General Secretaryship was not equivalent to the supreme party leadership and that the party had never had a chairman.[14] He was being mealy-mouthed. What he meant was that he himself would remain the one dominant leader. Lenin and Stalin had fallen out many times before, during and after the October Revolution.[15] This was the norm in the Central Committee. Lenin had confidence that he would not lose control of things.

Stalin agreed with the broad lines of the NEP. He did not see himself as a mere administrator and freely offered his opinions across the range of debates within the leadership; and, contrary to later depictions of him, his caution in foreign policy did not reconcile him to total abstention from taking risks abroad. Even after the Anglo-Soviet Treaty of March 1921, he favoured sending military instructors and supplies to Afghanistan with the objective of undermining the British Empire.[16] He also continued to regard the new Baltic states – especially Latvia and Estonia – as territories illegitimately torn away from Russia 'which enter our arsenal as integral elements vital for the restoration of Russia's economy'.[17] The idea is false that Stalin could hardly care less if the Soviet state remained permanently isolated. He accepted isolation as a fact of political and military life that could not yet be altered. In such a situation, he considered, it behoved the Politburo to get on with post-war reconstruction as best it could until such time as fresh revolutionary opportunities abroad arose. This remained his attitude in subsequent years.

But Stalin, like Lenin, wanted to avoid trouble for the foreseeable future. Lenin saw a chance for the Soviet state to come to an understanding with Germany. Talks among the European powers had been convened at Genoa in northern Italy. The RSFSR and Germany were treated as pariah states, and Lenin made overtures for a separate commercial treaty between them. This was duly signed at nearby Rapallo in April 1922. Both states had more in mind than mere trade. Germany, prevented by the Treaty of Versailles from rearming itself, arranged to test military equipment and train army units secretly on Soviet soil. Others in the Politburo, especially Zinoviev, were reluctant to accept that the 'revolutionary upsurge' had subsided in Europe. Despite the Treaty of Rapallo, the Comintern in 1923 at Zinoviev's behest encouraged an armed rising against the German government on the sixth anniversary of the Bolshevik seizure of power in Petrograd. Stalin had nothing to do with such adventures.

Yet the working arrangement between Lenin and Stalin had already been put to an acute test. The occasion was the sudden deterioration in Lenin's health on 25 May 1922, when he suffered a massive stroke while recuperating from surgery to remove a bullet lodged in his neck since the attempt on his life in August 1918. Lenin lost mobility on the right side of his body; he could not speak clearly and his mind was obviously confused. Groups of doctors, including well-rewarded specialists brought from Germany, consulted among themselves on the nature of Lenin's illness. Opinion was divided. Among the possibilities considered were hereditary cardiac disease, syphilis, neurasthenia and even the effects of the recent operation on his neck. There were times when Lenin gave up hope entirely and thought his 'song was sung'. But, helped by his wife Nadya and sister Maria Ulyanova, he pulled himself together psychologically. He welcomed visitors to keep abreast of public affairs.

As General Secretary, Stalin was the most frequent of these. He was not a friend. Lenin did not think highly of him outside their political relationship. He told Maria that Stalin was 'not intelligent'. He also said Stalin was an 'Asiatic'. Nor could Lenin abide the way Stalin chewed his pipe.[18] Lenin was a fastidious man typical of his professional class; he expected comrades to behave with the politesse of the European middle class. He turned to the language of national superiority. Stalin was not merely a Georgian but an Oriental, a non-European and therefore an inferior. Lenin was unconscious of his prejudices: they emerged only when he was off his guard. These prejudices contributed to his failure until then to spot that Stalin might be a leading candidate to succeed him. When he thought of power in parties, Lenin had the tendency to assume that only those well grounded in doctrine stood much chance. He assumed that the sole figures worth consideration in any party were its theorists. The classic instance was his obsession with Karl Kautsky. Both before and during the Great War he overrated Kautsky's influence over the German Marxist movement. Although Kautsky was an influential figure, he was very far from moulding the policies of the German Social-Democratic Party.[19]

At any rate Stalin was Lenin's intermediary with the distant world of Kremlin politics while Lenin convalesced at the village of Gorki, twenty miles south of Moscow. When Stalin was set to arrive there for one of their conversations, Lenin would tell his sister Maria to fetch a bottle of decent wine for the guest. Stalin was a busy man; he needed to be treated properly. Maria had recently studied photography in order to catch Lenin on camera, and she snapped Stalin with him on one of his frequent visits.[20] The two of them got along fine and sat out on the terrace for their discussions. There were a few matters that in other circumstances would have been resolved in Lenin's favour at the Central Committee; his absence compelled him to entrust his cases to Stalin. But there was one request which caused Stalin much trepidation. Lenin before his stroke had asked Stalin to supply him with poison so that he might commit suicide if ever he became paralysed. He repeated the request on 30 May. Stalin left the room. Outside was Bukharin. The two of them consulted Maria. They agreed that Stalin, rather than refuse point-blank, should go back to Lenin and say that the doctors were offering an optimistic diagnosis which made suicide wholly inappropriate.[21] The episode passed, and Stalin resumed his trips to keep Lenin up to date with politics in the capital.[22]

Lenin was a cantankerous patient and sought Stalin's assistance in sacking those doctors who annoyed him:[23]

If you have left Klemperer here, then I at least recommend:
1) deporting him from Russia no later than Friday or Saturday

together with Förster, 2) entrusting Ramonov together with Levin and others to use these German doctors and establishing surveillance over them.

Trotski praised Lenin's 'vigilance', but – like the whole Politburo – he voted to reject the request. Eighty other leading Bolsheviks were being treated by the Germans. Deportation would have been a ludicrous measure.[24] Lenin's capriciousness grew. Exasperated by his comrades' refusal to accede to his preferences on policy, he proposed a total reorganisation of the Central Committee. His preposterous suggestion was to sack most of its members. The veterans should be removed forthwith and replaced by Vyacheslav Molotov, Alexei Rykov and Valeryan Kuibyshev. Out, then, would go not only Stalin but also Trotski, Kamenev and Zinoviev.[25]

Lenin's physical debility and political inactivity frustrated him. His tirades stemmed from irritation with what he heard about shifts in official policy. In each instance he found Stalin in disagreement with him. A dispute had been brewing about foreign trade since November 1921.[26] Although Lenin had promoted the expansion of the private sector under the NEP, he drew the line at ending the state's monopoly on commercial imports and exports. Others in the Central Committee, led by Finance Commissar Sokolnikov and supported by Stalin, regarded this as impractical. Sokolnikov had a point. The creaky state bureaucracy was incapable of pursuing all opportunities for trade abroad. The frontiers were not effectively sealed; smugglers were doing business unimpeded and untaxed by the authorities. If the purpose of the NEP was to regenerate the economy, then permission for a widening of the limits of legal private engagement in foreign trade would help. Lenin refused to listen. It had become an article of faith for him to turn the Soviet state into an economic fortress against infiltration by unsupervised influences from abroad.

Lenin had to seek friends outside his previous group. Sokolnikov was with him. Also strongly on his side was the People's Commissar for Foreign Trade Lev Krasin; but Krasin carried little weight in the Party Central Committee. The most influential advocate of a position similar to Lenin's was in fact the person who himself had argued that Lenin had removed too much state regulation from the running of the economy at home: Trotski.

The growing alliance of convenience between Lenin and Trotski came into existence only slowly. Suspicion persisted on both sides about current economic measures. But a second matter meanwhile unsettled Lenin's relationship with Stalin in summer 1922 when the constitutional discussions about the future of the Soviet state came to a head. To Lenin it seemed crucial that the Soviet republics established since 1918 should be joined on equal terms in a federal structure. Formally, the impression had to be given that, although the state would be run from Moscow, the communist rulers rejected all tendencies of 'Great Russian chauvinism'. The RSFSR, vast as it was, would be but one Soviet republic alongside the Soviet republics of Ukraine, Belorussia and the Transcaucasian Federation. Lenin wanted the new federal state to be called the Union of Soviet Republics of Europe and Asia. This had always been his goal. (He had explained this in his confidential correspondence with Stalin in mid-1920.)[27] Lenin was not aiming to run down the influence of the Bolsheviks in the Comintern. But his medium-term objective was genuinely internationalist, and he thought that the name and structure of the projected federal state ought to mirror this.

Stalin, however, wished to expand the RSFSR over the entire territory held by Soviet republics and to provide Ukraine, Belorussia and the Transcaucasus with the same status as existing 'autonomous republics' of the RSFSR such as the Bashkirian Autonomous Soviet Socialist Republic. The state would remain designated as the RSFSR. Stalin could argue that he was only proposing what the Bolsheviks had always said they would supply in their socialist state: 'regional autonomy'. Lenin and Stalin had long asserted, since before the Great War, that this would be the party's solution to the yearnings of the 'national minorities'. Stalin wanted to prevent the Soviet republics from privileging those nations after which each such republic had been named. It was for this reason that he had proposed that the Soviet republics formed in Azerbaijan, Armenia and Georgia in 1920–1 should be gathered together in a Transcaucasian Federation within the RSFSR. This was his device to stop local nationalisms getting further out of hand as had happened in previous years. He regarded Lenin's demand for a formal federal structure as having the potential to undermine the whole state order. With characteristic brusqueness he dismissed it as 'liberalism'.

Stalin continued to plan for 'autonomisation'. His associates Sergei Kirov and Sergo Ordzhonikidze successfully put pressure on the communist leaderships of Azerbaijan and Armenia to approve his scheme in September 1922. So did the Transcaucasian Regional Committee.[28] But the Georgian Central Committee, which had always disliked the scheme and knew it would diminish its low popularity in Georgia still further, rejected it. There were also signs that the Ukrainian and Belorussian communist leaderships – and even, in its quiet way, the Armenian one – accepted it only with great reluctance.[29] Stalin struck back, claiming that failure to follow his proposals would lead to a continuation of 'sheer chaos' in Soviet governmental affairs.[30] He pushed the scheme through a commission of the Party Orgburo on 23 September.[31] News of this reached Lenin, who spoke with Stalin directly on 26 September.[32] Lenin insisted that changes should be made to the draft accepted by the Orgburo commission. He called for an abandonment of 'autonomisation'. Lenin again demanded a Union of Soviet Republics of Europe and Asia; he continued to insist that Russia (in the form of the RSFSR) should join this federation on an equal basis with the other Soviet republics.[33]

Lenin had got his information from Budu Mdivani and other Georgian communists. Stalin was losing his grip. Mdivani had previously been in his good books; it was Stalin who had arranged for him to become Chairman of the Georgian Revolutionary Committee in July 1921 instead of Stalin's internal party critic Pilipe Makharadze.[34] Lenin began to take the side of the Georgian communist leaders when they disagreed with Stalin. Yet Lenin did not go all the way with Mdivani. He still supported Stalin on the need for a Transcaucasian Federation as a device to damp down the manifestations of nationalisms in the south Caucasus; and Stalin, from his side, retracted his demand for the RSFSR to 'autonomise' the other Soviet republics. He did this reluctantly: when Kamenev advised compromise, he replied: 'What is required, in my view, is firmness against Ilich.' Kamenev, who knew his Lenin, demurred and argued that this would merely make matters worse. Stalin at last conceded to Kamenev: 'I don't know. Let him do as he thinks sensible.'[35] The agreed name of the state was to be the Union of Soviet Socialist Republics (or USSR). Stalin did not like the idea but he ceased to raise objections.

He had cause to feel let down by Lenin. The matters dividing them were not of primary importance despite what was said by Lenin at the time (and despite what was written by historians ever after).[36] Stalin and Lenin agreed about basic politics. Neither questioned the desirability of the one-party state, its ideological monopoly or its right to use dictatorial and terrorist methods. They concurred on the provisional need for the NEP. They had also reached an implicit agreement that Stalin had an important job in the central party apparatus to block the advance of the Trotskyists and tighten the whole administrative order. Lenin had trusted him with such tasks. Stalin had also been the comrade in whom he had confided when he wanted to commit suicide. Whenever toughness or underhandedness was needed, Lenin had turned to him. Not once had there been a question of basic principle dividing them, and they had worked well together since the trade union dispute. Lenin had been behaving bizarrely in summer 1922 before he fell out with Stalin. But it was Stalin who had to deal with him. His difficulties with Lenin would have tested the patience of a saint.

Their quarrels about Georgia and about the state monopoly of foreign trade touched matters of secondary importance. Lenin was not demanding independence for Georgia; his pleas on behalf of Georgian communists related to the degree of autonomy they should be permitted: it was almost a dispute about political cosmetics. Stalin also had a reasonable case that the Georgian communist regime had been far from even-handed in its treatment of the non-Georgians. The Transcaucasian Federation was a plausible scheme to prevent national oppression in Georgia, Armenia and Azerbaijan. The foreign trade dispute, too, was nowhere near as clear-cut as Lenin claimed. The state monopoly had failed to thwart the growth of smuggling and currency speculation; and Stalin and his supporters had a point that this led to a loss of state revenues. Yet although Stalin resented Lenin's intervention, he could not stop the Old Man of Bolshevism carrying on as he liked to the extent that his physical condition permitted.

18. NATION AND REVOLUTION

It was galling for Stalin that Lenin had turned against him on the national question. Their collaboration in trying to solve it had begun before the Great War, and Lenin could not have coped without him. Although Stalin did not look for gratitude, he had cause to expect a more reasoned exchange of opinions. Disagreements between them about policy were not new.[1] But Lenin and Stalin had concurred about the strategic orientation of rule in the Soviet multinational state. Stalin was the People's Commissar for Nationalities' Affairs and the Politburo's specialist on the nexus of matters touching on nationhood, religion and territorial boundaries throughout the Civil War. As his military duties ended, he maintained control over decisions on the nationalities. When the leadership began to plan the country's permanent constitutional structure, he was given a central role. The task was taken up in earnest in 1922.

Sovnarkom had long ago settled its viewpoint on several aspects of 'national' policy. Non-Russians were allowed their own schools and press and promising young supporters of the Bolsheviks of each national and ethnic group were trained to occupy leading political positions. Stalin supervised the policy even though, during the Civil War, he was often away from Moscow. Meetings of the People's Commissariat for Nationalities' Affairs collegium in his absence had been chaotic. Sometimes they were also noisy and over-long when he was present. His deputy Stanislaw Pestkowski recalled:[2]

> It is hardly surprising that he sometimes lost patience. But on no occasion did he show this at the meetings themselves. In those instances where his supply of patience had been exhausted as the result of our interminable arguments at our gatherings he would suddenly vanish. He used to do this extraordinarily deftly. He would say: 'I'll be back in a minute.' Then he would disappear from the room and go off and hide in one of the cubby holes of the Smolny [Institute] or the Kremlin.

The time had not arrived when anticipation of Stalin's displeasure caused all to shiver in their boots. Stalin was but one Bolshevik leader among others. Only Lenin with his greater personal prestige could get away with rebuking miscreants.

When Stalin got very fed up he crept out of Sovnarkom itself. (So much for the myth of the grand bureaucrat with inexhaustible patience.) Pestkowski, who knew Stalin's habits better than most, would receive instructions to flush him out of his lair: 'I caught him a couple of times in comrade-sailor Vorontsov's apartment where Stalin, stretched out on a divan, was smoking his pipe and thinking over his theses.'[3] There were times when Stalin longed to be reassigned to the fronts of the Civil War and get away from the palaver in his Commissariat.

The cardinal decisions on the national question had anyway been taken by the central party leadership. As the Red Army reimposed central authority over the outlying regions of the former Russian Empire, the Kremlin leadership needed to clarify and disseminate policy in order to maximise its appeal to non-Russians. This was a difficult task. In 1917 it had been the workers and soldiers of Russia who had voted most strongly for the Bolsheviks. The Red Army on the rampage failed to allay suspicions about Russian imperialism, and the stream of decrees from the People's Commissariat for Nationalities' Affairs took time to have a positive impact. A further problem was caused by the international situation. Although the Western Allies pulled out of the former Russian Empire at the end of 1919, regional powers in eastern Europe and western Asia continued to pose a military threat, and the Politburo was concerned that Britain and France might use such powers to overthrow Soviet communism. Turkey, Finland and Poland were feared as potential invaders. In these circumstances the Central Committee and Politburo in 1919 set up independent Soviet states in Ukraine, Lithuania and Belorussia – and in 1920–1 in Azerbaijan, Armenia and Georgia. Communist leaders in Moscow hoped by such means to prove that their commitment to national self-determination was genuine.

The division of Azerbaijan, Armenia and Georgia into separate states had occurred because of inter-national enmities in the anti-Bolshevik Transcaucasian Federation established after the October Revolution. Before the pan-Turkic Musavatist party came to power in Baku in 1918 there had formally been no such place as Azerbaijan.[4] The frontiers of Azerbaijan, Armenia and Georgia remained contentious under the early Soviet administration. Yet rudiments of statehood had been acquired. The invading Bolsheviks intended to build on them.

It had been Stalin who drew up the decrees recognising the Soviet republics in Estonia, Latvia and Lithuania in December 1918.[5] He accepted them as a temporary expedient; later he referred to this as a policy of 'national liberalism'.[6] Practical implementation was tricky. There was a shortage of local Bolshevik leaders and activists, and often those Bolsheviks who came from the locality were Jewish rather than of the titular nationality. Stalin was brought into the discussion even when he could not attend sessions in the capital. He was given the right of personal veto over whether to designate the Hümmet organisation as the new Communist Party of Azerbaijan. Only Stalin was thought to know whether the Hümmetists could be trusted as the territorial power.[7] As the Civil War drew to an end, the question arose of the permanent constitutional future. Stalin had no doubt. Until then there had been bilateral treaties between the RSFSR and the Soviet republics. These had been tilted in favour of the RSFSR's hegemony; and in any case the Party Central Committee controlled the communist parties in those other republics.[8] A centralised state run from Moscow was already a reality. Stalin wished to bring the governmental structures into line with those of the party by incorporating the Soviet republics in the RSFSR.

Initially he got his way. The 'union treaty' negotiated between the RSFSR and the Ukrainian Soviet Socialist Republic after the Civil War unified their People's Commissariats in military, economic and transport affairs – and the RSFSR People's Commissariats were given authority over the Ukrainian ones. Yet the Central Committee stopped short of approving his fundamental objective of comprehensive incorporation.[9] Kamenev was his chief opponent on that occasion. But Lenin too became a critic. A fault-line in their long-lasting collaboration was being disclosed. Lenin had drawn the conclusion from the history of the Civil War that the formal constitutional concessions to the borderlands had to be maintained. Soviet republics in Ukraine and elsewhere had to be preserved. What Stalin desired was to expand the RSFSR and turn Ukraine into one of its internal 'autonomous republics'. An immense dispute was in the making.

The establishment of autonomous republics had begun in the Civil War, and the policy was widely implemented from 1920 as the national-territorial principle of local government was extended to the Bashkirs, the Tatars, the Kirgiz, the Chuvash, the Mari, the Kalmyks, the Vots and the Karelian Finns.[10] This was not achieved without controversy. The granting of authority to indigenous national and ethnic groups annoyed the Russian inhabitants of autonomous regions and provinces who felt they were being reduced to second-class status as citizens of the RSFSR. Yet the Politburo bent over backwards to be seen to enhance conditions for non-Russians. Not a few towns with a mainly Russian population were included in an autonomous republic specifically so that the republic might become economically and administratively self-standing.[11] All this made for complex discussions in Moscow, and easy answers were seldom on offer. The Bolsheviks were trying to de-imperialise an old empire without allowing its disintegration into separate nation-states. There were no models to copy. They were setting the precedent, and Stalin was the Politburo's acknowledged specialist in this matter.

His involvement was often a troubled one. The Tatar–Bashkir Republic, installed in the RSFSR in 1919, had quickly come to grief. The Tatars and the Bashkirs were not the best of friends, and the local Russian residents disliked feeling excluded from influence. Inter-ethnic violence scarred the entire region. The Red Army had to be deployed to restore order and Stalin reasonably decided that the Tatars and Bashkirs should have separate national-territorial units. The basic orientation of policy was maintained. Stalin went on establishing autonomous republics even if this meant offending the local Russians.[12]

No region presented him with trickier problems than did his native Caucasus. The ethnic intermingling – on both the north and south sides of the mountain range – was intense and the chronic rivalries were acute. Stalin could not deal with this exclusively from the Kremlin and on 14 September the Politburo assigned him a mission to the north Caucasus. After the disappointments of the Soviet–Polish War, he was given much scope for initiative.[13] This was the kind of mission he liked. Reaching the region, he gave approval to the existing Mountain Republic: he liked its capacity to unite Chechens, Ossetians, Kabardians and others. But he did not include the Cossacks.[14] Much of the trouble in the north Caucasus derived from the Imperial practice of settling Cossacks, descendants of Russian peasant refugees, in villages as a means of controlling the indigenous nations. A Mountain Republic with their participation would scarcely be effective. Stalin boasted to Lenin in October 1920 that that he had meted out 'exemplary punishment to several Cossack settlements' for their rebellious activity.[15] Despite his later reputation, Stalin had no special fondness for Russians and his continuation of the ethnic cleansing of the Cossacks reflected this.[16]

Attending the Congress of Peoples of the Terek in November 1920, Stalin considered future constitutional arrangements:[17]

What type of autonomy is going to be given to the Mountain Republic? ... Autonomy can be diverse: there's administrative autonomy such as is possessed by the Karelians, Cheremis, Chuvash and Volga Germans; there's also political autonomy such as the Bashkirs, Kirgiz and Tatars have. The Mountain Republic's autonomy is political.

He clearly meant that the peoples of the north Caucasus would be allowed not only to manage their own territorial units but also to pursue their national and ethnic interests within them.

Stalin explained his policy to the Tenth Party Congress in March 1921 when introducing the debate on the national question. His speech contrasted western Europe where nation-states were the norm and eastern Europe where the Romanovs, Habsburgs and Hohenzollerns had ruled vast multinational states. Stalin exaggerated the national homogeneity of states in the West but he was right that the mixture of nations was denser to the East. At any rate he declared that the anti-imperial struggle had intensified after the Great War as Turkey in particular supported movements for national liberation in the colonies of the European powers. But supposedly only Soviet Russia could do anything practical. Stalin declared:[18]

The essence of the national question in the RSFSR consists in eliminating the backwardness (economic, political, cultural) of nationalities which has been inherited from the past in order to give an opportunity to backward peoples to catch up with central Russia in relation to statehood, culture and economy.

He identified two dangers. The first was obvious to anyone like himself from the borderlands of the Russian Empire. This was 'Russian great-power chauvinism'. The other was the nationalism of non-Russians outside Russia, and Stalin stressed that it was a nationalism widely shared by local communists. Both dangers had to be confronted by the Russian Communist Party.

'Under the Soviet federative state,' Stalin declared, 'there are no longer either oppressed nationalities or ruling ones: national oppression has been liquidated.'[19] The speech was uncharacteristically vague in content. Stalin may have been too busy to prepare it properly while organising the Leninist faction in the trade union controversy. He was also suffering from agonising stomach pains.[20] Then again, he had a huge capacity for work and had always summoned up the strength for a big speech. The probability is that, knowing how quickly passions were ignited by the national question, he sought to damp things down.

If this was his intention, it was unsuccessful. Critics lined up to attack. They assailed Stalin for making an abstract report 'outside time and space' and for yielding too much to 'petit-bourgeois' nationalist demands while not struggling hard enough against Russocentrism.[21] In fact Stalin had problems regardless of what he said. Some delegates wanted decentralisation and greater room for national self-expression. Others, wanting firmer centralisation in Moscow, attacked the alleged indulgence shown to nationalism since the October Revolution. Stalin himself was accused of 'artificially implanting Belorussian nationhood'. This comment roused him to fury. His reply went:[22]

> This is untrue because Belorussian nationhood does exist; it has its own language which is different from Russian, in view of which it's possible to raise higher the culture of the Belorussian people only in its own language. Such speeches were given five years ago about Ukraine, about Ukrainian nationhood. And it's not so long ago that people used to say that the Ukrainian republic and Ukrainian nationhood were a German invention. Meanwhile it's clear that Ukrainian nationhood exists and that the development of its culture constitutes a duty for communists.

Stalin was not going to allow the entire policy developed by himself and Lenin to be derided, defamed or ditched.

His arguments were demographic and political. The towns of Ukraine, he predicted, would soon cease to be Russian when flooded with Ukrainian newcomers, just as Riga had once been predominantly a German city and had gradually been Latvianised. Secondly, he maintained that if ever the message of Marxism was to be accepted in the borderlands of the former Russian Empire, it had to be conveyed in languages which were comprehensible and congenial to the recipients. The idea that Stalin was a 'Great Russian chauvinist' in the 1920s is nonsense. More than any other Bolshevik leader, including Lenin, he fought for the principle that each people in the Soviet state should have scope for national and ethnic self-expression.

Yet it was fiendishly difficult to turn principle into practice. The Caucasus continued to worry the Politburo; and whatever general scheme was applied to it would have consequences for the entire constitutional structure of the Soviet state (or states). When Georgia fell to the Red Army in March 1921, the Bolsheviks had reclaimed as much

of the former Russian Empire as they would possess until the annexa-
tions of 1939–40. Poland had thrown back the Reds at the battle of the
Vistula. Estonia, Latvia and Lithuania had abolished their Soviet republics and grasped their independence. The Politburo was determined that
this should not happen in the Caucasus. Soviet republics in Azerbaijan,
Armenia and Georgia had been established and Moscow steadily
increased its control over the region. All the old problems, however,
were replicated there. Veteran Bolsheviks were few and popular support
for the communist regimes was frail. Religious traditions were strong.
Customary social hierarchies were tenacious. What is more, the Red
Army had marched into a region which had been tearing itself apart
with vicious armed conflict since 1918. There had been wars across
borders. There had also been persecution of national and ethnic minorities within each state. Ethnic cleansing had been perpetrated.[23] The
Politburo had yet to bring about a final settlement.

There were several possibilities. Each little area could have been
transformed into a province of the RSFSR. This would have the advantage of administrative neatness and centralist control. Another option
would be to establish several Soviet republics on the model of Ukraine
in the Civil War. Not only Georgia, Armenia and Azerbaijan but also
Abkhazia, Dagestan, Chechnya and other parts of the north Caucasus
could have been handled in this fashion. Yet another possibility was to
resurrect the short-lived anti-Bolshevik Transcaucasian Federation of
1918 as a pro-Soviet entity – and, perhaps, to add the north Caucasus to
its composition. No plan existed before or after the October Revolution.
Stalin in 1920–1, though, came to advocate placing the north Caucasus
inside the RSFSR; he also aimed to maintain the Soviet republics of
Georgia, Armenia and Azerbaijan while compelling them to enter a
Transcaucasian Federation (which itself would become a subordinate
part of the RSFSR). He never spelled out why he excluded the north
Caucasus from his scheme for the rest of the Caucasus. But probably he
wanted a defensible border for the RSFSR against a potential invasion by
the Turks or the Allies. The reason why he inclined towards a Transcaucasian Federation is easier to understand: it was a device to ensure an
end to the inter-state and inter-ethnic conflicts in the region. Georgia,
Armenia and Azerbaijan were not to be trusted as separate Soviet
republics.

In summer 1921 Stalin, who had been convalescing in Nalchik in the
north Caucasus,[24] paid a trip at last to the south Caucasus. Until then
the affairs of the region had been handled by himself in the Kremlin and

by the Party Caucasian Bureau based in Tbilisi. The Bureau's leaders were his friends Sergo Ordzhonikidze and Sergei Kirov, and Ordzhonikidze insisted that Stalin's presence was required if the many pressing problems were to be resolved.[25] It was his first visit to Georgia since before the Great War. He had no illusions about the kind of welcome he would receive. Even many among Georgia's Bolsheviks had always disliked him, and his identification with the 'Russian' armed forces of occupation – the Red Army – did little to improve his standing among Georgians in general. But Stalin was undeterred. If Ordzhonikidze and Kirov as the Kremlin's representatives could not do this, Politburo member Stalin would force through the necessary decisions.

The Caucasian Bureau had been divided over various territorial matters. As well as the recurrent pressures from the Georgian communist leadership to incorporate Abkhazia in the Georgian Soviet Republic there was a demand from the Azerbaijani communist leadership in Baku for Karabagh, an Armenian-inhabited enclave butting into Azerbaijan, to be made part of Azerbaijan; and the Armenian communists fiercely opposed this on the ground that Karabagh should belong to Armenia. Ruling the Caucasus was never going to be easy after the wars fought between the Azeris and Armenians from 1918. But on balance it was Stalin's judgement that the Azerbaijani authorities should be placated. Revolutionary pragmatism was his main motive. The Party Central Committee in Moscow gave a high priority to winning support for the Communist International across Asia. Bolshevik indulgence to 'Moslem' Azerbaijan would be noted with approval in the countries bordering the new Soviet republics. In any case, the Turkish government of Kemal Pasha was being courted by Moscow; armies of Turks had rampaged into Georgia, Armenia and Azerbaijan in recent years and continued to pose a threat to Soviet security: the appeasement of Azerbaijan was thought an effective way of keeping Istanbul quiet.

This stored up trouble for the future. If the matter had been decidable without reference to the situation in the rest of Asia, Stalin would probably have left Karabagh inside Armenia despite Azerbaijani protests. He would also, if he had had his way at the same meeting of the Caucasian Bureau, have handed Abkhazia to Georgia with rights of internal autonomy.[26] But Abkhazian Bolshevik leaders Yefrem Eshba and Nestor Lakoba, who had negotiated a treaty between the RSFSR and Kemal Pasha's Turkey,[27] had lobbied hard in Moscow and set up their Abkhazian Soviet Republic. Georgia's Menshevik government had annexed Abkhazia and maltreated its people. Eshba and Lakoba insisted that their country's reincorporation in Georgia would cast an odour of unpopularity on Bolshevism; and faced with this campaign, Stalin backed down and allowed them their Soviet republic. He could only do this, however, at the cost of annoying the Georgian Party Central Committee (which likewise argued that Bolshevism would incur popular hostility if he gave in to Eshba and Lakoba).

He was given proof of this when he addressed the Party City Organisation in Tbilisi on 6 July. This audience was already angry with him and his speech made everything worse. Stalin argued that the Georgian economy was incapable of post-war recovery without the specific assistance of Russia.[28] This was both untrue and offensive; for Western investment and trade could have helped to regenerate industry and agriculture in the country. Intellectually he was on firmer ground when he asserted:[29]

> Now, on arriving in Tiflis [Tbilisi], I've been struck by the absence of the old solidarity among the workers of the various nationalities of the Caucasus. Nationalism has developed among workers and peasants and distrust has been strengthened towards comrades of a different nationality; anti-Armenian, anti-Tatar, anti-Georgian, anti-Russian and any other nationalism you like to mention.

But this argument, too, failed to go down well. Essentially Stalin was warning the Georgian communist leaders and activists that they had to show themselves worthy of Moscow's support. Abkhazians, Ossetians and Adzharians had indeed suffered under the Menshevik government, which had treated their lands as provinces of historical Georgia. They had insisted that the Abkhazians were a Georgian tribe despite the fact that their language is entirely unrelated. If harmony was to be attained, the Georgian communist leadership had to set an example.

Stalin ran into still worse trouble at a workers' mass meeting he addressed in Tbilisi. Georgia's returning son was heard in silence as he explained the case for Sovietisation. This contrasted with the attitude to Isidore Ramishvili, the deposed Menshevik Interior Minister and old personal enemy of Stalin, who was greeted with a lengthy ovation.[30] Stalin's temper had a fast fuse and, protected by his Cheka guards, he stormed out. His entire political career in Tbilisi had been full of rejections. This latest episode was one humiliation too many. As usual he sublimated his resentment by attacking others. He held Pilipe Makharadze, Chairman of the Georgian Revolutionary Committee, personally responsible for the fracas. Makharadze was sacked and replaced by Budu Mdivani.[31] At the time Stalin felt he had promoted a more loyal and compliant Bolshevik to power in Georgia. And of course he misjudged his man. Mdivani turned out to be a far from pliable appointee; and it was he who had agitated Lenin into action from his sickbed against Stalin on the national question.

The tempestuous dispute between Lenin and Stalin in 1922–3 tended to hide the fact that Stalin stood by the general agreement they reached after he had made the concessions that Lenin demanded. The decision to form the Union of Soviet Socialist Republics was ratified on 31 December 1922 and the new Constitution came formally came into force at the beginning of 1924. The federal system was a mere screen. The Politburo of the Russian Communist Party took the main decisions about each Soviet republic. Stalin had his own growing bias in favour of Russia and the Russians. Yet the grant of authority, prestige and enhancement to the other peoples remained intact. The Soviet republics were conserved and the autonomous republics proliferated. National and ethnic groups enjoyed the freedom to run presses and schools in their own languages – and Stalin and his associates gave resources for philologists to develop alphabets for the languages of several small peoples in the Caucasus and Siberia so that schooling might commence. The party also tried to attract indigenous young recruits to the party. Stalin spelled this out to a conference held by the Central Committee with 'national' republican and provincial communist leaders in June 1923.[32]

It was an extraordinary experiment. The Politburo, while setting its face against the possibility that any region of the USSR might secede, continued to try to demonstrate to everyone at home and abroad that the October Revolution had set the conditions for the final solution of the national problems. Stalin was not just following policy. He believed in it and was one of its most committed exponents. His Georgian origins and early Marxist activity had moored him to the idea that the peoples of the former Russian Empire needed to be schooled, indoctrinated and recruited if Marxism was to take root among them. He and Lenin had got together about this in 1912–13. Stalin was not just playing with such ideas. Since before 1917 he had understood the importance of national languages and national personnel for the advancement of communism. He had sloughed off some early ideas but continued to insist that Marxism had to incorporate a serious commitment to solving the national question. His altercations with Mdivani and the Georgian communist leadership derived not from 'chauvinism' (as Lenin had claimed at the time and Trotski repeated later) but from a specific set of objections to Mdivani's reckless disregard for the wishes of Moscow and the interests of the non-Georgians in Georgia.[33]

Official measures on the national question had always been distasteful to many communist leaders, and it was Stalin who had to shoulder the bulk of the opprobrium. Trotski, Zinoviev and Kamenev agreed with the official line. Being Jews, however, they felt inhibited from taking a prominent role in debates about nationhood. Although Bukharin made the occasional comment, he too kept out of the spotlight. And so Stalin, despite Lenin's accusation that he was a Great Russian chauvinist, remained chiefly responsible for party policy. Mdivani and other Georgian communist leaders quickly fell out with him. The imposition of a Transcaucasian Federation was too bitter a cup for them to drink from, and Stalin's manipulations in 1922 permanently offended them. Not for the first time since 1917 he was undertaking uncongenial tasks which others shunned.

19. TESTAMENT

Tensions between Stalin and Lenin went on rising in autumn 1922. Stalin was not in a conciliating mood. He rebuked Lenin for garbling the contents of party policy in an interview for the *Manchester Guardian*:[1] the pupil was telling off his teacher. No Politburo member except Trotski wrote so bluntly to Lenin. These niggles added to Lenin's set of concerns about the General Secretary, and he became agitated about leaving the communist party to Stalin. As his hope of physical recovery slipped away, he dictated a series of notes to be made public in the event of his death.[2] They were headed 'Letter to the Congress' because he wanted them to be read out to the next Party Congress. These are the notes known to history as Lenin's Testament.

The gist lay in the sentences he composed on 25 December 1922 about fellow party leaders Stalin, Trotski, Zinoviev, Kamenev, Bukharin and Pyatakov. Molotov was one of the leaders peeved to have been left out of the list:[3] Lenin was leaving a record for history. In fact the Testament's main concern was with two individuals on the list:[4]

> Comrade Stalin, having become General Secretary, has concentrated boundless power in his hands and I am not convinced that he will always manage to use this power with adequate care. On the other hand comrade Trotski, as has been shown by his struggle against the Central Committee in connection with the People's Commissariat of the Means of Communication, is distinguished not merely by his outstanding talents. He surely is personally the most able individual in the current Central Committee but he has an excessive self-confidence and an excessive preoccupation with the purely administrative side of affairs.

Lenin dwelt on rivalry between Trotski and Stalin:[5] 'These two qualities of the two outstanding leaders of the present Central Committee have the capacity to bring about an unintended split [in the party], and unless the party takes measures to prevent this, a split could happen unexpectedly.' A split in the party, he argued, would imperil the existence of the Soviet regime.

Lenin went on: 'Our party rests upon two social classes and this is what makes possible its instability and makes inevitable its collapse unless agreements can take place between these two classes.'[6] The danger he had in mind was that Trotski and Stalin would promote policies favouring different classes – the working class and the peasantry – and that this would induce strife that would undermine the regime.

To many party officials who were privy to the Testament this seemed an eccentric analysis. They recognised the isolation of the Soviet state in the international system and had not forgotten about the foreign intervention in the Civil War. They could also understand why Lenin picked out Trotski as someone who might bring disunity to the central party leadership. But Lenin's preoccupation with Stalin caused surprise. Popular opinion, according to reports of the GPU (as the Cheka had been known since 1921), suggested Trotski, Zinoviev, Kamenev, Rykov, Bukharin or even Dzierżyński as the likeliest winner of the contest for the political succession.[7] Even within the ruling group Stalin was still not taken as seriously as he should have been. Lenin, though, had at last got his measure; and on 4 January 1923, as the dispute over Georgia grew bitter, he dictated an addendum to his characterisation:[8]

> Stalin is too crude; and this defect, which is wholly bearable inside our milieu and in relations among ourselves, becomes intolerable in the post of General Secretary. I therefore make a proposal for comrades to think of a way to remove Stalin and in his place appoint someone else who is distinguished from comrade Stalin in all other respects through having the single superior feature of being more patient, more loyal, more courteous and more attentive to comrades, less capricious, etc.

Lenin's meaning pierced its way through his shaky syntax: he wanted to remove Stalin from the General Secretaryship.

His scheme was limited in scope. He was not proposing Stalin's removal from the central party leadership, still less from the party as a whole. Such an idea would have been treated with the disdain which had met his request in July 1922 to dismiss most members of the Central Committee.[9] Nor was Lenin the perfect political astrologer of his time. There was absolutely nothing in the Testament predicting the scale of terror which ensued in the years from 1928. Lenin, the leading proponent of state terror in the Civil War, failed to detect Stalin's potential to apply terror-rule still more deeply in peacetime. The Testament of 1922–3 was limited to an effort to deprive Stalin of his most important administrative post.[10]

Files on the Georgian Affair were brought out for Lenin to examine. He had made up his mind about the verdict: Stalin and his associates were guilty of Great Russian chauvinism even though Stalin, Ordzhoni-kidze and Dzierżyński themselves were not Russians. Already at the end of the previous year, in an article on the national question, Lenin had acknowledged:[11]

> I am, it seems, immensely guilty before the workers of Russia for not intervening sufficiently energetically and sufficiently sharply in the notorious question of autonomisation, officially known, it seems, as the question of the union of soviet socialist republics.

He also dictated an article on bureaucracy in the organs of party and government, making strong criticisms of the Workers' and Peasants' Inspectorate. It was obvious to informed observers that Stalin, who headed the Inspectorate, was his principal target. *Pravda*'s editors blunted Lenin's article in its published form;[12] but the general intent was conserved. Lenin composed a further article, 'Better Fewer But Better', demanding the immediate promotion of ordinary industrial workers to political office. His rationale was that they alone had the attitudes necessary to create harmony in the Party Central Committee and put an end to bureaucratic practices. Once again it was a message that was meant to damage Stalin.

Lenin went on giving dictation to Maria Volodicheva and Lidia Fotieva. Although he seems to have stopped mentioning sensitive matters in front of Nadya Allilueva, he took no other precaution beyond telling his secretaries to keep everything to themselves and to lock up his papers. This was how he plotted the downfall of an individual whom he considered the greatest danger to the Revolution. Lenin's excessive self-confidence – the very defect he ascribed to Trotski – had not left him.

He would have been less insouciant if he had known his secretaries better. Volodicheva was disconcerted by the contents of his dictated notes on 23 December and she consulted her colleague Fotieva, who advised her to take a copy to none other than Stalin. Stalin was shocked but not deterred. He had had an altercation with Krupskaya the previous day on discovering that she had been helping Lenin to communicate with Trotski and others about current politics. Krupskaya's behaviour contravened the Politburo's orders, and Stalin, who had been asked to ensure observance of the regimen specified by Lenin's doctors, directed verbal obscenities at her. Krupskaya declared that she alone knew what was medically best for Lenin. If Lenin were to be denied political contact with other leaders, his recovery would be delayed still further. She wrote in these terms to Kamenev, adding that nobody in the party had ever addressed her as foully as Stalin. But she did not tell Lenin for fear of upsetting him; and Stalin had not sought to withhold the right to dictate from Lenin. He resented being picked out for blame when he was only carrying out Politburo orders;[13] but he reasonably assumed that the matters dividing him from Lenin were amenable to eventual resolution.

Some weeks later, however, Krupskaya blurted out to Lenin how Stalin had behaved towards her. Lenin was infuriated. Although he himself often swore,[14] he drew the line at the verbal abuse of women. Stalin's comportment offended him, and on 5 March 1923 he dictated a sharp letter:

> You had the uncouthness to summon my wife to the telephone and swear at her. Although she has even given you her agreement to forget what was said, this fact has nevertheless become known through her to Zinoviev and Kamenev. I do not intend to forget so easily what has been done against me, and it goes without saying that I consider something done against my wife to be something also done against me. I therefore ask you to consider whether you agree to retract what you said and apologise or you prefer to break relations between us.

Stalin was stupefied. He had tried to mend bridges with Lenin by letting him continue dictating and researching even though the resultant articles hurt him. He had asked Lenin's sister Maria Ulyanova to plead his case: 'I love him with all my heart. Tell him this in some way.' With the letter in his hands Stalin tried to tell himself: 'This isn't Lenin who's talking, it's his illness!'

He scribbled out a half-hearted compromise. 'If my wife had behaved incorrectly and you had had to punish her,' he wrote, 'I would not have regarded it as my right to intervene. But inasmuch as you insist, I am willing to apologise to Nadezhda Konstantinovna.' On reflection Stalin redrafted the message and admitted to having bawled at Krupskaya; but he added that he had only been doing his duty as given him by the Politburo. He added:

Yet if you consider that the maintenance of 'relations' requires me to 'retract' the above-mentioned words, I can retract them, while nevertheless refusing to understand what the problem is here, what my 'guilt' consists of and what in particular is being demanded of me.

Whenever he started to apologise, he ended up rubbing salt in the wound. How on earth Stalin thought such a message would placate Lenin is hard to imagine. But he was a proud man. He could not bring himself to show any greater contrition, and was on the point of paying dearly.

Yet this did not happen. On 10 March, agitated by the dispute, Lenin suffered a heart attack. Suddenly Stalin no longer needed to concern himself about Lenin directly leading a campaign against him. Lenin was taken off to the Gorki mansion outside Moscow, never to return. He was a helpless cripple tended by his wife Nadya and sister Maria; and although the doctors told them that all was not lost, Nadya ceased to believe them. His medical condition remained subject to security surveillance. The reports of GPU operatives to the Kremlin let Stalin know he was in the clear: Lenin was beyond recovery; it was only a matter of time before he died.

Lenin's dictated thoughts, however, remained a threat. The dying leader had had them typed up in multiple copies and their existence was known to Politburo members and to the secretaries in Lenin's office. Not everyone in the Politburo was friendly to Stalin. Relations between Trotski and Stalin had never been good, and Stalin could expect trouble from that quarter. What counted in Stalin's favour, though, was that Kamenev, Zinoviev and others anticipated a strong bid from Trotski for supreme power. Stalin was a valuable accomplice whom they were disinclined to remove from the General Secretaryship. They knew his defects as well as Lenin did; they were also less aware of his capacities and ambition than Lenin had become: they therefore underestimated the difficulty they might have in handling him in the years ahead. This meant that if Stalin played his hand skilfully, he might yet survive the storm. The next Party Congress – the Twelfth – was scheduled for April 1923. The Politburo aimed to show that the regime could function effectively in Lenin's absence. Trotski was offered the honour of delivering the political report on behalf of the Central Committee, but refused. Instead it was Zinoviev who gave it. Among themselves Zinoviev, Kamenev and Stalin arranged the rest of the proceedings in advance.

Stalin, though, gave the organisational report. Cleverly he accepted

Lenin's proposal for structural reforms to the Party Central Committee and the Central Control Commission; but whereas Lenin had wished to promote ordinary workers to membership of these bodies, Stalin gave preference to local party leaders of working-class origin who no longer worked in factories or mines. By this means Stalin would control the process and emasculate Lenin's intentions.

He also delivered the report on the national question. He crafted his words with cunning and spoke like a man on the attack. He condemned both Great Russian nationalism and the nationalisms of the non-Russian peoples. He suggested that party policy had been correct in doctrine, policy and practice – and by implication he suggested that he was merely progressing along a line marked out by Lenin. Budu Mdivani got up to say that Stalin and his associates had handled affairs unfairly.[15] By then, however, Stalin had had time to organise his defence and to get leaders from the south Caucasus to put Mdivani under fire. Zinoviev, too, rallied to Stalin's side, demanding that Mdivani and his supporters should dissociate themselves from Georgian nationalism. Bukharin asserted the need to avoid giving offence to non-Russian national sensibilities; but he too failed to indicate that Stalin had acted as an obstacle to the success of official policy. Even Trotski refrained from an open attack on the General Secretary despite the encouragement he had been given by Lenin. Yet the pressure on Stalin had been intense, and with a degree of self-pity he claimed he had not wanted to deliver the report on the national question. As usual he represented himself as simply carrying out duties assigned to him by the leadership.

And he survived the ordeal. He paid a price: he had to accept several amendments to the draft resolution and most of these gave greater rights to the non-Russians than he liked. Yet the Georgian case was rejected and Stalin survived the Congress. The Testament remained under lock and key. It could have been revealed to the Congress, but his allies Zinoviev and Kamenev had blocked such a move.[16] For a general secretary who had been on the brink of being removed from the Central Committee this was worth celebrating as a victory. Zinoviev, Kamenev and Stalin appeared to run party and state like a triumvirate.

Trotski passed up his opportunity to cause an upset. In subsequent years his supporters criticised his failure to grab his chance at the Twelfth Party Congress. Undoubtedly he had little tactical finesse in internal party business. Yet it is questionable whether he would have done himself a favour by breaking with the rest of the Politburo. Too many leaders at the central level and in the provinces had identified him as the

Bonaparte-like figure who might lead the armed forces against the Revolution's main objectives. His anti-Bolshevik past counted against him. His Civil War record, which involved the policy of shooting delinquent Bolshevik leaders in the Red Army, had not been forgotten. Furthermore, several of his admiring subordinates in the Revolutionary-Military Council of the Republic had – like him – not belonged to the Bolsheviks before 1917; and some of them had not been revolutionaries at all. Trotski had an intermittent tendency towards nervousness in trials of strength in the party. He was also aware that any attempt to unseat a Politburo member would have been interpreted as a bid for supreme power even before Lenin had passed away. Trotski decided to wait for a better chance in the months ahead.

Rivalry in fact grew among his enemies as soon as the Congress was over. Kamenev and Zinoviev had protected Stalin because they wanted help against Trotski. But they were disconcerted by the individual initiatives taken by Stalin in the weeks since Lenin's heart attack. Zinoviev, based in faraway Petrograd, objected to decisions being taken without consultation. In the Civil War and afterwards it had been normal for Lenin to seek the opinion of Politburo members by phone or telegram before fixing policy. Stalin had gone ahead with his preferences on the *Pravda* editorial board, on the national question in the USSR, on the Middle East and on the Comintern. He was getting too big for his Tsaritsyn boots, and Zinoviev aimed to treat him firmly. While in Kislovodsk in the north Caucasus, Zinoviev called a meeting with other leading Bolsheviks on vacation near by. These included Bukharin, Voroshilov, Lashevich and Yevdokimov. Although Lashevich and Yevdokimov were his trusted supporters working with him in Petrograd, Voroshilov was a client of Stalin who was likely to relay the content of the conversations to the General Secretary. Perhaps (as most have supposed) Zinoviev was naïve. More likely, though, he thought that Voroshilov would be the intermediary who would carry the message back to Stalin that he had to change his behaviour or suffer the negative consequences.

On 30 July he wrote to Kamenev:[17]

> You're simply letting Stalin make a mockery of us.
> Facts? Examples?
> Allow me!
>
> *1) The nat[ional] question.*
> . . . Stalin makes the appointment of the Central Committee plenipotentiaries (instructors)

2) The Gulf Convention. Why not consult the two of us and Trotski about this important question? *There was sufficient time.* By the way, I'm meant to be responsible for the People's Commissariat for Foreign Affairs . . .

3) Comintern . . .
V.I. [Lenin] dedicated a good 10 per cent of his time to the Comintern . . . And Stalin turns up, takes a quick look and makes a decision. And Bukh[arin] and I are 'dead souls': we're not asked about anything.

4) Pravda
This morning – and it was the last straw – Bukharin learned from Dubrovski's personal telegram that the ed[itorial] board had been replaced without informing him or asking Bukh[arin] . . .
    We won't tolerate this any longer.
    If the party is doomed to go through a period (probably *very* brief) of Stalin's personal despotism, so be it. But I for one don't intend to cover up all this swinish behaviour. All the platforms refer to the 'triumvirate' in the belief that I'm not the least important figure in it. In reality there's no triumvirate, there is only Stalin's dictatorship.

According to Zinoviev, the time to act was overdue.
    He exaggerated the power of the General Secretary. A simple vote in the Politburo, chaired by Kamenev, could still restrain Stalin; and when Zinoviev was unable to attend sessions, it would not have been difficult to insist on preliminary consultation of his opinions. Yet he was right about Stalin's growing desire to get his way without reference to fellow Politburo members. Stalin saw the need for tactical retreat. He agreed to – and indeed appeared to encourage – changes in the composition of central party bodies. His critics had seen how often he had placed his supporters in posts of authority outside Moscow. He sat through Orgburo meetings which decided such matters. The solution was obvious. Trotski, Zinoviev and Bukharin were appointed to the Orgburo. They could oppose Stalin's schemes whenever they wanted.[18]
    It made little difference. The reason usually given is that Trotski and Zinoviev failed to appreciate the importance of attending the Orgburo whereas Stalin was a contented participant. Yet the basic question is why Trotski and Zinoviev, having identified the source of Stalin's bureaucratic power and demanded Orgburo membership for themselves, failed to follow through with their action against him. This question, though,

begs yet another one. Was Stalin's willingness to sit through meeting after meeting the most important reason for his capacity to defeat them? The answer must surely be no. It was not as if Trotski, Kamenev and Zinoviev spent their time untroubled by the duty to attend bureaucratic meetings. The entire Soviet order was bureaucratic, and meetings of administrative officials were the norm. The leading organs of the Central Committee had been recomposed mainly with a view towards administering a shock to the General Secretary. His fellow Politburo members thought they could get on with their individual campaigns to succeed Lenin. Each expected to run his administrative hierarchy without interference from the others. Stalin's career had not been extinguished but his political capital had been reduced to a minimum.

He was helped by events. All Politburo members, including Trotski, wanted to keep unity in the central party leadership. Isolated and resented across the country outside the party, they eagerly presented a front of agreement in public. Lenin was not yet dead even though leaders in the Kremlin knew that his chances of recovery were remote. Stalin's adversaries in the Politburo did not want to rock the communist party boat by trying to throw Stalin overboard.

Yet the disagreements continued behind the scenes. They were exacerbated by the handling of economic policy by Kamenev, Zinoviev and Stalin. In mid-1923 there was suddenly a deficit in food supplies to the towns. This was the result of what Trotski called the 'scissors crisis'. Prices of industrial goods had increased three times over prices paid for agricultural products since 1913. Thus the blades of the economy's scissors opened. Peasants preferred to keep grain in the countryside rather than sell to government procurement agencies. They hoarded some of their harvest. They fed themselves and their animals better. They made more vodka for themselves. What they refused to do was to give way to the Bolsheviks, who had made the goods of manufacturing industry so expensive. The members of the Politburo majority gave ground to rural demands and reduced industrial prices. The wheels of exchange between town and village started to move again. Trotski did not fail to criticise his rivals for economic mismanagement; he saw them as having fulfilled his fears about the NEP as a potential instrument for turning away from the objectives of the October Revolution and towards the requirements of the peasantry.

Trotski's fellow leftists in the party made a move against the developing nature of the New Economic Policy in October 1923. Yevgeni Preobrazhenski and others signed the Platform of the Forty-Six, criticising the organisational and economic policies of the ascendant party leadership. They demanded wider freedom of discussion and deeper state intervention in industrial development. In November 1923 Trotski joined the dissenters with a series of articles entitled 'The New Course'. The Thirteenth Party Conference in December had arraigned this Left Opposition for disloyalty. The ascendant leaders needed Stalin more than ever as a counterweight to Trotski; all the criticisms of the summer were mothballed – and Zinoviev no longer talked of the need to restrain Stalin's administrative autonomy. The suppression of factional activity in the provinces, they thought, was best left in his hands. They also entrusted him with putting the case against Trotski at the Conference. For once they did not want this honour. They knew that Stalin could look Trotski in the eye and smack him politically in the face – and perhaps they calculated that Stalin would do himself no favours by appearing divisive while they seemed above the demands of factional struggle.

Stalin was more than willing to oblige with a castigation of Trotski. His words were incisive:[19]

> Trotski's mistake consists in the fact that he has counterposed himself to the Central Committee and put about the idea of himself as a superman standing above the Central Committee, above its laws, above its decisions, so that he gave grounds for a certain part of the party to conduct their work in the direction of undermining confidence in the Central Committee.

The Conference was a triumph for Stalin. Lenin ailed while Trotski wavered and Kamenev and Zinoviev applauded. Stalin had secured his rehabilitation.

And although the Testament had warned against a split between himself and Trotski, Stalin had gone ahead and denounced Trotski. Lenin, if he had recovered, would not have accepted Stalin's excuse that he was only doing what the rest of the Politburo had asked. Yet Stalin had never prostrated himself before Lenin and had reason to feel wronged by him. He had kept a grip on his resentment at his treatment; this was not a comportment he often displayed. Presumably he understood that the chances were that Lenin was too ill to make a physical recovery; and anyway he continued to feel a genuine admiration for the sinking Leader. Stalin limited himself to monitoring what went on at the Gorki mansion, where bodyguards and nurses were reporting to Dzierżyński, who in turn kept him informed.[20] Stalin was not yet out of trouble. Nadezhda Krupskaya could be up to her old tricks by reading out the *Pravda* editorials on the divisive proceedings at the Thirteenth Conference. By this means it would be possible for Lenin to learn that his predicted spat between Stalin and Trotski had already occurred. Yet Stalin was registering an impact. Proud of his performance at the Conference, he was a supreme Leader in the making and was beginning to stand tall.

20. THE OPPORTUNITIES OF STRUGGLE

Lenin died of a heart attack on 21 January 1924. Stalin, who was given the honour of organising the funeral, gained further security in his post. The Politburo had decided on extraordinary treatment of the corpse. It was to be embalmed and put on permanent display in a mausoleum to be erected on Red Square. Krupskaya objected in vain to the quasi-religious implications. Stalin was determined upon the 'mausoleumisation' of the founder of Bolshevism. Several scientists volunteered their services and the race was joined to find a chemical process to do the job. Trotski enquired whether he should come back from Tbilisi, where he had arrived *en route* for Sukhum on the Black Sea to convalesce from a severe bout of influenza. Stalin telegraphed that his return was neither necessary nor possible since the funeral would be held on 26 January. The advice had hostile intent: Stalin knew Trotski would attract all the attention if he appeared in Moscow for the ceremony. Trotski travelled on to Sukhum, where Stalin's supporter Nestor Lakoba welcomed him. Dzierżyński, who had taken Stalin's side in the Georgian Affair, had already sent instructions that nobody should bother Trotski during his stay at the state dacha.[1]

Much has been made of Stalin and Dzierżyński's wish to keep Trotski out of the way. Purportedly Trotski's absence from the funeral ruined his chances of succeeding Lenin as supreme party leader whereas Stalin's leadership of the funeral commission put him at a crucial advantage. This is unconvincing. Although Trotski years later was to complain about Stalin's trickery, he did not claim it had made much difference. Placing his premium on his own convalescence, Trotski stayed in Sukhum for weeks before making the train journey back to Moscow.

In fact the funeral took place on 27 January, and Stalin was a pallbearer with Kamenev, Zinoviev, Bukharin, Molotov, Dzierżyński, Tomski and Rudzutak. He turned out in his quasi-military tunic. Along with others he gave a speech. It included a series of oaths ending with the words:[2]

Leaving us, comrade Lenin left us a legacy of fidelity to the principles of the Communist International. We swear to you, comrade Lenin, that we will not spare our own lives in strengthening and broadening the union of labouring people of the whole world – the Communist International!

He was not alone in using religious imagery[3] and his delivery was still not that of a polished orator. The significance of the speech lay elsewhere. Stalin was at last talking like someone who could speak to the party as a whole. Indeed he spoke as if on the party's behalf. He was emerging on to centre-stage – and he had the nerve to drape himself in a flag of loyalty to the man who had wished to shatter his career. Few had imagined he would act with such aplomb.

The Central Committee put aside its disputes, at least in public. Bolsheviks had often talked about the threat posed by other political parties. This was an exaggerated fear after the Civil War; organised opposition to Bolshevism was at its nadir. Yet GPU head Felix Dzierżyński and Stalin did not drop their guard, believing that Mensheviks, Socialist-Revolutionaries or even 'Black Hundreds' (who had organised anti-semitic pogroms before the Great War) might arrange 'counter-revolutionary' outbreaks against the Bolsheviks.[4] Their attitude mirrored the beleaguered, suspicious outlook of the communist leaders. They had surprised their opponents by seizing power in the October Revolution and were concerned lest something similar might happen to themselves.

Stalin had worked closely with the GPU since returning from the Soviet–Polish War.[5] This reflected the interdependence of party and police as well as his personal preoccupation with considerations of security. The Soviet dictatorship was maintained by repression, and no Bolshevik – not even 'softer' ones like Kamenev and Bukharin – failed to appreciate the regime's dependence on the GPU. As Stalin began to show his confidence, Lenin's widow Krupskaya temporarily changed her behaviour towards the General Secretary. She no longer said what she thought of him. Nor could she prevent historical confections about his career from appearing in print. Her authority in the People's Commissariat for Enlightenment was on the wane.[6] In order to reassert herself she presented herself as the prime annalist of Lenin in his time. She undertook this also as a means of coping with bereavement: she had written a sketch for Lenin's biography within weeks of his death. In May she sent it to Stalin asking what he thought of her project.[7] Stalin, who had his own reasons to build a bridge towards her, wrote back approvingly. Certainly he read the piece carefully since he took the trouble to correct a mistaken date.[8]

Stalin and Krupskaya were setting themselves up as the high priest and priestess of the Lenin cult. Lenin's image was ubiquitous. Petrograd was renamed Leningrad and books and articles on him were produced in vast quantities. Paradoxically this new cult required the censoring of Lenin's works. Comments by Lenin at variance with Stalin's policies were banned. Lenin could not be allowed to appear as having ever made mistakes. An example was the speech to the Ninth Party Conference in which Lenin admitted that the Polish War had been a blunder and declared that 'Russian forces' alone were insufficient for the building of communism in Russia.[9] It was withheld from publication. Stalin also censored his own works so as to enhance his reputation for consistent loyalty. At Lenin's fiftieth-birthday celebration in 1920 Stalin's eulogy had included a reference to past failures of judgement. A decade later when Stalin was approached for permission to reprint the speech, he refused: 'Comrade Adoratski! The speech is accurately transcribed in essence although it does require some editing. But I wouldn't want to publish it: it's not nice to talk about Ilich's mistakes.'[10] Christianity had to give way to communism and Lenin was to be presented to society as the new Jesus Christ. He also had to be displayed as quintessentially Russian if communism's appeal was to spread among the largest national group. Stalin forbade mention of Lenin's mixed ethnic ancestry – the fact that Lenin's great-grandfather had been Jewish was kept secret.[11]

Meanwhile Stalin was eager to put himself forward as a theorist. He had had no time to write a lengthy piece since before 1917; and no Bolshevik leader was taken seriously at the apex of the party unless he made a contribution on doctrinal questions. Despite the many other demands on his time and intellect, he composed and – in April 1924 – delivered a course of nine lectures for trainee party activists at the Sverdlov University under the title *Foundations of Leninism.*

Quickly brought out as a booklet, it was a work of able compression. Stalin avoided the showiness of similar attempts by Zinoviev, Trotski, Kamenev and Bukharin, who in private liked to disparage him. The rumour was also put about that, in so far as Stalin's words had merit, he had plagiarised the contents of a booklet by a certain F. Xenofontov. In fact Stalin was a fluent and thoughtful writer even though he was no stylist. His exegesis of Lenin's doctrines was concise and to the point and his lectures were organised in a logical sequence. He was doing what

Lenin had not undertaken on his own behalf, and by and large he succeeded in codifying the ragbag of writings, speeches and policies of Lenin's lifelong *oeuvre*. He denied that Bolshevik ideas were applicable exclusively to 'Russian reality'. For Stalin, Lenin had developed a doctrine of universal significance: 'Leninism,' he proclaimed,[12]

> is the Marxism of the epoch of imperialism and proletarian revolution. More precisely, Leninism is the theory and tactics of proletarian revolution in general and the theory and tactics of the dictatorship of the proletariat in particular.

Stalin contended that Lenin was the sole great heir to the traditions of Marx and Engels.

He laid out Lenin's 'teaching' with catechistic neatness. It was this quality which provoked his rivals' condescension; but it elicited approval from the young Marxists listening to the lectures. Not that the booklet was unambiguous in content. Stalin's summary of Leninist theory indeed displayed a veritable precision of vagueness. He emphasised certain topics. Quoting from Lenin, he argued for the 'peasant question' to be solved by a steady movement towards large-scale farming co-operatives.[13] He urged the party to ignore the sceptics who denied that this transition would end with the attainment of socialism. He also looked at the national question, maintaining that only the establishment of a socialist dictatorship could eliminate the oppression of nations. Capitalism allegedly disseminated national and ethnic hatreds as a means of dividing and ruling the planet.

Stalin had little to say about topics of conventional significance for Marxists. He seldom referred to the 'worker question'. He offered just a few brief comments on worldwide socialism. But he had started again, for the first time since before the Great War, to make his mark as a contributor to Marxist theoretical discussions. He was making progress in his career. Yet there was a fly in the ointment. Lenin had laid down that his Testament should be communicated to the next Party Congress in the event of his death. Krupskaya, despite her reconciliation with Stalin, felt a higher duty to her husband's memory and raised the question with the central party leadership.[14] The Thirteenth Party Congress was scheduled for May 1924. Stalin had reason to be concerned. Even if Krupskaya had not made a move, the danger existed that Trotski would see tactical advantage in doing it for her. Stalin could not automatically rely on support from Kamenev and Zinoviev: the

Kislovodsk saga had showed as much. All his gains over the past few months would be lost if an open debate were to be held at the Congress and a resolution was passed to comply with Lenin's advice to appoint a new general secretary.

Stalin was lucky since the Party Central Committee, with the encouragement of Kamenev and Zinoviev, ruled that the Testament should be read out only to the heads of the provincial delegations. If Kamenev and Zinoviev had not still been worried about Trotski, they might have done for Stalin. But instead they spoke up for him. Stalin sat pale as chalk as the Testament was revealed to the restricted audience. But the sting was extracted from Stalin's political flesh. Trotski, scared of appearing divisive so soon after the death of Lenin, declined to take the fight to the 'troika' of Stalin, Zinoviev and Kamenev. Zinoviev's *amour propre* was coddled by the decision that he should deliver the Central Committee political report which had regularly been given by Lenin until his final illness. Thus was lost the best opportunity to terminate Stalin's further rise to power. Perhaps Stalin would have defended himself effectively. Zinoviev and Kamenev were not very popular and Stalin's behaviour was not widely in disrepute in the party at this stage. Yet Stalin liked to fight from a position of strength and he was at his weakest in those few days at the Congress. The notion that he owed his survival to his antics as a trapeze artist is wrong. What saved him was the safety net provided by provisional allies Zinoviev and Kamenev and Trotski's failure to attack.

His own moments of prominence were few. He gave the organisational report with the usual dour assemblage of structural and numerical details; but he made no interventions in the rest of the open proceedings. The most perilous time occurred when he reported on the national question at lengthy closed sessions. Now that leading delegates knew about Lenin's deathbed criticisms this was a sensitive topic. His Georgian communist enemies were lining up to take pot-shots at him. Yet Stalin did not flinch. Rather than apologise, he gave a spirited apologia of official policy.

The sense of hurt diminished but did not disappear. The internal strains of the troika irked him: he knew that Zinoviev and Kamenev looked down on him and that, given a chance, they would ditch him. His health, too, was poor. Feeling humiliated, Stalin followed his usual course: he requested release from his duties. In a letter to the Central Committee on 19 August 1924 he pleaded that 'honourable and sincere' work with Zinoviev and Kamenev was no longer possible. What he needed, he claimed, was a period of convalescence. But he also asked the Central Committee to remove his name from the Politburo, Orgburo and Secretariat:[15]

> When the time [of convalescence] is at an end, I ask to be assigned either to Turukhansk District or to Yakutsk Province or somewhere abroad in some unobtrusive posting.
>
> All these questions I'd ask the Plenum to decide in my absence and without explanations on my part since I consider it harmful to the cause to give explanations apart from those comments which have already been given in the first section of this letter.

He would be going back to Turukhansk as an ordinary provincial militant and not as the Central Committee leader he had been in 1913. Stalin was requesting a more severe demotion than even the Testament had specified.

He was psychologically complex. That he contemplated going back to northern Siberia may be doubted. But he was impulsive. When his pride was offended, he lost his composure. Even by offering his resignation, he was taking a huge risk. He was gambling on his exhibition of humility inducing the Central Committee, which included some of his friends, to refuse his request. He needed to put his enemies in the wrong. The ploy worked perfectly.

The Central Committee retained him as General Secretary and the final settling of accounts among Stalin, Kamenev and Zinoviev was yet again postponed. Coming back from vacation in the autumn, he had recovered his self-possession. In advance of Politburo meetings he consulted Kamenev and Zinoviev. If Zinoviev was in Moscow, the three of them met privately and then, in conspiratorial fashion, arrived at the Politburo separately. Stalin brazened it out, shaking hands with his arch-enemy Trotski as they greeted each other. He also restrained any display of personal ambition. Kamenev, not Stalin, chaired the Politburo after Lenin's death.[16] Yet already Stalin was taking care of his future. When his rivals fail to join him in the Orgburo, he was free to replace them with appointees more to his liking. The Stalin group formed itself under his leadership; it was like the street gang which he had been thwarted from leading as a boy in Gori.[17] None was more important than Vyacheslav Molotov and Lazar Kaganovich. Both were Secretaries of the Central Committee; they also intermittently headed one or another of its departments and helped Stalin in the Orgburo. And when Ukrainian communist politics became troublesome for the Kremlin in April 1925,

Kaganovich was dispatched to Kiev to become First Secretary of the Communist Party of Ukraine.

Stalin also built up a retinue of supporters in the Central Committee. Among them were Sergo Ordzhonikidze, Kliment Voroshilov, Semën Budënny, Sergei Kirov and Andrei Andreev. All these men were loyal to him without being servile and called him Koba.[18] Some had had disputes with him in the past. Molotov had fallen out with him in March 1917. Kaganovich had criticised the Central Committee's organisational policy in 1918–19 and Ordzhonikidze could never button his lip when he had something on his mind.[19] Andreev had even been a Workers' Oppositionist. Budënny and Voroshilov had served under him in Tsaritsyn; Ordzhonikidze and Kirov had been his subordinates in the Caucasus. Andreev had impressed him with administrative work in the early 1920s. The gang took time to coalesce, and Stalin never allowed its members to take their positions for granted. Even the Tsaritsynites needed to keep proving their worth in his eyes. Sergei Minin and Moisei Rukhimovich, cronies on the Southern Front, came to seem as useless as hardened paint. Minin sided with the opposition to the ascendant party leadership and Stalin had nothing more to do with him. Minin committed suicide in 1926. When Rukhimovich's incompetence at organising transport was exposed, Stalin sacked him as 'a self-satisfied bureaucrat'.[20]

He demanded efficiency as well as loyalty from the gang members. He also selected them for their individual qualities. He wanted no one near to him who outranked him intellectually. He selected men with a revolutionary commitment like his own, and he set the style with his ruthless policies. None earned disapprobation for mercilessness towards enemies. He created an ambience of conspiracy, companionship and crude masculine humour. In return for their services he looked after their interests. He was solicitous about their health. He overlooked their foibles so long as their work remained unaffected and they recognised his word as law.

This is what Amakyan Nazaretyan wrote about working 'under Koba's firm hand':[21]

> I can't take offence. There's much to be learned from him. Having got to know him at close hand, I have developed an extraordinary respect towards him. He has a character that one can only envy. I can't take offence. His strictness is covered by attentiveness to those who work with him.

On another occasion he added:[22]

He's very cunning. He's hard as a nut and can't be broken at one go. But I have a completely different view of him now from the one I had in Tiflis. Despite his rational wildness, so to speak, he's a soft individual; he has a heart and knows how to value the merits of people.

Lazar Kaganovich shared this endorsement:[23]

In the early years Stalin was a soft individual . . . Under Lenin and after Lenin. He went through a lot.

In the early years after Lenin died, when he came to power, they all attacked Stalin. He endured a lot in the struggle with Trotski. Then his supposed friends Bukharin, Rykov and Tomski also attacked him . . .

It was difficult to avoid getting cruel.

For Kaganovich, Stalin's personality responded to circumstances not of his making.

He discouraged attention to his national origin. In the provinces his supporters played up the fact that his main opponents – at first Trotski and then Kamenev and Zinoviev – were Jews. He himself never mentioned this, but he did not stop others from bringing it up.[24] He had his own reasons for caution. Not only Jews but also Poles, Georgians and Armenians had a presence in the Bolshevik party central and local leadership out of proportion to the USSR's demography, and there was growing resentment of the fact in the country. Stalin, moreover, still spoke with a heavy accent. Trotski put this with typical cattiness: 'The Russian language always stayed for him not only a language half-foreign and improvised but – much worse for his awareness – conventional and strained.'[25] Snubs about his linguistic facility were not uncommon in the 1920s.[26]

Yet no one else in the ascendant central leadership set himself up quite so effectively. Bukharin had a following in the party but no consolidated network of clients. Zinoviev had such a network but most of his clients were based in Leningrad. Kamenev had never been much of a patron. The sole leader to match Stalin's ability in forming a cliental group was Trotski. He still appealed to members of the Inter-District group which had joined the Bolsheviks in May 1917, and he had attracted admirers in the Civil War as People's Commissar for Military Affairs. The Left Opposition, when attacking the Politburo in the last quarter of 1923, looked to him for inspiration. Among them were Yevgeni Preobrazhenski, Leonid Serebryakov, Nikolai Krestinski, Adolf Ioffe and Christian Rakovski. Yet Trotski lacked Stalin's day-to-day accessibility. He had the kind of hauteur which peeved dozens of potential supporters. He was also devoid of Stalin's tactical cunning and pugnacity, and there was a suspicion among Trotski's followers that their idol's illnesses at crucial conjunctures of factional struggle had a psychosomatic dimension. Yet he had a large enough following to take on and beat Stalin if the situation had been different. The trouble was that Trotski had lost the early rounds of the contest. He was always coming from behind on points.

Stalin continued to box warily. The defeat of the Left Opposition in the winter of 1923–4 had been achieved in open combat. Trotski and the Left Opposition had attacked and Stalin, Zinoviev, Kamenev and Bukharin had retaliated. Stalin had had little need to sack Trotskyists and replace them with individuals loyal to the ascendant party leadership.[27] Yet the Orgburo and the Secretariat – as well as the Politburo in the highest instance – used their right to change postings in the following months. The ascendant party leadership manipulated the various administrative levers to its advantage. Steadily the Left lost its remaining key jobs in party, government, army and police. The sackings were accompanied by demotions which frequently involved relocation to distant parts of the USSR. This was really a light form of exile whereby the ascendant leadership consolidated its grip on power. The Left was also doctrinally undermined. The Agitprop Department of the Secretariat publicised past disputes between Lenin and Trotski. Its various adjuncts printed dozens of anti-Trotski pamphlets; and Stalin as an avid reader scribbled an *aide-mémoire* on the cover of a work on the October Revolution: 'Tell Molotov that Tr[otski] lied about Lenin on the subject of ways to make an insurrection.'[28]

He was highly conspiratorial. According to Politburo secretary Boris Bazhanov, Stalin's desk had four telephones but inside the desk was a further apparatus giving him the facility to eavesdrop on the conversations of dozens of the most influential communist leaders. He could do this without going through the Kremlin switchboard, and the information he gathered must have alerted him to any manoeuvres being undertaken against him.[29] Personal assistants such as Lev Mekhlis and Grigori Kanner carried out whatever shady enterprise he thought up.[30] He was ruthless against his enemies. When Kamenev asked him about the question of gaining a majority in the party, Stalin scoffed: 'Do you know what I think about this? I believe that who votes how in the party is unimportant. What is extremely important is who counts the votes and how they are recorded.'[31] He was implying that he expected the central party apparatus to fiddle the voting figures if ever they went against him.

This sort of remark gave Stalin the reputation of an unprincipled bureaucrat. He revelled in his deviousness when talking to his associates. But there was much more to him. He had the potential of a true leader. He was decisive, competent, confident and ambitious. The choice of him rather than Zinoviev or Kamenev to head the charge against Trotski at the Thirteenth Party Conference showed that this was beginning to be understood by other Central Committee members. He was coming out of the shadows. From the last months of 1924 he showed a willingness to go on attacking Trotski without keeping Zinoviev and Kamenev at his side. Kamenev had made a slip by referring to 'nepman Russia' instead of 'NEP Russia'. The so-called nepman was typically a private trader who took advantage of the economic reforms since 1921 and who was resented by Bolsheviks. Stalin made a meal of Kamenev's slip in the party press. Around the same time Zinoviev had described the Soviet regime as 'a dictatorship of the party'. Stalin as Party General Secretary vigorously repudiated the term as a description of political reality.[32] Kamenev and Zinoviev were put on notice that they should look out for themselves. In autumn 1924 Stalin moved against their leading supporters. I. A. Zelenski was replaced as Moscow City Party Secretary by Stalin's supporter Nikolai Uglanov.[33]

Strategic factors were coming between Stalin on one side and Zinoviev and Kamenev on the other. Stalin wanted to defend the case for the possibilities of 'building socialism' in the USSR even during the NEP. This countered Trotski's argument, fleshed out in *The Lessons of October* in 1924, that the October Revolution would expire unless sustained by co-operation with socialist regimes in Europe. Trotski was extending his pre-revolutionary ideas about the need for 'permanent revolution'. To Stalin his booklet seemed both anti-Leninist in doctrine and pernicious in practice to the stability of the NEP. Bukharin, an arch-leftist in the Bolshevik leadership in the Civil War, agreed with Stalin and was rewarded with promotion to full membership of the Politburo after the Thirteenth Party Congress. He and Stalin began to act together against Zinoviev and Kamenev. Bukharin, as he pondered party policy after Lenin, believed that the NEP offered a framework for the country's more peaceful and evolutionary 'transition to socialism'. He disregarded traditional party hostility to kulaks and called on them to 'enrich themselves'. He sought a moderation of repressive methods in the state's handling of society and wished to put the emphasis on indoctrinating the urban working class. He saw peasant co-operatives as a basis for 'socialist construction'.

Stalin and Bukharin rejected Trotski and the Left Opposition as doctrinaires who by their actions would bring the USSR to perdition. The leftist push for a more active foreign policy might provoke a retaliatory invasion by the Western powers. Trade would be ruined along with Soviet capital investment plans. The Trotskyist demand for an increased rate of industrial growth, moreover, could be realised only through the heavier taxation of the better-off stratum of the peasantry. The sole result would be the rupture of the linkage between peasants and working class recommended by Lenin. The recrudescence of social and economic tensions could lead to the fall of the USSR.

Zinoviev and Kamenev felt uncomfortable with so drastic a turn towards the market economy. They still feared Trotski. They also wanted to maintain the peasant–worker linkage. But they were unwilling to give their imprimatur to Bukharin's evolutionary programme; they disliked Stalin's movement to a doctrine that socialism could be built in a single country – and they simmered with resentment at the unceasing accumulation of power by Stalin. Zinoviev and Kamenev were vulnerable to the charge of having betrayed the Bolshevik Central Committee in October 1917. They had to prove their radicalism. It was only a matter of time before they challenged their anti-Trotski allies Stalin and Bukharin. Stalin was ready and waiting for them. To most observers he seemed calmer than during those earlier disputes when he had flown off the handle in internal party disputes. But this was not the case. Stalin was just as angry and ferocious as ever. What had changed was that he was no longer the outsider and the victim. Stalin dominated the Orgburo and the Secretariat. With Bukharin he led the Politburo. He could afford to maintain an outward tranquillity and catch his enemies unawares.

He continued to act in such a fashion. He had survived Lenin's criticism by the skin of his teeth. He had to show others that he was not as black as he had been painted. His gang in the central party leadership would help him. But he had to watch out for others. Dzierżyński did not owe him any favours. Krupskaya, after her early overtures to Stalin, kept her own counsel. Bukharin himself was not dependable; he went on talking amicably to Trotski, Zinoviev and Kamenev even while castigating their policies. Bolshevik politics were in dangerous flux.

21. JOSEPH AND NADYA

The struggles among the communist party factions were also a contest for individual supremacy. Trotski, Zinoviev, Bukharin and Stalin each felt worthy to succeed Lenin, and even Kamenev had ambition. Stalin was tired of seeing his rivals strutting on the public stage. He accepted that they were good orators and that he would never match them in this. Yet he was proud – in his brittle, over-sensitive way – that his contribution to Bolshevism was mainly practical in nature: he thought *praktiki* like himself were the party's backbone. The *praktiki* looked up to Lenin as the eagle who scattered his opponents like mere chickens. Stalin seemed unimpressive to those who did not know him and indeed to many who did; but he was already determined to fly into history as the party's second eagle.[1] He did not just scatter his rivals for the succession: whenever possible, he swooped down and tore them to bits. Chatting to Kamenev and Dzierżyński in 1923, he had explained his general attitude: 'The greatest delight is to pick out one's enemy, prepare all the details of the blow, to slake one's thirst for a cruel revenge and then go home to bed!'[2]

Such was the man who had taken Nadya Allilueva as his wife after the October Revolution. There had been no wedding ceremony, but their daughter Svetlana was told that her parents lived as spouses from some unspecified time before the Soviet government's transfer from Petrograd to Moscow in 1918. (Apparently the official registration did not take place until 24 March 1919.)[3] Nadya was less than half his age at the time and he was her revolutionary hero; and she had yet to learn that the harsh features of his character were not reserved exclusively for the enemies of communism.

At first things went well. Alexandra Kollontai, who got to know Nadya in the winter of 1919–20, was impressed by her 'charming beauty of soul' as well as by Stalin's demeanour: 'He takes a great deal of notice of her.'[4] But trouble was already in the air. Joseph wanted a wife who took household management as her priority; this was one of Nadya's accomplishments which had caught his eye in 1917.[5] Nadya, however, wanted a professional career. As the daughter of a Bolshevik veteran, she had carried out important technical tasks on the party's behalf in the Civil War. Although she had no professional qualifications, she had a grammar school education and proved a competent clerk at a time when politically reliable secretaries were few.[6] She soon learned how to decode telegrams transmitting confidential information among Soviet leaders, including her husband.[7] Lenin employed her on his personal staff.[8] Joseph was more often absent on campaign than at home until autumn 1920, leaving Nadya to devote herself to her Sovnarkom duties. She became so close to the Lenins that if Nadezhda Krupskaya was going away on a trip, she would ask her to feed their cat. (Lenin could not be depended upon.)[9] Nadya joined the party, assuming that her involvement in Bolshevik administration at the highest level would continue.

Her hope was dashed when Joseph returned from the Soviet–Polish War and family chores increased. Joseph wanted a settled domesticity at the end of his working day, whenever that might be. Matters came to a head late in the winter of 1920–1. Nadya, pregnant since June 1920, had gone on working while carrying the child. Joseph himself had fallen badly ill. In the Civil War he had frequently complained of his aches and pains as well as his 'exhaustion'.[10] No one had taken him seriously because he had usually done this when trying to resign in high dudgeon. Brother-in-law Fëdor Alliluev, seeing him before the Tenth Party Congress, remarked how tired he looked. Stalin agreed: 'Yes, I'm tired. I need to go off to the woods, to the woods! To relax and have a proper rest and sleep as one ought!'[11] He took a few days off. It was only when he retired to his bed after the Congress that medical attention became an obvious necessity. Professor Vladimir Rozanov, one of the Kremlin doctors, diagnosed chronic appendicitis. Rozanov said the problem might have existed for a dozen years; he could barely believe Stalin had been able to stand upright. Instant surgery was vital.

Operations for appendicitis in that period were often fatal. Rozanov worried that the procedure could infect Stalin's peritoneum; he also thought him dangerously thin.[12] Initially a local anaesthetic was administered because of his weakened condition. Yet the pain became unbearable and the operation was not completed until after a dose of chloroform. Allowed home afterwards, Stalin lay on a divan reading books and convalesced over the next two months. As he got better, he went out in search of company. By June he had been passed fit. Coming upon Mikhail Kalinin in discussion with other Bolsheviks about the NEP, he announced his return to work: 'It's oppressive to lie around by yourself and so I've got up: it's boring without one's comrades.'[13] This sentiment might easily have been included in any collection of memoirs about Stalin; but the rest of Fëdor Alliluev's story was too embarrassing for Stalin to allow publication. He would not permit people to discover that he had ever been anything but tough in mind and body.

Joseph's illness and recuperation coincided with the arrival of their first child. Vasili Stalin was born in Moscow on 21 March 1921. Delight at his safe delivery was tempered for Nadya by the fact that Joseph increased pressure on her to dedicate herself to domesticity. No one on her side of the family helped her out: all of them, including her mother Olga, were immersed in political activity. Olga was anyway hardly a model for child rearers. When Nadya and the other Alliluev children had been young, they had often had to fend for themselves while their parents went about their professional lives and revolutionary activity.

Nadya could not turn for help to the other side of the family: Joseph's mother Keke adamantly refused to move to Moscow. In June 1921, after recovering from the appendicitis operation, Stalin had headed south on party business to Georgia and visited Keke. The son greeted his mother without the warmth that might have been expected after their long separation.[14] She knew her own mind and did not flinch from enquiring: 'Son, there's none of the tsar's blood on your hands, is there?' Shuffling on his feet, he made the sign of the cross and swore that he had had no part in it. His friend Sergo Ordzhonikidze expressed surprise at this religious recidivism; but Stalin exclaimed: 'She's a believer! I wish to God that our people believed in Marxism as they do in God!'[15] They had been apart from each other for many years; and even though he had wriggled out of answering her straightforwardly, her question to him showed she knew a gulf of belief would continue to keep them apart. As a Christian Keke had reason to tell her son that the Red Kremlin was no place for her. For her safety and comfort, Stalin moved her into one of the servants' apartment in the old Viceroy's palace in Tbilisi. Budu Mdivani commented that the local authorities increased the guard on her: 'This is so that she doesn't give birth to another Stalin!'[16]

But Joseph did not come back unaccompanied. In Georgia he also sought out his son Yakov by his first wife Ketevan. Yakov had been looked after by Ketevan's brother Alexander Svanidze and his wife Maria. Joseph hardly knew the thirteen-year-old Yakov but wished to take him at last into his care – or at least into Nadya's. Nor was this the end of the family's expansion. The leading Bolshevik F. A. Sergeev, alias Artëm, perished in a plane crash in July 1921 leaving a young son. It was the custom in the party for such orphans to be fostered by other Bolsheviks, and this is what the Stalins did. The lad Artëm Sergeev lived with them until manhood (and became a major-general in the Red Army in the Second World War).[17] Stalin also interested himself in the upbringing of Nikolai Patolichev, the son of a comrade who reportedly had died in his arms in the Soviet–Polish War of 1920.[18] Young Patolichev was not brought into the family. Nevertheless in the space of a few months the Stalin household had grown in number from two to five.

Nadya brought in domestic assistance while her busy husband focused his energies on politics. She hired a nanny for Vasili; she also employed servants. She herself was like a terrier in getting raw materials for the kitchen. The Kremlin administrative regime, run by Stalin's old friend Abel Enukidze, assigned a quota of food products for each resident family. Joseph, whose health had troubled him throughout the Civil War, had been recommended a diet with plenty of poultry. As a result he had acquired the monthly right to fifteen chickens, a head of cheese and fifteen pounds of potatoes. By mid-March 1921, days before the new baby was due, the family had already eaten its way through ten of its fifteen chickens. (Either the birds were unusually small and thin or the Stalins had the appetite of horses.) Nadya wrote a request for an increased quota.[19] (Even before she married Joseph she had known how to handle the Soviet bureaucracy: in November 1918, after the Alliluevs moved to Moscow, she wrote to Yakov Sverdlov asking for a better room for them.)[20] In later years she made further pleas. One of them was a request for a new kindergarten; she was turned down on that occasion.[21]

Nadya's wish to work outside the home was conventional among young Bolshevik women, who combined a dedication to the revolutionary cause and to women's emancipation. She did not object to supervising household management so long as she had servants and could continue to be employed in Lenin's office. The double role was very heavy and the lack of support from Joseph made it scarcely bearable. He was frequently late in getting back to the Kremlin flat. He was uncouth in manners and had an obscene tongue when irritated. Nor was his language confined to phrases like 'Go to the Devil!' Hating to be contradicted, he used the foulest swear-words on his wife. His rough manner was extreme, and it cannot be discounted that he was compensating to some degree for personal insecurities. After hurting his arm as a boy, he had been unable to join in the normal rough-and-tumbles of childhood. He had been rejected on physical grounds by the Imperial

Army in the Great War. Stalin wanted to be thought a man's man. In fact, according to his grand-nephew Vladimir Alliluev, he had carefully manicured nails and 'almost a woman's fingers'.[22] Did he have some residual doubts about his manliness by contemporary criteria? If he did, it was Nadya who paid the price.

Like most of his male contemporaries, Stalin expected a wife to obey. Here he was disappointed, for Nadya refused to be meek. Disputes between them were frequent more or less from the start of their sustained cohabitation. She too had her moods. Indeed it is now clear that she had mental problems. Perhaps they were hereditary. Schizophrenia of some kind seems to have affected previous generations of her mother's side of the family; and her brother Fëdor, after an acutely traumatic event after the Civil War when the former bank robber Kamo stage-managed a scene in which he threatened to shoot him, had a breakdown from which he never recovered.[23] Nadya had a volatile temperament and, although she remained in love with Joseph, the marriage continued to be rancorous between the patches of tranquillity.

Someone in the central party apparatus decided that Nadya was unsuitable for party membership. The rumour was that it was none other than Joseph. In December 1921 she was excluded from the party: this was a disgrace for anyone working as she did in the offices of Sovnarkom. Eventually she could have lost her job. The charge was that she had not passed the various tests applied to all party members and had not bothered to prepare herself for them. Nor had she helped with mundane party work; this was all the less acceptable inasmuch as she was 'a person of the intelligentsia'. Only one Central Control Commission member spoke up for her even though Lenin himself had written warmly in her support.[24] Nadya begged for another chance and promised to make a greater effort in the way that was demanded. Initially the decision was made to 'exclude her as ballast, completely uninterested in party work'; but finally the Central Control Commission allowed her to keep the secondary status of a 'candidate' party member.[25] She could have done without this contretemps in a year full of problems; but at least the eventual decision enabled her to go on working for Lenin's office without a blemish on her record.

It cannot be proved that Joseph had been behind the move to take away her party card; and Nadya never expressly blamed him. But he belonged to the Politburo and the Orgburo and was already intervening in the Secretariat's work in 1921:[26] he could have put in a good word for her if he had wanted. But she had survived. Stalin accepted the situation and avoided interfering with her professional aspirations again. She functioned as one of Lenin's secretaries even while Lenin and Stalin were falling out. Krupskaya even asked her to liaise with Kamenev on Lenin's behalf about the Georgian Affair.[27] It would be strange if Nadya kept this a secret from her husband. Perhaps he at last began to see the advantages of having a working wife.

At home Nadya was a severe mother and denied to the children the open affection she directed at Joseph. Strict standards of behaviour were enforced. Yakov, who hardly knew his father before moving to Moscow, reacted badly to this. Joseph's work kept him away from the apartment and the bond between them never solidified. Such interest as he took in his son tended to involve pressure. He pushed books at him and expected him to read them. 'Yasha!' he wrote on the cover of B. Andreev's *The Conquest of Nature*, 'Read this book without fail!'[28] But it was Nadya who had to handle Yakov on a daily basis and, as her letter to Joseph's mother in October 1922 indicated, she found him exasperating:[29]

> I send you a big kiss and pass on greetings from Soso: he's very healthy, feels very well, works hard, and remembers about you.
>
> Yasha [i.e. Yakov] studies, plays up, smokes and doesn't listen to me. Vasenka [i.e. Vasili] also plays up, insults his mama and also won't listen to me. He hasn't yet started smoking. Joseph will definitely teach him to since he always give him a puff on his *papiroska*.

A *papiroska* is a cigarette with an empty tube at the end which acts like a cigarette-holder to allow smoking while wearing gloves in sub-zero temperatures. It was in character for Joseph to expect Nadya to enforce discipline while he himself disrupted it.

Life nevertheless had its pleasant side. The Stalins lived in two places after the Soviet–Polish War: their Kremlin flat and the dacha they called Zubalovo near the old sawmill at Usovo outside Moscow. By a bizarre coincidence, the dacha's owner had belonged to the Zubalishvili business family which had built the hostel that became the Tiflis Spiritual Seminary. Probably it tickled the fancy of Stalin and his neighbour Mikoyan that they were living in homes put up by an industrialist from the south Caucasus against whom they had once helped to lead strikes.[30]

Several dachas were made state property in the same district in 1919 and the Stalins occupied Zubalovo-4. Stalin, who had never had a house of his own,[31] cleared the trees and bushes to turn his patch into a spot to his liking. Near by was the River Moskva, where the children could swim in the summer. It was a beautiful spot which might have appeared in the plays of Anton Chekhov; but whereas Chekhov described how the old rural gentry were supplanted by the *nouveaux riches*, this was a case of the *nouveaux riches* being expelled by revolutionaries. While gloating over the Zubalishvilis' forced departure, Stalin had no inhibition about creating a style of life that was similarly bourgeois. When they could, the entire Stalin family went out to Zubalovo. They gathered honey. They searched for mushrooms and wild strawberries. Joseph took pot-shots at pheasants and rabbits and the family ate what he killed. The Stalins kept open house and visitors stayed as long as they wanted. Budënny and Voroshilov often popped over to drink and sing with Joseph. Ordzhonikidze and Bukharin were others who spent time there. Gentle-mannered Bukharin was a particular favourite with Nadya and the children: he even brought a tame grey fox with him and did a painting of the trees by the dacha.[32]

In the summers they holidayed in the south of the USSR, usually in one of the many state dachas by the Black Sea. Stalin had material couriered to him whenever he needed to be consulted. But he knew how to enjoy himself. There were always plenty of Caucasian dishes and wines on his table and the visitors were many. Georgian and Abkhazian politicians queued to ingratiate themselves. His Moscow cronies, if they were staying in nearby dachas, called on the family; and picnics were arranged in the hills or by the seaside. Although Stalin could not swim, he loved the fresh air and the beach as well.

He also used the vacations as a time to allow his body to recuperate. Joseph's health had always troubled him and since 1917 he had resorted to various traditional cures. The rheumatism in his arm and his bothersome cough – probably caused by his pipe-smoking – figured often in his letters.[33] Once he had stopped at Nalchik high up in the north Caucasus. It was a place visited by tuberculosis patients.[34] But Stalin's specific complaints were different; and for his rheumatism, which affected his arm every spring, he was advised by Mikoyan to try the hot baths at Matsesta near Sochi on the Black Sea coast.[35] Stalin tried this and found the waters at Matsesta to work 'a lot better than the Essentuki muds'.[36] Essentuki was one of the spa towns of the north Caucasus famous for the medical benefits of its soil. Stalin mostly, in any case, preferred to go to Sochi for his summer vacations.[37] From 1926 he put himself in the hands of Dr Ivan Valedinski, a great believer in 'balneology'. When Stalin made his way south in the summer, he pocketed instructions from Valedinski: he was told to take a dozen baths at Matsesta before returning home. Stalin asked for permission to enliven his stay with a glass or two of brandy at weekends. Valedinski was stern: Stalin could take a glass on Saturdays but definitely not on Sundays.[38]

Perhaps the doctor forgot that Sundays were not sacred for an atheist. In any case Stalin was never a trusting patient; he had his own pack of medicines and used them as he saw fit regardless of advice from doctors.[39] It is doubtful that he went along with everything that Valedinski specified. But undoubtedly he felt better than earlier. The hot baths eased the pain in his joints and the aspirin prescribed by Valedinski reduced the pain in his neck. A heart check-up in 1927 confirmed him as generally robust.[40]

More worrisome to Stalin than his recurrent ill health were his growing difficulties with Nadya. Periods of calm and tenderness were interrupted by explosions of mutual irritation. Nadya and the children spent time with him in the south; and she and Joseph wrote to each other if for some reason she could not stay there.[41] Her absence became normal once she started a student's course at the Industrial Academy: the beginning of term coincided with her husband's annual holiday leave. Their letters to each other were tender. He called her Tatka and she called him Joseph. She was solicitous about him: 'I very much beg you to look after yourself. I kiss you deeply, deeply, as you kissed me when we said goodbye.'[42] She also wrote to his mother on Joseph's behalf, giving news of the children and passing on little details about life in Moscow. Stalin himself wrote to Georgia only infrequently. He was too preoccupied with political business, and anyway he had hardly bothered about his blood relatives for many years. Usually his letters to his mother were brief to the point of curtness and ended with a phrase such as 'Live a thousand years!'[43] Nadya was doing her best for him, but she could never get the appreciation and understanding from her husband that she craved.

His harshness would have demoralised the most optimistic spirit. Nadya's mental condition worsened and she was given to episodes of despair. Stalin's flirtations with other women probably played a part in this. On the secretarial staff of the Politburo was a beautiful young woman, Tamara Khazanova, who befriended Nadya; she came round to the Kremlin flat and helped with the children. At some point it would seem that Stalin took a fancy to her and pursued his interest.[44]

Nadya descended into gloom. She expressed her thoughts in a letter to her friend Maria Svanidze, the sister of Joseph's first wife:[45]

> You write that you're bored. You know, dearest, that it's the same everywhere. I have absolutely nothing to do with anyone in Moscow. Sometimes it seems strange after so many years to have no close friends, but this obviously depends on one's character. Moreover, it's strange that I feel myself closer to non-members of the party (women, of course). The obvious explanation is that such people are simpler.
>
> I greatly regret tying myself down again in new family matters. In our day this isn't very easy because generally a lot of the new prejudices are strange and if you don't work, then you're looked upon as an 'old woman'.

'New family matters' was Nadya's odd way of referring to her latest pregnancy. Because of this she had to delay getting the requisite qualifications for professional employment. Enrolment on some training course remained her ambition. She told Maria to take the same attitude or else spend her time running errands for others.[46]

The child she was expecting was born on 28 February 1926; it was a girl, and they named her Svetlana. Nadya, however, remained determined to free herself of domesticity and in autumn 1929 she got herself enrolled at the Industrial Academy in central Moscow on a course specialising in artificial fibres. The Stalin household was left to servants and nannies.

Each morning she left the Kremlin and made for the Industrial Academy. She left behind all privilege. She was also leaving a middle-aged environment and joining people of her own age. Most of the students were unaware that Nadya Allilueva was the wife of the Party General Secretary – and even if they knew this, they did not act much differently towards her. Off set Nadya without chauffeur or bodyguard, taking the same forms of transport as her fellow students. She wrote to Joseph about a very tedious journey on 12 September 1929:[47]

> Today I can say that things are better since I had an exam in written maths which went well but in general everything is not so successful. To be precise, I had to be at the I[ndustrial] A[cademy] by nine o'clock and of course I left home at 8.30, and what happens but the tram has broken down. I started to wait for a bus, but there wasn't one and so I decided to take a taxi so as not to be late. I got into it and, blow me, we'd only gone 100 yards and the taxi came to a halt; something in it as well had gone bust.

While claiming to find this catalogue of service breakdowns funny she pleaded a bit too hard for this to convince. Nadya had high standards in everything and was annoyed by the deterioration in conditions. She was making sure that Joseph learned something about the kind of life facing ordinary metropolitan inhabitants: the noise, mess and disorder.[48]

Even Joseph sometimes encountered such unpleasantness for himself. On one occasion in the late 1920s he and Molotov were walking outside the Kremlin on some business or other. Molotov never forgot what ensued:[49]

> I remember a heavy storm; the snow was piling up and Stalin and I were walking across the Manège. We had no bodyguard. Stalin was wearing a fur coat, long boots and a hat with ear-flaps. No one knew who he was. Suddenly a beggar stuck to us: 'Give us some money, good sirs!' Stalin reached into his pocket, pulled out a ten-ruble note and handed it to him, and we walked on. The beggar, though, yelled after us: 'Ah, you damned bourgeois!' This made Stalin laugh: 'Just try and understand our people. If you give them a little, it's bad; if you give them a lot, it's also bad!'

But generally he was insulated from experiences of this kind.

What worried Nadya, though, was that he had cut himself off from a sustained family commitment. He was bad-tempered and domineering at home. She suspected him of having flings with attractive women who came his way. And he otherwise seldom thought of anything but politics. He felt fulfilled not in their Kremlin flat or at Zubalovo but in his office a few hundred yards across Red Square on Old Square. This was where the Central Committee was situated from 1923. He had his office on an upper floor near Molotov, Kaganovich and others.[50] Stalin spent most of the day and often a large part of the evening there. Nadya did not nag him about being left on her own, but she did feel that his behaviour at home – when he was there – left a lot to be desired. Her unhappiness was understandable. Stalin had no interests outside work and study apart from the occasional hunting expedition. Unlike Molotov and his other cronies, he did not play tennis or skittles. He did not even go to the cinema. The marriage of Joseph and Nadya looked like a divorce waiting to happen.

22. FACTIONALIST AGAINST FACTIONS

The year 1925 brought the disputes in the Politburo to a head. Personal bickering became all-out factional conflict as Zinoviev and Kamenev moved into open opposition to Bukharin and Stalin. They wrangled over the party's internal organisation as well as over international relations. Official agrarian measures were also highly controversial. Bukharin in his enthusiasm for the New Economic Policy had said to the more affluent peasants: 'Enrich yourselves!'[1] This hardly coincided with Lenin's comments on kulaks over the years. Even in his last dictated articles Lenin had envisaged a steady movement by the peasantry towards a system of farming co-ops; he had never expressly advocated the profit motive as the motor of agricultural regeneration. Stalin's ally Bukharin appeared to be undermining basic Leninist ideas, and Zinoviev and Kamenev were not just being opportunistic in castigating this. They generally objected to the growing compromises of the New Economic Policy as it had been developed. Stalin and Bukharin stuck together to see off their factional adversaries. Having fought against Trotski and the Left Opposition, they battled against Zinoviev and Kamenev when they called for a more radical interpretation of the 'union of the working class with the peasantry'. The survival of the NEP was at stake.

Clashes occurred at the Central Committee in October 1925. Zinoviev and Kamenev had arrived with assurances of support from Grigori Sokolnikov, the People's Commissar of Finances, and Lenin's widow Nadezhda Krupskaya. Stalin and Bukharin carried the majority on that occasion. But neither Zinoviev nor Kamenev had lost their following at the party's highest level. Stalin therefore decided to attack them openly at the Fourteenth Party Congress in December 1925. He did this deftly by revealing that they had once tried to get him to agree to Trotski's expulsion from the party. Sanctimoniously disclaiming his own propensity for butchery, Stalin announced:[2]

We are for unity, we're against chopping. The policy of chopping is repugnant to us. The party wants unity, and it will achieve this together with comrades Kamenev and Zinoviev if this is what they want – and without them if they don't want it.

Although his own personality had been criticised by Lenin as crude and divisive, he contrived to suggest that the menace of a party split was embodied by what was becoming known as the Leningrad Opposition.

Kamenev put things starkly:[3]

We're against creating a theory of 'the Leader' [*vozhdya*]; we're against making anyone into 'the Leader'. We're against the Secretariat, by actually combining politics and organisation, standing above the political body. We're for the idea of our leadership being internally organised in such a fashion that there should exist a truly omnipotent Politburo uniting all our party's politicians as well as that the Secretariat should be subordinate to it and technically carrying out its decrees ... Personally I suggest that our General Secretary is not the kind of figure who can unite the old Bolshevik high command around him. It is precisely because I've often said this personally to comrade Stalin and precisely because I've often said this to a group of Leninist comrades that I repeat it at the Congress: I have come to the conclusion that comrade Stalin is incapable of performing the role of unifier of the Bolshevik high command.

This warning appeared extravagant to the supporters of Stalin and Bukharin. But Kamenev had a point. He understood that, beneath the surface of amity between Stalin and Bukharin, Stalin aspired to become the party's unrivalled leader.

Zinoviev repaid Stalin for breaching the secrecy of their conversations by divulging details of the Kislovodsk episode, when even some of Stalin's friends had discussed the desirability of trimming his powers;[4] but he was relying on his rhetorical flourishes to get his way and the usual applause was no longer forthcoming. Although Zinoviev had been outmanoeuvred, he could not blame all his misfortune on the General Secretary. It had been Zinoviev who had started up the engine of mutual suspicion. If anyone had shown overweening ambition it was him. As yet he had little to counterpose to the policies of the Stalin–Bukharin duumvirate running the Politburo. Zinoviev and Kamenev might mumble about the inadequacies of the regime, but they had until recently been pillars supporting its pediment. When Zinoviev delivered a co-report to Stalin's official report for the Central Committee, he complained about his treatment at Stalin's hands and warned against the further compromises with the peasantry promoted by Stalin and Bukharin. But quite what he would do in their place was not made clear.

Zinoviev and Kamenev had put themselves in the wrong with most party leaders and militants. They had restored factionalism to the party at a dangerous time. Scarcely had Trotski been defeated than they split the ascendant party leadership. The party was insecure across the USSR. Its victory over the Whites in the Civil War left it without illusions about its isolation in the country. Workers outside the Bolshevik ranks were widely disgruntled. Peasants were far from being grateful to the Bolsheviks for the NEP; a deep resentment existed about the continuing attacks on the Russian Orthodox Church. Many members of the technical professions, while operating in Soviet institutions, yearned for the very 'Thermidorian degeneration' which the party feared. Thermidore had been the month in 1794 when the Jacobins who had led the French revolutionary government were overthrown and radical social experiments were brought to an end. Most creative intellectuals continued to regard Bolshevism as a plague to be eliminated. Many non-Russians, having experienced independence from Russia in the Civil War, wished to assert their national and ethnic claims beyond the bounds allowed by the USSR Constitution. 'Nepmen' made big money during the NEP but yearned for a more predictable commercial environment. The richer peasants – the so-called kulaks – had the same aspiration. In the shadows of public life, too, lurked the legions of members of the suppressed political parties: the Mensheviks, Socialist-Revolutionaries, Kadets and the many organisations established by various nationalities.

The party felt surrounded by enemies in its own country, and the Soviet communist leadership – including Stalin – was acutely aware that the imposition of a centralised one-party state had not yet led to a revolutionary change in attitudes and practices at lower levels of the party, the state and society. Policies were formulated largely without consultation outside the Kremlin. Overt opposition was restricted to the successive internal Bolshevik party oppositions. Other tendencies, whenever they came into the open, were suppressed with vigour by the OGPU (as the GPU was renamed in 1924). Politburo members without exception were aware that they presided over a state with imperfect methods of rule. Social, national and religious antagonism to Bolshevism was widespread. Even the party had its defects: factional strife and administrative passive disobedience as well as a decline in ideological fervour at the very lowest echelons was evident. Whoever won the struggle to succeed Lenin would immediately face a graver task: to make the governance of the USSR denser and irreversible. Stalin had power over the formulation of policy and the choice of personnel; he had managed to trounce his main individual enemies in the party. He had not yet turned the Soviet order into a system of power enshrining pervasive obedience and enthusiasm.

The sense that at any time a capitalist 'crusade' might be declared against the USSR added to his fundamental concern. Foreign states had intervened in Soviet Russia in 1918–19 and might do so again. Admittedly the USSR had trade treaties with the United Kingdom and other states. It had signed the Treaty of Rapallo with defeated Germany. The Comintern was gradually building up the number and strength of affiliated communist parties. Ostensibly there was no threat to peace. Even the French, who had made trouble over the Soviet renunciation of the debts of Nicholas II and the Provisional Government, were in no mood to start an invasion. Yet so long as the USSR was the sole socialist state in the world, there would be diplomatic tension which could abruptly turn the situation on its head and the Soviet Union could be invaded. Bolsheviks were on the alert for military outbreaks on their borders. They believed that the Poles would not have moved into Ukraine in 1920 unless the incursion had been instigated by the Western Allies (and although this was untrue, there was indeed military collusion with French military advisers and diplomatic negotiation with the British). If the British and French themselves did not crusade against the USSR in the 1920s, Bolsheviks thought, they might well arm and deploy proxy invading armies. The armed forces of Poland, Finland, Romania and even Turkey were regarded as candidates for such a role.

Yet it was in such a situation, with the USSR pressed by enemies from within and outside its frontiers, that Zinoviev and Kamenev were choosing to take the path already trodden by Trotski. Even without Stalin's speeches against them, they appeared menacingly disloyal. In 1925 there were 1,025,000 Bolsheviks in a population of 147 million.[5] As Bolsheviks conceded, they were a drop in the ocean; and it was admitted that the mass recruitment campaigns during and after the Civil War had created a party which had a few thousand experienced leaders and militants and a vast majority which differed little in political knowledge and administrative expertise from the rest of society. Zinoviev and Kamenev seemed to be self-indulgently ambitious and they were about to pay the price.

Stalin continued to issue works explaining his purposes. He had to prove his ideological credentials; and among his various accomplishments was a sequel to his lectures at the Sverdlov University: in 1926 he published *On Questions of Leninism*. (This is conventionally translated as *Problems of Leninism*.) Its contents did little to change the consensus among leading Bolsheviks that Stalin was an unimaginative interpreter of Lenin's doctrines. The more exploratory pamphlets and articles were produced by others. Trotski wrote on problems of everyday life, Preobrazhenski on economic development, Bukharin on epistemology and sociology. There was scarcely anything in *Problems of Leninism* that could not easily be found in the main published works of Lenin. It was indeed a work of codification and little else. Just one ingredient of the book held attention at the time: Stalin's claim that socialism could be constructed in a single country. Until then it had been the official Bolshevik party assumption that Russia could not do this on its own. Indeed it had been taken for granted that while capitalism remained powerful around the globe, there would be severe limits on the achievability of immense social and economic progress in even the most advanced socialist country.

Such had been Lenin's opinion, and he had expressed it in his foreign policy. Whenever possible, he had tried to spread Revolution westwards by propaganda, financial subsidy, advice or war. Repeatedly he had urged that Russian economic reconstruction would be a chimerical objective unless German assistance, whether socialist or capitalist, were obtained. Consequently his programme involved Bolsheviks beginning to build socialism in Russia in the expectation that states abroad, especially Germany, would eventually aid the task of completing the construction. In September 1920 he stated this at the Ninth Party Conference. 'Russian forces' alone, Lenin insisted, would be inadequate for that purpose; even economic recovery, far less further economic development, might take ten to fifteen years if Soviet Russia were to remain isolated.[6]

Stalin, however, argued that the construction of socialism was entirely feasible even while no fraternal socialist state existed. The great codifier had to engage in subterfuge here. He had to misquote Lenin's published texts and, using his organisational authority, prevent embarrassing unpublished speeches and writings from appearing. Such was the contempt in which his enemies held his writings that they did not deign to expose his unorthodoxy; and indeed it is only in retrospect that his heretical teaching came to have any practical significance. In the 1920s it had no direct impact on practical politics. All supporters of the NEP took it for granted that the USSR had to get on with 'socialist construction' on its own at a time when no other socialist state existed. The question of how far the Bolsheviks would be able to succeed in this seemed unnecessarily abstract.

The other contenders for the leadership also produced books explaining Leninism to the rest of the party: Trotski, Zinoviev, Kamenev and Bukharin. Each invoked the authority of Lenin and claimed to have produced a coherent Leninist strategy. There was nothing intellectually astounding in any of these works, but each author had the knack of giving the impression of being an outstanding intellectual. Trotski, when bored in the Politburo, would pull out a French novel and read it to himself ostentatiously. He was arrogant even by the Politburo's standards. But his contempt for 'ignorant' and 'ill-educated' Stalin was universally shared. What they failed to understand was that *Problems of Leninism*, apart from the heretical point on 'socialism in one country', was a competent summary of Lenin's work. It was well constructed. It contained clear formulations. It was a model of pedagogical steadiness: ideas were introduced and carefully explained from various angles. Nearly all the main themes of Lenin's life's work were dealt with. The book's succinct exposition was recognised at the time, and it went into several subsequent printings.

Stalin's rivals quite underestimated his determination to prove them wrong in their low opinion of him. He understood where his deficiencies lay. He knew little German, less English and no French. He therefore resumed his attempt to teach himself English.[7] He had no oratorical flourish. He therefore worked hard on his speeches and let nobody write them for him or edit his drafts. His Marxism lacked epistemological awareness. He therefore asked Jan Sten to tutor him on a weekly basis in the precepts and methods of contemporary Marxist philosophy.[8]

Stalin was meanwhile marking out a distinct profile for himself at the apex of the party. His idea about 'socialism in one country, taken separately' was poor Leninism; but it struck a chord with many party committee members who disliked Trotski's insistence that the October Revolution would wither and die unless socialist seizures of power took place in other powerful countries on the European continent. Stalin, steady advocate of the NEP, contrived to suggest that he deeply believed in the basic potential of progress in the USSR without foreign assistance. Socialism in one country was an exposition of ideological inclination.[9] Equally important were certain tendencies in Stalin's thought. His commitment to the NEP was increasingly equivocal. He never followed Bukharin in giving it a rousing endorsement; and increasingly he stipulated the need for higher levels of investment in state industry and for ever heavier taxation of the more affluent peasants. He also continued to insist that workers should be promoted from the factory into administrative posts; his detestation of 'bourgeois specialists' remained constant.[10] In line with official party policy he made appointments to party posts on the basis of demonstrable allegiance to Bolshevism before 1917.[11]

The point is that this configuration of tendencies in ideology and policy had growing appeal for party leaders in Moscow and the provinces. Stalin did not rise to supreme power exclusively by means of the levers of bureaucratic manipulation. Certainly he had an advantage inasmuch as he could replace local party secretaries with persons of his choosing. It is also true that the regime in the party allowed him to control debates in the Central Committee and at Party Congresses. But such assets would have been useless to him if he had not been able to convince the Central Committee and the Party Congress that he was a suitable politician for them to follow. Not only as an administrator but also as a leader – in thought and action – he seemed to fit these requirements better than anyone else.

Stalin and Bukharin prepared themselves for a last decisive campaign against the internal party opposition. They had always hated Trotski and, in their private correspondence, they took delight in their growing success in humbling him. But they also retained a certain fear of him. They knew him to be talented and determined; they were aware that he had kept a personal following in the party. Trotski remained a dangerous enemy. They had less respect for Zinoviev but saw that he too was still a menace. Even more perilous was the effect of the rapprochement of Trotski and Zinoviev. As Zinoviev criticised Bukharin and Stalin from a left-wing position, the differences among the oppositionists lessened. A United Opposition was formed in mid-1926. When Stalin heard that Krupskaya had sympathies with Zinoviev, he wrote to Molotov: 'Krupskaya's a splitter. She really needs a beating as a splitter if we wish to conserve party unity.'[12] Two years earlier he had welcomed her support as he defended himself against the effects of Lenin's Testament. Having survived that emergency, he intended to deal with her as severely as with other leading members of the United Opposition.

By mid-1926 the scene was set for the settling of accounts and Stalin was spoiling for a fight. When Trotski muttered to Bukharin that he expected to have a majority of the party on his side, the General Secretary wrote to Molotov and Bukharin: 'How little he knows and how low he rates Bukharin! But I think that soon the party will punch the snouts of Tr[otski] and Grisha [Zinoviev] and Kamenev and will turn them into renegades like Shlyapnikov.'[13] He accused them of behaving even less loyally than Shlyapnikov's Workers' Opposition. They needed to be confronted. Zinoviev should be sacked from the Politburo. The ascendant party leadership need have no fear: 'I assure you that this matter will proceed without the slightest complications in the party and the country.'[14] Zinoviev should be picked off first. Trotski could be left for later.[15]

The Stalin group in the leadership was by then well organised. Stalin himself could afford to stay by the Black Sea while, on 3 June 1926, a terrific dispute raged for six hours about theses proposed by Zinoviev.[16] Stalin wanted total control of his group. He wanted to be kept abreast of developments and relayed regular instructions to his subordinates. But he had created a system which permitted him to be the master even while he was on vacation. He asserted himself to an ever greater extent. In September 1926 he wrote to Molotov indicating substantial reservations about his ally and supposed friend Bukharin: 'Bukharin's a swine and surely worse than a swine because he thinks it below his dignity to write a couple of lines.'[17] Around that time he also said of his associate Mikoyan: 'But Mikoyan's a little duckling in politics, an able duckling but nevertheless a duckling.'[18] From all this it appeared that Stalin saw himself as the single indispensable force in the campaign against the United Opposition. In his own eyes, no one else could successfully co-ordinate and lead the ascendant party leadership in the coming factional conflicts. He made it his aim to send Trotski and Zinoviev down to permanent defeat.

Yet the strain of constant polemics took its toll on him. Free in his accusations against the United Opposition, he was hurt by the tirade of personal abuse he himself had to endure. He was an extremely sensitive bully. When the situation got too much for him, he followed his pattern in the early years after October 1917 and sought to resign. On 27 December 1926 he wrote to Sovnarkom Chairman Alexei Rykov saying: 'I ask you to release me from the post of Central Committee General Secretary. I affirm that I can no longer work at this post, that I'm in no condition to work any longer at this post.' He made a similar attempt at resignation on 19 December 1927.[19] Of course he wanted to be persuaded to withdraw such statements of intent – and indeed his associates did as he wished. But the mask of total self-control and self-confidence had slipped in these moments.

Stalin's vacillation was temporary and fitful. The United Opposition had yet to be defeated and he returned to work as Party General Secretary with the pugnacity for which his associates admired him. Stalin and Bukharin were ready for the fight (although Bukharin had the disturbing tendency to go on talking to their opponents in a friendly fashion). The political end for Trotski, Zinoviev and Kamenev came surprisingly quickly. In spring 1927 Trotski drew up an ambitious 'platform', signed by eighty-three oppositionists (including himself), offering a fulminating critique of the sins of the ascendant party leadership. He demanded a more 'revolutionary' foreign policy as well as more rapid industrial growth; and whereas previously he had expressed concern about the 'bureaucratisation' of the party, he and his supporters now insisted that a comprehensive campaign of democratisation needed to be undertaken not only in the party but also in the soviets. The claim was made that only through such a set of measures would the original goals of the October Revolution be achievable. For the United Opposition, then, the Politburo was ruining everything Lenin had stood for. A last-ditch fight was required for the re-elevation of the party's principles to the top of the current political agenda.

Stalin and Bukharin led the counter-attacks through the summer of 1927. Their belligerent mood was strengthened by their acute awareness that the United Opposition, while hurling accusations about the Politburo's dereliction of revolutionary duty, was also indicting its members for simple incompetence. The Politburo was determined to hold firm as international complications intensified. The British Conservative government had been looking for a scrap for some months and when a police search of the Anglo-Soviet trading company Arcos came up with compromising evidence, the United Kingdom broke diplomatic relations entirely and expelled the Soviet ambassador in May. Next month the Soviet ambassador to Poland was assassinated. Not for the first time there were war scares in the USSR. The OGPU reinforced its vigilance against subversion and sabotage. Troubles came thick and fast. In mid-July the news had come from China that the nationalist leader Chiang Kai-shek had massacred communists in Shanghai in April. Whereas nothing which happened in London and Warsaw was the Politburo's fault, Stalin and Bukharin were directly responsible for the policies imposed by the Comintern on the Chinese communist leadership. Until recently they had insisted on an alliance with Chiang Kai-shek against the wishes of the Chinese communists; now, in August 1927, they licensed them to organise an uprising against Chiang Kai-shek. The United Opposition upbraided the Politburo for a total lack of effective supervision of the USSR's foreign policy.

Stalin, however, went off as usual to the south for his vacation. His assumption was that he could leave the Central Control Commission, chaired by Ordzhonikidze, to handle the disciplining of the Opposition. Papers were couriered to him regularly. What he read threw him into a rage. Somehow Zinoviev and Trotski had succeeded in turning the Central Control Commission's enquiries into an opportunity to challenge the Central Committee. And Ordzhonikidze seemed to have lost control of developments. 'Shame!' wrote Stalin to Molotov in anticipation of a more aggressive stance being taken by the men he had left in charge of Moscow.[20]

In June and July he peppered his letters with detailed instructions on both Britain and China.[21] Yet he did not lift his eyes from the internal threat: Trotski had to be dealt with. Stalin raised with Molotov and Bukharin the question of whether their enemy would be best deported to Japan.[22] The decision was taken to proceed in stages. At the joint plenum of the Central Committee and the Central Control Commission in October 1927, some of Trotski's followers shouted out that the Politburo was burying Lenin's Testament. Stalin was ready for them:[23]

> The Opposition is thinking of 'explaining' its defeat by personal factors: Stalin's crudity, the uncompromising attitude of Bukharin and Rykov and so on. It's a cheapskate explanation! It's less an explanation than superstitious nonsense . . . In the period between 1904 and the February [1917] Revolution Trotski spent the whole time twirling around in the company of the Mensheviks and conducting a campaign against the party of Lenin. Over that period Trotski sustained a whole series of defeats at the hands of Lenin's party. Why? Perhaps Stalin's crudity was the cause of this? But Stalin was not yet secretary to the C[entral] C[ommittee]; [Stalin] at that time was cut off and distant from foreign parts, conducting the struggle in the underground whereas the struggle between Trotski and Lenin was played out abroad. So where exactly did Stalin's crudity come into that?

His handling of the plenum was a masterpiece of persuasion. He reminded the Opposition that previously he had rejected calls for the expulsion of Trotski and Zinoviev from the Central Committee. 'Per-haps,' he waspishly suggested, 'I overdid the "kindness" and made a mistake.'

The joint plenum excluded Trotski, Zinoviev and Kamenev from the Central Committee. On 14 November 1927 Trotski and Zinoviev were expelled from the party entirely, and this decision was ratified by the Fifteenth Party Congress in December. The Stalin–Bukharin axis had triumphed. Their version of revolutionary policies at home and abroad had prevailed after a decade of constant factional strife among Bolshe-viks. Bukharin maintained friendly relations with his defeated adversar-ies. But Stalin refused to compromise. At the Fifteenth Party Congress the further exclusion of seventy-five oppositionists, including Kamenev, was announced. Stalin and Bukharin had seen off the acute threat to the NEP. No one imagined that within a month the political settlement would be destroyed and that the two victors would become enemies. In January 1928 the New Economic Policy was about to be torn apart by the Party General Secretary.

PART THREE

DESPOT

23. ENDING THE NEP

Suddenly at the end of the 1920s Stalin trampled on the New Economic Policy like an angry bull. The economic compromise inaugurated by Lenin's Politburo seven years earlier was rejected. Massive violence was used to introduce a system of collective farms. Forced-rate industrialisation began. Persecution of kulaks, nepmen and 'bourgeois specialists' was intensified. Politics too underwent change. The internal party regime was further tightened and show trials were resumed against surviving leaders of the moribund rival parties. An offensive began against every kind of nationalist tendency.[1] The boundaries of cultural expression were drastically reduced and organised religion became the object of violent assault. The controversial settlement that had held since 1921 fell apart.

Stalin initiated the changes after the shortfall in grain supplies became critical at the end of 1927. On 6 January 1928 the Secretariat sent out a secret directive threatening to sack local party leaders who failed to apply 'tough punishments' for grain hoarders.[2] Stalin let his feelings show in a letter to Sergei Syrtsov and the Siberian party leadership:[3]

> We hold that this is the road to panic, to the raising of prices – the very worst form of barter when it is plainly impossible to meet the needs of a countryside full of peasants with marketable grain stocks: it strengthens the capacity of the powerful stratum of the country-side to resist . . . The peasant will not hand over his tax on the basis of a *Pravda* editorial – compulsory schedules are crucial for him.

Siberian communists were put on notice that an immediate increase in grain procurements was demanded. Unlike Ukraine and the north Caucasus, Siberia – which had supplied a third of Soviet wheat exports – had experienced a warm summer. Stalin was determined to extract the grain from its kulak owners. He and a select group of party functionaries set off by train from Moscow on 15 January 1928. Politicians like Mikoyan, Kirov, Zhdanov, Shvernik, Postyshev and Kosior made similar trips, accompanied by thousands of party officials, to the agricultural regions of the USSR.[4]

State grain procurements had tumbled to only 70 per cent of the total obtained a year before. The difficulties had arisen from the Politburo's mishandling of the economy. Since 1926 several measures had been introduced to squeeze additional revenue from the private sectors. A class tax was levied on the kulaks: fiscal revenue from them rose by over 50 per cent in 1926–7. 'Evil-intentioned' hoarding of industrial and agricultural products was in 1926 made a criminal offence under Article 107 of the Criminal Code. Surcharges were imposed on the traffic of private goods on the railways. The government expropriated many private flour-mills. These measures followed the reorientation of immediate economic objectives proposed by Stalin and Bukharin at the Fourteenth Party Congress in December. Party policy was being geared to an accelerated pace of industrialisation through a steady expansion of state capital accumulation. This emphasis was reaffirmed in July 1926. Gosplan – the State Planning Committee, which was responsible for drawing up a plan for the country's economic development – was told to prepare for a situation where enterprises would become subject to greater instruction and supervision. Moves were made towards bringing the entire economy under central governmental authority.[5]

Politburo members became impatient about the NEP; and as they turned policy in the direction of radical change they committed themselves to the socialist and industrialising aims of the makers of the October Revolution. In opting for rapid and fundamental change they were intensifying the transformation of the USSR in the direction of 'modernity'. The vestiges of the old order were to be eradicated. Irked by Trotski, they wished to demonstrate their credentials. They also knew that the slow pace of economic transformation made fertile soil for the United Opposition's propaganda among party leaders in the provinces[6] – and despite the ceaseless political centralisation since mid-1918 there was reason for the ascendant leaders to fear a sudden flaring up of resistance to their supremacy. But they believed in what they were doing. Stalin lived for Bolshevism; but he combined ideological adherence with feelings towards his rivals – jealousy, rancour and vengefulness – that were far from pure.

The predictable consequence of the economic measures from 1926 was the disruption of the market economy. Even before hacking at the roots of the NEP, Stalin – together with Bukharin until the expropriations of January 1928 – had been giving them a serious bruising. They had disturbed the garden still earlier by lowering prices for products from state-owned factories as a means of resolving the 'scissors crisis' in 1923. The effect was cumulative. A shortage of goods was reported as traders bought up what was available. Three years later Stalin and Bukharin also brought down prices they were willing to pay for grain. The result was a decline in the marketing of the cereal harvest. The two leading individuals in the Politburo had competed with each other in incompetence. Only one of them, Bukharin, saw the error of his ways by indicating to the Central Committee that retail prices needed to be raised to avoid calamity. Stalin faced him down. He had had enough: the NEP in its early years had restored the economy but could not secure industrial advance at a pace rapid enough for Politburo members. The Central Committee plenum in February 1927 backed the measures taken in the previous year.

Stalin and Bukharin had tipped the economy downhill, and Stalin refused to recognise their stupendous blunder. What was he thinking of in 1927? Stalin never explained his strategy in detail. Some have suggested that he merely wanted power and had to pick a fight with Bukharin on terrain where he could count on him taking a stand out of line with opinion in wider party circles. This is a possibility. But the more plausible explanation is that Stalin, having agreed with Bukharin on a more militant approach to industrialisation, refused to back down. He had a blunted faculty of judgement. The NEP had always left a bad taste in the mouth of Stalin and many leading Bolsheviks at the centre and in the provinces. The recurrent emergencies had kept them edgy. There had been the terrible famine in 1922 and the 'scissors crisis' in commerce in 1923. The party had tried to squeeze more out of the workers in factories and mines by rationalising the process of production. But this was never enough to satisfy the critics on the political left. In their diverse ways the oppositionists – the Democratic Centralists, the Workers' Opposition, the Left Opposition, the Leningrad Opposition and the United Opposition – made the Politburo edgy by castigating it for ideological cowardice and betrayal.

The NEP had achieved more than its critics allowed. The volume of industrial and agricultural output by 1926–7 by most estimates had wholly or nearly reattained the level of the last year before the Great War; and the Soviet state was raising its rate of investment in capital projects. The NEP appeared capable of generating a moderate pace of economic development in the years ahead. There was also much political and social stability. Party, OGPU and Red Army held unchallengeable

power. A Georgian uprising occurred in 1924; there were also disturbances in central Asia. But otherwise there was tranquillity. The clampdown on public dissent was effective.

The question remained whether the pace of economic development
was sufficient for the USSR to protect itself against potential external
enemies. By the late 1920s the main dangers were thought to be Britain
(which broke diplomatic relations in May 1927), France (which continued to demand the repayment of Russia's old state loans) and Japan
(which greedily eyed Soviet possessions in the Far East). It was doubtful
that the Red Army was well enough equipped to deal with any of them
in a war. Although industrial development was proceeding, the technological gap between the Soviet Union and the West's most advanced
economies was growing. The Bolsheviks had come to power as firm
believers in the vital necessity of science and engineering as vehicles of
socialist progress. A decade after the October Revolution nothing had
happened in the USSR which suggested that the gap could soon be
closed. The USA and Germany were racing ahead. Stalin and his
associates were concerned about the Soviet regime's persistent failure.

The party's mood did not rest only on calculations of economic
development. Nepmen made fortunes while manufacturing little. A
wealthy stratum of peasants, whom the Bolsheviks referred to as the
kulaks, again emerged in the countryside. Priests, imams and rabbis
spread the word of God. Marxist–Leninist atheism was unpopular.
Sections of the intelligentsia, especially among the non-Russian peoples,
were cultivating nationalist ideas. Concessions on the national question
had been promoted since the October Revolution and reinforced under
the NEP. In Ukraine there was a systematic campaign of 'Ukrain-
ianisation' of schools, press and public personnel. Similar drives were
undertaken in other Soviet republics. Yet nationalism was on the rise
everywhere in the USSR and was outmatching the spread of socialist
consciousness. The basic policy of Lenin and Stalin was backfiring
spectacularly. Moscow responded in 1926 by endorsing measures to
deport a number of religious and tribal leaders in Azerbaijan.[7] The
handling of the national question grew harsher at the same time as
severity increased in economic policy. Stalin's associate Kaganovich, who
headed the Communist Party of Ukraine in 1925–6, mooted measures to
deport Poles from the western borderlands to the USSR's internal
regions. His purpose was to prevent Ukraine being infiltrated by
Piłsudski's intelligence agencies.[8]

The same party which had made the October Revolution in the name of the working class and the poorest peasants looked out on a society where capitalism, religion and nationalism were growing in strength. Even the ranks of the party caused concern. Membership in 1927, after an intensive recruitment campaign, rose to 1,200,000. Although this was a substantial total, it disguised official worries that the quality of recruits in terms of ideological fervour and educational accomplishment left much to be desired.[9]

It was against this background that the destabilising economic measures had been introduced from the mid-1920s. Stalin had long had a penchant for economic autarky. Unless state policy produced indigenous industrial growth, he assumed, it was inappropriate. He had written to Molotov in June 1925:[10]

> Either we resolve [this serious question] correctly in the interests of the state and of the workers and the unemployed, whom it would be possible to set up in expanded production or else, if we don't resolve it correctly, we'll lose tens of millions – apart from everything else – to the benefit of foreign manufacturers.

Whereas Bukharin advocated industrialisation at a slowish pace and tried to discourage demands for acceleration, Stalin displayed increasing frustration. The partnership of Stalin and Bukharin was disintegrating without either of them yet anticipating that a decisive rupture was about to occur. They still got on well in the Politburo. They also saw each other socially. But Stalin's ideas were hardening. In December 1926 he denied that the USSR would take fifty or more years to match the volume of the economics of foreign capitalist powers. Indeed he declared that 'giant steps' forward could and should be taken.[11]

Stalin's contribution to discussions of economic policy until January 1928 had been of a measured nature and – apart from his licensed attacks on the internal party oppositions – his outward behaviour had been calm since Lenin's death. His rivals had some excuse for misreading the situation; but it was not a mistake they were going to be able to repeat without pain. Stalin was acting craftily. He breathed not a word to Bukharin about the war on the countryside he was about to start. Closeted for two days on the Trans-Siberian Railway with his aide Alexander Poskrëbyshev and others, though, he was in a pugnacious frame of mind. (Poskrëbyshev was the latest of Stalin's personal assistants and was to remain in post until 1953.) Anybody who got in Stalin's way on his trip was going to receive ferocious treatment. On arrival in Novosibirsk, he ordered arrests of 'anti-Soviet' kulaks. Grain procurement quotas were to be fulfilled. The campaign started to 'expand the establishment' of collective farms.[12] Squads were assembled in west Siberia and the Urals to collect the quotas set for grain collection. They travelled out to the farms armed to the teeth and grabbed whatever produce they discovered. As in 1918–20, Bolsheviks entered villages, summoned peasant gatherings and demanded immediate compliance at gunpoint.

Stalin returned to Moscow on 6 February 1928 with wagons of grain seized from 'hoarders'. *Pravda* celebrated the achievement.[13] It seemed that Stalin's line had triumphed without resistance in the central party leadership. He and the other leaders insisted that the 'middle peasants' as well as the kulaks needed to be coerced into releasing their harvests.[14] Bukharin was outraged. The change in policy had been undertaken in the provinces without prior sanction by the Politburo or the Central Committee. There was no precedent in the party's history. Stalin had arrived in Moscow like a thief with his loot; instead of acknowledging his crime, he expected to have his virtue commended. The Politburo was in uproar. Its members stopped speaking to each other outside official meetings. When challenged about his policies, Stalin grew angry and imperious. Bukharin complained to him about his demeanour on 16 April. Stalin wrote back: 'You won't force me to stay quiet or hide my opinion by your shrieks about "*my wanting to teach everybody*". Is an end ever going to be put to the attacks on me?'[15] These words combined self-righteousness and over-sensitivity in a pugnacious mixture.

Stalin understood how to exploit the situation. He wanted faster agricultural collectivisation and state-planned industrialisation. Most party officials had never felt comfortable with the NEP. They itched to go over to a more 'revolutionary' line. In the Komsomol – the party's youth organisation – there were also many militants who yearned for the Politburo to abandon compromise. This trend was also found in the OGPU: many police officials were eager to enforce a regime with greater control over an unruly society. The Red Army had leading commanders eager for economic transformation and an end to the constriction of their budgetary opportunities.[16] Although agriculture had been the focal point of Stalin's initiative in January 1928, he associated himself with a much larger agenda. Like his supporters in the party and other public bodies, he wanted to accelerate and deepen the country's transformation. Industry, schooling, urban construction and socialist indoctrination were to be prioritised. The state was to become more penetrative and traditional attachments to religion and nationhood were to disappear.

The USSR was to turn itself into a military power which could defend itself.

Moving beyond agricultural policy, Stalin organised a trial of engineers and 'industrial specialists', including several foreigners, from Shakhty in the Don Basin. They were charged with deliberate sabotage. Officially the OGPU under Genrikh Yagoda was conducting an independent enquiry. In reality it was Stalin who was accuser and judge. Investigative procedures were ignored. The Party General Secretary ordered the arrested individuals to be beaten into confessing to imaginary crimes. He was resetting the machinery of Soviet politics. He was cracking the resistance of industrial specialists – managers, engineers and planners – to demands for quicker industrial growth. Through the Shakhty plaintiffs he established a case of widespread sabotage. The shadow of suspicion fell over specialists throughout the USSR.

Stalin had let others do his dirty business. He avoided calling for the execution of the accused in the Shakhty Affair. He manoeuvred so as to get his results while protecting a pure reputation.[17] Meanwhile Gosplan was preparing directives for the USSR's entire economy. Sovnarkom had given instructions to this effect in June 1927 and the work was coming to completion in summer 1928. The first variant of the Five-Year Plan was scheduled for inauguration in October. The output targets were astonishingly high: capital goods were projected to increase by 161 per cent and consumer goods by 83 per cent.[18] All sectors of the economy were to be subjected to state control. Although priority was given to the development of heavy industry, the Politburo anticipated that the popular standard of living in the towns would simultaneously improve. There was also an expectation that a hundred thousand tractors would be manufactured for use in agriculture and put at the disposal of the collective farms which were about to be created. Revenues for this overoptimistic scheme were to come from the main beneficiaries of the NEP. Stalin wanted to exact a tribute from the better-off peasantry. Bukharin described this as 'idiotic illiteracy'.

Bukharin in April secured a decision at the Central Committee plenum condemning 'excesses' in recent practices in procurement. When the Central Committee met again on 4 July, its official resolution gave a commitment to the NEP and even promised a rise in grain prices.[19] The problem for Bukharin, though, was the failure of his measures to restore economic stability. Peasants refused to release grain stocks. The violence had exacerbated relations between the villages and the administrative authorities. In any case the shortage of industrial products for purchase gave no incentive for the peasantry to return to the market.[20] The Politburo had hoped to alleviate problems by importing wheat; but this was too little and too late to terminate the food-supplies deficit. Nor did it do anything about the difficulties with the peasants. Meanwhile the towns remained short of grain and vegetables. The Politburo could not ignore the monthly reports: the USSR faced a winter of urban malnutrition.

What Bukharin had not bargained for was the reaction of several powerful leaders. He had expected Voroshilov and Kalinin to criticise what had happened in the Urals and Siberia.[21] Even Ordzhonikidze was sometimes disloyal to Stalin behind the scenes.[22] Bukharin remained hopeful that he could win over individuals such as OGPU leader Yagoda as well as the rest of the party. The reversion to War Communism had to be exposed for what it was.[23] Yet Stalin won all of them to his side. (It was said that Kalinin's weakness for ballerinas allowed Stalin to put pressure on him.) By summer 1928 Bukharin was becoming frantic. He even started to worry that Stalin would bring Kamenev and Zinoviev back into public politics as useful allies. Bukharin made overtures to Kamenev to prevent this. 'The disagreements between us and Stalin,' he told him, 'are many times more serious than all the ones we had with you. The Rightists ... wanted Kamenev and Zinoviev restored to the Politburo.'[24] Bukharin's overtures were a sign of panic. He could not assemble sufficient support at the highest party levels. His sole prominent allies against the General Secretary were Rykov, Tomski and Uglanov.

Yet Bukharin believed that the 'Urals-Siberian method' would be disowned and that the market mechanisms of Lenin's NEP restored. Initially his optimism seemed justified. The 'excesses' reported in the expropriation campaign were officially castigated and denials were issued that the 'extraordinary measures' implied an abandonment of the NEP. Although Stalin successfully insisted that a stronger commitment to early collectivisation also be inserted into public statements, the feeling was widespread that he had damaged himself politically.

Bukharin did not give up. Having written inscrutable prose for most of his adult life, he came down to earth and published 'Notes of an Economist'. Bukharin castigated ideas of 'super-industrialisation'. According to him, these were Trotskyist and anti-Leninist. He claimed that only a balanced, steady relationship between the interests of industry and agriculture would secure healthy economic development.[25] There was nothing in the 'Notes' that jarred against anything Stalin had said up to 1928; and since Stalin still avoided disowning the NEP, Bukharin did not need special permission to publish what he wanted in the hope of neutralising a politician whom he had come to regard as the USSR's Genghis Khan.[26] But he also misjudged Stalin by assuming that all that interested him was to keep power.[27] What had started as a crisis over food supplies had acquired other dimensions. Stalin's group in the Politburo and Central Committee were not going to be satisfied by changes to agricultural measures. They wanted fast industrial progress and military security. They wished to crush nationalism and religiosity. They aimed to eradicate hostility to the Soviet regime, and the remnants of the old propertied classes were to be got rid of. Cities, schools and cinemas had to be established. Socialism was to be spread as an idea and a practical reality.

Stalin and Bukharin clashed every time they met. In his condition of heightened expectancy, Stalin applied his programme to international relations. He now denied that 'capitalist stabilisation' prevailed, and he declared that the world economy was facing yet another fundamental emergency. He resolved that this should be reflected in the world communist movement. Before the Comintern's Sixth Congress in July 1928, Stalin declared that anti-communist socialists in Europe – members of labour and social-democratic parties – were the deadliest enemies of socialism. He called them 'social-fascists'. Bukharin was horrified: he understood the dangers posed by the European far right. Appreciating the qualitative difference between conservatism and fascism, he wanted Hitler's Nazis to be the main object of the German Communist Party's political attack. But Stalin amassed the support required in the Politburo for a change of policy in the Comintern. The internal breach with the NEP obtained an external aspect. Until then it had been the official line that world capitalism had stabilised itself after the Great War. Now Stalin insisted that a 'third period' had commenced as capitalism entered its terminal crisis and that revolutionary opportunities were about to present themselves in Europe.

This had been under discussion in the Politburo for a year or two but no serious alteration of the Comintern's practical instructions to Europe's communist parties had followed. Wanting to do down Bukharin, Stalin had a personal interest in changing policy. But there was probably more to it. Stalin had had doubts about 'European socialist revolution' in 1917–18. Yet his scepticism was absolute and sometimes his Bolshevik instincts took him over. Aiming at the transformation of the USSR, he might have been reverting to radical type. From mid-1928, however, Stain's group ordered communists throughout the continent to adopt the stance taken by the Bolsheviks in 1917. Extreme radicalism became dominant again and the Comintern, at the Politburo's instigation, purged the doubters and vacillators – as well as the Trotskyists – from the ranks of its parties. World communism was being readied for the imminent revolutionary upheaval.

Stalin, while insisting that revolutions were about to break out in Europe, continued to stipulate that the Russian Communist Party should concentrate on building 'socialism in one country'. His enemies took this as proof that Stalin was a hypocrite or a bungler. Trotski reminded everyone of Stalin's cack-handed instructions to the Chinese Communist Party in 1927; Bukharin was baffled by the turn in policy. There was no fundamental paradox in Stalin's change of policy. His controversial commitment to socialism in one country did not imply a basic disregard for the necessity of international revolution. Stalin had never ceased to accept that the USSR would face problems of security until such time as one or more of the globe's great powers underwent a revolution of the Soviet kind. This did not mean, however, that he was willing to risk direct intervention in Europe; he still feared provoking a crusade against the USSR. But he no longer sought to restrain the communist parties in Germany, France and Italy which had made no secret of their frustration with the Comintern's insistence that they should collaborate with social-democratic and labour parties in their countries.

He seldom did anything for one sole reason. When allied to Bukharin before 1928, Stalin left a lot of the handling of the Comintern to him. Bukharin had many supporters in leading positions in the foreign parties. By altering policy and expelling dissenters, Stalin could bring his own people to the top. Prone to moodiness, Bukharin contemplated resigning as a means of putting pressure on Stalin.[28] Stalin had frequently offered his own resignation from posts since the October Revolution; but he would not have treated Bukharin with the indulgence which he himself had received. His only idea of victory involved crushing and humiliating the enemy.

Much ground had already been prepared for him. In moving forward to comprehensive state ownership and regulation, the ascendant party leadership was moving backwards towards the Soviet economic system of the period of the Civil War. The Supreme Council of the People's Economy had been established to supervise all economic activity after the October Revolution.[29] The banking and industrial sectors had been seized by the state in the Civil War and much had subsequently been retained. Gosplan had been created in February 1921. After starting the

First Five-Year Plan, Stalin and his associates suggested that they were initiating a calculated strategy from this transformation. The word 'plan' implied that this was the case. No such strategy in any definitive form existed and there were many zigzags on the route to transformation. Policies were modified and sometimes abandoned. Once announced, targets for economic growth were frequently altered. Yet Stalin was not without a compass when he threw the NEP overboard. Although he lacked a calculated strategy, he always possessed a set of operational assumptions, and these assumptions were shared by many in the central and local party leaderships.

Sooner or later, as even Nikolai Bukharin thought, the market had to be eliminated from the economy and the social elements hostile to socialism – the kulaks, the nepmen, clergy, 'bourgeois specialists', nationalists and supporters of all other political and cultural trends – had somehow to disappear. The need for a wholly state-owned economy and state-directed society was the shared objective of leading Bolsheviks. They did not flinch at the use of force. Hardened by their experiences before and after the October 1917 Revolution, they were more than willing to ensure compliance by crude methods. The frustrations of the NEP were immense. The military threat from abroad did not fade and the technological gap between the USSR and the West was growing. Loyal supporters of the ascendant party leadership, moreover, were embarrassed by oppositionists who declared that they had betrayed the objective of the Revolution led by Lenin. Such a mentality offered a framework of assumptions inside which it was possible for Stalin to make his piecemeal proposals from 1928 and to count upon substantial support in the wider party.

Stalin started with basic assumptions about the world. These came from his peculiar and distorted reaction to his Georgian background, to his experience of the revolutionary underground and to the Bolshevik variant of Marxism. Whatever the matter to be decided, he was never perplexed to the point of vacillation. His axioms did not prescribe policy in detail. By thinking and commanding according to his fundamental ideas, he could be instantly decisive. Any given situation might sometimes require much study – and Stalin worked assiduously even after the Second World War at keeping himself well informed. But most situations could be decided without a great deal of work; indeed Stalin could afford to leave them to his subordinates and demand reports on what had been decided. He surrounded himself with persons such as Molotov and Kaganovich who shared his assumptions, and he promoted others who could be trained to internalise them (or to go along with them out of ambition or fear). It is this inner world of assumptions which gives the clue about Stalin's otherwise mysterious capacity to manoeuvre in the changing situations of the 1930s.

During the First Five-Year Plan the USSR underwent drastic change. Ahead lay campaigns to spread collective farms and eliminate kulaks, clerics and private traders. The political system would become harsher. Violence would be pervasive. The Russian Communist Party, OGPU and People's Commissariats would consolidate their power. Remnants of former parties would be eradicated. 'Bourgeois nationalists' would be arrested. The Gulag, which was the network of labour camps subject to the People's Commissariat of Internal Affairs (NKVD), would be expanded and would become an indispensable sector of the Soviet economy. Dozens of new towns and cities would be founded. Thousands of new enterprises would be created. A great influx of people from the villages would take place as factories and mines sought to fill their labour forces. Literacy schemes would be given huge state funding. Promotion of workers and peasants to administrative office would be widespread. Enthusiasm for the demise of political, social and cultural compromise would be cultivated. Marxism–Leninism would be intensively propagated. The change would be the work of Stalin and his associates in the Kremlin. Theirs would be the credit and theirs the blame.

24. TERROR-ECONOMICS

Stalin in 1929 was determined to alter the USSR's economic structures and practices. Gosplan was put under a political clamp and told to produce ever more ambitious versions of the First Five-Year Plan. The Politburo resolved that targets should be hit inside four rather than five years, and the officials of Gosplan were commanded to carry out the gigantic task of amending schemes involving the country's industry, agriculture, transport and commerce. Warnings by experts against hyper-optimism were ignored. Whole new cities such as Magnitogorsk were constructed. Digging began of the White Sea–Baltic Canal. Engineering plants in Moscow and Leningrad were expanded; new mines were sunk in Ukraine, the Urals and the Kuznets Basin. Peasants in their millions were attracted into the expanding labour force. Skilled workers became managers. Factories were put on to a seven-day working week. American and German technology was bought with revenues which accrued from the rise in grain exports. Foreign firms were contracted to establish new plants and help train Soviet personnel. Educational facilities were expanded. Youth was promoted. A vast economic transformation was put in hand.

Industrial wages were meant to rise by about a half, but the skyrocketing of food prices discounted any such gain, especially after the introduction of bread rationing in early 1929. Housing construction lagged far behind the needs of the expanded urban population. Having aimed to build a hundred thousand tractors, security considerations turned the Politburo and Gosplan towards raising the proportion of the budget devoted to armaments. The needs of consumers were also downgraded as the requirements for coal, iron, steel and machinery were increased.[1]

Having forcibly extracted grain from the hands of the peasantry since January 1928, the Politburo ignored Bukharin's call for a reversion to the New Economic Policy and began to designate his ideas as a Right Deviation from Marxist–Leninist principles. In 1929 it resolved upon the mass collectivisation of agriculture. There had been many sorts of collective farms in the 1920s. Stalin selected two types to be introduced. The 'higher' type was the sovkhoz, whose land was owned by the state and whose workers were simply the rural equivalent of the hired factory labour force. The other type was the kolkhoz. This stood for 'collective farm' in Russian; the difference from the sovkhoz was that kolkhozes formally rented the land from the state and agreed to deliver a fixed quota of the harvest to the state. Whereas sovkhoz workers were paid a regular wage, workers on a kolkhoz were paid according to the number of days they contributed to the farm. The real difference was minimal for peasants. The Politburo's policy as publicly announced was that entrance to either type of collective farm should be on a voluntary basis. Local party committees were ordered to conduct propaganda to encourage the phenomenon. Once Bukharin had been ejected from the Politburo in November 1929, Stalin stiffened the campaign.[2]

The Politburo repeatedly raised the tempo of implementation. The process quickened even in summer as the authorities strove to procure the required grain from the villages at prices resented by the peasants. An article by Stalin on 7 November, the anniversary of the October Revolution, contended that many rural households saw the advantage of collective farms without the need for the state to compel them; and it drew a contrast with the proposals of the United Opposition.[3] A Politburo commission was established to work out implementation. The purpose was to prioritise the setting up of collective farms in the lower Volga region (which was famously fertile). Russia's Far North was to be the last region to undergo total collectivisation in 1933. It was a short schedule but it became shorter. Central and local cadres who argued for a delay were firmly overruled. Instructions were kept confidential and vague; and party and governmental functionaries, concerned that they might be judged lacking in obedience, set about imposing total collectivisation with immediate effect.[4]

In July 1929 it stayed official policy that terror should be avoided and that kulaks as well as the majority of the peasantry ought to be enlisted in the collective farms. Stalin, however, wanted none of this. In December 1929 he announced that kulaks should be banned from becoming collective farm workers. His words were blunt:[5]

> Now we have the opportunity to carry out a resolute offensive against the kulaks, break their resistance, eliminate them as a class and replace their production with the production of kolkhozes and

sovkhozes ... Now dekulakisation is being undertaken by the masses of the poor and middling peasant masses themselves, who are realising total collectivisation. Now dekulakisation in the areas of total collectivisation is not just a simple administrative measure. Now dekulakisation is an integral part of the creation and development of collective farms. When the head is cut off, no one wastes tears on the hair.

On 30 January 1930 the Politburo chillingly approved the liquidation of kulaks as a class. A Central Committee directive was sent out in February. Three kulak categories were designated. The first consisted of individuals to be sent to concentration camps, the second to distant parts of the USSR and the third to other parts of their province. The Politburo called for religious bodies to be simultaneously targeted.[6] The OGPU was managed in the same way as the economy. Quotas were assigned to regions for dekulakisation, and destinations in the north Urals and Kazakhstan were prescribed. The Politburo handed down the schedule for operations.[7]

Stalin, like other Bolsheviks, detested the kulaks. He seems to have sensed that the peasantry would not join the sovkhozes and kolkhozes unless they were afraid of the consequences of resistance. Repression of a sizeable minority would bring this about – and anyway he probably genuinely believed that the kulaks would seriously disrupt the operation of collective farms. Over 320,000 households were subjected to dekulakisation by July 1930. The violence was immense. The superior force of the authorities, aided by the suddenness of the campaign, prevailed. A whole way of rural life was being swept into oblivion.[8]

Already in 1927 the Politburo had sanctioned the use of forced labour to expand the mining of gold. This initiative was translated in the following year to timber hewing.[9] Stalin gave rulings on the use of concentration camps not just for the social rehabilitation of prisoners but also for what they could contribute to the gross domestic product in regions where free labour could not easily be found. He had never been reluctant to contemplate such camps as a central component of communist party rule; and he did not flinch from ordering arrests and ordering OGPU chief Vladimir Menzhinski to create the permanent organisational framework. Among the victims were categories of persons whom he feared and resented. Members of outlawed political parties were high on the list. Stalin also had 'bourgeois nationalists', priests and private traders in his sights as well as recalcitrant economic experts. His method was a continuation of the techniques developed at Shakhty. Leading individuals and groups in 'anti-Soviet' categories were put on show trial. The objective was to intimidate all their followers and sympathisers into giving up thoughts of opposition in case they too might be arrested.

A succession of such trials occurred in 1929–30. These involved much political inventiveness with Stalin supplying the main momentum. Historians Sergei Platonov and Yevgeni Tarle were arrested and included in the so-called Academy of Sciences Affair which led to the condemnation of the non-existent All-People's Union for the Struggle for Russia's Regeneration in July 1929.[10] The fictitious Industrial Party, including the engineer Leonid Ramzin, was brought to court in November 1930. The Labouring Peasant Party, also non-existent, was arraigned in December 1930; the main defendants were the economists Alexander Chayanov and Nikolai Kondratev.[11] The so-called Union Bureau of the Mensheviks was tried in February and March 1931 with Nikolai Sukhanov as the leading plaintiff.[12] Outside the RSFSR there were trials of nationalists. Many of them had until recently been figures of the political establishment. But wherever Stalin and his associates caught a whiff of nationalism they resorted to judicial procedures. Ukraine, Belorussia and the Caucasus, north and south, were subjected to similar proceedings. Torture, outlandish charges and learned-by-rote confessions became the norm. Hundreds of defendants were either shot or sentenced to lengthy terms of imprisonment.[13]

Stalin's strategy was to bring about a massive increase in political control as his general revolutionary assault was reinforced. His zeal to subjugate all strata of 'specialists' was heightened. Industrial managers, lawyers, teachers and military officers fell foul of him. The Red Army narrowly escaped a trial of its commanders but the interrogations alone, which involved Stalin in person, were enough to scare the living daylights out of the officer corps. Individual generals, though, were persecuted. Like the Red Army, the Russian Orthodox Church – as well as the other Christian denominations and indeed Islam, Judaism and Buddhism – escaped a show trial. But this did not mean that repression was withheld. Attacks on religious leaders became so frequent and systematic that the League of the Militant Godless expected belief in deities to be eradicable within a few years. Persecution was extreme, and only a twelfth of the Russian Orthodox Church's priests were left functioning in their parishes by 1941.[14]

Meanwhile promotions of newly trained workers and peasants took place as the administrative stratum was widened. Volunteer collectivisers were found among young workers. Armed and indoctrinated, these so-called '25,000-ers' set out for the villages to deal with the 'class enemy'.[15] Recruitment to the party expanded. By 1931 it had 1,369,406 full members.[16] Literacy and numeracy spread. There was a reprise of revolutionary spirit as the regime gave out the message that socialism was being created in the USSR while abroad capitalism was entering its final crisis. The Wall Street Crash of October 1929 made this a plausible message at the time. Unconditional enthusiasts for the Politburo's policies existed everywhere. Even many who detested the violence and vilification were willing to believe that a new and better world was being created. In the party there was relief that action at last was being taken. Bukharin's group had so little organised support that it did not merit the name of the Right Opposition. The end of the NEP was welcomed. Local party secretaries became mini-Stalins making all the fundamental decisions across the range of public policy – and the fact that nearly all the economy was somehow or other taken into the hands of the state meant that their powers had never been greater.[17]

While promoting industrialisation and collectivisation, Stalin did not overlook the fact that he ruled a former empire. In a speech to a conference of industrial functionaries on 4 February 1931 he declared: 'In the past we didn't have and couldn't have a fatherland. But now that we have overthrown capitalism and power is in our hands, the people – and we – have a fatherland and we will protect its independence.'[18] Patriotism was making its way back on to the list of official priorities. While society was being split asunder by policy initiatives from the late 1920s, Stalin recognised that some cement was needed to keep the people of the USSR together.

The range of changed policies was large, and in every case Stalin's intervening hand was felt. Even on the 'philosophical front' he was active. On 9 December he visited the Institute of Red Professors. Several of the academics, including Abram Deborin, were known as supporters of Bukharin. Stalin demanded greater militancy from his own followers in the party cell at the institute: 'Everything written here by you is correct; the problem is that not everything has yet been said. In the critical part it's possible to say much more. You've given the correct evaluation here but it's too soft and unsatisfactory.' Then he added: 'Do you have the forces? Will you be able to cope? If you have the forces, you need to do some beating.'[19] Stalin was determined to crack the nut of intellectual resistance to his policies. He spoke of Deborin's group:[20]

They occupy the dominant positions in philosophy, in natural science and in several fine questions of politics. You've got to be able to grasp this. On questions of natural science the Devil knows what they're doing; they are writing about Weismannism, etc., etc. – and this is all presented as Marxism.

It's necessary to scatter them and dig over all this dung which has accumulated in philosophy and natural science.

Stalin treated the philosophers in the party cell as troops to be deployed in a campaign against the enemy.

The motif was manifest: 'What sort of Marxism is this which separates philosophy from politics, theory from practice?'[21] Stalin was somewhat incoherent. Elsewhere in his commentary he accused Bukharin and Deborin of cloaking their politics in philosophical argumentation. But he was not worried by his contradictions. He wanted cultural life cleared of every trace of opposition to his policies. Narrowness, rigidity and ritualism were to be introduced. Lenin was to be raised as the unchallengeable totemic figure in the campaign. His *Materialism and Empiriocriticism*, that crude work on epistemology which Stalin had dismissed when it appeared in 1909, would be elevated to the status of a philosophical classic and all philosophers would have to take its postulates as axiomatic.[22]

Yet even Stalin could not totally ignore the huge disruptions to agriculture caused by his policies. Forewarned of the fate awaiting them, peasant communities in Ukraine, the north Caucasus, south Russia and central Asia took up arms. The urban squads of collectivisers were met with violent opposition. The Red Army, despite early official concerns about the loyalty of its conscripts, successfully suppressed such risings; and nowhere did the rebels manage to organise themselves across a broad territory as they had at the end of the Civil War. But the imposition of collective farms led to deep resentment. Antagonism to the authorities was ineradicable and the millions of peasants who were forced to give up their property and customs withdrew co-operation. Productivity fell away. A system proposed as the permanent solution to the problems of the rural economic sector might have yielded more grain for the towns but this was happening at the point of a rifle, and the perils of continuing mass collectivisation at the current rate became obvious.[23]

Several in Stalin's entourage witnessed on the trips around the country the appalling consequences of this policy. (They did this without

calling for a reversal of the general line: they were not Bukharinists.)
Stalin was unbudgeable from the general line of agrarian policy. The
most he would concede was that local implementation had been excessive and that officials in the provinces had misunderstood central policy.
On 2 March 1930 *Pravda* printed an article by him, 'Dizzy with Success',
which castigated over-zealous collectivisers:[24]

> It follows that the task of the party is to consolidate the achieved
> successes and to use them in a planned fashion for further move-
> ment forward.
>   But the successes have their dark side, especially when they
> are achieved 'easily' and, so to speak, through the mode of
> 'unexpectedness'.

He deceitfully insisted that it had always been his intention that collectivisation should be conducted on the voluntary principle. By then the
proportion of the USSR's agricultural households herded into collective
farms had risen to about 55 per cent.[25] Stalin maintained that local party
officials were guilty of 'excesses' and 'distortions'. Unlike the United
Opposition, he declared the central party leadership had not intended to
impose collectivisation by force and by decrees.

'Dizzy with Success' involved gargantuan hypocrisy. Although he was
primarily culpable for the recent acceleration, Stalin did not admit
blame. For a whole year he had goaded party officials to bully peasants
into collective farms. He had issued fearsome directives on dekulakisation. He had sacked and disgraced politicians who criticised the pace of
collectivisation; even his cronies in the Politburo had attracted his ire.
But he had a highly developed instinct for political self-preservation.
Embitterment against him was intense in society. The time had come to
place the blame on those who had faithfully implemented his wishes. He
got away with this. Confused lower-level officials allowed many millions
of households to revert to traditional land tenure. Quickly the percentage
of collective farms in the USSR's agriculture started falling: by early June
it was only twenty-three.[26] Yet Stalin, while willing to retreat tactically,
was fixed on his strategy: Soviet farming was to be forced into the
collectivist mould in short order. After the summer the campaign for
total collectivisation was resumed and in 1932 about 62 per cent of the
households engaged in agriculture belonged to collective farms. The
percentage was to rise to ninety in 1936.[27] This was achieved by means of
massively increased force applied with greater precision than before. The

result was turmoil in the countryside. The combination of violent seizure of grain stocks and violent reorganisation of farm tenure and employment resulted in famine across vast areas.

The economic premise of policy was not publicly revealed, but Stalin made it plain in an instruction to Molotov: 'Force up the export of grain to the maximum. This is the core of everything. If we export grain, credits will be forthcoming.'[28] A few days later, in August 1930, he repeated the message in case its content had not been fully accepted. Mikoyan had reported complacently about the level of wheat procurement across the USSR. This to Stalin was insufferable. The point was to go on raising that level and to 'force up' the grain export trade 'wildly'.[29] Nothing less than a hysterical campaign to collect and sell wheat abroad would satisfy him.

Again and again he reverted to tactical, temporary retreats such as had happened with 'Dizzy with Success'. On holiday by the Black Sea in August 1931 he saw enough for himself to know that collectivisation had reduced 'a series of districts in west Georgia *to starvation*'. But characteristically he blamed the resident party and OGPU officials: 'They don't understand that the Ukrainian methods of grain procurement, necessary and sensible in grain districts, are imprudent and harmful in non-grain districts which, moreover, have *no* industrial proletariat.' He even deplored the arrest of hundreds of people – not a reaction normally found in Stalin's career.[30] Stalin recommended that grain be shipped forthwith into west Georgia. Contrary to what is often thought, the Politburo under his leadership frequently made such decisions on emergency relief. But always the main strategic objective was kept in mind and eventually reapplied. Industrialisation and collectivisation were two sides of the same coin. The state needed to seize grain for export in order to finance the expansion of mining and manufacturing output. Stalin left no one in the Kremlin in doubt about this.

He barked out the case for driving the economic transformation at a frenetic pace in a speech to a conference of industrial officials and managers on 4 February 1931:[31]

To slacken the tempos would be to fall behind. And the backward get beaten. We don't want to be beaten. No, that's not what we want. The history of old Russia consisted, among other things, in her being ceaselessly beaten for her backwardness. She was beaten by the Mongol khans. She was beaten by the Turkish beys. She was beaten by the Swedish feudal rulers. She was beaten by the Polish–

Lithuanian lords. She was beaten by the Anglo-French capitalists. She was beaten by the Japanese barons. Everyone gave her a beating for her backwardness. For military backwardness, for cultural backwardness, for state backwardness, for industrial backwardness, for agricultural backwardness. They beat her because it was profitable and could be done with impunity. You remember the words of the pre-revolutionary poet: 'You are wretched, you are abundant, you are mighty, you are powerless, Mother Russia.'

The language had an emotional intensity he had not used since Lenin's funeral. The sonorous phrases hit home like a hammer. The patriotic appeal was unmistakable. The simple metaphor of 'beating', repeated again and again, conveyed the urgency of the struggle ahead.

Stalin warned his audience: 'Such is the law of the exploiters: beat the backward and the weak. The wolf's law of capitalism. You are backward, you are weak – so you are in the wrong and therefore you can be beaten and enslaved.'[32] The solution, he insisted, was irresistible:[33]

We have fallen behind the advanced countries by fifty to a hundred years. We must close that gap in ten years. Either we do this or we'll be crushed.

This is what our obligations before the workers and peasants of the USSR dictate to us.

He had no doubt about what could be achieved. At a May Day reception in 1933 he was to declare:[34]

If the Russians are armed with tanks, aircraft and a marine fleet, they're invincible, invincible.

But they cannot advance badly armed in the absence of technology, and the whole history of old Russia is summed up in this.

The Leader's voice in his 1931 speech to the industrial officials and managers had confirmed that there would be no vacillation. The course of rapid industrialisation and collectivisation had been set and there would be no deviation from it. Leader, party and state were wholly determined to reach the plotted destination. Firmness and courage were required. But Stalin was confident. In a sentence that was quickly picked up by official propagandists he declared: 'There are no fortresses that could not be stormed by Bolsheviks.' Looking across the audience, he moved to the finale of his speech:[35]

We have carried out a series of the hardest tasks. We have over-thrown capitalism. We have constructed large-scale socialist indus-try. We have turned the middle peasant on to the path of socialism. We've done the most important thing from the viewpoint of construction. There's still a little left to do: to learn technology and to master science. And when we do that, we'll have tempos which at present we daren't even dream about.

And we'll do that if we really want to!

Stalin was a bureaucrat, conspirator and killer and his politics were of a monstrous species. Yet he was also inspiring. Nobody listening to him on that occasion could fail to be impressed by his performance.

He was summoning his subordinates, in the republic and the provinces as well as in Moscow, to effect a gigantic political and economic transmutation. He knew that he could not know everything that went on. He was adept at getting thousands of officials to show the required zeal by setting out a general policy or handing down fixed delivery quotas. Many subordinates were appalled by the 'excesses'. But many others – out of conviction, fear or ambition – co-operated eagerly. Once the project had been formulated in 1928–9, officialdom in all Soviet institutions competed with each other to obtain a share of the increased resources. They also aspired to the power and privileges dangled as a bait in front of them. The direction of policy had been made abundantly clear and they wanted to take advantage of the journey about to be embarked upon.[36]

His summons was successful. The First Five-Year Plan, scheduled to last to the end of 1933, was completed a year ahead of schedule. National income had nearly doubled since the tax-year 1927–8. Gross industrial output had risen by a remarkable 137 per cent. Within industry, the output of capital goods registered a still more impressive increase of 285 per cent. The total employed labour force had soared from 11.3 mil-lion under the New Economic Policy to 22.8 million. The figures have to be treated with caution. Stalin and his associates were never averse to claiming more for their achievements than they should have done; and indeed they themselves derived information from lower echelons of party and government which systematically misled them. Disruption was everywhere in the economy.[37] Ukraine, south Russia and Kazakhstan were starving. The Gulag heaved with prisoners. Nevertheless the econ-omic transformation was no fiction. The USSR under Stalin's rule had been pointed decisively in the direction of becoming an industrial, urban society. This had been his great objective. His gamble was paying off for him, albeit not for his millions of victims. Magnitogorsk and the White Sea–Baltic Canal were constructed at the expense of the lives of Gulag convicts, Ukrainian peasants and even undernourished, overworked factory labourers.

25. ASCENT TO SUPREMACY

Stalin had once paraded before the party as the paladin of Lenin's New Economic Policy. As Party General Secretary he had ordered searches of the archives and exposed every disagreement between his enemies – Trotski, Kamenev, Zinoviev and Bukharin – and Lenin. Stalin himself had fallen out badly with Lenin in 1922–3. Yet when Trotski's American supporter Max Eastman published documents on that dispute in 1925, Stalin got the Politburo to command Trotski to reject them as forgeries. Implicitly he was making the claim that he alone loyally tended the flame of Lenin's memory.

Prudence held him back from announcing the NEP's abandonment. In economics, moreover, there was more than a hint of Trotski's ideas in his new measures. Better for Stalin to pretend that he was building up the legacy of Lenin. At the same time, though, he wanted to assert his status as supreme party leader. It was no longer enough to appear as his master's voice: Stalin had to impose his own persona. A fine chance came with his fiftieth-birthday celebrations in December 1929.[1] *Pravda* fired a barrage of eulogies about his past and present contribution to the revolutionary cause. There had been nothing like it since Lenin's fiftieth birthday in April 1920 when Stalin had been among the leading eulogists. Stalin could gloat. He had survived the storms of censure about Lenin's Testament and subsequent public criticism in the decade. At the banquet in Stalin's honour he listened to the series of speeches itemising his virtues and achievements. The underestimated General Secretary had scaled the peak of the All-Union Communist Party, the Soviet state and the Communist International.

He behaved imperiously. Earlier he had been renowned for his common touch and had seemed so 'democratic' in comparison with most other party leaders.[2] A young Nikita Khrushchëv never forgot the impression Stalin made on him at the Fourteenth Party Congress in 1925. His Ukrainian delegation asked Stalin to have his photograph taken with them. Petrov the photographer shouted instructions about the pose he wanted. Stalin quipped: 'Comrade Petrov loves to order people around. He orders people around even though that's now prohibited here. No more ordering people around!'[3] Khrushchëv and his friends were entranced: Stalin appeared one of their own sort. It was a proletarian revolution, they thought, and a working-class fellow was running the party which had made it. But the gap between him and his followers was widening. He demanded complete obedience and often interfered in their private lives. Taking a dislike to Kaganovich's beard, he ordered him to shave it off and threatened to do the job himself with his wife Nadya's scissors.[4] Probably Stalin wanted the Politburo to be identified with beardless modernity, but he had a crusty way of obtaining his purposes.

He had clambered up the ziggurat of power whose apex was the Politburo. Its members took the great decisions on political, economic, national and military policy. The Politburo's agenda regularly included items on culture, religion and law. Stalin had no rivals among its members. These included Vyacheslav Molotov, Lazar Kaganovich, Anastas Mikoyan and Sergo Ordzhonikidze. Though dominant in the Politburo, Stalin did not chair it. The tradition persisted that the chairman of Sovnarkom should perform this task.[5] Stalin understood the instincts of the party. Like the Roman emperor Augustus who avoided awarding himself the title of king (*rex*) while founding a monarchy, he sacrificed personal vanity to the reality of supreme power. His main title was Party General Secretary – and sometimes he just signed himself as Secretary.[6] His most important supporters were Molotov and Kaganovich. Both were determined and ideologically committed politicians – and Stalin had steadily imposed his will on them. They referred to him as the Boss (*Khozyain*). (They did this out of his hearing. Although he allowed a few old comrades to call him Koba, his growing preference was for fellow politicians to use 'comrade Stalin' or 'Iosif Vissarionovich'.) Scarcely an important Politburo matter was settled in contradiction of his wishes.

He never stopped working even on holiday by the Black Sea. His personal assistants went with him and he dealt with important matters requiring his immediate adjudication by telegram. Molotov and Kaganovich kept in regular contact. Stalin himself continued to consult other communist leaders on the coast: they queued to have meetings with him. But this was a sideshow to the main drama. Moscow was Stalin's preoccupation and he ensured that the two men he left in the capital shared his general vision of what kind of revolution was desirable. He had chosen well.

When he was in Moscow, too, Stalin devolved much responsibility to Molotov and Kaganovich. He bothered ever less frequently to convoke the Politburo. From seventy-five sessions in 1924 the number declined to fifty-three in 1928 and down again to twenty-four in 1933. Decisions were taken by polling the members by telephone, and this facilitated his ability to manipulate and control.[7] It was usually Kaganovich who chaired the Orgburo and Secretariat. In September 1930 Stalin wrote to Molotov about the need to get rid of Rykov and for Molotov to take his place.[8] Others in Stalin's entourage felt unhappy – and perhaps also jealous – about the plan for Molotov's promotion, and Voroshilov suggested that Stalin himself should take over Sovnarkom so as to bring about the 'unification of leadership'. Molotov lacked 'the gifts of a strategist'.[9] Having enjoyed the praise, Stalin rejected the advice and gave the post to Molotov. He wanted to concentrate his own energies on the party and on the Comintern while knowing that Molotov would loyally carry out the tasks given to him.

The Orgburo, Secretariat and Sovnarkom dealt with matters which had to be referred to the Politburo if internal dispute arose. Stalin was kept informed about everything impinging on general policy or his personal interests. The three leaders anyway had to stick together. The Soviet economy had been exposed to the maelstrom of forced-rate industrialisation and forcible mass collectivisation. Popular disturbances were commonplace. The internal party opposition had been crushed but not liquidated, and the concern remained that Zinoviev, Kamenev, Bukharin or even Trotski might return to exploit the situation.

Stalin's supporters also ran the various People's Commissariats and other state institutions. No room was allowed for half-heartedness. If supporters wished to keep their posts they had to comply to the full. In September 1929 his Chekist brother-in-law Stanisław Redens brought the news to Stalin's attention that OGPU chief Vladimir Menzhinski had disciplined his officials for 'diseased phenomena' in their work. This was an attempt to put a brake on the implementation of official policies. Stalin wanted zeal and results, not procedural regularity. He wrote to Menzhinski indicating the 'evil' of his ways.[10] Menzhinski's deputy Genrikh Yagoda risked similar reproof a year later when he wrote to Stalin about the 'crude compulsion of poor and middling peasants to enter the kolkhozes'.[11] Stalin also kept up the pressure on the Party Central Control Commission. This was the body which adjudicated cases of disobedience to party policies; it was also meant to protect Bolsheviks against an over-mighty central party apparatus but this function had passed into desuetude. Stalin used the Central Control Commission under Ordzhonikidze to bully the oppositionist groups out of existence – and he was not slow to upbraid his ally Ordzhonikidze for lack of zeal in prosecuting troublemakers.[12]

Joint meetings of the Central Committee and the Central Control Commission were also used as a means of getting Stalin's favoured policies validated. He pulled this trick whenever he thought he might meet with criticism in the Central Committee. The result was satisfactory for him. The OGPU, Central Control Commission and Central Committee were bodies which supervised all Soviet public life, and they were held under the authority of Stalin and his leading group.

Having defeated the Left Opposition and Right Deviation, Stalin allowed individual oppositionists back into public life on strict terms. If they petitioned for rehabilitation he demanded that they should recant like an accused heretic before the Spanish Inquisition. Abject public self-criticism was demanded and, often enough, obtained. Many Trotskyists in particular were attracted by the high priority accorded to fast industrial growth; never having been principled democrats, they forgot their demands for the restoration of democracy to party and soviets and joined the Stalin group. Pyatakov and Preobrazhenski were among them. Not that Stalin was going to trust them regardless of what they said in public. In September 1930 he wrote to Molotov:[13]

> Careful surveillance needs to be maintained for a while over Pyatakov, that genuinely rightist Trotskyist (a second Sokolnikov) who now represents the most harmful element in the composition of the block of Rykov–Pyatakov plus the Kondratevite–Defeatist mood of bureaucrats from the Soviet apparatus.

Stalin remained uneasy about factional regrouping. His operational code was: once an oppositionist, always an oppositionist. If given reason to re-expel adversaries from public life, he was unlikely to take a kindly approach.

This tendency to see conspiratorial linkages among those who were not on his side was detectable in a note he sent to Ordzhonikidze in 1930. The OGPU had conducted interrogations of a large number of former Imperial Army officers and discovered that several had put their political hopes in Mikhail Tukhachevski. Although not a scintilla of proof was found that Tukhachevski planned a *coup d'état*, Stalin's suspicion deepened:[14]

At any rate, Tukhachevski has turned out to be captive to anti-Soviet elements and has been especially worked over by anti-Soviet elements from the ranks of the Rightists. That's what comes out of the materials [of the interrogations]. Is this possible? Of course it's possible once it has failed to be excluded. Obviously the Rightists are ready to go to the lengths of a military dictatorship if only this would free them from the C[entral] C[ommittee], from kolkhozes and sovkhozes, from Bolshevik rates of development of industry.

Stalin was in no doubt: Tukhachevski, Kondratev and Bukharin were leading figures in this disloyal 'camp' of the Rightists.[15] Only after the OGPU had done its work did he allow himself to believe that Tukhachevski was '100% clean'.[16]

He drove his ideas like iron bolts into the minds of his associates. Molotov, Ordzhonikidze, Kaganovich, Voroshilov and a few others were his confidants, and his implicit objective was to form a fanatical Kremlin gang devoted to himself as boss. Anyone who got in his way was expelled. In October 1930 he took offence at the People's Commissar for Finances. He wrote to the Politburo ordering: 'Hang Bryukhanov by the balls for all his present and future sins. If his balls hold out, consider him acquitted in court; if they don't hold out, drown him in the river.'[17] Stalin drew a picture of Bryukhanov suspended in the air and attached to a pulley by a rope which was tugging his penis and testicles back through his legs. Sometimes, though, he aimed his ridicule at himself. Writing to Voroshilov in March 1929, he mocked his own grandiose image: 'World Leader [*Vozhd*]? Go fuck his mother!'[18]

Yet although Stalin could chaff himself in this fashion, he let no gang members do the same to him: his dignity mattered a great deal to him. So too did his authority. It was he who decided who could join and who should leave the gang. He also told the gang who its enemies were. He cajoled the members to regard their critics as the worst renegades. Indeed by 1932 he told Kaganovich to get *Pravda* to 'curse crudely and sharply' not only Mensheviks and Socialist-Revolutionaries but also Right Deviationists and Trotskyists as being advocates of the restoration of capitalism.[19] The intention was evident. Stalin and the Kremlin gang were to regard themselves as the sole repository of political wisdom and socialist commitment. The people of the USSR should be led to believe that only the ascendant party leadership would truly try to supply society with material and social welfare and that anti-Stalinists would drag the country down and back to the bad old days of greedy factory owners, bankers and landlords. Vilification of opponents should therefore be taken to the point of the fantasy that Bukharin and Trotski were in league with the capitalist West.

Stalin turned all criticism of himself into a drama. Slight divergence from his wishes was treated as personal betrayal and political treason. He transmitted this attitude to his followers and got them to gang up on those whom he wished to topple. On vacation in September 1929, he sent a furious note to Politburo members Molotov, Voroshilov and Ordzhonikidze:[20]

> Have you read Rykov's speech? In my opinion it represents the speech of *a non-party Soviet bureaucrat* disguised by the tone of someone 'loyal' and 'sympathetic' to the Soviets. Not a word about the party! Not a word about the Right Deviation! Not a word about the party's achievements which Rykov dirtily accredits to himself but which in fact were made through struggle with the Rightists, including Rykov himself . . . I have discovered that Rykov is continuing to act as [Politburo] *chairman* for you on Mondays and Thursdays. Is this true? If it's true, why are you permitting such a comedy? Who needs it and for what purpose?

Molotov instantly obeyed: 'It's obvious to me . . . that St[alin] is right. My only disagreement is that we're "sheltering" Rykov. We must, however, correct the matter as proposed by St[alin].'[21]

It was easy for Stalin, the Soviet political counterpart of Al Capone, to find new gang members.[22] As his previous supporters were found wanting in zeal or efficiency, he promoted others. Some were among the most unappealing figures in Soviet public life. Andrei Vyshinski, a former Menshevik, became Chief Prosecutor in 1935. His basic proposition that confession (which could be obtained by torture) was the queen of the modalities of judicial proof was music to Stalin's ears. Lavrenti Beria, First Party Secretary of the Transcaucasian Federation until his promotion in 1938 to the leadership of the NKVD (which incorporated the OGPU from 1934), had a penchant for beating his prisoners personally. Nikolai Yezhov, promiscuous bisexual and alcoholic, was even quicker to jump to the worst conclusions about individuals than Stalin was. Stalin was to make him NKVD chief in 1936. Others such as Nikita Khrushchëv, who headed the Moscow City Party Committee from 1935, had a decent side; but this did not stop him from doing his share of killing in the Great Terror.

Stalin did not overlook the Comintern. Bukharin had supervised its

Executive Committee on the Politburo's behalf since Zinoviev's demise. With the falling out between Stalin and Bukharin in 1928, this body became an area of contention, and Bukharin was ejected from the Executive Committee in April 1929. For some time Stalin relied upon Dmitri Manuilski and Osip Pyatnitski to run the show for him in the Comintern. They held the main European communist parties to account. A tight hierarchy controlled what went on in German, Italian and French communism. The system of command was reinforced by the presence in Moscow of leading and trusted leaders on secondment from their native countries. Among them were Ernst Meyer, Palmiro Togliatti and Maurice Thorez. But the Comintern did not limit itself to long-distance control. Agents were sent on lengthy missions. Thus the Hungarian Eugen Fried was dispatched to Paris and kept in regular contact with the Politburo of the French Communist Party; and communists in France attempted little without prior sanction being obtained from him.[23] The Comintern had been strictly controlled since its foundation in 1919; but the degree of interference rose in the 1930s as Stalin sought to ensure that nothing done by communists abroad would damage the interests of what he was attempting in the USSR.

It did not come easily to Stalin to offer a reasoned critique. In fact it did not come to him at all. He was a political streetfighter: no holds were barred. He believed this was what the situation required. Although he confected a risible image of his enemies, his worries about the position of himself and his associates were not entirely unrealistic. They had jerked the rudder of policies away from the NEP and set a course for rapid and violent economic transformation. The gang had to take responsibility for the consequences. They could expect no mercy unless they could guarantee an increase in economic and military capacity. It made sense to blackguard the critics in case things went wrong. Citing Lenin's words at the Tenth Party Congress in 1921, Stalin told Kaganovich that factional dissent from the ascendant leadership's line would result in the emergence of 'White Guard' tendencies and 'the defence of capitalism'.[24] Lenin had said no such thing. But this did not matter to Stalin: he wanted to sharpen the siege mentality already experienced by his fellow Politburo members and the repetition of outlandish accusations suited this desire.

While rehabilitating several repentant members of the United Opposition, Stalin showed no indulgence to the unapologetic Trotski. In January 1929 the Politburo discussed what to do with the man who was capable of causing them most trouble. From exile in Alma-Ata, Trotski was producing ripples in Moscow. His remaining supporters tended his memory in hope that his restoration to power would not long be postponed. Even members of Stalin's entourage urged him to bring Trotski back since the basic official economic orientation was what Trotski had long recommended (and Aaron Solts said to Ordzhonikidze that Trotski would bring greater intelligence to the policies).[25] Trotski offered no word of compromise to Stalin, who for his part feared that until he got rid of his old enemy there would always be a danger that Trotski would exploit whatever difficulties arose in the First Five-Year Plan.

Yet Stalin did not yet call for his physical liquidation. No veteran Bolshevik had been executed for political dissent. The alternative to Alma-Ata was deportation from the USSR. Already in summer 1927 Stalin had considered sending him to Japan.[26] The Politburo came to its decision on 10 January 1929 and Trotski was expelled for 'anti-Soviet work'.[27] Turkey was the destination chosen. Trotski and his family set sail across the Black Sea on the steamship *Ilich*. The Politburo calculated that he would be shunned by the parties of the Comintern (as he was) and ignored by the world's capitalist powers (as he was). But Trotski was not finished. He started to publish a regular *Bulletin of the Opposition* from abroad. Expelled from party and country, he had nothing to lose. What was disconcerting to Stalin was that Trotski's contact with the USSR remained unbroken. The *Bulletin* reported on controversies in the central party leadership. Trotski knew the Moscow political gossip; he also dredged his memory for instances of Stalin's stupidity and nastiness and described them in his autobiography[28] – and he knew that Stalin hated being ridiculed or criticised. Distribution of the *Bulletin* was clandestine, but this had also been the case with the Bolshevik faction before 1917. Deportation was not the cure for the ills of Trotskyism.

Stalin did not repeat the gaffe of letting an oppositionist leader out of his clutches. In summer 1929 he learned that Vissarion Lominadze and a few other second-rank Bolsheviks were criticising the style and policies of his leadership. In the following year there was further trouble. Lominadze had been talking also to the Chairman of the RSFSR Sovnarkom, Sergei Syrtsov. Stalin drew the worst possible conclusion, writing to Molotov:[29]

I'm sending you the two communications of [the interrogated informer] Reznikov about the anti-party – and essentially Right-Deviationist – factional Syrtsov–Lominadze grouping. Inconceivable

vileness. All the details point to Reznikov's communications corre-
sponding to reality. They were toying with a *coup d'état*, they were
playing at being the Politburo, and they've ended up in a complete
collapse.

Stalin's suspicions were too fantastic even for Molotov, and Lominadze
and Syrtsov were simply dismissed from the Central Committee.

The atmosphere of a political witch-hunt was thickening. Nikolai
Bauman was sacked from the Central Committee Secretariat for being
mildly conciliatory to the former members of the United Opposition.
Stalin, Molotov and Kaganovich were edgy. Their policies involved a
huge gamble. In seeking to consolidate the regime and to deepen the
Revolution they were attacking a wide front of enemies in politics, the
economy and society. This required the vigorous deployment of party,
armed forces and the OGPU. The leaders of these institutions had to be
trustworthy. Each institution had to be strengthened in personnel and
material resources to carry out its tasks. But, as the state's power was
increased, the danger arose that such leaders had a growing capacity to
undermine the Politburo. Lukewarm followers were of no use to Stalin.
Unequivocal support alone would do.

The firmness shown by Stalin in 1930–1 failed to discourage confidential criticism in the upper echelons of the party. Although the
Syrtsov–Lominadze group had been broken up, other little groupings
sprouted up. One consisted of Nikolai Eismont, Vladimir Tolmachev
and A. P. Smirnov. Denounced by informers in November 1932 and
interrogated by the OGPU, they confessed to verbal disloyalty. But this
was not enough for Stalin. The joint plenum of the Central Committee
and the Central Control Commission in January 1933 condemned the
leaders for having formed an 'anti-party grouping' and took the opportunity to reprimand Rykov and Tomski for maintaining contact with
'anti-party elements'.[30] Yet no sooner had one grouping been dealt with
than another was discovered. Martemyan Ryutin, a Moscow district
party functionary, hated Stalin's personal dictatorship. He and several
like-minded friends gathered in their homes for evening discussions and
Ryutin produced a pamphlet demanding Stalin's removal from office.
Ryutin was arrested. Stalin, interpreting the pamphlet as a call for an
assassination attempt, urged Ryutin's execution. In the end he was
sentenced to ten years in the Gulag.[31]

Stalin never forgot a slight or missed a chance to hit back. He would
wait as long as necessary to take his chance. Every tall tree he chopped

down satiated an ego which had been injured by years of underappreciation and mockery. His memory was extraordinary, and he had his future victims marked down in a very long list. He extended his distrust to his allies and subordinates. Stalin demanded total loyalty. His daughter Svetlana, writing a reverential memoir in 1967, recalled:[32]

> If he cast out of his heart someone who had been known to him for a long time and if in his soul he had already translated that person into the ranks of 'enemies', it was impossible to hold a conversation with him about that person.

This was his way. Once an enemy always an enemy! And even if he was compelled for internal party reasons to show mercy, he always intended to slake his thirst for vengeance in due course.

Bukharin belatedly appreciated this. Until 1928 he had been content to have his rough, aggressive comrade at his side. When he fell out with Stalin, he knew it would be hard to get back into his favour. Still he went on trying to arrange his readmission to public life. He wrote pleading letters to Stalin. He continued to visit and stay in Stalin's dacha at Zubalovo, talking at length with Nadya Allilueva and playing with their children. Foolishly, however, he went on blabbing about his genuine opinions to other oppositionist leaders. He sometimes did this on the telephone. Little did he suspect that the OGPU provided Stalin with transcripts of its phone-taps. Bukharin, Kamenev and Zinoviev were providing material which would make Stalin's ultimate retaliation truly terrible. He knew their flattery and obeisance were insincere.

His close associates were equally determined to consolidate the authority of their gang. But almost always in the course of the First Five-Year Plan it was Stalin who took the initiative in persecuting or suppressing the group's enemies. No one was more suspicious and aggressive. Yet his maladjusted personality was not the only factor at work. Although he exaggerated the scale of immediate menace to the leading group, he and his associates had cause for anxiety. Trotski was active abroad. Bukharin became editor of the government's newspaper *Izvestiya* ('News') in 1934; Zinoviev and Kamenev returned to prominence around the same time. An alternative leadership in waiting had re-formed itself. The Bolshevik party's experience in 1917 showed how quickly a small political group could turn a country upside down. Stalin had to watch out. The fact that lesser fry among his own supporters – Lominadze, Syrtsov, Eismont, Tolmachev and Smirnov – had proved disloyal made him still edgier.

Furthermore, expressions of disgust about 'peasant questions' were commonplace in the Red Army. Since the armed forces were imposing official agrarian policy, this had to be a cause for concern. Soldiers widely hated the collective farms. Rumours were rife. In 1930 a story flew around the Moscow Military District that Voroshilov had killed Stalin.[33] The implication was obvious: a yearning existed for a change in policy. Having identified himself as the protagonist of radical change, Stalin had made himself the target of unpopularity.

At every level of authority in the USSR there was discontent. The regional party officials felt a growing concern about Stalin's unpredictable and violent inclinations; they did not warm to the possibility that he might go on putting pressure on them for increased rates of economic growth – and the First Five-Year Plan had made such officials more powerful than under the NEP. The party had been the vanguard institution of the Five-Year Plan. As the state took private economic sectors into its ownership and as the whole economy expanded, so each regional party official acquired enormous authority. With this authority, though, there came massive responsibility. Many officials, harassed by the Kremlin's imposition of production quotas and acquainted with the enormous disorder and discontent across their regions, yearned for a period of retrenchment rather than continued rapid transformation. The leadership of several People's Commissariats in Moscow and the provinces felt similar unease about Stalin and the Politburo. The Soviet state, while gaining much from the policies of the First Five-Year Plan, was far from being reconciled to unthinking acceptance of whatever policies were handed down from on high.

Below the stratosphere of party and governmental officialdom there were millions of malcontents. Oppositionists in their thousands were waiting for Stalin's fall. Outside the ranks of Bolshevism there were still more irreconcilables. Most Socialist-Revolutionaries, Mensheviks and Kadets had ceased political activity; but they were willing to start operating again if the opportunity arose. The same was true of Borotbists, Dashnaks, Musavatists and the many other national parties which had been suppressed in the Civil War. Then there were the priests, mullahs and rabbis who had suffered persecution by the Bolsheviks, and, although up to three million people had emigrated after the October Revolution, there remained plenty of former aristocrats, bankers, industrialists, landowners and shopkeepers who continued to long for the Soviet state's collapse.

Years of state violence and popular hardship had deepened the reservoir of anger with the regime. Kulaks and their supporters had been killed and deported. Industrial managers and other experts had been persecuted. 'Bourgeois nationalists', including Russian ones, had been imprisoned. Remaining religious leaders had been persecuted. Show trials had been organised in Moscow and the provinces. The labour-camp system held a million convicts. Whole zones in north Russia, Siberia and Kazakhstan were inhabited by involuntary colonists who lived and worked in conditions scarcely better than prison. Hostility to the regime was not confined to those who had suffered arrest or deportation. Peasants on the collective farms, especially in the famine areas, hated the agricultural system imposed on the villages. Workers were annoyed by the failure of the authorities to fulfil their promise to raise the popular standard of living. Even the newly promoted administrators in politics and the economy contained many who disliked the harsh practices of the regime. The display of obedience did not tell the whole truth. A multitude of individuals suffered from the punitive, arbitrary workings of the Soviet order and might be counted on to support almost any movement against Stalin and his policies.

This was not the way the official propagandists presented the situation, and fellow travellers around the world replicated their triumphal complacency; indeed the idea that Stalin had no external reason for feeling insecure has become the standard view upon the condition of Soviet politics by the early 1930s. Dictatorships, however, are not immune to political instability, and the Bolshevik leaders sensed that the important strata in society would oust them if the opportunity ever offered itself. Stalin had won several victories. He had instigated forced-rate industrialisation and collectivisation to the accompaniment of massive repression. He had imposed the aims of 'socialism in one country'. He had harried the former internal party oppositions. He had become the dictator of the USSR in all but name. He and his associates were not without support. Promotees enjoyed their new privileges. Members of the Komsomol and young party activists were enthused by the project of revolutionary transformation. Cultural activists admired the anti-illiteracy campaign. Military personnel relished the strengthening of the armed forces. There was an appreciation that while the Western economies were being disrupted by the effects of the Wall Street Crash, the USSR was making a great industrial advance.

Stalin and his associates would not have lasted in office without such support. It was not yet clear whether the support outweighed the hostility in state and society. For the moment no one could challenge Stalin. He had reached the coveted summit of power. But the summit was an exposed spot, and it remained to be seen whether he would pay for having attained this position of eminence.

26. THE DEATH OF NADYA

Stalin became ever more isolated from daily life in the USSR as concern for his personal security grew. He no longer kept open office in the Secretariat. He visited no collective farm. While on vacation in Abkhazia allegedly he once went to inspect a market; but the Sukhum authorities, eager to impress him, got the stallholders to lower their prices for the duration of his visit: thus he was prevented from discovering the high cost of living.[1] In any case, he never inspected the factories and mines being constructed; and when he went to inspect the White Sea Canal, his trip was announced in the press only days after it had taken place.[2] The OGPU had picked up a potential assassin, Yakov Ogarëv, outside the Kremlin in November 1931. Ogarëv, however, had been so surprised by Stalin's unexpected appearance on Red Square that he failed to pull out his revolver.[3] Security concerns alone did not explain Stalin's withdrawal from view. The fact was that he had set up a political structure which no longer required him to get out and about. Whether in the Kremlin office or at his dachas, he could give his orders and prod his subordinates into carrying them out.

Political cloistering did nothing to lessen the strains in his family. His son Yakob tried to kill himself in 1929; it was a botched attempt which earned Stalin's contempt rather than sympathy. Marital relations with Nadya were tense. He was extremely gruff to her and never admitted to fault. Quite possibly Stalin continued to have the odd fling with young communists; and, even if he was faithful to Nadya, she did not always believe him and was driven mad with jealousy. Yet it had never been his way to compromise in personal relationships, least of all with women. Joseph's attitudes were not the only reason why she got angry. Another factor was her mental condition. Although its precise nature remains unclear, probably it would nowadays be categorised as some kind of schizophrenia. Days of quietude alternated with explosive aggression. Stalin could never be sure what awaited him in the Kremlin flat or at the Zubalovo dacha – and his insensitivity to her plight was driving her to despair. Nadya had always been strong-willed. Stalin had been the love of her life, and, unlike others in her family, she did not have extra-marital dalliances. Feeling rejected and underappreciated, she could take it no more in 1926 and decamped to Leningrad, intending to divorce Joseph.[4]

Yet she yielded to his pleadings and gave the marriage another try. She wanted no more children; according to her daughter, she had already had two abortions.[5] Stalin had not obstructed her from registering as a student at the Industrial Academy. Letters between husband and wife were tender. His routine was established: every summer he would go to the south of the RSFSR. Usually the destination was Sochi on the north-east coast of the Black Sea. Nadya filled her letters with news of the children, the household, the weather and her progress as a student.

The Stalins decided to consult over her mental condition with foreign medical experts. Since the Treaty of Rapallo in 1922 it had been normal for members of the Soviet elite to go to German clinics and spas. Stalin was one of the few who spurned this privilege; distrusting doctors and disliking foreign countries, he never considered travelling abroad for his healthcare. Georgi Chicherin, his Foreign Affairs Commissar, rebuked him: 'How good it would be if you, Stalin, were to change your appearance and travel for a certain time abroad with a genuine inter-preter rather than a tendentious one. Then you'd see reality!'[6] But Stalin approved of Nadya's trip. No less than his wife, he urgently wanted her to get cured. Even for her, however, permission had to come from on high. The Party Orgburo and Secretariat took from April to July 1930 to process her request, supported by her physicians in Moscow, to spend a month in Germany. The final sanction was signed by Stalin, Molotov, Kaganovich and I. N. Smirnov.[7] Stalin arranged for Nadya to send him personal letters through the diplomatic post.[8] She met her brother Pavel and his wife Yevgenia on her trip; and after seeing the doctors she returned in time for the start of the Industrial Academy term in September.[9]

The medical papers are missing;[10] but according to Nadya's niece Kira Allilueva the diagnosis was a fusion of the cranial seams.[11] Joseph wrote affectionate letters to her. Throughout these months – before, during and after her journey – he used the sentimental code they had developed over the years, dropping particular letters from phrases like 'deep kisses many times'.[12]

Her health, though, did not improve. In 1932 she turned to Soviet physicians for advice on what appear to have been abdominal complaints. It has been mooted that they resulted from an earlier abortion.[13] What seems to have happened is that a planned surgical operation was postponed on medical grounds. This was what she confided to her Kremlin maid Alexandra Korchagina.[14] Nadya fretted as much as ever; and although she made no further attempt to break free from her husband, the marriage remained an unsettled one. He could hardly be bothered with her. In a period where he and his propagandists were touting the importance of films, Joseph did not bestir himself by taking her to the cinema. When he was not drinking with his uncouth comrades, he went on flirting with women. The children brought no solace to Nadya. Severe and demanding, she gave them little of the cuddling normal in other families. Only when they were apart did Joseph and Nadya get back on affectionate terms. This was little comfort for a woman who was expected to give the maximum of psychological support to her husband without ever being able to count on his reciprocation.

Nadya did not limit her assistance to family matters but also supported him politically. Stories spread that, like her confidant Bukharin, she detested the agricultural collectivisation campaign. In fact she was a wife who jealously guarded her husband's political position. On 2 May 1931 she wrote to Sergo Ordzhonikidze about Industrial Academy affairs. Her claim was that Stalin's injunction for the right sort of 'technical specialists' to be trained was being ignored. Yet she insisted that her fellow students were not to know and the letter was to be destroyed.[15] She was snitching on people in the Industrial Academy in support of the line of the country's ruling clique.

Yet the dual problems of her medical condition and her relationship with Joseph had her on the brink of eruption. The only surprise is that no one properly understood this. Close friends like Tamara Khazanova (by now married to Andrei Andreev) and Molotov's wife Polina Zhemchuzhina knew of her troubles but failed to understand the depths of her misery. Nadya felt terribly lonely. She found certain kinds of social situation very disturbing. She tended to get distressed when Joseph got together with his cronies and their wives. The ruling group's tradition was to gather for supper at the Voroshilovs' Kremlin flat for a celebration of the October Revolution anniversary on 7 November. (Sovnarkom had adopted the Gregorian calendar in 1918, moving the date by thirteen days and thereby changing the month in which the Revolution had taken place.) Always there was excessive drinking and a lot of crude banter. In 1932 Nadya made a special effort to dress up to look her best. It made no difference to Joseph's behaviour. Late in the evening he flirted with the wife of Alexander Yegorov, who had served with him in the Soviet–Polish War. Natalya Yegorova was wearing a glamorous frock and behaving coquettishly. Apparently he did his crude trick of rolling a bit of bread into a ball and flicking it at her. Nadya was seized with jealousy, and stormed out of the gathering. Witnesses dismissively put this down to her 'Gipsy blood'.[16]

There are other versions of what happened before she left. One story has it that Stalin yelled across at Nadya using the familiar 'you' form in Russian and that she took exception to this. Another is that he threw a lighted cigarette at her. But the likeliest version is that he was indeed making eyes at Natalya Yegorova and that Nadya could take it no longer. What happened next is more definitely recorded. Polina Zhemchuzhina ran after her into the cold night air. Nadya was extraordinarily tense and Polina walked her around the Kremlin grounds in an attempt to calm her down. Then Nadya went by herself to the family flat while Polina went back to the party.[17]

Nadya's thoughts plunged into existential darkness. Some years previously her brother had made her the present of a gun; despite looking like a toy pistol (as Stalin later recalled), it was a lethal weapon.[18] Seating herself on the bed, she pointed it at her heart and shot herself. Her corpse was found by the morning maid. The panicking household staff made a call to Abel Enukidze. As Central Committee member and administrator of the Kremlin site, he would have the authority to decide on appropriate action. As it happened, Enukidze was also Nadya's godfather.[19] Without hesitation he ordered that Stalin should be roused. The Stalins had taken to sleeping in separate rooms and Joseph was seemingly unaware of the consequences of his misbehaviour the night before. Doctors were summoned to ascertain the cause of death. This was not going to be a lengthy task: Nadya had shot herself through the heart. When Professors Rozanov and Kushner carried out the post-mortem after midday, the body was laid out on the bed. Near by was the small revolver. Death must have been instantaneous and, they concluded, had occurred eight to ten hours previously. Nadya had taken her own life. Rozanov and Kushner started to write their brief report at one o'clock.

The politicians were deciding what to reveal to the public.[20] It was thought inappropriate to tell the truth for fear of diminishing Stalin's prestige. Instead *Pravda* was asked to state that Nadya had died of the effects of appendicitis. Wives of the most prominent leaders signed a letter of condolence to Stalin. This too was published in the newspaper.

A funeral commission was selected, headed by Avel Enukidze. There was to be a cortège behind a horse-drawn carriage carrying her coffin. The mourners would gather on Red Square at three o'clock in the afternoon on 12 November and would walk across the city to the Novodevichi Monastery Cemetery. Such occasions were cause for official concern, and the OGPU was put in charge of the organisation and security of the proceedings. Orchestras were to be supplied by the OGPU and the Red Army. A short ceremony was to take place at the graveside. There would be two speakers: Kaganovich as Moscow City Committee Party Secretary and Kalashnikov, a representative from the Industrial Academy where she had been studying.[21] Stalin left the details to others. His public appearance on the day of the funeral was going to be an ordeal, and he did not volunteer to give a eulogy before the coffin was interred.

Despite what many subsequently suggested, he attended the ceremony. The cortège of mourners made its way on foot through the city. It was a day without snow. Crowds lined the streets. At the cemetery the open coffin was taken from the carriage and lowered into the hard earth. Kaganovich's oration briefly mentioned the deceased and ended with a request that communist party members should carry out the duties falling to them as a consequence of Stalin's personal loss. Kalashnikov gave a eulogy to Nadya as a fine and dedicated student.[22] The funeral was over within minutes. Stalin and his comrades returned by limousine to the Kremlin. A simple tombstone was erected over Nadya's grave, where it remains to this day.

When the Industrial Academy approached Stalin for permission to examine her working materials, he immediately consented and asked Anna Allilueva, Nadya's sister, to expedite this. Not for Stalin the usual possessiveness of the widower. He told Anna to inspect the safe with the assistance of Tamara Khazanova.[23] Nadya's daughter Svetlana was to claim that a suicide note was left behind; but Svetlana learned only many years later that her mother had died by her own hand, and her memoirs are anyway not always reliable. It anyway can hardly be assumed that such a note would necessarily explain everything. What is clear is that the official clampdown on information in 1932 served only to feed the growth of rumours. In diplomatic circles it was bruited that she had committed suicide.[24] Gossip was intense within the walls of the Kremlin. This was dangerous activity. Alexandra Korchagina, the maid of Joseph and Nadya, was denounced by other Kremlin domestic staff for saying that Stalin had killed her; she was sentenced to three years' corrective labour on the White Sea–Baltic Canal. Korchagina claimed that it was her own denouncers who had made such a statement about Stalin.[25] The denouncers themselves were arrested in the 1935 clear-out of Kremlin auxiliary staff.[26]

Indisputably Stalin was deeply shaken. 'I was a bad husband,' he admitted to Molotov: 'I never had time to take her to the cinema.'[27] This was hardly a full recognition of the scale of assistance he would have needed to give Nadya. But it signalled a degree of remorse. Significantly it also implied that circumstances, rather than his own demeanour, determined his contribution to the tragedy. He was also thinking as much about himself as about his deceased wife. His self-centredness grew. Within a few weeks he was blaming her directly and worrying about the fate of their children. The attempt on his own life by young Yakov Dzhughashvili came back to mind, and at a dinner with his friends he blurted out: 'How could Nadya, who so much condemned Yasha for such a step, go off and shoot herself? She did a very bad thing: she made a cripple out of me.' Alexander Svanidze, his brother-in-law by his first marriage, tried to mollify him by asking how she could leave her two children motherless. Stalin was angry: 'Why the children? They forgot her within a few days: it's me she made a cripple for life!' But then he proposed: 'Let's drink to Nadya!'[28]

Steadily he came to take a less charitable view of Nadya's suicide:[29]

> The children grew up without their mother, that was the trouble. Nannies, governesses – however ideal they might have been – could not replace their mother for them. Ah, Nadya, Nadya, what did you do and how much I and the children needed you!

He focused his thoughts on the harm done to the children and, above all, to himself. Sinking into introspection, he confided in no one. He told the children that their mother had died of natural causes. Tough and icy though he was in outward behaviour, Stalin's inner mood was touchy.

For some weeks there were worries that he too might do away with himself. He was pale and inattentive to his daily needs. His characteristic earthy sense of humour disappeared. It was weeks before he started to pull himself around. Seeking companionship, he turned to his Politburo associates. Kirov was a particular chum. Whenever Kirov was on a trip from Leningrad, he went to see the Ordzhonikidzes; but frequently Stalin called him over to his place and Kirov slept there overnight.[30] Mikoyan was also frequently invited. This caused embarrassment for Mikoyan, whose wife Ashken was not easily persuaded that he really was staying where he said. Soon Mikoyan had to start declining Stalin's requests, and Stalin turned to Alexander Svanidze.[31] He sorely needed the reassurance and company of familiar individuals. The Soviet Union's ruler was a lonely widower. According to Lazar Kaganovich, he was never the same man again. He turned in on himself and hardened his attitude to people in general.[32] He drank and ate more, sometimes sitting at the table for three or four hours after putting in a full day in his office.[33]

Yet he did not yet take things out on the family and friends of his late wife. (That came later.) The Alliluevs tried to stay in touch with him without presuming too much upon his time and convenience. Nadya's father Sergei wrote to him to ask whether he might still go and stay at the Zubalovo dacha. He was in poor health and hoped to convalesce in the countryside.[34] The request, written two months after Nadya's death, tugged Stalin out of his self-absorption. Indeed it exasperated him: 'Sergei! You're a strange person! What sort of "permission" do you need when you have the full right to come and reside in "Zubalovo" without any "permission"!'[35] He welcomed other members of the Alliluev family, and Yevgenia – Nadya's sister-in-law – made efforts to see that he had a social life. The Svanidzes too popped by to see him whenever they could. Blood ran thicker than water both for Stalin and them.

Yet Zubalovo offered reminders of his married years. Another dacha outside Moscow seemed a sensible idea, and Stalin discovered an architect with ideas he found congenial. Miron Merzhanov designed country houses with thick, gloomy walls as if they were intended to stand as impregnable fortresses. Without Nadya to dissuade him, Stalin commissioned a residence serving better as a work place than as a family home. A rural spot was found near Kuntsevo, west of Moscow. It was only seven miles from the Kremlin and could be reached within minutes by official limousine. Stalin got the dacha he wanted. There was a large hall for meetings as well as several bedrooms and rooms for afternoon tea, billiards and film-shows. The construction was complete by 1934; Stalin quickly set himself up there and ceased to sleep in the Kremlin flat. The dacha became known as Blizhnyaya ('Nearby Dacha'). Another was built further out and called Dalnyaya ('Distant Dacha'), but Blizhnyaya was his favourite. Merzhanov had to be patient with his patron. No sooner had Blizhnyaya gone up than Stalin demanded alterations, even to the extent of requiring a second storey to be added.[36] He was forever thinking of ways to make the little rural castle into his dream.

His was a restless and unhappy spirit. Although he lived by choice apart from his family, he was not comfortable with being on his own;

and Moscow, where he had spent most years of his second marriage, was never going to allow him to forget the past. He looked forward keenly to his vacations in the south. Although he and Nadya had holidayed there together, her student obligations had latterly kept her in Moscow. State dachas already existed along the coast between Sochi and Sukhum, and Merzhanov was kept busy with commissions to design new ones.

Nearly all Stalin's vacations after 1932 took place in Abkhazia. Although he lived alone in the various local dachas, he spent his time convivially. The wine flowed and his tables groaned with food. His boon companion was Nestor Lakoba. In the factional disputes of the 1920s Lakoba had kept the Communist Party of Georgia clear of oppositionist influence. He had fought in the Civil War and was a crack shot with a hunting rifle; it amused Stalin that Lakoba put the Red Army commanders to shame when they went out hunting in the mountains.[37] Lakoba, moreover, had been an orphan and – like Stalin – had had a difficult childhood; and he too had studied at the Tiflis Spiritual Academy.[38] He was a bluff Caucasian who saw to it that Stalin was given the leisure to enjoy the delights of the Caucasus: the scenery, the wildlife, the wines and the cuisine. Even when Stalin stayed in Sochi, over the Abkhazian border in the RSFSR, Lakoba would come to visit. In 1936 when Lakoba got into political trouble with higher party authority in the Transcaucasian Federation and was stripped of the right to leave Sukhum without permission, Stalin was furious. Whatever might be the local political intrigues, he wanted the company of Nestor Lakoba.[39]

The first holiday after Nadya's death was memorable in more ways than one. On 23 September 1933 Stalin and his bodyguards took a boat trip off Sukhum. Suddenly they were subjected to rifle fire from the coast. His chief bodyguard Nikolai Vlasik threw himself on top of Stalin to protect him and requested permission to return fire. Meanwhile the boatman steered away from the area. The immediate assumption was that this had been an attempt at assassination; but the truth turned out to be more mundane. The Abkhazian NKVD had been suspicious of a boat which did not come from the locality and assumed that foreigners were up to no good. The coastguards owned up and pleaded for mercy, and Stalin recommended that they should suffer only disciplinary measures. (In the Great Terror the case was dug up and they were either shot or sent to forced-labour camps.)[40]

Stalin's power and eminence attracted attention from politicians in the south Caucasus. His presence was a heaven-sent opportunity to impress him. Among those who yearned to be taken up by Stalin was

Lavrenti Beria. In 1933 he was First Secretary of the Party Transcaucasian Committee and one bright summer's morning found an excuse to visit Stalin before breakfast at a Black Sea dacha. Beria was too late. Stalin was already down in the bushes below the buildings and, when Beria caught his first glimpse of him, he saw to his chagrin that Stalin was accompanied by Lakoba. Not that this inhibited Beria from toadying. After breakfast Stalin remarked: 'That wild bush needs clearing out, it gets in the way of the garden.' But efforts to remove the roots failed until Beria, snatching an axe off a Muscovite visitor, applied himself. Beria made sure Stalin heard him saying: 'I can chop under the roots of any bush which the owner of this garden, Joseph Vissarionovich, might point to.'[41] He was almost volunteering himself as a purger for Stalin. Few of these convivial encounters were without political content. Stalin, even on holiday, could not insulate himself from the ambitions of intriguers.

Yet most of his visitors were party and government functionaries of the region. No one, not even Molotov or Kaganovich, was a chum as Kirov had been; and Lakoba was more like a seasonal landlord than a genuine intimate. Having put up barricades against psychological intrusion, Stalin restricted himself to playful recreation. He took nieces and nephews on his knee. He sang Orthodox liturgical chants by the piano. He went hunting, challenged visitors to games of billiards and welcomed the presence of female relatives. But he had got harder as a personality. Ice had entered his soul. Molotov and Kaganovich, who immensely admired him, could not work out what made him tick. They later said that he changed a lot after Nadya's death. But the same works emphasise what made him exceptional: will power, clarity of vision, endurance and courage. Always Molotov and Kaganovich were observing him from the outside. They were in awe of Stalin. While they too were wilful and determined, they appreciated someone who had these qualities to a unique level of intensity. When he acted oddly, they gave him the benefit of the doubt. They thought he had earned the right to any psychological peculiarity by the services he had rendered to the USSR.

Most of them until the late 1930s felt no reason to query the mental condition of their Leader. Doubtless Stalin had previously driven them to distraction with orders to intensify political and economic campaigns. Yet the policies had been those of the ascendant party leadership and the negative side of Stalin's personality was largely overlooked. Earlier acquaintances had been more perceptive. Fellow pupils in Gori and Tbilisi as well as many party comrades before 1917 had remarked on his hypertrophied sense of importance and his excessive tendency to take offence. And when Lenin used him as Political Commissar in the Civil War or as Party General Secretary, he knew that Stalin would need careful handling if his volatility and crudity were not to damage the interests of the Revolution. Then in the early 1930s Stalin started to demand capital punishment for his adversaries in the communist party. If Nadya's suicide changed him, it was only to push him down a road he had been travelling his whole life long.

27. MODERNITY'S SORCERER

Stalin and his associates aimed to turn the USSR into an industrial and military megalith. They were militants. They wrestled to change society from top to bottom. They fought for 'cultural revolution'. Their campaign, as they saw it, required the entire syndrome of attitudes and behaviour in the country to be transformed in the spirit of the Enlightenment in general and Marxism in particular. War was waged upon customary ideas. Religion was to be eradicated and nationalist affiliations dissolved. The intelligentsia in the arts and sciences was to be battered into submission or else discarded. The objective was for communism to become the generally accepted ideology and for Stalin's variant of Marxism–Leninism to be installed as its core. He had not suddenly discovered this inclination. In the 1920s he had urged that young communists be trained to take up positions of authority and spread the party's ideas.[1] The entire generation of Bolshevik veterans shared his standpoint. They believed that the achievement of socialism required a fundamental rupture with the old society and the elites who had formed opinions in it.

Stalin, like every communist, insisted that culture was not confined to the poems of Pushkin but covered literacy, numeracy, hygiene, shelter, food, conscientiousness and efficiency. There was an almost religious ecstasy in the political sermons he and his fellow leaders delivered on the 'cultural front'. Writers were designated as 'engineers of human souls'. His Marxist faith was fused with a warlike spirit. No one underestimated the difficulties of the campaign as Stalin urged the cultural combatants to rise to the task in hand. At the Seventeenth Party Congress in January–February 1934 he declared that fierce battles still lay ahead:[2]

> The enemies of the party, opportunists of all colours, national-deviationists of every kind have been crushed. But the remains of their ideology live on in the heads of individual party members and

often give evidence of their existence ... And the soil for such
inclinations undoubtedly exists in our country if only because we
still have intermediate strata of the population in town and countryside who represent a nutritive environment for such inclinations.

Fervour and pugnacity were demanded: Stalin had begun a war he was
determined to win.

Most observers have assumed that his ultimate aim was merely to
'catch up' with the West. This is to underestimate his purposes. He had
a much more comprehensive project, and the atmosphere of his rule,
which engendered much popular enthusiasm, is incomprehensible without that project. When Stalin spoke about the need for the introduction
of 'modernity' (*sovremennost*') to the USSR, what he had in mind was
something more than blind imitation of the advanced capitalist
countries. Soviet-style modernity in his estimation would be of an
altogether superior kind.

He and the rest of the Politburo were Marxist believers. The utopian
strain in their thought was to the fore in the early 1930s; they thought
that Soviet modernity would raise humanity to a higher plane of
existence not just by eliminating the bad old traditions in Russia but also
by doing things unparalleled in the West. Unemployment had already
been eradicated and soon the gap in material conditions between town
and countryside would be closed.[3] Universal provision of food, shelter,
education and healthcare would be guaranteed. Bolsheviks had always
claimed that capitalism was an inherently wasteful economic system
in comparison with socialism. Marx and Lenin had written that industrialists and bankers inevitably developed an interest in doing down
competitors and in blocking technological advance at the expense of
popular aspirations and requirements. Resources were not going to be
unproductively expended in Stalin's USSR. A virtue was claimed for the
standardisation of products and services. The higher good was the
principle of common availability. Stalin was hostile, at least in public, to
the maintenance of manufacturing sub-sectors dedicated to luxury
goods. Individualisation of choice was consciously downplayed. The
priority was for the 'new Soviet person' to accept the obligations of
membership of 'the collective'.

Stalin advocated ideas of this kind in speeches and articles. He
embodied them in his public appearance and comportment. His soldierly
tunic, his avoidance of the word 'I', his issuance of orders in the name
of the respective party organs rather than in his own, even his lack of

oratorical tricks: all these features helped to convey the message that Soviet modernity would ultimately triumph and bring unprecedented benefit to toiling humanity.

The ascendant party leadership had cleared a lot of the ground for cultural transformation. The First Five-Year Plan was accompanied by vicious campaigns against religion, and the Red Army and the 25,000-ers arrested clerics and kulaks with equal eagerness. Religion was to be stamped out. Many churches, mosques and synagogues were shut down. Out of 73,963 religious buildings open before 1917, only 30,543 were allowed to function by April 1936.[4] Nationalism of every stripe was also trampled underfoot. The elites of the various national and ethnic groups were objects of intense suspicion, including even many people who had aligned themselves with the communists in previous years. Show trials of leading 'bourgeois nationalists' were held from 1929. The League of the Militant Godless was given sumptuous funding. When Mykola Skrypnik, a Bolshevik Ukrainian leader who had strongly promoted the interests of his nation, committed suicide, no official regret was expressed. The times had changed, and the USSR was being pointed towards transformations which according to veteran Bolsheviks were overdue. Private printing presses were closed down. Travel between the USSR and foreign countries became impossible unless political and police organs gave their sanction. The ascendant leaders tried to insulate the country from all ideological influences but their own. Basic cultural assumptions of Bolshevism were at last going to be realised.

Such assumptions had been more pluralistic before the October Revolution than later. Bolshevism's regimentative side won out over its other tendencies after 1917, and the extremism of Stalin and his cronies prevailed over attitudes once sponsored by the rest of the Politburo. The violence and crudity of the new campaign in the 'cultural revolution' was remarkable.

Nor was high culture overlooked as an arena of struggle. Stalin's interventions had previously been of a confidential nature, and in the 1920s it had been Trotski and Bukharin who were known for their contacts with the creative intelligentsia. Trotski had written *Art and Revolution*. Stalin was now seeking to impose himself. In 1930 he gave a ruling on the political history of Bolshevism before 1914.[5] Increasingly his subordinates interfered in the arts and sciences through the Agitation and Propaganda Department of the Secretariat. Long gone was the period when Anatoli Lunacharski (who died in 1933) or Nadezhda Krupskaya could fix the main lines of policies through the People's

Commissariat of Enlightenment. Stalin was determined to get the kind of culture, high and low, appropriate to the state and society he was constructing. He increased his contacts with intellectuals. He watched plays and the ballet more than previously. He kept on reading novels, history books and conspectuses of contemporary science. He got his associates to do the same. Cultural transformation had to be directed just as firmly as the basic changes in economics and politics.

He welcomed a few intellectuals as his occasional companions. This too was a change from previous years when only his political cronies, apart from the poet Demyan Bedny, got near him. Maxim Gorki, whom he had tempted back from a self-imposed exile in 1931, frequented Stalin's dacha. Other visitors included the novelists Mikhail Sholokhov and Alexei Tolstoi.

However highly he valued Gorki as a writer, however, reasons of state were never far from his mind. Gorki was famous in the West and could be turned into an embellishment of the USSR. He was fêted on his return as a great proletarian intellectual. Stalin wanted something for all this. In 1929 he persuaded Gorki to visit the Solovki prison camp; he even cajoled him into becoming co-author of a book on the building of the White Sea Canal.[6] Gorki was duped into believing that humanitarian efforts were being made to rehabilitate the convict labourers. He also presided over the First Congress of Writers in 1934 and lent a hand in the formation of the Union of Writers. Gorki's approval helped Stalin to bring the arts in the USSR under tight political control. The price Stalin had to pay was to have to listen to the writer's complaints about the maltreatment of various intellectuals by the authorities. But fortunately for Stalin, Gorki died in summer 1936. The rumour grew that the NKVD poisoned him for importuning the General Secretary a little too often. However that may have been, his death freed Stalin to transform Gorki into an iconic figure in the official arts of the USSR.

Sholokhov and Tolstoi too had dealings with Stalin. *Quiet Flows the Don* by Sholokhov was one of the few good pieces of Soviet inter-war prose which did not assail the premises of communism. Set in the Cossack villages of south Russia and crammed with regional idioms, the novel was a saga of the Civil War. Its first edition contained episodes thought to be indulgent to the Whites. Sholokhov, after modifying the text as required, entered the classical canon of the regime. He also produced a sequel, *The Virgin Soil Upturned*, about the collectivisation campaign. This was aesthetically less impressive; it also strengthened the suspicion that he had purloined most of the chapters of *Quiet Flows the*

Don from a deceased Cossack writer.[7] Even so, Sholokhov was not a servile hack. He was horrified by what he witnessed in the countryside as the Cossacks were brutally herded into collective farms. Repeatedly he wrote to Stalin pointing this out. As famine grew in south Russia, the correspondence became heated on both sides.[8] Sholokhov's letters testify to his courage; Stalin's engagement with him signals a recognition that loyalist intellectuals performed a useful function for him by raising difficult questions without ever threatening his political position. No politician got away with such impertinence.

Another writer who had Stalin's ear was Alexei Tolstoi, the patriotic novelist and nephew of the nineteenth-century author. Tolstoi had come to think that the Bolsheviks had discharged the historic task of reuniting Russia, seeing off its external enemies and undertaking its overdue industrialisation. The novelist fed ideas to Stalin about the continuities between Imperial and communist patterns of rule. According to Tolstoi, it was the Party General Secretary's duty to stand firm in the tradition of Ivan the Terrible and Peter the Great. Ivan and Peter had used brutal methods in pursuit of the country's interests. Tolstoi was knocking at an open door: Stalin, an eager student of Russian history, already saw the connections with the reigns of Ivan and Peter.[9]

He knew what he liked in the arts as well as in historical scholarship. At the theatre he had admired Mikhail Bulgakov's *The Days of the Turbins* since its première in 1926. This was a play about the shifting allegiances in Ukraine during the Civil War. Stalin's devotion showed a willingness to understand the fighting in terms much less simplistic than in official history textbooks: Bulgakov depicted not only the Reds but also the Whites in sympathetic tones. At the ballet Stalin preferred Chaikovski's *Swan Lake* to newer pieces of music and choreography. The significance of this is a matter of speculation. Perhaps he simply wanted to identify himself as an enthusiast for classical dance and anyway found nothing very attractive in Soviet choreography. It was the same with music. Although he began to attend symphonies and operas, few contemporary composers engaged his admiration. Poetry by living writers too was of small interest to him. The poet Vladimir Mayakovski, who committed suicide in 1930, was turned – like Gorki – into an artistic totem of the regime. Stalin paid only lip-service to his memory. (Lenin had claimed it was scandalous at a time of paper shortage to allocate resources for his poems.) The General Secretary had an enduring love for the Georgian poetical classics to the exclusion of Soviet contemporary verse.

Down the years he was mocked as someone without feeling for the arts. His enemies consoled themselves in defeat by drawing attention to his intellectual limitations. They went too far with their ridicule. Stalin also had himself to blame, for he had deliberately drawn the curtains over his educational level, poetical achievement and range of intellectual interests,[10] and his verbal exchanges with most writers and painters usually turned on political questions.

In fact the flame of Stalin's genuine aesthetic appreciation had not gone out. He displayed it especially when questions arose about the arts in his native Georgia. When Shalva Nutsubidze compiled and translated an anthology of Georgian poetry into Russian in the mid-1930s, Stalin could not resist taking a look at the typed draft. Back flowed his lifelong enthusiasm for poetry, and he pencilled proposed amendments in the margins.[11] Nutsubidze and Stalin made for an odd pair. Nutsubidze was a scholar who had refused to join the party; his very project to produce a Georgian literary anthology might have served as a pretext for arresting him. But the two men got on well and Nutsubidze appreciated Stalin's suggestions as real improvements.[12] Stalin did not allow his assistance to be publicised. Nor did he give permanent approval to attempts to resuscitate his fame as a minor Georgian poet. Some of the early verses crept into print and this cannot have happened without his sanction. But second thoughts prevailed. The poems were not widely reprinted in his time in power and did not appear in his multi-volume *Works* published after the Second World War. Reasons of state prevailed over vanity. Stalin had probably concluded that the romantic poetry of his youth would disfigure his image as the Man of Steel. Presumably he also wanted to set the literary tone for the times. Culture was to be judged by the yardstick of current political requirements.

Literature, painting and architecture were arts more easily analysed in this reductive fashion than music. Stalin wanted two things at once. He desired culture for the 'masses'; he also aimed to disseminate high culture. He wished the USSR's attainments to outmatch any achieved abroad. Insisting on Russia's centuries-old greatness, he assimilated Russian writers and composers of the nineteenth century – Pushkin, Tolstoi, Glinka and Chaikovski – to the socialist project after 1917. He had a private enthusiasm for Dostoevski, whom he judged a brilliant psychologist;[13] but Dostoevski's overt reactionary politics and mystical religious faith proved too much even for Stalin to approve republication of his works. The librettos of Glinka's operas were rewritten and many of Pushkin's and Tolstoi's writings were banned. Even so, much of the pre-revolutionary artistic heritage with its conservative, liberal and apolitical elements was made available to the public. Stalin's cultural programme was an unstable mixture. He could kill artists at will and yet his policies were incapable of producing great art unless he either deliberately or unconsciously overlooked, at least to some extent, what his artists were really doing.

Culture in general attracted his occasional – and unpredictable – interventions. Stalin's aide Lev Mekhlis rang up *Pravda* cartoonist Boris Yefimov in 1937 and told him to come immediately to the Kremlin. Suspecting the worst, Yefimov feigned influenza. But 'he' – Stalin – was insisting; Yefimov could postpone the visit at most by a day. In fact Stalin simply wished to say that he thought Yefimov should cease drawing Japanese figures with protruding teeth. 'Definitely,' replied the cartoonist. 'There won't be any more teeth.'[14] Stalin's interventions were equally direct in film production. Boris Shumyatski, the People's Commissar in charge of Soviet cinema until his arrest in 1938, understood that the General Secretary was the sole reviewer who had to be taken seriously.[15] Stalin had screening facilities set up in his dachas outside Moscow and by the Black Sea. Films such as *Lenin in October* were among his favourites; but he liked audiences to be entertained as well as indoctrinated. He did not object to an escapist melodrama like *Circus*; and as propaganda came to stress patriotism, Stalin applauded the films *Ivan the Terrible* and *Alexander Nevski* directed by Sergei Eizenshtein. It was a favour which Eizenshtein both relished and feared: he knew that Stalin would pounce with fury upon any scenes he deemed to conflict with current official politics.

Such artistic works of distinction as were created in the 1930s – with very few exceptions – came into being despite him. The works of Anna Akhmatova, who composed her wonderful elegiac cycle of poems *Requiem* in 1935–40, were banned from the press. (Only in the Second World War, when her verses were useful for raising public morale, did Stalin somewhat relent.)[16] That masterpiece of Russian prose, *The Master and Margarita* by Mikhail Bulgakov, remained in his desk drawer at his death and was not published in full in the Soviet Union until 1975. Stalin even terrorised the genius of mid-century Russian classical music Dmitri Shostakovich, who was denounced for writing pieces which nobody could whistle. Shostakovich was constrained to 'confess' his errors; indeed his Fifth Symphony in 1937 became known as 'A Soviet Artist's Reply to Just Criticism'. Music, however, was less harshly treated than the other arts. Terrified though he had been, Shostakovich went on

writing and having his symphonies performed. Just a few fine literary
pieces were printed. Among them were Sholokhov's two novels and
some of Andrei Platonov's short stories. But generally Stalin's rule spread
a blight over the already damaged artistic environment of the USSR.

The Great Terror of 1937–8 was to scare most intellectuals into co-
operating overtly with the state or else just keeping their heads down.
Just a very few of them challenged authority. Osip Mandelshtam in 1934
read out an anti-Stalin poem to a private soirée:[17]

> We live, deaf to the land beneath us,
> Ten steps away no one hears our speeches,
>
> But where there's so much as half-conversation
> The Kremlin man of the mountains will be mentioned.
>
> His fingers are as fat as grubs
> And the words, final as lead weights, fall from his lips,
>
> His cockroach whiskers leer
> And his boot tops gleam.
>
> Around him a rabble of thin-necked leaders – fawning
> Half-men for him to play with.
> They whinny, purr or whine
> As he prates and points a finger,
>
> One by one forging his laws, to be flung
> Like horseshoes at the head, the eye or the groin.
>
> And every killing is a treat
> For the broad-chested Ossete.

The last line reproduced the (unproved) rumour that Stalin was of
Ossetian ancestry.

The listeners that evening included an informer, and the poet was
arrested. Even Stalin, though, was unsure what to do with him. His
instinct was to execute him; but instead he telephoned another great
poet, Boris Pasternak, and asked whether Mandelshtam's was a truly
wonderful talent. Pasternak was in acute embarrassment: if he said yes,
he too might be arrested; but to say no would be to condemn his friend
and rival to the Gulag. Pasternak gave an equivocal answer, prompt-
ing Stalin to comment sarcastically: 'If I had a poet friend who was in
trouble, I'd throw myself at a wall to save him!'[18] Mandelshtam was sent
to the Gulag in 1938. The list of fine artists who were shot or incarcerated

is depressingly long. More great intellectuals perished in the 1930s than survived. Isaak Babel, writer of wonderful short stories about the Red cavalry in the Soviet–Polish War of 1920, was a victim. So was the theatre director Vsevolod Meyerkhold. Even Mikhail Bulgakov, whose plays had pleased Stalin in the 1920s, was ushered into the pits of depression. He perished a broken man in freedom in 1940. Anna Akhmatova suffered despite never being arrested: her son Lev was taken by the police in her place. Unlike Bulgakov, she endured her situation with lasting fortitude.

The repression came also to scholarship and the natural sciences. Among the victims of the show trials in 1929–31 were historians such as Sergei Platonov who were accused of Russian nationalist activity. Yevgeni Tarle, who later became one of Stalin's favourite historians, was locked up. Literary criticism was another dangerous scholarly area. Although Stalin enlisted nineteenth-century poetry and prose in his programme for cultural revolution, he was not going to permit the publication of unorthodox interpretations. Scientific teaching and research were also persecuted whenever he saw them as a threat to the regime. The list of outstanding figures who were repressed is a long one. It included the biologist Nikolai Vavilov, the aircraft designer Andrei Tupolev and the physicist Lev Landau.

This treatment of the country's scientists clashed with the official campaign to put the USSR in the vanguard of scientific progress. Yet the Soviet Union was a political despotism and Stalin had prejudices which he imposed even on areas of human enquiry where he had no expertise whatever. He also had a bias in favour of scientists who came from the working class or peasantry and, regardless of their limited education, challenged conventional ideas. He was further attracted to any scientific idea which appeared congenial to the crude version of Marxist episte- mology and ontology which he espoused (and which he wrote up in the chapter on dialectical materialism in the *History of the All-Union Com- munist Party (Bolsheviks): A Short Course*.[19]) The most notorious case was Timofei Lysenko, a self-styled geneticist who claimed to be able to breed new strains of plant by changing their climatic environment. Trained geneticists such as Vavilov protested that Lysenko ignored decades of proof that plants did not pass on their environmentally acquired characteristics from one generation to another. Lysenkoism was a bastard form of the Lamarckian propositions of natural selection. Vavilov failed to interest Stalin; Lysenko captivated his enthusiasm. The result was a catastrophe for Soviet genetics and the consignment of Vavilov to a forced-labour camp.

Many of the scientists, scholars and artists who thrived under Stalin were third-raters. Chairman of the USSR Writers' Union was the talentless Alexander Fadeev, not Bulgakov or Pasternak; and it was the mediocre Tikhon Khrennikov rather than the musical genius Dmitri Shostakovich who led the USSR Union of Composers. Political reliability was what counted with the Agitprop Department of the Party Secretariat. The organisations gave the permits for individuals to function in the Soviet Union; they could make or break the careers of their members. They disposed of funds, food packs, sanatoria and holiday dachas. Their leaders – the Fadeevs and the Khrennikovs – went to social gatherings hosted by Stalin. Each Soviet republic had its own unions. The Kremlin conferred awards and medals. Not only scholars but also aviators, footballers, opera singers and even circus clowns hoped to win them. The annual Stalin Prizes brought prestige and a handsome cheque in the bank account. Stalin was the architect of this system of control and reward. He carried through the cultural revolution of his choice, and was proud of the achievements under his rule.[20]

By 1939 about 87 per cent of Soviet citizens between the ages of nine and forty-nine were literate and numerate. Schools, newspapers, libraries and radio stations proliferated. Factory apprenticeships had hugely expanded in number. The universities teemed with students. An agrarian society had been pointed in the direction of 'modernisation'. The cultural revolution was not restricted to the dissemination of technical skills; it was also aimed at spreading science, urbanism, industry and Soviet-style modernity. Attitudes and manners were to be transformed.[21] Schools, newspapers and radio trumpeted this official priority. Soviet spokesmen – politicians, scholars, teachers and journalists – asserted that the USSR was a beacon of enlightenment and progress. Capitalist states were depicted as forests of ignorance, reaction and superstition. Physics, the ballet, military technology, novels, organised sport and mathematics in the USSR were touted as evidence of the progress already made.

The USSR had in many ways dragged its society out of the ruts of traditionalism. But the process was not unidirectional. Marxism–Leninism, despite its pretensions to 'scientific analysis', rested on assumptions inherited from earlier centuries. This was particularly true of Stalin's way of thinking. He had never eradicated the superstitious worldview he had encountered as a small boy; and his attitudes were transferred to cultural life as a whole once he had supreme power. Official Soviet thought, consolidated in the Civil War, postulated the existence of alien, maleficent forces acting against the common weal. Conspiracies were supposedly being formed everywhere. The appearance of sincerity had always to be queried. Foreign agencies were alleged to be ubiquitous in the USSR. Such thinking did not begin with Stalin. Lenin during the Kronstadt Revolt and on other occasions had ascribed outbreaks of dissent and resistance to the activity of capitalist powers abroad. Under Stalin, though, this mode of perception became an ever more cardinal feature. The testing of political and economic assertions against empirical evidence fell into desuetude; open discussion on the scientific model ceased. Pronouncements from the Kremlin served as the regime's kabbalah. Anyone refusing to accept the existence of fiends using diabolical methods to overturn the regime was liable to be treated as an infidel or heretic deserving summary punishment.

A corpus of magical writ was purveyed. Its texts were not the works of Marx, Engels or even Lenin. Soviet culture from the late 1930s was dominated by *The History of the All-Union Communist Party (Bolsheviks): A Short Course* and the official biography of Stalin. Excerpts from both were accorded quasi-Biblical authority. Marxism–Leninism in general, and Stalin's version of it in particular, was reproducing a mentality characteristic of peasant traditionalism. Customs in the countryside were associated with belief in spirits, demons and sorcerers. Witchcraft was a normal phenomenon and spells were regularly employed to ward off evil (or to inflict it on enemies). This syndrome suffused Stalinism and its culture. Without using the term, Stalin suggested that black magic had to be confronted if the forces of good – Marxism–Leninism, the communist party and the October Revolution – were to survive and flourish. Not every novelist, scholar or scientist went along with such idiocy. Quite the contrary: the best cultural achievements under Stalin were devoid of it. But in key sectors, especially the schools and the print and broadcast media, he could impose the pattern very effectively. Despite its achievements in twentieth-century culture, the USSR was being dragged back to older modalities of thought. Stalin, far from being the clean-limbed titan of modernity, was a village sorcerer who held his subjects in his dark thrall.

28. FEARS IN VICTORY

Even as the First Five-Year Plan had neared completion in 1932, the strains in the economy and in society were becoming intolerable. The famine deepened in Ukraine, south Russia, the north Caucasus and Kazakhstan. Rural rebellions had not been completely suppressed. Attacks on collectivisation squads, OGPU officials and local soviets continued. Having been bludgeoned into joining kolkhozes, hundreds of thousands of peasant families left the countryside rather than endure further hardship.[1] Trouble started to spread to the towns. Strikes and demonstrations against the regime were organised in the textile city of Ivanovo.[2]

Like Lenin in 1921, Stalin saw the need for a temporary economic retreat. The difference was that, whereas Lenin had introduced the New Economic Policy mainly for fear of a universal revolt by the peasantry, it was the workers who brought Stalin to his senses. If industrialisation were to be disrupted, the foundations of his power would be undermined. There was recognition that the problems in the towns and villages were linked. From May 1932 the peasants were permitted to trade their agricultural surplus at so-called kolkhoz markets. Between August 1932 and February 1933 the state's planned collection quotas for grain were reduced from 18.1 to 14.9 million tons.[3] The industrial component of the retreat took shape in a slackening of the tempo of capital investment during the Second Five-Year Plan. The rampant dash for expanded output in factories and mines was to be slowed.[4] The living conditions of citizens were at last given prominence. Industrial consumer products were planned to increase by 134 per cent and agricultural output by 177 per cent in 1933–7. Housing space was to expand by two fifths.[5] Apparently he was beginning to see sense. The objective was to avoid a second headlong dash for growth in capital projects and to consolidate the gains already won.

There was more discussion in the Politburo about industry than about agriculture. Stalin knew his mind about the countryside even though he felt the need to make concessions. Industrial policy put him in a quandary, and he listened to the debate in the Politburo as Molotov and Kaganovich argued for a slowing down against the wishes of Ordzhonikidze in the People's Commissariat of Heavy Industry. Stalin's instincts tugged him towards Ordzhonikidze but he moved increasingly against him. At the January 1933 Central Committee plenum Stalin announced a lowering of the industrial growth target to 13–14 per cent.[6]

The pressure on society was only moderately relieved. The reduced agricultural collections did little to stave off starvation since the 1932 harvest, badly affected by the weather, was a poor one. Stalin's concessions to the peasants had their limits; and the insistence on keeping up grain exports was maintained. The penal sanctions for disobedience were made more severe than ever. On 7 August, at his personal instigation, peasants who stole even a handful of grain became liable to the death sentence or a minimum of ten years' imprisonment.[7] At a time when peasants in several regions were so desperate that some turned to cannibalism, this was a decree of extraordinary ferocity even for Stalin. The yeast in the bread of reform was repression. He also instructed the OGPU to see that kulaks and 'speculators' did not take advantage of the concessions being made.[8] Police, army and party were used to ensure that the basic economic and political changes introduced since 1928 would stay intact. Stalin was completely in charge of economic policy. The slightest sign of disagreement from communist leaders in Moscow or the provinces earned his instant rebuke. The result was that not once after the second half of 1932 did a fellow Politburo member dare to challenge any of his decisions.[9]

At times Stalin seemed baffled by the abuses and chaos he had caused through his policies. Writing to Kaganovich and Molotov in June 1932, he mentioned that party committees in Ukraine and the Urals were crudely dividing the centrally assigned quotas for grain procurement among the lower territorial units of each province. He asked why such committees did not take local peculiarities into account.[10] But in order to fulfil the quotas imposed from Moscow there was little that provincial administrators could do but use rough and ready methods. They were only doing at the local level what Stalin was doing in the Kremlin. Being cut off from rural and administrative realities, he assumed that the problem was local incompetence or mischief.

Yet reports on the poor harvest and spreading famine caused even Stalin, comfortably on vacation by the Black Sea, to lighten Ukrainian grain collections in mid-August; and once his sanction had been secured, the Politburo halved its quotas to alleviate the hardship.[11] (Not that he stopped feeling let down by the republican party leaders in Kiev: he kept his promise to the Politburo that eventually they would be removed.)[12] Stalin also allowed a lowering of procurement quotas in the Volga, the Urals and Kazakhstan after the 1933 harvest.[13] But his indulgences were temporary and partial. When Kaganovich in September 1934 requested yet another lowering of the Ukrainian grain quotas, Stalin retorted:[14]

> I consider this letter an alarming symptom since it shows that we can slip on to an incorrect path unless we switch the matter to a firm policy on time (i.e. immediately). The *first* lowering was necessary. But it is being used by our officials (not only by peasants!) as a first step, which has to be followed by a second step, towards putting *pressure* on Moscow for a *further* lowering.

Politburo member Kaganovich was being reminded that the general orientation of policies was to be sustained.

The palliative measures of 1932–3 had little immediate effect. Even the lowered collection quotas left the peasantry with less wheat and potatoes than they needed for subsistence. They ate berries, fungi, rats and mice; and, when these had been consumed, peasants chewed grass and bark. Probably six million people died in a famine which was the direct consequence of state policy.[15] Further measures were announced. The Kolkhoz Model Statute, introduced in 1935, allowed each household between a quarter and a half of a hectare for its private plot.[16] This additional incentive to the economy's non-state sector was a signal of the terrible conditions for Soviet consumers. Without private agricultural production, albeit in a very restricted framework, conditions would have been still worse. Peasants eked out their existence in the most severe circumstances even after the famine ended in 1933. But life was only a little better for most workers in the towns. Urban wages remained lower in real terms than before the First Five-Year Plan. Industrialisation and collectivisation had thrown society into the maelstrom of hunger, migra-tion and the Gulag. But Stalin and his Politburo had pulled back from the most extreme of their policies for economic transformation, and many officials and most citizens were hoping that the frenzied chaos of 1928–32 had been terminated.

The Seventeenth Party Congress of January and February 1934 was hailed in advance as the Congress of Victors. On the surface there was unanimity among the delegates. No direct criticism of the ascendant party leadership was made. Stalin's Central Committee report was met with rapturous acclaim; its contents ranged confidently across both foreign and internal policy. He took pride in the 'victories' achieved since 1928. Rapid industrialisation and agricultural collectivisation had been imposed. Bolshevik oppositions on the left and the right had been crushed. Priority had been given to socialism in one country. The Central Committee was distinguished more by its listing of long-term objectives than by its specification of immediate policy.

Delegates confined themselves in public to making pleas on behalf of particular localities or economic sectors. Some asked for adjustments of existing measures; but there was no overt discussion of the Ukrainian famine or general industrial policy.[17] Behind the scenes, however, there were grumbles about Stalin's methods and ambitions. Republican and provincial party officials had had a rough time in recent years as they strove to implement the demands of the Politburo and Gosplan. They had no objection to the additional powers and privileges all this had brought. But the perspective of a regime of permanent pressure was undesirable for them. Quite apart from their personal interests, they believed that a period of consolidation was required. In the absence of open opportunities some of them – at least according to a few sources – approached Politburo member Sergei Kirov and asked him to consider taking over the General Secretaryship from Stalin. Other memoirs suggest that, when the vote for the Central Committee took place, Stalin did badly and that Kaganovich, who was in charge of the counting, had to fiddle the results to secure Stalin's re-election. If this was true, then the call of the arrested Ryutin was being answered, and Stalin stood in danger of political oblivion.[18]

Stalin gave grounds for worry that the flames of his severity had not been extinguished. While agreeing on the need for economic consolidation, he did not fail to argue the need for vigilance and repression whenever enemies of the people were discovered. He declared that internal party oppositionists had 'descended into the camp of livid counter-revolutionaries and wreckers in the service of foreign capital'.[19] Former oppositionists had only recently been readmitted to the party. It seemed from Stalin's Central Committee report than he was not entirely convinced that the settlement should be permanent – and he menacingly linked internal party opposition to traitorous activity at the level of the state. It is no wonder that many delegates thought it dangerous to leave him in post as General Secretary.

Events behind the scenes at the Congress remain mysterious. Those intimately involved in them – Kirov and Kaganovich – never divulged the details. Most of the lesser participants were to disappear in the Great Terror and no formal record was made of what had happened at the Congress. Kirov was to acquire a posthumous reputation as a political moderate in the Politburo. There is little to sustain this beyond a few gestures in the direction of increasing bread supplies in Leningrad where he was City Party Secretary.[20] All Politburo members tended to protect their sectors of work against the ravaging effects of general policy, and Kirov was no exception. And if indeed Kirov was approached at the Congress, he is likely to have told Stalin of the kind of support he was receiving from delegates. Kirov did not comport himself as a Leader in the making and gave no sign of this ultimate ambition. It cannot be demonstrated beyond doubt that the Congress vote for the new Central Committee humiliated Stalin. All that may confidently be said is that many officials were disenchanted with him and that they may have registered this on their ballot papers. Stalin for his part had cause to worry regardless of the stories about Kirov and the Central Committee vote. Having won victory on all fronts in the First Five-Year Plan, he had learned that a multitude of fellow victors refused to give him carte blanche to proceed however he wished.

For a while he did little in reaction, and the more moderate face of official policy was maintained. It was made more difficult for the police arbitrarily to arrest specialists working in the economy. The OGPU, moreover, was incorporated in the People's Commissariat of Internal Affairs. Some contemporary observers hoped that this would lead to a taming of the repressive zeal of the Chekists. Thousands of individuals arrested in the late 1920s started to return from the labour camps and resume a free life. The economy was steered steadily towards the achievement of the goals of the Second Five-Year Plan in an atmosphere untainted by the previous hysteria.

But then something happened which disrupted the political calm. On 1 December 1934 Kirov was shot by an assassin. Leonid Nikolaev, probably annoyed by Kirov's dalliance with his wife, walked into the Smolny Institute and killed him stone dead. The Leningrad NKVD had already been reported for sloppiness in September 1934,[21] and its subsequent incompetence belonged to a pattern. Stalin was shocked white and rigid – or at least this was how he appeared to others at the time. Nikolaev was listed as a former Zinovievite. He was quickly interrogated, including a session in Stalin's presence, and then shot. Mysterious accidents swiftly occurred to his police handlers – and although the NKVD leadership in Leningrad was disciplined for its oversights, the punishment was far from severe for most of them.[22] Stalin issued a decree sanctioning the formation of *troiki* which could mete out summary 'justice' without recourse to the courts. The basis was laid for an extension of state terror. Former oppositionists were arrested and interrogated. Zinoviev privately speculated that Stalin would use the murder as a pretext to undertake his own campaign of repression on the model of Hitler's activity in Germany.[23] Stalin attended Kirov's funeral looking grim and determined. Even his close associates wondered how he was going to deal with the situation; but everyone assumed that severe measures would be applied.

Instantly the rumour spread that Stalin had connived in Kirov's liquidation. He was known for a preference for repressive action, and stories abounded that Kirov had been touted as his replacement as General Secretary. Supposedly Stalin was behind the killing. In fact all the evidence is circumstantial and no proof has ever been found. What is undeniable is that Stalin had no compunction about drastic measures. He had not yet killed a close associate but the assassination of Kirov could have been the first such occasion; and even if he did not order the killing, it was he who most benefited from it. Kirov's death permitted him to treat the former oppositionists as he had implied he wanted to in his Central Committee report to the Seventeenth Party Congress.

Zinoviev and Kamenev were taken into the NKVD's custody in Moscow and accused of having organised a terrorist conspiracy with their oppositionist followers. Stalin had never ceased to worry about the capacity of the oppositions of left and right to return to power, especially if their ideas had resonance among current party officials. The suppression of successive groupings under Lominadze, Eismont and Ryutin gave no cheer. There could easily be others lurking in Moscow and the provinces. What is more, Stalin knew that Bukharin, Kamenev and Zinoviev had not lost hope of restoration to power. He maintained surveillance over them through the eavesdropping facilities of the political police.[24] He knew that they hated and despised him. Bukharin, while professing respect for Stalin to his face, was privately denouncing him. Kamenev and Zinoviev were contemptuous in the extreme. And Trotski was at liberty abroad editing the *Bulletin of the Opposition* and sending his emissaries into the USSR. Stalin was aware that, despite what they pretended, his party enemies felt they had a lot in common with each other. There was a distinct possibility that they would establish a clandestine coalition to undermine Stalin and his Politburo. Trotski's capacity to maintain contact was well established. When sixty-eight of his supporters were arrested in Moscow in January 1933, the OGPU discovered a cache of Trotski's latest articles.[25]

There was also a surge of resentment throughout society at the effects of Stalin's policies. Peasants had been battered into the collective farms and detested the new agricultural system, and hundreds of thousands of kulak families had been badly abused. Workers who failed to be promoted to managerial posts experienced a drastic deterioration in their conditions. Wages, food and shelter were seldom better than rudimentary. Higher up the social system too the bitterness was intense: engineers, intellectuals, economic experts and even managers bore a grudge about the harassment they suffered. The sense of civic disgruntlement was deep and widespread. Former members of other parties as well as defeated communist oppositionists were rancorous about the hostile sanctions applied against them. Whole national and religious groups prayed for a miracle that would remove the burden of Stalin's policies from their shoulders. There was plenty of human material across the USSR which could, if conditions changed, be diverted into a coup against his Politburo.

Zinoviev and Kamenev refused to 'confess' to conspiratorial organisation. But faced with a long prison sentence as well as permanent separation from involvement with communism, they cracked and admitted political and moral responsibility for Nikolaev's action. The Politburo – or rather Stalin – decided that Zinoviev was the more dangerous of the two. Zinoviev was given ten years, Kamenev five. The NKVD did not stop at that. Six hundred and sixty-three past supporters of the Leningrad Opposition were rounded up and exiled to Yakutia and other parts of eastern Siberia.[26] The incrimination of former internal oppositions continued. Trotski was regularly reviled in *Pravda* and *Izvestiya*. At the same time as the verdict was passed on Zinoviev and Kamenev it was announced that an exchange of party cards was to take place. The purpose was to sieve out party members who had failed to carry out the minimum of their duties or had behaved improperly or even had once belonged to internal party oppositions. No judicial consequences were anticipated for those who were to have their membership cards withdrawn. But a signal was being given that a campaign of persecution which had as yet been confined to ex-oppositionist leaders and their supporters was not to stop at the gates of the party. All had to prove themselves loyal to the Politburo or risk expulsion and demotion.

The menacing nature of the exchange of party cards was embodied in a secret directive sent out by the Party Secretariat on 13 May 1935.[27]

Stalin was rampant. The Secretariat explained that adventurers, enemies of the party and outright spies had got hold of such cards. The party had been infiltrated by alien and anti-Soviet elements. On 20 May the Politburo intervened with a directive specifying that all former Trotskyists outside prison or labour camp without exception should automatically be dispatched to forced labour in the Gulag for a minimum of three years.[28] Stalin's revenge on his old adversaries and detractors had been years in coming. Now it was revealed in its primitive fury. On 20 November a further stage was reached when the imprisoned Zinoviev and Kamenev as well as the deported Trotski were charged with espionage on behalf of hostile foreign powers.

Members of Stalin's group were identifying historic oppositional activity with current state treason. Veteran heroes of the communist party were being denounced as mercenary agents of Western interests. They were like rabbits rigid with fear as the fox approaches. Flight was anyway impossible. All they could hope for was that the rest of the Politburo would somehow restrain the General Secretary.[29] But the political mood was not encouraging. Stalin had quietly returned to the assumption that the surest way of strengthening both his personal position and the buoyancy of economic development was to exert heavy pressure on Gosplan and the People's Commissariats for raised industrial tempos. Anticipating opposition, he strove to exploit efforts made by individual workers to challenge the conventional methods of production. In the Don Basin the miner Alexei Stakhanov was reported as having hewed 102 tons of coal in a single six-hour stint in August 1935. This was fourteen times the norm set by the mine's managers. Stalin took this as demonstration that passive resistance to the Second Five-Year Plan persisted. Stakhanov was summoned to Moscow and showered with honours and gifts. The Stakhanovite movement was spread to all sectors of the economy, even to farms and to the railways.

Stakhanovites could not break records without managers making special arrangements for them. Other workers were compelled to give auxiliary support. This disrupted the pattern of general production and output was negatively affected. Moreover, the Stakhanovites cut corners in their efforts. Broken machinery was often the result. Yet Stalin ignored the evidence. Scientific approaches to production were abandoned as the enthusiasm for getting workers to earn privileges by increased output prevailed.[30]

Things could have turned out badly for the specialists in the economy – the managers, foremen, engineers and planners – if ever the suspicion of them encouraged by the Stakhanovite movement had taken the penal form applied to former oppositionists. It was a close-run thing. Stalin in 1935 did not confine his persecuting passion to the dual repression of former party oppositionists and current suspect party members. He also turned his anger upon whole social categories of citizens. The NKVD was ordered to clear Leningrad of people who by virtue of their occupation or status before 1917 were deemed intrinsically hostile to the USSR. Aristocrats, landlords, businessmen and their families in their thousands were expelled to smaller towns and villages with just the minimum of personal possessions. Over eleven thousand individuals were deported by the end of March from Leningrad,[31] and the policy was reproduced in the other large cities. The Politburo under Stalin's leadership was beginning to purge the cities of alleged anti-Soviet elements in much the same way as it had done to the rural areas by means of dekulakisation from 1929.

Yet the current specialists, although they were harassed at work, were not strongly persecuted unless they visibly obstructed official measures. They benefited from the desire of individuals in Stalin's entourage to hang on to them. Ordzhonikidze, People's Commissar for Heavy Industry since 1932, protected his managers and planners not only because he thought they were being defamed but also because he recognised that he would not fulfil his institution's quotas for the Five-Year Plan without their expertise.

The benefits of economic consolidation were anyway beginning to be demonstrated. Steel output in 1935 was over double the amount for 1932.[32] The Second Five-Year Plan, like the First, was recurrently altered as it was being implemented. Among the inevitable modifications was an increase in the budget for armaments production after Hitler became German Chancellor in January 1933 and the USSR had to assume that war with the Third Reich might soon occur.[33] This obviously involved a deferment of achieving the goals set for consumer goods. But generally the Kremlin was satisfied with the progress being achieved. Although policy was made and announced in an atmosphere of crisis, Politburo members including Stalin gave no impression in their correspondence or discussions that they thought that there was serious active resistance to their purposes or that advances in economic development were not being made. The progress continued into 1936 and beyond. Gross industrial output in 1937, the final year of the Second Five-Year Plan, had increased by three fifths over output in 1932. Even agriculture began to recover from the traumas of collectivisation. Gross agricultural output rose by about a half in the same period.[34]

Stalin's own activity was still ambiguous. In 1935–6 he oversaw the elaboration of a new USSR Constitution. He involved many leading figures in politics and culture in the work; even Bukharin at his editorial offices in *Izvestiya* contributed to the early variants.[35] Ultimate authority, however, stayed with Stalin and the Politburo. In practice this meant Stalin. And Stalin, the relentless persecutor of ex-oppositionists and the so-called 'former people', sanctioned the granting of full civic rights under the Constitution to all Soviet citizens regardless of their social, religious or political backgrounds. Universal equality of treatment was proclaimed. Soviet citizens were guaranteed pay, food, education, shelter and employment. No other constitution in the world was so expansive in the benefits it proffered. At a time when all his political manoeuvres were at their most opaque Stalin presented a baffling persona to observers in 1936. The Constitution was so comprehensively benign in most of its clauses that some thought he was engaged in subterfuge. Perhaps it was designed mainly for gullible foreign eyes in the interests of the USSR's international relations. Possibly he also intended it as propaganda at home without seriously intending to realise its contents in the foreseeable future. Stalin had a long record of disguising oppression and exploitation in the Soviet Union and claiming the country as a paradise for most of its citizens.

Introducing the Constitution in November 1936, Stalin proclaimed: 'Socialism, which is the first phase of communism, has basically been achieved in our country.' Breaking with his earlier idea that resistance to communism grew fiercer as the accomplishments of the regime mounted, he welcomed the revocation of the 1918 disfranchisement of the old political, economic, social and religious elites. But he brooked no challenge to the orientation of the Politburo. The Constitution defined the USSR as 'a socialist state of the workers and peasants'. Despite their constitutional rights, citizens would not be permitted to overturn the Soviet order. Stalin, glossing various clauses, openly stated that there would be no weakening of the communist dictatorship.

Some citizens, however, failed to understand the practical limits to the Constitution's realisability. Complaints and denunciations were sent to the Kremlin on the assumption that the authorities had a genuine commitment to comprehensive civic rights.[36] Of course most people saw through the illusion. The according of full civil rights to 'former people' meant that they at best gained the rights of the oppressed remainder of Soviet citizens – and there was no official intention to reform this basic situation. The USSR was ruled arbitrarily and with massive repression. Most people expected little from the new Constitution. At a funeral meeting someone shouted: 'One dog – Kirov – has been killed. That still leaves another dog, Stalin, alive.'[37] Resentment was dire in the country-side.[38] Few citizens expected much advantage to accrue to them from the Constitution. Although the communist party was not mentioned in any of its clauses, the party's political monopoly was plainly going to be maintained so long as Stalin remained in power. The electoral system was as much a fiction as its Soviet predecessor. The NKVD laid its reports on Stalin's desk. Whatever he had been planning by means of the Constitution, he was left in no doubt that he had not fooled most people. Everyone knew that the party and police intended to exercise as fierce a dictatorship as before.

Other events in the second half of 1936 signalled that Stalin was far from content with political conditions. His measures, always brutal, were descending to the depths of depravity. On 29 June 1936 a secret message went from the Secretariat to local party bodies alleging the discovery of the 'terrorist activities of the Trotyskist–Zinovievite block'. Evidently the judicial sentences in the previous year had not satisfied Stalin, and Zinoviev and Kamenev were arraigned in August in a Moscow show trial. They duly confessed to having led, in concert with Trotski abroad, an Anti-Soviet Trotskyist–Zinovievite Centre which systematically carried out assassinations in the USSR. Budënny idiotically suggested getting the Comintern to capture Trotski and ship him back for trial with the two main defendants.[39] Zinoviev and Kamenev were already broken men before their miserable appearance in court. At Stalin's behest they were subjected to continual revilement and mockery throughout the proceedings. The verdict was execution by shooting. Zinoviev and Kamenev had been told that, if they confessed to involvement in the Kirov 'conspiracy' in 1934, their sentences would be commuted. But Stalin had tricked them. Early next morning, before any judicial appeal could be considered, they were hauled out of their cells and shot.

Just as ominous was the change in personnel in the NKVD. Neither Genrikh Yagoda nor his predecessor Vladimir Menzhinski had always pleased Stalin. He had had to goad them into the extreme forms of action which he advocated from the late 1920s. They were not his placemen even though they never ultimately failed to carry out his commands. Yagoda tried to ingratiate himself by telling Stalin every time a fresh cache of Trotskyist material was found.[40] But it was not enough for Stalin. He wanted someone at the head of the NKVD who would be able to anticipate his wishes rather than respond to them, sometimes slowly and not very efficiently.

On 26 September 1936 he thought he had found that man in Nikolai Yezhov. Yagoda was sacked by Politburo decision and Yezhov took his place. Yezhov was a party official who had risen steadily through the ranks since 1917. He joined the Assignments and Records Department of the Party Secretariat in 1927, becoming its head in 1930. At the time of his appointment as People's Commissar of Internal Affairs he was both Secretary of the Party Central Committee and Chairman of the Party Control Commission. Stalin had seen him at work and appreciated his fanatical commitment to rooting out and annihilating the adversaries of the ascendant party leadership. In 1935 Yezhov, with Stalin's encouragement and editorial assistance, had produced a 'theoretical work', never published, on the internal party oppositions. Entitled 'From Factionalism to Open Counter-Revolution', it intensified the menace to everyone – especially the leaders – who had ever failed to accept Stalin's line of policy. To have been an oppositionist in the past had become the same as to be guilty of treason in the present.[41] On being appointed People's Commissar of Internal Affairs, Yezhov was asked to devote nine-tenths of his time to the NKVD.[42]

Since December 1934 Stalin had had the legislative and organisational basis for an expanded state terror in the form of the *troiki*. He had practised terror widely but fitfully in 1935–6. He had also shown a degree of self-restraint as had his associates, and his rule was increasingly characterised by economic advance and social quiescence. But resentment was deep in society even though active resistance had been quelled. Although oppositionists and 'former people' were being hunted down, many had escaped capture. Links remained between Trotski and his followers; Bukharin was not the sole leading ex-oppositionist leader who hoped for a change of personnel and politics at the apex of Soviet politics. As yet Stalin's victims, at least in the course of the Second Five-Year Plan, fell into restricted categories. But there was no guarantee that this would always remain the case.

Stalin's earlier career, especially in the Civil War and during the First Five-Year Plan, pointed to the dangers of the situation. He was always tempted to settle accounts violently with 'enemies', and he was angry when his entourage failed to identify them to him. He never lacked eagerness to take the initiative. He was at his most dangerous when he sensed peril for himself and the Soviet order. Sooner or later, Stalin, the most determined driver of the vehicle of terror, would again grasp the steering wheel and turn the key. The years from the end of 1932 through to late 1936 witnessed occasional ignition and abrupt forward movement. The machinery responded fitfully to Stalin's guidance. When he turned the key the result was unpredictable. Sometimes the battery was flat and needed topping up. On other occasions the plugs were too damp and all he could achieve was a brief, sputtering sound. But in fact the vehicle was roadworthy; and when the circumstances were more favourable in 1937, the driver would be able to start and keep it running at full speed until he decided to bring it to a halt a year later.

29. RULING THE NATIONS

The communist party administered a multinational state. Russians constituted 53 per cent of the population and Stalin tried to associate himself with the Russian nation.[1] This tendency of his had grown over the 1920s and early 1930s. Stalin and Lenin had fallen out when Lenin demanded gentler treatment for the Georgian communist leadership than Stalin approved.

Young Vasili Stalin once said to his sister Svetlana: 'But you know, our father *used to be* a Georgian.'[2] The boy had been brought up in Russia speaking Russian and thought of his father as a Russian. Vasili was making a childish error: Stalin had not magically become a Russian. It is true that Stalin once referred to himself as a 'Russified Georgian Asiatic' and denied that he was a 'European'.[3] This was a rare attempt at national self-description after the October Revolution, but it has to be treated with circumspection. Georgia, according to the geographers, belongs to Asia since it lies to the south of the peaks of the Caucasus. Consequently the combination of 'Georgian' and 'Asiatic' is perplexing. Presumably it stemmed to some degree from a Georgian sense of cultural superiority over the peoples of the East. Stalin in any case used the phrase not in public but at a private dinner party in Voroshilov's apartment. He blurted it out in a light-hearted apology to the Bulgarian communist Georgi Dimitrov for interrupting his speech to the guests. By calling himself an Asiatic, a pejorative term among Europeans, Stalin was using humour to lighten the atmosphere. As always his comments must be interpreted in the light of the circumstances of their expression.

Yet there was a core of intrinsic plausibility in Stalin's quip. Born a Georgian, he retained habits and attitudes of his homeland and continued to cherish Georgian classical poetry. But he was also impressed by the rulers of the great Asian empires. He read avidly about Genghis Khan. His experience with Russia too had imprinted itself on his consciousness. He admired Russian nineteenth-century literature. He was proud of Russia's past and present power. He resented the loss of those territories such as Sakhalin which had belonged to the Russian Empire. He liked to be among Russians as well as among Georgians. The likelihood is that his subjective identity was neither exclusively Russian nor exclusively Georgian but a fluid, elusive mixture of both. This is not an unusual condition. Many people who travel from country to country semi-assimilate themselves to new cultures without abandoning the culture of their upbringing. Stalin, moreover, was a socialist inter-nationalist. As a Marxist he considered ideas of nationhood to be a temporary and contradictory phenomenon: they both enhanced and vitiated their societies. It is doubtful that Stalin felt a need to fix a national identity for himself in his own mind. Rather his priorities were focused upon ruling and transforming the USSR and securing his personal despotism.

These priorities nudged him towards a change of policy on the national question regardless of the complexities of his own identity. Despite arresting individuals for Russian nationalism in the course of the First Five-Year Plan, he simultaneously ordered the media to avoid offending the national feelings of ordinary Russians and issued a confidential rebuke to the poet Demyan Bedny for poking fun at Russian popular proclivities.[4] Stalin and Kaganovich, when ordering the demolition of the Cathedral of Christ the Saviour in central Moscow in 1932, specified that this should be done without public announcement and at night: they did not want it getting about that a Georgian and a Jew had given the command.[5] When Stalin's official biography appeared in 1938, there was no reference to his Georgian background after the second sentence in the book.[6]

He had reason to be worried about Russian popular resentment at being ruled by alien politicians. Although the NKVD – and previously the OGPU – seems to have reported little on this, Stalin had a lifelong sensitivity to such matters. A clandestine poster had an image of two bands of warriors facing each other across the river. One was a Jewish band led by Trotski, Kamenev and Zinoviev, while the other was Georgian and commanded by Stalin, Ordzhonikidze and Enukidze. Below the image was the inscription: 'And the Slavs fell into dispute about who was to rule in Old Russia.'[7] Stalin indeed had several non-Russians in his entourage and not all of them were Georgians. Prominent among them in the early 1930s were Kaganovich (a Jew) and Mikoyan (an Armenian). Consequently Stalin remained wary of popular opinion. The battering of Russia's peasantry, its Orthodox Church and its village ways of life induced vast hostility to the regime. What is more, the emphasis of official propaganda was on the importance of Stalin in the shaping of policies. This left no doubt about his personal responsibility. Peasants hated him, and no amount of propaganda could mollify their feelings.[8]

By then the regime had abandoned many of its original objections to Russian traditions. The doyen of Soviet historical scholarship in the 1920s had been Mikhail Pokrovski, who had depicted the centuries before 1917 as an epoch of Russia's oppression of other peoples in the empire. No emperor or general had been accorded any positive qualities. The entire social system was treated as a blockage to social progress. From the mid-1930s all this changed. Ivan the Terrible and Peter the Great were lauded as initiators of administrative order, economic advance and external influence. The commanders Alexander Suvorov and Mikhail Kutuzov were hailed as rescuers of Russia and Europe from French tyranny. Whereas the Caucasian rebels had once been treated as heroes, historians began to stress that Russian Imperial rule conveyed much benefit to the borderlands. Russian scientific and cultural achievements were also highlighted. The chemist Mendeleev and the physiologist Ivan Pavlov (who died only in 1936) were said to be superior to their foreign counterparts. Russian nineteenth-century literary classics were produced in enormous print-runs, and the centenary of Alexander Pushkin's death was celebrated with pomp in 1939. It was no longer acceptable to mock or denigrate Russia and the Russians in Stalin's USSR.

With Zhdanov and Kirov Stalin oversaw production of appropriate historical texts.[9] The new orthodoxy was that the USSR was enhancing the best customs of Russian Imperial patriotism and enlightenment without reproducing the negative features of tsarism. Pride in country was to be fostered. Much of this was cynical propaganda to win favour with Russians. But it probably played on chords by then congenial to Stalin. After the October Revolution twentieth-anniversary parade in 1937 he spoke at a private dinner in Voroshilov's Kremlin flat attended by a couple of dozen leading politicians and military commanders:[10]

> The Russian tsars did many bad things ... But there's one good thing they did: they created an immense state from here to Kamchatka. We've been bequeathed this state. And for the first time we, the Bolsheviks, have rendered this state cohesive and reinforced it as a unitary and indivisible state not in the interests of the great landowners and the capitalists but rather to the advantage of workers and of all the peoples that constitute this state.

Stalin was an able actor and may not have believed a word of this. But the likelihood is that the statement with its peculiar mixture of Marxist–Leninist and Russian Imperial sentiments reflected his genuine opinion.

He was also responding to the currents swirling in the political air. Individuals of Russian nationality tended to take the place of the defeated adversaries of the Stalin faction. Jews lost out. In the light of his continued association with Jewish friends (if indeed anyone could be called his friend), it would be difficult to call him an anti-semite; yet the fact remained that his principal enemies Trotski, Zinoviev and Kamenev – prominent members of Lenin's Politburo – were Jewish by origin. Throughout the hierarchies of state administration the Russians were being promoted. Even in non-Russian Soviet republics they were securing posts. By contrast non-Russians seldom rose to high office outside areas where their nation did not constitute the majority of the local population. From the mid-1930s the Gulag system of camps contained 'bourgeois nationalists' of all national and ethnic groups except the Russians. The Russian language was honoured. It became compulsory in all schools and offices even though the Soviet republics were simultaneously allowed to go on teaching the local language too. The alphabets of other languages were altered. Latin and Arabic scripts gave way in most languages to ones based on the Cyrillic model.[11]

Many suggested that Stalin, frustrated with merely distorting Marxism–Leninism, had effected its abandonment. The émigré Russian fascist leader Konstantin Rodzaevski, becoming convinced that Stalinism and fascism were identical, returned from Harbin to the USSR after the Second World War. (This was not Rodzaevski's wisest move: he was shot on arrival in Moscow.)[12] So was Stalin objectively a Russian nationalist even if he did not subjectively advocate such a posture? Undoubtedly from the mid-1930s he engineered the elevation of the Russians over the other nations of the Soviet Union. Russians were preferred for appointment to high public office. The Russian language was given pride of place in the school curriculum. Russian writers, commanders and even certain emperors were eulogised by the media. The conquest of those other nations by the forces of the Russian Empire was treated as a boon for their general development.

The extolling of Russia and the Russians was accompanied by brutal maltreatment of several other peoples of the USSR. Ukrainians and Kazakhs believed that Stalin was inflicting genocide on them. Both suffered extremes of hardship through the violent collectivisation of agriculture imposed from Moscow. Kazakhs, a nomadic people, were forced to settle in kolkhozes. Ukrainians had always been an agricultural people. Abruptly their villages had been invaded by the OGPU and the 25,000-ers and, after the deportation of kulaks, the remainder of the inhabitants were forced into the collective farming system. The Kazakhs and Ukrainians suffered worse than Russians in most areas of Russia. The reason was similar: the Kazakhs had a culture which had not yet accepted agriculture, much less collective farming; the Ukrainians included many households with a notable commitment to the benefits of private farms. Kazakhs and Ukrainians were bound to be hit deliberately hard by the collectivisation campaign started at the end of the 1920s.

Initially there was an economic and cultural motivation to the Politburo's treatment of both peoples rather than a national one. But once the campaign got under way, Stalin and his associates were alert to any possibility that 'bourgeois nationalists' might put themselves at the head of the rural resistance. Kazakh tribal and religious leaders were constantly persecuted. Repression was also applied in Ukraine not only against kulaks but also against priests, writers and scholars.

Ukraine, however, continued to present Stalin with causes for political concern even though he was willing in 1932–3 to lower the grain-collection quotas across the republic. As collectivisation and dekulakisation proceeded and material conditions worsened, peasants in their hundreds of thousands sought to flee to regions of the USSR where the food supply was more secure. Among the refugees were Ukrainians who, according to the OGPU, carried the bacillus of nationalism. The Politburo's reaction, instigated by Stalin, was to instruct the Ukrainian communist authorities to close the Republic's frontiers to human traffic from 22 January 1933. The same policy of closure was applied to the Kuban area of the north Caucasus where many Ukrainians had settled in earlier years: Stalin wanted to stop them from spreading nationalist ideas outside their villages.[13] In the previous month, on 14 December 1932, the Politburo had decreed that the traditional party policy of recruiting mainly Ukrainian cadres to party and government in Ukraine and in Ukrainian-inhabited areas elsewhere had been applied much too mechanically. The alleged result was the penetration of the state by 'bourgeois-nationalist elements'. The Politburo commanded that a much more rigorous political sieving of promotees should be undertaken.[14]

Coming after the arrests and trials of Ukrainian cultural figures from the late 1920s,[15] these measures were brutal and discriminatory; and although Stalin did not seek the extermination of all Ukrainians and

Kazakhs, he certainly aimed to extirpate all opposition real and potential from among them. The ultimate objective, though, was to turn Ukraine and Kazakhstan into economically efficient Soviet republics. He therefore allowed both peoples to retain their culture, albeit in a much more restricted form than in the decade after the October Revolution. If the Ukrainian Soviet Socialist Republic could be made an integral part of the USSR, it would constitute a economic model which would win admirers for communism in eastern Europe.[16] Fertile Kazakhstan could also become a republic envied abroad, especially by Moslems. Collectivisation, dekulakisation, declericalisation and neglect of famine were appalling ways to raise Ukraine and Kazakhstan as models of the communist order, but they made a modicum of sense within the worldview of Stalin's Marxism–Leninism.

Not all interpretations of Stalin as a nationalist have him as a Russophile. Some think his indulgences to the Russians were a blind to his drive to enhance the prestige and conditions of the Georgian nation. Supposedly, far from being a Russian nationalist, he had maintained the patriotic enthusiasms of his youth. He had never approved Abkhazia's separation from Georgia in the constitutional arrangements of 1921–2, despite delighting in taking his vacations on the Abkhazian coast.[17] In 1931 he compelled his friend Nestor Lakoba to accept the incorporation of Abkhazia in the Georgian Soviet Republic. Most Georgians regarded Abkhazia as a province of historical Georgia and many of them felt grateful to Stalin for his action. Once incorporated, Abkhazia was exposed to a Georgianising cultural offensive, especially after the murder of Lakoba in December 1936.[18] The Abkhaz alphabet was compulsorily changed to a system based on the Georgian script. Abkhaz-language schooling was restricted. Georgian officials were transferred to the Abkhazian party, government and police. Demographic restructuring took place as Mingrelians, living in western Georgia, were allotted housing and jobs in Abkhazia from 1937.[19]

Stalin himself kept up his interest in the cultural pursuits of his youth. He fostered the publication of the old Georgian literary classics. He continued to read the great thirteen-century epic *Knight in the Panther's Skin* by Shota Rustaveli. He permitted the reprinting of Alexander Qazbegi's *Patricide*, the tale of mountain banditry which had inspired him as a boy. It was this cultural interest that had led Stalin to spend time reading and amending Shalva Nutsubidze's anthology of Georgian poetry.[20]

Yet these phenomena do not signify that Stalin was a Georgian nationalist. Such an interpretation would fit ill with his policies at the end of the Civil War, with the conquest of Georgia in 1921, with the persecution of the Georgian communist leadership in 1922 and above all with the attacks on Georgia's peasants, priests, cultural figures and politicians from the late 1920s through to the late 1930s. The fact that many Georgians subsequently forgot about this does not alter this record. Stalin's attitude can probably be best explained by reference to his long-known approach to the national question in general. Since *Marxism and the National Question* in 1913, his axiom had been that peoples without a vigorous press and literature should not be described as nations.[21] His premise was that such peoples should be brought to a higher cultural level by being associated with adjacent sophisticated nations. This role could be fulfilled in Abkhazia by increasing the Georgian influence; and whereas he wanted to see the Ukrainians and Belorussians pulled higher by the introduction of Russian culture, his personal experience told him that Georgians, being non-Slavs, could not sensibly be handled this way: Georgian national consciousness was too strongly developed for this to be possible.

Stalin elevated the status of Russians in the USSR and favoured some nations more than others; and he did this for a mixture of ideological and pragmatic reasons. The USSR was a state undergoing an economic and social transformation. Stalin had preconceptions about how to deal with the resultant problems. But he also had to react to circumstances that neither he nor anyone in his entourage had anticipated. Through the 1930s he found provisional solutions to the problems old and new.

Yet Stalin was no more likely to amputate Marxism–Leninism than to cut off his own fingers. What he was doing was more like shaving his beard; for the essential ideology was left largely intact. Stalin was idiosyncratic in the aspects of Russian national identity he chose for approval. He declined to include aspects which had figured prominently in the ideology of most professed nationalists in the nineteenth and early twentieth centuries. These had praised the religious faith of the Russian people, their rural customs and the simplicity and beauty of their villages. Russia's peasantry – its unsophisticatedness, endurance and lack of regard for the rest of the world – had been at the core of historical nationalism. None of this appeared in a positive light in Stalin's thinking. He dredged the Russian past for precedents for the communist preoccupation with state power, strong rulers, terror, industrialisation, towns and cities, secularism and organisational gigantism. There had been trends in this direction in some intellectual circles before 1917, but not in exactly the same form. The version of Russian nationalism which he allowed emerged largely from his own head.[22]

There of course existed another ideology which hymned dictatorship, militarism, cities, gigantism and distrust of the West and derided peasant, village and Christianity. That ideology was Marxism–Leninism. What Stalin had done was to strip back the various versions of Russian national identity to a single, very peculiar one – and it was one which maximised the overlap with Marxist–Leninist notions as they had evolved since 1917. Russians were encouraged to enjoy a sense of nationhood but were severely dissuaded from exploring it. The authorities felt they knew what national identity was good for the Russian people, and punished attempts to offer alternatives.

Russians, furthermore, were expected to be as much Soviet as Russian. Just as the Romanov tsars had fostered popular allegiance to the Russian Empire more than to any national idea, so Stalin induced a mingling of multinational pride in the USSR more than unequivocal nationalism.[23] He gave an impromptu speech at the dinner in Voroshilov's flat on 7 November, and among other things he declared:[24]

> Old Russia has now been turned into the USSR where all peoples are equal. The country is strong through its own power, army, industry and collective farm agriculture. Among the equal states and countries in the USSR it is the Russian nation which is the most Soviet and the most revolutionary.

He did not explain why Russians were more loyal than other nations to the October Revolution and the Soviet Union. But two factors stood out. One was that the Soviet Union was founded on a Russian territorial core. Another was that the Russian people were given advantages denied to others. Nevertheless Stalin did not want them turning into nationalists. He still feared the Russians. Consequently while other peoples had their own communist parties, he withheld this from the RSFSR. Their national feelings were to be channelled into a fusion of Soviet and Russian identities. By this means he would be able to enlist their support without letting the uncontrollable genie of nationalism into the open.

What is also clear is that Russification had its limits in the other Soviet republics. The USSR remained a multinational state and Stalin stayed committed to inducing non-Russians to assimilate themselves to the Soviet order. For this he needed schools and press to use local languages and for access to be open for the promotion of local national groups. National pride had to be fostered. Thus the Ukrainian poet

Taras Shevchenko, who died in 1861, was celebrated the length and breadth of the Soviet Union. Similar trends occurred in Georgia and other Soviet republics in the south Caucasus as national literary figures were acclaimed. The process of getting the peoples of central Asia to assimilate their sentiments to the territorial units demarcated by the boundaries of Kazakhstan, Kirgizstan, Tajikistan, Uzbekistan and Turkmenistan also continued; and the Belorussians, whose national consciousness had been weakly developed before 1917, continued to possess their own schools and press.

This immense conglomeration of peoples, held together in the framework of a revolutionary state, required new forms of rulership. Stalin is wrongly depicted as simply a tsar in Red clothing. In several ways he could not have been more different from Nicholas II. It is true that both Stalin and Emperor Nicholas, apart from a few trips to the ballet, rarely appeared in public except on occasions of great state ceremony. But Nicholas and his wife regularly went to the places favoured by peasants for Christian pilgrimage. They passionately enjoyed attending the reburial of St Serafim of Sarov deep in Russia's countryside in summer 1903.[25] Stalin went nowhere regularly unless to his dacha or on holiday. He did not deign to receive groups of peasant petitioners as the tsars had done. Lenin had understood that such activities helped him to keep in touch with what was happening in the country at large and to enhance his popularity. This practice was shunned by Stalin long before he started to worry about his personal security: he must have known that peasants – and probably most workers too – would have given him an earful of complaints about the dreadful conditions in the country.

There was an exception to his seclusion. Sister-in-law Maria Svanidze jotted down an account in her diary of an incident on his daughter's birthday in November 1935. Svetlana wanted to take a ride on the new Moscow Metro and Maria was set to accompany her and her brother Vasili. At the last minute Stalin said he would join them together with Molotov. Kaganovich was flummoxed. Although he had ordered ten tickets in advance, he was alarmed by the security implications of the news that Stalin was going to be involved. When they arrived at Crimea Square, the walls of the newly opened Metro station had not yet dried out but normal passengers were already using it. Bystanders spotted Stalin while arrangements were being made for him and his companions to travel in a separate carriage with its own engine, and when they got out at Okhotny Ryad, the station nearest to the Kremlin, there were ovations from fellow passengers. Resuming their places in the carriage,

they travelled onward on the Ring Line until Stalin decided it was time
to return home.[26]

Such an excursion might have been undertaken by Nicholas II if he
had still been on the throne. But usually Stalin's behaviour contrasted
with his practice. He gave speeches and wrote articles on Soviet and
world politics whereas the Romanovs left it to their bishops to give
sermons: tsars did not characteristically write conspectuses of their
intentions. Nicholas II was a Christian believer; he felt no need as a ruler
to explain his faith to those outside his family. Stalin was of a different
mould. He spent much time in the 1920s and 1930s working on
manuscripts. It was hard, unremitting work. He dispensed with the
services of shorthand typists: he thought they fidgeted too much. He
wrote laboriously in his own hand rather than suffer distraction. No
emperor since Catherine the Great had such a zest for writing – and
Empress Catherine had written mainly to confidential correspondents
such as Voltaire and Diderot: Stalin composed his literary stuff for the
world. The Romanovs were by and large considerate to their ministers.
Stalin enjoyed humiliating his subordinates; he traumatised and killed
many of them. He was seldom courteous and never unmenacing. (Often
when he turned on the charm, he made them wonder what devilishness
he was preparing.) He scared his entourage witless. Not since Ivan the
Terrible and Peter the Great had there been a Russian ruler who set out
to have this effect.

A further point of difference between Stalin and the tsars in their
styles of rulership was of a social nature. Repeatedly, he insisted at
private gatherings that his political success was attributable to the
support of 'the masses':[27]

> I don't deny that leaders have an importance; they organise and
> lead the masses. But without the masses they're nothing. People
> such as Hannibal and Napoleon perished as soon as they lost the
> masses. The masses decide the success of every cause and of
> historical destiny.

Tsars did not talk this way. Indeed in June 1937 Stalin went further.
Being used to toasting the health of People's Commissars, he wanted
respect to be given to 'the tens of thousands' of small and medium
leaders: 'They're modest people. They don't push themselves forward
and are barely discernible. But it would be blindness not to notice
them.'[28]

He gave sharp expression to this attitude on 7 November 1937 at the

October Revolution anniversary dinner, where he delivered a speech unrecorded in the press. The *praktiki*, he declared, were the intermediaries who maintained the link between the Kremlin and the masses. His rivals in the Soviet leadership in the 1920s had been more popular; but they overlooked the need to nurture the careers of functionaries in the lower ranks. When Dimitrov and others tried to praise him personally, he countered with a eulogy of the *praktiki*.[29] His belief was that the defeat of the internal party oppositions, followed by the purges of recent months, had got rid of those leaders from higher echelons in pre-revolutionary society. He had said this in June 1937 to military commanders after the arrest and execution of Tukhachevski.[30] Stalin was eager to prove that he and his surviving associates were better able than the privileged former émigrés to understand the needs of the working class and the peasantry. They themselves were from the lower depths – or at least many of them were. No Romanov emperor boasted of having no genealogical excellence.

Yet there was a moment in the Moscow Metro episode when minds turned back to the Imperial epoch. At Okhotny Ryad station Stalin's group left the train to try out the escalator. Meanwhile the passengers on the platform thrust forward into his carriage and stayed when Stalin returned and the train moved on:[31]

> Everything was very touching. J[oseph] was gently smiling the whole time, his eyes were kind [*dobrye*], kind and gentle. I think what touched him, for all his sobriety, was the love and attentiveness shown by the people for their leader [*vozhd*]. There was nothing artificial or formal about it. He sort of said about the ovations given to him: the people need a tsar: i.e. a person to whom they can bow low and in whose name they can live and work.

This remark does not seem to refer exclusively to the Russians;[32] probably Stalin had all the masses of the former Russian Empire in mind when he said it. Nevertheless he had revealed something important about his understanding of rulership in the USSR. To Stalin's eyes, the mentality of most Soviet citizens not yet been transformed by the October Revolution. They needed to be ruled, at least to some extent, in a traditional way. And this meant they needed a 'tsar'.

Stalin was an avid reader of books about Ivan the Terrible and Peter the Great. He admired their forceful methods and condoned brutality in pursuit of the interests of the state. Evidently some tsars were more congenial as models than others. Even Ivan the Terrible fell short of being the apple of his eye. For Stalin, Ivan was too unsystematic in repressing his enemies. More generally, though, he adopted certain techniques of rulership from the tsars. Most Romanov rulers maintained an aura of mystery. Too much exposure to public view might have derogated from the dignity and authority of the Imperial throne. Stalin adhered to this tradition. Possibly he did this because he knew he did not sound entirely Russian. In fact there were Romanov emperors who had had the same problem: Catherine the Great was a German princess of the houses of Anhalt and Holstein. In Stalin's case the difficulty was made greater by the fact that he, a Georgian ruling Russia, had an entourage with many who were also not Russians. Stalin, furthermore, had modified his political style. No longer did he have open office hours when ordinary party militants could come and consult him. He did not have his photograph taken with provincial delegations at Party Congresses; he did not submit his ideas to discussion on public occasions.

Just a few traces of his 'common touch' persisted. Despite his enormous workload, Stalin still found time to pen personal notes to individuals who wrote to him about all manner of small matters. When the peasant woman Fekla Korshunova, aged seventy, sent a letter asking permission to present him with one of her four cows, he replied:[33]

> Thanks, mother [*matushka*], for your kind letter. I don't have need of a cow since I don't have a farm – I'm totally a state employee [*sluzhashchii*], I serve the people as best I can, and employees rarely have farms. My advice to you, mother, is to hold on to your cow and keep it in memory of me.

This little response is a feather in the scale of his virtues; it is massively outweighed by the scale holding the records of his murderous misanthropy. But it shows that even in the terror years he was capable of kindness to strangers.

Despite rationing the number of his public appearances, Stalin could not avoid giving speeches and having them recorded for Soviet newsreels. The party's customs could be emasculated but not entirely abandoned. In order to confirm his legitimacy as Lenin's successor he had to get up at Party Congresses and deliver the keynote addresses just as he was obliged to write articles and booklets explaining the latest versions of Marxist–Leninist doctrine. He never became an outstanding orator. He lacked a sense of timing; often he seemed to quicken up or slow down without a feeling for what he was saying.[34] When he emphasised something, he did this with clumsy severity. Yet his primitiveness as a speaker also worked for him. Stalin wrote his own words; his message was always carefully considered. He delivered a speech with brusque directness. He was more like a general addressing his troops than a politician – or at times he was akin to a priest reading out a piece of liturgy whose details had ceased to engage his whole attention. Efforts to enliven such occasions were few. If ever there was humour, it was heavily sarcastic; and anecdotes drawn from his direct experience were notable for their rarity.

Nor indeed did he adopt a paternalistic manner. No Romanov, not even the wilder ones such as Peter the Great, was so lacking in the social graces on public occasions. Stalin to the end of his life preserved the unrefined demeanour of the stereotypical veteran Bolshevik. No Bolshevik was more tsar-like than he; but he was still a Bolshevik.

30. MIND OF TERROR

Stalin frequently lied to the world when he was simultaneously lying to himself. If ever he called somebody a traitor, it was not only the minds of others he was manipulating. Needing to believe the worst of specific individuals or groups, he let his language slip from established fact to desired reality. This is detectable in the message he sent to Kaganovich in August 1934 after an abortive mutiny by the divisional artillery commander Nakhaev:[1]

> He is, of course (of course!), not on his own. He should be shoved against a wall and forced to tell – to divulge – the whole truth and then punished with total severity. He – he has to be – a Polish–German agent (or a Japanese one). The Chekists are becoming ridiculous when they discuss his 'political views' with him (and this is called *interrogation!*).

Stalin was on vacation by the Black Sea at the time, hundreds of miles from Moscow. His sole knowledge of the Nakhaev incident had come through telegrams. He had been told that Nakhaev had tricked his troops into an insurrection; there was no evidence to incriminate Nakhaev in a wider plot. As for Nakhaev's operating as a 'Polish–German agent', this was fanciful speculation. Stalin had confected a story for himself and others and then tried to apply a coating of feasibility.

He seldom exposed his mental processes in public. He did not keep a diary, and the letters to his wife Nadya add little to what is known about his innermost thinking: at most he would refer briefly to his health, mood or the weather. More clues to his calculations emerge from his correspondence with Molotov, Kaganovich and other politicians. Often the contents were suspicious, conspiratorial and vengeful.[2] He disbelieved that trouble happened by accident or by mistake. Plotters were at work everywhere, he assumed, and had to be discovered and punished.[3] Stalin's correspondence showed him imperious in pursuit of his purposes. When issuing instructions to Politburo members, he rarely asked for their opinions but always demanded total compliance. While believing in communism, he did not trust or respect communists.

Trotski put down his recollections (and this became one of his main activities after being deported from the USSR in 1929). Molotov, Kaganovich and Mikoyan wrote informative memoirs.[4] Stalin's daughter and some of his in-laws also recorded their experiences.[5] Sometimes Stalin blurted out something in their presence that gives us a piece of his mental jigsaw. This could be a casual statement to Molotov or to a close relative; it could equally be an improvised speech or a toast at a private banquet.[6] Of course it would be foolish to forget that, when he spoke, he usually concealed something. Stalin watched people always as if they might be his enemies. Constantly he presented himself to individuals with a purpose in mind. He decided in advance what he wanted from them and adjusted his behaviour to this. He rarely raised his voice and his self-control was legendary among his associates.[7] Even many of the intimate files are ambiguous evidence on the workings of Stalin's mind. Yet he gave himself away in dribs and drabs; enough is available for subsequent generations to make plausible guesses.

What has always been intriguing is how an undemonstrative bureaucrat of the 1920s turned into a mass killer.[8] This puzzle results from analytical laziness. Even anti-communist scholars copied Trotski's brilliant portraiture of Stalin.[9] Yet Trotski gave a self-serving account. Remembering the Civil War, he stressed in particular how Stalin had conspired against party policy on the Red Army's organisation; he failed to mention the vicious terror perpetrated by Stalin at that time. Trotski himself was an enthusiastic perpetrator of terror in the Civil War and had no incentive to castigate behaviour which he too displayed. He also disliked admitting that he should have been able to predict how Stalin might behave in the 1930s.

Stalin's propensity for violence, excessive even by Bolshevik norms, was observable soon after the October Revolution. In the Civil War he had put whole villages to the torch near the Southern Front in order to inspire fear among the peasantry.[10] He had arrested Imperial Army officers in the Red forces on the slightest pretext and loaded them on to a barge on the River Volga: only a last-minute intervention from Moscow prevented him from drowning them.[11] Even the ordinary conscripts in the Red Army had had grounds to be afraid. Stalin and his comrades on the Southern Front were reckless in their operational dispositions: the human losses in the forces under their command were unjustifiably high. Lenin, while confessing that he was no military expert, rebuked him for this at the Eighth Party Congress in March 1919.[12] A handful of ruthless comrades gathered around him as if he was their gang leader. His friends plotted together and stuck up for each other whenever the gang's interests were threatened. Stalin was willing to pay any price in lives to attain his objectives. In all lives except his own. For Stalin the supreme criterion of political judgement was the need to protect and enhance his personal power.

He was in his element when functioning in a chaotic environment. The trick he perfected in the Civil War had been the concoction of an atmosphere of suspicion and fanaticism unrestrained by moral scruple. He issued general objectives without specifying how they were to be attained. His supreme stipulation was that the objectives would be met; and if the measures involved heads being broken, he did not mind. While the world spun wildly, Stalin alone stayed tranquil and unmoved. This is how Stalin had liked it in the Civil War. His record as a political and military leader had been known at that time but subsequently ignored.

Yet although Stalin was ruthless and cynical, he was also optimistic in his own peculiar way. He regularly got rid of associates who queried his policies. His assumption was that people could always and easily be found to replace those who were deliberately slaughtered or who were inadvertently lost in the mayhem. 'When the people makes its wishes clear,' he said in a characteristically Delphic pronouncement, 'people start to appear.'[13] He was an eager promoter of the young and talented, and assumed that recruits from the working class and the peasantry could quickly master most specialised tasks. Middle-class experts in his opinion were a bane, and none were worse than the officers in the Imperial Army. Trotski stipulated that promotion should be given only on the basis of professional criteria; Lenin wavered from time to time, but he too was loath to get rid of individuals merely because of their class origins if genuine expertise was needed. Stalin was the real enthusiast in the party leadership for choosing on the premise of class. He took seriously the Leninist nostrum that communist leaders should release the potential of the lower social orders in the old society and that the tasks of socialist management were in fact simpler than the 'bourgeois specialists' contended.

This outlook was not unique among Bolsheviks, even though Stalin held to it with a fanaticism such as no other Bolshevik exhibited. Not only Molotov and Kaganovich but also his other close associates shared his general attitudes. They had joined Stalin as they scrambled up the slippery pole of Soviet politics in the 1920s and 1930s. His enemies were theirs too, and they knew that their fate would be sealed if he tumbled from power. Like Stalin, they saw factional opponents as 'swine' and 'scum'; and they began to compete in demanding severe sanctions. Voroshilov in a letter to Stalin in 1934 referred to Trotski, Kamenev and Zinoviev as 'horrible little individuals, traitors, finished people'; and he added, 'This poisonous and miserable scum ought to be annihilated.'[14]

The enthusiasm of Stalin's associates for political repression stemmed from the traditions of Bolshevism. The discourse of the Soviet state had always been extremist in tone and content. Terms such as 'anti-Soviet elements' and 'enemies of the people' had been in common use from the Civil War. The notion that whole social categories deserved harsh persecution was widespread. Terrorist methods had been approved and 'theorised' by Lenin and Trotski.[15] Show trials and the systematic fabrication of charges had been commonplace since the Socialist-Revolutionary leaders were arrested and sentenced in 1922.[16] The practice of accusing those who opposed the Bolsheviks of having direct links with foreign governments and their intelligence agencies had been rife since the suppression of the Kronstadt Mutiny in 1921. The campaign of arrests during the First Five-Year Plan resuscitated such tendencies. The sense that people had to choose to be either for or against the October Revolution was universal among Bolsheviks; and all of them knew that the Soviet state was beleaguered by the forces of world capitalism. Stalin and his associates were a brutal lot. But a party lacking in gentility had produced them.

His associates were not just ingratiating themselves with Stalin when they used such language. Certainly they strove to please the Boss, and several were careerists. But many of them served and respected him also because they shared many of his ideas. This was especially true of Molotov and Kaganovich. The Great Terror, while being instigated by the single-minded leadership of Joseph Stalin, was also a reflection – however distorted a reflection – of the mind-set of Bolshevism as it had been imposed on the party by the mid-1930s. The group around Stalin had its jargon and attitudes. Its members made proposals within a particular ambience. Stalin gathered further associates who were closely in line with his basic orientation. Yezhov, who started working in the Central Committee Secretariat in 1930, was a noteworthy example. Even careerist newcomers probably came to imbibe several of the basic tenets.

Yet Stalin was the moving spirit in the coterie. He was proud of his position in the USSR; and when he looked abroad, there were few individuals he regarded with admiration. Adolf Hitler was one of the few. The occasion for Stalin to express his esteem came in June 1934 when the Führer ordered the German armed forces – the Wehrmacht – to arrest and kill the members of the SA. This was an act of political mass murder. The SA had been the paramilitary arm of the Nazi Party in its rise to power and its leader was Hitler's associate Ernst Röhm. When Röhm started to criticise Hitler's collusion with the German political and economic establishment, he signed the death certificate for himself and his organisation. Stalin relished the news of the Night of the Long Knives: 'What a great fellow! How well he pulled this off!'[17] It took one to know one. But he said this in a casual chat with Mikoyan: the significance of Stalin's remark only seemed sinister to him in retrospect. Perhaps others in the gang talked in a similar fashion. What was characteristic about Stalin is that he meant every word he said about Hitler with passionate intensity, and was willing to act in the same fashion when the opportunity arose.

The psychological and intellectual scaffolding for Stalin's proclivities was occluded from the public. He greatly admired Lenin. But among the other objects of his admiration was Ivan the Terrible. Most educated people in the USSR would have been horrified by this. Tsar Ivan was associated with arbitrary rule and terror as well as an erratic personality. But Stalin thought differently. For years he brooded over the life and rule of the fifteenth-century tsar.

At a Kremlin reception on 8 November 1937 Stalin accused the leading oppositionists of planning the territorial disintegration of the USSR in league with Germany, Britain, France and Japan. He vowed to destroy all of them. If anyone sought to detach the smallest piece of Soviet territory, he declared, 'he is an enemy, an accursed enemy of the state and the peoples of the USSR'. Then came the climax:[18]

> And we will annihilate every such enemy, even if he were to be an Old Bolshevik! We will annihilate his entire clan, his family! We will mercilessly annihilate everyone who by his actions and thoughts (yes, thoughts too) assails the unity of the socialist state. For the total annihilation of all enemies, both themselves and their clan!

This was hardly Marxist in style or content. Was it perhaps a residue of Stalin's extreme attitude to his upbringing in Georgia where, at least in the mountains, the traditions of the blood feud persisted? This cannot be the exclusive explanation. Although Georgian traditions may have encouraged him to seek revenge for any damage, they did not involve the assumption that the destruction of entire extended families was desirable.[19] A more plausible influence was Stalin's reading of early Russian history – he had long been an enthusiastic reader of R. Vipper's biography of Ivan the Terrible.[20] Dedicating himself to exterminating not only individual leaders but also their relatives, Stalin was reproducing the attitudes of Ivan the Terrible.

He continued to ponder the springs of human endeavour. He put one trait of character above all others: 'Lenin was right to say that a person lacking the courage to act at the crucial moment cannot be a true Bolshevik leader.'[21] He wrote this in a letter to Kaganovich in 1932. Two years later a similar sentiment surfaced in one of his brief messages to his mother: 'The children send their respects to you. Since Nadya's death, of course, my personal life is heavy. But so be it: a courageous person must always stay courageous.'[22] Probably Stalin was expressing himself sincerely. (Perhaps he was also trying to convince himself that he was valorous.) All acquaintances were impressed by his will power. Even the wilful Kaganovich was bendable to his purposes. But this was not enough for Stalin, who wanted to appear not merely strong-minded but also courageous. Such a virtue was to remain a dominant theme in his thinking; he was to emphasise the need for it in the very last speech he improvised to the Central Committee in October 1952, just months before his death.[23]

His style of thinking can be glimpsed in the jottings he made in the 1939 edition of Lenin's *Materialism and Empiriocriticism*. Stalin studied this dour work on epistemology despite all the practical matters of state he had to decide. He scattered a commentary in the margins. Stalin savoured Lenin's polemical attacks, scribbling down phrases such as 'Ha! Ha!' and even 'Oi Mama! Well, what a nightmare!'[24] His mental fixation with Lenin was evident from the way he repeatedly copied out Lenin's name in Latin script.[25] Yet the most intriguing thing is what he wrote on the flyleaf at the end of the book:[26]

NB! If a person is:
1) strong (spiritually),
2) active,
3) intelligent (or capable),
then he is a *good* person regardless of any other 'vices'.

1) weakness,
2) laziness,

3) stupidity
are the only thing [*sic*] that can be called vices.

Of all the reactions to Lenin's *Materialism and Empiriocriticism* this is
surely the oddest. It is hard to believe that it was the reading of the book
that provoked Stalin's comments; probably he simply used the flyleaf as
a convenient space for ideas that came to mind.

Stalin, communing with himself, used the religious language of the
spirit and of sin and vice. Human endeavour apparently could be
encapsulated only in such terms: evidently Marxism would not fulfil this
task by itself. Stalin was reverting to the discourse of the Tiflis Spiritual
Seminary; his early schooling had left an indelible imprint.

The content of the commentary, though, is deeply unChristian; it is
reminiscent more of Niccolò Machiavelli and Friedrich Nietzsche than
of the Bible. For Stalin the criterion of goodness was not morality but
effectiveness. Individuals were to be judged for their inner strength,
assiduity, practicality and cleverness. Any blemishes on the escutcheon
of a career were forgivable if accompanied by substantial achievements
in the service of the cause. Furthermore, the fact that the characteristics
despised by Stalin were weakness, idleness and stupidity is revealing.
Stalin the mass killer slept easily at night. Not for him the uneasiness of
wearing the crown of state: he adored power. But he was also self-
demanding. He wanted action and wished it to be based on sound
judgement, and he could not abide sloth and lack of intelligent commitment. He was offering himself the plaudits of history. Judging his own
long and bloody career in revolutionary politics, he found nothing to
reproach. But like a sixteenth-century Calvinist he felt the need to keep
asking himself whether he really met his own exacting standards. Gruff
and blunt as he was among his associates, he had episodes of introspection. But he did not torment himself. The very process of laying out the
criteria of judgement apparently allayed such doubts as he had about
himself. He grew into his own myth.

The fact that he jotted down his remarks in a copy of a work by
Lenin may not have been an accident: Stalin measured himself by Lenin's
standard.[27] The influence was not merely ideological. Stalin had seen
Lenin at close quarters and abidingly respected and even revered his
memory. But the language used in the jottings was not especially
Leninist. Possibly Stalin's style of amoralism came not from Marxism–
Leninism but from a much earlier set of ideas. He read Machiavelli's *The
Prince* and annotated his own copy of it. (Alas, the copy has disappeared

from the archives.)[28] His insistence on the importance of courage could well have derived from Machiavelli's supreme demand on the ruler: namely that he should show *vertù*. This is a word barely translatable into either Russian or English; but it is identified with manliness, endeavour, courage and excellence. Stalin, if this is correct, saw himself as the embodiment of Machiavellian *vertù*.

His was a complex mind. He had a personality prone to mistrustful fantasy and, tragically, he had the opportunity to act out his own psychological damage by persecuting millions of his people. He perceived enemies everywhere; his whole cognitive tendency was to assume that any slight problem in his personal or political life was the result of malevolent human agency. He was also drawn to suspecting the existence of plots of the widest nature. He did not limit this attitude to the USSR. Contemplating the anti-British Indian National Congress in 1938, he assured a reception of newly elected USSR Supreme Soviet delegates in 1938 that more than half were 'agents bought up by English money'.[29] That the British government possessed paid informers is beyond dispute. But the idea that so large a proportion were regularly denouncing Mahatma Gandhi is without substance although it may indicate the state of mind of its advocate. In the USSR, where his word was law, Stalin was seldom content to allow for the possibility that a particular victim might have been acting alone. His preference was to link his 'enemies' with a conspiracy spread out across the world and connected with the intelligence services of hostile foreign powers. His associates reinforced his propensities. They had always felt politically besieged.

It was a feeling that increased after they drove out the party oppositions and undertook campaigns of immense brutality in the country. They treated all people who resisted or simply criticised them as rubbish to be annihilated. Not all of them lusted after terror, yet some did and many more were willing collaborators. Every one of these associates had reason to be fearful. The deep resentment across Soviet society was real, and they could not be confident that an alternative political leadership would not arise and overthrow them.

Stalin did not suffer from a psychosis (which is the word nowadays preferred by doctors for madness). Unlike people who are classified as mentally ill, he did not experience episodes which stopped him functioning with day-to-day competence at work. He was not a paranoid schizophrenic. Yet he had tendencies in the direction of a paranoid and sociopathic personality disorder. There was something very odd about him, as his close comrades sooner or later discerned: he was not fully in control of himself. Unease in his presence was not a new phenomenon. From boyhood onwards his friends, while recognising his positive qualities, had noted a deeply uncongenial side. He was extraordinarily resentful and vengeful. He coddled his grievances for years. He was supremely casual about the effects of the violence he commissioned. In 1918–20 and from the late 1920s he had terrorised mainly people who belonged to social groups hostile to the October Revolution; from the mid-1930s he began to victimise not only such groups but also individuals known personally to him – and many of them were veteran party comrades. His capacity to turn on friends and subordinates and subject them to torture, forced labour and execution manifested a deeply disordered personality.

There were factors in his earlier life which must have pushed him down this road. He had a Georgian sense of honour and revenge. Notions of getting even with adversaries never left him. He had a Bolshevik viewpoint on Revolution. Violence, dictatorship and terror were methods he and fellow party veterans took to be normal. The physical extermination of enemies was entirely acceptable to them. Stalin's personal experiences accentuated the tendencies. He never got over them: the beatings in his childhood, the punitive regime of the Seminary, the disregard for him as a young activist, the deprecation of his talent in Revolution and Civil War and the assault on his reputation in the 1920s.

This is not the whole story. The environment around him in the 1930s really was a threatening one. His own policies had of course made it so. Nevertheless he had plenty of reason to feel that he and his regime were under menace. At the end of the 1920s he had introduced an order which was widely and deeply detested across the country. His speeches had left no doubt that official policies were of his making. His cult confirmed the impression. Kulaks, priests and nepmen had suffered under the First Five-Year Plan. It was not at all outlandish to presume that millions of victims, if they had survived, thirsted after the removal of Stalin and his regime. He knew that his rivals wanted rid of him and thought him unreliable, stupid and dangerous. He got used to planning on his own and to discarding associates at the least sign that they refused to go along with him. He saw enemies everywhere and intended to deal with all of them severely, however long he might have to wait. The situation was immensely dangerous. Stalin was an oddball. Culture, life-experience and, probably, basic personality made him dangerous too.

For all his sociability, moreover, Stalin was a lonely man – and such friends as he made were either found wanting in loyalty or died. He no longer had domestic stability or permanent emotional support. His first wife had died young. His life as a clandestine party organiser had been disrupted and unsatisfactory, and he had found it next to impossible to make friends in exile. (Not that he had tried very hard.) His second wife had killed herself; and, among his best friends in power, Kirov had been assassinated and Ordzhonikidze had eventually opposed his strategic ideas. Solitary again, Stalin had no peace of mind. He was a human explosion waiting to happen.

There was a vicious circle in the interaction between what was happening in the country and what he thought about it. His policies had produced a ghastly situation. Millions had died in the course of collectivisation in Ukraine, south Russia, the north Caucasus and Kazakhstan. Repression had been massive in town and countryside. The popular standard of living had plummeted. Resistance had taken the form of rural revolts and industrial strikes, and the ascendant party leadership could not depend entirely even upon the armed forces. Yet rather than change his policies Stalin introduced greater violence to the tasks of governance. Violence in turn bred stronger resentment and this induced Stalin, already a profoundly suspicious and vengeful ruler, to intensify and broaden the application of state coercion. The situation brought out the worst in him. In fact he had plenty of badness in him to be brought out long before he held despotic power. To explain is not to excuse: Stalin was as wicked a man as has ever lived. His was a mind that found terror on a grand scale deeply congenial. When he had an opportunity to implement his ideas, he acted with a barbaric determination with few parallels in world history.

31. THE GREAT TERRORIST

If Stalin's mind had a predisposition towards mass terror, it remains to be explained why he abruptly intensified and expanded repressive measures in the last months of 1936. For two years he had been gearing up the machinery of state violence. He had crushed active critical groupings. He had arrested thousands of former members of the United Opposition and killed Zinoviev and Kamenev. He had deported tens of thousands of 'former people' from the large cities. He had filled the Gulag system of camps to bursting point with real and potential enemies of the regime. His personal supremacy was unchallenged. He suborned his entourage into accepting his main demands in policy; and when he sensed a lack of total compliance, he replaced personnel with ease. The procedural mechanisms had been simplified since Kirov's assassination. Stalin still formally consulted the Politburo but its members were merely asked to ratify measures which the NKVD proceeded to apply through its *troiki*. Party rule had ceased to function in its customary fashion.

A further step in the direction of what became known as the Great Terror was taken at the December 1936 Central Committee plenum.[1] Stalin let his dogs off the leash and set them on Bukharin and the veteran Rightists. Yezhov led the pack, declaring that Bukharin had known all about the terrorist plans and actions of the (non-existent) Trotskyist–Zinovievite block. The scheme was obvious. Yezhov had been sanctioned to widen the net of former oppositionist victims and to brand all of them as being in league with each other and working for foreign powers. Bukharin for months had been living in fear of something like this happening. When it occurred, it took him by surprise. He was still editor of *Izvestiya*. He had written pieces which, if read between the lines, could be interpreted as warnings about the effects of Stalin's policies; but he had kept out of contact with the survivors of the Left Opposition. He had had nothing to do with Zinoviev and Kamenev for years. Yet Stalin and Yezhov were hunting him down. Bukharin demanded to confront those of Yezhov's prisoners who were incriminating him. This was arranged in the presence of Stalin and the Politburo. Dragged out of the Lubyanka, Yevgeni Kulikov claimed that Bukharin had headed a Union Centre.[2] Georgi Pyatakov went further, claiming that Bukharin had liaised regularly with known Trotskyists like himself.[3]

Bukharin was not yet arrested, but from December 1936 through to July 1937 the net of repression was cast ever wider and reached its full list of victim-categories. The NKVD arrested followers of oppositions of both Left and Right. It seized existing holders of office in party, government, army and all other public institutions. It moved against large groups in society which had connections with the pre-revolutionary elites. It apprehended members of former anti-Bolshevik parties, clergy and ex-kulaks. It picked up and deported several national and ethnic groups in the USSR's borderlands. Having identified the categories for repression, the NKVD's terror machinery was kept working at full pace until November 1938.

One thing is sure: it was Stalin who instigated the carnage of 1937–8, although there was a current of popular opinion in the USSR that it was not essentially his fault. Supposedly his associates and advisers had persuaded him that only the most extremes measures would save the state from destruction; and in later decades this notion continued to commend itself to a handful of writers.[4] But this was self-delusion. Stalin started and maintained the movement towards the Great Terror. He did not need to be pushed by others. He and nobody else was the engineer of imprisonment, torture, penal labour and shooting. He resorted to terror on the basis of Bolshevik doctrines and Soviet practical precedents. He also turned to it out of an inner psychological compulsion.[5] Yet although he did not need much temptation to maim and kill, he had a strategy in mind. When he acted, his brutality was as mechanical as a badger trap. Stalin knew what he was hunting in the Great Terror, and why. There was a basic logic to his murderous activity. It was a logic which made sense within the framework of personal attitudes which interacted with Bolshevism in theory and practice. But he was the despot. What he thought and ordered had become the dominant factor in what was done at the highest level of the Soviet state.

Chief among his considerations was security, and he made no distinction between his personal security and the security of his policies, the leadership and the state. Molotov and Kaganovich in their dotage were to claim that Stalin had justifiable fears about the possibility of a 'fifth column' coming to the support of invading forces in the event of war.[6] Stalin gave some hints of this. He was shocked by the ease with which it had been possible for General Franco to pick up followers in the Spanish Civil War which broke out in July 1936.[7] He intended to prevent this from ever happening in the USSR. Such thinking goes some way to explaining why he, a believer in the efficacy of state terror, turned to intensive violence in 1937–8. Yet he would probably have felt impelled towards terror even without the pressures of the international situation. He felt the impulse to terror before the late 1930s. Inside the party there was much discontent with him and his policies, and indeed massive anger existed across the country. Although his power was enormous, he could never allow himself the luxury of complacency. The possibility of the bitter discontent bursting into a successful movement against him could not be discounted. Stalin's revolutionary break with the NEP had caused tremors which were far from dying down. Beneath the surface of calm and obedience there boiled a deep resentment in state and society which had already given him cause for anxiety.

So if his reaction to the Civil War in Spain was the match, the entire political and social situation in the USSR over the past few years was the tinderbox. Stalin had come close to saying this in the message he and Zhdanov sent from the Black Sea to Kaganovich and Molotov on 25 September 1936:[8]

> We consider it an absolutely necessary and urgent matter to appoint com[rade] Yezhov as People's Commissar of Internal Affairs. Yagoda has clearly shown himself not up to the task of unmasking the Trotskyist–Zinovievite bloc. The OGPU is four years behind in this matter.

In lighting the match, Stalin did not necessarily have a predetermined plan any more than he had had one for economic transformation at the beginning of 1928. Although the victim-categories overlapped each other, there was no inevitability in his deciding to move against all of them in this small space of time. But the tinderbox had been sitting around in an exposed position. It was there to be ignited and Stalin, attending to all the categories one after another, applied the flame.

Trotski's former ally Georgi Pyatakov had been arrested before Yezhov's promotion. Pyatakov had been working efficiently as Ordzho-nikidze's deputy in the People's Commissariat of Heavy Industry. Ordzhonikidze, in discussions after the December 1936 Central Com-mittee plenum, refused to believe the charges of terrorism and espionage laid against him. This was a battle Stalin had to win if he was to proceed with his campaign of repression. Pyatakov was placed under psychological pressure to confess to treasonous links with counter-revolutionary groups. He cracked. Brought out to an interview with Ordzhonikidze in Stalin's presence, he confirmed his testimony to the NKVD. In late January 1937 a second great show trial was held. Pyatakov, Sokolnikov, Radek and Serebryakov were accused of heading an Anti-Soviet Trots-kyist Centre. The discrepancies in evidence were large but the court did not flinch from sentencing Pyatakov and Serebryakov to death while handing out long periods of confinement to Radek and Sokolnikov. Meanwhile Ordzhonikidze's brother had been shot on Stalin's instruc-tions. Ordzhonikidze himself fell apart: he went off to his flat on 18 February 1937 after a searing altercation with Stalin and shot himself. There was no longer anyone in the Politburo willing to stand up to Stalin and halt the machinery of repression.[9]

Ordzhonikidze's suicide happened in the course of a Central Com-mittee plenum that lasted into March 1937. Stalin, without hiding behind Yezhov, asserted that the Trotskyist–Zinovievite bloc had installed an agency for espionage, sabotage and terrorism working for the German intelligence services.[10] Yezhov repeated that Trotskyists, Zinovievites and Rightists were operating in a single organisation, and Stalin with the plenum's consent instructed him to carry out a thorough investigation.[11] Stalin also threatened those who held posts in the party. He aimed to break up the clientelist system which inhibited the operation of a vertical administrative hierarchy:[12]

> What does it mean if you haul a whole group of pals along with you? It means you've acquired a certain independence from local organisations and, if you like, a certain independence from the Central Committee. He has his own group and I have my own group and they're personally devoted to me.

The alarm bell was being rung for a party and police purge. Bukharin was arrested on 27 February, Yagoda on 29 March. Mass expulsions meanwhile took place from the party through to the summer. Marshal Tukhachevski was arrested on 27 May along with most members of the Supreme Command. The armed forces had been added to party and police as suspect institutions. Tukhachevski was shot on 11 June; he had signed a confession with a bloodstained hand after a horrific beating.

The tall poppies of the USSR were being cut down. Yet another Central Committee plenum was convoked on 23 June. Yezhov reported on his investigations. Shamelessly fabricating the evidence, he reported that a Centre of Centres had been uncovered uniting Rightists, Mensheviks,

Socialist-Revolutionaries, the Red Army, the NKVD, Zinovievites, Trotskyists and provincial party leaders. This was an alleged conspiracy on the
grandest scale. Not only anti-Bolsheviks and former Bolshevik oppositionists but also current party leaders were said to have plotted to
overthrow Stalin and his comrades; and Yezhov implied that only his
own vigilance had prevented a coup from occurring.[13]

Stalin managed the process cunningly. He contrived again to hide
behind Yezhov's initiatives and pretend that he himself had nothing to
do with the planning of repression. But as the moves were made against
Central Committee members, it was unfeasible for him to say nothing;
and in any case he was easily thrown into a bad temper by open criticism
of the arrests. At the June 1937 plenum of the Central Committee G. N.
Kaminski, People's Commissar of Health, objected: 'This way we're
killing off the entire party.' Stalin barked back: 'And you don't happen
to be friends with these enemies!' Kaminski had taken his stand on
principle and stuck to it: 'They're absolutely not my friends.' Stalin came
back at him: 'Well, in that case it means you're a berry from the same
field as them.'[14] Another brave individual was Osip Pyatnitski, a leading
Soviet functionary in the Comintern, who vehemently opposed the
proposal to execute Bukharin and accused the NKVD of fabricating its
cases. Stalin suspended the proceedings and assembled the Politburo
to discuss the outburst. Voroshilov and Molotov went to Pyatnitski to
persuade him to retract. Pyatnitski refused. When the Central Committee
reconvened, Yezhov denounced Pyatnitski as a former Okhrana agent,
and Pyatnitski's days were numbered. Stalin drew the plenum to a close
on 29 June. He had crushed all opposition and called on the Central
Committee to expel thirty-five full and candidate members from its
ranks. The shocked Central Committee voted in favour.[15]

Equipped with the Central Committee's troubled approval, the
Politburo on 2 July decided on a decree to carry out a definitive purge
of 'anti-Soviet elements'. Not only the alleged leadership of the (entirely
fictitious) Centre of Centres was to be eliminated but even whole social
categories were to be savaged.[16] It would affect former kulaks, Mensheviks, Socialist-Revolutionaries, priests, Bolshevik oppositionists, members
of non-Russian parties, White Army soldiers and released common
criminals. Order No. 00447 was drawn up by Stalin and Yezhov and
sanctioned by the Politburo on 31 July. The campaign was set to start on
5 August, and Stalin signalled his intention to oversee it by not taking
his regular vacation by the Black Sea. Yezhov, consulting him frequently,
had established a USSR-wide quota for people to be condemned. With

Above.
Stalin gives daughter Svetlana a cuddle.

Left.
Stalin's first son Yakob Dzhughashvili after being taken prisoner by the Wehrmacht.

Below.
Stalin's son Vasili at the controls of his aircraft.

Stalin in 1932.

'Stalin's Pipe'. The smoke coils around wreckers and kulaks.
Drawn by V. N. Deni, it appeared in *Pravda* on 25 February 1930.

Top. Mikhail Kalinin, Lazar Kaganovich, Sergo Ordzhonikidze, Stalin, Kliment Voroshilov and Sergei Kirov at a celebration of Stalin's fiftieth birthday.

Above. Anastas Mikoyan gesticulates to Maxim Gorki and Kliment Voroshilov.

Stalin together with Vyacheslav Molotov.

Line drawing by V. N. Deni: Stalin stands in Napoleonic pose with modern industrial structures and a banner of Lenin in the background.

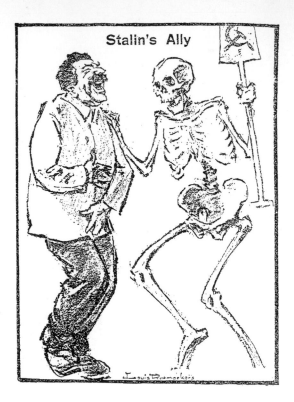

Stalin's Ally

'Stalin's Ally': cartoon
in the *Daily Telegraph*,
6 October 1939.

Below.
'The Plutocratic-
Bolshevik Wedding':
Nazi cartoon in
Preussische Zeitung,
16 July 1941. A Hasidic
Jew unites Stalin and
Churchill in marriage.
Molotov and Halifax stand
behind them.

Opposite top.
Stalin's work desk in
the carriage.

Opposite below.
Stalin's rail carriage
FD 3878.

Stalin, Roosevelt and Churchill at the Yalta Conference in February 1945.

elaborate precision he determined that 268,950 individuals should be arrested. The procedures would involve judicial farce; the victims were to be hauled before revolutionary *troiki* of party and police and, without right of defence or appeal, found guilty. It was also indicated exactly how many should be dispatched to forced labour: 193,000 individuals. The rest, 75,950, were to be executed.

The fact that he ordered the killing of nearly three out of every ten people arrested under Order No. 00447 invalidates the suggestion that Stalin's mass purges in mid-1937 were motivated mainly by the quest for slave labour.[17] Undoubtedly the NKVD's enterprises needed such labour to fulfil their targets for building, mining and manufacturing. But the Great Terror, while having an economic purpose, was systematically wasteful of human resources. The mass killings demonstrate that security interests were at the forefront of Stalin's mind.

On 25 July 1937 he and Yezhov had also put forward Order No. 00439, which spread a net of terror across a further category of people. German citizens and Soviet citizens of German nationality were to be arrested. The order did not designate a quota: the NKVD was charged simply with getting on with the operation on its own initiative. In fact 55,000 people received punitive sentences and these included 42,000 executions.[18] Stalin had decided that some types of foreigner were just as dangerous to him as kulaks and other 'anti-Soviet elements'. He did not stop with the Germans resident in the USSR. After them came the Poles, the former émigrés in the Chinese city of Harbin, the Latvians and several other peoples. 'National operations' of this nature continued through the rest of 1937 and all 1938.

The conclusion is inescapable. Stalin had decided to deal with the objects of his security worries in a sustained burst of NKVD mass arrests and murders. Additions were recurrently made to the quotas set for the operation against 'anti-Soviet elements' and to the list of nationalities marked down as hostile. Leaders in the provinces were not discouraged from applying for permission to raise the number of victims to be seized. Stalin wrote telegrams fostering the murderous enthusiasm. No document survives of his having gone the other way and trying to stem the flood of arrests, torture and killing. When the Krasnoyarsk Party Regional Committee wrote to him about a fire in a grain store, he simply replied: 'Try the guilty persons in accelerated fashion. Sentence them to death.'[19] There was no injunction to local leaders to exercise care in repressing the 'correct' people. His emphasis was always upon getting his subordinates to carry out the Great Terror with zeal. Thick, bloody slices

were cut from the personnel of party, government and all other institutions. The word went forth that the only way to save your life, if it was
at all possible, was to comply eagerly with orders for repression.

Even Kaganovich had to plead his case before him when Stalin
objected to his past association with 'enemy of the people' Marshal Iona
Yakir. Kaganovich plucked up courage to point out that it had been
Stalin who had recommended Yakir to him a decade before.[20] Nikita
Khrushchëv, Moscow Party Committee Secretary, was similarly threatened when Stalin accused him of being a Pole. At a time when Polish
communist émigrés in Moscow were being routinely shot, Khrushchëv
was understandably keen to prove that he was a genuine Russian.[21]

Stalin's involvement remained direct and deep as his envoys went to
the main centres to preside over the sackings and arrests of local leaders.
One of these envoys was Politburo member Andreev, a repentant
member of the Workers' Opposition whose past made it imperative to
carry out orders implicitly. He went to cities such as Chelyabinsk,
Krasnodar, Samara, Saratov, Sverdlovsk and Voronezh as well as Soviet
republics such as Belorussia, Tajikistan, Turkmenistan and Uzbekistan.[22]
Andreev quickly decided whom to arrest and whom to replace them
with. But he consulted Stalin before going ahead with his plans. From
Stalinabad in Tajikistan he reported that 'enemies have been working
here in a basic fashion and have felt fairly free in doing this'. Stalin
telegraphed back on 3 October 1937:[23]

> We sanction Protopopov as [Party] First Secretary, Iskanderov as
> Second, Kurbanov as Ch[airman] of the Sovnarkom, Shagodaev
> as Ch[airman] of the Central Executive Committee.
>
>   Ashore and Frolov ought to be arrested. You need to leave in
> time to be back here in Moscow for the Central Committee plenum
> of the All-Union Communist Party on 10 October.
>
>   Let Belski proceed to Turkmenia in a few days' time to carry
> out a purge. He will receive his instructions from Yezhov.

Andreev, Malenkov, Zhdanov and others toured the various regions
carrying out their master's policy.

Although it was physically impossible to ratify each and every
operation carried out in particular localities, Stalin still managed to
examine 383 'albums' of proposed victims brought to him by Yezhov in
the Great Terror. These albums alone contained the names of about
44,000 people. The higher the status of the victim, the more likely it was
that Yezhov would seek Stalin's signature before proceeding. Stalin, a

busy man, was expected to go through the lists and tick off recommended sentences whenever he spotted a name he knew and had a preference for what should be done. He did this with his usual assiduity; there is no sign that he objected to doing things in the 'album fashion'. All the time, too, he bound the rest of the Politburo to the process. Molotov, Kaganovich and Voroshilov and others were asked for their approval, and they frequently added their rhetorical flourishes to their names. 'Give the dog a dog's death!' was one of Molotov's touches. Stalin was still avoiding incurring exclusive responsibility. Obviously he retained a residual worry that he would not get away with the outrages he was organising. Having bludgeoned his comrades into condoning the measures, he wanted their continuing formal complicity.

The fact that Stalin targeted millions of persons who had broken no law had operational consequences. So too did his determination to purge every single public institution. In this situation it was crucial to obtain assent and co-operation from officials in party, government and police who might otherwise have disrupted the process – and as things turned out, many of them were doomed to pay for their compliance with their own lives. It was presumably for this reason that Stalin needed the trials, however spurious and brief they were, to take place. Not only that: he felt constrained to obtain proofs of crime. Somehow he had to demonstrate to the survivors of the Great Terror, including the individuals he promoted from obscurity, that the dreadful state violence had been justified. A comparison with Nazi Germany is apposite. When the German security agencies rounded up Jews, Roma, homosexuals and the mentally disabled there was no secret about the regime's antagonism towards them. Hitler kept quiet about the scale of the arrests and the fate of those who had been arrested; but this coyness was aimed at avoiding unnecessary opposition among citizens of the Reich: he had no need as he saw things to pretend that the victims were spies or saboteurs. They had been arrested exactly because they were Jews, Roma, homosexuals or mentally disabled.

Such an approach would not do for Stalin. Kulaks, priests, Mensheviks, Germans, Harbinites and Trotskyists lacked the popular antagonism towards them that Hitler had whipped up against his victims. They had to be shown to be a malignant presence in respectable, loyal Soviet society. Stalin was running a terror-state. Yet the requirement existed even for him to keep the confidence of the office-holders whose lives he spared. It did not greatly matter that his case against the victims was inherently implausible. What counted was that stenographers could record that, as far as the state was concerned, due legal process had taken place. Perhaps there was a personal edge to this. Stalin had characteristically seen the world in black-and-white terms. Intermediate colours did not exist for him, and he implicitly believed that those persons whom he felt he could not trust were indeed working actively and conspiratorially against him and his policies. For psychological reasons, then, he too required that his victims could be shown to have done wrong; and since the NKVD lacked material evidence, the sole option was for the alleged spies and saboteurs to be brought to admit their guilt. Interests of state came together with the aberrant purposes of an unbalanced Leader.

Ostensibly he acted as he did because evidence was brought to him that 'enemies of the people' – imperialist agents, subversives and counter-revolutionaries – had been exposed by the NKVD. Stalin was so suspicious that he probably persuaded himself that many of those whom he condemned to the Gulag or to execution were genuinely guilty of such crimes against the state. The nearest he came to witnessing the result of his barbarism was when he held confrontations between some broken leader willing to 'confess' and some other leader who was being denounced but had not yet been arrested. At the confrontation with Kulikov in December 1936, Bukharin was like a butterfly seeing the needle about to pin him to a board.

Yet although Stalin apparently derived satisfaction from such confrontations, he organised them only in the period when he still needed the sanction of his Politburo comrades for particular verdicts. After early 1937 he dropped them as being no longer necessary. Throughout the last months of 1937 the purges continued. They affected both central and local functionaries as well as 'ordinary' people. Awards were announced for the heroic butchers in the NKVD. Yezhov's name became second only to Stalin's in official esteem. On 16 December it was the turn of Abel Enukidze and fellow defendants to be tried by a Military Collegium as spies, bourgeois nationalists and terrorists. This was done in secret and in quick order. They were all shot.[24]

In March 1938 it was the turn of Bukharin. Along with him in the dock were three others who had belonged to the Party Central Committee in Lenin's time: Alexei Rykov, Nikolai Krestinski and Christian Rakovski. Yagoda was also a defendant, as were several lesser figures. The third great show trial was organised by those leading figures in the NKVD who had as yet survived the Great Terror. The charges were as bizarre as before. Bukharin in particular was said to have plotted in 1918 to murder Lenin and Stalin and seize power. He parried this particular accusation while accepting political responsibility for the anti-Stalin conspiracies alleged to exist in the late 1930s. Krestinski was less co-operative. At his first appearance in court he retracted his prison testimony. Next day, looking still more haggard, he reverted to the testimony agreed with his captors. Nearly all the accused had been savagely beaten. Bukharin was spared this but was visibly a broken man. From his prison cell he had written a note to Stalin: 'Koba, why is my death necessary for you?' But Stalin wanted blood. Constantly consulted by Chief Prosecutor Andrei Vyshinski and Vasili Ulrikh at the end of the court's working day, he ordered that the world's press should be convinced of the veracity of the confessions before sentences were passed.[25] Many Western journalists were indeed hoodwinked. The verdict was announced on 13 March: nearly all the defendants were to be shot.

Two days later Stalin approved a further operation to purge 'anti-Soviet elements'. This time he wanted 57,200 people to be arrested across the USSR. Of these, he and Yezhov had agreed, fully 48,000 were to be rapidly tried by *troiki* and executed. Yezhov, by now practised at the management of such operations, attended to his duties with enthusiasm. Through spring, summer and autumn 1938 the carnage continued as the NKVD meat-grinder performed its grisly task on Stalin's behalf. Having put Yezhov's hand at the controls and ordered him to start the machine, Stalin could keep it running as long as it suited him.

Stalin never saw the Lubyanka cellars. He did not even glimpse the meat-grinder of the operations. Yezhov asked for and received vast resources for his work. He needed more than his executive officials in the NKVD to complete it. The Great Terror required stenographers, guards, executioners, cleaners, torturers, clerks, railwaymen, truck drivers and informers. Lorries marked 'Meat' or 'Vegetables' took victims out to rural districts such as Butovo near Moscow where killing fields had been prepared. Trains, often travelling through cities by night, transported Gulag prisoners to the Russian Far North, to Siberia or to Kazakhstan in wagons designed for cattle. The unfortunates were inadequately fed and watered on the journey, and the climate – bitterly cold in the winter and monstrously hot in summer – aggravated the torment. Stalin said he did not want the NKVD's detainees to be given holiday-home treatment. The small comforts that had been available to him in Novaya Uda, Narym, Solvychegodsk or even Kureika were systematically withheld. On arrival in the labour camps they were kept constantly hungry. Yezhov's dieticians had worked out the minimum calorie intake for them to carry out heavy work in timber felling, gold mining or building construction;

but the corruption in the Gulag was so general that inmates rarely received their full rations – and Stalin made no recorded effort to discover what conditions were really like for them.

Such was the chaos of the Great Terror that despite Stalin's insistence that each victim should be formally processed by the *troiki*, the number of arrests and executions has not been ascertained with exactitude. Mayhem precluded such precision. But all the records, different as they are about details, point in the same general direction. Altogether it would seem that a rough total of one and a half million people were seized by the NKVD in 1937–8. Only around two hundred thousand were eventually released. To be caught in the maw of the NKVD usually meant to face a terrible sentence. The *troiki* worked hard at their appalling task. The impression got around – or was allowed to get around – that Stalin used nearly all of the arrestees as forced labourers in the Gulag. In fact the NKVD was under instructions to deliver about half of its victims not to the new camps in Siberia or north Russia but to the execution pits outside most cities. Roughly three quarters of a million persons perished under a hail of bullets in that brief period of two years. The Great Terror had its ghastly logic.

32. THE CULT OF IMPERSONALITY

The Lenin cult glistened like a film of oil over the dark ocean of Soviet reality in the late 1930s. Stalin had always presided over its rites. It had been he who arranged for the corpse of the Soviet leader to be displayed in the Mausoleum. He organised the publication of Lenin's memoirs and helped to set up an Institute of Lenin. He vowed undying allegiance to Lenin's ideas and practices. During the New Economic Policy he claimed to be a mere pupil of the great man.

The 'biography' by Lenin's aide Ivan Tovstukha in 1927 was really just a catalogue of his arrests, places of exile, main publications and official posts. Although it mentioned Stalin's support for Lenin against Kamenev and Zinoviev in October 1917, there was no reference to subsequent factional campaigns, and he was listed as being merely 'one of the secretaries of the Party Central Committee from 1922': his full title of General Secretary was omitted.[1] With Stalin's rise to political supremacy at the end of the 1920s all this started to change. After sending Bukharin and the Right Deviation down to defeat, he demanded appreciation as more than a party administrator. On 21 December 1929 Stalin's (supposed) fiftieth birthday was celebrated with the fanfares of a ceremony of state.[2] Even if he had been bashful (and in fact he was wary of making himself look ridiculous by permitting excessive praise),[3] political self-interest dictated the need for media acclaim in a period when oppositionist leaders were making scathing criticisms. Stalin aspired to his own personal cult.

He continued to express admiration for his predecessor. Although he allowed others to use the term 'Marxism–Leninism–Stalinism', he himself avoided it. Stalin even refused to sanction a complete edition of his collected works (whereas Trotski had already published twenty-one volumes of his writings before falling from grace). Addressing a large Moscow conference on propaganda in 1938, he condemned attempts to put him on the same level as Lenin as a party theorist. His *Foundations of Leninism*, Stalin insisted, was only a work of exegesis. The originality of thought lay with Lenin, which was why it made sense to talk of Marxism–Leninism and not just Marxism. But the teacher ought not to be confused with the pupil.[4]

Nevertheless he often allowed his light to outshine the aureole surrounding his predecessor. Comparisons of the two men began to be made at Lenin's expense. The party historian Yemelyan Yaroslavski opined that Stalin was the more decisive of the two leaders and that the reason lay in the excessive number of years spent by Lenin in emigration.[5] But usually the downgrading of Lenin was done in a visual fashion rather than in texts. On New Year's Day in 1931 *Pravda* carried a line drawing of Stalin on its front page – and Lenin appeared in it only as a name printed on a banner.[6] A similar picture was used to emphasise Stalin's greatness in the annals of Soviet communism on New Year's Day in 1937.[7] Line drawings continued to be preferred to cartoons. *Pravda* had always avoided carrying humorous representations of the party's leaders. (Foreign anti-communist politicians, though, were thought fair game.) This tradition endured through the 1930s. No levity was permitted to infringe Stalin's dignity; and whenever his image appeared in Soviet newspapers, it was in contexts that corroborated his supreme status. Commissioned pictures had to convey the impression of an inspiring genius with the determination and wisdom to change the face of state and society in the USSR, and both editors and censors were careful to comply.

Photographs were frequently carried. Among the most famous was one taken as he scooped little Gelya Markizova into his arms when she presented a bouquet to him.[8] Her bright smiling face adorned many books in following years. Little did readers know that her parents perished in the Great Terror soon after her big day. But Stalin got what he wanted. He was able to have himself represented as the warmest friend to all children in the country.

He strove to identify himself with young people in general. *Pravda* reproduced many photos of him greeting heroes of labour, science or exploration. Astutely he did not always monopolise the publicity. The typical front page of newspapers gave pride of space to young heroes of the moment: Stakhanovite miners or metalworkers, record-breaking milkmaids, geographical explorers or long-distance aviators. Citizens were invited to believe that the state led by Stalin had a dynamic orientation towards science, education, meritocracy and patriotism. Aviators had a special attraction for Stalin. When a celebratory book appeared on his meetings with individuals of outstanding achievement,

Soviet flyers were given greater space than any other category of person. He loved to meet them: 'You know how I'll fight like a tiger so that no one may give offence to our flyers!';[9] and they were understandably pleased by his attentiveness and by the medals they received from him.[10] By sharing the plaudits with Soviet citizens beyond the inner circle of powerful political leaders he enhanced his image as a modest man of the people. For Stalin, aviators and explorers had the advantage of operating far away from the public gaze. By contrast industrial managers and party bosses were widely unpopular and indeed Stalin routinely castigated them whenever (his own) policies caused resentment. Culpable subordinates served as a lightning conductor that deflected political damage on to others.

Stalin also aimed to associate himself with leaders of official organisations and enterprises at lower levels of the Soviet state. While arresting a multitude of the older post-holders in the 1930s, he issued appeals to those younger ones who took their place. Having long represented himself as a *praktik*, he declared at a Kremlin reception for metallurgical and coal-mining functionaries on 30 October 1937:[11]

> I'm going to propose a somewhat peculiar and unconventional toast. Our custom is to toast the health of the [Kremlin's] leaders, chiefs, heads and people's commissars. This of course isn't a bad thing. But apart from the big leaders there also exist middle-size and small leaders. We have tens of thousands of them, these leaders – both small and middling. They are modest people. They don't push themselves forward and they're practically invisible. But it would be blind of us not to notice them. For the fate of production across our entire people's economy depends on these people.

He chose his words subtly so as to avoiding reducing himself to the level of his audience. He left no doubt that he was one of the 'big leaders', and the cult of the Vozhd confirmed that he was the biggest of them. This mixture of self-assertion and modesty won friends and influenced the Kremlin elite, the party and the people.

Stalin liked to be seen to be restricting the cultic extravaganza. Worship had to be fulsome but not totally ridiculous in its extent. He frequently reprimanded his underlings if, unable to guess his opinion, they overstepped the mark of flattery. He was made angry by an attempt to publish his articles from the years before the Great War. Stalin wrote to Kaganovich, Yezhov and Molotov in August 1936 – while he was on holiday by the Black Sea – seeking their help in preventing publication.[12]

(Obviously he could have given a direct order and it would have been instantly obeyed; but Stalin also wanted to impress on the Politburo that he remained a member of a political team.) He continued to comment scathingly on what was written about him. Stalin exclaimed to one of his physicians, M. G. Shneidorovich, about the inaccuracies in Soviet newspapers: 'Look, you're an intelligent man, doctor, and you must understand: there's not a word of truth in them!' The physician was beginning to feel he had the Leader's confidence until Stalin added that doctors were just as unreliable as journalists – and doctors had the means and opportunity to poison him![13]

Beria could nevertheless publish a history of Bolshevik party organisations in the Transcaucasus. This had gained Stalin's sanction. Beria's book controverted the received opinion that only the Marxists of St Petersburg or the emigration had had a decisive impact on the fate of the party. Although the contents were mostly a historical fiction, the theme of the historical importance of the borderlands was overdue its attention. (Beria, though, was not the authentic author: he commissioned and appropriated the text and then shot the writers.) Beria's great Caucasian rival, Nestor Lakoba, produced an account of Stalin's experiences along the Black Sea littoral after the turn of the century.[14] Some memoirs also appeared about Stalin in Siberian exile.[15] Yet there was little detail about the episodes in his rise to prominence in the Russian Social-Democratic Workers' Party before the Great War and the circumstances of his co-optation to the Central Committee in 1912. Much remained hidden, and Stalin kept it that way. Mystery served his purpose: people would naturally be inclined to assume that he had been more important than was true. He enlarged the space for this to occur by removing his enemies from the history of Bolshevism. Steadily those other Bolsheviks who had been close to Lenin before the October Revolution were eliminated from the textbooks – and in most cases they were physically liquidated.

The grandiose acclaim kept on growing. At the Sixteenth Party Congress in June 1930 Stalin was greeted by 'stormy, prolonged applause extending into a lengthy ovation'. The Congress rose to its feet shouting 'Hurrah!' The same occurred at the Seventeenth Party Congress in January 1934, when there was a tremendous ovation and shouts of 'Long live our Stalin!' By the Eighteenth Party Congress in March 1939, after the Great Terror, even this was thought inadequate. Congress organisers had arranged chants of 'Hurrah for our Leader, Teacher and Friend, Comrade Stalin!'

Stalin biographies had been appearing thick and fast. The French writer Henri Barbusse's 1935 life of the General Secretary was translated into Russian and placed on sale in the USSR.[16] It was Barbusse who put into circulation the phrase: 'Stalin is the Lenin of today.' But not even Barbusse entirely pleased Stalin. It was this displeasure that led him in 1938 to get the Central Committee to commission *Stalin: A Biography*, which narrated his life from birth in the little town of Gori to the present day. His towering importance in Bolshevik theory and practice was affirmed. The *History of the All-Union Communist Party (Bolsheviks): A Short Course* appeared in the same year and covered the periods of communist party history through to the late 1930s. For years there had been competing versions of the history of Soviet communism. Several had enjoyed the approval of the Central Committee, and their authors – Nikolai Popov, Yemelyan Yaroslavski and Andrei Bubnov – had earned large royalties. Yet a single official statement was required when unflinching orthodoxy was a matter of life and death. A team of writers was assembled under V. G. Knorin, Y. M. Yaroslavski and P. N. Pospelov to provide such a work.

Stalin too worked on it behind the scenes; he not only wrote a chapter in the *Short Course* but also edited the book's entire text five times.[17] A line of legitimate succession was traced from Marx and Engels through Lenin to Stalin. Tendentiousness and mendacity were the book's hallmarks. For every point where disputes had arisen among Marxist revolutionaries it was suggested that only one authentic expression of Marxism was available and that Lenin and his follower Stalin had consistently adopted it. Soviet communism's history was treated in Manichean terms. There were the forces of rectitude led by Leninism and the forces of deceit and betrayal under the anti-Bolshevik parties – the Socialist-Revolutionaries, Mensheviks, Anarchists and nationalists of all types – as well as, subsequently, the Bolshevik factions hostile to Stalin. The *Short Course* deplored 'the Trotskyists, the Bukharinites, nationalist deviators and other anti-Leninist groups'. Not once had Lenin made a mistake in doctrine or strategy. By good fortune a man equally infallible, Stalin himself, succeeded him.

The two leading characters of the *Short Course* were treated differently. It is usually assumed that the book enabled Stalin to supplant Lenin in the mythology of Soviet communism.[18] This is untrue. Despite creating his own cult, he still found it useful to acknowledge the superiority of Lenin.[19] This was obvious in the handling of the party's early history. Whereas the official biography gave attention to Stalin's career as a young revolutionary, his name hardly appeared in the opening chapters of the *Short Course*.[20] In the entire book there were forty-nine citations of Lenin's works but only eleven of those by Stalin. Evidently Stalin still sensed a continuing need to cloak himself with the mantle of Lenin's memory.[21] The treatment of the October Revolution is remarkable in this respect. Its pages on the seizure of power avoided any reference to Stalin.[22] (Later generations of historians have missed this; indeed one wonders whether they have bothered to read the *Short Course*.) The point is that Stalin in the late 1930s, despite dominating the Soviet political scene, saw the desirability of placing a few limits to the worship of his own greatness. Even the Leader had to be cautious.

What is more, there was little in the writings about Stalin which gave a vivid impression of him. Usually the official eulogies are ascribed to a 'cult of personality' since this was the term used by Nikita Khrushchëv when he posthumously denounced Stalin in 1956. A more accurate translation from the Russian would be 'cult of the individual'. Thus the 1938 biography recited the barest details of the first half of Stalin's life before proceeding to catalogue his actions at the level of policy. There was scant attention to the family, school and native town of his boyhood. Accounts of his career in the clandestine Bolshevik committees before the Great War were discouraged; even his career in the October Revolution, the Civil War, the NEP and the Five-Year Plans was hardly covered in either the biography or the *Short Course*. He discouraged all historical and literary attempts to explain how he came to think what he thought or do what he did before the onset of his despotism. He strove instead to get writers, painters and film-makers to present him as the embodiment of the party rather than as a credible actor in history. Despite the preoccupation of the state media with Stalin, extremely little was allowed into the public domain telling of his ancestry, education, beliefs, demeanour or calculations.

His private existence too remained especially secluded. Before 1932 it was never mentioned in the newspapers that he was a married man. When he appeared on top of the Lenin Mausoleum, he was accompanied solely by fellow leading politicians. *Pravda* had made only a brief announcement of Nadya's death.[23] The same attitude was taken with Stalin's mother. *Pravda* carried short articles about his visit to her in 1935 shortly before her death, and her funeral too was reported.[24] Otherwise his privacy was closely guarded. A few exceptions existed. In 1939 a series of articles appeared by V. Kaminski and I. Vereshchagin about Stalin's early life, and these included brief memoirs by some of his schoolboy friends and documents referring to his education.[25] Some personal documents also appeared about Stalin's periods of arrest and imprisonment.[26]

The continued austerity of the Stalin cult invites comment. One possibility is that he recognised that most aspects of his past and present life were unlikely to commend him to others – and so he drew the curtains across them. This is conceivable but unlikely. Stalin was a maestro of historical fabrication, and mere facts would not have inhibited him from inventing a wholly fictional biography. Another possibility is that Stalin was simply unimaginative; and since he, unlike Hitler who had Goebbels, was his cult's main artificer, this may explain the situation. But Stalin was surrounded by associates who yearned to prove their usefulness to him. It is not credible that alternative ideas were not proposed to him. The most plausible explanation is that Stalin still believed that austerity was what best suited Russia's cultural ambience as well as the sensibilities of the world communist movement. After the Seventeenth Party Congress in 1934, he had stopped being called General Secretary but instead was designated Secretary of the Party Central Committee. Until 6 May 1941, furthermore, he resolutely refused to become Sovnarkom Chairman despite the fact that this had been Lenin's job. He could not even be tempted to create the post of Chairman for himself in the Party Politburo. Nor was Stalin head of state. That position continued to be held by Mikhail Kalinin as Chairman of the Central Executive Committee of the Congress of Soviets. Letters to the ascendant communist leadership were often addressed not to Stalin but to Kalinin or to both of them.[27]

Yet he dominated the central public life of the USSR. People lived or died according to his whim. Political, economic, social and cultural activity was conditioned by his inclinations of the day. He was the masterful guide of men and manager of affairs in the Soviet state. But Stalin had always been cunning. He had learned of the advantages of a display of modesty. Better, he concluded, to let it be thought that he was thirsty neither for power nor for prestige. Did his interest in the career of Augustus, first of the Roman emperors, influence him? Augustus would never accept the title of king despite obviously having become the founder of a dynastic monarchy.[28]

Stalin of course wanted adulation and the cult was extravagant in his praise; the restrictions imposed by him were pragmatically motivated. He discerned that he would gain more admirers if he stopped himself – and was seen to stop himself – short of making the very extreme claims put forward by Kremlin sycophants. Control of the process was crucial to him. He remained alert to the danger of letting people praise him on their own initiative and – bizarre as it might seem – banned discussion circles (*kruzhki*) from looking at either the *Short Course* or his official biography. The reason he gave was that he did not want citizens, tired after a day's labour, to have to turn out in the evening. In an exchange with a Leningrad party propagandist he ordered: 'Let them have a quiet life!'[29] But this was disingenuous. Party members had to go to post-work meetings as a political duty. Stalin's real aim was surely to restrict debate altogether. The texts of the two books were fairly straightforward in themselves and could quickly be studied by individuals reading alone. And once they had read and digested the texts, they could join in the ceremonies and festivals which were organised by the authorities with scrupulous care on the streets, in factories and at offices.

The cult certainly had its successes. A seventy-one-year-old woman textile worker was invited to the October Revolution celebrations on Red Square in 1935 but because of short-sightedness did not catch a glimpse of Stalin. Bumping into Ordzhonikidze, she cried: 'Look, I'm going to die soon – am I really not going to be able to see him?' Ordzhonikidze told her she was not going to die and, as she walked on, a car drew up and out got Stalin. She clapped her hands: 'Hey! Look who I've seen!' Stalin smiled and said modestly: 'What a good thing! A most ordinary human being!' The old woman burst into tears: 'You are our wise one, our great one ... and now I've seen you ... now I can die!' Stalin, thinking on his feet, replied: 'Why do you need to die? Let others go and die while you go on working!'[30]

The little episode shows that many citizens, especially those who felt grateful to the authorities, had a compulsive urge to revere him. (It also indicates that Stalin, even if he liked such flattery, reacted pretty brusquely: his main concern was to coax the old woman to go on toiling years beyond the age of retirement!) Moreover, people were much more likely to engage in his worship when they were in a crowd affected by the officially created atmosphere. Not only unsophisticated citizens but also many politicians and intellectuals experienced an inner need to extol him. They counted themselves blessed even if they only briefly met him or caught a glimpse of him. The writer Konstantin Chukovski was hardly a natural Stalinist. Disconcerted by the kind of literature demanded of authors by Stalin, he retreated into writing tales for children. Even so, his diary from 1936 records the following impression at a congress:[31]

Suddenly there appeared Kaganovich, Voroshilov, Andreev, Zhdanov and Stalin. What on earth happened to the hall! And HE stood
still, somewhat tired, pensive and magnificent. One could sense the
immense habituation to power, the force and at the same time
something feminine and soft . . .

That Chukovski was charmed by Stalin's 'graceful smile' says much for
the impact of the cult.

Yet the success was not as large as Stalin had hoped. Among the
peasantry in particular there was pervasive dislike of him and many
villagers regarded him – a Georgian, an atheist, an internationalist – as
the very Antichrist. So desperate was rural opinion by the late 1930s that
many peasants seriously hoped for war with Germany on the assumption
that only military invasion would dislodge Soviet communism from
power and bring about opportunities for decollectivisation.[32] Such hostility was not confined to rural inhabitants. A misspelled and ungram-
matical letter of protest dispatched to him and Kalinin by fifty Leningrad
workers in March 1930 had stated:[33]

No one has sympathy for Soviet power and you are considered
hangmen of the Russian people. Why should we undertake the
Five-Year Plan so abruptly when we have become poor after such
richness as we had in Russia – let's just take the example of sugar,
which used to be fed to pigs and which now can't be found even
for money, and meanwhile our children are starving and there's
absolutely nothing to give them to eat.

The period of the First Five-Year Plan was directly associated with Stalin
in the popular mind. He had claimed credit for the industrial and
cultural revolution of those years. The result was that everyone knew
who was to blame for the hardships.

Exactly how widespread and deep was such hatred is a question
which will never be satisfactorily answered. The NKVD supplied regular
reports on popular opinion, but their language and orientation left much
to be desired. Security agencies had an interest in alarming Stalin. Their
power and prestige rested on their capacity to persuade him that it was
only their vigilance which protected the state against its millions of
internal enemies. (Not that he usually took much persuading.)

Yet undoubtedly many Soviet citizens, like the woman textile worker,
loved the Leader. Conditions did not worsen for everyone in the 1930s.
Jobs became available offering improved salary, housing and consumer

goods for promotees. Stalin's rejection of the egalitarian principle for the Soviet order created an attractive prospect for them. Usually coming from working-class or peasant backgrounds, his beneficiaries could hardly believe their luck. They replaced the elites which were being butchered on his orders. The propaganda was crude but it worked with the grain of the self-interest of the promotees. They were ambitious, bright and obedient young men and women who wanted to get on in the world. The school system reinforced the message that Stalin had moved the USSR on to the tracks of universal progress. Needless to say, even the promotees might have had their doubts. It was possible to like some aspects of him and his policies and to disapprove of others. Many people hoped against all the evidence that the terror policies would eventually be abandoned. Perhaps, they thought, Stalin would soon see the need for reform – and some thought the violence would stop when he discarded the advisers who were misleading him.[34]

Stalin depended on this naïveté. He could hardly induce a purged kulak, priest or party oppositionist to love him. He could not expect a lot of undernourished, overworked factory labourers or kolkhozniki to sing his praises. But indisputably some of them did admire him. And, above all, members of the new administrative stratum wished to stick with him since he had given them their place in the sun. He had transformed the economy and built a military power. He was the Vozhd, the Leader, the Boss. Great was the name of Stalin in the minds of beneficiaries of the Stalinist state order.

33. BRUTAL REPRIEVE

The Great Terror came suddenly to an end on 23 November 1938. The occasion was marked unofficially by the removal of Yezhov from the NKVD and the advent to office of his deputy Lavrenti Beria. Until then there had been no serious attempt to stop the carnage. Everyone near Stalin had known that the campaign of arrests, tortures and executions had his active support: it was perilous to advocate a change of policy while he seemed fixed in purpose.

Signs had already appeared that some in Stalin's entourage wanted to halt the machinery of terror. Malenkov began the attempt at the Party Central Committee plenum in January 1938; he did this subtly by deploring the large number of mistakes in expulsions from the party in the previous year.[1] Direct criticism of arrests and executions was avoided. Holding to the theme of internal party procedures, Malenkov rebuked local leaders for throwing innocent communists out of the party. Everyone knew that more was involved than the loss of a party membership card. Expelled Bolsheviks were invariably sent to the Gulag or shot. Malenkov later claimed that he was putting pressure on Stalin to see the light. If so, it would have been the only time he did so. Malenkov was Stalin's creature and it is inconceivable that Stalin did not sanction Malenkov's initiative; and in any case, apart from a decision to handle expulsions more carefully, no brake was yet applied to the machinery of terror. Nevertheless Stalin evidently had growing doubts about Yezhov. He made this manifest in a typically indirect fashion when, on 21 August 1938, Yezhov was given the People's Commissariat of Water Transport in addition to his existing duties. This implicitly warned him that he would have the NKVD taken away from him if he failed to satisfy the Leader.

Yezhov understood the danger he was in and his daily routine became hectic; he knew that the slightest mistake could prove fatal. Somehow, though, he had to show himself to Stalin as indispensable. Meanwhile he also had to cope with the appointment of a new NKVD Deputy Commissar, the ambitious Lavrenti Beria, from July 1938. Beria had until then been First Secretary of the Communist Party of Georgia; he was widely feared in the south Caucasus as a devious plotter against any rival – and almost certainly he had poisoned one of them, the Abkhazian communist leader Nestor Lakoba, in December 1936. If Yezhov tripped, Beria was ready to take his place; indeed Beria would be more than happy to trip Yezhov up. Daily collaboration with Beria was like being tied in a sack with a wild beast. The strain on Yezhov became intolerable. He took to drinking heavily and turned for solace to one-night stands with women he came across; and when this failed to satiate his needs, he pushed himself upon men he encountered in the office or at home. In so far as he was able to secure his future position, he started to gather compromising material on Stalin himself.

Quite how Yezhov could ever have made use of such documents is hard to imagine. His behaviour indicated how desperate he, the Iron Commissar, had become. Knowing he could be arrested at any time, he was sent daily into hysteria. His fate depended on whether Stalin wanted to alter policy or change personnel. If he was to survive, the NKVD chief needed Stalin to commit himself to permanent state terror with Yezhov still in charge.

A further decline in Yezhov's influence was detectable on 23 October 1938, when the writer Mikhail Sholokhov gained an audience with Stalin to complain about being investigated by the NKVD.[2] Stalin humiliated Yezhov by requiring him to attend. On 14 November an order came from Stalin to purge the NKVD of individuals 'not worthy of political confidence'. Next day the Politburo confirmed a directive of party and government to terminate cases currently under investigation by the *troiki* and the military tribunals. On 17 November the Politburo decided that enemies of the people had infiltrated the NKVD.[3] Such measures spelled doom for Yezhov. He drank more heavily. He turned to more boyfriends for sexual gratification. He spoke incautiously about politics.[4] He was psychologically collapsing as Stalin increasingly treated Lavrenti Beria as NKVD chief-in-waiting. The wolves were gathering. At an evening meeting with Stalin, Molotov and Voroshilov on 23 November, Yezhov confessed to his incompetence in catching enemies of the people; his resignation was accepted.[5] Yezhov kept his other posts in the Central Committee Secretariat and the People's Commissariat of Water Transport for some months. But his days of pomp and authority were over.

Beria was charged with restoring order in the NKVD and submitting it to the party's control. Ruthless and competent, he could be trusted to clear up the mess left behind by Yezhov. Beria was no angel. Unlike Yezhov, he took an active part in beatings and kept canes for use in his office. Yet he had a steadier character than his predecessor, and Stalin and he instigated a set of reforms. Approval of torture in interrogations was not revoked but restricted, according to a January 1939 directive, to 'exceptional' cases.[6] A dossier was assembled on Yezhov, who appeared in public for the last time on 21 January 1939. He was arrested in April and executed the following year. The entire system of *troikis* was dismantled. The nightmare of 1937–8 was ended; it was popularly referred to as the 'Yezhovshchina'. This suited Stalin, who wanted the blame removed from his own shoulders. Yet although the terror-procedures were reduced, they were not abolished. The party did not control the NKVD at central and local levels on a daily basis. Torture continued to be used. The frantic atmosphere of the Great Terror had been dissipated but Stalin's USSR remained a murderous madhouse – and most of the leading madmen were confirmed in power.

Yezhov's removal came after Stalin started to allow discussion in his entourage about abuses of power. Two years of arrests and executions had occurred, and it was known that a high proportion of the victims did not belong to the categories of people describable as 'anti-Soviet elements'. It is quite possible too that Yezhov misled Stalin about aspects of the process. Yezhov's career and life depended on his ability to persuade Stalin that genuine anti-Soviet elements and enemies of the people were being arrested and eliminated. Yezhov's activity put everyone at risk.

Just as many people at the time and a few subsequent commentators surmised that the Great Terror had not been started on Stalin's initiative,[7] so the idea got about that the process was entirely out of his control once it had begun. Stalin may well have failed to anticipate the catastrophic excesses of the NKVD under Yezhov. What is more, local police organs undoubtedly bothered less about arresting individuals who fell into the designated social categories than in meeting the numerical quotas assigned to them. Repressions in 1937–8 were constantly accompanied by 'wrongful' arrests. Abuses and excesses were ubiquitous. It is also true that many truly anti-Soviet individuals survived the Great Terror and put themselves at the disposal of the German occupation regime in 1941. Hitler's forces had little difficulty discovering kulaks, priests and other anti-Soviet elements which had been intended for elimination by Soviet terror operations. To that extent it is true that

Stalin's purposes had been frustrated. The 'cleansing' of the USSR of all its enemies, real or potential, had not been completely successful despite one of the most thorough repressive projects in world history.

Yet his failure to achieve all his objectives in their entirety is scarcely proof that he did not succeed to a very large degree. The fact that a multitude of people were wrongly arrested was neither here nor there. Essentially Stalin was applying to the judicial system what he had already developed for the economic system. The management of most sectors of public affairs in the USSR was chaotic. Policy was imposed and quantitative targets were set with dire punitive sanctions in the event of failure to hit the targets. This had been how the industrial growth rates were administered in the First Five-Year Plan. Agricultural collectivisation had been directed in the same way. The point was that the entire administrative system operated on the premise that lower-level officials had to be given precise numerical indicators. Stalin and the Politburo knew that the information reaching them from the localities was frequently unreliable. Misinformation was a basic defect of the Soviet order. Just as waste occurred in industrial production, so unnecessary human losses could be accepted in the Great Terror. So long as Stalin achieved the ultimate aim of eradicating most of that mass of disgruntled individuals who might remain a menace he had no compunction about the mayhem he caused.

Unmistakably he had become the country's despot. He had eliminated foes in every institution. Not even the party had restrained him. Among the main results of the Great Terror had been drastic reduction in the party's power and status. Stalin had turned himself into the unchallengeable individual locus of state authority. His was a most personal autocracy. He had come closer to total despotism than almost any monarch in history. He held sway over the Soviet state; no state institution could push him into decisions which he found uncongenial. Grand policy was firmly in his grasp and, by unpredictable interventions in smaller affairs of state, he caused all holders of office to try and anticipate his wishes. The state, moreover, kept its people in a condition of traumatic subservience. Civil society barely existed. Only the Russian Orthodox Church kept the slightest vestige of autonomy from the state – and it was scarcely much of an autonomy when tens of thousands of priests had been murdered. Every other institution and association was subject to the requirements of the central political authorities. Stalin had stabilised his despotism and its structures by means of the Great Terror, and the pervasiveness of control by the one-party state was deep and irresistible.

Yet this was not a totalitarian dictatorship as conventionally defined because Stalin lacked the capacity, even at the height of his power, to secure automatic universal compliance with his wishes. He could purge personnel without difficulty. But when it came to ridding the Soviet order of many informal practices he disliked, he was much less successful. In such cases he was like someone trying to strike a match on a block of soap.

Constraints continued to exist upon his rule. In 1937 he had told the Party Central Committee that he intended to eradicate the network of political patronage in the USSR. Yet cliental groups survived. The politics of the USSR continued to involve patronage – and in many parts of the country this meant links based on families and clans. There were also local 'nests' of functionaries leading the party, soviets and other public institutions. Technical and social obstacles to a neat vertical system of state power remained. Functionaries promoted in the late 1930s, however much they admired Stalin, saw it was vital to be cautious in messages to Moscow. Misinformation from below remained a basic local requirement for self-protection. The press, judiciary and market had countervailed only weakly against provincial political establishments under the NEP; they had massively less weight – if indeed they had any weight at all – after 1928. The situation changed little after 1938. Stalin's clique could not know everything with the desired accuracy. Promoted functionaries were keen to enjoy their privileges. Stalin needed to treat them well materially; he could not permanently rely on terror alone.

He had a clear understanding of this. He had deliberately promoted the young and working-class cadres to high postings. Whereas in France and Britain the old clung to power, Stalin had brought on a fresh generation to replace the ageing veterans of the October Revolution – and he was pleased with his achievement.[8] He had promoted young adults to all rungs on the ladder of party and government. This had long been one of his objectives, and he had attained it by the most brutal methods. At the end of the Great Terror he sought to keep the promotees on his side. The system of graduated perks and privileges was maintained. The higher the rung, the greater the reward. Stalin bribed them into murderous complicity. The administrative beneficiaries of the purges had a fixed higher income and guaranteed access to goods and services denied to the rest of society. Even if they did not literally step into dead men's shoes, they certainly took possession of their apartments, dachas, paintings, carpets and pianos. They hired their tutors, chauffeurs and nannies. The promoted officials belonged to a privileged elite.

Stalin wished to sedate the minds of officials still fearful that he might resume the terror. At the celebratory Eighteenth Party Congress in March 1939, his general report picked up the theme:[9]

The correct selection of cadres means:

Firstly to value cadres like the gold reserve of party and state, to cherish them, to show them respect.

Secondly to know the cadres, to make a careful study of the virtues and defects of each cadre official, to know how to facilitate the official's capacities.

Thirdly to cultivate the cadres, to help each growing official to rise higher, not to begrudge time in handling these officials patiently and hastening their growth.

Fourthly to promote new, young cadres boldly and in a timely fashion, to avoid letting them stand around in the same old place or letting them go stale.

His appeal to the recent promotees was fervent. Unnamed discussants, he declared, thought it better for the state to 'orientate itself to the old cadres' with all their experience. But Stalin insisted that the wiser course was the one he had chosen.[10] Not for the last time he gave the impression that the promotees had no firmer friend than himself.

Having created a new administrative elite, he wanted their allegiance. It was for them more than for any other group in society that he had ordered the publication of the *Short Course*. Indeed the whole 'technical–scientific intelligentsia' was in his sights. Recognising that they had limited time to do any reading at the end of the working day, he had supplied them with an easily assimilated text which explained and justified the existence of the Soviet order.[11] This was also the group in society which, after the Great Terror, he and Zhdanov sought to recruit to the party. No longer were workers to be given privileged access to membership. Recruitment should take place on merit and usefulness for the socialist cause.[12]

A technocratic imperative was being proclaimed, and Stalin was putting himself forward as the Leader of the newly reformed USSR. With typical false modesty – and even self-pity – he pretended that the burden of individual leadership had somehow been thrust upon him. At times he complained about this. While other Soviet leaders tended the business of their assigned institutions, he gave consideration to the entire range of affairs. At a supper party in 1940 he was quite mawkish:[13]

But I *alone* am occupied with all these questions. Not one of you even thinks about it. I have to stand *alone*.

Yes, I can study, read, follow things up each day. But why can't you do that? You don't like to study, you go on living complacently. You waste Lenin's legacy.

When Kalinin protested that they were always short of time, Stalin exclaimed: 'No, that's not the point! People wet behind the ears don't want to study and re-study. They listen to me and then leave everything as it was before. But I'll show the lot of you if I lose my patience. And you know how I can do that!' This was a charade: Stalin would have locked up any Politburo members poking their noses into what he regarded as exclusively his business.

While wanting his policies to be followed, however, Stalin demanded that his subordinates should give frank, instant opinions. Every so often he got each of them on his own and enquired about options. For Stalin, Politburo members were useless unless they could come up with ideas for fresh measures. His period of rule was characterised by constant emergency. This made for an arena of discussion which would have driven most men crazy. Stalin was incessantly looking for signs of weakness or treachery. If they seemed shifty, he told them so; and he had a knack of catching them off guard. Always Stalin was querying whether a subordinate was 'sincere'. He could not abide what official propaganda referred to as 'double-dealing'. His ideal communist party associate was ruthless, dynamic, straightforward and utterly loyal. He liked, too, individuals who came 'from the people'. Not all his subordinates, even after the Great Terror had spent itself, were working class or peasant in origin. Indeed Molotov, Zhdanov and Malenkov were distinctly middle class by parentage. But the general tone in Stalin's entourage was never genteel, and all his subordinates had to join in displays of the crude masculinity which the Boss liked.

Like all bullies, Stalin acted out his fantasies. If ever any of these Soviet leaders was insincere in his behaviour to his intimates, it was the Boss himself. His was the least straightforward personality of all of them. He would have hated to be asked the piercing questions with which he skewered others. In identifying personal treachery as the most heinous offence, he was externalising a worry about his subordinates reflecting a cardinal feature of his own character. At last his gross personality disorder was functioning without restraint. He could indulge his paranoiac, vengeful proclivities to the utmost and nothing except a successful internal coup, military conquest or his premature death could save others from his murderous whims.

Across the 1930s Stalin had dominated the Politburo and the rest of the Soviet political leadership; but the Great Terror had elevated him to an unprecedented height above the other leaders. In all but name he was despot. His associates continued to respect him, even to admire him. But they also existed in mortal dread. Few dared to contradict him even in private conversation. Only Molotov had sufficient confidence to disagree with him about policies – and even he had to exercise caution in his phrasing and demeanour. The others were even more circumspect. It was a fiendishly difficult task because Stalin often deliberately disguised what he really thought. Politburo members were compelled to reveal their opinions without foreknowledge of his intentions. Always they were kept edgy by the master of intimidation and mystification. He had killed Kaganovich's brother Moisei and demoted Molotov's wife from office. He went on to arrest her as well as the wives of Kalinin and Andreev. Physical danger did not disappear from the Politburo. By devouring other members of their families, the Kremlin shark signalled that his appetite for victims had not been satisfied. They could take nothing for granted.

Most of those associates who survived the Great Terror succeeded in living out the natural term of their lives. Molotov, Kaganovich, Mikoyan, Voroshilov and Zhdanov had been with Stalin since the 1920s and were kept by his side at least until he started to move against some of them after the 1940s. The promoted newcomers – Malenkov, Khrushchëv, Vyshinski and Beria – stayed with him to the end of his life. The ruling group began to settle down. From the end of 1938 no Politburo member was arrested until Voznesenski was put away in 1949. No Red Army general was taken into custody, moreover, before the defeats of June 1941. But the memory of what had happened earlier did not vanish. All the rulers were acutely aware that they stayed in post solely at the whim of their supreme master.

He acted on his own. Among the arcana of Soviet administrative correspondence is a report of the NKVD in 1940 which Beria relayed to Stalin. The main conclusion was that the Gulag more than paid for itself as a sector of the Soviet economy: 'The entire system of camps and labour colonies is fully paying its way and no subsidy for the prisoners (1,700,000 persons), their guards or the camp apparatus is needed.'[14] Beria was on the make and may already have known that the opposite was true. But the regime was being consolidated; Stalin would not consider any basic alteration of what he had built. He was powerful and confident. He was overworked. He had strengthened the state as the prime lever of political and economic change. He had never believed in ⱽ the spontaneous positive potential of the people. He wanted workers and peasants to support the regime, to work to their physical limit and to denounce 'enemies'. He was jovial about the usefulness of the camps and executions. At the Eighteenth Party Congress he exulted that whereas 98.6 per cent of voters had supported the regime after Tukhachevski's trial in mid-1937, the proportion increased to 99.4 per cent after Bukharin had been sentenced in March 1938.[15]

This was the comment of a man who felt he had largely succeeded. He had achieved enough of his objectives to know that his personal despotism and his design for the Soviet order were secure at least for the foreseeable future. He and the Politburo were to make minor modifica-tions in future years as they sought to bind the walls together in the face of unanticipated storms. The basic design stayed intact; and those observers who have interpreted the modifications in terms of fundamen-tally separate periods are scarcely convincing. If it makes sense to talk of 'late Stalinism' or 'high Stalinism', the date of demarcation should be set at the end of the Great Terror in 1938. Stalin went on tinkering with his architect's drawings. Relations among party, people's commissariats and armed forces underwent alteration before, during and after the war. He fiddled with the scope allowed for Russian national identity and for cultural and religious expression; he also adjusted his cult to the social atmosphere of the time. Economic policies were repeatedly modified. Foreign policy was frequently amended. Stalin did not refer to his architecture as Stalinist but was not averse to others using the term. This order prevailed until the day he died – and in many respects it was to outlive him.

PART FOUR

WARLORD

34. THE WORLD IN SIGHT

Stalin the Leader was multifaceted. He was a mass killer with psychological obsessions. He thought and wrote as a Marxist. He behaved like the more ruthless Russian rulers of earlier centuries. He was a party boss, administrator, editor and correspondent. He was a paterfamilias and genial host at his dacha as well as a voracious reader and intellectual autodidact. Depending on circumstances, he displayed all these aspects at once or hid some while exhibiting others. He had the capacity to divide and subdivide himself. Stalin's multitude of forms left his associates impressed, baffled and fearful – and indeed this was one of the secrets of his success in maintaining dominance over them.

His record as an international statesman has always been controversial. The jury of history has offered a majority verdict that his preoccupation with Soviet economic development and political consolidation deflected his attention from foreign affairs. Some have accused Stalin of knowing and caring nothing about events abroad. The building of 'socialism in a single country' was among his main slogans, and the General Secretary's advocacy of this priority fostered the misperception, both at the time and later, that he was not bothered by what happened in the rest of the world. The general assumption has been that he and his Politburo comrades had ditched the project of worldwide socialist revolution. His opponents Trotski and Bukharin said this, and their view has attracted the nodding heads of most subsequent commentators. About Stalin's concentration on the situation inside the USSR there is no doubt. But this did not mean he overlooked foreign policy. Nor did he allow it to be formulated without his active intervention: he continued to give it the high priority it had had for him in the 1920s.

Stalin had always thought hard about international relations and Soviet external security. During the Civil War he had had responsibility for policy in the Caucasus and the Baltic region. In 1920 he discussed with Lenin the future of a Europe under socialist administration. Stalin offered his thoughts on military and political aspects of the Red Army's campaign in Poland; he also came to the fore with proposals for expanding Soviet influence along the entire frontier from Turkey to Afghanistan. Under the New Economic Policy, far from being preoccupied with factional and bureaucratic matters, he took an active leading part in the Politburo's decisions on Britain, Germany and China.

Detailed elaboration of policy was still left to institutions with the necessary expertise: the People's Commissariat of External Affairs and the Comintern. When Georgi Chicherin retired through ill health in 1930, Maxim Litvinov took his place despite having no recent affiliation with Stalin;[1] and when the post of Secretary-General of the Executive Committee of the Comintern was created after the Seventh World Congress in 1935, Stalin turned not to an adjutant such as Molotov or Kaganovich but to the Bulgarian communist Georgi Dimitrov, whom he barely knew but who had worldwide fame after being put on trial in Nazi Germany. Stalin in public mentioned foreign policy in his political reports on behalf of the Central Committee but wrote no substantial piece on the subject. Yet when items of importance cropped up, an internal group of the Politburo consulted among themselves.[2] Stalin watched, regulated and directed. He sent instructions. No important decision was taken before he had given his approval. Yet he did not usually roll up his sleeves and get involved in the minutiae of implementation as he did in internal affairs.

This detachment from the day-to-day running of the People's Commissariat and the Comintern as well as the confidentiality of discussions at the highest level (which was maintained for decades after Stalin's death)[3] sustained the mystery about the Politburo's intentions. Abroad, speculation was rife. The USSR's military might was growing at a steady rate. Each May Day parade indicated that the Soviet state was recovering its position as a European and Asian power of importance.

Yet what did Stalin want to do in the world? If he is judged by his own speeches and articles, he looked upon global politics through the lens of Marxism–Leninism and rejected any suggestion that Soviet foreign policy was based on the selfish pragmatism of the USSR as a single state. Repeatedly he declared his indebtedness to the ideas of Vladimir Lenin. At Congresses he cited this as the party's main legacy. Lenin had argued that, so long as capitalism survived around the world, imperialist rivalries would recur. Economic competition between advanced industrial powers would inevitably spill over into diplomatic conflicts and outright wars. Those powers lacking overseas colonies and informal dependencies were bound to seek access to the markets of their more fortunate rivals. A Second World War – and possibly further global wars – would be the inevitable result. In his address to the Eighteenth Party Congress, Stalin picked up this theme. The diplomatic and military conflicts of the 1930s appeared to him as confirmation of Lenin's analysis in every detail: capitalism was inherently incapable of maintaining peace around the globe.

From this viewpoint the treaties signed at the end of the Great War were a prescription for future military explosion. Germany had been humbled at Versailles in 1919 and its determination to reassert itself would cause ceaseless trouble. The USA, victorious in the First World War, had an interest in dismantling the British Empire and in restricting Japanese influence in the Pacific region. Throughout Europe and Asia there were suppurating sores in international relations which could lead to wars. Supposedly the problem lay with the persistence of the global capitalist economy. The USSR meanwhile remained a pariah state. When the League of Nations met for the first time in January 1920, it withheld a seat from the Soviet regime. The post-war treaties, moreover, created successor states in eastern Europe hostile to the October Revolution. The perceived danger for the Politburo was that somehow this volatile situation might result in a crusade against the USSR.

For Stalin, as had been true for Lenin before him, the primary aim of Soviet security policy was to stay clear of entanglement in conflicts between capitalist powers. Since the mid-1920s Stalin had emphasised a concern with building 'socialism in a single country'. This did not mean that he urged pacifism or envisaged permanent abstention from military activity; indeed he looked forward to the possibility that the Red Army might exploit difficulties among capitalist powers as a result of their wars. He had never revoked his statement in *Problems of Leninism* that more revolutions were needed for the Soviet state to secure itself against the possibility of foreign military intervention and overthrow.[4] For the most part he emphasised another aspect of Lenin's thought, namely that the USSR should seek to stay out of world wars. As he put it, he and his fellow leaders were not going to 'pull chestnuts out of the fire' on behalf of capitalist powers.

Such considerations conditioned Soviet foreign policy in the inter-war period. But they were of a generalised nature and led many contemporary politicians and diplomats – and subsequent writers – to suppose that Stalin was a pragmatist who had put ideology behind him. This is a tricky topic. It is true that, if account is taken of the somersaults in Soviet diplomatic activity, Lenin and Stalin showed little consistency.

In Lenin's time the Treaty of Brest-Litovsk had been signed in 1918 and some observers, including a lot of communists, treated this as an abandonment of Bolshevik revolutionary goals. Yet the Red Army invaded Poland in 1920 and engaged in 'revolutionary war'. Similar inconsistency was evident from the late 1920s. At first Stalin used the Comintern to instruct communist parties in Europe to regard social-democratic and labour parties as their greatest enemies; but he then insisted that communists should join 'popular fronts' with such parties. Of course the Marxist–Leninist stress on the importance of flexibility in Soviet foreign policy was hardly distinctive: it is an almost universal characteristic of diplomacy regardless of time, place or political orientation. Marxism–Leninism after 1917 was reinventing the ancient wheel of international relations.

And even when Stalin appeared 'ideological', he never overlooked practical considerations. The USSR was an isolated state whose structure of politics and economy posed a challenge to the world's capitalist powers. Hostility to the Soviet Union had led to military intervention in the Civil War; this put the Politburo on constant alert for a possible repetition. Stalin and his associates had a pragmatic interest in ending their international isolation; they looked for opportunities for revolutionary self-assertion. There were few ways to alter the fundamental situation short of demolishing the legacy of the October Revolution. At the very least the USSR would have had to reintroduce the market economy and recognise the debts owed by Russian governments before October 1917.

Nothing about Stalin suggested that he would contemplate such a step. Accused by Trotski of betraying the October Revolution, he indeed distorted and eliminated much of Lenin's legacy. But a Leninist of a sort he remained while introducing a personal dimension to his handling of international relations. He acted as if politics were fundamentally a matter of unmasking and neutralising conspiracies at home and abroad. Lenin had not been averse to impugning the motives of foreign states; he had not failed to trump up the charge in March 1921 that the Kronstadt mutineers were in league with governments hostile to the Soviet state. Stalin, moreover, made little distinction between types of capitalist state. He was equally ready to deal with fascists, liberal democrats and socialists in governments abroad; the popular-front policy was premised on pragmatic judgement rather than ideological preference. Yet this was no different from the attitude struck by Lenin, who in 1920 had urged the German communists to form an alliance with the German extreme right as a means of undermining the Weimar Republic and tearing up the Treaty of Versailles. Trotski in exile exaggerated the discrepancy between the viewpoints on Soviet foreign policy taken by Lenin and Stalin.[5]

But how could Stalin translate these principles into action? In the early 1930s he had no constructive programme of foreign policy except for his aim to enable the USSR to survive. He did not shape events but instead reacted to them. This remained true while few options for alliance were available to a Soviet state whose very existence was a challenge to the world's other powers. The best Stalin could hope for was to neutralise the threats of a crusade against the USSR. He was agitated by signs of expansionism on his borders. To the north and south there was little menace, but the omens were dire to the east. In December 1931 the Japanese invaded Manchuria and installed the puppet state of Manchukuo under the heel of the Kwantung Army. Militarism held sway in Tokyo. The Kremlin was concerned lest this might be the prelude to an attack on the USSR through Siberia.

During the First Five-Year Plan Stalin saw reasons to be hopeful about developments to the west. There was in fact much congruence between policy at home and policy abroad: at the beginning of the 1930s it was extremely radical in both cases. Communist parties across Europe were encouraged to go on to the political attack against their govern-ments. Ultra-leftist campaigns were approved. The Comintern, which had tended towards caution in Germany after the failure of revolution to occur there and had eliminated leftist leaders who sympathised with Trotski, started to campaign against those whom it accused of 'rightism'. The basis for Stalin's optimism was the acute trouble in the world economy. The Wall Street Crash in 1929 created havoc in every capitalist country. While the Politburo and Gosplan planned and achieved a massive increase in Soviet industrial output, the markets in North America and Europe fell into disarray – and no country was more economically disrupted than Germany. Communists in the main German cities took political advantage, claiming that the Great Depression signalled the final crisis of capitalism around the globe. Stalin agreed with this interpretation, which fitted Bolshevism's long-standing predictions and analyses.

Thus it came about that during the Reichstag electoral campaign in July 1932 he instructed the Executive Committee of the Comintern to order the German Communist Party to treat the social-democrats rather than Hitler's NSDAP as the main enemy. Hegemony over the political left was to be given precedence over struggling against Nazism. This egregious mistake is taken as evidence that he had no serious perspective on the general situation in Europe. German communist leaders were alarmed by his instruction and a delegation was sent to him. When they pleaded that the danger from the Nazis was a most urgent one, he retorted that he had taken this into account. Stalin understood that Hitler might do well in the elections. His riposte to his visitors, who included Franz Neumann, was blunt. He argued: 'Don't you think, Neumann, that if the nationalists come to power in Germany, they'll be so completely preoccupied with the West that we'll be able to build up socialism in peace?' By this he seemed to mean that the Nazis as fundamental adversaries of the Treaty of Versailles would cause havoc in Europe. He appeared to believe that the result would probably be to the advantage of the Comintern in the cause of spreading revolution westwards from Russia.[6]

In fact the defeated leader of the Right Deviation, Bukharin, had anticipated that Hitler would be a much more aggressive and effective leader than Stalin supposed; and this prognosis was vindicated when the Führer, building on his electoral success, became German Chancellor in January 1933. He tore up the Treaty of Rapallo. He withdrew the Wehrmacht from its collaboration with the Red Army. He fulminated against the Bolshevik political and ideological menace to Europe. The contents of *Mein Kampf* were shown to have been no aberration as Hitler asserted himself in Europe. Stalin's assessment of German political trends had been proved dangerously naïve. The threat from the West had become as acute as the threat from the East, and Germany and Japan became the twin focus of changes in Soviet foreign policy for the rest of the decade. Stalin took little note of North America beyond encouraging closer commercial links between the USSR and the USA. About South America, Africa and the rest of Asia he had little to say. The Politburo continued to avoid risky revolutionary initiatives. Armaments production was kept as a high priority. Discussions were held in Moscow to elaborate a foreign policy adequate to deal with German expansionism.

The Politburo, shocked by Hitler's success in Germany, took steps to increase Soviet security. One such improvement was achieved that same year when the USA announced its decision to give diplomatic recognition to the USSR. This suited the interests of American business abroad. Having spent years enhancing Soviet influence in Europe, Stalin had acquired a window on to the New World.[7]

Meanwhile the Red Army was reinforced in the Far East in case

Tokyo should try to use its Manchurian quasi-colony as the base for an invasion of the USSR. Stalin had not forgotten about the Japanese incursions into eastern Siberia before the Bolsheviks won the Civil War in Russia. As regards Germany, there was greater room for manoeuvre. People's Commissar of External Affairs Maxim Litvinov argued that rapprochement with all Europe's anti-fascist parties and the formation of popular fronts were essential for Soviet interests. This had the support of Georgi Dimitrov, who had been released from a German prison in February 1934 and given political asylum in the USSR. Dimitrov objected to the official characterisation of the leaders and members of other socialist parties as 'social-fascists'.[8] Although the ideas originated with Litvinov and Dimitrov, sanction had to come from the Politburo and in particular from Stalin. France was recognised as the country in Europe which needed to be pulled into the Soviet embrace. Like the USSR, France felt threatened by Hitler's foreign policy; it was reasonable for Stalin to assume that a reconciliation between the USSR and France would suit both governments.

Stalin also accepted advice from Litvinov to adopt a policy of 'collective security'. At the Seventeenth Party Congress in January 1934 he expressed satisfaction at the improvement in diplomatic relations with France and Poland. Although he denied this implied a reversal of the USSR's antagonism to the Treaty of Versailles, he objected to the stated anti-Soviet pretensions of Nazi leaders and offered no olive branch to Germany. His hopes at that time lay with the USA (and even in Japan, which he thought could be induced into co-operating with the USSR). 'We stand', said Stalin,

> for peace and for the cause of peace. But we're not afraid of threats and we're ready to respond blow for blow to warmongers. Anyone wanting peace and seeking businesslike links with us will always have our support. But those who are trying to attack our country will receive crushing retaliation to teach them in future not to push their pigs' snouts into our Soviet garden patch.
>
> That's what our foreign policy is about.[9]

But he omitted to say how these aims could be achieved. What was clear was that Soviet leaders were seeking a way out of their isolation.

The formation of popular fronts was a new term but not a wholly new policy: it had been tried in the mid-1920s. Yet the threat from Nazi Germany was at last recognised as being of a unique order. Dimitrov argued that the Comintern had to be reorganised to deal with this. In

October he argued that the Comintern was over-centralised. Communist parties abroad, he wrote to Stalin, should be given the latitude to react autonomously to national conditions.[10] This did not mean that the foreign communist parties would have a choice about whether to set up popular fronts. They were peremptorily told to set them up.[11] Dimitrov was writing about secondary matters; he wanted the parties to handle day-to-day affairs without constantly referring them upwards. He was hoping for pies in the sky. While calling for independence for these parties, he did not break the chains of their continued subjection.

Stalin approved these ideas of Dimitrov without much modification. Dimitrov was proving a fertile source of ideas for allowing the USSR and Europe's communist parties to adapt to fast-changing political and military realities. Stalin failed to come up with novel ideas of his own. Nevertheless such changes as were made to foreign policy had to have his personal permission; and while giving Dimitrov his head in the Comintern, he and Litvinov had other fish to fry. Stalin did not limit the USSR's initiatives in international relations to contacts with left-of-centre parties. He also wanted reconciliation with the French government of Gaston Doumergue. Steadily the Soviet leadership was edging its way to a policy founded on treaties of 'collective security'. With this in mind, Stalin permitted his diplomats to apply for and secure the USSR's entry into the League of Nations in September 1934. Not only France but also Czechoslovakia and Romania were the object of Soviet overtures.[12] Stalin was aided by the general fear of a Germany resurgent under Hitler. The existence of the Third Reich scared these states, and all of them were considering surmounting their fundamental distaste for dealing with the USSR. The Red Army's potential as an anti-Nazi force in eastern and central Europe made negotiations with the Kremlin more attractive than at any time since the October Revolution.

There was much disagreement among observers about Stalin's purposes. To some it seemed that he was steadily moving towards a more traditional Russian agenda in foreign policy. The particular treaties and alliances did not matter for them: such things always changed in each generation. But the idea was gaining currency that Stalin had abandoned the internationalist objective of Leninism and wished for the USSR's recognition as a great power with no interest in the overturning of the world political and economic system. Others accepted this as true but qualified the judgement. To them it seemed obvious that both the geopolitical position of the Soviet Union and Stalin's personal preference dictated an inclination towards rapprochement with Germany at the expense of good relations with the United Kingdom and France. Yet such an analysis was challenged by those who felt that Stalin lacked the mental preparation to be anything else than reactive as a global statesman.

They underestimated his thoughtful adaptiveness and the extent of his break with Marxism–Leninism. Equally clearly he was eager to avoid the mistakes made under Lenin's leadership. He told guests at a dinner party attended by Georgi Dimitrov that Lenin had been wrong to call for a European civil war during the Great War.[13] He also set about studying the history of international relations, and much scholarly research on this was published at his instigation in Moscow in the 1930s. While thrusting this information into the frame of his worldview, he retained a readiness to keep Soviet foreign policy flexible. Lenin had come to power with this attitude. Stalin had been impressed and sought to emulate him. Just as Lenin had confronted and survived the deadly diplomatic trial of strength with Germany in 1917–18, Stalin was determined to prove his mettle in the contests of the 1930s. As the threats in Europe and Asia grew, he wanted to be intellectually prepared. Without such knowledge, he knew, he could be caught out of his depth; and he had no desire to put himself as an innocent into the arms of the People's Commissariat of External Affairs or of the Communist International.

Civil war had broken out in Spain in July 1936 when the fascist general Francisco Franco revolted against the Republican coalition government of Diego Barrio (who derived authority from a popular front). Franco appealed for assistance from Germany and Italy. Both complied, and Hitler's Luftwaffe was given experience in bombing towns and villages. Meanwhile France and the United Kingdom, while sympathising with the elected government, maintained a position of neutrality. The Spanish government rallied all the forces it could on the political left. Spain's communists in particular stood by it.

In Moscow the time had come for a decision on whether or not to intervene as Hitler and Mussolini had already done. Deployment of Red military units was not feasible at such a distance. But the revolutionary tradition impelled Stalin to look favourably on the request from Madrid for help. So too did the awareness that if no resistance to German assertiveness were shown, Europe as a whole would be exposed to the expansionist aims of the Third Reich. Failure to act would be taken as a sign that the policy of the popular front had no substance. Finance and munitions were dispatched by boat to Spain from Leningrad. Simultaneously the Communist International sent the Italian Communist

Party leader Palmiro Togliatti under the alias Ercoli to direct the activities of the Spanish communists. Togliatti and his fellow political and military emissaries found a chaotic scene. At Stalin's command they sought to turn the Spanish Communist Party into the leading force on the left without actually entering the government coalition. The policy of the popular front was maintained and Moscow frowned on all talk of a communist seizure of power. Dimitrov came into his own by leading the implementation of the general line agreed in the Kremlin: he knew it was not safe to ignore his master's voice.[14]

As the Republic's armed forces were pushed on to the retreat by Franco, the Spanish government pressed for the communists to enter the coalition. Stalin had to be phoned for consent and then Dimitrov sent the tactical instructions to communist leader José Diaz. Eventually the socialist party chief Largo Caballero emerged as head of government. By March 1937 Stalin had become distinctly edgy about being drawn into a military struggle of internal significance without being able to control the consequences, and reports about the effectiveness of the coalition and its army were not encouraging. His instinct was to pull out of Spain and disband the International Brigades in the event that Germany and Italy were also to withdraw; but for the moment he insisted on a merger of the communist and socialist parties in Spain.[15] This immediately became Comintern policy. Yet the inter-party negotiations in Spain made little progress: years of mutual antagonism could not be discounted overnight. Nor did Stalin help the situation by deploying NKVD agents to seek out and liquidate Spanish Trotskyists. Distrust on the political left grew rapidly as members of the POUM, loyal to Trotski's ideas, were rounded up. Remorselessly the Spanish Communist Party reinforced its influence in the government.

The situation changed from month to month and the socialists refused to do the bidding of the Spanish Communist Party. By February 1938 Stalin had concluded that the communists should resign from the government. Dimitrov in Moscow and Togliatti in Spain complied with the decision despite the disarray it was bound to cause in the anti-Franco alliance.[16] The political tensions on the left were not concocted out of nothing by Stalin. But he made them murderously worse than they need have been; and if anyone thought that his accusations against internal victims in the USSR were merely an instrument of despotism without genuine importance for him, they were disillusioned by events in Spain. Exactly the same political persecutions were put in train. Stalin was determined that the far-left elements on the Republican side should be liquidated before they could infect the Spanish Communist Party with their diseased purposes. Of course there were plenty of leftists in Spain who by their own profession were Trotskyists, anarchists or independent communists. Stalin had no need to ponder the options: he knew he had to cauterise the wound of far-left pluralism. Spain was going to be helped on the terms of his political homicidalism.

The Civil War had by then turned decisively in Franco's favour. By March 1939 it was over. The Republicans had lost the protracted struggle against reactionary forces backed by German and Italian fascism. Stalin's policy was criticised by Trotski as excessively cautious. For Trotski, the Spanish Civil War offered one of those regular opportunities to spread revolution west of the USSR and to undermine the political far right across Europe. Stalin, though, was mindful of the risks he would run with any strong intervention. Always he dreaded thrusting the French and British governments into the arms of General Franco. Too obvious a communist hegemony over the Spanish government coalition might easily have brought this about. But he and the Comintern at least did something, and it is hardly likely that the Republicans would have held out so long if he had not sanctioned the Spanish Communist Party's participation. His Trotskyist critics accused him of excessive pragmatism in his management of Soviet foreign policy. They ignored the limited resources available to the USSR. Economically, militarily and – above all – geographically there was no serious chance for him to do more than he achieved at the time.

If he could not have done much more to help, however, he could certainly have done less to hinder. His behaviour towards the Spanish political left, especially in the suppression of the POUM, rightly earned him the opprobrium of George Orwell in *Homage to Catalonia*. For Stalin acted within the cage of his assumptions. He could not imagine how a revolutionary movement could be properly mobilised unless it was purged of untrustworthy elements. At the very same time as he was getting rid of such people in the USSR he was determined to eliminate them from the ranks of the Comintern. The cause of the Revolution would rest on the inner health of the political far left. Trotskyists were infectious vermin. Stalin's Comintern agents fought for the cause of Soviet internal politics in the mountains and plains of distant Spain.

35. APPROACHES TO WAR

Domestic politics, state security and foreign policy were knotted together in the late 1930s. Stalin arrested hundreds of thousands of harmless Soviet citizens who were of an awkward national ancestry. Poles, Finns, Chinese and Koreans resident in border areas next to the states of their co-nationals were routinely deported to other distant regions of the USSR. Even the Greeks living in the Soviet republics by the Black Sea, hundreds of maritime miles from Greece, suffered this fate.[1] Soviet state security policy had a national and ethnic dimension. While promoting the press and schooling for non-Russians in the Soviet multinational state, Stalin showed an intense hostility to some among them. What has become known as ethnic cleansing was not new to the USSR. The Politburo had practised such a policy against Cossacks in the north Caucasus at the end of the Civil War.[2] Proposals for cleansing on the basis of nationality resurfaced at the start of the Five-Year Plan.[3] But Stalin's deportations, arrests and executions during and after the Great Terror mounted to a higher scale of national and ethnic repression.

The application of this policy did not exclude card-carrying communists in the Soviet Union. Stalin's zeal to make the country safe from subversion from abroad went to the point of the extermination of the Communist Party of Poland exiles in Moscow. Polish communists were especially suspect to him. Several of their leaders had sympathised with Soviet internal oppositions in the 1920s. Earlier still, many of them had sided with the Polish Marxist leader and theorist Rosa Luxemburg against Lenin before the Great War. Stalin had anyway always fretted about the menace posed by Poland to the USSR. He was easily convinced by reports from Yezhov's NKVD that the Polish exile community had been infiltrated by the intelligence agencies of the Western capitalist powers. Stalin was in no mind in November 1937 to treat people on an individual basis: he demanded the entire party's dissolution. Dimitrov, himself a Bulgarian exile in Moscow, docilely complied and wrote to Stalin for procedural advice. Stalin replied with the blunt demand that

Dimitrov should show a sense of urgency: 'The dissolution is about two years late.'[4] Already several Polish communist leaders were in the Lubyanka. The NKVD swiftly picked up the remainder, and most of the prisoners were shot.

Dimitrov's obedience did not save the Comintern from Stalin's suspicions. Scores of functionaries in its Executive Committee as well as its various departments were executed. No exemption was given to emissaries serving in Spain who were loyally slaughtering the POUM. Stalin and Yezhov tricked many of them back from Madrid and had them killed. Stalin was blunt to Dimitrov, raging that 'all of you in the Comintern are hand in glove with the enemy'.[5] In Moscow he could carry out the purge he desired. Abroad he got Dimitrov to compel the freely operating communist parties – few though they had become – in France, Spain, Italy, the United Kingdom and the USA – to expel members who refused to support the official line or who had sympathised with Stalin's opponents in the past. This punitive atmosphere pervaded the worldwide communist movement. Stalin wanted only such support abroad as was unmistakably loyal.

As the Republicans went down to defeat in the Spanish Civil War, Stalin's interest reverted to the French Communist Party and its policy toward Léon Blum's socialist government. French communist leader Maurice Thorez, like his counterparts elsewhere in Europe, had been wary of the turn towards the popular front; but, having accepted it, he proposed to join Blum's cabinet in 1936. Permission had to be sought in Moscow. When Moscow demurred, Thorez obeyed Moscow.[6] Always the Kremlin kept tight tutelage and Stalin was in command. The chief restriction on his manoeuvres was the quality of information reaching him from the Executive Committee of the Comintern as well as from France and other countries; and leaders such as Thorez, much as they strove to please Stalin, draped their messages in the cloth of their political preferences. Stalin had confidence in the system of decision-making he had established. He also functioned according to his general assumptions about global developments. While recognising the importance of international relations, he could not afford to spend most of his time on them if he was to secure the kind of internal transformation he sought – and in the late 1930s the carrying through of the bloody mass purges remained his first priority. Only an extraordinarily decisive Leader could operate as he did on the European and Asian political stage.

This was obvious in his intervention in the affairs of the Chinese Communist Party. Stalin continued to demand that Mao Tse-tung maintain the alliance with Chiang Kai-shek. Although Mao thought that Stalin overrated the Chinese nationalist movement – the Kuomintang – led by Chiang Kai-shek, he sorely needed financial and political assistance from Moscow. 'United front' tactics were demanded by Stalin, and Mao had to accede. Since being suppressed by the Kuomintang in 1927, the Chinese Communist Party had regrouped. The Long March had been undertaken in 1934 to the north of China, where Mao consolidated the party's support in the villages. The Kuomintang and the Chinese Communist Party remained intensely hostile to each other. Mutual suspicion spilled over into sporadic violence. Civil war was prevented only by the external threat posed by militarist Japan. The Japanese, who had occupied Manchuria in 1931 and set up the Manchukuo puppet state, plainly contemplated further territorial expansion. To Stalin, who as usual thought in broad geopolitical categories and desired to enhance the immediate security of the USSR, it seemed best for Mao and Chiang to put aside their rivalry; this was the advice supplied by the Comintern to the Chinese communists throughout the mid-1930s.

Mao continued to wriggle away from the Comintern line. No foreign communist party leader before the Second World War displayed such contumacy (as Stalin regarded it). Mao's men, far from allying themselves with Chiang, took him captive. Moscow ordered his immediate release. Mao was exasperated by the meddling; he wanted to kill the enemy leader who had come close to suppressing his entire party in 1927. Yet he had to comply or face losing crucial military supplies from the USSR. Communist discipline had prevailed.[7]

The situation changed in July 1937 when the Japanese invaded China proper. Beijing and Shanghai fell quickly to their forces. The Chinese Red Army resumed a more co-operative attitude towards the Kuomintang in the national interest. Yet China's joint forces were no match for Japan. Down the country swept the conquering army, carrying out massacres of civilians in the cities. Stalin pledged weapons and finance to the Chinese communists. He also reorganised his own borderlands. It was in these years that Stalin ordered ethnic purges of Koreans and Chinese living in the Soviet Far East. The regional leadership of the NKVD was replaced and the Red Army was put on alert for any menace from Japan's Kwantung Army in Manchukuo. The two sides, Soviet and Japanese, kept each other guessing about their geopolitical pretensions. Frequent border skirmishes aggravated the situation and on 25 November 1936 the Japanese signed the Anti-Comintern Pact with Germany and Italy. Concern in the Kremlin was acute. Stalin saw no point in diplomatic concessions, and when the Kwantung Army clashed with Soviet forces in May 1939 at Nomonhan, he met fire with fire. War broke out. The Red Army in the Far East was reinforced by tanks and aircraft. Commander Georgi Zhukov was dispatched to lead the campaign.[8]

The maps in east, south and west were being redrawn by militarism. The League of Nations had proved ineffective as Japan overran first Manchuria and then China. International protests failed to save Ethiopia from Italian conquest; and Germany, after intervening actively in the Spanish Civil War, annexed Austria and Czechoslovakia. Yet until Nomonhan the Red Army had seen more action against Soviet peasant rebels than against the foreign enemies of the USSR. The great test of Stalin's industrial and military preparations was at last taking place.

Despite the lacerations of the Great Terror, the Red Army acquitted itself well. Just as the Russians had expected an easy victory over an inferior enemy in 1904, the Japanese anticipated a Soviet military collapse. Intelligent and adaptive, Zhukov had learned much from the German training programmes observed on the soil of the USSR until 1933. Like Tukhachevski, he identified tank formations as essential to contemporary land warfare. His arrival in the Far East energised the Soviet offensive strategy. He had witnessed Stalin's destruction of the Supreme Command and knew that nothing short of comprehensive victory over the Japanese would keep the NKVD off his back.[9] His sole advantage was that Stalin, as had been the case since the Civil War, did not stint in the granting of men and equipment to his commanders. Zhukov plotted to outmatch the enemy in resources before taking them on. By August 1939 he had amassed such a force and could start his planned offensive. Stalin watched warily through the prism of reports reaching him from army commanders and the military intelligence agency. While Zhukov needed Stalin's trust, Stalin needed Zhukov's success in the campaign.

Stalin himself was being courted by Britain and France as their governments sought ways to restrain Hitler by means of an agreement with the USSR. Yet there was little urgency in the overtures. The British Foreign Office sent out a middle-ranking official by steamship to Leningrad instead of flying him out, and the official was not allowed to take any diplomatic initiative. Stalin, hedging his bets in European diplomacy, took the drastic step of letting Berlin know that he would not be averse to an approach from the Germans.

He had already expended a load of precious resources on extending the internal state terror to foreign parts. The extermination of Trotskyists and anarchists in Spain was just part of his repressive zeal. Assassinations were carried out against anti-communist Russian émigrés in Europe. Individual communist critics of Stalin were also targeted. The greatest quarry of all was Trotski. Huge priority was accorded by the Soviet intelligence organs to funding and organising attempts on his life. Shunted from one country to another, he had finally found refuge in Coyoacán on the outskirts of Mexico City. No longer a fundamental threat to Stalin in the Kremlin, Trotski had infuriated him by publishing the *Bulletin of the Opposition* and organising the Fourth International. The first attack on him in Coyoacán was led by the mural artist David Alfaro Siqueiros. It failed, and Trotski reinforced his security precautions. But Stalin was obsessed with his wish to kill him. The second attack was more subtly arranged. NKVD agent Ramón Mercader managed to infiltrate the Trotski household by posing as a follower of his. On 20 August 1940 he had the opportunity he had awaited in the villa and plunged a mountaineering ice-pick into Trotski's head.

The hunting down of Stalin's mortal enemy had involved a large diversion of resources from other tasks of espionage.[10] Nevertheless the Soviet spy network was not ineffective in the 1930s. Communism was seen by many European anti-fascists as the sole bulwark against Hitler and Mussolini. A small but significant number of them volunteered their services to the USSR. Stalin and the NKVD could also count on regular reports from communist parties in Europe and North America.

This provided the Soviet leadership with the information to formulate its foreign policy on the basis of sound knowledge about the likely response from abroad. In Japan, Germany and the United Kingdom the NKVD had high-level spies with extraordinary access to state secrets. The problem was not the provision of information but its processing and distribution. Stalin insisted on restricting the reports from diplomatic and espionage agencies to a tiny handful of associates. An inner group of the Politburo was established to monitor, discuss and decide. But such was his suspicion towards fellow politicians in the Kremlin that he often let no one else inspect the available reports. As crises in international relations multiplied and deepened before 1939, this meant that the actions of the USSR depended crucially, to a much greater extent even than in Germany, on the lonely calculations of the Leader. Simultaneously he was also examining reports on the entire gamut of internal policies on politics, security, economy, society, religion, nationhood and culture. His time for scrutinising the material flowing from abroad was finite. The reportage was always contradictory in content; it was also of diverse degrees of reliability. Stalin's mistrust of his associates meant that he wasted the advantages supplied by his intelligence network.[11]

He was culpable too for reducing the People's Commissariat of External Affairs to a shadow of its former self. The Great Terror had removed hundreds of qualified personnel. Jews in particular were repressed. The result was that after 1937–8 every functionary in Moscow and the embassies avoided saying anything that might conceivably cause trouble. Strong, direct advice to Stalin was eschewed.

Nerves of steel were required for Stalin and his Politburo associates as they followed events in Europe and Asia in 1939. His personal interventions in diplomatic affairs were becoming ever more frequent, and on 5 May 1939 he formalised the situation by changing the leadership of Sovnarkom. Stalin installed himself as Chairman for the first time. This was a step he had until then resisted; since 1930 he had been content to let Molotov run the government. The darkening picture of international relations induced a change of mind. Molotov, though, was not discarded but assigned to the People's Commissariat of External Affairs. Maxim Litvinov was eventually, in 1941, appointed ambassador to the USA. His known preference for a system of collective security against the fascist threat in Europe had appeared to limit Soviet diplomatic options in mid-1939. The door was opened for a more flexible foreign policy towards Nazi Germany if the opportunity arose. (The fact that Litvinov was Jewish was a further impediment to conciliation with Hitler.) Molotov was Stalin's senior henchman as well as a Russian. Yet another signal was being given that Stalin believed highly important developments to be in the offing.

This has led to speculation that he was playing a long-term hand with a view to a deal with Germany. This was a tradition in Soviet foreign policy. When socialist revolution failed to break out in Berlin after October 1917, Lenin persistently sought to regenerate the Soviet economy by means of German concessionaires. Without German assistance, whether socialist or capitalist, he saw little chance of restoring industry and agriculture across the country. The Treaty of Rapallo in 1922 went some way in this direction. Did Stalin have a similar orientation? It is surely most unlikely. He had introduced the First Five-Year Plan so as to liberate the USSR from dependency on all foreign support, even if, for a few years, imports of American and German technology had to continue.

Stalin's observation of the world since the Wall Street Crash confirmed his set of ideas. To him, capitalism appeared inherently unstable. It was also, however, still dangerous. Until such time as the Red Army was an unchallengeable force on two continents it behoved Soviet diplomacy to manoeuvre towards agreements with foreign powers. Even Germany, despite being ranged on the opposite side in the Spanish Civil War, was not necessarily irreconcilable. Like Japan, Germany was a constant geopolitical factor to be taken into account in his calculations. But increasingly he felt that the USSR's industrial and military achievements were allowing a more active foreign policy. In the 1920s, when military commanders Mannerheim and Piłsudski held power in Finland and Poland, the Politburo was perpetually worried about their depredatory intentions. In the following decade these fears diminished. The Red Army was a power to be reckoned with. In 1939 its forces were at war with Japan and holding their own. The People's Commissariat of External Affairs could deal with bordering states – Finland, Estonia, Latvia, Lithuania, Poland, Romania and Bulgaria – from a position of strength. Their potential to cause damage to the USSR would only be realised if they concerted their efforts. But after Hitler's rise to power they were more concerned about being conquered by the Germans than exercised by thoughts of bringing down Bolshevism in Moscow.

Germany, though, could act independently. Its successive campaigns of expansion had been condoned by the United Kingdom and France. Soviet diplomatic attempts to organise resistance had been rebuffed. Stalin had offered assistance to Czechoslovakia before its destruction in March 1939. Whether he was seriously intending to commit the Red Army is doubtful. He was making a public statement of the USSR's anti-fascism in the knowledge that the British and French were most unlikely to take a stand against Hitler. The Czechoslovaks themselves were reluctant to have Soviet armed units on their soil. In spring and summer 1939 Hitler increased the pressure on Poland. He evidently had his eyes on Danzig on the Baltic coast. Poland was under military threat, and yet its politicians refused to ally with the USSR. Soviet–Polish enmity was an irremovable feature of Warsaw's calculations. In these circumstances it was hardly surprising that Stalin began to consider whether a deal with Hitler might be preferable to standing wholly outside developments in eastern Europe.

Stalin relied primarily upon military power, intelligence reports and diplomatic finesse to see him through. The Comintern was a weak source of assistance. The Chinese communists were incapable of defeating the Japanese and had yet to crush the Kuomintang. The German communists were dead or in concentration camps – and a few were émigrés in the USSR. Communism as a political force in central and eastern Europe was on its knees. In Spain and Italy too it was battered. In the rest of the world, including North America, it still counted for little. In the United Kingdom it was a minor irritant to the status quo, mainly to the British Labour Party. In only one country, France, did the communist party retain a mass following. But the French communists were but one party on the left. Although they could organise industrial strikes and political demonstrations, they were chiefly a disruptive factor in national politics. Stalin was often criticised, especially by Trotski's Fourth International, for turning away from the Comintern in the 1930s. The reality was that the world communist movement offered little hope of making revolutions.

Even if a revolution had broken out, there would have been complications for Soviet military and security policy. The USSR had few options in the last years of the decade. Stalin, who had always been sceptical about forecasts of a European revolutionary upsurge, reposed his immediate confidence in the activity of the Soviet state. This did not mean that he had abandoned belief in the inevitability of socialist revolution around the world. The global 'transition', he thought, would eventually take place as had been predicted by Marx, Engels and Lenin. But he was realistic about the current weakness of the world communist movement; and being a man who liked to operate with a broad programmatic scheme at any given time, he put his trust in his army, in his intelligence agencies and – above all – in himself and his subordinate partner Molotov.

Stalin and Molotov, with their limited diplomatic experience, assumed dual responsibility; and although Molotov occasionally stood up to Stalin in matters of ideology,[12] they never clashed about foreign policy. But this commonalty increased the country's jeopardy. Stalin could scarcely have fashioned a more perilous arrangement in which decisions of state might be taken. He alone took the supreme decisions. On his mental acuity depended the fate of his country and peace in Europe and the Far East. Most leaders would have lost sleep over this burden of responsibility. Not Stalin. He was supremely self-confident now that he had liquidated those prominent intellectuals who had made him feel edgy and – deep down in his mental recesses – inadequate. He learned fast and prided himself on his mastery of detail. He had never lacked will power. The rest of the Politburo, terrified by the purges of 1937–8 and immersed in their other vast functions of governance, left foreign policy to the Boss. Steadily the inner group was left out of discussions. Yet its members remained impressed by his competence and determination. This was a situation which beckoned to disaster. Disaster was not long in paying a visit.

36. THE DEVILS SUP

An event occurred in the early hours of 24 August 1939 which shocked the world when the USSR and Germany sealed a ten-year non-aggression pact. The ceremony took place in Molotov's office in the Kremlin with Stalin in attendance,[1] and the two foreign ministers – Molotov and Ribbentrop – appended their signatures. Six years of mutual vilification between the Soviet Union and the Third Reich ended. *Pravda* ceased to excoriate Hitler and Nazism in its editorials and Hitler stopped criticism of 'Judaeo-Bolshevism'. Anti-German films were withdrawn from Soviet cinemas; anti-Soviet pamphlets and books were taken down from the shelves of German bookshops. Two dictatorships which had supported opposite sides in the Spanish Civil War embraced each other.

Stalin in his dog-eared tunic looked over Molotov's left shoulder as he signed the document. Like Lenin with the Treaty of Brest-Litovsk, he kept back in case things turned out badly. Stalin was delighted with the way things had turned out since Ribbentrop's arrival at the Central Aerodrome on the previous day. Ribbentrop had come to the Kremlin in mid-afternoon, where Stalin and Molotov met him. For Ribbentrop, this was a sign that the Soviet leadership really had a serious interest in a deal with the Third Reich. Diplomatic notes had passed between Berlin and Moscow for three weeks. Ribbentrop had come to propose an agreement to settle the Soviet–German relationship from the Baltic Sea down to the Black Sea. Hitler's immediate objective was an invasion of Poland, but the enterprise would be perilous without the USSR's collusion. The Führer authorised Ribbentrop to arrange a non-aggression treaty between the Soviet Union and Nazi Germany. The proposed treaty anticipated the division of the northern regions of eastern Europe into two zones of Soviet and German influence; it also laid down a scheme to increase mutually beneficial trade. Ribbentrop had flown to Moscow to stress that Hitler, despite being the author of *Mein Kampf*, was in earnest.

The willingness of Stalin to enter such an arrangement with Nazi

Germany had been strengthened by the half-heartedness of diplomatic efforts by alternative powerful partners. By mid-August the prospect of alliance with Britain and France had disappeared, and each day made any German offer more tempting. Molotov on Stalin's instructions sent a confidential note agreeing to diplomatic talks. Germany's impatience was growing. Hitler needed to invade and subjugate Poland before winter set in. On 19 August Stalin intimated that Moscow was ready to receive Ribbentrop. Such was the haste of the rapprochement that Hitler had no time to attend – or perhaps he would not have gone to Moscow in any case.

Stalin, though, was pleased. Three hours of quiet negotiation in the afternoon of 23 August left just one divisive matter. This involved the fate of Latvia. Hitler had instructed Ribbentrop to keep Latvia, with its influential German minority, in Germany's zone of influence. But Stalin and Molotov were intransigent. The old Imperial frontiers were something of a preoccupation for Stalin. There was also the factor of strategic security. If Hitler were to overrun Latvia, he would have a territorial wedge cutting into the USSR's borderlands. Talks were adjourned at 6.30 p.m. for Ribbentrop to withdraw to consult his Führer. Hitler quickly conceded, and Ribbentrop went back to the Kremlin to tell Stalin the news. Stalin, who was normally as impassive as stone when he wanted to be, could not stop shaking. But he got a grip on himself and as the two groups finalised the text of a treaty, Stalin brought out the bottles and proposed a toast 'to the Führer's health'. Ribbentrop reciprocated on the Führer's behalf.[2] Deep in the night the formal ceremony took place with Stalin grinning at Molotov's shoulder. Teetotaller Hitler was told at his Eagle's Nest retreat above Berchtesgaden and allowed himself a small glass of champagne.[3]

Hitler had need of the assurance that the USSR would not oppose his conquest of most of Poland. This was a temporary compromise: he had not dropped his objective of an eventual invasion of the USSR. But what about Stalin himself? In the light of what happened in 1941, when Hitler ordered Operation Barbarossa, was he prudent to do what he did in 1939?

This begs the question of whether Stalin had a realistic alternative. Evidently the reconciliation with Germany was his personal decision after consultation with Molotov. Staff in the People's Commissariat of External Affairs were given no advance warning and were not asked to prepare background briefings.[4] There had been no hint in the central daily newspapers. Apart from Molotov, the foreign-policy group in the

Politburo which included Malenkov, Beria and Mikoyan was left in the dark about the matter.[5] If ever there was proof that Stalin was willing to take immense risks, the Nazi–Soviet agreement provided it. Having reached the decision, moreover, he did not deign to explain his calculations to others. In truth there were at the time only two basic options for Soviet foreign policy: an agreement with Hitler or an agreement with France and the United Kingdom. Peace with Hitler would give Stalin a period of respite to go on building up Soviet military strength. By contrast it was not clear that the French and British were seriously interested in a deal. The fact that the British had sent only a middle-ranking Foreign Office official to conduct talks in Moscow in summer 1939 was deeply discouraging to the Kremlin.

Stalin, fearing dangerous isolation, believed a deal with Germany was the only option on the table. He had to surmount ideological inhibition: the Nazis were the greatest enemy of world communism. Yet Stalin did not let doctrine impede him. Marxist–Leninism anyway made no fundamental distinction between types of capitalist states. For Stalin, all such states – whether liberal-democratic or fascist – were fundamentally deplorable. When he moved towards the policy of the popular front in 1934, he was merely making the practical calculation that the Third Reich posed an immediate threat to the USSR in Europe. This had not ruled out the ultimate possibility of a treaty with Hitler any more than Lenin had excluded the possibility of temporary armed collusion with German proto-Nazis in mid-1920.[6] Furthermore, Lenin too had wanted the Soviet state to avoid entanglement in a world war among capitalist states. The basis of the USSR's policy should be for the great powers to fight any future world war among themselves and for the Red Army to exploit whatever situation might result. If it took a non-aggression treaty to keep Hitler's hands off the USSR and to induce Germany to move its armed forces against France and the United Kingdom, Stalin was willing to take the step.

He did not believe that a mere treaty would secure peace for the Soviet Union. He also knew that Hitler was a formidable potential enemy. Molotov was to recall:[7]

> It would be wrong to say that he underestimated him. He saw that Hitler had somehow managed to take only a short time to organise the German people. There had been a large communist party and yet it had disappeared – it was wiped out! And Hitler took the people with him and the Germans fought during the war in such a

way that this was palpable. So Stalin with his dispassionate approach to the consideration of grand strategy took all this very seriously.

This has the ring of truth. In public it was necessary for a Marxist to stress that Nazism was supported mainly by the middle class. Yet Stalin knew that he was up against a Führer whose people were behind him. He also had no reason to believe that Hitler would quickly crush the armies of the French after defeating Poland. Like most observers, Soviet leaders assumed that the Third Reich would be enmired in difficulties in the West and that this would enable the USSR to go on preparing for war rather than having to fight one against the Wehrmacht.

There were two sections to the Treaty of Non-Aggression: one was public, the other secret. The public section stipulated that the USSR and the German Reich agreed not to make war on each other either individually or in concert with other powers. Disputes between them were to be settled by negotiations or, if this proved ineffective, by an arbitration commission. The treaty entailed that, if either party became engaged in war with another power, no support should be forthcoming to that other power. The treaty was to remain valid for ten years with provision to extend it for five years. The USSR and Germany were to increase their trade on a mutually advantageous basis. Yet the treaty's secret section was still more significant. Its clauses demarcated 'spheres of interest' for the Soviet and German regimes in eastern Europe. Germany was recognised as having freedom of action from its existing eastern frontier across to Lithuania. Influence in Poland was to be divided between the USSR and the Third Reich. Without expressly saying so, Hitler and Stalin intended to occupy their 'spheres' and reduce them to direct political subservience.

Hitler quickly realised his geopolitical objective. On 1 September 1939 a Blitzkrieg was started against Poland. Within days the Polish military resistance had been crushed. Warsaw fell on 27 September. The British and French governments, somewhat to Hitler's surprise, delivered an ultimatum to Berlin on the first day of the war. Hitler ignored it. To German dismay, Stalin at first refused to sanction the movement of the Red Army into the territory agreed as falling within the Soviet sphere of interest. The reason was that the USSR and Japan remained at war in the Far East, and the military risk of deploying forces in eastern Poland was too great until the two countries agreed to make peace on 15 September. The Red Army moved into Polish territory two days later. A second agreement – the Treaty of Friendship, Co-operation and

Demarcation – was agreed on 28 September. Stalin demanded not only Estonia and Latvia but now also Lithuania as part of the Soviet sphere. He aimed both to recover the land of the Russian Empire and to secure a compact area of defence for the USSR. Hitler, who already was thinking about attacking France, quickly acceded.

Stalin's established procedures for dealing with 'enemies of the people' came into effect. Political, economic and cultural leaders were rounded up. Army officers too were arrested. Some were shot, others were sent to labour camps in Siberia and Kazakhstan. The NKVD, learning lessons from the Great Terror, had prepared itself carefully with lists of people to be seized. Stalin wanted to be sure that police action hit exactly those groups which he had identified as hostile to Soviet interests. He and Beria did not confine themselves to persecuting individuals. Whole families were arrested and deported. Poland was the first country to suffer.[8] Estonia, Latvia and Lithuania were next on the agenda as Stalin and Molotov ordered their governments to sign pacts of mutual assistance. A similar command was conveyed to Finland. The consolidation of the entire region under Soviet hegemony was pursued. The problem was that Finland, which was diplomatically close to Germany, was unwilling to lie down. Negotiations ceased. Stalin set up a government-in-waiting with Moscow-based Finnish communists and, on 30 November, the Red Army attacked confident that it would soon reach Helsinki.

The Finns, however, held steadfast. The Reds, racked by the effects of the Great Terror, fought hard but incompetently. The Winter War turned into a bloody stalemate in the northern snows. The Finnish government was aware that the total defeat of the Red Army was beyond it. Discussions were resumed and a peace treaty was signed in March 1940. The realistic Finns gave up much territory and several military bases. The Soviet frontier with Finland was moved hundreds of miles to the north of Leningrad. Stalin had achieved his ends but at a terrible price. One hundred and twenty-seven thousand Red Army soldiers perished.[9] More importantly for Stalin (who cared nothing for the number of deaths), the military might of the USSR had been exposed as weaker than the world had thought. If the Soviet armed forces could not crush Finland, what would they be able to do against the Third Reich if ever war broke out with Hitler?

The shock was general in the Kremlin. With so large a force, the Red Army had been expected to thrust back the Finns without difficulty and enable the establishment of a Finnish Soviet Republic which would apply for incorporation in the USSR. Stalin was beside himself with fury. He rebuked Voroshilov. Drink and old friendship loosened Voroshilov's tongue. Despite the Great Terror, he kept a sense of personal honour and was unwilling to accept criticism from the Leader who had supervised every large decision about security and defence in recent years. Voroshilov had had enough: he picked up a plate of suckling pig and crashed it down on the table.[10] This sort of outburst would have condemned most men to the Gulag. (They would usually have gone to the Gulag long before they got round to shouting at the Leader.) The war, though, gave Stalin reason to take stock strategically and necessitated a reorganisation of the Red Army. Stalin dismissed the inadequate Voroshilov and appointed Semën Timoshenko, a professional commander, to lead the People's Commissariat of Defence.

The urgency of the task was demonstrated in summer 1940 as the Wehrmacht raced through the Low Countries into France, forcing Paris's capitulation and the emergency evacuation of British forces from the beaches of Dunkirk. The fall of the United Kingdom seemed imminent. Timoshenko, with Stalin's consent, restored a sense of pride to the Soviet officer corps. Political education was reduced as a proportion of required military training. Plans were put in hand for a new line of defence works to be constructed along the boundaries separating the German and Soviet spheres of interest. In order to realise this aim it appeared necessary to bring Estonia, Latvia and Lithuania under the USSR's control. There was to be no repetition of the Finnish débâcle. A brief charade was played out. Incidents of 'provocation' were arranged for the Kremlin to have a pretext to intervene. Baltic politicians had to be intimidated. Ministers were summoned from the capitals of Estonia, Latvia and Lithuania. Stalin and Molotov were bullies with decades of experience. The visitors to Moscow were given no choice but to accept annexation. Molotov snarled to the Latvian Foreign Minister: 'You're not going to return home until you give your signature to your self-inclusion in the USSR.'[11] The three governments were militarily helpless. Resistance would lead to national disaster.

Compliance, of course, would also bring disaster since Estonia, Latvia and Lithuania would undoubtedly undergo the same treatment as eastern Poland. In fact the bully-boy methods did not immediately result in signed requests for incorporation in the USSR. The Red Army therefore moved in force to secure Stalin's aims, and NKVD units – some of which had been operating in Poland – were close behind. A façade of constitutionalism was maintained. Politburo member Andrei Zhdanov, closely liaising with his master Stalin, was sent to the Baltic region to carry out his orders behind the scenes. Police arrests took place under the cover of a news black-out. Executions and deportations ensued as the Soviet-dominated media announced fresh elections. Only candidates belonging to the communists, or at least supporting them, were allowed to stand. Parliaments assembled in Tallinn, Riga and Vilnius in July and declared total agreement with Moscow's wishes. All petitioned, as Stalin had demanded, for incorporation in the USSR. For form's sake Stalin declined to admit the three on the same day. Lithuania entered the USSR on 3 August, Latvia two days later and Estonia a day after that.

Stalin was playing the geopolitical game for all it was worth. Communist political prospects in Europe had vanished. For Stalin, an inveterate opportunist, this was no problem. While not ceasing to believe in the superiority of communism over capitalism, he waited for the next chance to promote his kind of dictatorship abroad. Lithuania, Latvia and Estonia were not the only places he had in his sights as lying within the zone of the USSR's special interest. Stalin and his representatives persistently specified Romania and Bulgaria in this way. Nor did he fail to argue that Turkey fell within the Soviet zone of hegemony. And Stalin, while delivering abundant quotas of grain and oil to a Germany at war with France and the United Kingdom, demanded German technology in exchange. Berlin had to sanction the sale of Messerschmitt fighters, a Panzer-III tank and the cruiser *Lutzow*; it also showed the construction plans for the battleship *Bismarck* to Soviet specialists.[12] Stalin has the reputation of having been gulled by Hitler. This was not how things appeared to Berlin in 1939–40. Stalin had driven a hard bargain and insisted on its complete fulfilment. As he pushed his case at the risk of raising tension between Moscow and Berlin, Hitler described him as a 'cold-blooded blackmailer'.[13]

What changed Stalin's attitude was nothing that happened in eastern Europe or the Far East. France's collapse in summer 1940 transformed everything. Soviet military planning had been based on the assumption that Hitler would encounter more effective resistance from the French armed forces than had been met in Poland. Geopolitics in Europe were turned upside down. Few observers gave the United Kingdom much chance of survival in the following months. For Stalin, the implications were dire. The Wehrmacht looked as if it was close to completing its tasks in the West. It would no longer face a two-front war if it turned its power against the USSR. Stalin's relations with Hitler immediately reflected the consequences of France's collapse. Truculent since August 1939, he began to appease. War with Germany had to be averted at any cost.[14]

Appeasement was practised without any express declaration of a change in stance. But Stalin's statements behind the scenes, recently made available, reveal his worries. At the October Revolution anniversary dinner in the Kremlin on 7 November 1940 he indicated his shock at the military developments. He did not limit himself to the French débâcle. The Soviet–Japanese War had indicated weaknesses in the country's air force if not in its tanks. The Winter War with Finland had gone much worse for the USSR, revealing gross defects in organisation and planning. Then Germany had overwhelmed France in the summer campaign and driven the British back over the Channel. Stalin was blunt: 'We're not ready for war of the kind being fought between Germany and England.'[15] Molotov was to recall him concluding around that time that 'we would be able to confront the Germans on an equal basis only by 1943'.[16] The diplomatic ramifications were enormous. Hitler had to be reassured that Soviet military intentions were entirely peaceful. His requests for raw materials had to be met even if German technology was not immediately available in exchange: late delivery, once complained about, was now forgivable.

As the diplomatic world darkened in the first half of 1941, Stalin revised several of his political judgements. Already he had added to the Russian national ingredients in Marxism–Leninism. Steadily, as he looked out on the countries of Europe under the Nazi jackboot, he reached the conclusion that the Comintern's usefulness had come to an end. If communism was going to appeal to broad popular opinion, it had to be regarded as a movement showing sensitivity to local national feelings. Perhaps Stalin also urgently wanted to reassure Hitler that Soviet expansionism was a defunct aspiration. He mentioned this to Dimitrov in April 1941; communist parties, he asserted,[17]

> should be made absolutely autonomous and not sections of the Comintern. They must be transformed into national communist parties with diverse denominations: workers' party, Marxist party, etc. The name is not important. What is important is that they put down roots in their people and concentrate on their own specific tasks ... The International was created in Marx's time in the expectation of an approaching international revolution. The Comintern was created in Lenin's time at an analogous moment. Today,

national tasks emerge for each country as a supreme priority. Do not hold on tight to what was *yesterday*.

Dimitrov had virtually been told that his job was obsolete.

This did not mean that Stalin had given up faith in the ultimate worldwide success of communism; but what Dimitrov was hearing, in an indirect way, was a judgement that the military situation in Europe had become so complex and dangerous that it was no longer to the USSR's advantage to maintain a co-ordinated communist movement under the direction of the Comintern. Stalin had not abandoned hope of controlling the activity of other communist parties. Instead he had made the provisional judgement that his policy of appeasing Germany would be enhanced if he put distance between his government and the Comintern. Only the outbreak of war with Germany delayed Stalin's dissolution of the Comintern.

Yet Stalin, while seeking to appease Hitler, wanted to keep up the morale of his own Red Army. On 5 May 1941 he addressed the ceremony for graduates of military academies in Moscow. His words, unreported in the press at the time, were combative. Instead of the reassuring words he issued to the media about Germany, he declared:[18]

> War with Germany is inevitable. If com[rade] Molotov can manage to postpone the war for two or three months through the M[inistry] of F[oreign] Affairs, that will be our good fortune, but you yourselves must go off and take measures to raise the combat readiness of our forces.

Stalin urged the Soviet armed forces to prepare for war.[19] He explained:[20]

> Until now we have conducted a peaceful, defensive policy and we've also educated our army in this spirit. True, we've earned something for our labours by conducting a peaceful policy. But now the situation must be changed. We have a strong and well-armed army.

Stalin continued:

> A good defence signifies the need to attack. Attack is the best form of defence ... We must now conduct a peaceful, defensive policy with attack. Yes, defence with attack. We must now re-teach our army and our commanders. Educate them in the spirit of attack.

Was this – as some have suggested – the index of an intention to attack Germany within the near future? Undeniably he had no scruples about stabbing friends and allies in the back. Hitler felt and acted the same way, and Nazi propaganda about *Lebensraum* and Slavic *Unter-menschen* had not been forgotten in the Kremlin. It would have made strategic sense for Stalin to strike down Hitler before Hitler could invade the USSR. It is also true that Zhukov and Timoshenko were sketching plans for such an offensive.

Yet none of this proves that Stalin genuinely contemplated his own offensive in the immediate future. A military graduation ceremony in the Europe and Asia of mid-1941 was hardly an occasion for a political leader to moderate the combat mentality of future officers. They needed to be readied for war; they also had to see that they had a political leadership willing to wage war. Moreover, it would have been remiss of Stalin to fail to instruct Zhukov and Timoshenko to plan for an offensive. All armies need to undertake multiple planning and the Red Army was no exception. Stalin wished to be able to deal with every possible contingency. He was realistic about the need for at least a couple of years before his forces could take on the Germans. He did not exclude the possibility of attacking Germany if and when the Wehrmacht seemed weak. The Marxist–Leninist tradition in foreign policy prescribed that the USSR should exploit the political, economic and military rivalries among capitalist powers. This was how states of all kinds had behaved since time immemorial. If Germany looked weak, the Soviet mountain eagle would swoop down and take its prey.

Consequently Stalin's priority in May and June 1941 was to avoid giving Hitler a reason to start a war. The General Staff had yet to complete a definitive comprehensive plan for defence.[21] Diplomatic and economic appeasement remained foremost in Stalin's mind. The analyses of military professionals in Berlin and Moscow had pinpointed the importance of beginning such hostilities in early summer in order to shatter the USSR's defences before the onset of winter; and Stalin was hoping that all this was correct. Hitler had been prevented from invading the Soviet Union at the appropriate time because of trouble in Yugoslavia since the spring. But the secret decision had already been taken in Berlin: Hitler was going to attack as soon as he had amassed sufficient forces in German-occupied Poland. His confidence rested on ignorance of Soviet military capacity. Stalin's secretiveness meant that the Germans had been kept in the dark about the USSR's true strength. By the time such information started to reach Berlin, it was too late to persuade Hitler to call off the invasion.[22]

Stalin hoped against hope that his diplomatic manoeuvres were paying off as midsummer approached. He ignored the rising mountain of information that Hitler was up to no good on his borders. Zhukov was becoming frantic. In mid-June he made one of his recurrent attempts to snap Stalin out of his policy of appeasement. Stalin angrily pounced on him: 'What are you up to? Have you come here to scare us with the idea of war or is it that you really want a war? Haven't you got enough medals and titles?'[23] This was a punch below the belt that made Zhukov lose his temper even with Stalin. But the moment passed and the appeasement policy was maintained. Thus the conditions for the greatest military disaster of the twentieth century were unwittingly prepared by the supremely confident Leader in the Kremlin.

37. BARBAROSSA

In the hour before dawn on 22 June 1941 the German armed forces started Operation Barbarossa. There was no warning from Hitler; this was a classic Blitzkrieg and Stalin was in bed at the time in his Blizhnyaya dacha. In the diplomatic crisis of recent weeks he had judged that intelligence sources predicting a German invasion were just a provocation. Timoshenko as People's Commissar of Defence and Zhukov as Chief of the General Staff thought him mistaken and had stayed up on duty all that last night. At 3.30 a.m. they received reports of heavy shelling along the Soviet–German frontier. They knew this for what it was: the beginning of war. Timoshenko ordered Zhukov to call Blizhnyaya by telephone. Zhukov obediently asked a sleepy Vlasik, the chief of Stalin's bodyguard, to rouse the Leader.[1]

Like a schoolboy rejecting proof of simple arithmetic, Stalin disbelieved his ears. Breathing heavily, he grunted to Zhukov that no countermeasures should be taken.[2] The German armies had had no more compliant victim. Stalin's only concession to Zhukov was to rise from his bed and return to Moscow by limousine. There he met Zhukov and Timoshenko along with Molotov, Beria, Voroshilov and Lev Mekhlis.[3] (Mekhlis was a party bureaucrat who had carried out many tasks for Stalin in the Great Terror.) Pale and bewildered, he sat with them at the table clutching an empty pipe for comfort.[4] He could not accept that he had been wrong about Hitler. He muttered that the outbreak of hostilities must have originated in a conspiracy within the Wehrmacht. Always there had to be a conspiracy. When Timoshenko demurred, Stalin retorted that 'if it were necessary to organise a provocation, German generals would bomb their own cities'. Ludicrously he was still trying to persuade himself that the situation was reversible: 'Hitler surely doesn't know about it.' He ordered Molotov to get in touch with Ambassador Schulenburg to clarify the situation. This was clutching at a final straw while Armageddon erupted. Schulenburg had in fact already requested an interview with Molotov in the Kremlin. In the meantime

Timoshenko and Zhukov went on imploring Stalin's permission to organise armed counter-measures.[5]

Schulenburg, who had sought to discourage Hitler from invading, brought the unambiguous military news. Molotov reported back to Stalin: 'The German government has declared war on us.' Stalin slumped into his chair and an unbearable silence followed. It was broken by Zhukov, who put forward measures to hold up the forces of the enemy. Timoshenko corrected him: 'Not to hold up but to annihilate.' Even then, though, Stalin continued to stipulate that Soviet ground forces should not infringe German territorial integrity. Directive No. 2 was dispatched at 7.15 a.m.[6]

The Germans swarmed like locusts over the western borderlands of the USSR. Nobody, except perhaps Stalin, seriously expected the Red Army to push them back quickly to the river Bug. A military calamity had occurred on a scale unprecedented in the wars of the twentieth century. Stalin had not yet got a grip on himself. He was visibly distraught and could not focus his mind on essential matters. When Timoshenko returned from the People's Commissariat of Defence to confer, Stalin refused to see him. Politics, even at this moment, had to come first and he insisted that a Politburo meeting should take precedence. Finally at nine o'clock in the morning Timoshenko was allowed to present a plan for the creation of a Supreme Command. The Politburo meanwhile gave Molotov the task of speaking on radio at midday.[7] Stalin still felt disoriented. If he had wanted, he could have given the address himself. But shock and embarrassment deflected him. He was determined to stay at the centre of things, however – and he knew that Molotov would not let him down at the microphone. Stalin was not wasting time with resentment about what Hitler had done to him. War had started in earnest. He and the USSR had to win it.

How had he let himself be tricked? For weeks the Wehrmacht had been massing on the western banks of the River Bug as dozens of divisions were transferred from elsewhere in Europe. The Luftwaffe had sent squadrons of reconnaissance aircraft over Soviet cities. All this had been reported to Stalin by his military intelligence agency. In May and June he had been continuously pressed by Timoshenko and Zhukov to sanction the dispositions for an outbreak of fighting. Richard Sorge, the Soviet agent in the Germany embassy in Tokyo, had raised the alarm. Winston Churchill had sent telegrams warning Stalin. The USSR's spies in Germany had mentioned the preparations being made. Even the Chinese Communist Party alerted Moscow about German intentions.[8]

Yet Stalin had made up his mind. Rejecting the warnings, he put faith in his own judgement. That Stalin blundered is beyond question. Yet there were a few extenuating circumstances. Stalin expected there to be war with Germany sooner or later. Like military planners everywhere, he was astonished by Hitler's easy triumph over France. The success achieved by the Wehrmacht in the West was likely to bring forward any decision by the Führer to turn eastwards and attack the USSR. But Stalin had some reason to believe that the Germans would not risk an attack in the year 1941. Although France had been humbled, Hitler had not dealt a fatal blow to the British. His armed forces had also met difficulties in the Balkans in the spring when action against the German occupation of Yugoslavia diverted troops needed for Operation Barbarossa. Stalin continued to hold to the belief that a successful invasion of the USSR would have to be started in early summer at the latest. Napoleon's fate in 1812 had shown the importance of beating Russians without having to trudge through snow. By mid-June 1941 it looked as if the danger of a German crusade had faded.

Some Soviet intelligence agents were also denying that a German attack was imminent. A fog of reports befuddled Stalin's calculations.[9] He made things worse by insisting on being the sole arbiter of the data's veracity. The normal processing of information was disallowed in the USSR.[10] Stalin relied excessively on his personal intuition and experience. Not only fellow politicians but also People's Commissar of Defence Timoshenko and Chief of the General Staff Zhukov were kept in the dark about reports from embassies and intelligence agencies.[11] The Germans took advantage of the situation by planting misinformation; they did much to induce Stalin to believe that a military campaign was not in the offing. Thus Stalin in the early months of 1941 moved along a dual track: he scrupulously observed the terms of his pact with Nazi Germany while telling gatherings of the Soviet political and military elite that, if the Germans attacked, they would be repulsed with ferocious efficiency. He had been taking a massive gamble with his country's security. Cautious in so many ways, Stalin trusted in his ability to read the runes of Hitler's intentions without discussing the evidence with anyone else.

Stalin was shocked by Operation Barbarossa, but Molotov always defended the Boss against the charge that he collapsed under the strain:[12]

> It can't be said he fell apart; certainly he was suffering but he did not show it. Stalin definitely had his difficulties. It would be stupid

to claim he didn't suffer. But he's not depicted as he really was – he's represented as a repentant sinner! Well, of course, that's absurd. All those days and nights, as always, he went on working; he didn't have time to fall apart or lose the gift of speech.

Stalin's visitors' book confirms that he did not lapse into passivity.[13] Zhukov too insisted that Stalin's recovery was swift. By the next day he had certainly taken himself in hand, and over the next few days he seemed much more like his old self. His will power saw him through. He had little choice. Failure to defeat the German armed forces would be fatal for the communist party and the Soviet state. The October Revolution would be crushed and the Germans would have Russia at their mercy.

On 23 June Stalin worked without rest in his Kremlin office. For fifteen hours at a stretch from 3.20 a.m. he consulted with the members of the Supreme Command. Central military planning was crucial, and he allowed his political subordinates to get on with their tasks while he concentrated on his own. Then at 6.25 p.m. he asked for oral reports from politicians and commanders. Molotov was with him practically the whole time. Stalin was gathering the maximum of necessary information before issuing further orders. Visitors are recorded as having come to him until 1.25 a.m. the next morning.[14]

The Supreme Command or Stavka – the term used under Nicholas II in the First World War – had also been established on 23 June. Stalin was initially disinclined to become its formal head. He was not eager to identify himself as leader of a war effort which was in a disastrous condition. So it was Timoshenko who as Chairman led a Stavka including Stalin, Molotov, Voroshilov, Budënny, Zhukov and Kuznetsov. The others also tried to persuade Stalin to permit his designation as Supreme Commander. He refused even though in practice he acted as if he had accepted the post. The whole composition of Stavka was shaped by him,[15] and it was noticeable that he insisted that leading politicians should belong to this military body. Not only Molotov but also Voroshilov and Budënny were basically communist party figures who lacked the professional expertise to run the contemporary machinery of war. Timoshenko, Zhukov and Kuznetsov were therefore outnumbered. Stalin would allow no great decision to be taken without the participation of the politicians, despite his own gross blunders of the past few days. He called generals to his office, made his enquiries about the situation to the west of Moscow and gave his instructions. About his supremacy there was no doubt.

He drove himself and others at the maximum pace until the early hours of 29 June, when Molotov, Mikoyan and Beria were the last to leave him. (V.N. Merkulov, who had headed the state security organisation for several months, had departed some minutes before.)[16] At that point he started to behave mysteriously. His visit to the Ministry of Defence two days earlier had been a difficult one. When Timoshenko and Zhukov showed him the operational maps, he was shocked by the extent of the disaster for the Red Army. Having surmounted his bewilderment about Operation Barbarossa on 21 June, he suffered a relapse. Fellow members of the Politburo, Sovnarkom and Stavka had no idea what had happened to him. When calls were put through to the Blizhnyaya dacha, his chief aide Poskrëbyshev claimed not to know where he was. Yet he was indeed skulking at that dacha. Commanders and politicians were left to get on with the war with Germany as best they could. No one outside Blizhnyaya knew whether he was alive or dead.

The German advance quickened across the Soviet borderlands. Trained by Stalin to accept his whims, his military and political subordinates tried to run their institutions as if nothing strange was occurring. But they worried about doing anything without clearing it with him beforehand. The situation was changing by the hour. Stalin's sanction had been essential for years and Stavka needed his presence at the centre of things. What was he doing? One possibility was that his morale had fallen so low that he felt incapable of continuing at his post. He had much reason to feel bad about his recent performance. Another possibility is that he was seeking to impress upon his subordinates that, however poorly he had performed, he remained the irreplaceable Leader. Stalin was an avid reader of books on Ivan the Terrible and to some extent identified himself with him. Tsar Ivan had once abandoned the Kremlin and withdrawn to a monastery; his purpose had been to induce boyars and bishops to appreciate the fundamental need for him to go on ruling. After some days a delegation came out to the Tsar to plead with him to return to the Kremlin. Perhaps Stalin was contriving a similar situation.

The truth will never be known since Stalin never spoke of the episode. His subordinates eventually plucked up courage to find out what was going on. Nikolai Voznesenski, the rising star in state planning bodies, was visiting Mikoyan when a call came through from Molotov for them to join him. Malenkov, Voroshilov and Beria were already with Molotov, and Beria was proposing the creation of a State Committee of

Defence. Mikoyan and Voznesenski agreed. This State Committee of Defence was envisaged as supplanting the authority of both party and government and as being headed by Stalin. It was the first great initiative for years that any of them had taken without seeking his prior sanction.[17]

The snag was to get Stalin to agree. The group resolved to drive out to Blizhnyaya to put the proposal to him directly. When Molotov raised the problem of Stalin's 'prostration' in recent days, Voznesenski stiffened his nerve: 'Vyacheslav, you go first and we'll be straight behind you.' Mikoyan interpreted this as more than a travelling plan. Voznesenski was saying that, if Stalin could not pull himself together, Molotov should take his place. Arriving at the dacha, they found him slumped in an armchair. He looked 'strange' and 'guarded', quite unlike the Leader they were used to. 'Why,' he muttered, 'have you come?' Mikoyan thought Stalin suspected that they were about to arrest him. But then Molotov, his old comrade, spoke for everyone by explaining the need for a State Committee of Defence. Stalin was not yet reassured, and asked: 'Who's going to head it?' Molotov named Stalin himself. Even then Stalin appeared surprised and simply said: 'Good.' The ice was melting. Beria suggested that four Politburo members should join him in the State Committee: Molotov, Voroshilov, Malenkov and Beria. Stalin, recovering his confidence, wanted to add Mikoyan and Voznesenski.[18]

Beria objected that Mikoyan and Voznesenski were indispensable for work in Sovnarkom and Gosplan. Voznesenski rose angrily against Beria. Stalin was in his element: his subordinates were more interested in arguing with each other than in rivalling him. Agreement to a State Committee of five members was obtained with wide powers for Mikoyan to organise supplies and for Voznesenski to co-ordinate armaments production.[19] The decision was confirmed in the press on 1 July.[20] And Stalin was back in charge. The suggestion that Molotov might be substituted for Stalin could have been the death of all of them; it was kept secret from him. It was anyway an occasion which Stalin was unlikely to forget. Beria believed that sooner or later the visitors to the dacha would pay the price just for having seen him in a moment of profound weakness.[21]

On 10 July, after being prodded by Zhukov among others, Stalin allowed himself to be appointed Supreme Commander. He was cautious even about this and the acquisition of the title was withheld from the media for several weeks. His reason for this fumbling was not disclosed and he never discussed it with his intimates. But it is hard to avoid the conclusion that Stalin had wanted to avoid too close an association in the popular mind with the catastrophe at the front. If the defeats continued, he would make other heads roll. He took even longer to take official charge of Stavka. Not until 8 August did he agree to become its Chairman. Was this yet another sign that he had learned from biographies of the first Roman emperor, Augustus, that real power mattered more than titles? Whatever it signifies about Stalin's attitude to his image, it is clear evidence that at last he thought that the Red Army had recovered from its disastrous first days in the field against the Germans. The beginnings of an effective defence were being organised, and order and efficiency were replacing chaos: Stalin could at last take the risk of assuming full supreme responsibility; and indeed failure to do so would raise questions about his commitment.

Someone who paid the ultimate price for annoying Stalin even without having seen him in his depressed mood at the dacha was Western Front commander Dmitri Pavlov. Placed in an impossible situation by Stalin's military mismanagement before and on 22 June 1941, Pavlov was being made the scapegoat for the German military success. To err is human and Stalin had erred on a stupendous scale. He forgave himself but not others; and when he made a mistake, it was others who got the blame. Pavlov was arrested, tried by court martial and sentenced to death. Quite what Stalin thought he was achieving by this is hard to understand. The sentence was not given wide publicity. Most probably Stalin was just doing what had become his normal practice, and he wanted to keep his commanders in fear of him. But perhaps he also discerned the need to avoid causing a collapse in the morale of the entire officer corps. Hence he opted for compromise. He obtained his victim but refrained from the pre-war scenario of torture, show trial and forced confession. This was little consolation to the hapless Pavlov, but it was the earliest frail sign that Stalin understood the need to adjust his behaviour in the furnace of war.

Hitler's Wehrmacht meanwhile continued to rampage deep into Soviet territory. The German strategic plan was to motor across the plains and marshes of the western borderlands of the USSR and, within a few weeks, occupy the main European regions. They seemed about to fulfil every expectation of the Führer. Experienced tank formations rolled over vast territory encountering brave but ineffective defensive operations. Minsk, Belorussia's capital, fell on 29 June, Smolensk on 16 July. No great urban centre lay between Smolensk and Moscow. Despairing of the existing command on his Western Front, Stalin released Timoshenko and Zhukov to reorganise things on the spot and stiffen resistance. Some deceleration of the German advance was achieved against Army Group Centre. But Panzer formations were simultaneously smashing their way towards Leningrad in the north and Kiev further south. Already all Poland, Lithuania and Belorussia was subject to rule by the General Government appointed by Hitler. It seemed that nothing could save 'Soviet power'. Operation Barbarossa was undertaken by armed forces which had conquered every country in Europe they had attacked. Over three million men had been amassed for the campaign against the USSR. At Hitler's disposal were more than three thousand tanks and two thousand aircraft. Security forces followed in the path of their victories: Einsatz-kommandos extirpated all those thought hostile to the New Order. Everything had been planned and supplied to evident perfection.

Panic seized Moscow and Leningrad as thousands of inhabitants tried to leave before the Germans arrived. The refugees included party and government functionaries. Stalin was merciless. Beria, who had been given general oversight of security matters in the State Committee of Defence, was empowered to set up barrier detachments on the capital's outskirts and mete out summary justice to those who sought to flee. Strategic dispositions were made as the State Committee established high commands for the North-Western, Western and South-Western Fronts. Stalin's confidence in military professionalism had not matured. Although he appointed Timoshenko to the Western Front, he stipulated that Voroshilov should head the North-Western Front while Budënny took the South-Western Front.[22] Voroshilov and Budënny, his comrades in the Civil War, had won no laurels in the Soviet–Finnish War and yet Stalin stood by them. Party committees and soviet executive committees in the provinces were brought directly under the State Committee's leadership and ordered to stiffen the spirit of resistance. The conscription of men for the Red Army was to be intensively undertaken. Armaments production had to be boosted, labour discipline tightened and food supplies secured from the villages. How this was done was a matter of indifference to Stalin. He cared only for results.

An immense number of prisoners-of-war fell into German hands: more than 400,000 Red Army troops were seized in the battle for Minsk alone. The Soviet air force in the western borderlands had been destroyed, mainly on the ground, in the first two days of hostilities. The linkages of transport and communications had been shattered. When Smolensk was occupied, the party headquarters had no time to incinerate its documents. The USSR lost its Soviet republics in the western borderlands as Ukraine, Belorussia, Lithuania, Latvia and Estonia were subjected to German rule. The USSR had lost half its industrial and agricultural capacity and almost the same proportion of its population. Morale was low in the unoccupied zones. Civil administration was chaotic. German bombers continued to wreck places of habitation many miles beyond the lines of the Wehrmacht's advance. In Moscow there was gathering panic. Many government officials tried to flee. Neither Molotov's speech on 22 June nor Stalin's eleven days later convinced most people that successful defence was possible.

Nor did the USSR lack citizens who were pleased with what seemed to be happening. Many in the western borderlands welcomed Wehrmacht troops as liberators. Ukrainian peasants greeted them with the traditional bread and salt. Stalin's aim to extirpate the possibility of a fifth column by means of the Great Terror proved ineffective. All he had achieved was a stoking up of the fires of embitterment with his rule. The peasantry longed to be freed from the torments of the collective-farm system. They were not the only ones. In towns and cities, especially among people who were not Russians or Jews, there was much naïveté about Hitler's purposes. This was not surprising since German occupation policy had yet to be clarified, and some Nazi functionaries saw advantage in seeking voluntary co-operation in the conquered regions of the Soviet Union by dismantling the entire order constructed since 1917. Churches were reopened. Shops and small businesses began to operate again. Hitler foolishly overruled any further proposals in this direction. All Slavic peoples were to be treated as *Untermenschen*, fit only for economic exploitation on behalf of the Third Reich. Wehrmacht and SS were instructed to squeeze labour and raw materials out of Ukraine as if the country was a lemon.

The war effort in the USSR began to be co-ordinated. Party functionaries were ordered to address factory meetings and to tell the workforces that the Germans were about to be halted. Huge demands were to be made of Soviet citizens. Working hours were lengthened, labour discipline tightened still further. The menace of Nazism would be dispelled. The USSR was going to win and the Third Reich, despite current appearances to the contrary, to lose. The Soviet regime would act as ruthlessly in war as it had done in peace.

Yet it was difficult to believe the few real optimists. Official spokesmen were assumed to be saying only what they had been ordered to say. The Luftwaffe was bombing Moscow by 21 July. A month of fighting had brought the Soviet Union to its knees. Army Group North was approaching Leningrad and, with the fall of Moscow apparently imminent, Hitler and his generals began to contemplate switching forces to Army Group South to secure the coming conquest of Kiev. The Soviet refugees streaming into central Russia brought with them tales of German military success which undermined *Pravda*'s insistence that the Red Army was ceasing to retreat. What Hitler was achieving was what German commanders Ludendorff and Hindenburg had threatened to do if Lenin and the communists had failed to sign a separate treaty at Brest-Litovsk in early 1918. Vast economic resources had come under German occupation for use in the war against the USSR. Evacuation of factories and workforces was attempted on Stalin's orders; and Red troops and the NKVD, as they retreated, implemented a scorched-earth policy to minimise the benefit to the Wehrmacht. Hitler prepared himself to be master of the East.

38. FIGHTING ON

Autumn 1941 was grim for the Russians. The United Kingdom had stood alone against Germany for over a year and now the USSR joined it in even greater peril. The British could not send much aid in finances, armaments or troops. Although the front between the Wehrmacht and the Red Army was but one of the fronts in the Second World War, it was at this time virtually a separate war. The front had yet to be stabilised by effective Soviet defence. In October the German forces, having lunged across the plains and marshes to the east of the River Bug, were massing outside Moscow for a final thrust at the USSR's capital. Critical decisions needed to be taken in the Kremlin. The initial plan was for the entire government to be evacuated to Kuibyshev on the Volga. Stalin was set to leave by train – and Lenin's embalmed corpse, reinfused with chemicals, was prepared for the journey to Tyumen in west Siberia. Moscow appeared likely to fall to the invader before winter. Not since Napoleon's invasion in 1812 had the Russian capital faced such a plight – and Stalin, unlike Alexander I, could scarcely expect that Hitler would grant him his life in the event of the increasingly probable German victory.

Yet the line held. Zhukov, Stavka's Chief of Staff, was transferred to the field for the defence of Moscow. At the last moment Stalin decided to stay in the capital. While sanctioning the departure of several People's Commissariats to Kuibyshev, he decided that Zhukov might pull off victory and instructed the leading politicians to remain with him in the capital. He could not have dreamed up a better piece of propaganda. The word got out that the Leader was refusing to forsake the capital. Resistance was going to be shown by everyone from Stavka members down to the ordinary infantryman and factory worker.

The first test of Stalin's resolve came towards the end of the year with Stavka's discussion about deep defence. Zhukov was a natural forward-mover; he was never more content than when organising Red forces to attack the Wehrmacht. But he was also a professional military man. The strategic chances of resisting German forces advancing on Kiev were minimal, and Zhukov – like the other commanders – concluded that the abandonment of the Ukrainian capital would conserve human and material resources which could be used at a later stage in the war. He put this to Stalin at his predictable peril. Stalin was angry. 'How,' he asked, 'could you even think of giving up Kiev to the enemy?' Still Zhukov stood his ground: 'If you think the Chief of Staff can't talk anything but absolute nonsense, he's got no business here.'[1] Nevertheless Stalin stayed with his own impulses and the order was given that Kiev should be defended to the last. Timoshenko, usually timid about offending Stalin, considered withdrawing from Kiev without telling Stalin. (This, obviously, would have been a suicidal measure for Timoshenko.) Attack, attack and attack: this was Stalin's way to repel the Nazi invasion. So at Stalin's insistence the armed forces in the capital were ordered to prepare for decisive action. Civilians were told to stay behind.

The Wehrmacht moved forward. What astounded its commanders were Soviet pluck, determination and flexibility. They had been taught to regard the Russians as *Untermenschen* but discovered that the peoples of the USSR, including the Russians, were far from being primitives. Stalin would not yet budge on strategy. Abandonment of great cities was anathema to him. He had yet to learn that strategic withdrawal could facilitate an indispensable regrouping. He acted like a military ignoramus just as he had been proved a diplomatic one in mid-1941. Inevitably Kiev fell to the larger and better-organised forces of the Wehrmacht on 19 September.

The Red Army's strategic options were few. While the Wehrmacht held the initiative, Stavka had to react to German moves. Commanders were ordered to hold their present positions. Stavka decided which sectors most needed reserves to be rushed to them. While Zhukov worked on a plan of campaign, Stalin harassed his politicians into expanding output for the armed forces. Astonishing feats were performed in the USSR in 1942. The factories and workforces evacuated from the western regions of the USSR were restored to operation in the Urals. Meanwhile the industrial enterprises of central Russia were intensifying activity. The grievous losses of 1941 were being made good. This was done with Stalin's customary ruthlessness. The slogan 'Everything for the Front!' was realised almost to the letter. Industry, already heavily tilted towards military needs before 1941, produced virtually entirely for the needs of the armed forces. Consumer goods ceased to be manufactured. Soviet economic might was so successfully dedicated to the war effort that in the last six months of 1942 it reached a level of production which the Germans attained only across the entire year. The numbers were remarkable. In that half-year the USSR acquired fifteen thousand aircraft and thirteen thousand tanks.[2]

The price was paid by other sectors of the economy. Resources were denied to agriculture. As young men were conscripted into the armed forces and young women left for jobs in the factories, conditions on the collective farms sharply deteriorated. Many farms fell out of production or else were run by the labour of women long past their time of youthful vigour. Yet the government procurement quotas were maintained so that the soldiers and workers might be fed. The result was the deeper impoverishment of the countryside. The state administrative order which reported massive achievements in turning out tanks and aircraft was a disaster for agriculture. Stalin's propagandists – and many later commentators – emphasised that his policies had proved themselves wonderfully in war; they could do this only by keeping silent about farms in the unoccupied regions.

Yet the patriotic spirit was unquenchable. Propaganda stiffened the resistance by publishing details of German atrocities. *Pravda* did not become a 'paper of record', yet it did not have to concoct falsehoods about the Wehrmacht and the SS. Once the Soviet military resistance began to stiffen, Moscow's media concentrated effectively on German atrocities. Jews, Roma and communists were being shot out of hand. Murder and pillage were ravaging the USSR's western borderlands. Although the Germans allowed most churches and some private shops to be reopened in Ukraine, they generally treated the country as a place for plunder. Harvests were routinely seized, and the German occupiers found the collective farms too useful an instrument of grain procurement to be abandoned. Early in Operation Barbarossa there had been debate in Berlin about policies of occupation. Several officials had urged the prudence of seeking to neutralise opposition in the western regions of the USSR by granting economic and social concessions. Hitler quashed this talk. For him, the whole purpose of the invasion was to realise his ideological dream. The Wehrmacht, SS and civilian administration were ordered to treat the Slav *Untermenschen* as a human resource exploitable to the point of death.

This apparently had no effect on Stalin. He had failed to anticipate the intensity of Nazi brutality; but even when reports reached him from behind the German lines, he held his tongue about them. He spoke only in general terms about German atrocities (whereas Churchill and Roosevelt emphasised the massive disregard for international laws on war). Stalin himself waged war, as he conducted politics, with his own immense savagery. The NKVD had rampaged across Estonia, Latvia and Lithuania killing or arresting whole strata of the population. It was through Operation Barbarossa that for the first time since the Civil War he confronted an enemy as willing as he was to use terror against innocent non-combatants.

Stalin in any case gave little thought to the matter.[3] Calling on his compatriots to fight a bitter war regardless of cost, he had no interest in focusing attention on the horrific strength and ruthlessness of the Wehrmacht. He and Stavka got on with planning, organising and supervising the war effort. They were hard men by any standards. Those communist leaders with a soft side to their thinking – Bukharin, Kamenev, Tomski or Ryazanov – had perished in the Great Terror. There were no such spirits in Stavka or the State Committee of Defence. If any of them had reservations about Stalin's severity towards his own forces, they kept quiet about them. Both sides in the German–Soviet conflict went at each other without regard to the Geneva Convention. Prisoners-of-war were treated atrociously. Strategy and tactics were developed which spared neither soldier nor civilian. The restraints which characterised the fighting between Germany and the Western Allies never prevailed on the front with the Red Army. Warfare reverted to the colossal brutality last seen in Europe in the religious wars of the seventeenth century, and Stalin was in his element.

The USSR's survival of that first terrible winter of 1941–2 seemed a miracle at the time. The USA entered the war against Germany in 1941. Stalin's Western Allies, despite their public bravado, had not given him much of a chance; and although Washington promised arms and other supplies through the system of Lend-Lease (which postponed any payment till the end of hostilities), little reached the USSR until the later months of 1942. The Soviet Union had had to cope with Nazi Germany on its own, while Hitler could draw upon increasing support from Italy, Hungary, Romania and Slovakia.

Sober assessment was less unfavourable to Stalin's chances. The pre-war analysis, shared in Berlin and Moscow held that the Germans needed to attack by early summer if they were to conquer. The actual military campaign validated this analysis. The Wehrmacht, after massive advances into the western borderlands of the USSR, was halted outside Leningrad and Moscow; it had failed to overrun the Russian heartland, oil-rich Baku and the Volga transport routes. The USSR retained adequate human and material resources to go on resisting the aggressor. The Wehrmacht operated in bleaker conditions than Hitler had anticipated. The last months of 1941 were bitterly cold. German lines of communication and supply were overstretched: Hitler had not got far enough to have final success but had gone too far to maintain his armed forces in a decent condition. Germany's military equipment, moreover, had not been built to specifications for the rigours of the Russian winter. The odds began to turn in the USSR's favour despite the enduring impact of Stalin's miscalculations about Operation Barbarossa.

Stalin had gained his second wind even though the immediate situation was deeply discouraging. The Wehrmacht prowled like a panther outside Moscow and Leningrad. Supplies of food in the unoccupied parts of the USSR had fallen by a half as a result of German control of Ukraine. The Don Basin too had been seized, and with it had vanished three quarters of the country's access to coal, iron and steel. Other metal deposits lay in the territories held by Germany; these included copper, manganese and aluminium. Potential conscripts to the Red Army were reduced by the speed and depth of the Wehrmacht's advance. In the Soviet-held territories, moreover, there was much chaos. Millions of refugees streamed into central Russia. Trains reached Moscow from the west with wagons piled high with the machinery of factories that had been evacuated.

The Supreme Commander reverted to instinct. Attack, he insisted to his exhausted generals, was preferable to defence. Even Stalin acknowledged that this was impossible near Moscow and Leningrad. But he thought his maps indicated German weakness in the Don Basin. Generals and commissars warned him that logistics and geography were unpropitious; but they got nowhere. Stalin argued – or rather he assumed and did not care about what others argued against him – that almost any action was better than passivity. In April 1942, as the snow gave way to mud, Stalin overrode Stavka and compelled its military specialists to organise an offensive in eastern Ukraine with the objective of seizing Kharkov. This would be the first serious Soviet counter-attack. It was planned with egregious indiscretion and German intelligence agencies had prior knowledge. The Wehrmacht had made its arrangements and was waiting; it also knew in advance about Stalin's plan to retake the Crimea. A strategic trap was sprung. Despite the objections from his advisers, Stalin insisted on the offensives and the Red Army drove its tanks straight into the jaws of defeat.

Hitler had dealt a juddering blow to the Soviet armed forces, and

Kharkov stayed in the hands of the enemy. Hitler continued to think in grandiose terms. The war was going well for German forces in north Africa and it was not unreasonable to suppose that the Wehrmacht, coming from the south and the north, would soon overrun the entire Middle East and take possession of its oil. The Japanese, Hitler's allies, were moving fast down the western rim of the Pacific Ocean. No country could hold out against Japan; the European imperial powers – Britain, France and Holland – were being worsted in the Asian struggle. Hitler confidently chose Stalingrad (formerly known as Tsaritsyn) as his next target.

Stalin ordered the city to be held at all costs. There is much unwarranted commentary that both he and Hitler exaggerated Stalingrad's strategic significance. Stalin had been based there for some months in 1918 and his propagandists had treated the Tsaritsyn campaign as crucial to the outcome of the Civil War. Hitler, it is said, was drawn to attacking Stalingrad because the city bore Stalin's name. Sentiment and symbolism may well have contributed to the German determination to take Stalingrad and the Soviet will to resist. But the primary reason for Hitler's decision was strategic. Stalingrad lay in an area vital for the logistics of the USSR's war effort. German control over the mid-Volga region would cut the USSR off from its oil supplies in Baku and Grozny. Its possession would also permit the Germans to break across the Volga to south-eastern Russia and dangerously reduce Moscow's access to grain and potatoes. The alternative would have been to concentrate on the capture of Moscow so as to dominate the centre of transport and administration for the entire USSR. But Hitler's decision was sound even if it was not the sole option available to him.

Germany and its allies started the Stalingrad campaign on 28 June 1942. Quickly they reached and took Voronezh. Then Rostov fell. Stalingrad seemed doomed and a confident Hitler split the attacking forces so as to seize the oil of the north and south Caucasus. The reports to Moscow made painful reading for Stavka. Panic gripped the inhabitants of Russia's south. To prevent any repetition of the kind of panic which had disrupted the capital in July 1941, Stalin issued Order No. 227, 'Not a Step Backward!', on 28 July 1942. Its terms, read out to troops in the field but withheld from the Soviet media, demanded obedience on pain of severe punishment. Retreat, unless it had clear sanction from the Kremlin, was to be treated as treason. Soviet-held territory was to be defended at all costs. 'Panickers' and 'cowards' were to expect summary treatment: they would either be shot on the spot or transferred to the so-called penal battalions (where they stood little chance of survival). Order No. 227 had been edited and signed by Stalin. No serving soldier was left in doubt of his determination to compel the Red Army to fight without giving an inch.

Yet when Stalin refused to send reinforcements to Stalingrad, he was not relying on Order No. 227. He was fearful about diverting his reserves from Moscow and Leningrad. German commander Friedrich Paulus's forces moved unrelentingly on Stalingrad. Stalin turned again to Zhukov. Implicitly he recognised that he had been making misjudgements in Ukraine and southern Russia which at last he called upon his most dynamic officer to rectify. As a reward for his achievements Zhukov was made Deputy Supreme Commander. After a swift visit to the front, Zhukov stood out for a changed set of military dispositions. In particular he called for the dispatch of reserves to Stalingrad. This plan was agreed in September 1942, and Zhukov and the new Chief of Staff Alexander Vasilevski worked out the details with Stalin. Gradually the Supreme Commander was learning how to work with fellow Stavka members. The plan for a wide counter-offensive – Operation Uranus – was elaborated. Reserves were assembled and the defenders of Stalingrad, cut off by the Germans, were ordered to hold out for the duration. Whole districts of the city were reduced to rubble by the constant bombing raids of the Luftwaffe. Vasili Chuikov was appointed the new Soviet commander, but Hitler believed that Paulus would soon have possession of Stalingrad.

Zhukov and Vasilevski conferred with Stalin and other commanders at each stage of their planning. This was the outcome of Stalin's growing respect for their professional expertise. Zhukov reported to Stalin on his direct observations near the front. When he made recommendations about operational defects, he had to put up with Stalin expatiating on contemporary warfare.[4] Yet generally Stalin behaved himself. He proposed that Operation Uranus should be postponed if preparations were not fully in place.[5] This was not a Stalin seen earlier in the war.

Final decisions on Operation Uranus were taken on 13 November. Zhukov and Vasilevski took comfort from the fact that Romanian rather than German troops would stand across the line of the Soviet advance; they also had numerical superiority in men and armaments. Stalin listened attentively, slowly puffing on his pipe and stroking his moustache.[6] Members of the State Defence Committee and the Politburo came in and out. The general plan was gone over several times so that all leaders might understand their responsibilities. Zhukov and Vasilevski, while advocating this counter-offensive, reminded Stalin that the

Germans would almost certainly transfer troops from Vyazma to strengthen Paulus's forces. They therefore suggested a synchronised counter-offensive by the Red Army to the north of Vyazma. Stalin gave his consent: 'This would be good. But who of you is going to take up this matter?' Zhukov and Vasilevski divided the responsibilities between them, and Stalin ordered Zhukov to leave next day for Stalingrad to oversee the last arrangements before Operation Uranus. Stalin left the date for the start of the campaign to Zhukov.[7] Zhukov and Stalin were almost as confident as they were determined. This time the Germans would be beaten.

Operation Uranus had initial success on 19 November but then got held up by the German defence. Stalin, according to Zhukov, sent dozens of telegrams hysterically urging his commanders to crush the enemy.[8] This was his old way with subordinates: they had to be kept functioning at a frantic pace or Stalin would get angry. Hitler meantime transferred Erich von Manstein, one of his best generals, to break through the Soviet lines around Stalingrad. But Stalin had also learned patience. It helped that the geography of the region was well known to him. This made it less likely that he would impose manifestly impractical ideas. But still Stalin displayed 'excessive nervousness' in Stavka.[9]

In December 1942 he decided in the State Defence Committee to put Konstantin Rokossovski in sole command of the front. Stalin had until then been exercising a degree of self-restraint at planning sessions, and the surprised Zhukov fell silent. Stalin exclaimed: 'Why are you keeping quiet? Or is it that you don't have your own opinion?' Zhukov, who had spent weeks assembling a command group at Stalingrad, pointed out that these commanders, especially Andrei Yeremenko, would take offence. But Stalin had made up his mind: 'Now is not the time to be offended. Ring up Yeremenko and tell him the State Defence Committee's decision.'[10] Yeremenko indeed took it badly, but Stalin refused to speak to him. The plan and the personnel were at last in place. The fighting around Stalingrad had reached a peak of intensity. The city had been turned into a lunar landscape; hardly a building remained intact. Ammunition and food were running out. The icy Volga winter made conditions hardly bearable for soldiers on both sides: frostbite and malnutrition affected many of them. Soviet forces, however, were somewhat better supplied than the Germans and their allies. Hitler had failed to remedy the problem of stretched lines of communication. Unmistakably the Red Army had the edge.

Hitler was altogether too casual about the difficulties in Stalingrad until Paulus had been cut off by Konstantin Rokossovski's Don Front and Nikolai Vatutin's South-Western Front. Paulus's only option was to attempt a break-out; but Hitler, who thought that the Luftwaffe would keep German forces supplied until such time as Manstein could make a crushing advance, overruled him. Zhukov and Vasilevski had anticipated all this. They filled the gap between Paulus and Manstein with a mass of armoured divisions. From this position they intended to deliver two strategic blows. Operation Saturn aimed to retake Rostov-on-Don while Operation Circle would complete the closure of Stalingrad and the destruction of Paulus's forces. This dual scheme was too ambitious. It allowed Manstein to stabilise his front and threaten the Soviet besiegers of Stalingrad. By themselves Zhukov and Vasilevski might have reacted more flexibly. But they had Stalin looking over their shoulders. Once he had the scent of victory, he could not contain himself. The result was that the Reds were needlessly fighting to the point of exhaustion – and the Germans were given a second chance.

Yet Soviet forces regrouped. Manstein failed to smash down their defences, and Rokossovski was able to turn his divisions on Paulus. The Wehrmacht experienced the fate it had customarily meted out to its enemies. German soldiers had been convinced by Nazi propaganda that they were going to fight a rabble of *Untermenschen* in the name of European civilisation; they were instead being reduced to a piteous condition by a superior power which was well armed, well organised and well led.

Other war leaders might have gone down to witness some of the action. Stalin resolutely stayed put in Moscow. The reality of war for him was his conversations with Zhukov, his inspection of maps and the orders he shouted down the telephone line at frightened politicians and commanders. He neither witnessed nor read about the degradation among Paulus's forces. They froze and starved and caught rats and chewed grass and tree bark for food. The end was approaching, and Paulus was invited to surrender. The street fighting pinned him deep into the city. Hand-to-hand combat continued until Paulus gave himself up, and on 2 February 1943 German resistance ceased. Stalingrad was a Soviet city again. The German losses were greater than in any previous theatre of the Second World War: 147,000 of them had been killed and 91,000 taken captive. The Red Army had lost still more men. But it had gained much more in other ways. The myth of the Wehrmacht's invincibility had been discredited. Hitler had visibly lacked basic skills of generalship. Whereas Soviet citizens had once doubted whether the Red Army could win the war, now everyone thought it might have a chance.

Stalin was generous to his commanders. Zhukov and five others were awarded the Order of Suvorov, 1st class. Stalin made himself Marshal of the Soviet Union. He convinced himself that he had been tested in the heat of battle and had achieved everything demanded of him. His real role had been as a co-ordinator and instigator. He drew together the military and civilian agencies of the Soviet state. The expertise was supplied by the commanders in Stavka, and the courage and endurance came from the officers and men of the Red Army in conditions of almost unbelievable privation. The material equipment was produced by poorly fed factory workers who toiled without complaint. Food was provided by kolkhozniks who themselves had barely enough grain and potatoes to live on. But Stalin was unembarrassed by self-doubt. Whenever he appeared in public and whenever pictures of him appeared on newsreels or in the press after Stalingrad, he donned the marshal's uniform.

39. SLEEPING ON THE DIVAN

The German invasion deprived Stalin of the presence of his family. His sons Yakov and Vasili were on war service. Yakov was a lieutenant in the 14th Armoured Division, Vasili a very young air force commander. Yakov suffered a terrible fate. Captured near Vitebsk by the Wehrmacht in 1941, his identity was discovered and he was kept as a prized prisoner. Hitler sanctioned an offer to ransom him for one of the leading German generals. The Germans interrogated him in the hope of hearing things which might be used to embarrass his father. Yakov, despite his youthful misdemeanours, proved a stoical inmate and stood up for Stalin and the USSR. Stalin endured the situation and refused the German proposal point blank. Yet the situation deeply troubled him; he asked Svetlana to stay in his bedroom for several successive nights.[1] Only Zhukov dared to enquire after Yakov. Stalin walked about a hundred paces before replying in a lowered voice that he did not expect Yakov to survive captivity. Later at the dining table he pushed aside his food and declared with a rare intimacy: 'No, Yakov will prefer any death to the betrayal of the Motherland. What a terrible war! How many lives of our people has it taken away! Obviously we'll have few families without relatives who have perished.'[2]

Order No. 270, which had been edited and sharpened by Stalin,[3] prohibited Soviet servicemen from allowing themselves to be taken prisoner. Red Army POWs were automatically categorised as traitors. Yet Stalin exempted his son Yakov from blame. Nevertheless the iron was in his soul: he wanted the policy of no surrender to be taken seriously and could not afford to be seen indulging his son.

The relationship between Stalin and his sons had been poor long before the war. Yakov had continued to annoy his father, even refusing to join the communist party. Stalin sent for him and remonstrated: 'And you are my son! What do I look like? Me, the General Secretary of the Central Committee? You can have all the opinions you wish, but do think of your father. Do it for me.' This argument got through to Yakov and he joined the party.[4] But they saw little of each other and Stalin was never slow to issue reprimands. It was a similar situation with his younger son Vasili, who took more than the normal time to qualify for the officer corps in the Soviet air force (which was the favourite section of the armed forces for the offspring of Politburo members). It is said that Stalin complained: 'You should long ago have got your diploma from the Military Academy.' Vasili is reported to have lashed back: 'Well, you haven't got a diploma either.'[5] Perhaps the story is apocryphal. But it has the sound of psychological truth. Stalin was always trying to impress others as a man who understood armies and military strategy. Only his son would have dared to point out the amateurish foundations of his military knowledge.

Until the war Svetlana had been the apple of his eye. Nadya's strict standards of behaviour were relaxed after her death,[6] and Svetlana was fussed over by tutors and housekeeper Katerina Til. A nurse combed her hair. The general oversight of her daily schedule, though, was handed to Stalin's chief bodyguard Nikolai Vlasik.[7] Stalin was too busy to see a lot of her; in any case his opinion was that 'feelings were a matter for women'.[8] What he wanted from his children was that they should be a delight for him on those occasions when they spent time together. He in turn wished to be fun for them. Yakov and Vasili did not meet these specifications: neither of them worked hard at school or behaved with the mixture of respect and levity that he required. But Svetlana fitted the bill. He penned letters to her pretending to be her 'first secretary comrade Stalin'. She wrote out orders to him such as 'I hereby command you to permit me to go to the theatre or cinema with you.' To this he replied: 'All right, I obey.'[9] As Maria Svanidze, Stalin's sister-in law from his first marriage, recorded in her diary for 1934, Svetlana adored him: 'Svetlana rubbed against her father the whole time. He stroked her, kissed her, admired her and fed her from his own spoon, lovingly choosing the best titbits for her.'[10]

Relations between father and daughter deteriorated after Operation Barbarossa. By her mid-teens she was interested in men, and this brought out his ill-tempered side. When she showed him a photograph of herself in clothes he thought immodest (and he had strict ideas on this subject), he snatched it from her and ripped it up.[11] He hated her wearing lipstick. When she wanted to stay overnight at the Berias' dacha, where she was a frequent visitor, he ordered her to return home immediately: 'I don't trust Beria!'[12] Stalin was aware of Lavrenti Beria's proclivities towards young women. Although it was Beria's son Sergo she was visiting, Stalin took no chances and attached a security official – known to Svetlana as Uncle Klimov – to act as her chaperone.

Svetlana's discomfort was increased by what she learned about her family's history. Her aunt Anna told her, when she reached the age of sixteen, that her mother Nadya had not died of natural causes but had committed suicide. Svetlana was shocked by what she heard; her father had always avoided the topic.[13] Anna did not tell Svetlana much more: she had already taken a large risk in breaching Stalin's confidence. Svetlana proceeded to ask her father for further information. According to Sergo Beria, in whom she confided, Stalin's response was hurtful. He resented the way Svetlana kept on examining pictures of Nadya. When she asked him whether her mother had been beautiful, he replied more insensitively: 'Yes, except that she had teeth like a horse.' He added that the other Alliluev women had wanted to sleep with him. This too may well have been true, but it was a painful message for Svetlana. He finished by explaining: 'At least your mother was young, and she really loved me. That's why I married her.'[14]

It was around this time that Svetlana started going out with film-writer Alexei Kapler. A more unsuitable boyfriend could not be imagined. Kapler was a womaniser who had had a string of affairs. He was over twice Svetlana's age. He was also Jewish – and Stalin even before the war had been trying to identify himself and his family with the Russians. Kapler was incredibly indiscreet. He acquired Western films such as *Queen Christina* (starring Greta Garbo) and Walt Disney's *Snow White and the Seven Dwarfs* and showed them to Svetlana. He passed on books by Ernest Hemingway, who was then unpublished in the USSR. Kapler handed her – a girl who loved literature – copies of poems by Anna Akhmatova who had been in official disgrace before the war.

Kapler made Svetlana feel desirable as a woman, and she fell head over heels in love with him.[15] Stalin, on hearing about developments from Vlasik, knew how things might turn out. Hadn't he himself seduced girls in Siberia? Hadn't he taken a woman half his age off to Tsaritsyn in 1918 and exploited his mature charms? Something had to be done. Stalin decided that the best thing – for once – was not to have the man arrested but to send him as a *Pravda* correspondent to the front at Stalingrad.[16] It was mere coincidence that Kapler was to be sent to Stalingrad where Stalin and Nadya Allilueva had spent several months. Stalin wanted to give Kapler a fright by assigning him to the vicinity of direct military conflict. After the Great Terror such an intervention from the Kremlin was enough to scare the daylights out of anyone, but Kapler carried on regardless. Far from crumbling under the pressure, he sent articles to Moscow with obvious hints at his relationship with Svetlana. 'At the moment in Moscow,' he wrote in one of them, 'doubtless the snow is falling. From your window is visible the jagged wall of the Kremlin.' Such recklessness brought Svetlana to her senses and she cut contact with Kapler.[17]

But her heart remained with him and when he returned from Stalingrad they started to see each other again. They kissed and cuddled despite being accompanied by Uncle Klimov. Poor Klimov felt damned if he reported this and damned if he didn't. On hearing what was happening, Vlasik angrily sent an official to order Kapler out of Moscow. Extraordinarily enough, though, Kapler told him to go to hell.

Stalin at last intervened. 'I know everything,' he said to Svetlana. 'All your telephone conversations, here they are!' He tapped his pocket, which was full of transcripts. He had never spoken so contemptuously to her. Glaring into her eyes, he shouted: 'Your Kapler is an English spy; he's been arrested!' Svetlana shouted: 'But I love him!' Stalin lost his self-control and sneered: 'You *love* him!' He slapped her twice in the face. 'Just think, nanny, what's she's come to! There's such a war going on and she's tied up with all this!' A torrent of obscenities flowed from his lips until his anger had subsided.[18] She broke with Kapler, and her father seemed to have got his way. But his victory was illusory. No sooner had she dropped Kapler than she turned her attention to Beria's son Sergo. Sergo's father and mother were horrified by the dangers which could arise from such a relationship, and told him to keep away from her. Sergo's mother Nina was frank with Svetlana: 'You are both young. You must get a job first. And he looks on you as a sister. He'll never marry you.'[19] Svetlana recognised reality and looked elsewhere. In spring 1944, after a brief courtship, she married one of her brother Vasili's friends, Grigori Morozov. This time Stalin was more restrained. Although he refused to invite Morozov to the Blizhnyaya dacha, he let the marriage go ahead.

He could not control absolutely everything and, while a war was going on, did not try. Disappointed in his family, he let his thoughts turn back to Georgia and to his boyhood friends. He had never forgotten them despite years without direct contact. From the thousands of rubles in his unopened pay packets he made a money transfer to Petr Kapanadze, Grigol Glurzhidze and Mikhail Dzeradze. (He was characteristically precise: 40,000 rubles for the first and 30,000 each for the others.) The Supreme Commander signed himself Soso.[20]

He had gone on seeing old friends and relatives after Nadya's suicide, but everyone noticed how lonely he was becoming. He welcomed the Alliluevs and Svanidzes to the Blizhnyaya dacha until the late 1930s. The Great Terror changed this. Stalin had Maria Svanidze arrested in 1939 and sent to a labour camp. Her husband Alexander Svanidze also fell victim to the NKVD: he had been arrested in 1937 and was shot in 1941. Alexander behaved with extraordinary courage under torture and refused to confess or beg for mercy. Although Stalin did not yet touch the closest relatives of his deceased second wife, their spouses were not so lucky. Stanisław Redens, Anna Allilueva's husband, was arrested in 1938.[21] Anna got permission to plead his case along with her parents in the presence of Stalin and Molotov. But on the day of their meeting her father Sergei Alliluev refused to go with them. Stalin took this badly and Redens's fate was sealed.[22] Even those among Stalin's outer family who escaped incarceration lived in continuous dread of what might happen to them. Yet like everyone in the Kremlin elite, they were moths flying near to the light source; they were incapable of pulling themselves out of their orbits.

During the war there would have been little time for family conviviality even if Stalin had not already ravaged the lives of his relatives. Such hours as he got for relaxation – and they were few – were spent in the company of the commanders and politicians who happened to be at hand. These occasions were predominantly male affairs, and the drink was as lavishly provided as the food. Yet he rationed the evenings he devoted to pleasure. He focused his waking energies on leading the war effort.

That Stalin managed to cope with the intense physical pressures is remarkable. Through the 1930s he had experienced bouts of ill health. His neck artery went on troubling him. His blood circulation was monitored by a succession of doctors; but he distrusted nearly all of them: he had persuaded himself that hot mineral baths were the best cure for any ailments. In 1931 he had a bad throat inflammation just after taking the waters in Matsesta and had a temperature of 39°C. A streptococcal infection followed five years later. His personal physician Vladimir Vinogradov was worried enough to go off and consult other specialists about desirable treatment. Stalin was too sick to join in the New Year celebrations in 1937. Again in February 1940 he was struck down by a raging high temperature and the usual problem with the throat.[23] Until 1941, however, he could count on lengthy breaks for recuperation. Usually he had spent several weeks by the Black Sea, giving his body time to recover from the punishing schedule he set himself in Moscow. This was not possible after Operation Barbarossa. Throughout the hostilities, except when he travelled to Yalta and Tehran to confer with the Allied leaders or when he made a much-publicised trip to the proximity of the front,[24] Stalin stayed in Moscow or its environs. And he worked himself like a dog.

The strains were manifest. His hair turned grey. (Zhukov unreliably said it was white.)[25] His eyes were baggy from insufficient sleep. Excessive smoking aggravated the growing problems of arteriosclerosis. Not that he would have listened to doctors' advice to change his style of life. Tobacco and alcohol were his consolation, and anyway the medical experts who saw him are not known to have counselled an alteration in the way he lived. They feared to do this – or possibly they did not see much wrong with his behaviour: not every doctor in that period was as severe as their present-day successors. Relentlessly, therefore, Stalin was driving himself to an earlier grave than biological inheritance had prescribed for him.[26]

Stalin lived an odd life after his wife's suicide, but others in his entourage had even odder ones. Beria was a rapist of young girls. Others in the Kremlin had a taste for women even though outright physical coercion was not involved. Abel Enukidze, executed in 1937, had been notorious for employing attractive young women whom he took to bed. Kalinin had a penchant for ballerinas, Bulganin for opera divas. Khrushchëv was said to chase women on a regular basis. The sexual history of the Soviet elite included promiscuousness on the part of several leaders, and a few of them had not confined themselves to intercourse with women. Yezhov had been bisexual and found comfort sometimes with both the husband and wife in a marriage. Such individuals were using their political power to secure gratification. As they knew, they could be arrested at any time. Many of them also found relief in drink. Zhdanov and Khrushchëv were boozers on a heroic scale. An evening for them was not complete without a skinful of vodka and brandy, and Yezhov had often been drunk by the late morning. Terror brought odd individuals to the apex of the Soviet order and the pressure made them still odder.

It may seem surprising that they managed to function at all as politicians. But this would miss the point. Although they would have engaged in sexual and alcoholic excess even if they had not become Soviet politicians, undoubtedly they were also driven in this direction by the pressures – and dangers – of their jobs.

Stalin's existence before Operation Barbarossa had been stolid by comparison, but it was not devoid of female companionship or heavy drinking. A plausible piece of gossip was that Stalin took a fancy to his deceased wife Nadya's sister-in-law Yevgenia. She saw quite a lot of him in the months after the suicide. Another who did so was Maria Svanidze.[27] This was not approved by Maria's husband Alexander, who thought that it might lead to hanky-panky. Maria made no secret of the fact that she 'loved Joseph and was attached to him'.[28] She was good-looking and worked on stage as a singer:[29] she could hardly help attracting Stalin's attention. But it was Yevgenia who was most gossiped about. In fact Yevgenia, whose husband Pavel Alliluev died in 1938, quickly married an inventor called Nikolai Molochnikov. Although it is doubtful that she and Stalin had a sexual relationship, there remains the suspicion that Yevgenia went off with Molochnikov as a way of avoiding becoming more closely involved with Stalin. Her daughter Kira has said opaquely: 'She got wed so as to defend herself.'[30] But filial piety discouraged her from stating whether it was Stalin's attentions that she wanted to escape. What is known is that Stalin subsequently rang her several times and that during the Second World War he asked her to accompany Svetlana and other relatives as they were evacuated from Moscow. Yevgenia refused his request on the ground that she had her own immediate family to think about.[31]

Rumours had other candidates as his lovers in the late 1930s; it was even said that he secretly married again. The person said to have been his wife was named as Rosa Kaganovich. This allegation was peddled by the German Nazi media. Supposedly Rosa was Lazar Kaganovich's beautiful sister. It was a pack of lies. Lazar Kaganovich had only one sister, Rakhil, who died in the mid-1920s.[32] Another suggestion was that it was Lazar Kaganovich's daughter Maya whom Stalin took to bed. Certainly she was good-looking. But there is no credible evidence. Lazar Kaganovich was not a prude and had no reason as a pensioner to pretend that his daughter had had no relationship with Stalin if this was not true.[33]

What is beyond doubt is the kind of life enjoyed by Stalin among his male friends. He loved to sing with Molotov and Voroshilov accompanied by Zhdanov on the piano. Molotov came from a musical family and could play the violin and mandolin. When he had been in administrative exile in Vologda before the Great War, he had supplemented his convict's allowance by joining a mandolin group which went round the local restaurants and cinema. Zhdanov too had a cultural hinterland and joined in the fun at the dacha, and Voroshilov had a decent voice. All had memorised church music as youngsters and, ignoring their atheistic commitment, performed the hymns they loved.[34] Stalin's voice had held up well and he could still take the baritone's parts.[35] He also sang to his daughter Svetlana and his Alliluev nephews and nieces. Kira Allilueva recalled him dandling her on his knee and giving renditions of his favourite tunes.[36] Despite later being imprisoned and exiled by his police, she continued to hold her uncle in affection. His joviality in private surroundings had not vanished with his wife's suicide.

Another form of recreation was billiards. When the Alliluevs visited, Stalin sometimes played against Nadya's elder brother Pavel. Usually it was a convivial occasion, but not always. Pavel had grown wary of Joseph. The house rule was that losers in any match had to crawl under the table afterwards. One evening in the 1930s Pavel and Joseph lost a match to Alexander Svanidze and Stanisław Redens. Pavel anticipated dangerous resentment and ordered his sons to do the crawling on behalf of himself and Stalin. But Pavel's daughter Kira was present. 'This,' she cried with childish righteousness, 'is against the rules. They've lost, let them crawl under!' A frightened Pavel strode across to her and struck her with his cue. Stalin could not be allowed to feel humiliated.[37]

Indulgence also had to be shown him at his dinner parties. He himself liked to flirt with women and probably he bedded some of them. It would be astounding if such an egotist had failed to take his opportunities with at least some of the many women who made themselves available. But he disapproved of public licentiousness (which is one of the reasons why his sex life after 1932 remains mysterious). His hypocritical prudery about women, though, was accompanied by an open relish for sessions of heavy drinking. He virtually forced brandies and vodka on his guests – and then stood back and waited for them to blurt out some secret while under the influence of alcohol. He himself took the precaution of drinking wine in the same size of glass that the others had for vodka. Another of his tricks was to imbibe a vodka-coloured wine while others drank spirits. (He admitted this stratagem to Ribbentrop in 1939.)[38] Having put his guests uncomfortably at their ease, he wanted to watch and listen rather than to get drunk. He liked practical jokes and dirty anecdotes, and there was trouble for anyone who declined to join in. Among his more childish tricks was to put a tomato on the seat of a Politburo member. Always the squelching sound brought tears of laughter to his eyes.

Such parties continued to be held after 1941 even though they happened less frequently. They belonged to the secret life of the Kremlin's rulers. The only witnesses, apart from the small number of servants, were communist emissaries from eastern Europe who reached Moscow in the closing years of the war. Brought up to imagine Stalin as an austere character, they were always stupefied by the vulgarity of the scene. Stalin must have suspected that this would be the reaction of most people. Although he ordered lots of drink for Churchill and Roosevelt, he never got up to the usual japes in their presence.

He also dressed up for meetings with the Allied leaders. But this was exceptional. With other visitors he saw no need to look smart. He continued to shuffle around the grounds of the Blizhnyaya dacha in his favourite Civil War coat which had fur on both its inside and outside. Alternatively he might put on his ordinary fur coat (which had also been acquired after the October Revolution). When servants surreptitiously tried to get rid of it, he was not fooled: 'You're taking the opportunity to bring me a new fur coat every day but this one has another ten years in it.' He was no less attached to his old boots.[39] Zhukov noted that he stuffed his pipe not with any special tobacco but with the filling of the Herzegovina Flor cigarettes available in all kiosks. He unravelled the cigarettes himself.[40] One rising young official, Nikolai Baibakov, was taken aback by his shabbiness. His boots were not only decrepit; they even had holes in the toes. Baibakov mentioned this to Stalin's personal assistant Poskrëbyshev, who told him that Stalin had cut the holes to relieve the friction on his corns.[41] Anything to avoid submitting himself to a doctor's regular inspection!

Although he occasionally let his hair down, Stalin spent most of the war overladen with work. Most nights were passed in his makeshift office deep below the Mayakovski Metro station. The days were long and exhausting, and usually he slept not in a bed but on a divan. Not since Nicholas I, that most austere of Romanovs, had a ruler of the Russians been so frugal in his habits. Stalin was aware of the precedent,[42] and turned himself into a human machine for the winning of the Great Patriotic War.

40. TO THE DEATH!

Victory at Stalingrad in February 1943 made the defeat of the Wehrmacht possible but not yet certain. Hitler's forces in the East were determined and well-equipped. They kept Leningrad under siege. The Ice Road linking the city to the rest of Russia was under constant bombardment. Moscow too remained in peril. Any strategic mistake or diminution of patriotic commitment would have baleful consequences for the USSR.

The Red Army strove to follow up Stalingrad with total victory. Stalin's growing readiness to listen to advice in Stavka and the State Defence Committee paid dividends. It was as well that he changed his ways, if only for the war's duration. Manstein was hastily reassembling the divisions of the Wehrmacht after the Stalingrad defeat for a campaign which he designated Operation Citadel. Pushing up from Ukraine, he aimed to confront the Red Army at the large bulge in its south-facing front near Kursk on the Russo-Ukrainian border. Manstein was planning rapid action. But he was prohibited by Hitler from opening his offensive and taking Stavka by surprise. Hitler had learned like Stalin that the careful preparation of each campaign was crucial; inadvertently he gave the Reds time to think and react. This should have played into Stavka's hands. Unfortunately, though, Stalin's caution was only intermittent. The instinct to attack at every opportunity had not died in him. Learning that the Wehrmacht was holding back, he could not help himself: he demanded that Stavka organise a massive offensive without delay.

Zhukov would have none of this; he delivered a report to Stavka insisting that defence in depth was the better option: bloody but dependable attrition was preferable to a bloodier and riskier attack – and Zhukov predicted that Kursk would be the place where the decisive battle would take place.[1] On 12 April a Stavka conference was held. Stalin gruffly gave way to Zhukov's proposal, which was backed by his military colleagues Alexander Vasilevski and Alexei Antonov.[2] German intentions quickly became clear as fifty of Hitler's best divisions were moved into an attacking position where Zhukov had predicted. Stalin, though, had second thoughts in May and argued again in favour of a pre-emptive offensive. Zhukov, Vasilevski and Antonov held firm and carried opinion in Stavka with them.[3] Stalin accepted the result and rushed Zhukov and Vasilevski to take direct command. By 4 July the imminence of the German attack was obvious to Zhukov, who ordered Rokossovski to put the agreed plan into operation. Stalin was informed of the decision without prior consultation. It was a bold gesture of autonomy by Zhukov but he got away with it. Stalin received the news without his usual rancour: 'I'll be in Stavka awaiting the development of events.'[4]

When hostilities started early next morning, Zhukov was immersed in the task of reacting to unexpected dispositions made by the Germans. It was Stalin who rang him rather than the other way round: 'Well, how's it going? Have they started?' Zhukov simply replied: 'They've started.'[5] Stalin had to bide his time and control his nerves. The fate of the USSR was in the hands of the Red Army, and there was no longer anything he could do from Moscow that could affect the outcome of battle.

Wehrmacht tanks made ground in the first two days, but then the Soviet lines held. Zhukov and Manstein struggled to outwit and out-punch each other. Zhukov's ruthless tactics were effective. Instead of waiting for his artillery to batter the enemy before throwing his tanks at them, he undertook both actions simultaneously. Soviet losses were immense; but although the Germans suffered fewer, they could ill afford them in the light of their increasing shortage of men and supplies. Zhukov by his own estimation had 40 per cent more troops, 90 per cent more weaponry, 20 per cent more tanks and 40 per cent more aircraft.[6] Wasteful though he was of his resources, he had calculated that the Germans faced disaster unless they carried off a speedy victory. German success was never likely. In accordance with the long-elaborated plan, the Red Army counter-attacked from both the Bryansk Front and the Western Front. The Wehrmacht was pummelled backwards. Stalin could not resist demanding the intensification of offensive operations, and as usual it fell to Zhukov to get him to allow time for physical recovery and tactical regrouping. Disputes proliferated and Stalin made plenty of wounding accusations.[7] But Zhukov was made of strong stuff and was sustained by confidence in imminent triumph. In August he had his moment of glory when he was able to report his final success to Stavka.

The Germans had failed to win the battle of Kursk. The Red Army had not won in a conventional sense because the Wehrmacht conducted a planned and orderly retreat. Thus there was no definitive end to the battle. But Hitler had sustained strategic defeat simply by not having been able to win. After Kursk the Wehrmacht was pushed steadily westwards. Red Army morale rose as German spirits dipped. The USSR conscripted its vast reservoir of peasant soldiers while the Germans and their allies were running out of fighting men. Soviet factories reached a peak of production and were accelerating at a faster rate than Germany's industrial capacity. Stalin and his Stavka believed that the reverses suffered by German arms at Kursk signalled the beginning of the end for Hitler's New Order in Europe.

Soviet commanders were right that Stalin had contributed less than themselves to the victory at Kursk. Yet they saw only the military side of his activity: they had little cognisance of his other interventions in the USSR's war effort. Stavka had nothing to do with foreign policy, political organisation, cultural and social policy or economic mobilisation. Stalin interfered in all these sectors and his impact was deep. In 1941–2 this had already led to several adjustments which he thought necessary to the interests of the USSR. The massive territorial losses in the war's early months precipitated a collapse in food supplies as Ukrainian wheat, potatoes and sugar beet fell into the hands of the Germans. Although no directive was issued, the authorities slackened off their efforts against the black market in agricultural produce. The exceptions were cities under siege such as Leningrad where the NKVD punished anyone caught trading on the street. But market economics more widely crept back into the Soviet order as party and municipal government accepted that peasants bringing sacks of vegetables for sale helped to alleviate urban malnutrition;[8] and Stalin, who had fulminated against the flouting of trading laws in the 1930s, kept silent about this during the war.

He also understood the need to widen the limits of cultural expression. Many intellectuals who had been suspect to the authorities were told that the state welcomed their creative services. Notable among them were the poet Anna Akhmatova and the composer Dmitri Shostakovich. Akhmatova had been married to the poet Nikolai Gumilëv, who had been killed as an anti-Soviet militant in 1921; her son Lev still languished in prison and her writings had not been published for years. But well-read members of society remembered her with affection. It was in Stalin's interest to allow her work to be read over the radio and at concerts. This permission was not indiscriminate. Preference was given to those of her poems which emphasised the achievements of the Russian people. Shostakovich had learned the lesson of his troubles before the war and given up accompanying his music with words. He wrote the score of his Seventh (Leningrad) Symphony while working as a night fire warden. The piece was recognised for its greatness by the first-night audience in 1942.

Cheap editions of the Russian classics were distributed at the front. Stalin as writer also belonged to the Soviet literary pantheon and the commissars gave his pamphlets to the troops; but he was not in fact a favourite author for men on active service. The regime recognised this and moderated its insistence on placing his *oeuvre* at the centre of its propaganda.

Stalin also dropped the Internationale as the USSR state hymn (or national anthem) and held a competition for a new one. The winner was Alexander Alexandrov with a melody which stirred the soul. Words were added by Sergei Mikhalkov and Garold El-Registan and they were among the most effective items in the armoury of official propaganda. The first verse went:[9]

> The indestructible union of free republics
> Was bound together by Great Rus.
> Long live the united, the powerful Soviet Union
> Created by the will of the people!

The second verse moored patriotism in allegiance to the October Revolution:

> Through the storm the sun of freedom shone on us
> And the great Lenin lit up the way for us:
> Stalin brought us up – he inspired us towards loyalty to the people,
> Towards labour and towards heroic feats!

The hymn had a genuine emotional resonance for the wartime generation; it was hardly a cultural 'concession' since it contained a paean to Stalin; but it indicated that the authorities understood that cosmopolitanism, as embodied in the Internationale, did little to make Russians fight for the Motherland.

Still more important were Stalin's decisions on the Russian Orthodox Church. By 1939 there were only around a hundred places of worship still open to believers.[10] No monastery had survived the Soviet years. Tens of thousands of priests had been slaughtered in the Civil War, the First Five-Year Plan and the Great Terror. People nevertheless believed in God. When the USSR census took place in 1937, some 55 per cent of the population rejected the aspirations of the atheistic state and declared themselves religious believers – and naturally the true proportion of the faithful must have been much greater.

Stalin, former pupil of the Tiflis Spiritual Seminary, welcomed Acting Patriarch Sergei's patriotic stance. He was also pleased by the offertories collected in churches for the production of armaments. The Dmitri Donskoi tank column came from this source. It suited Stalin nicely that the Russian Orthodox Church was stiffening the military commitment of its congregations. Buildings were quietly allowed to be reopened for religious purposes. Stalin formalised the position by inviting Acting Patriarch Sergei to a meeting with him in the Kremlin on 4 September 1943. Sergei arrived, wondering what exactly awaited him.[11] Stalin acted as if no contretemps had ever taken place between the Soviet state and the Russian Orthodox Church. Jovially he enquired of Sergei why he had come with so few priests. Sergei overcame the temptation to say that he could easily have mustered more clergy if Stalin had not spent the previous decade arresting and executing them. Yet the atmosphere was lightened by Stalin's proposal that in return for the termination of persecution and for a measure of freedom to hold services of worship the Church should acknowledge the legitimacy of the Soviet state and avoid criticism of its internal and external policies.[12]

The timing of this concession was never explained by Stalin; he did not even allow *Pravda* to make a public announcement. Yet it was a concordat in all but name. This has led to speculation that foreign policy might have been the motivating factor. Stalin was about to meet Roosevelt and Churchill at the Tehran Conference. It has been suggested that a demonstrable diminution of anti-religious persecution was thought likely to enable him to squeeze a better deal out of the Western Allies.[13]

This would be more plausible if he had simultaneously lessened the pressure on the other Christian denominations, especially those with organisations in the West. But Stalin openly privileged the Russian Orthodox Church. The explanation is probably connected to his calculations about rule in the USSR. The meeting with the Acting Patriarch occurred shortly after the battles of Stalingrad and Kursk. The Red Army was about to start offensives to retake the western borderlands. Hitler had permitted Christian denominations, including the Ukrainian Auto-cephalous Church, to function under German occupation. Religious freedom, having been tasted again, would be hard to suppress quickly. While restoring limited autonomy to the Russian Orthodox Church, Stalin enabled it to resume charge of buildings which had not belonged to it since the 1920s. As the Soviet armed forces fought their way into Ukraine and Belorussia, churches were transferred into the possession of the Russian Orthodox Church. Evidently Stalin judged that Christian believers would be more easily controlled if Sergei, who was elected Patriarch at the Synod held in September 1943, was presiding over them. Stalin left nothing to chance. He appointed G. Karpov to the Governmental Council on the Russian Orthodox Church to oversee relations with it. Stalin wanted his pound of flesh.

Another change in policy occurred in the international communist movement. Stalin reverted to his inclination in early 1941 to abolish the Comintern. Turning to Dimitrov, he instructed him to organise the necessary formalities. At meetings of the Comintern Executive Committee in May 1943 the foreign communist leaders meekly agreed to Stalin's demands.[14] He claimed to have concluded that it had been mistaken to try – as Lenin had done – to run the world communist movement from a single centre. He himself had repeated the error, and the result had been that communist parties had been accused by their enemies of being directed by the Kremlin. Stalin wanted them to be able to appeal to their respective parties without this albatross round their necks.[15]

It hardly needs to be stressed that Stalin was being disingenuous. He had not the slightest intention of releasing his political grip on foreign communist parties. While allowing them the appearance of autonomy, he aimed to keep them on a short lead. Comintern Secretary-General Georgi Dimitrov would simply be transferred to the International Department of the Central Committee Secretariat of the All-Union Communist Party. His duties would be kept secret and essentially unchanged. Dimitrov had always been expected to advise and obey Stalin in relation to the world communist movement, and the same situation persisted after the Comintern's dissolution. This gives a clue to Stalin's reasons for the astonishing decision. There was speculation at the time and subsequently that he was trying to reassure the Western Allies about his intentions. But it can hardly have been the main motive. The period when Stalin most needed to call upon their trust had already passed. The USSR had been at its weakest before Stalingrad and Kursk, when the Wehrmacht had hopes of winning the war. Yet Stalin had done nothing for two years. He had bided his time until victory for the Red Army started to appear likely.

The timing is unlikely to have been accidental. Stalin and his advisers were making plans for Europe after the war. Ivan Maiski and Maxim

Litvinov, removed as ambassadors to London and Washington, gave their ideas. Dimitrov added his. Molotov was constantly available. All were thinking hard about what could be done to maximise the security and power of communism to the west. Clandestine communist groupings had been scratching out an existence in the early years of the Soviet–Nazi military conflict. While the USSR was on the defensive, anything that could be done by the foreign parties of the Comintern to sabotage Hitler's New Order in Europe was welcomed. But in mid-1943 these limits on ambition had to be lifted. Stalin wanted to build up support for communist parties in eastern and east-central Europe. The parties themselves were frail – and he had not helped the situation by exterminating as many Polish comrades as possible in 1938. The Red Army was poised to recover the western borderlands of the USSR, as its territory had stood before the Nazi–Soviet diplomatic agreement of August 1939. Indeed, it was about to overrun most countries to the east of Germany and Stalin knew that their communists were regarded as agents of Moscow. It was vital for them and him to pretend that they were not Moscow's stooges. The Comintern's dissolution was a basic precondition.

This meant that communist parties should find ways to identify themselves not only as internationalists but also as defenders of the national agenda. Stalin ensured that this was understood among the foreign communist leaders resident in Moscow as well as among those who had maintained contact from their own countries. Heroes, symbols, poems and songs of a nationalist resonance had to be grasped by communism; and in this way, he assumed, the local appeal of communist parties would be enhanced. This had been undertaken for Russians in the USSR; it needed to be repeated in countries which the Red Army was about to conquer. Communism was neither just an international movement nor just a Russian one; it was seeking, at Stalin's behest, to acquire a diversity of national colours.[16]

This was a concession masking militant aims. Other shifts of policy in the second half of 1943 were less covertly introduced. Among them was the reassertion of Marxism–Leninism. Russian national feeling was far from being rejected. Heroes of old Russia – the ones acceptable to the regime – were retained: Ivan the Terrible, Peter the Great, Suvorov, Lomonosov, Pushkin and Tolstoi. But the limits had to be respected. And as the war was drawing to a close, the Kremlin began to emphasise Soviet motifs. Patriotism was put forward as a greater value than internationalism, and the 'fraternal friendship' of the Soviet peoples was affirmed. Cosmopolitan became a dirty word. Any sign of admiration for the societies and cultures of the West was severely punished. The Soviet armed forces' dependence on jeeps, explosives and other military equipment supplied to the USSR by the USA under the terms of Lend–Lease was the object of Stalin's suspicion. The influx of high-quality foreign products could undermine official Soviet boasts. In 1942 the crime 'praise of American technology' was added to the USSR's legal code and people could be thrown into the Gulag camps simply for expressing appreciation of a jeep.[17] Stalin was aiming at the reinsulation of the Soviet mind from foreign influences at the very time when hopes were growing for the convergence of the Red Army with its Western Allies in Germany for the defeat of Nazi power.

Ideas were tried out to increase the Red Army's appeal in eastern and east-central Europe. Among them was Panslavism. This was the notion that the Slavs, regardless of nationality, politically and culturally had much in common. Alexander III and Nicholas II had exploited it so as to increase the Russian Empire's influence in Bulgaria and Serbia. Stalin let groups be formed dedicated to the unification of the Slavs in the struggle against Hitler.[18] He gave the non-Marxist historian Yevgeni Tarle a platform to promote the idea. For Stalin, the USSR – unlike the Russian Empire – was practising Panslavism (or Slavophilia as he referred to it) on a unique basis: 'We, the new Slavophile Leninists – the Slavophile Bolsheviks, communists – stand not for the unification of Slavic peoples but for their union.' For Stalin, such a union was crucial if the Slavs were to solve the age-old problem of protecting themselves against the Germans.[19]

The intent was obvious: the conquest of the eastern half of Europe would be eased if the USSR could count on sympathy in those countries beyond the usual constituency of communist parties. This had been done by the last two Romanovs with much success in diplomatic relations with Bulgaria and Serbia, and Stalin counted on using it similarly. It contained damaging flaws, however, which were exposed almost as soon as he played the Panslavist card. Not all Slavs were of the Orthodox Church or had a traditional feeling of linkage with Russians. Poles and Czechs, being Catholic, remembered centuries of antagonism. Furthermore, not all peoples in eastern and east-central Europe were Slavs. Panslavism was a downright threat to Hungarians, Romanians and Germans. (It did not commend itself to Estonians, Latvians and Lithuanians, but they were anyway going to be re-annexed to the USSR.) Stalin persisted with the policy until after the defeat of Nazi Germany. It was a sign of his wrong-headedness. Not all his wartime shifts in policy were successful. It also exhibited an acute perception that the campaign to win the peace had to be worked up long before the war was over. Stalin had no illusions about the difficulties ahead.

Proof that his Panslavism had ulterior motives lies in the development of Soviet internal policy. The motif of the Motherland dominated official statements, and steadily the coarseness of anti-internationalism increased. Alexander Fadeev, Chairman of the USSR Union of Writers, roundly condemned 'rootless cosmopolitanism'. [20] Stalin did not comment publicly on this initiative; but the fact that Fadeev's provocative article became the unchallengeable party line is proof that this chauvinistic version of patriotism had Stalin's approval and indeed had been instigated by him. Among those groups most clearly threatened by the accusation of cosmopolitanism, of course, were Soviet Jews. Stalin was already playing with one of the grubbiest instruments of rule: anti-semitism.

This deserves consideration by those who want to make sense of Stalin and Soviet politics. Public life in the wartime USSR was not homogeneous. Nor was there a sudden break in 1945. Of course Stalin made concessions in the war; but several of them – especially as regards the Orthodox Church and the Comintern – really belonged to an agenda of increased rather than decreased state pressure. Stalin conceded when he had to, but snatched back his limited compromises as soon as he had the chance. His behaviour was mysterious to those who surrounded him. To them it appeared that he was more open than in the past to military advice and to the country's religious and cultural traditions. They hoped that some kind of conversion had taken place and that this behaviour would continue after the war had been won. They fooled themselves. There were plenty of signs in 1943 and even earlier that Stalin had given ground only tactically. Those who knew him intimately, especially fellow members of the State Committee for Defence, noticed nothing to indicate that the Boss wanted reform; they understood that the recent relaxations might not necessarily be permanent. They were right.

Yet the rest of Soviet society – or at least those of its members who wanted to think the best of him – were kept in the dark. War left them no time to ponder. They were fighting, working and looking for food. The relief of pressures was welcomed by them, but they expected much more. Indeed thousands of Russian POWs, once removed from the grip of Stalin's regime, decided that Stalin too was an enemy and volunteered to help the Germans defeat him under the leadership of Lieutenant-

General Andrei Vlasov. But the vast majority of those captured by the Wehrmacht refused to cross sides.[21] Like other citizens of the USSR, they hoped against hope that deep reforms would take place at the end of the war. Rigours which had been bearable in the battles against Nazism would be regarded as unnecessary and intolerable once Germany had been defeated.

People were deluding themselves. Stalin had made only those concessions vital for the prosecution of a successful military effort. The basic Soviet order remained intact. Since the start of Operation Barbarossa Stalin had ordered the NKVD to mete out merciless punishment to military 'cowards' and labour 'shirkers'. Any sign of deviation from total obedience invoked instant retaliation. The state planning agencies diverted available resources to the armed forces at the expense of civilians, who were left with barely enough for subsistence. The vertical chains of command were tightened. Central and local political leaderships were required to carry through every decree from the Kremlin to the letter. The one-party dictatorship was being put to the ultimate test and was reorganised so as to use the powers at its disposal to the maximum effect. The party in particular acquired importance as an organisation co-ordinating relations between the Red Army and the governmental institutions in each locality; it was also the party which devised the propaganda to stiffen the morale of soldiers and civilians. Yet the USSR remained a terrifying police state and the basic structures of coercion stayed in place. No informed citizens should have expected anything different from Stalin. He had ruled by fear for too long for there to be doubt about how he would behave on the resumption of peace.

41. SUPREME COMMANDER

The man with the gammy left arm rejected for conscription in the First World War and criticised for military bungling in both the Civil War and the Soviet-Polish War commanded a state at war with Nazi Germany. Stalin in Moscow confronted Hitler in Berlin. In the minds of both men this was a personal duel as well as a clash between ideologies and state-systems. Neither of them lacked self-belief in directing his war effort.

The Soviet war leader took time to judge how to handle public opinion. Molotov made the initial announcement about the war on behalf of the political leadership on 22 June 1941. Another hero of the day was the radio announcer Isaak Levitan, whose rich bass voice epitomised the popular will to resist the German invasion at any cost. When at last Stalin made his broadcast to Soviet citizens on 3 July, eleven days after the start of military hostilities, he adjusted his language to the wartime emergency. These were his opening words:[1]

> Comrades! Citizens!
> Brothers and sisters!
> Fighters in our army and navy!
> It is to you I appeal, my friends!

Many have noted that Stalin was reverting to traditional Russian discourse by addressing himself to 'brothers and sisters'. This is true. But what is usually missed is that he started his speech by appealing to comrades and citizens (and at least one listener noted a caesura between 'Citizens! Comrades!' and 'Brothers and sisters').[2] Nor did he seek to identify himself exclusively with Russians. When listing the peoples threatened by Germany, he mentioned not only the Russians but also 'the Ukrainians, Belorussians, Lithuanians, Latvians, Estonians, Uzbeks, Tatars, Moldavians, Georgians, Armenians, Azerbaijanis and the other free peoples of the Soviet Union'.[3]

Listeners were grateful for signs that resolute defence was being prepared. The writer Yekaterina Malkina heard the speech and was inspired by it; and her house servant was so moved that she broke down in tears. Malkina wrote to a friend:[4]

> I forgot to tell you further about Stalin's speech that, as I listened to it, it seemed that he was very upset. He talked with such large pauses and frequently drank a lot of water; you could hear him pouring it out and swallowing it. All this served to strengthen the emotional impact of his words. That very day I went and signed up with the volunteer army.

Few persons who heard him that day forgot the experience.

Groping his way towards an appropriate mode of communication, he sometimes succeeded brilliantly:

> How could it happen that our glorious Red Army gave up to the fascist forces a number of our towns and districts? Surely the German fascist forces are truly invincible forces, as the boastful fascist propagandists constantly trumpet?
>
> Of course not! History shows that invincible armies don't exist and have never existed. Napoleon's army was considered invincible but it was crushed in turn by Russian, English, German forces. Wilhelm's German army during the first imperialist war was also considered an invincible army, but it suffered defeat several times at the hands of Russian and Anglo-French forces and, finally, was defeated by Anglo-French forces. The same has to be said about the present German fascist army of Hitler. This army has not yet met serious resistance on the continent of Europe. Only on our territory has it met serious resistance.

These words were delivered in an unyielding tone which confirmed that the fight would be taken to the Germans. The challenge was flung back at Hitler and the Wehrmacht.

Stalin's rhetoric was woefully unrealistic about the kind of enemy facing the Red Army. He warned people that enslavement to 'German princes and barons' awaited them in the event of the USSR's failure to beat the Wehrmacht.[5] He ignored the specific nature of Nazism's New Order. Not princes and barons but Gauleiters and the SS were the Third Reich's enforcers. Racial violence, mobile gas-wagons and concentration camps were installed in the East and yet not once did Stalin refer to them. The First World War remained imprinted on his mind. He was also transfixed by the memory of the Civil War. In his speech on Red

Square on 7 November 1941 – the anniversary of the October Revolution – he rambled on about foreign 'interventionists' as if they and the Nazis were threats to the Soviet state of equal importance.[6] Equally adrift from the facts was his claim that Germany was racked by 'hunger and impoverishment'.[7] Stalin was dredging up outdated clichés of Bolshevik party pronouncements. As Soviet soldiers and civilians came into direct contact with the Wehrmacht and SS, they learned for themselves that Nazism had methods and purposes of unique repulsiveness. Stalin's reputation as a propagandist was greater than his performance.

There were limits indeed to Stalin's adaptability. Winston Churchill's regular parliamentary speeches and Franklin Roosevelt's weekly radio broadcasts stood in contrast with Soviet practice. Stalin delivered only nine public wartime addresses of any length. He did not write for the newspapers. Although he could have got others to compose pieces for him, he refused to publish in his own name what he himself had not written. Information in general about him was scanty. He passed up opportunity after opportunity to inspire people outside the format of his preferred modalities.

Pravda continued to mention him with cultic reverence. Photographers were seldom allowed to take his picture; it was mainly old photos which were published in the press, and even these were used sparingly.[8] It was as if the decision was taken to treat him as a disembodied symbol of the USSR's war effort rather than the living Supreme Commander. Posters, busts and flags continued to be produced. Booklets of his best-known articles and speeches were on sale at cheap prices. Commissars in the armed forces gave lectures on political policies and military strategy as well as on Stalin's personal leadership. He let no details of his activities be aired in the mass media. He continued to handle his public image on his own terms, and he had never felt comfortable with the frequent communing with society which the leaders of the Western Allies found congenial. Nor did he change his mind on letting a subordinate – as Hitler did with Goebbels – manufacture a public image for him. As before the war, Stalin kept direct control of what was said on his behalf.

Yet his reclusive tendency retained at least some advantages and was not as harmful to the regime as it would have been elsewhere. Many Soviet citizens inferred that a wise patriarch commanded the political and military agencies of the state. This may have helped more than it hindered the war effort. Stalin was inept at tasks of self-endearment or public reassurance. His characteristic inclination at large gatherings and in radio broadcasts was to project ferocity. If people had seen him more often, the illusion of his well-meaning sagacity could have been dispelled. His seclusion allowed them to believe in the sort of Stalin they wanted. They might persuade themselves that all the troubles of the inter-war period would be resolved once the Germans had been defeated. There was immense popular expectation that a victorious Stalin would sanction a relaxation of the Soviet order. People in their millions had got him wrong. But their mistake helped them to fight on for victory despite the horrific rigours.

Abroad his reclusiveness worked even better. Little was known about him. He had baffled even many Moscow-based diplomats before the war.[9] Interest had been greatest among communists, but loyal members of the Comintern did not stray beyond the pieties offered in the official biography; and renegades such as the Trotskyists, who knew a lot more, were a vociferous but ignored minority. The general public in the West were hardly better informed after the Nazi–Soviet pact in August 1939. David Low, cartoonist for London's *Evening Standard*, produced wonderful images of Stalin and Hitler embracing while each hold a dagger behind the other's back. Stalin was represented as a baleful tyrant. Yet it was Hitler rather than Stalin who held the attention of Western commentators. This remained the situation until Operation Barbarossa. It was then that Stalin became the hero of the anti-Nazi belligerent countries. The same fact reduced the incentive to pry into the dark corners of Stalin's career. If his Red Army was fighting back, he had to be supported and his communist loyalists in Western countries needed to be treated as patriots rather than subversives. British diplomats and journalists ceased any criticism. Stalin was their new idol.

When the USA entered the war in December 1941, the adulation crossed the Atlantic. In the following year *Time* magazine named Stalin its Man of the Year. The commendation noted brightly:[10]

> The trek of world dignitaries to Moscow in 1942 brought Stalin out of his inscrutable shell, revealed a pleasant host and an expert at playing his cards in international affairs. At banquets for such men as Winston Churchill, W. Averell Harriman and Wendell Wilkie, Host Stalin drank his vodka straight, talked the same way.

More generally the editorial declared:

> The man whose name means steel in Russian, whose few words of English include the American expression 'tough guy', was the man of 1942. Only Joseph Stalin fully knew how close Russia stood to

defeat in 1942, and only Joseph Stalin fully knew how he brought Russia through.

This comment set the tone for Western descriptions of him for the rest of the war. He had already won *Time* magazine's accolade as Man of the Year at the beginning of 1940.[11] But whereas earlier he had been praised as a master of clever, pragmatic manoeuvres, the current emphasis was upon straightforwardness and steadfastness. He was being hailed as a statesman with whom the West could do business. Churchill kept his reservations to himself in the interests of the Grand Alliance. The cult at home acquired its affiliate shrines in the lands of capitalism – and it was just as vague and misleading in the West as it was in its homeland.[12]

Beyond the public gaze Stalin was as complex an individual as ever. An accomplished dissembler, he could assume whatever mood he thought useful. He could charm a toad from a tree. The younger public figures promoted in the late 1930s were particularly susceptible. One such was Nikolai Baibakov. What struck Baibakov was Stalin's 'businesslike approach and friendliness'. While discussion took place in his office, he would pace around and occasionally direct a penetrating gaze at his interviewees. He had several tricks up his sleeve. One of them was to set up a debate between experts without revealing his preference in advance. Baibakov also recalled that Stalin never held discussions until he had studied the available material. He was well informed about many matters. He seldom raised his voice and scarcely ever bawled at anyone or even expressed irritation.[13]

Baibakov was looking back through rose-tinted spectacles; the rest of his account indicates that interviews could be terrifying affairs. Stalin, when putting him in charge of the oil installations of the Caucasus, spelled out his terms:[14]

> Comrade Baibakov, Hitler is bursting through to the Caucasus. He's declared that if he doesn't seize the Caucasus, he'll lose the war. Everything must be done to prevent the oil falling into German hands. Bear in mind that if you leave the Germans even one ton of oil, we will shoot you. But if you destroy the installations prematurely and the Germans don't grab them and we're left without fuel, we'll also shoot you.

This was hardly the most 'businesslike and friendly' of injunctions; but Baibakov in retrospect thought that circumstances required such ferocity. Plucking up courage in Stalin's presence, he had quietly replied: 'But you leave me no choice, comrade Stalin.' Stalin walked across to him, raised his hand and tapped his forehead: 'The choice is here, comrade Baibakov. Fly out. And think it over with Budënny and make your decision on the spot.'[15]

Another incident was overheard by General A. E. Golovanov in October 1941. He was at Stavka when Stalin took a phone call from a certain Stepanov, Army Commissar on the Western Front. Stalin's telephone receiver had a built-in amplifier and Golovanov was able to listen to the exchange. Stepanov, on behalf of the Western Front generals, asked permission to withdraw staff headquarters to the east of Perkhush-kovo because of the proximity of the front line. This was the sort of request which enraged Stalin, and the conversation went as follows:[16]

> *Stalin:* Comrade Stepanov, find out whether your comrades have got spades.
> *Stepanov:* What's that, comrade Stalin?
> *Stalin:* Do the comrades have spades?
> *Stepanov:* Comrade Stalin, what kind of spades do you mean: the type used by sappers or some other?
> *Stalin:* It doesn't matter which type.
> *Stepanov:* Comrade Stalin, they've got spades! But what should they do with them?
> *Stalin:* Comrade Stepanov, pass on to your comrades that they should take their spades and dig their own graves. We here are not leaving Moscow. Stavka will remain in Moscow. And they are not going to move from Perkhushkovo.

He did not usually have to bother with sarcasm. The memory of the Great Terror was enough to discourage most military and political personnel from making such an approach to him.

The atmosphere of fear and unpredictability choked nearly everyone into compliance with whatever Stalin was demanding. Just a few Soviet leaders dared to object to what he said. Two of these were Georgi Zhukov and Nikolai Voznesenski. Yet Stalin intimidated even Zhukov. He also exasperated him. Stalin, Zhukov noted, had taken time to understand the need for careful preparation of military operations by professional commanders. He was like a 'fist-fighter' in discussion when better results could have been obtained by more comradely methods.[17] He was also arbitrary in his appointment and replacement of command-ers, acting on the basis of partial information or of mischievous suggestions. The morale of commanding officers would have been higher if he had not meddled in this way.[18]

Stalin's other subordinates had learned to keep their heads down. 'When I went to the Kremlin,' said Ivan Kovalëv about his wartime experience in the post of People's Commissar of Communications,

> Molotov, Beria and Malenkov would usually be in Stalin's office. I used to feel they were in the way. They never asked questions, but sat there and listened, sometimes jotting down a note. Stalin would be busy issuing instructions, talking on the phone, signing papers . . . and those three would go on sitting there.[19]

Stalin's visitors' diary makes it clear that these three saw him more frequently than any other politicians. Mikoyan had a theory about this. He hypothesised that Stalin kept Molotov in his office because he feared what Molotov might get up to if he was allowed to be by himself.[20] Mikoyan had a point even if he exaggerated it. Stalin had to include others in affairs of state and they in turn had to know what was afoot. Needless to add, he did not give a damn that the main state leaders would be dog-tired by the time they got to their People's Commissariats and started at last to deal with their own business.

He trusted none of his politicians and commanders. Even Zhukov, his favourite military leader, was the object of his disquiet: Stalin instructed Bogdan Kobulov in the NKVD to put a listening device in his home. Seemingly the same was done to Stalin's old comrades Voroshilov and Budënny. His suspicions were boundless.[21] Having ordered Dmitri Pavlov's execution in the early days of the war, Stalin was little more satisfied with Ivan Konev, Pavlov's successor on the Western Front. Konev's failure to bring an immediate halt to the German advance was reason enough to question his loyalty. Stalin was all for shooting him. Zhukov was no friend of Konev's but thought such a fate completely undeserved. He had had to plead with Stalin to relent.[22] Zhukov was being taught that absolutely no commander was secure in post and life.

Stalin knew he could not do without Zhukov from October 1941. German tank corps had reached the outskirts of Moscow and German bombers flew over the city. Soviet regular forces were hurried out to meet the threat. Panic seized the minds of ordinary citizens, and the NKVD rounded up those who tried to flee. The factories and offices hardly shut for the duration of the battle. Stalin and Zhukov conferred:[23]

Stalin: Are you convinced that we'll hold on to Moscow? I ask you
  this with a pain in my soul. Tell me honestly as a communist.
Zhukov: We will definitely hold on to Moscow.

Having assured the Supreme Commander that Moscow would not fall,
Zhukov had to fulfil his commitment regardless of difficulties.

When sending telegrams to Stalin and phoning him from the field,
Zhukov addressed him as 'Comrade Supreme Commander'.[24] The
nomenclature was a typical Soviet mishmash: Zhukov had to refer to
him as a fellow communist as well as a commander. Stalin kept up the
proprieties in return. Even in emergencies he often avoided giving orders
in his own name. Phoning through to his generals on the various fronts,
he was inclined to say some such phrase as 'the Committee of Defence
and Stavka very much request the taking of all possible and impossible
measures'.[25] Zhukov remembered these evasive niceties many years later.

He also recalled how Stalin delighted in using pseudonyms. There
were patches of comradeliness between them when the fighting was
going in the USSR's favour and he held Zhukov in esteem (despite
keeping him under surveillance). Zhukov and he worked out an agreed
code for their exchanges by land line or telegram: Stalin was 'Vasilev'
and Zhukov 'Konstantinov'. Stalin had used this pseudonym before 1917,
and perhaps it signalled some kind of self-identification with Russia.
False names were in any case a bit of a game: there was little chance of
the German intelligence agencies being fooled by a pseudonym, especially
one which had been used by Stalin in the past. Yet Stalin ought not to
be judged too harshly. (There are abundant other reasons to indict him
without artificially inflating the number.) The pressures on the two of
them were immense, and it is no surprise that 'Comrade Supreme
Commander' consoled himself with nicknames. In his lighter moments
he knew how to encourage as well as how to terrify his military subordinates.

He would not be induced, however, to witness conditions at the
front; indeed he scarcely left Moscow apart from completely unavoidable trips to the Allied conferences at Tehran and Yalta. While urging
audacity upon his commanders, he took no risks with his personal
security. There was one exception and it was much trumpeted in the
press. In 1942 he made a journey to the front, ostensibly to monitor the
progress of the campaign. When he got to within thirty or forty miles of
active hostilities, he was greeted by military commanders on the Minsk
Chaussée who advised him that they could not guarantee his safety if he

travelled further. Stalin must have known that they would say this. This was the nearest he approached to any point of direct action in the war. He never saw a shot fired. But he made much of the conversation with his commanders and, after due display of disappointment, returned to the Kremlin. Much was made of the journey in official propaganda. *Pravda* reported it as if Stalin really had reached the front and given much needed orders on strategy and tactics to the frontal command.

Mikoyan told a less flattering tale of the journey. 'Stalin himself,' he wrote, 'was not the bravest of men.' Allegedly Stalin, as he talked with his commanders, felt an urgent call of nature. Mikoyan speculated that it might have been mortal fear rather than the normal effects of digestion. Stalin anyway needed to go somewhere fast. He asked about the bushes by the roadside, but the generals – whose troops had not long before liberated the zone from German occupation – could not guarantee that landmines had not been left behind. 'At that point,' Mikoyan recorded with memorable precision, 'the Supreme Commander in sight of every-one dropped his trousers and did his business on the asphalt. This completed his "reconnoitring of the front" and he went straight back to Moscow.'[26]

Avoidance of unnecessary risk was one thing, and Stalin took this to an extreme. But it is scarcely fair on Stalin to claim that he was a coward. Probably his behaviour stemmed rather from an excessive estimate of his own indispensability to the war effort. He looked on his military and political subordinates and thought they could not cope without him. Nor was he afraid of personal responsibility once he had got over the shock of 22 June 1941. He lived or died by his success in leading army and government. He exhausted every bone in his body for that purpose. And Zhukov credited Stalin with making up for his original military ignorance and inexperience. He went on studying during the fighting, and with his exceptional capacity for hard work he was able to raise himself to the level where he could understand most of the military complexities in Stavka. Khrushchëv later caricatured Stalin as having tried to follow the campaigns on a small globe he kept in his office, and this image has been reproduced in many subsequent accounts. In fact Stalin, while scaring his commanders and often making wholly unrealis-tic demands upon them, earned their professional admiration.

Not only military dispositions but also arrangements about the entire civilian sector of society and economy were in Stalin's hands. He kept a watch on all resources and wrote down details in a little notebook. He was always keen that his subordinates should husband the resources already in their possession. Everything from tank production to foreign currency reserves was recorded by him, and he was miserly in making additions to what was already assigned to institutions. His leading associates were instructed to take the same approach to their own underlings: Molotov for tanks, Mikoyan for food supplies, Kaganovich for transport, Malenkov for aircraft and Voznesenski for armaments. The little notebook ruled their lives.[27] Stalin was the linchpin of the Soviet war effort. The two sides of that effort, the military and civilian, were kept separate. Stalin did not want the commanders to interfere in politics and the economy nor the intervention of politicians in Stavka; and when he held meetings of the State Committee of Defence it was he who brought the two sides together.

42. THE BIG THREE

Vital interests of the USSR, the USA and the United Kingdom coincided after the events of June and December 1941. Churchill offered assistance to Stalin as soon as the German–Soviet war broke out. An agreement was signed on 12 July 1941. A British delegation headed by Lord Beaverbrook and accompanied by American diplomat Averell Harriman flew out for talks with Stalin in September. Negotiations ensued between Washington and Moscow when war started between Germany and the USA in December. A Combined Chiefs of Staff committee was created to co-ordinate American and British operations. The leaders of the Allied countries – Churchill, Roosevelt and Stalin – were soon as known as the Big Three.

The Grand Alliance was racked by mutual suspicions. A global war was being fought and the distribution of resources between the battle-fields of Europe and Asia had yet to be agreed. There also had to be consultation about strategic operations. As the fighting continued between the Third Reich and the USSR, the Americans and British needed to decide when to open a 'second front' in western Europe. There was also the question of mutual assistance. Both the USSR and the UK looked to the USA, the world's largest economic power, as a source of equipment, food and financial credit. The governments had to agree on the terms for this. War aims too had to be clarified. There was ceaseless tension between the Americans and the British since Washington had no desire to prop up the British Empire in the event of Allied victory. Similarly neither the Americans nor the British wished to give Stalin a free hand in his dealings with eastern Europe. Nor had the Allies discussed what to do with Germany after Hitler. Such were the dilemmas which would eventually necessitate the involvement of the supreme leaders.

The Big Three kept in contact by means of telegrams and embassies. Direct negotiations, however, were also desirable. The problem was that Roosevelt was physically disabled, and frequent long air-trips were too gruelling for him. Churchill, though, was an enthusiastic voyager. The British Prime Minister crossed the Atlantic to meet Roosevelt in Placentia Bay in August 1941 and in Washington the same December. He made still more dangerous flights to hold talks with Stalin in Moscow in August 1942 and October 1944 (which involved stop-overs in Gibraltar, Cairo, Tehran and the airfield at Kuibyshev).

Stalin, obsessively wishing to control everything in Moscow and being unwilling to risk journeys by air, held out against any such trips whenever he could possibly avoid them. Molotov as People's Commissar of External Affairs had been dispatched to Berlin in 1940. He also flew to the UK over the Baltic and across the North Sea in May 1942; such was his distrust of perfidious Albion that he slept with a revolver under his pillow. Stalin egocentrically expected others to take the risks. His immobility exasperated Roosevelt and Churchill. Roosevelt described the splendours of the Ghiza pyramids to persuade the Soviet leader to fly to Cairo.[1] As he pointed out, he himself was willing to travel even though the USA Constitution restricted the time a president could spend abroad.[2] Stalin could not put off a meeting of the Big Three indefinitely; and after turning down Cairo, Baghdad and Basra, he agreed to Tehran in November 1943. It was not far from the USSR and he had assured himself that the Soviet embassy in the Iranian capital could guarantee safety. Otherwise he refused to travel outside the territory of Soviet jurisdiction. The next conference was held at Yalta in the south of the RSFSR in February 1945. Stalin had got used to working at night and sleeping for most of the day. He had to go back to a more conventional schedule for meetings with Roosevelt and Churchill.[3]

Stalin had made his own preparations for travel. In 1941 he ordered the fitting out of a special railway carriage which would enable him to carry on working while travelling. At eighty-three tons, it was heavily armoured. Inside it had every facility – study, sitting room, toilet, kitchen and bodyguards' compartment – fitted out in the solid style he favoured. There was nothing luxurious about the carriage; the heavy wood and metal of its interior bespoke a leader who disliked frippery and demanded to be guaranteed conditions of regular work. Carriage FD 3878 was like a mobile Kremlin office.[4]

Agreements with the Western Allies were put into place long before Stalin used his new facility. The USSR urgently needed supplies. Churchill had offered assistance after the start of Operation Barbarossa and military convoys were sent to the Arctic Ocean. But the British themselves relied on American supply ships. It was therefore important for the Soviet government, once Hitler had declared war on the USA, to seek help from Roosevelt. In fact it was in the American interest to comply with such requests if this meant that the Wehrmacht would be weakened by the strengthened resistance of the Red Army. The Lend–Lease arrangement already in place with the United Kingdom was extended to the USSR. Loans, military equipment and food were earmarked for Soviet use. Shipments to the USSR were made by Arctic convoys to Murmansk or else across the frontier with Iran. The war with Japan in the Pacific ruled out the other routes. Steadily, though, American jeeps, spam, sugar and gunpowder filled vital gaps in production. Destruction of British vessels was frequent under attack from German submarines but Stalin took the rate of loss as undeserving of comment when the Red Army was giving up the lives of millions of its troops against the Germans.

The other thing agitating Stalin left him even less satisfied. He wanted the Western Allies to organise the opening of a second front in Europe as a means of relieving the pressure on his own armed forces. He never lost a chance to demand greater urgency from the USA and the UK. Fresh to the anti-Hitler military struggle, the Americans talked airily about managing this by the end of 1942. Churchill was more circumspect and, on his Moscow visit in August 1942, pulled out a map of western Europe to explain the vast logistical difficulties of a seaborne invasion from Britain. Stalin continued to bait him: 'Has the British navy no sense of glory?'[5] Churchill was on the point of leaving for London without further discussion. He had had enough of the Soviet leader's angry demands. Seeing that he had gone too far, Stalin invited him to yet another convivial dinner and the crisis faded. Roosevelt and his advisers, when they acquainted themselves with the military logistics, accepted the cogency of Churchill's argument; and Stalin had to recognise that until they were ready and willing to launch their ships across the English Channel, there was nothing he could do to make them hurry.

Although Stalin went on rebuking Churchill and Roosevelt in his correspondence, he could also be tactful. To Roosevelt, on whom he was dependent for finance and military supplies, he wrote on 14 December 1942:[6]

Permit me also to express confidence that time has not passed in vain and that the promises about opening the second front in Europe, which were given to me by you, Mr President, and Mr

Churchill in relation to 1942, will be fulfilled and will anyway be
fulfilled in relation to spring 1943 . . .

It made no difference. The Americans and the British refused to rush
their preparations.

Their stubbornness increased the urgency for Stalin to accede to
their invitation to a meeting of the Big Three. Thus the Tehran
Conference was organised. Churchill knew his Allied partners well by
that time but Stalin and Roosevelt had never met. The Soviet and
American leaders set about charming each other. They hit it off well.
Stalin was on his best behaviour, impressing the President as someone
he could have dealings with. Both Stalin and Roosevelt wanted to see the
British Empire dissolved, and Roosevelt said this when they were alone
together. Roosevelt prided himself on understanding how to handle
Stalin, who appeared to him a crude but reliable negotiator; it did not
occur to him that Stalin was capable of turning on his own bonhomie to
suit his purposes. Roosevelt was ailing by the middle of the war. His
energy and intellectual acumen were running out. At the Tehran and
Yalta Conferences Stalin made the most of his friendly relationship with
Roosevelt and tried to hammer a wedge between him and Churchill. He
did not always succeed. But he did well enough to prevent Churchill
from insisting on a firmer line being taken against Soviet pretensions in
eastern Europe.

Yet Churchill too had to be conciliated. Churchill had been the
world's loudest advocate of a crusade against Soviet Russia in the Civil
War. He had referred to the Bolsheviks as baboons and had called for
the October Revolution to be 'strangled' in its cradle. Stalin brought up
the matter in a jovial fashion. Churchill replied: 'I was very active in the
intervention, and I do not wish you to think otherwise.' As Stalin
contrived a smile, Churchill ventured: 'Have you forgiven me?' Stalin's
diplomatic comment was that 'all that is in the past, and the past belongs
to God'.[7]

The Western leaders of the Grand Alliance could at any rate count
on royal treatment à la soviétique when they made journeys to meet
Stalin. It was Churchill who got the most sumptuous welcome by dint
of going to Moscow. In October 1944 Molotov as People's Commissar
for External Affairs put on an enormous party at which the tables heaved
with food and wine. The British official group ate heartily before leaving
for a concert in the Chaikovski Hall. The orchestra played Chaikovski's
Fifth Symphony and Rakhmaninov's Third. Stalin had agreed to dine

that night at the British embassy. Churchill and he were getting on well at the dinner party, and such was Stalin's bonhomie that he came through to the lower rooms so that the rest of the visiting Britons could see him. They toasted him before he went back to a further bout of eating and drinking. Usually Stalin staved off inebriation by drinking a vodka-coloured wine while others drank spirits. He had admitted this stratagem to Ribbentrop in 1939.[8] But that night he allowed himself to become well oiled before leaving the den of Anglo-Saxon capitalist reaction at four o'clock in the morning.[9] By custom Stalin was wide awake at that hour; but his British hosts did not know that: they were left with the impression of a genial guest who had shared in the mood of the occasion.

There had been similar hospitality at the Tehran Conference and this created the atmosphere among the Big Three for agreement on large decisions. Stalin, Roosevelt and Churchill were determined to prevent Germany from ever again becoming a menace to world peace. The most effective step, they concurred, would be to break up the state,[10] and some in Roosevelt's entourage wished to go as far as the compulsory deindustrialisation of the country. Borders in eastern and central Europe also attracted attention at Tehran. Stalin's concern with Soviet security induced Churchill to propose a redrawing of the European map. He demonstrated this with the aid of three matchsticks. Apparently he thought that without a visual aid he would not get his point across to the Caucasian. Churchill wanted to shift both Poland and Germany westward.[11] The western edge of the USSR in his estimation should end at the line proposed in mid-1920 by Lord Curzon (which, as Anthony Eden pointed out, was virtually the same as what was known in the West as the Ribbentrop–Molotov frontier – Molotov did not demur).[12] The USSR would be expanded at Poland's expense. Poland would be compensated by acquisitions in eastern Germany.[13] To guarantee his continental security Stalin also demanded that the city-port of Königsberg should pass into the possession of the USSR, and Roosevelt and Churchill agreed.[14]

Stalin had to adjust his daily timetable to achieve his goals; for whereas he could intimidate all leading Soviet politicians and commanders into adopting his nocturnal work-style, he could not expect Roosevelt and Churchill to negotiate by candlelight. Stalin played his hand with an aplomb sustained by a secret advantage he held over his interlocutors in Tehran: he had their conversations bugged. Beria's son Sergo wrote about this:[15]

At 8 a.m. Stalin, who had changed his habits for the occasion (usually he worked at night and got up at 11 a.m.), received me and the others. He prepared himself carefully for each of our sessions, having at hand files on every question that interested him. He even went so far as to ask for details of the tone of the conversations: 'Did he say that with conviction or without enthusiasm? How did Roosevelt react? Did he say that resolutely?' Sometimes he was surprised: 'They know that we can hear them and yet they speak openly!' One day he even asked me: 'What do you think, do they know that we are listening to them?'

Even though the Western delegations worked from the premise that Soviet intelligence agencies might be listening to them, Stalin may have been less baffled about Roosevelt and Churchill than they were by him.

On Churchill's trip to Moscow in October 1944 there was an acute need to talk further about the future of Europe. Churchill broached the matter deftly: 'The moment was apt for business, so I said: "Let us settle our affairs in the Balkans."' Churchill took the bull by the horns and scribbled out his proposal on a blank sheet of paper. He suggested an arithmetical apportionment of zones of influence between the USSR on one side and the United Kingdom and the USA on the other. This was the notorious 'percentages agreement':[16]

	%	
Rumania	90	Russia
	10	The others
Greece	90	Great Britain (in accord with USA)
	10	Russia
Yugoslavia	50–50	
Hungary	50–50	
Bulgaria	75	Russia
	25	The others

Stalin waited for the translation, glanced at the paper and then took his blue pencil from a bronze pot and inscribed a large tick. There followed a long pause: both men sensed they were deciding something of historic importance. Churchill broke the silence: 'Might it not be thought rather cynical if it seemed we had disposed of these issues, so fateful to millions of people, in such an offhand manner? Let us burn the paper.' But Stalin was untroubled, and said: 'No, you keep it.'[17]

Churchill, talking later to the British ambassador, referred to his proposal as the 'naughty document'. Stalin had second thoughts about details and asked for greater influence in Bulgaria and Hungary. In both cases he demanded 80 per cent for the USSR. British Foreign Secretary Anthony Eden, with Churchill's consent, agreed to this amendment in a session with Molotov.[18] Mythology has descended upon the agreement on percentages. The legend grew, for example, that Stalin and Churchill had carved up all Europe between them and that their conversation predetermined all the territorial and political decisions subsequently taken by the Allies. In reality the 'naughty document' was a provisional bilateral accord for action in the immediate future. It left much undiscussed. No mention was made of Germany, Poland or Czechoslovakia. Nothing was said about the political and economic system to be installed in any country after the war. The intended post-war order in Europe and Asia had yet to be clarified, and the percentages agreement did not bind the hands of the USA. Unconsulted, President Roosevelt could accept or reject it as he wished. Yet such in fact was his desire to keep the USSR sweet until Germany's defeat that he welcomed the 'naughty document' without demur.

By the time the Big Three met at Yalta on 4 February 1945 it was urgent for them to grasp the nettle of planning post-war Europe and Asia. For Stalin it was also an occasion for the Soviet authorities to show off their *savoir faire*. Each delegation stayed in a palace built for the tsars. This cut no mustard with the aristocratic British Prime Minister. Churchill said that 'a worse place in the world' would not have been discovered even with a decade's exploration. The length of the journey can hardly have annoyed this inveterate traveller. Yalta is on the Crimean peninsula. Before 1917 it was one of the favourite spots for holidaying dignitaries of the Imperial state. Stalin loved the entire shore from Crimea down to Abkhazia – and it is hard to resist the observation that Churchill was indulging in English snobbery.

The Yalta Conference took decisions of enormous importance and Stalin was at his most ebullient. He asked to be rewarded for promising to enter the war against Japan after the coming victory over Germany. In particular, he demanded reparations to the value of twenty billion dollars from Germany. This was controversial, but the Western leaders conceded it to Stalin. More hotly debated was the treatment of Poland. At the insistence of Roosevelt and Churchill the future Polish government was to be a coalition embracing nationalists as well as communists. Yet they failed to pin down Stalin on the details. The wily Stalin wanted a free hand in eastern and east-central Europe. Roosevelt and he were on friendly terms and sometimes met in Churchill's absence. As the junior partner of the Western Allies Churchill had to put up with the situation while making the best of it; and when Stalin demanded south Sakhalin and the Kurile Islands – known to the Japanese as their Northern Territories – in return for joining the war in the Pacific, Churchill was as content as the American President to oblige. Stalin and Churchill also acceded to Roosevelt's passionate request for the establishment of a United Nations Organisation at the war's end. For Roosevelt, as for Woodrow Wilson after the First World War, it was crucial to set up a body which would enhance the prospects for global peace.

The Western Allies were not in an enviable position. Although Germany was on the brink of defeat, there was no telling how long Japan might hold out. The American and British forces in Europe, moreover, had been told they were fighting in alliance with the Red Army. Not only *Pravda* but also the Western establishments buffed up Stalin's personal image. No sooner had the USSR entered the war with the Third Reich than the British press replaced criticism with praise. On the occasion of Stalin's birthday in December 1941 the London Philharmonic Orchestra, not previously known as a communist front organisation, played a concerto in his honour.[19] Public opinion more widely in the West was acutely grateful to the Red Army (as well it might have been) and, less justifiably, treated Stalin as its brave and glorious embodiment. A military confrontation by the Western Allies with the USSR would have been politically as well as militarily difficult. More could have been done nevertheless to put pressure on Stalin; and although Churchill was firmer than Roosevelt, even he was too gentle.

In fact the worst contretemps among the Big Three at Yalta occurred not during the formal negotiations. Roosevelt after a drink at lunch told Stalin that in the West he was known as Uncle Joe.[20] The touchy Soviet leader felt himself the object of ridicule: he could not understand that his nickname indicated a high degree of grudging respect. Needled by the revelation, he had to be persuaded to remain at table. The use of nicknames was anyway not confined to Stalin: Churchill called himself 'Former Naval Person' in telegrams to the American President.[21] Stalin was not averse to taking a dig at Churchill. At one of the Big Three's meals together he proposed that to prevent a resurgence of German militarism after the war the Allies should shoot fifty thousand officers and technical experts. Churchill, knowing Stalin's bloody record, took him at his word and growled that he would rather be shot himself than 'sully my own and my country's honour by such infamy'. Roosevelt tried to lighten the atmosphere by saying that the execution of forty-nine thousand members of the German officer corps would be quite sufficient. Churchill, nauseated by the banter, made for the door and had to be brought back by Stalin and Molotov, who apologised for what they claimed had been a joke.[22]

The British Prime Minister remained unconvinced that Stalin had been jesting; but not for a moment did he contemplate withdrawal from the Yalta Conference. As at previous meetings, he – like Stalin and Roosevelt – saw that the Allies had to stick together or hang separately. When personal insults, however intentionally, were delivered to one of them, the others had to smooth ruffled feathers. In fact it was one of Churchill's entourage, General Alan Brooke, who had the worst verbal exchange with Stalin. This had happened at a banquet at the Tehran Conference when Stalin rose to accuse Brooke of failing to show friendship and comradeship towards the Red Army. Brooke was ready for him and replied in kind that it seemed that 'truth must have an escort of lies' in war; he went on to assert that he felt 'genuine comradeship' towards the men of the Soviet armed forces. Stalin took the riposte on the chin, remarking to Churchill: 'I like that man. He rings true.'[23]

Clever though he was, Stalin was no diplomatic genius. Yet the Big Three had conflicting interests and he took advantage. Stalin had been given his inch and aimed to take a mile. Already the idea had formed in his mind that the USSR should conquer territory in the eastern half of Europe so as to have a buffer zone between itself and any Western aggressor. Stalin had a decent working partnership with the exhausted Roosevelt; and although he and Churchill did not trust each other, they felt they could go on dealing across the table. Many in Poland and elsewhere felt that this co-operation was taken to excessive lengths. The Polish government-in-exile warned about Stalin's ambitions, but in vain. On 12 April, however, Roosevelt died. Stalin, a man scarcely prone to sentimental outbursts, sent a warm letter of condolence to Washington. It was not so much the death of a fellow member of the Big Three as the collapse of a working political relationship that he mourned. Personal diplomacy had obviated many snags which could have disrupted the tripartite military alliance since 1941. Stalin had enjoyed being taken seriously as a politician by Churchill and Roosevelt for the duration of hostilities, and their meetings had enhanced his self-esteem. Roosevelt's successor, Vice-President Harry Truman, had a more right-wing reputation. Stalin anticipated rougher modes of deliberation on world affairs in the time ahead.

43. LAST CAMPAIGNS

At last in summer 1944 the Western Allies were ready to open the second front. Operation Overlord began on 6 June, when American, British, Canadian and other forces under the command of Dwight Eisenhower landed on the beaches of Normandy in northern France. It was an amphibious operation of immense daring and cleverness. Having fooled the Wehrmacht about the precise spot, the Allied armies pushed the Germans into retreat. If Stalin had been beginning such an offensive in the East, he would have demanded that the Western Allies attack the Germans simultaneously. Yet he did not hurry his preparations any more than the Americans and the British had done in earlier years. The Eastern counterpart was to be Operation Bagration. The name was not chosen accidentally: Bagration was one of Alexander II's most successful commanders in 1812; he was also a Georgian like the USSR's Supreme Commander. Massive German forces remained in the east, 228 divisions as compared to the 58 facing Eisenhower and Montgomery. On 22 June, after months of preparation by Zhukov and Vasilevski, Operation Bagration was begun. It was exactly three years after the Germans had crashed over the River Bug in Operation Barbarossa. Deep, complex combinations of tanks and aircraft were deployed across the long front.[1] In East and West it was clear that the final battles of the war in Europe were imminent.

The Pripet marshes between Belorussia and Poland were the next fighting ground, and Stalin basked in the glory obtained by the success of his military professionals. On 22 July Rokossovski's forces crossed the Bug. Stavka concentrated the Red Army's advance in the direction of Warsaw and Lwów. Stalin had last been involved in battles over the territory in 1920, and this time he was in total charge of the Red Army's activities. When Lwów fell on 27 July, the Wehrmacht pulled back across the River Vistula. Neither Hitler nor his generals had a serious strategy to reverse the fortunes of the Third Reich. German forces faced the prospect of war against formidable enemies on two massive fronts. The

Western Allies were grinding their way towards the Ardennes, while the Red Army could see Warsaw through their binoculars.

The Wehrmacht stood across the Red Army's advance not only in Poland but also in every country of eastern Europe. The obvious temptation, after the Red Army crossed the Bug, was to order the pursuit of the enemy to Warsaw. Against this was the calculation that Soviet forces had not yet completed the reconquest of the Baltic states and that a massive defence had been prepared by Hitler in Poland itself. There were reasons for Stavka to allow the Red Army to be rested and resupplied for the arduous crossing of the Vistula. Stalin also needed to be assured that any thrust at Warsaw would not expose his forces to a wheeling movement by the Germans from Romania. Although he had driven the Wehrmacht off Soviet territory, he recognised that a serious military campaign lay ahead.[2] A further problem was the weakness of Soviet intelligence in respect of the Polish situation. Stalin was largely to blame for this. By annihilating thousands of Polish communists in Moscow in the Great Terror, he had deprived himself of agents who could have been infiltrated behind the lines in 1944. And his murderous behaviour towards fleeing Poles in 1939–41 had added to the general suspicion of him in Poland.

In fact the Polish anti-German resistance had secretly been preparing an uprising in Warsaw, and plans were at an advanced stage. Nationalists, far from wanting to welcome the Red Army, hoped to overturn Nazism in Warsaw without Soviet interference. The purpose was to prevent Poland falling prey to the USSR after liberation from Germany. The military organisation was led by the Home Army, and the Warsaw Uprising began on 1 August. It was a brave but doomed endeavour. The Germans brought in the Wehrmacht and steadily the rebels were picked off and defeated. The fighting was over by 2 October.

The Red Army's lengthy period of recuperation and re-equipment caused much adverse comment both at the time and in subsequent years. The Home Army, while planning to defeat the Germans in Warsaw by Polish efforts, pleaded desperately for Soviet support and received almost nothing. Not that the question of earlier military intervention failed to be raised in Moscow; indeed there had been no angrier discussion in Stavka since before the battle of Kursk. Unfortunately almost nothing is known about who said what until the Warsaw Uprising was over. Zhukov, the military professional, was still arguing the need for a prolonged pause in early October. Molotov took the opposite side, demanding an immediate offensive. Beria made mischief among the disputants, delighting in pitting one member of Stavka against another. Stalin predictably leaned towards Molotov: action was his preference. But Zhukov persisted. Eventually Stalin gave way, albeit with his customary lack of grace.[3] Zhukov had won the debate at the expense of piling up problems for his relations with Stalin at the war's end. The Red Army drew itself up on the eastern bank of the Vistula and stayed put for the rest of the year.

What Stalin said to Zhukov was probably not the full extent of his thinking. The weary condition of the Red Army was only one of the factors to be weighed in the balance. Stalin was already looking for ways to secure political dominance over Poland during and after the war. His experience in the Soviet–Polish War of 1920 had convinced him that Poles were untrustworthy because their patriotism outweighed their class consciousness. 'Once a Pole, always a Pole' might have been his motto in dealing with them and their elites. He was determined that whatever Polish state emerged from the débris of the war would stay under the hegemony of the USSR. This meant that the émigré government based in London was to be treated as illegitimate and that any armed organisation formed by the Poles in Poland would be treated likewise. Stalin felt no incentive to handle Poles sympathetically. He had ordered the murder of thousands of captured Polish officers in April 1940 in Katyn forest in Russia. He no more wanted the survival of Poland's political and military elite than he aimed to preserve the elites in Estonia, Latvia and Lithuania – and he was long practised in the art of solving public problems by means of the physical liquidation of those who embodied them.

Stalin also had objective strategic reasons for refusing to start an early offensive across the Vistula. Hitler and his commanders in August had treated the Red Army as the most urgent enemy and left the suppression of the Warsaw Uprising to their security units while the Wehrmacht massed by the river to repulse any attempt at a crossing by Rokossovski. The German authorities were confident they could easily suppress Polish insurgents. What was militarily inexcusable in Stalin's behaviour, however, was his rejection of all Polish pleas for assistance once the Warsaw Uprising had begun on 1 August 1944. Churchill detected the dirty work and rebuked the Kremlin.[4] British aircraft based in Italy were dispatched to drop supplies to the Poles. But Stalin was immovable and the Red Army did not budge.

The Warsaw Uprising was neither soon nor easily suppressed. While the Red Army took the opportunity for rest, recovery and resupply, the Home Army of the Poles got about its business. The insurgents were flexible, well organised and utterly determined. The Germans had no idea how to contain them until the order was given to raze the districts of insurgence to the ground. Stalin might have had justified doubts that aid for the Polish rebels by means of an amphibious assault across the Vistula would decisively weaken the Wehrmacht. But if it had been a large group of Russian or Ukrainian partisans rising against the Third Reich, he would surely have dropped guns and food for their use and bombed the Germans. His prevention of assistance to Warsaw involved a calculated decision about Poland's future. Already Stalin had set up a Provisional Government. This was the cabinet, appointed by the Kremlin and beholden to it, which he intended to put into power after Germany's defeat. Other Polish leaders, however popular they might be across the country, were to be kept away from the centre of events. Stalin aspired to rule Poland through his communist stooges. The more insurgents were wiped out by the Germans, the nearer he would come to his objective. Churchill's imprecations about Stalin's military and political measures were justified ones.

Nevertheless Churchill was to impress on Stalin at their Moscow meeting in October 1944 that he held no suspicion that the Red Army had been deliberately held back.[5] The cohesion of the Grand Alliance took precedence. The Wehrmacht, despite being on the defensive in East and West, had not lost its resilience. The Allies knew they had a fight on their hands as Germans, despite grumbling about Hitler's military and economic failures, stood by their Führer. Churchill and Stalin understood the importance of getting to Berlin first. The conquest of territory would put the conqueror in a position to prescribe the terms of peace. Roosevelt and Eisenhower felt differently; their strategy was premised on the desire to minimise casualties on their side rather than join a race to reach Berlin first. Stalin was determined to win the race even if the Americans declined to compete. He was worried that the USA and the United Kingdom might do a deal with the Germans for an end to the fighting. This could lead to a joint crusade against the Soviet Union; and even if this did not happen, the Germans might surrender to the Western Allies and deprive the Soviet Union of post-war gains. Stalin selected his finest field commanders – Rokossovski, Konev and Zhukov – to reinforce the campaign to seize the German capital.

The Red Army on his orders started the Vistula–Oder Operation on 12 January 1945. Although his Red Army outnumbered the Wehrmacht by three to one, the German will to resist had not faded. Konev's 1st Ukrainian Front burst forward on the southern wing of a military force which stretched across the length of the Polish lands. Zhukov's 1st Belorussian Front advanced in the north. As German defences crumbled, Zhukov could report that he held the banks of the River Oder. The pockets of Germans who had not retreated were caught in a trap. Königsberg and its population were cut off. On its way through Poland the Red Army came across terrible sights as it entered the concentration camps. Evidence of mass murder had been obliterated at Belzec, Sobibor and Treblinka, but at Auschwitz (Oswiecim) the fleeing Germans had not had time to disguise the incarceration, forced labour, starvation and murder. Soviet soldiers would have acted furiously even without such an experience. German atrocities in the USSR had been systematic from the beginning of Operation Barbarossa, and Soviet wartime propaganda had dulled any lingering sensitivities towards the Germans as a people. As it moved into central Europe, the Red Army went on the rampage; its troops pillaged and raped with almost no restraint by its commanders.

Red troops acted with almost no discrimination about nationality. Not only Germans but also other peoples were brutally treated and Stalin refused to punish the offenders. The Yugoslav communist leader Milovan Djilas complained to him in vain. 'Well, then,' Stalin replied:[6]

> imagine a man who has fought from Stalingrad to Belgrade – over a thousand kilometres of his own devastated land, across the dead bodies of his comrades and dearest ones. How can such a man react normally? And what is so awful in his having fun with a woman, after such horrors? You have imagined the Red Army to be ideal. And it is not ideal, nor can it be . . . The important thing is that it fights Germans.

Djilas, who had fought in the Balkans and was not noted for sensitivity, could hardly believe his ears.

Careless about how his soldiers behaved off-duty, Stalin was determined that they should take the German capital. He deceived the Western Allies about his intention. On 1 April 1945, as he was settling his military plans in Moscow, he telegraphed Eisenhower, agreeing that Soviet and Western forces should aim to converge in the region of Erfurt, Leipzig and Dresden; and he added: 'Berlin has lost its previous strategic significance. Therefore the Soviet Supreme Command is thinking of assigning second-level forces to the Berlin side.'[7] Compounding the lie, he proposed that the 'main blow' should be delivered in the second half of May. Simultaneously he ordered Zhukov and Konev to hurry forward their preparations.[8] Churchill became ever more concerned. Politically, in his view it was vital to meet up with the Red Army as far to the east as was possible. But he failed to get a positive response from Roosevelt before the Soviet forces were on the move again. On 19 April they threw down the Wehrmacht defences between the river Oder and the river Neisse. On 25 April they had reached the outskirts of Potsdam outside Berlin. This was on the same day that Konev's divisions made direct contact with the First US Army at Torgau on the River Elbe. Yet the Reds got to Berlin first. Zhukov prevailed over Konev in their race. On 30 April Hitler, recognising the hopelessness of his position, committed suicide. Unconditional surrender followed.[9]

Many divisions of the Wehrmacht surrendered to the American and British forces on 8 May, whereas Zhukov received such offers only the next day. The collapse of German military power permitted Stalin to turn his face eastwards. The USSR could never be secure while an aggressive Japan sat on its borders. He was to refer to the 'shame' heaped upon the Russian Empire through defeat in the naval battle of Tsushima in 1905. Tokyo had put forces into the Soviet Far East in the Civil War. Japan had invaded Manchuria in 1931 and signed the Anti-Comintern Pact in 1936. War had exploded between Japan and the USSR in 1938, involving the largest tank battles yet seen in the world. It was not until mid-1941 that Japanese rulers decided to undertake expansion southwards along the rim of the Pacific rather than westward through Siberia.

The Western Allies, having to husband their human and material resources, continued to need help from the Red Army. There was every sign that the Japanese were readying themselves to defend their territory to the last soldier. Stalin at Yalta had exacted the promise from Roosevelt and Churchill that the USSR would receive the Kurile islands in the event of Allied victory. This was still Stalin's objective after the victory in Europe. Rapid preparations were made by Stavka for the Red Army's entry into the war in the Pacific. Having suffered from Japanese expansionism in the 1930s, Stalin intended to secure a peace settlement that would permanently protect the interests of the USSR in the Far East. Nearly half a million troops were transferred along the Trans-Siberian railway to the Soviet Far East. Yet the Kuomintang under Chiang Kai-shek refused to accept the terms which had been put by Stalin to the Western Allies. Stalin conducted further negotiations with the Chinese and made an unadorned case for concessions from China and territory from Japan. Otherwise, he asserted, the Japanese would remain a danger to its neighbours: 'We need Dairen and Port Arthur for thirty years in case Japan restores its forces. We could strike at it from there.'[10]

By 16 July 1945, however, the Americans had successfully tested their A-bomb at Alamogordo. It had also become clear that the Japanese would fight for every inch of their islands, and President Truman saw nuclear weapons as a desirable means of avoiding massive loss of lives among the invading American forces. He no longer saw any reason to encourage Soviet military intervention. Having seen how Stalin had tricked Roosevelt over Berlin, he was not going to be fooled again. American policy towards the USSR was in any case getting steadily sterner. What Truman would not do, though, was retract Roosevelt's specific promises at Yalta to Stalin about China and Japan: he did not want to set a precedent for breaking inter-Allied agreements. Stalin did not know this. He had yet to test Truman's sincerity as a negotiating partner. He sensed that, unless the Red Army intervened fast, the Americans might well deny him the Kurile Islands after Japan's defeat. Stalin wanted total security for the USSR: 'We are closed up. We have no outlet. Japan should be kept vulnerable from all sides, north, west, south, east. Then she will keep quiet'[11] The race for Berlin gave way to the race for the Kuriles.

Stalin, Truman and Churchill came together at the Potsdam Conference from 17 July. This time there was no argy-bargy about the choice of venue; the leaders of the Big Three wanted to savour victory at the centre of the fallen Third Reich. While Stalin took his train from Moscow, Truman made the long trip across the Atlantic and joined Stalin and Churchill in Berlin. Meetings were held in the Cecilienhof. The wartime personal partnership was already over, with Roosevelt's replacement by Truman. Perhaps Roosevelt would anyway have ceased to indulge Stalin in the light of American global ambitions after the world war. Certainly Truman already felt this way.

The other great change in the Big Three occurred in the course of the Potsdam Conference. On 26 July the British elections swept the Labour party to power. Churchill ceded his place at the negotiations to his Deputy Prime Minister Clement Attlee. The new government was no gentler on Stalin than Churchill, and the Potsdam Conference turned into a trial of strength between the USA and the USSR with the British regularly supporting the Americans. Several topics were difficult: the Japanese campaign; the peace terms in Europe; and Poland's frontiers and government. The Americans, buoyed by their monopoly of nuclear-weapons technology, were no longer eager for Soviet military assistance in the Far East. This time it was Stalin who stressed the need for the USSR's participation. On Europe there was agreement on the Allies' demarcation of zones of occupation. But wrangles remained. It was decided to hand over the details for resolution by the Council of Foreign Ministers. Poland, though, could not be pushed aside. The Conference at Stalin's insistence listened to the arguments of the USSR-sponsored Provisional Government. The Americans and British complained repeatedly about Soviet manipulation and about political repression in Warsaw. The Western Allies expected Stalin to respect Polish independence and to foster democratic reform.

Both Truman and Stalin knew that the American A-bomb was ready for use, but Truman did not know that Stalin knew. In fact Soviet espionage had reported accurately to Moscow, and on this occasion Stalin did not disbelieve his agents. When Truman informed him about the American technological advance, Stalin had prepared himself to be unperturbed – and Truman was astounded by his sangfroid. In the same period Stalin buttonholed his commanders, urging them to bring forward the Soviet offensive against Japan. But technical reasons obstructed any change in schedule, and Stalin restrained an inclination to insist on the impossible. Increasingly the Western Allies ignored him. Truman, Churchill and Chiang Kai-shek issued their own ultimatum to the Japanese government from Potsdam. Nobody consulted Stalin.[12]

Arriving back in Moscow, Stalin kept pestering Vasilevski in Stavka. The response from Vasilevski was that Soviet forces would be ready to attack the Japanese no later than 9 August. But even this was too late. Truman had taken his decision to instruct American bombers to undertake their first military operation with nuclear weapons. On 6 August a B-29 took off from Tinian island to drop a bomb on Hiroshima. A fresh stage in human destructiveness had been reached as an entire city was reduced to rubble by a single military overflight. Still Stalin hoped to include himself in the victory. On 7 August he signed the order for Soviet forces to invade Manchuria two days later. But again he was pre-empted. The failure of the Japanese to sue for peace led Truman to sanction a further bombing raid by B-29s on 8 August. This time the target was Nagasaki. The result was the same: the city became an instant ruin and the population was annihilated. The Japanese government, at the behest of Emperor Hirohito, surrendered on 2 September 1945. Stalin had lost the race for Tokyo. The Manchurian campaign still went ahead as planned in Moscow and the Kwantung Army was attacked. But really Japan's fate lay in the hands of President Truman.[13]

The only lever left to Stalin in diplomacy was his impassivity. At a reception for Averell Harriman and the diplomat George Kennan on

8 August he made a point of seeming unconcerned about the fate of Hiroshima and Nagasaki. He also displayed knowledge about the German and British attempts to build A-bombs. Evidently he wished to let Truman know that Soviet spies were briefing the Kremlin about the development of military nuclear technology worldwide. He deliberately let slip that the Soviet Union had its own atomic-bomb project.[14] Stalin acted his chosen role to perfection. American diplomats knew very well that the Soviet political elite had been depressed by the bombing of Hiroshima and Nagasaki. The USSR's pre-eminence with the USA and the United Kingdom as a victorious power had been put into question, and the immense sacrifices offered across the Soviet Union in 1941–5 could soon prove to have brought little benefit to its citizens. Stalin had won many hands without having the aces to finish the game.

44. VICTORY!

In the early hours of 9 May 1945 radio announcer Isaak Levitan read out the news everyone had been greedy for. The war with Germany was over. Popular excitement had been growing for days. When the moment came, the celebrations were tumultuous; they occurred across the USSR and in all the countries which had fought Hitler's New Order. The Soviet government had arranged a fireworks display for the evening in Moscow, but people had started their festivities hours earlier. Millions thronged the central districts. Everywhere there was dancing and singing. Any man in the green uniform of the Red Army stood a fair chance of being hugged and kissed. A crowd gathered outside the US embassy as the chant went up: 'Hurrah for Roosevelt!' The American President was so much identified with the Grand Alliance that few remembered he had died in April. Behaviour was unrestrained. Prodigious drinking occurred; the police overlooked young men urinating against the walls of the Moskva Hotel. Restaurants and cafeterias were packed with customers where food was scarce but vodka plentiful.[1] There was joy that Nazism had been crushed under the tank tracks of the Red Army.

Stalin's daughter Svetlana phoned him after the radio broadcast: 'Papa, congratulations to you: victory!' 'Yes, victory,' he replied. 'Thanks. Congratulations to you too. How are you?' The estrangement of father and daughter melted in the warmth of the moment.[2] Khrushchëv was less lucky. When he made a similar phone call, Stalin rebuked him. 'He made it known,' Khrushchëv suggested, 'that I was taking up his valuable time. Well, I simply froze to the spot. What was this about? Why? I took it all badly and cursed myself thoroughly: why had I phoned him? After all, I knew his character and could have expected no good whatever to come of it. I knew he would want to show me that the past was already a stage we had gone through and that he was now thinking about great new matters.'[3]

Stalin delivered an 'address to the people' starting: 'Comrades! Men and women compatriots!'[4] Gone were the gentler vocatives of his radio broadcast at the start of Operation Barbarossa. The USSR had been saved and the 'great banner of freedom of peoples and peace between peoples' could at last be waved. The Great Patriotic War was over.[5] But, if his style was solemn, it was also gracious at least for his Russian listeners. At a banquet for Red Army commanders on 24 May he declared:[6]

> Comrades, allow me to propose one last toast.
>
> I would like to propose a toast to the health of our Soviet people and, above all, of the Russian people because it is the outstanding nation of all the nations forming part of the Soviet Union.
>
> I propose this toast to the health of the Russian people because in this war it earned general recognition as the leading force of the Soviet Union among all the peoples of our country.

Previously he had never unequivocally endorsed one nation out of the many which composed the USSR. To many Russians it seemed that the oven of war had smelted the base metals out of him and produced a stainless Leader who deserved their trust and admiration.

These were canting words since Stalin was as much afraid of Russians as proud of them. But it suited him to put the Russian people on an even higher pedestal of official esteem than before the war. Intuitively, it would seem, he understood that he needed to grant legitimacy to a national patriotism less qualified by Marxism–Leninism. At least he did this for a while. (And perhaps even Stalin got a bit carried away by the euphoria of the moment.) What had appeared completely inconceivable in summer 1941 had come to pass. Hitler was dead. Nearly all the eastern half of Europe was under Soviet military control. The USSR was treated by the USA and the United Kingdom as co-arbiter of the fate of the world.

Allegedly Stalin had wanted Hitler caught alive and was annoyed by his suicide, and there was a story that Zhukov had vowed to parade him in a cage on Red Square. This may indeed have been how a commander might have bragged to his political master. But it is improbable that Stalin would have allowed such a spectacle: he still wished to avoid giving unnecessary offence to his allies. The goal of the USA and the United Kingdom was the methodical de-Nazification of German public life, and they hoped to persuade Germans to abandon their affection for Hitler. Conquerors had last humiliated their enemy leaders in such a fashion during the triumphs granted to successful Roman commanders. Cheated of catching his quarry alive, Stalin instructed his intelligence agencies to bring him the physical remains. This was done in deadly secrecy; once it had been ascertained that the charred parts of a burnt corpse outside Hitler's bunker were those of the Führer, they were conveyed to the Soviet capital. Stalin's sense of urgency derived from political concerns. Nothing was to be left on German soil which could later become a focus for pro-Nazi nostalgia.

In a peculiar way this was an involuntary gesture of respect for Hitler, as Stalin was implying that his dead enemy was still dangerous. Towards most other leaders in the world apart from Churchill and Roosevelt he felt condescension at best. (What he thought about Mussolini remains mysterious, but the only Italian he took seriously was the communist party leader Palmiro Togliatti.) Churchill's successor Clement Attlee made little imprint on his consciousness. Even Truman failed to impress him. Whereas Roosevelt had aroused his personal curiosity, he barely gave his successor a second thought. There is nothing in the records of Stalin's conversations to indicate an appreciation of Truman's talents. He was more appreciative of Churchill. Yet the United Kingdom, as Stalin's economic experts such as Jeno Varga demonstrated to him, was no longer the force in world affairs it had once been. Churchill could huff and puff, but the house of the USSR would not fall down. Stalin saw himself as one of history's outstanding figures. When he came across domineering characters of his own type such as Mao Tse-tung, he refused to treat them decently. Mao arrived in Moscow in December 1949 after seizing power in Beijing, and he was told none too politely that the USSR expected massive concessions from China. In any case Stalin, mounting to his crest of post-war grandeur, had no intention of allowing a fellow communist to rival his prestige. Master of world communism and leader of a triumphant state, he desired to bask alone in the world's acclaim.

The day set aside to celebrate the triumph over Nazism was 24 June 1945. There was to be a parade on Red Square in front of tens of thousands of spectators. Victorious regiments which had returned from Germany and eastern Europe were to march in triumph before the Kremlin Wall. It was put to Stalin that he should take pride of place, riding a white horse in the traditional Russian mode. (This was how Russia's generals had headed military parades through Tbilisi.) An Arab steed was found which Stalin tried to mount. The result was humiliation. Stalin gave the stallion an inappropriate jab with his spurs. The stallion reared up. Stalin, grabbing the mane ineffectually, was thrown to the ground. He injured his head and shoulder and was in a vile mood as he got to his feet. Spitting in anger, he declared: 'Let Zhukov lead the parade. He's an old cavalryman.'[7] Some days before the parade he summoned Zhukov, who had returned from Berlin, and asked whether he could handle a horse. Zhukov had belonged to the Red Cavalry in the Civil War; but his first instinct was to remonstrate that Stalin should head the parade as Supreme Commander. Without revealing his equestrian difficulties, Stalin replied: 'I'm too old to lead parades. You're younger. You lead it.'[8]

The ceremonial arrangements were meticulously realised on the day itself. While Stalin and other political leaders stood on top of the Lenin Mausoleum below the Kremlin Wall, Marshal Zhukov rode across Red Square to salute him. The entire Soviet military effort between 1941 and 1945 was acclaimed. A regiment from each front in the war marched behind Zhukov. All saluted Stalin. The packed crowd, drawn from people whom the authorities wanted to reward, roared approval. The climax of the ceremony came when the banners of the defeated Wehrmacht were carried over the cobbled space to be cast down directly in front of Stalin. The weather was not at its best; there had been an earlier downpour.[9] But the applause for Stalin and the troops of the Soviet armed forces cancelled the gloom. He had risen to the apex of his career and was being recognised as father of the peoples of the USSR.

All went to plan on 24 June apart from the unseasonable rain, and the Soviet order seemed stronger than ever. The Red Army dominated to the River Elbe. Eastern and east-central Europe were subject to Soviet military and political control and, while the war in the Pacific continued, Red forces were being readied to take part in the final offensive against Japan. Secretly, too, the USSR was intensifying its research on the technology needed to make an atomic bomb. Already its armaments industry was capable of supplying its military forces with all they needed to maintain Soviet power and prestige. The political and economic system consolidated before the Second World War remained intact. Party, ministries and police had firm authority, and the tasks of peaceful reconstruction of industry, agriculture, transport, schooling and health-care seemed well within the USSR's capacity to discharge. Hierarchy and discipline were at their peak. Morale in the country was high. Stalin's despotism appeared an impregnable citadel.

Next day at the Kremlin reception for participants in the Victory Parade he was triumphant:[10]

I offer a toast to those simple, ordinary, modest people, to the 'little cogs' who keep our great state mechanism in an active condition in all fields of science, economy and military affairs. There are a lot of them; their name is legion because there are tens of millions of such people.

The 'people' for him were mere cogs in the machinery of state and not individuals and groups of flesh and blood with social, cultural and psychological needs and aspirations. The state took precedence over society.

Yet Stalin, while masterminding an image of omnipotence for the Soviet state, did not himself believe in it. The USSR had daunting problems. He ordered the security agencies to collate information with a view to making the Soviet case for reparations when the Allies next conferred. Catalogues of devastation were compiled. Twenty-six million Soviet citizens had perished in the Second World War. Stalin was not innocent of blame: his policies of imprisonment and deportation had added to the total (as had his disastrous policy of agricultural collectivisation, which impeded the USSR's capacity to feed itself). But most victims died at the front or under Nazi occupation. Some 1.8 million Soviet civilians were reportedly killed by the Germans in the RSFSR; double that number was recorded for Ukraine.[11] The dead were not the only human losses in the USSR. Millions of people were left badly wounded or malnourished, their lives having been wrecked beyond repair. Countless children had been orphaned and fended for themselves without public support or private charity. Whole districts in the western borderlands had been depopulated so drastically that farming had ceased. The Soviet Union had paid a high price for its victory, and it would take years to recover.

As the NKVD completed its cataloguing tasks (while not ceasing to discharge the duty of arresting all enemies of Stalin and the state), the scale of the catastrophe was made clear. In the zone of the USSR previously under German occupation scarcely a factory, mine or commercial enterprise had escaped destruction. The Wehrmacht was not the sole culprit: Stalin had adopted a scorched-earth policy after 22 June 1941 so as to deprive Hitler of material assets. Yet the subsequent German retreat in 1943–4 had taken place over a lengthier period, and this had provided the Wehrmacht with time to carry out systematic destruction. The record put together by NKVD almost defies belief. No fewer than 1,710 Soviet towns had been obliterated by the Germans along with around seventy thousand villages. Even where the Wehrmacht failed to set fire to entire townships, it succeeded in burning down hospitals, radio stations, schools and libraries. Cultural vandalism was as near to comprehensive as Hitler could make it. If Stalin had a crisis in the availability of human resources, he faced an equally appalling set of tasks in consequence of the devastation of the material environment.

Not only that: the structure of administrative control was much more shaky than it had been before the war. Displaced persons were everywhere; and as the troops came back from Europe, the chaos increased. No picture of this was permitted to appear in the newspapers or the newsreels. The emphasis continued to fall upon the bravery and efficiency of the Red Army in Germany and the other occupied countries of central and eastern Europe. The reality was very different. The Soviet order was most easily restored in the larger cities, especially those which had never been under German rule. But the intense concentration on military tasks in the Great Patriotic War had led to the running down of those aspects of civilian administration which were not narrowly connected with the fight against the Germans. In the zone previously occupied by the Wehrmacht the shambles of organisation was acute. In places it was hard to believe that the Soviet order had ever existed as peasants reverted to a way of life which predated the October Revolution. Private trade and popular social customs had reasserted themselves over communist requirements. Stalin's writ was unchallengeable in Moscow, Leningrad and other conurbations, but in smaller localities, especially the villages (where most of the population still lived), the arm of the authorities was not long enough to affect daily lives.

And despite the Red Army's triumph in Europe there were problems in several countries under Soviet occupation. The military, security, diplomatic and political agencies of the USSR, already stretched to the limit before 1945, had somehow to cope with the responsibilities of peace. Yugoslavia was unusual in as much as its own internal forces under Tito had liberated it from the Germans. Elsewhere the Reds had played the crucial part in defeating the Wehrmacht. Victory proved simpler than occupation. Few people in central and eastern Europe wished to be subject to communist rule. Stalin and the Politburo knew how effectively the communists had been eradicated by Hitler and his allies and how little support the national communist leaders in Moscow-based emigration had in their homelands.

Somehow Stalin had to devise a way of gaining popular sympathy in these occupied countries while solving a vast number of urgent tasks.

Food supplies had to be found. Economies had to be regenerated and post-Nazi administrations set up. Functionaries had to be checked for political reliability. The shattered cities and damaged roads and railways had to be restored. At the same time Stalin was determined to gain reparations from the former enemy countries, not only Germany but also Hungary, Romania and Slovakia. This was bound to complicate the task of winning popularity for himself and for communism. The Western Allies were another difficulty. An understanding existed with them that a rough line ran from north to south in Europe separating the Soviet zone of influence from the zone to be dominated by the United States, Britain and France. Yet there was no clarity about the rights of victor powers to impose their political, economic and ideological models on the countries they occupied. Nor had the victors specified what methods of rule were acceptable. As the ashes of war settled, tensions among the Allies were rising.

The global rivalry of the Allies was bound to increase after they had crushed their German and Japanese enemies. Stalin's armies had taken the brunt of the military burden in Europe, but American power had also been decisive and was growing there. In the Far East the Red Army contributed little until the last few days. The United States, moreover, was the world's sole nuclear power. The management of the post-war global order posed many menaces to Soviet security – and Stalin was quick to comprehend the danger.

If his regime was unpopular abroad, it was not much more attractive to Soviet citizens. There was a paradox in this. Undoubtedly the war had done wonders to enhance his reputation in the USSR; he was widely regarded as the embodiment of patriotism and victory. Even many who detested him had come to accord him a basic respect – and when defectors from the Soviet Union were interviewed it was found that several basic values propagated by the authorities found favour. The commitment to free education, shelter and healthcare as well as to universal employment had a lasting appeal. But the haters in the USSR were certainly numerous. Armed resistance was widespread in Estonia, Latvia, Lithuania, western Belorussia and western Ukraine. These were recently annexed areas. Elsewhere the regime was much more durably in control and few citizens dared to organise themselves against Stalin and his subordinates. Most of those who did were young people, especially students, who had no memory of the Great Terror. Small, clandestine groupings were formed in the universities. Typically they were dedicated to the purification of Marxist–Leninist ideology and behaviour from

Stalinist taint: state indoctrination had got the brightest youngsters to approve of the October Revolution. These groupings were easily penetrated and dissolved.

More worrisome for the authorities was the hope prevailing across society that immense political and economic changes would follow the achievement of military victory. Stalin was a student of Russian history; he knew that the Russian Imperial Army's entry into Paris in 1815 after the defeat of Napoleon had led to political unrest in Russia. Officers and troops who had experienced the greater civic freedom in France were never the same again, and in 1825 a mutiny took place which nearly overthrew the Romanovs. Stalin was determined to avoid any repetition of that Decembrist Revolt. The Red Army which stormed Berlin had witnessed terrible sights in eastern and central Europe: gas chambers, concentration camps, starvation, and urban devastation. Nazism's impact was unmistakable. But those serving soldiers had also glimpsed a different and attractive way of life. Churches and shops were functioning. Goods were available, at least in most cities, which in the USSR were on sale only in enterprises reserved for the elites. The diet was more diverse. Peasants, if not well dressed, did not always look destitute. The pervasive regimentation of the USSR, too, was absent from the countries over which they had marched. This included Germany itself.

Stalin did not receive explicit reports on this: the security agencies had long since learned that they had to give him the truth in ideologically acceptable terms, and Stalin did not want to hear that life was more congenial abroad. What he was told by the agencies was alarming enough. Booty brought back by soldiers included all manner of goods from carpets, pianos and paintings to gramophone records, stockings and underwear. Red Army soldiers had made a habit of collecting wristwatches and, as often as not, wearing all of them simultaneously. Even civilians who had not moved beyond the old Soviet frontiers but had been held under German military rule had had experience of a different way of life which had not been in every way uncongenial. Churches, shops and small workshops had been restored after the initial success of Operation Barbarossa. Such Soviet citizens had neither war booty nor the experience of foreign travel; but their expectation that things would change in the USSR was strong. Across the entire Soviet Union, indeed, there was a popular feeling that it had been worth fighting the war only if reforms were to ensue.[12]

And so beneath the draped red flags of victory there lurked danger and uncertainty for Stalin and his regime. He understood the situation more keenly than anyone near to him in the Kremlin. It was this awareness as well as a perennial grumpiness that had made him so curt with Khrushchëv after the fall of Berlin. He saw that critical times lay ahead.

Yet he would not have been human if warmer feelings had not occasionally suffused him. At the spectacular ceremonies he puffed out his chest. The stream of foreign dignitaries coming to Moscow at the end of the Second World War caught the sense of his mood. On such occasions he let pride take precedence over concern. Stalin, the Red Army and the USSR had won the war against a terrible enemy. As usual he compared current conditions with those which had prevailed under his admired predecessor. This was obvious from what he said to Yugoslav visitors:[13]

> Lenin in his time did not dream of the correlation of forces which we have attained in this war. Lenin reckoned with the fact that everyone was going to attack us, and it would be good if any distant country, for example America, might remain neutral. But it's now turned out that one group of the bourgeoisie went to war against us and another was on our side. Lenin previously did not think that it was possible to remain in alliance with one wing of the bourgeoisie and fight with another. This is what we've achieved . . .

Stalin was proud that he had gone one stage further than Lenin had thought possible. Whereas Lenin had hoped to preserve the Soviet state by keeping it out of inter-capitalist military conflicts and letting the great capitalist powers fight each other, Stalin had turned the USSR into a great power in its own right. Such was its strength that the USA and the United Kingdom had been obliged to seek its assistance.

How long, however, would the alliance hold after the end of hostilities with Germany and Japan? On this, Stalin was quietly definite when he met a Polish communist delegation:[14]

> Rumours of war are being put about extremely intensively by our enemies.
>
> The English [sic] and Americans are using their agents to spread rumours to scare the peoples of those countries whose politics they don't like. Neither we nor the Anglo-Americans can presently start a war. Everyone's fed up with war. Moreover, there are no war aims. We aren't getting ready to attack England and America, and they're not risking it either. No war is possible for at least the next twenty years.

Despite what he said in public about the warmongering tendencies of the Western Allies, he expected a lengthy period of peace from 1945. The Soviet Union and the states friendly to it in eastern Europe would not have an easy time. Devastation by war and the complications of post-war consolidation would exert the minds and energy of the communist movement for many years. But the USSR was secure in its fortress.

For many, especially those who were unaware of Stalin's homicidal activities, there would have been no Soviet victory in the Second World War but for his contribution – and perhaps Germany would permanently have bestridden the back of the European continent. In the USSR, too, the acclaim for him had intensified although it would be wrong to think that the exact degree of approval for him is ascertainable. Nor would it be right to assume that most citizens had uncomplicated feelings about him. Throughout the war he had held back from identifying himself with specific political and social policies. He had made that mistake during agricultural collectivisation in the late 1920s, and the self-distancing manoeuvre of 'Dizzy with Success' had not succeeded in saving him from the peasantry's opprobrium. Quite who was responsible for the avoidable horrors of Soviet wartime measures was therefore not clear to everyone. Millions of citizens were willing to give him the benefit of the doubt: they wanted a relaxation of the regime and assumed that this would come about as the war came to an end.

Stalin was more widely loved than he had any right to expect. In his more relaxed moods he liked to compare himself with the Allied leaders. His qualities, he told others, included 'intelligence, analysis, calculation'. Churchill, Roosevelt and others were different: 'They – the bourgeois leaders – are resentful and vengeful. One ought to keep feelings under control; if feelings are allowed to get the upper hand, you'll lose.'[15] This was rich coming from the lips of a Leader whose own violent sensitivities were extreme. But Stalin was in no mood for self-criticism. In a confidential meeting with Bulgarian communists he derided Churchill for failing to anticipate his defeat in the British parliamentary elections in July 1945 – and Churchill, according to Molotov, was the foreign politician whom Stalin respected the most. The conclusion was obvious: Stalin had become convinced of his own genius. He was master of a superpower beginning to fulfil its destiny. His name was as glorious as the victory being celebrated by the communist party and the Red Army. World renown had settled upon the cobbler's son from Gori.

PART FIVE

THE IMPERATOR

45. DELIVERING THE BLOW

Stalin's mind was a stopped clock. There was no chance in 1945 that he would satisfy popular yearnings for reform. His assumptions about policy had hardened like stalactites. He knew what he was doing. If he had relaxed the regime, he would have imperilled his personal supremacy. This consideration counted more for him than evidence that his mode of rule undermined the objective of durable economic competitiveness and political dynamism. Stalin thought strictly within the frame of his worldview and operational assumptions. The habits of despotism had anaesthetised him to human suffering. The man who digested a daily multitude of facts disregarded information he found uncongenial.

Only his death or drastic physical incapacitation might have moved the mechanisms towards reform. He might easily have died in the first half of October 1945 when the condition of his heart gave him problems.[1] The years were catching up with him. He had had patches of ill health since the Revolution, and the Second World War had levied a heavy toll. At the age of sixty-six he was long past his physical prime. His cardiac problem was kept a state secret and he took a two-month vacation;[2] but this had been nothing unusual for him in the inter-war years. Not even the members of his entourage were initiated into the details of his condition – they were simply left to surmise that he was suffering from an illness of passing significance. Apart from his physician Vladimir Vinogradov, no one had an inkling of the medical prognosis. Politburo members knew they had to desist from any display of inquisitiveness. It would have been dangerous for Stalin to think they were aware of his growing frailty. He would instantly have suspected that a coup against him was in the offing. He needed only a scintilla of doubt about individuals to flash in his mind before consigning them to the security police.

Despite his bodily decline, he could go on ruling the USSR through the existing institutions, personnel and procedures. Stalin's personal supremacy rested upon the maintenance of the one-party dictatorship.

Ideocracy and terror remained indispensable instruments of his despotism – and he never wavered in his determination to sustain it. He did not retreat from his intentions towards the wider world and aimed at a further strengthening of the USSR's position as a great power. He reinforced Soviet hegemony over countries on the western borders: the zone of Europe conquered by the Red Army was to be held tightly within his grasp; and opportunities were to be sought to extend the USSR's influence in Asia. Having won the war against the Third Reich, Stalin did not intend to lose the peace to the Western Allies. At a meeting with his intimates, he ordered them 'to deliver a strong blow' against any suggestion of the desirability of 'democracy' in the USSR.[3] In Stalin's opinion, democratic aspirations in Soviet society were the unfortunate consequence of co-operation with the USA and the United Kingdom from 1941. Western politicians after 1917 had feared the spread of the revolutionary bacillus from Russia; Stalin from 1945 dreaded his USSR becoming afflicted with counter-revolutionary infections: parliaments and markets to his mind were the diseased products of the capitalist order which had to be stopped from leaching their poison into his country.

He cultivated peaceful relations with his Western allies and sought economic benefit through increased trade and loans. He allowed a widening of the scope of public debate after the war. He contemplated measures to expand the provision of industrial consumer goods. Yet already he made such any such orientation subsidiary to the achievement of other priorities. Stalin let nothing get in the way of the enhancement of the country's military might and security – and he set about dedicating vast resources to the acquisition of his own A-bomb and to the subjugation of eastern and east-central Europe to the Kremlin. The question was not whether Stalin would rule moderately or fiercely, but how fiercely he would decide to rule. The connection between internal and external policies was intimate. Ferocity in the USSR had ramifications abroad. Equally important was the likelihood that any expected deterioration in relations with the Western Allies would induce him to reinforce repressive measures at home.

Stalin had deported several Caucasian nationalities to the wilds of Kazakhstan in 1943–4. He had arrested the various elites of Estonia, Latvia and Lithuania when he reannexed those states in 1944; the victims were either shot, thrown into the Gulag or dumped in Siberian settlements. Dekulakisation and declericalisation were bloodily imposed and 142,000 citizens of these new Soviet republics were deported in 1945–9.[4]

Stalin set the intelligence agencies to work at catching anyone disloyal to himself and the state. He put Soviet POWs through 'filtration' camps after their liberation from German captivity. An astonishing 2,775,700 former soldiers in the Red Army were subjected to interrogation upon repatriation, and about half of them landed up in a labour camp.[5] Everywhere the police and party were looking out for insubordination. Marxist–Leninist propaganda had regained prominence toward the end of the war, and this emphasis continued after 1945. Citizens of the USSR were to be left with no illusions: the pre-war order was going to be reintroduced with a vengeance.

The Soviet armed forces and security agencies had their hands full inside the USSR's own borders. Even the task of feeding the army was difficult.[6] Resistance was intense in those regions which had lain outside the USSR before the Second World War. Partisan warfare in defence of nationhood, religion and social custom was intense in Estonia, Latvia, Lithuania, western Belorussia and western Ukraine. Stalin was not alone in the Kremlin leadership in thinking that massive retaliation was required. The word went forth that the new borders of the USSR were permanent and non-negotiable and that its citizens would have to accept the fact or suffer the punitive consequences. Stalin was turning the country into a military camp. By assuming the title Generalissimus – like one of his heroes, Suvorov – on 28 June 1945 he signalled the regimentation he was going to imprint on Soviet public life. Uniforms, conscription and armaments were lauded. *Pravda* editorials were full of injunctions to obey party and government. The need for state defence was regularly conveyed by the media. There was no sense that peacetime would last long. The official media insisted that further sacrifices would be required of society.

Across the half of Europe it controlled, meanwhile, the USSR reinforced the victory achieved over Nazi Germany. The Red Army and the NKVD confined the 'liberated' peoples to a framework of policies favourable to the local communist parties. Stalin had been preparing for this outcome for a couple of years. Former diplomats Maxim Litvinov and Ivan Maiski, whom he had sacked when he deemed them altogether too soft on the Western Allies, continued to be charged with preparing confidential papers on the future of both Europe and the Grand Alliance.[7] Germany's defeat made it urgent to lay down practical guide-lines for the USSR's hegemony over eastern Europe. Stalin adopted a differentiated strategy. In Germany he aimed to maximise his influence in Prussia, which lay in the Soviet occupation zone, without causing diplomatic conflict with his allies. In the other countries he had greater flexibility but still had to tread carefully. Communists were few outside Yugoslavia and had only a small following. At first Stalin moved cautiously. While inserting communists into coalition ministries, he eschewed the establishment of undiluted communist dictatorships.

Stalin's foreign policy beyond the countries under the Soviet Union's direct control was complex. It never stopped evolving. He hesitated to annoy the other members of the Grand Alliance; he did not want to jeopardise his gains in eastern and east-central Europe while lacking the military capacity to match the Americans. He was also eager to get the most out of the wartime relationship with the USA. The wreckage of the war left little scope for the USSR to export grain, oil and timber to pay for imports of machinery and technology, as Stalin had done in the 1930s. An American state loan would help enormously, and for a couple of years this remained one of his prime objectives.

Simultaneously he and Molotov intended to maximise Soviet influence around the world. The blood of the Soviet wartime dead in their opinion had earned Moscow the right to assert itself just as Washington and London did. The eastern half of Europe was not the limit of their pretensions. After Mussolini's Italian Empire collapsed, Stalin instructed Molotov to press for newly liberated Libya to be declared a Soviet protectorate. Nor was he quick to withdraw the Red Army from northern Iran, where Azeris were the majority of the population. There was talk in the Kremlin of annexing the territory to Soviet Azerbaijan – the Azerbaijani communist leadership were especially keen on this.[8] Whether Stalin seriously expected the Western Allies to give way is unknown. Perhaps he was just chancing his arm. He was anyway realistic enough to see that the USSR would not dent the 'Anglo-American hegemony' in most parts of the globe until his scientists had developed bombs of the type dropped by the US Air Force on Hiroshima and Nagasaki. Like Hitler, Stalin had failed to understand the destructive potential of nuclear weapons. He intended to rectify the situation by putting Politburo member Beria in charge of the Soviet research programme. The task was to enable the USSR to catch up with the Americans without delay.

The Kremlin's other inmates were no less brutal than Stalin; they would no longer have had their posts if they had not proved themselves by his amoral standards. Yet their knowledge of conditions in the USSR made several of them doubt the desirability of pre-war policies. Stalin eventually witnessed how bad things were. In summer 1946 he went by car to the Black Sea. His caravan of vehicles made slow progress. The roads were in a terrible state and Stalin and his guests, together with hundreds of guards, stopped over in many towns. He was greeted by local communist leaders who fell over themselves to show their prowess in regenerating the country after the destruction of 1941–5. In Ukraine, where the shortage of grain was already turning into famine, Stalin was served exquisitely prepared food. Each evening his table groaned with meat, fish, vegetables and fruit. But the attempts at camouflage did not work. With his own eyes he could see at the roadsides that people were still living in holes in the ground and that wartime debris lay everywhere – and this, according to his housekeeper Valentina Istomina, made Stalin nervous.[9] If he had travelled in his railway carriage FD 3878, he would have missed seeing this.

He got over such concerns. He was not going to alter policies merely because most citizens, after a gruelling war, were hungry and destitute. He was confident that he could continue to impose a state budget that minimised attention to popular well-being. Politburo members soon understood this. If they wanted to influence the programme of party and government, they had to be wary about how they presented their ideas to the Leader – and sometimes they overestimated his level of tolerance. Several ideas were put into public discussion after 1945. Politburo members had to do this with caution if they were to survive not just politically but also in a physical sense. But they were also useless to Stalin if they failed to offer a strategic view on the USSR's difficulties. He demanded this of his subordinates; they were not allowed merely to administer existing policies. Stalin had a talent for getting them to reveal what was in their minds. This was not very difficult since he had the power of life and death over them. At the same time they knew this and yet had to pretend to him and to themselves that they did not. While Stalin remained alive, they had to play the game according to his rules.

Several of them – Beria, Malenkov and Khrushchëv – later showed an understanding that the degree of the regime's repressiveness was counter-productive. There was an economic aspect to this. When the annual accounts were drawn up, it became crystal-clear that the Gulag forced-labour system cost the state more than it earned in revenues; and monetary incentives began to be introduced to raise productivity in the camps.[10] This was hardly surprising. The wretches who worked with inadequate food and medical care in Siberia and northern Russia did not operate with the efficiency of free men and women. In order to hold them captive, moreover, a vast legion of administrators, guards, railwaymen and secretaries was required. This system of unofficial slavery was not the most cost-effective way to obtain timber, gold and uranium. But nobody could afford to say this directly to the Leader for fear of joining the slave-gangs. But the truth of the Gulag was known in the supreme ruling group.

Other parts of Stalin's programme also gnawed at the minds of several Politburo members. Malenkov was later to espouse the cause of light industry; he especially advocated the need to increase industry's commitment to the production of consumer goods. Beria was subsequently concerned that official policy continued to offend those who did not belong to the Russian nation; he also objected to the extreme controls over cultural self-expression. Khrushchëv, with his sense of the rudimentary requirements of most citizens, felt that agrarian reform was vital. About foreign policy it was even more dangerous to express an opinion; and after the initial debate about the chances of the world communist movement Stalin clamped down: it remained for leading Soviet politicians on Stalin's death – again it was Beria and Malenkov – to insist that a Third World War would be a disaster for the human race. Beneath the surface of official politics there was appreciation that something had to change. Several Politburo members understood that the rigidities of Marxism–Leninism–Stalinism after the war provided no permanent solution. Things had to change not only for the good of the members of the Politburo but also in order to conserve the power and prestige of the USSR.

While Stalin lived, however, his policies were unchallengeable. He was not completely inflexible and some wartime 'compromises' remained in place. He did not abandon the wartime understanding with the Russian Orthodox Church. Those churches which had been reopened in the war continued to function, and the Patriarch agreed to act as unofficial ambassador for the 'peace policy' of the Soviet government – and the Russian Orthodox Church avidly occupied buildings which had previously belonged to other Christian denominations.

Stalin also persisted with the ideological favour shown to the Russians in wartime. This was obvious in historical textbooks. Before 1941 it was still acceptable to show respect for those who resisted the expansion of the Russian Empire. Shamil, the Moslem cleric who fought the armies of Nicholas I and Alexander II in Dagestan and Chechnya, was given his due as an anti-tsarist hero. After the Second World War his reputation was consistently blackened. Indeed each and every figure in the pre-revolutionary past who had failed to welcome the armies of the tsars was condemned as reactionary. Russia had allegedly brought culture, enlightenment and order to its borderlands. The treatment of Shamil was a litmus test of the development of policy on the national question. So too was the visual symbolism of the urban landscape. For the octocentenary celebration of Moscow's foundation in September 1947, Stalin commissioned a statue of Prince Yuri Dolgoruki for erection on Gorki Street. Its chain-mailed muscularity was designed to induce awe at the greatness of medieval Muscovy.[11] Stalin's toast to the Russian nation on 24 May 1945 had been no fleeting fancy.

Even the limits of cultural expression were as wide as they had been in the war. In the arts and scholarship the situation remained marginally freer than before the Great Patriotic War. The composer Shostakovich and the poet Akhmatova still wrote pieces for public performance. Scholars, too, went on benefiting from a working environment which was less stringent than before the war.

The level of material provision for Soviet citizens continued to exercise the minds of Stalin and his government; they remained cognisant of the high level of expectations among the peoples of the USSR once the war had been won. Initially Stalin did not plan for an economy of shortage. Although he imposed heavy control over politics, he still aimed to expand the supply of food and industrial products through the retail trade. Several governmental decrees confirmed this purpose in 1946–8.[12] There was much talk about stimulating the production and distribution of consumer goods, and it was recognised that some reorganisation of commercial structures would be needed.[13] For this to happen there also had to be an end to wartime inflation. In December 1947 party and government abruptly announced a devaluation of the ruble. The savings of citizens were automatically reduced to a tenth of what they had been. A decree was passed in the same month to terminate the ration-book system: Soviet citizens had to buy what they could with the rubles in their pocket or under their mattress.[14]

The USSR was not the only state to take drastic action for post-war economic regeneration. Yet few governments behaved with so little regard for the difficulties posed for consumers. Announcements were made suddenly and without warning. Stalin had always ruled that way. He expected 'the people' to accept docilely what he demanded. Although he irritated millions of citizens by devaluing the currency, he scarcely induced their ruination: the reason they had had so much money was that they could not find the goods to spend it on. His own savings were depreciated by the devaluation decree; but he had never been a materialistic man. Unopened pay-packets were found at his Blizhnyaya dacha when he died. What mattered to Stalin was not wealth but power. In any case he and his close subordinates were protected by the network of special shops from any untoward financial effects. Stalin had for a long time intimidated those reporting to him into playing down news of hardship. It was in 1947 that a terrible famine occurred across Ukraine. Khrushchëv had to deal with it as party boss in Kiev. While appealing to the Kremlin for assistance, he was careful lest Stalin should conclude that he had gone soft. Stalin therefore did not hear how bad the situation was.[15]

Yet even Khrushchëv's cautious words got him into trouble: 'Stalin sent me the rudest, most insulting telegram which said I was a suspect person: I was writing memoranda to try and show that Ukraine could not fulfil its state procurement [quotas], and I was requesting an outrageous amount of ration-cards to feed people.'[16] Stalin was not responsible for the drought that had ruined the 1946 harvest. But he remained the founder and director of the collective-farm system and his ferocious rejection of the request for aid to Ukraine makes him culpable for the deaths of millions of people in the famine of the late 1940s. Cases of cannibalism occurred. The experience seared itself into Khrushchëv's consciousness. He had come to understand the idiotic brutality of the Soviet economic order. Stalin was incapable of such a reaction. Like Lenin, he hated any sign of what he regarded as sentimentality; and both Lenin and Stalin tended in the first instance to assume that any reports of rural hardship were the product of peasants tricking urban authorities into indulging them.[17]

Not that Stalin and his central subordinates controlled everything. They concentrated on restoring authority over those sectors of state and society where authority had prevailed before 1941. Sometimes, but not always, this involved a shift in the content of policy. Yet this hardly makes it sensible to call this a period of 'high Stalinism' even though several Western scholars have liked to claim that the post-war years were unique. In fact Stalin's actions were mostly reactionary: he was reverting the Soviet order to the template he had more or less imposed before Operation Barbarossa. Yet society in Russia and its borderlands had never been completely regulated by the Kremlin. The old amalgam of regimentation and chaos persisted. Several groups in society were more overt in asserting their wishes than before the war. Most obvious, of course, were the partisans in the newly annexed territories in the west of the USSR. The Gulag too was no longer quiescent. The arrest of Ukrainian and Baltic dissenters introduced into the labour camps an intransigent element, sustained by religious faith and national pride, which had hardly been noticed in the Gulag complex before the war.

If a totalitarian state could not stop protests and strikes in its detention zones, something was wrong – and several of the Kremlin leaders were aware of this even if they kept the knowledge secret from Stalin. The unrest in the Gulag happened despite the intensification of repressive campaigns. Even in the more established parts of the USSR there were aspects of belief and behaviour which remained stubbornly unamenable to political manipulation. The coercive agencies in the war had concentrated their efforts on eradicating defeatism. Yet many people, especially youngsters, simply wanted to get on with their personal lives without the state's interference. Western music and, in some instances, even Western clothes fashions were adopted by young people.[18] The alienation of Muscovite students in particular was pronounced. And skilled workers also refused to be gulled by official propaganda; they knew their value to industrial enterprises which were under instructions to raise production sharply. Labour discipline, no longer backed by legal sanctions as severe as in the pre-war years, was seldom enforceable.

It was dangerous to present Stalin with reports on phenomena which he might blame on the person who was reporting. His associates censored themselves in communication with him.[19] He ruled through the institutions and appointees he himself had put in place. He never visited a factory, farm or shop in the post-war years (apart from a trip to a market in Sukhum; this had also been no different in the 1930s).[20] He received no visitors from outside the political milieu except for the brief sojourn of his childhood friends at one of his Black Sea dachas.[21] He experienced the USSR and the world communist movement on paper in the form of decrees, reports and denunciations. He could not know everything.

Stalin's inability to eradicate apathy, chaos and disobedience continued. His was the primary responsibility for the decision to deliver a blow against popular aspirations to some permanent relaxation of the Soviet order. Assumptions that changes would be put in hand at the end of the war were crudely disappointed. The question arises of whether the life of workers, kolkhozniks and administrators would have been radically different if Stalin had died at the moment of military victory. The answer can only be guessed at, but it is difficult to see how such a regime could have remained in power if it had failed to continue to apply severe repression. The ruin of cities, villages and whole economic sectors placed a vast burden on the state budget. Things were made worse by security concerns. The race to develop nuclear weaponry was bound to be extremely costly for the Soviet Union. Although friendly diplomatic relations with the USA and even American financial assistance could have alleviated the situation, the essential problem would have remained: society below the level of the central and local elites was therefore likely to be asked to shoulder the burden in the form of a delay in improving living conditions – and without the Gulag and the security police agencies this was a situation which could not have been maintained.[22]

Stalin's associates needed to conserve the powers of repression if they wanted to survive. The moderation of many policies was not excluded by this; and in fact his associates quietly suggested a number of modifications to economic, national and foreign policy. But none of them was a procedural democrat or an advocate of a market economy. Stalin had them in personal thrall. But it was not just his terrifying nature which stopped radical reform from being attempted. The Soviet order had its own internal imperatives. It had never been as adaptive as capitalist societies in the West, and the conditions after the Second World War rendered its inflexibilities stronger than ever. Stalinism would outlast Stalin.

46. THE OUTBREAK OF THE COLD WAR

The USSR's relationship with the world of capitalism was always volatile. The October 1917 Revolution shook the global order like an earthquake and the tremors were registered in the politics and diplomacy of both the Bolsheviks and their enemies in the West. No government thought the rivalry could forever remain unresolved. The axiom was that permanent coexistence was impossible and that one side or the other would eventually triumph. Yet the communist leaders concurred that direct military conflict should be avoided. Truman, Attlee and Stalin agreed on this without the need to discuss it; and when Stalin was asked his opinion by visiting foreign communists, he insisted that the Third World War which he and they as Marxist–Leninists regarded as inevitable was not going to happen. He thought his will and judgement superior to those of his counterparts in the West. He also believed in the greater internal strength of the communist order in a potential conflict with capitalist states. Communism had spread fast in Europe and Asia. Nuclear-weapon technology had been a sector of Soviet weakness but he was doing something about this. He had allocated the resources to acquire parity for his armed forces and aimed to catch up with the USA in military power.

The USSR's agreements with Western governments, from the commercial treaties of 1921 onwards, had been regarded by everyone on both sides as suspendable. Subsequent events confirmed this approach. In 1924 the United Kingdom tore up the treaty signed with Sovnarkom in 1921. The Japanese in 1938 and the Germans in 1941 went to war with the USSR despite earlier concordats. The coalition which Stalin formed with the United Kingdom and the USA in the Second World War had from the start been characterised by strain and suspicion. The leaders of the Grand Alliance had lived on their nerves. Only their common anti-Nazi interest had kept them on speaking terms. Communism and capitalism dealt uneasily with each other.

Yet this does not explain why the coalition broke down when and in the way it did. Stalin had spent the war ranting about the perfidy of his foreign partners; and Truman had few illusions about the ruthless ambitions of the Soviet leader. It was not just a question of clashing ideologies and personalities. The states of the Grand Alliance had divergent interests. The United Kingdom wished to preserve its empire intact while the USSR and the USA aspired to have it dismantled. The USA aimed at hegemony in Europe and the Far East: this was bound to agitate the Soviet political leadership after the protracted struggle against Germany and Japan. Yet the USSR had brought eastern and east-central Europe under its direct dominion despite the Grand Alliance's promise to liberate all nations from wartime subjugation. The fact that the Soviet economy, apart from its armaments sector, was in ruins strengthened Truman's confidence. The USA flexed the muscles of its financial and industrial might around the globe, and until 1949 the USA had atomic weapons and the USSR had none. This was a dangerous world situation. The practical moves of Stalin and Truman had to be calculated with care if military conflict was to be avoided.

Stalin was given an inkling of future difficulty even as the Germans were going down to defeat. Lend–Lease aid was stopped without warning on 8 May 1945, and the ships on the high seas were ordered back to the USA. The USSR had served its military purpose for the Americans; it now had to show it deserved any further assistance. American actions in western Europe conformed to this pattern. Both overt and clandestine support was given to political groups in France and Italy dedicated to undermining the growth of communist influence. A blind eye was turned to General Franco's advocacy of Hitler's cause as Spain too was brought under American hegemony. The British assisted royalist forces in Greece in crushing the large armed units of communists. The Truman administration pursued the military and economic interests of American capitalism on every continent. Air force bases were acquired in Africa and Asia.[1] Pro-Washington dictatorships were helped to power in Central and South America. The British and Americans intervened in the Middle East to guarantee their access to cheap oil and petrol. American general Douglas MacArthur was given plenipotentiary authority in Japan until such time as he could establish a state in line with the USA's political orientation.

The British Empire was in decline, and Stalin cannot have been surprised that the Americans were eager to expand their political and military hegemony over the maximum number of countries. As the United Kingdom's weakness was exposed, world politics became a contest between the USSR and the USA. Stalin had to manoeuvre carefully. Negotiations to found the United Nations Organisation had begun in San Francisco in April 1945. Stalin wished to have the USSR made a member of the Security Council and to secure a right of veto within it. Molotov negotiated on Stalin's orders. It was not a congenial experience as the Americans were no longer worried about the sensitivities of their Soviet interlocutors.[2]

The policies of the USSR became clearer in 1946. By then Churchill was out of office but his speech at Fulton, Missouri on 5 March rejected any attempt at conciliation. Churchill spoke of an 'iron curtain' drawn down the centre of Europe by Stalin and the communist leadership. Concessions to the USSR should cease. Churchill was summarising what Truman had said in piecemeal fashion since the outset of his Presidency. But this left a lacuna in Anglo-American strategic thought. It was filled by a telegram sent from Moscow by American diplomat George Kennan on 22 February. Kennan argued that the Western Allies should seek to 'contain' their global adversary rather than use military force. By their further development of nuclear weapons the Americans also could deter the USSR from adventurism and aggression. This was the core of American state doctrine over succeeding years, and any member of the USA's leadership who challenged it was removed. President Truman became ever more assertive in his diplomatic dealings. The British were helpmates rather than decision-makers, but they approved the new orientation; and Stalin, regularly supplied with information from his intelligence agencies, knew that limits had been placed on his activity in global affairs if he wished to avoid armed confrontation with a stronger enemy.

The year 1947 pivoted the Grand Alliance towards open disharmony. Several events increased the mutual antipathy. Every crisis strengthened the belief of leading politicians, including Truman and Stalin, that their chronic suspicion of the rival power and its leader had been justified. Resumed co-operation would be difficult. The Allies lurched into the Cold War. Truman and Stalin spoke fractiously about each other. Each felt empowered by military victory to enhance his state's influence in the world and to ensure that his rival – whether in Washington or in Moscow – did not get away with anything.

The USSR had gone on flexing its muscles after the Second World War without getting into a fight. Avoidance of a Third World War was the supreme immediate priority. Little was done in the Far East. Stalin accepted that the Americans had unchallengeable control of Japan and its political and economic development; he contented himself with possession of the Kurile islands obtained in accord with the Yalta agreements. He also concluded that prolonged occupation of northern Iran by the Red Army would endanger relations with the USA. The Western Allies repeatedly demanded the withdrawal of Soviet armed forces, and in April 1947 Stalin at last acceded to this. The Iranian government proceeded to suppress separatist movements in the north of its country. But the Soviet Army pulled back, never to return. Stalin simultaneously tried to put pressure on Turkey for territorial concessions. In this instance President Truman's robust defence of Turkish sovereignty saved the situation from developing into an emergency. Stalin's chimerical ambitions to turn Libya into a protectorate of the USSR were also quietly abandoned after British Foreign Secretary Ernest Bevin flew into a rage in negotiations with Soviet diplomats.[3]

The serious trouble started on 5 June 1947 when US Secretary of State George Marshall announced economic assistance to European countries which had suffered from Nazi aggression. The offer was also available to the USSR, and Stalin's original scheme had been for representatives of Bulgaria and Romania to attend the subsequent exploratory gathering in Paris with the purpose of disrupting it; but he had second thoughts, becoming convinced that a 'Western block against the Soviet Union' was being organised.[4] Marshall intended to undermine Soviet hegemony over the countries of eastern Europe by providing them with American financial help. The Ministry of External Affairs in Moscow explored whether funds really would be released to the USSR for its post-war recovery. The answer was that the Americans made open markets the condition for aid. As Truman and Marshall knew, there was never any chance that Stalin and his associates would accept such restrictions. The Marshall Plan was tied to the geopolitical objectives of the USA and these included the drastic reduction of the USSR's power in Europe. Even Jeno Varga, who had suggested the possibility of a parliamentary road to communism in Europe, saw the Marshall Plan as a dagger pointed at Moscow.[5] Moderation in Soviet foreign policy came to a halt. Thus began the Cold War, so called because it never involved direct military conflict between the USSR and the USA.

Having conquered eastern Europe, Stalin would not relinquish his gains. He held to a traditional view of security based on buffer states. This was an approach soon to be made obsolete by long-range bombers and nuclear missiles. It also overlooked the huge onus taken upon itself by the USSR in occupying these countries and becoming responsible for

their internal affairs. Most communist leaders in eastern Europe anticipated Stalin's reaction and broke off negotiations with the Americans in
Paris.

Yet the Czechoslovak government, which included communist
ministers, was eager to go to Paris to discuss Marshall's proposals. A
delegation led by Klement Gottwald was received in Moscow on 10 July
1947. Stalin was furious:[6]

> We were astonished that you had decided to participate in that
> gathering. For us this question is a question about the friendship of
> the Soviet Union with the Czechoslovak republic. Whether you
> wish it or not, you are objectively helping to isolate the Soviet
> Union. You can see what's happening. All the countries which have
> friendly relations with us are refraining from participation in this
> gathering whereas Czechoslovakia, which also has friendly relations
> with us, is participating.

Communist leader Gottwald left his liberal Foreign Minister Tomáš
Masaryk to twist in the wind. Masaryk asked Stalin to bear in mind
Czechoslovak industry's dependence on the West; he added that the
Poles had wished to go to Paris. But Stalin was unmoved. Resistance
crumbled, and Masaryk begged Stalin and Molotov to help the Czechoslovaks to formulate the text of their withdrawal from participation. Stalin
simply advised him to copy the Bulgarian model. Masaryk salvaged a
scrap of national pride by pointing out that the government would not
be meeting until the following evening; but the entire delegation ended
by thanking Stalin and Molotov for the 'necessary pieces of advice'.[7]

Stalin was flinging mud in the face of the USA, and the world was
his witness. Overnight it became easier for Truman to get his way with
governments which had doubts about the hardening American line
towards the USSR; he was also helped in his campaign to convince the
US Congress that financial aid at least to western Europe lay among
the objective interests of the USA. Stalin had been pushed to the point
of strategic decision. He confronted a definite challenge: the American
President wanted to pull the greatest possible number of European states
under his country's hegemony and to bring benefit to its industrial and
commercial corporations. The USSR's economy remained in a desperate
plight and the Americans had no objective incentive to facilitate its
recovery. Even so, Stalin could have handled the situation with more
finesse. Instead of tossing the terms back in Truman's face, he could
have drawn out the negotiations and proved to the world that the

apparent altruism of the Marshall Plan concealed American self-interest. But Stalin had made up his mind. He never again met Truman after Potsdam and did not seek to. Nor could he be bothered with negotiating with Western diplomats. The USA had thrown down the gauntlet and he would pick it up.

Even so, the Americans declined to go further in trying to detach eastern Europe from the USSR. The policy of containment was interpreted as involving acceptance that such countries fell within the zone of Soviet influence. The chance of liberating these countries had been at its highest in 1945. Western public opinion could be manipulated, but only to a certain extent two years later. The Americans and the British had been taught to respect 'Uncle Joe'; they had also been told that the war would be over when Germany and Japan had been defeated. It would not have been easy to induce British or American soldiers to start fighting in mid-1947.

Soviet retaliation against the American initiative was not long in coming. In September 1947 a conference of communist parties was convoked at Sklarska Poręba in Poland. Stalin did not deign to attend. Having ordered the creation of a tight system of co-ordination by telephone and telegram, he sent Zhdanov on his behalf. Zhdanov had been well briefed and contacted Moscow whenever anything unpredicted arose. The organisational objective was to form an Informational Bureau (or Cominform) to co-ordinate communist activity in the countries of eastern Europe as well as in Italy and France. As relations worsened with the USA, Stalin withdrew permission for a diversity of national transitions to communism. The call was made for an acceleration of communisation in eastern Europe; and, in western Europe, the French and Italian parties were reprimanded for their reluctance to drop their parliamentary orientation (even though it had been Stalin who had instigated it!). The completion of a rigid communist order was the goal to the east of the Elbe. Stalin also had his ambitions elsewhere. He intended to disrupt 'Anglo-American' hegemony in western Europe by the sole political means to hand: communist party militancy.[8]

Yet blatant American interference in the Italian elections through subsidies to the Christian-Democratic Party proved effective. In the two halves of Europe the armed camps of former allies confronted each other. Ambiguity, however, remained over Germany, where the USA, the USSR, the United Kingdom and France had occupying forces in their respective zones. Each of these powers also controlled its own sector in Berlin, which lay within the USSR's zone.

Stalin, annoyed and frustrated by developments, decided to probe Western resolve at an early opportunity. Soviet representatives proposed the formation of a united German government. The condition for this would be Germany's demilitarisation. Stalin seemed to want either a communist or a neutral Germany as his further aim. He also aspired to an increase in reparations to the USSR. On 24 June 1948 Stalin started a blockade of the American, British and French zones of the city. Unable to secure the kind of Germany he found acceptable, he opted to cut off the eastern zone under the USSR's occupation from the rest of the country. The Soviet Army patrolled the border. Confrontation was inevitable, but Stalin gambled on the Western Allies being unwilling to risk war. He miscalculated. The Americans and British flew in supplies to their sectors of Berlin, and it was Stalin himself who had to decide whether to begin military hostility. The Berlin airlift continued through to May 1949. Stalin gave up. Western resolve had been tested and found to be too firm. Relations between the USSR and the USA deteriorated. A Western initiative inaugurated the Federal Republic of Germany in September 1949. In October the Kremlin sanctioned the German Democratic Republic's creation in response.

This was a turbulent environment. Like everyone else, Stalin was surprised by particular events and situations, and much of his time was spent on reacting to successive emergencies. Yet nothing happened which challenged his general operational assumptions about global politics. He did not expect favours from the Americans, and the Marshall Plan confirmed his darkest suspicions. The phrase used by Zhdanov at the founding Cominform Conference about the existence of 'two camps' in perpetual, unavoidable competition appeared prophetic. First to form an overt military alliance was the capitalist camp. The North Atlantic Treaty Organisation (NATO) came into existence in April 1949. Under the USA's leadership it included the United Kingdom, France, Italy, Canada, Belgium, Holland, Portugal, Denmark, Norway, Iceland and Luxemburg. Greece and Turkey joined three years later and the Federal Republic of Germany in 1955. Most countries in North America and western Europe adhered to NATO: it was a mighty and coherent alliance with the obvious but unstated purpose of seeing off any Soviet attack; and for all its European members its great virtue lay in binding the American government and military forces into their endeavour to keep the Soviet Army behind the Iron Curtain. In 1936 there had been an Anti-Comintern Pact; in 1949 an Anti-Cominform Pact had been established in all but name.

Western security concerns were increased on 29 August 1949 when Soviet scientists successfully tested their own A-bomb. Beria had used the ebullient Igor Kurchatov as the technical chief of the project. Kurchatov assembled a team of capable physicists. Soviet intelligence agencies handed over secret material taken by their agents from the Americans, and this hastened progress. The quest for uranium was facilitated by the consignment of hundreds of thousands of repatriated POWs to the mines in Siberia. Few survived the experience. By mid-1949 the USSR, from its own mines as well as from deposits in Czechoslovakia, had acquired sufficient plutonium and uranium-235 to go ahead with the construction of a Soviet bomb.[9]

Stalin took an active interest. The main figures in the research project were called before him in a lengthy meeting. Each had to report on his progress, and Stalin fired questions at them. Mikhail Pervukhin had to explain to him the difference between heavy water and ordinary water.[10] He told Stalin what he needed to know. Not having studied physics at the Tiflis Spiritual Seminary, the Leader started with only the most rudimentary grasp of the scientific principles. His ignorance had earlier been downright dangerous for the scientists. Having recently re-read Lenin's *Materialism and Empiriocriticism*, he was convinced that space and time were absolute, unchallengeable concepts in all human endeavours. (This contrasted with his dismissal of the controversy over the same book before the First World War as 'a storm in a teacup'.)[11] Einsteinian physics were therefore to be regarded as a bourgeois mystification. The problem was that such physics were crucial to the completion of the A-bomb project. Beria, caught between wanting to appear as Stalin's ideological apostle and wishing to produce an A-bomb for him, decided he needed clearance from the Boss for the Soviet physicists to use Einstein's equations. Stalin, ever the pragmatist in matters of power, gave his jovial assent: 'Leave them in peace. We can always shoot them later.'[12]

Kurchatov and his team pulled it off in the desert outside Semipalatinsk in Kazakhstan – and to his amazement, as the mushroom cloud gathered on the horizon, he was hugged by Beria. Such a display of emotion was unprecedented. But Beria, who had spent the past four years threatening Kurchatov, had lived under the same shadow cast by Stalin. A failed bomb test could have led to his death sentence. Instead he could report success to the Kremlin. Stalin was also delighted. The USSR had entered the portals of the world's nuclear-powers elite, and

Stalin himself could come to any future diplomatic negotiations as the equal of the American and British leaders.

This in turn opened him to persuasion that the USSR should assume an assertive posture in world politics. There were other reasons for his ebullience. Not only had the communist subjugation of eastern Europe occurred without serious setbacks but also the Chinese Communist Party had seized power in Beijing in October 1949. Communism had acquired possession of a third of the world's land surface. Mao Tse-tung had won his victory in the teeth of Stalin's reluctance to support him against the nationalist Chiang Kai-shek. The revolutionary outcome in China did not soften Stalin's attitude to Mao: he expected the new communist state to submit itself to the higher interest of world communism as delineated by Moscow. In practice this meant accepting the priority of Soviet needs over Chinese ones. Stalin continued to regard it as the USSR's right to hold on to Port Arthur as a military base and to dominate Manchuria. The USSR's military superiority and its willingness to render economic assistance compelled Mao to bite his tongue when he made a lengthy visit to Moscow from December 1949. The direct talks between Mao and Stalin became tricky when Stalin made clear from the start that he would not repeal the Sino-Soviet treaty of 1945, which had been concluded at a moment of China's extreme weakness and before the communist seizure of power.[13]

Mao did not secure all the military and economic assistance he was after. Stalin assured him that China was not yet threatened by foreign powers: 'Japan is still not back on its feet and is therefore not ready for war.'[14] As usual he added that the USA was in no mood for a big war. Stalin, hoping to distract his Chinese comrade with a campaign which would not upset the Soviet–American relationship, advised that Beijing should confine itself to conquering Taiwan and Tibet. Mao's frustration grew. Having taken power in China only weeks before, he was almost under house arrest at a government dacha outside Moscow as Stalin and he conferred. But then on 22 January 1950 Stalin suddenly reversed his position and told Mao of his willingness to sign a new Sino-Soviet treaty.

The question arises as to who or what was to blame for the descent into the Cold War. President Truman played his part. His language was hostile to the USSR and communism. The Marshall Plan in particular was framed in such a way as to make it well nigh inconceivable that Stalin would not take offence. Yet at the start even Molotov was inclined to accept the aid.[15] Truman was determined to promote the American economic cause in the world; he also had a genuine concern about the oppression which his predecessor's deals with Stalin had spread across eastern Europe. The USA had an economy undamaged by war and a society which, apart from its soldiers, had no direct experience of it. Its state and people were committed to the economics of the market. Its economic interest groups sought access to every country of the world. It was a military power greater than any rival. The USA did not threaten to declare war on the USSR, but it acted to maximise its hegemony over world politics and the result was a set of tensions which could always spill over into diplomatic confrontation or even a Third World War.

There remained the speculation that, if the wartime negotiations had demanded more of Stalin, the situation might not have arisen; yet not only Roosevelt but also Churchill had made commitments to him which were difficult to overturn unless the Anglo-Americans were willing to break with Stalin entirely. Even Churchill was averse to a military incursion over the agreed boundaries between the hegemonic zones of the USSR and its Western allies. Churchill had a long memory. At the end of the First World War many socialist and labour militants had been active in opposing military intervention in Soviet Russia after the Civil War. But from 1945 it was Attlee who governed the United Kingdom, and no public figure of importance advocated an incursion over the River Elbe. Truman and Attlee might well have had trouble mobilising popular support for any such action. The troops of the USA and the UK had been trained to regard the Soviet forces as allies. Civilians had heard the same propaganda. Germany and Japan had been identified as the only enemies and the task of orientating public opinion towards active military measures would have been extremely difficult. The chance had been lost at Yalta, Tehran and Potsdam – and even at those three Allied Conferences it would have been a tricky feat to pull off without trouble at home.

The USA and USSR were great powers which assumed that permanent unrivalrous coexistence was an implausible prospect. Stalin, moreover, was more active than Truman in making things worse. He grabbed territory. He imposed communist regimes. He anyway took it for granted that clashes with 'world capitalism' were inevitable. Indeed he was mentally more ready for war than were the American and British leaders. The Cold War was not unavoidable but it was very likely. The surprise is that it did not become the Hot War.

47. SUBJUGATING EASTERN EUROPE

There was little interference with the USSR's actions in Soviet-occupied eastern Europe after the Second World War. Truman and Attlee grumbled but they did not act far outside the scope of the agreements at Tehran, Yalta and Potsdam. The tacit deal remained in place that the USSR could get on with its military occupation and political domination while the USA, the United Kingdom and France imposed their control in the West. Stalin had small acquaintance with his vast zone. He had been to Kraków, Berlin and Vienna on his trip before the First World War, but his subsequent interest had been limited to the internal affairs of the Comintern. Yet he was a fast learner when events drove the need for knowledge. Already in the Second World War, as Hitler occupied countries near the USSR, Stalin took account of the situation in consultation with Dimitrov and Litvinov. He also recognised that unless communist parties adopted a more obviously national image they would never succeed in appealing to their electorates. He had planned in 1941 to abolish the Comintern. In 1943 this aim was fulfilled. Behind the scenes, though, the International Department of the Party Central Committee Secretariat commanded the foreign communist parties everywhere. Once given, orders were obeyed.

Stalin's concern with countries of the region grew as the end of the war approached. In Moscow he received representatives of the communist parties. In January 1945 he discussed economic aid, military dispositions and even the official language, frontiers and foreign policy of the Yugoslav state with Tito's emissaries. Informed of their desire to form a huge federation with Bulgaria and Albania, he urged caution. Continually he cajoled the Yugoslav leaders, who were more cocksure than others in eastern Europe, to ask his opinion in advance of large-scale action.[1]

Regular reports and requests came to Moscow after the war, and Stalin went on meeting communist visitors. His ability to issue impromptu decisions was extraordinary. In 1946 he had even set the timing of the following year's elections in Poland.[2] Polish President

Bolesław Bierut prefaced his discussion with the following obeisance: 'We've journeyed to you, comrade Stalin, as our great friend in order to report our consideration on the course of events in Poland and check on the correctness of our evaluation of the political situation in the country.'[3] His control over eastern Europe was facilitated by the consolidation of communism's organisational network across the region with the protection of the Soviet armed forces. Years of subordination, enforced by terror, ensured compliance. Communist leaders, with the exception of the Yugoslavs and perhaps the Czechs, also knew how weak their support was in their countries: dependency on the USSR's military power was crucial for their survival. New police agencies were set up on the Soviet model, and Moscow infiltrated and controlled them. Soviet diplomats, security officials and commanders monitored eastern Europe as if it was the outer empire of the USSR.

Problems awaited the Kremlin across the region. Communists in eastern Europe had suffered persecution before and during the Second World War. Their organisations were frail, their members few. Most of their leaders were popularly regarded as Soviet stooges. Communism was envisaged as a Russian pestilence, and the Comintern's dissolution had not dispelled this impression. It did not help the cause of national communists that the USSR seized industrial assets as war reparations in Germany, Hungary, Romania and Slovakia. The presence of the Soviet security police and the Red Army – as well as the continuing gross misbehaviour of Soviet troops – exacerbated the situation. A further problem for communist parties was the high proportion of Jewish comrades in their leaderships. Anti-semitism in eastern Europe was not a Nazi confection, and Jews in the communist leaderships bent over backwards to avoid appearing to favour Jewish people: indeed they often instigated repression against Jewish groups.[4] Yet Stalin had no patience with the difficulties experienced by the foreign communist parties. He had set down a political line; and if problems arose, he expected Molotov or some other subordinate to resolve them.

Stalin and his underlings in the USSR and eastern Europe did not lack self-assurance. History helped them. While installing non-democratic political systems in eastern Europe, they proceeded in accordance with local tradition in most cases. Nearly all countries in the region had possessed authoritarian governments, even dictatorships, between the world wars. Czechoslovakia had been the exception; all the rest, even if they started with a democratic system after the First World War, had succumbed to harsh forms of rule.[5] It worked to the Kremlin's advantage that these countries had yet to remove the social and economic obstacles to meritocratic progress. Reactionary army corps and wealthy quasi-feudal landlords had held enormous power. Popular educational advance had been fitful. The Christian clergy lacked openness to 'progressive' ideas about social change. Poverty was widespread. Foreign capital investment had always been low and the Nazi occupation had brought about a further degradation in conditions. By releasing eastern Europe from the chains of this past, communist administrations could count on a degree of popular consent. Industrial nationalisation and educational expansion were widely welcomed. The possibilities of promotion at work for those who belonged to the lower social orders were eagerly greeted.

Thus there were fewer obstacles to communisation in eastern Europe than would have been the case in western Europe. Stalin was assured of finding support east of the River Elbe even though communist parties had until recently been fragile in the region. The assumption in the Kremlin was that, once the reform process got under way, communisation would develop a momentum of its own.

The communists in Yugoslavia, having won their civil war with little assistance from Moscow, shared power with no other party and encouraged the Albanian communists to behave similarly. The process developed slowly elsewhere. Monarchs were removed in Romania and Bulgaria, and in all the states of the region there was an insistence on the inclusion of communists in government; but in most cases the cabinets were coalitional. Poland was a sore spot. The Provisional Government set up by Stalin grudgingly accepted members from the London-based government-in-exile; but the communists continued to harass all its rivals. Stanisław Mikołajczyk's Peasant Party was constantly persecuted. Elections were held elsewhere with considerable resort to malpractices which allowed communists to do better. Communists ruled Romania under Petru Groza. In Hungary Stalin faced greater difficulty. The elections of November 1945 had returned a huge anti-communist majority headed by the Smallholders' Party. Communists, though, held many positions of power and, supported by the Soviet occupying forces, conducted arrests. Czechoslovakia was easier. President Beneš, a liberal, advocated friendly relations with the USSR, and at the 1946 elections the communists emerged as the largest single party with 38 per cent of the vote. Communist leader Klement Gottwald became Prime Minister.

Yet the events of 1947 – the Marshall Plan and the First Conference of the Cominform – changed the whole atmosphere. The Cold War broke out in its most intense form. The east European communist parties discovered how things had been transformed at the First Cominform Conference at Sklarska Poręba in Polish Silesia. Malenkov was sent as Stalin's chief representative, and gave a tedious introductory speech proclaiming that a million copies of the official biography of Stalin had been printed since the war.[6] Zhdanov also attended. He and Malenkov functioned as Stalin's mouth and ears at the Conference. Zhdanov made the decisive comment on behalf of the Kremlin when he stated that 'two camps' existed in global politics. One was headed by the USSR, the other by the USA. Supposedly the USSR led the world's progressive forces. The Americans had no interest in the industrial recovery of Europe; Truman aimed at nothing less than the subjugation of the continent to his country's capitalist magnates.[7] The Marshall Plan was a trick designed to achieve this objective for Wall Street; it was nothing less than a campaign to consolidate the global hegemony of the USA.[8]

The Conference proceeded with unpleasantness. The Yugoslavs complained that the Italians had not behaved with revolutionary firmness. They accused the Greeks of lacking a commitment to insurgency.[9] Obviously they acted in complicity with Moscow; Stalin was insisting on fixing the blame on the Italian and Greek parties even though they had been carrying out his orders. Malenkov and Zhdanov fulfilled his instructions to the letter. In Stalin's opinion the Marshall Plan ruined the possibility of a durable understanding with the USA, and the Americans, if they hoped to destabilise eastern Europe, would have to accept that the USSR would attempt the same in western Europe. The Cominform was not the Comintern reborn; but it embraced communist parties in countries where the threat to the desires of the Western Allies was acute: membership included not only the countries occupied by the Red Army but also Italy and France.

Stalin made the most of the available opportunities. He had demanded a daily briefing on the proceedings hundreds of miles away in Sklarska Poręba; and by sending Malenkov and Zhdanov, who were comrades but never friends and allies, he would have competing sources of information. He aimed to seize back the international initiative and disturb Washington's equanimity. A contest between the 'two camps' was declared. No word of dissent issued from the mouths of participants; fear of offending the absent Stalin was paramount. Amendments to resolutions arose mainly from changes of mind amid the Soviet leadership, and these changes needed and received Stalin's sanction. The focus was on Europe. Stalin dealt with the situation without upsetting the status quo elsewhere in the world. This was why he had curtly rejected the request of the Chinese communist leaders to attend. The purpose of the Cominform Conference was to respond to the challenge thrown down by the Marshall Plan. Having proceeded carefully in the first couple of years after the victory over Nazism, Stalin indicated to communists in western and eastern Europe that a more militant programme had to be adopted.

Although he had succeeded in his task with Yugoslav assistance, Yugoslavia troubled him within months of the First Conference. Tito would not limit himself to his country's affairs. He badgered Stalin for aid to give to the Greek communists in their civil war against the monarchists (who were abundantly supplied and militarily reinforced by the British); he also agitated for the creation of a Balkan federal state which he evidently expected to dominate. He demanded a more rapid transition to communist policies across eastern Europe than Stalin thought desirable. Stalin decided to expel him from the Cominform and to advertise his fate as a warning to those communists in eastern Europe tempted to show similar truculence. Stalin, using Molotov and Zhdanov as his spokesmen, started the anti-Tito campaign in earnest in March 1948. Yugoslav communists were accused of adventurism, regional overassertiveness and a deviation from Marxist–Leninist principles. Stalin also rebuked Tito for poking his nose into politics in Austria, where the Soviet Army was among the occupying powers.[10]

The hardened line was expressed in an increase in communist political militancy across the region. Polish elections were held to the accompaniment of intimidation and electoral fraud. Bolesław Bierut became President and the comprehensive communisation of the country proceeded. Władysław Gomułka, the Party General Secretary, was judged too resistant to Stalin's demands for more rapid installation of Soviet-style economic and social policies and was arrested as a Titoist. The communists absorbed the other socialist parties to form the Polish United Workers' Party. In Hungary the Smallholders' Party leaders were arrested and in 1947 fraudulent elections brought the communists to power. The Social-Democrats were eliminated by forcing them to merge with the communists in the Hungarian Working People's Party. In Czechoslovakia the communists manipulated the police to such an extent that the non-communists resigned from the government. Fresh elections were held and the communists, facing few surviving rivals, won an overwhelming victory. Beneš gave way to Gottwald as President in June 1948. In Bulgaria the Agrarian Union was dissolved and its leader Nikola Petkov executed. For most purposes the communists assumed a monopoly of power. Georgi Dimitrov, Prime Minister from 1946, died in 1949 and his brother-in-law Valko Chervenkov took his place. After the Soviet–Yugoslav split the Albanian communist leadership under Enver Hoxha aligned itself with Moscow and executed Titoist 'deviationists'.

All this took place against the background of Stalin's onslaught on the Yugoslavs. Tito's *lèse-majesté* was discussed at the Second Cominform Conference, which opened in Bucharest on 19 June 1948. The Yugoslavs were not present. Stalin again declined to attend, but Zhdanov and the other delegates followed his agenda to the letter. The project of a Balkan federation was dropped; Yugoslavia was to be held within its frontiers. There was no shortage of communist leaders keen to castigate the Yugoslavs. The French representative Jacques Duclos took revenge for the accusations aimed at him at the First Conference; Palmiro Togliatti from Italy, still smarting from Tito's demand to annex Trieste to Yugoslavia, chipped in with a charge of espionage.[11] Tito had been transformed from communist hero to capitalist agent. The Yugoslav question dominated proceedings and Stalin was kept in daily touch with Zhdanov. The result was a vituperative rejection of Tito and his party. Yugoslav communists were admonished for anti-Soviet, counter-revolutionary, Trotskyist (and Bukharinist!), opportunistic, petit-bourgeois, sectarian, nationalist and counter-revolutionary tendencies. They were castigated at every turn. They were declared to have placed themselves outside the family of fraternal communist parties and therefore outside the Cominform.[12]

Not a squeak of opposition to Stalin and the Kremlin was audible from the other communist parties. As the Soviet propaganda machine got going, Tito was depicted as a fascist in communist clothing and as Europe's new Hitler. The entire Yugoslav political leadership were soon called agents of foreign intelligence services.[13] The consequences of challenging Moscow were being spelled out. An Eastern Block was formed in all but name. With the exception of Yugoslavia the countries of Europe east of the River Elbe were turned into subject entities and all were thrust into the mould of the Soviet order. Political pluralism, limited though it had been, was terminated. Economic policy too underwent change. The pace of agricultural collectivisation quickened in most countries. Across the region, indeed, communist parties increased investment in projects of heavy industry. Close commercial links were forged with the USSR. The Eastern Block aimed at autarky with economic interests as designated by Stalin being given priority. The Council for Mutual Economic Assistance (Comecon) was formed in January 1949 to control and co-ordinate developments. The whole region, including the Soviet-occupied German Democratic Republic, was locked into a single military, political and economic fortress. The Eastern Block was the outer empire of the USSR.

In return for obedience the subject countries were supplied with oil and other natural resources below world market prices. But in general the other immediate benefits flowed towards the Soviet Union, and Stalin and Molotov did not hide their pleasure. Although they had excoriated Churchill's Fulton speech on the Iron Curtain, their actions fitted the description given by the former British Prime Minister. Just as the USSR had been put into quarantine before the Second World War, eastern Europe was deliberately cut off from the West in the years after 1945.

Communism was triumphant and its leaders celebrated their victory. A technical point, however, had to be clarified. No one had yet explained how the new communist states were to be fitted into a Marxist–Leninist scheme of historical stages. Stalin had insisted that they should remain formally independent countries (and he discouraged early proposals for them to be simply annexed to the USSR as had been done with Estonia, Latvia and Lithuania). He also wanted to stress that the USSR was the originator of the world communist movement and was at a more advanced point in its progress towards communism than the newcomers. This was the kind of message he was propagating on all fronts in Moscow. Stalin laid down that Soviet, especially Russian, achievements dwarfed those of every nation on earth. In his eyes, his military and political forces were the bringers of a superior form of civilisation to a region blighted by centuries of reactionary rule. Soviet pride, indeed arrogance, was at its zenith. The countries of the Eastern Block were meant to be fraternal states. But they were to be left in no doubt that they were younger and lesser brothers. Big Brother was the USSR.

It was also a tenet of Marxism–Leninism that revolutionary socialism usually – indeed universally, according to Lenin's *The State and Revolution* – required a dictatorship of the proletariat to eradicate the vestiges of capitalism. This is what had supposedly happened in Russia with the October Revolution. Such a dictatorship could expect fanatical resistance such as had been mounted by the Whites in the Civil War. For years it had been the contention of Soviet theorists that such a result was normal. In the late 1940s, however, the situation was different. The Red Army had brought revolution to eastern Europe with its tanks and aircraft in 1944–5. The middle classes in those countries had no realistic chance of restoring capitalism, and armed uprising against Soviet armed forces would have been suicidal. The Russian historical template had not been copied.

Stalin therefore opted to designate the new communist states differently. It was the sort of task he liked in his role as the principal ideologist of world communism, and seemingly he scarcely bothered to consult his associates in the matter. He introduced a crafty nomenclature. Instead of referring to these states as proletarian dictatorships, he introduced a new term: 'people's democracies'. By this he contrived to suggest that their path to socialism would be smoother than had been possible in Russia. He did not have only the prevention of civil wars in mind. He was also implying that the range of popular consent reached beyond the working class to many large social groups. Peasants and the urban lower-middle class had suffered under many pre-war regimes across the region, and communist-inspired reforms had considerable appeal. Land was redistributed. Free universal education was provided. The social privileges of the upper orders were eliminated and avenues of promotion were cleared for young people who might otherwise have suffered discrimination. A term such as 'people's democracy' served to stress the basic commitment of communist parties to introducing reforms which were long overdue; it was a masterstroke of ideological appeal.

Yet the term involved immense deceit. Imperfect though democracy is everywhere, it usually involves the practical provision of legal and peaceful electoral procedures. Such provision occurred nowhere in eastern Europe. Even in Czechoslovakia there was political violence before the communists achieved power. In those countries where communists continued to allow other parties to serve as junior members of governing coalitions, no fundamental derogation from the desires of the local communist leadership was permitted. There was massive electoral fraud. Although the communists had some popularity, it was always highly restricted. The accurate suspicion remained that such communists had anyway to comply with instructions issuing from the Kremlin.

As the harness of repression was imposed, Stalin strove to increase the degree of dependable compliance. He did this in line with his lurch into an anti-Jewish campaign in the USSR after he fell out with the Israeli government.[14] Communist parties were constrained to select a Jew from among their midst, put him on show trial and execute him. In the Cominform countries the sordid legal processes began and no doubt many communist leaders in the region calculated that action against Jews would gain them national popularity. Yet the ultimate verdict was decided in Moscow. László Rajk in Hungary, Rudolf Slánský in Czecho-slovakia and Ana Pauker in Romania: all were found guilty without the slightest evidence that they had worked for foreign intelligence agencies. All were shot. Soviet penetration of these states meant that the Soviet embassies, the MVD (which was the successor body to the NKVD) and the Soviet Army directed high politics as they pleased. Only one country remained aloof from the scheme. In Poland the pressure from Moscow was to put Gomułka on trial as a spy and shoot him. But the rest of the Polish communist leadership, having incarcerated him, refused to apply the death sentence. Not everything in eastern Europe followed precisely the path drawn for it by Joseph Stalin.

But what was Stalin up to? Certainly he had it in for Jews from 1949, and his behaviour and discourse became ever cruder.[15] But Gomułka was a Pole without Jewish ancestry – and the leaders who put him in prison included Jews such as Bierut and Berman. Probably Stalin was also moving against nationalist tendencies in the communist leaderships of eastern Europe. Gomułka had famously stood out against accelerating the process of communisation in Poland and insisted that Polish national interests should be protected whenever he could. But Rajk in Hungary, Slánský in Czechoslovakia and Pauker in Romania could hardly be accused of indulging nationalism. Probably it is foolish to probe for a particular set of political sins detected by Stalin. If the results of the show trials in Hungary, Romania and Czechoslovakia are taken as a guide, then he surely had intended the political subjugation of eastern Europe.

The choice of victims did not much matter so long as they were leading communists. Until then the priority had been for the communist leadership in each country of the outer empire to persecute those elements of society which opposed communisation. The old elites in politics, the economy, Church and armed forces had been selected for arrest followed by forced labour or execution. The communist parties had had to infiltrate their members into all public institutions. They had to copy the basic architecture of the Soviet state and maintain close bilateral relations with Moscow. Weak in numbers in 1945, they had had to turn themselves quickly into mass parties. Their task had been to indoctrinate, recruit and govern in a situation where they knew that the bulk of their populations hated them. Yet they themselves had always been suspect to the Leader in the Kremlin. Before the end of the Second World War he thought them too doctrinaire and ordered them to try and identify themselves with the interests of their respective nations.

Then as the basic communist architecture was established, his emphasis changed and he turned towards getting them to play down the national aspects of policy. Monolithism was to prevail in the Eastern Block. Total obedience would become the guiding principle, and an example had to be made – as Stalin saw things – of a few bright early stars of the Cominform.

The process was scrutinised by Stalin in the MVD reports he received from the capitals of eastern Europe. Tortures previously reserved for non-communists were applied to Rajk, Pauker and Slánský. The beatings were horrific. The victims were promised that their lives would be spared if only they confessed in open court to the charges trumped up against them. Here the expertise of the Lubyanka came into its own. Techniques developed against Kamenev, Zinoviev, Bukharin and Pyatakov were applied in the dungeons and courtrooms of Budapest, Bucharest and Prague. Not all Western journalists had seen through the lies of the Great Terror of the late 1930s. The mistake was not repeated after the Second World War. The media in North America and western Europe denounced the trials. Stalin was rightly accused as the real criminal in the proceedings.

The frightened communist leaders maintained outward compliance, and no one knew whether the show trials might prove a prelude to wider purges. In the meantime the Eastern Block offered fealty to the October Revolution, the USSR and its leader Stalin. Cities were named after him. His works appeared in all the region's languages. His policies were accorded official reverence. Yet beneath the surface the popular resentment was immense. The religious intolerance of the communist authorities caused revulsion. The refusal to divert sufficient resources to satisfy the needs of consumers annoyed entire societies. Cultural restrictions annoyed the intelligentsia. No communist government offered the realistic prospect of change and all of them were firmly regarded as Soviet puppet ensembles. Countries in western Europe displayed intermittent irritation at the USA's hegemony; but the anger at the USSR's rule was wider and deeper in eastern Europe. Without the Soviet military occupation and the penetration by the MVD, no communist regime would have endured more than a few days by the early 1950s. Stalin had acquired the regional buffer zone he craved, but only at the price of turning those countries into a region of constant repressed hostility to his purposes. His political victory in 1945–8 was bound in the end to prove a Pyrrhic one.

48. STALINIST RULERSHIP

Putting aside his Stavka work in 1945, Stalin had picked up the routines of his social life. His options had been narrowed by his own actions. In the mid-1930s he had turned for company to the extended families of the Alliluevs and Svanidzes. But then he had killed or arrested several of them, and the survivors were in a state of psychological shock not conducive to a dinner-party atmosphere.

The Germans had shot Yakov. Vasili was an over-promoted wastrel who irritated fellow officers in the Soviet Air Force and whose drunken parties earned ostracism from his father. Svetlana brought little joy. After breaking with Kapler she set out to inveigle Beria's son Sergo into marriage – an unlikely venture since Sergo was already married. Thwarted, she instead married Grigori Morozov against Stalin's wishes in 1943. The marriage was stormy and a divorce was agreed in spring 1947. That summer Stalin invited her to spend some weeks with him at Kholodnaya Rechka by the Black Sea.[1] He had a dacha built for her down the steep slope from his own much bigger dacha.[2] Although this was a pleasant gesture, they were not going to share an abode: they were edgy in each other's company. Soon she turned her attentions to Zhdanov's son Yuri, and the couple married in 1949. Stalin showed little enthusiasm even for this unexceptionable match and declined to attend the ceremony; and although he had Svetlana's children to the dacha, his interest in them was fleeting. Svetlana and Yuri quickly fell out and separated. She exasperated Stalin. Individuals whom he wanted to integrate in his emotional world had to comply with his expectations or be cast from his affections.

Stalin remained a needy person: solitude did not suit him. He coped by joking with his dacha bodyguards. He teased his bodyguard chief Vlasik and his chief aide Poskrëbyshev. He chatted with his housekeeper Valentina Istomina; and even if the rumours of her having been his mistress remain unproven, he derived comfort from her companionship.

Yet these contacts did not make him a happy man, and his thoughts reverted to earlier periods in his life. In 1947 he wrote to a certain V. G. Solomin whom he had known in Turukhansk District in the First World War:[3]

> I still haven't forgotten you and friends from Turukhansk and indeed must never forget them. I'm sending you six thousand rubles from my [Supreme Soviet] deputy's salary. It's not so great an amount but it will still be of use to you.

On vacation at Kholodnaya Rechka in autumn 1948, he got downright nostalgic and ordered arrangements to be made to enable his Gori schoolmates to stay with him. Peter Kapanadze, M. Titvinidze and Mikhail Dzeradze were invited. There was initial embarrassment when they arrived. Kapanadze broke the ice by expressing his condolence about the death of that 'poor boy', Stalin's son Yakov. Stalin replied that he was but one parent among millions who had lost a relative. Kapanadze, who had business to attend to, left after a few days. There was much singing on subsequent evenings but Titvinidze and Dzeradze got fidgety before a week was up. Stalin asked whether they were bored. Titvinidze replied that they knew he had much work to do. Stalin took the hint. Soon they were packing their bags and, after a warm farewell, were driven home to Georgia.[4] He recognised that the past could not be restored by artificial means, and he never saw his friends again.

His Politburo subordinates were keener guests by the Black Sea or at the Blizhnyaya dacha. His dinner parties were now nearly always all-male affairs. For the politicians, an invitation signified continued favour and prolonged life. Hours of eating and drinking would usually be followed by a film-show. Stalin also still liked to sing those Church trios with Molotov and Voroshilov – accompanied by Zhdanov at the pianoforte – even though his voice had lost its strength and accuracy.[5] Otherwise, though, the dinners were raucous. As previously, he tried to get his guests hopelessly pickled. Endless toasts would be given to distinguished visitors, and Stalin, despite his demurrals, liked to receive praise.

Yet the soft potency of hospitality at the dachas could harden in an instant. As his political guests knew all too well, the Boss used occasions of hospitality to loosen tongues. Many needed little encouragement. *Pravda* editor Leonid Ilichëv never forgot the last occasion he went to Blizhnyaya. Stalin had called him at midnight, inviting him over to discuss a forthcoming article. There he came upon Beria, Malenkov and Molotov relaxing with the Leader. After an hour's work all moved to a lavishly prepared dinner table. Ilichëv was poured a glass of Georgian wine while Beria helped himself to a brandy and proposed a toast to Stalin. Prudently, because he had not yet eaten, Ilichëv swigged only half the glass and picked up a bite to eat. But Beria had spotted a breach of etiquette: 'You should drain your glass when drinking to comrade Stalin.' When Ilichëv muttered his excuse, Beria exclaimed in a tragic tone: 'Comrade Stalin, will you permit me to drink your health by draining his glass?' Stalin's eyes glistened derisively but he said nothing. Ilichëv gripped his glass tight. Beria tried to snatch it off him shouting: 'I wish to drink to comrade Stalin!' But Ilichëv held on to the glass and drank its contents.

Stalin acidulously announced that the next toast should be to Beria and asked why Ilichëv appeared reluctant to join in. The *Pravda* editor was speechless with fear. 'Well, then, comrade Ilichëv,' ventured the teasing Stalin, 'I'll drain your little glass and drink to our much respected friend Lavrenti.' Ilichëv could not afford to stay out of the toasting round and, after getting plastered, became the butt of everyone's ridicule. As light dawned, Malenkov helped him into his coat and his waiting car.

Stalin asked the Politburo members what they thought of Ilichëv as an editor. He was using tomfoolery to make a professional assessment. Beria opined that Ilichëv talked too freely; Malenkov added that a 'more solid' kind of person was needed. After sobering up, the editor found he had been sacked.[6] Yet he never blamed Stalin; he failed entirely to understand that it was by this social device that Stalin scrutinised and demeaned his minions. Those closer to Stalin were more aware of what was going on. So long as he kept the Politburo divided, his dominance was secure. Jealousy, misunderstanding and dispute were in the despot's regular tool-kit. Politburo members understood all this but could do nothing about it short of assassinating him. If ever such a thought crossed the mind of his subordinates, they swiftly dismissed it. The gamble would have been altogether too risky because he was guarded by men personally devoted to him. Even if a group of the politicians had got together in a conspiracy, there was always the probability that the others would gang up against them. Arrest would have been certain.

Stalin's actions remained brutal regardless of attempts to placate him – and he systematically undermined the position of those who had authority and prominence after the war.[7] His methods were characteristically devious. Molotov's wife Polina Zhemchuzhina was arrested in 1949. Zhemchuzhina was Jewish and Stalin objected to the warmth of her welcome for Israeli envoy Golda Meir in Moscow.[8] Molotov abstained in the Politburo vote on her expulsion from the party, but then apologised to Stalin:

> I declare that, having thought over this question, I vote for this Central Committee decision which corresponds to the interests of party and state and teaches a correct understanding of party-mindedness. Moreover, I confess my heavy guilt in not restraining Zhemchuzhina, a person close to me, from erroneous steps and links with anti-Soviet Jewish nationalists like Mikhoels.[9]

Molotov was not the only leader deprived of his marital partner. Yelena Kalinina and Tamara Khazan – wife of Andrei Andreev – had long been in labour camps (although Kalinina was released in time for her husband's death).[10]

Soviet politicians had to become masters of ingratiation. After a contretemps with Stalin in December 1945, Molotov assured him: 'I shall try by my deeds to become worthy of your trust, a trust in which every honourable Bolshevik sees not only personal trust but the party's trust which is dearer to me than my life.' His 'crude, opportunistic mistake' had consisted in allowing excerpts from Churchill's speeches to be reproduced in Moscow.[11] The matter was hardly of great importance but Stalin had refused to see it that way. 'None of us', he barked by telegram from Abkhazia, 'has the right to undertake a unilateral disposition involving alteration of our course of policy. Yet Molotov has arrogated that right to himself. Why and on what grounds? Is it not because such tricks enter his plan of work?'[12] Mikoyan too had to humble himself when Stalin was angered by decisions on grain procurement:[13]

> I and others of course can't pose questions in the way you can. I'll make every effort to learn from you how to work properly. I'll do everything to draw the necessary lessons from your severe criticism so that it will help me in future work under your fatherly leadership.

Some father! Some sons! The hands of Molotov and Mikoyan were steeped in the blood of the victims of Soviet state policies, and yet they too had to grovel. They knew they had to approach Stalin as if he were the USSR's stern but fair patriarch – and just possibly they might survive.

Stalin's paternal functions involved regular humiliation, and he was inventive in going about this. Molotov asked the Polish communist leader Jakub Berman for a waltz at one of Stalin's soirées. This infringement of manly convention pleased and suited Stalin. Molotov led the fumbling Berman while Stalin presided at the gramophone. Berman was to put a positive gloss on the episode: the waltz with Molotov had been a chance not to whisper sweet nothings to the Soviet Minister of Foreign Affairs but to mumble 'things that couldn't be said out loud'.[14] He contrived to forget how he and Molotov had been degraded for Stalin's delight.

The Leader's dominion involved chronometric regulation. Lunch was taken in the late afternoon around four or five o'clock and dinner was arranged for no earlier than nine o'clock. Stalin lived like this, and the entire ruling group had to adjust its collective body-clock to his habits.[15] Kaganovich aped him to the minute.[16] Molotov coped by taking little naps in daytime; such was his self-control that he was known to announce to his aides: 'I'm now going to take a rest in the next room for thirteen minutes.' He got up from the divan like an automaton and returned precisely thirteen minutes later.[17] All knew that the Leader worked from the early evening onwards; everyone in the upper strata of the Soviet elite had to do the same – and their families had to put up with this as the price to be paid for sustaining life and privilege. With the communisation of eastern Europe the schedule of the working day changed there too. Throughout the USSR and across to Berlin, Tirana and Sofia the leading figures in party and government dared not stray from the proximity of the phone. Stalin could ring at any time of the night through to the early hours of the morning.[18]

As Stalin's vacations in the south became longer, he resorted frequently to telegrams. He could not control the entire machinery of state in detail. This had long been obvious to him. 'I can't know everything,' he said to Ivan Kovalëv, Minister of Communications after the Second World War. 'I pay attention to disagreements and to objections, and I work out why they've arisen and what they are about.'[19] Stalin explained that his subordinates constantly kept things from him and that they always concocted a compromise behind the scenes before they reported to him. To him this was tantamount to conspiracy. Only Voznesenski stood out against such practices – and Stalin admired him for this. Stalin hated the 'insincerity' of other Politburo members. He might not detect particular cases of trickery but he knew they could trick him, and he functioned on the assumption that they were not to be trusted. The result was that Stalin, depleted in energy, looked for discrepancies between the accounts of one leader and another.[20] Any disagreement was likely to lie across fault-lines in policy. Stalin had hit upon an economical way of penetrating the secrets of what was being done in the corridors of the Kremlin.

Information also came to him by secret channels. The 'organs' – known as MGB from March 1946 and kept separate from the MVD – regularly reported on their eavesdropping of conversations among the Soviet leaders. Other Politburo members, he knew, were personally ambitious; and since they had repressed millions on his orders, he assumed they could form a violent conspiracy against him. Throughout the war with Germany he had ordered listening devices to be installed in the apartments of military personnel. The practice was applied to a growing list of civilian politicians. Even Molotov and Mikoyan were being bugged by 1950.[21]

Another of his modalities was to cultivate jealousy among his subordinates. There was constant bickering, and Stalin alone was allowed to arbitrate. He seldom allowed the highest political leaders to stay in a particular post for long. Nothing was left settled in the Kremlin: Stalin saw that job insecurity among his potential successors aided his ability to dominate them. The Moscow political carousel flung off some individuals from time to time, and the survivors regularly had to dismount and move from one seat to another. This was not enough by itself. Stalin's ill health barred him from undertaking the detailed supreme supervision he had exercised in the 1930s and during the Second World War. He needed a dependable individual to act as his eyes and ears in the leadership just as Lenin had turned to him for help in April 1922. Stalin operated with cunning. At any given time after 1945 he had a political favourite, and he sometimes hinted that the favourite was his chosen successor. But such favour was never formally bestowed, and Stalin raised up individuals only to hurl them down later. No one could grasp the levers of power in such a fashion as to acquire the capacity to supplant Stalin.

There were many levers. In 1946 the Council of Ministers (as Sovnarkom was redesignated in the same year) had forty-eight ministries and committees, each being responsible for a large sector of state functions.[22] Stalin ceased chairing it. Instead he increased the emphasis on 'curatorship'. This was a system whereby every leading associate of Stalin was assigned responsibility for a group of institutions.[23] Stalin, while wanting flux and vagueness as an ultimate safeguard of his rule, needed to assure himself that the state complied with his declared intentions. Curators were his solution. They met him frequently and never knew when he might haul them over the coals because one of their institutions had given him grounds for disquiet. Each group of institutions was the object of rivalry. Politburo members wanted to have as many as possible; this was a token of Stalin's approval as well as a grant of real power. Reduction of the number signalled that a particular associate had fallen under the shadow of disapprobation – or even of the Leader's lethal suspicion. His associates were under constant, intense pressure. Always they feared that some silly slip by one of their own subordinates might have adverse consequences for themselves. This could happen at any time because the Leader cultivated jealousies among all of them.

He also harangued them into adopting his own ferocious style of leadership: at a Party Central Committee plenum in March 1946 he declared: 'A People's Commissar must be a wild animal; he must work and take direct responsibility for work.'[24] Rulership as Stalin recommended it to People's Commissars and their curators was nothing like the model of bureaucratic life described by sociologists since Max Weber and Roberto Michels. Even in his last years, when the Soviet order was stabilised and in many ways petrified, it retained a militant and dynamic quality.

Politics were a bear-pit. Politburo members could bite and claw each other as brutally as they liked so long as they produced the outcome demanded by Stalin. Only in Stalin's presence were they constrained to moderate their behaviour. The Politburo had ceased to convene in the war and the pre-war tradition was not resumed.[25] Stalin continued to consult other leaders by informal methods. Always he liked to have leading figures in the Politburo write, telegram or telephone their assent to his preferences into policy. The Orgburo and the Secretariat – as well as the Council of Ministers and its Presidium – deliberated in his absence. The Party Congress, which had supreme formal authority over all party bodies, was not called until 1952. Stalin expected to rule through unofficial channels; he knew that disruption of institutional regularity helped to prolong his personal despotism. He could intervene with an order at his whim. He deliberately inflicted a contradictory pattern of work on his subordinates. They, unlike him, had to observe administrative procedures punctiliously. At the same time they had to obtain practical results regardless of the rulebook. The pressure was unremitting. This was the way he liked things, and the other leaders dared make no objection.

The fact that Stalin was often away from Moscow led many contemporaries (and subsequent commentators) to surmise that he was losing his grip on power. This was a misperception. On the large questions of the international, political and economic agenda there was little that escaped his adjudication; and Kremlin politicians were altogether too fearful of him to try to trick him. The framework of rulership at the centre and in the provinces also continued to exercise his attention. At the end of the war four bodies had immense importance. These were the government, the party, the security police and the army. Stalin needed all of them. He also required a situation in which no institution became so dominant as to threaten his position. The most obvious menace after the Second World War was the Red Army, and the country's military hero Georgi Zhukov immediately came under his suspicion.

No sooner had Zhukov led the victory parade on Red Square and completed Allied military negotiations with Eisenhower and Montgomery in Berlin than he was pulled out of the limelight. Stalin had plenty of compromising material against him. The security agencies reported to the Kremlin that Zhukov had stolen a trainload of loot from Germany. The list was enormous, including 3,420 silks, 323 furs, 60 gilt-framed pictures, 29 bronze statues and a grand piano.[26] This was established custom in the Red occupying forces. Practically every commander could have been arraigned on similar charges. Stalin played with the idea of a trial but in June 1946 limited himself to relegating the victor of Kursk and Berlin to the Odessa Military District (from which he was in turn dismissed in February 1947). *Pravda* steadily ceased to give prominence to the names of marshals. The police were empowered to tighten surveillance over the officer corps. Undeniably the Red Army (redesignated the Soviet Army in 1946) remained vital to the tasks of maintaining political control in the USSR and eastern Europe; it was also the recipient of budgetary largesse as Gosplan increasingly skewed central economic planning in favour of military expenditure. Yet Stalin remained eager to hold the armed forces under his civilian control.

The security agencies too came under suspicion. Here Stalin's method was different. Beria in peacetime, unlike Zhukov, was too useful to discard. Yet it suited Stalin to replace him in the leadership of the police. Beria knew too much and had too many clients whom he had appointed to office. Stalin therefore put Beria in charge of the Soviet atom-bomb project and introduced younger men to the Ministry of State Security (MGB) and to the Ministry of Internal Affairs (MVD). The appointee to the MVD in December 1945 was Sergei Kruglov, and Alexei Kuznetsov was given oversight over security matters on the Politburo's behalf; Viktor Abakumov became head of the MGB in May 1946. Although continuity of administrative leadership was desirable in theory, Stalin's higher demand was his inviolable personal power. A police chief who settled into office could pose an acute danger to him, especially since the MGB had uniformed forces which could be deployed in the normal course of events. Stalin also retained his own parallel security agency in the form of the Special Department. He relied heavily on Poskrëbyshev to keep him apprised of anything important to his interests. He also ensured that his bodyguard chief Vlasik should be beholden to himself and to no one else. This was a police state where the ruler held his police in permanent mistrust.

Yet his simultaneous reliance on the MGB and MVD was intense. Without their operational efficiency it would have been difficult to reduce the standing of the Soviet Army leadership. The Soviet budget continued to allocate massive resources to the security agencies. The Gulag still produced a crucial proportion of the country's diamonds, gold and timber, and the uranium mines were developed after 1945 with convict labour. Indeed Stalin's reliance on the security agencies grew as he reinforced policies which frustrated the hopes of most citizens for political and economic relaxation. Coercion of society was hugely important.

Yet not even Stalin projected a future for the USSR when the MGB and MVD would be the effective government. The Council of Ministers retained that function. The increasing complexity of the economy required specialist knowledge lacking in the security agencies. The Council of Ministers also sought to free itself from excessive tutelage by party bodies: a technocratic imperative was pursued by several leading political figures. This was an old discussion that had exercised Stalin's mind throughout the 1930s. As previously, he moved between two solutions. One was to give way to the ministerial lobby and put a stop to the party's interference. This was the orientation espoused especially by Georgi Malenkov. The other solution was to extend and strengthen the powers of the party, if not to the pitch of the late 1920s then at least to the detriment of the Council of Ministers in the 1940s. Among the advocates of this orientation was Andrei Zhdanov. Stalin in the early years after the Second World War leaned positively in the direction of Zhdanov. But then Zhdanov fell into disfavour, and he began to give backing to Malenkov.[27]

The arguments, from a structural viewpoint, were finely poised. Zhdanov and his friends could indicate that the Council of Ministers, left to itself, could not guarantee Stalinist ideological rectitude. Without this, the October Revolution was undermined and the rationale of the USSR's existence was ruined. The Soviet Union could not survive on technocratic impulses alone. Yet the other side of the debate had an equally strong case. The USSR functioned in a world of intense military and economic competition. If party doctrinaires held the whip hand over ministerial specialists, the country's capacity to match the USA and its capitalist allies would be reduced. Pettifogging tutelage by the party would tie one of the Soviet Union's hands behind its back in a contest which placed the West at an advantage.

Stalin did not need to be persuaded that the USSR had to become more competitive or that ideological indoctrination and political control were important. His state could do without neither government nor party; and even when he gave preference to one of them over the other, he omitted to make the choice a definitive one. The institutional tension worked to his personal advantage. By locking the two bodies in rivalry, he strengthened his position as arbiter. But this in turn meant that he had to settle for a lower level of administrative efficiency that he would otherwise have liked. He started from the premise that each institution pursued its interests at the expense of others. Persistent rivalries led to systematic obstruction. The tangled competences of government, party and police produce a thicket of bureaucratic paperwork which slowed down the processes of deliberation and implementation. Dynamism was introduced when Stalin himself gave a direct order or when he allowed an influential group of subordinates to pursue a desired initiative. But Stalin knew he could not know everything. The network of central institutional bodies worked well to maintain his despotism; it was less effective in facilitating flexible, efficient rulership. Stalin paid a price for his despotism.

49. POLICIES AND PURGES

Stalin did not confine his Kremlin political activity to manipulating the existing central structures and playing the leading politicians off against each other. There had to be constant deliberation on policies in the dangerous post-war years. The external and internal situation was always in flux and Stalin could not cope without consulting his fellow leaders. He had to accept that limits existed to what he could learn about the world by his solitary efforts. Nor could he safely rely exclusively on his own judgement. It was pragmatic to sanction a degree of diversity of opinion among his subordinates before fixing policy. Disagreements among the leaders were not only inevitable: they were also desirable. There was no secret about this; Politburo members understood how they were being manipulated. But they also saw that if they failed to take a position when affairs were under discussion, Stalin might decide that they were no longer of any use to him. At the same time they had to avoid saying anything which would annoy him. Short of assassinating him, they remained at his mercy – and his scrupulous attention to the details of his personal security made it highly unlikely that an attempt on his life would be successful.

Stalin's leading associates were in any case simultaneously occupied with the discharge of their institutional duties. Immense responsibility fell to each of them and their power and privileges were at least some compensation for the subjugated condition of their work. They were also motivated by patriotic zeal and, in some cases, ideological commitment. They had operated under Stalin's control for years. It is hardly a surprise that he continued dominating and exploiting them just as they did their own subordinates.

And so Stalin frequently shuffled the pack of the leadership as individuals won or lost his trust in the battles he permitted over policy. One leader he demoted soon after the war was Vyacheslav Molotov. Alongside Kaganovich and Mikoyan, Molotov was his longest-serving subordinate. Initially all seemed well. When Stalin went south on vacation in October 1945, he left the foursome of Molotov, Beria, Mikoyan and Malenkov in charge of the Kremlin.[1] But almost certainly he was looking for a pretext to attack Molotov, and the incident over the publication of excerpts of Churchill's speeches gave him what he wanted. Stalin may have resented Molotov's wartime fame as well as his popularity as an ethnic Russian. The British press must have made the situation still worse by speculating that Molotov was flexing his muscles to assume power.[2] The beneficiaries of the demise of Molotov were Malenkov and Beria, who in March 1946 were promoted – at a rare Party Central Committee plenum – to full membership of the Politburo, and Malenkov's name came after Stalin's in the composition of the Orgburo and Secretariat.[3] Molotov was not sacked as Minister of External Affairs until March 1949 but his time as Stalin's deputy had already ceased.

Yet although Stalin was resentful and suspicious, even he did not yet wish to get rid entirely of Molotov. When Trygve Lie, Secretary-General of the United Nations Organisation, visited Stalin in Moscow in May 1950, Stalin recalled Molotov to take an active part in the discussions.[4] Molotov's expertise was as yet too useful to discard. His formal status had been undermined but his actual influence, despite having been reduced, was still far from negligible. He remained a Politburo member and, more importantly, a regular dinner guest at Stalin's dacha. Stalin was playing a long game.

For a counterweight to Malenkov's new authority he turned to Andrei Zhdanov, who was put in charge of the Propaganda Administration in the Party Secretariat in April 1946. Zhdanov's position was consolidated by the simultaneous appointment of Alexei Kuznetsov, who worked alongside him in Leningrad, to head the Secretariat's Cadres Administration. Malenkov knew he would need to look over his own shoulder.[5] Indeed scarcely had he risen than he was cast down. In May 1946 the Politburo sacked him from the Party Secretariat. Stalin blamed him for failing to improve the quality of aircraft production. N. S. Patolichev took his place.[6] Malenkov's time in the sun had been short; like Molotov, however, he was not entirely excluded from Kremlin activity (at least after his return from an assignment in the Soviet republics of central Asia). As yet the juggling of the personnel pack after the war did not involve much beyond the obvious loss of prestige and influence. Malenkov was not arrested but his clients in party and government were removed from posts and often replaced by individuals associated with Zhdanov at the time when he had worked in Leningrad. Zhdanov's star was in the ascendant.

Exactly why Stalin had suddenly changed his preferences remains mysterious. It may be that he was genuinely annoyed by the revelations of sloppy standards in the aircraft-production industry. Perhaps, however, he was looking for any pretext whatever to keep the entire Politburo on its toes – and there was no member of the Politburo who eventually failed to incur his disapproval. Possibly Stalin's fondness for Zhdanov also played a part; Molotov recalled: 'Stalin loved Zhdanov more than all the rest.'[7] With Zhdanov at his right arm, Stalin moved against Mikoyan. This was not their first contretemps in recent years. In 1944 Stalin had 'crudely' rejected Mikoyan's proposal to give grain seeds for winter sowing to the restored collective farms of Ukraine: he accused Mikoyan of acting in 'an anti-state fashion'.[8] In December 1946 this turned into permanent hostility on Stalin's part when he accused him of supporting moves to yield to the USA's conditions for increased mutual trade.[9]

No one was safe. The Party Central Committee at Stalin's request promoted Voznesenski, a Leningrader, to the Politburo in February 1947. But Stalin at the same time elevated Nikolai Bulganin to membership: he did not want a Leningrad group to enjoy unrivalled power at the centre. Indeed he never let a new balance rest for long. Agitation of the scales was a feature of his rule, and he was most unlikely to keep Zhdanov as his permanent favourite. Molotov and Mikoyan, however, faded from view. Invited to eat with Stalin in Myussery in 1948, they were hurt by a little scene involving Poskrëbyshev. In the middle of the meal, Poskrëbyshev suddenly turned to Stalin and said: 'Comrade Stalin, while you've been on vacation down here in the south, Molotov and Mikoyan in Moscow have been organising a plot against you.'[10] The two accused understood that Stalin had stage-managed the scene; and when they protested their innocence, Stalin accepted their protestations. But they never came back into his favour. According to Mikoyan, Stalin's 'capriciousness' became evident only from the last years of the war. Mikoyan fooled himself. He failed to recall that Stalin in power had always revelled in arbitrary methods. The difference was that Mikoyan, after a career of enjoying Stalin's favour, had only recently become a victim of them.

If Mikoyan had a point, it was that Stalin from the last years of the war began to act more oddly than ever towards his entourage in social surroundings. They had been fearful of him before 1941. They had never been able to predict whether they might be picked on by him and arrested. But as victory in the war approached and Stalin resumed convivial behaviour, he enjoyed toying with their feelings. They thought this a sign of deterioration rather than the gradual extension of an existing trend. They were political survivors but unsophisticated psychologists despite their expertise in handling his moods over several decades.

Kremlin politics began to favour Malenkov and Beria when, in August 1948, Zhdanov died after lengthy treatment in a clinic. Plagued by alcoholism and cardiac disease, he had been poorly for years. But a rumour spread that his doctors had killed him. One of the clinic's medical officers, Lidia Timashuk, filed complaints about the shoddy treatment he had received. Although Stalin's office received the dossier on Zhdanov, no action followed – he may not in fact have scrutinised it at the time. He had anyway ceased to show favour towards Zhdanov for some months, and now he empowered Malenkov and Beria to follow up his death with an investigation of the political situation in Leningrad. Malenkov, a baby-faced and overweight apparatchik with a terrifying record in the Great Terror, claimed to find evidence of a conspiracy aimed at Stalin and the Kremlin. Stalin was sufficiently convinced that the Leningraders had been insubordinate in policy to sanction a massive political purge throughout the city's party and government leadership. Executions followed in 1950. Malenkov returned to the Kremlin as Stalin's favourite for the next few years.

Not all Leningrad politicians had associated themselves with Zhdanov's quest for a widening of the party's political functions. But many had done so, and the city had a reputation for harbouring those who retained a commitment to the party's importance, to ideology and to the curbing of technocratic tendencies in the vast apparatus of the Council of Ministers.[11] Lined up against Zhdanov had been Malenkov and Beria, who advocated greater latitude for the ministries to take up the task of economic regeneration. In the mandatory opaque language they stressed a preference for putting specialists in charge of affairs. Expertise rather than ideology should predominate. The division between the two sides was not entirely clear-cut. Beria and Malenkov did not advocate the party's removal from the country's administration. Both were also associated with the organs of repression even though Beria ceased being the leader of the security organs from 1945. To some extent their opinions reflected the interests of the institutions they currently headed – and this had been true also for Zhdanov. But a dispute of intrinsic importance had divided them. Stalin would have to resolve it somehow.

The Leningrad Affair was the first blood-purge of the communist political elite since 1938. The deportations, arrests and executions after the Second World War had been aimed at specific social categories, especially leading figures in public and economic life in the newly annexed Baltic states. Stalin had also put returning prisoners-of-war to forced labour in the camps of the Gulag. But the incarceration of the Leningraders was different because the victims belonged to the highest echelons of officialdom in the USSR. This time he did not bother with show trials. Hundreds of party and government functionaries were thrown into prison and shot. Among them were Politburo member Nikolai Voznesenski, Central Committee Secretary Alexei Kuznetsov, RSFSR Prime Minister Mikhail Rodionov and Leningrad Party First Secretary Pëtr Popkov.

Although Stalin did not disclose his motives, those of Malenkov and Beria may easily be guessed. They had always resented Zhdanov's authority and his political clientele in Leningrad. Soviet public life was a snake pit and Malenkov and Beria were two of its anacondas. Their opportunity to suffocate Zhdanov's associates had arrived. But why did Stalin agree? Probably he had come to resent the way that Voznesenski had spoken up against him in wartime; Voznesenski was also the only Politburo member to write a best-selling book after the war. It may well be that his growing status as a politician irritated Stalin just as Zhukov had annoyed him as a commander. At any rate when Voznesenski was discovered to have mislaid important Gosplan data, there was a chance for Malenkov, who had always hated him personally,[12] to accuse him of irresponsible and even traitorous behaviour.[13] Voznesenski was also found to have withheld information on discrepancies between state economic plans and the real economic situation. Straight-talking Voznesenski was shown to be a deceiver. Although everyone in the political leadership was deceitful, Voznesenski had had the ill luck to be discovered. To Stalin's mind, a Politburo member could commit no fouler offence than fail to be honest with him.

Others in Leningrad had also offended Stalin. The leadership in Leningrad, 'hero-city' in the Great Patriotic War, had cultivated local patriotism. Capital of the Russian Empire since the reign of Peter the Great, it remained a rival to Moscow after the transfer of the seat of government to Moscow in March 1918. Leningrad's inhabitants thought they had survived the German onslaught more by their own determination than by assistance from the Kremlin. The city was starting to seem like Russia's capital in a Soviet multinational state – the USSR – based in Moscow.

The leadership of party and government in the city had begun to give signs of overstepping the limits Stalin had approved.[14] Much as he liked to incorporate the national pride of Russians in doctrine and policy, he never lost his concern about the possible growth of nationalism among them. The Leningrad political elite failed to comprehend the rules of the situation. Kuznetsov had organised a retail fair in Leningrad for all parts of the RSFSR without the Kremlin's permission and Rodionov had called for a special 'Bureau for the RSFSR'.[15] Voznesenski had not worked in Leningrad since before the war; but Stalin sensed a nationalist streak in him and told Mikoyan: 'For him not only the Georgians and Armenians but even the Ukrainians aren't real people.'[16] Furthermore, the Leningraders, including Zhdanov, had enthused about the Yugoslavs after the Second World War. Tito and the Yugoslavs advocated a more radical communisation of eastern Europe.[17] Stalin had not demurred at the time; but when he and Tito fell out, Zhdanov's known inclination – even if it had had Stalin's endorsement at the time – may have made him suspect that the USSR's 'second capital' was a nest of treachery. Voznesenski had been highly favoured in wartime, and Kuznetsov in 1948 had even been mentioned by Stalin as his possible successor.[18]

Stalin was not really threatened by them. No Leningrad leader was demonstrably eager to promote a Russian nationalist cause. The only serious source of worry was that they sought to dig autonomous foundations for the RSFSR within the USSR. But always extremely wary, Stalin left nothing to chance. The Leningraders were arrested, interrogated and shot. They had not been a cohesive group with a uniform and agreed programme; and some of them – notably Politburo member and Gosplan Chairman Voznesenski – had interests which conflicted with Zhdanov's emphasis on the virtues of the party. But enough of them were in agreement in the political discussions after the war for them to be regarded as a potential orientation inside the supreme ruling coterie.[19]

The Leningrad Affair did not halt dispute about policy. Certainly the position of the ministerial apparatus was consolidated to the detriment of the party, and trained specialists in economic and social sectors of public life – and indeed in political ones – were left undisturbed by party and police. Having toyed with measures to raise the popular standard of living, Stalin had reverted to older priorities. The Cold War imposed colossal budgetary strains on the already damaged Soviet economy. Dispositions were made to maximise heavy-industrial production and resources were devoted in abundance to the armed forces and the armaments factories as well as to the development of nuclear weapons.

Xenophobic statements were issued about world affairs; little remained of the restraints characteristic of the Grand Alliance. The wartime cultural relaxation was revoked and persecution of the creative intelligentsia was resumed. Things Russian attracted extravagant praise. Marxism–Leninism in its peculiar Stalinist variant was at the centre of the propaganda of press, radio and schooling. Punitive procedures were tightened; prisoners released at the end of their sentences in the Gulag were rearrested and either sent back to camps or transferred to special settlements.

Stalin liked the world to believe that debate about primary aspects of policy had ceased to be necessary and that a popular consensus existed in the USSR. Thus any reconsideration of the 'line of the day' was a waste of time at best and a heresy and danger to state interests at worst. Supposedly Stalin's ideas were exactly those of the party and of the working class. Nevertheless some members of his entourage felt that several sectors of public life required reform. Malenkov believed that light-industrial production should be prioritised notwithstanding the deterioration in relations between the USA and the USSR. Beria agreed (and after Stalin's death he co-operated with Malenkov in seeking to foster reconciliation between the former military allies). Probably Malenkov and Beria also concurred that the breach with Yugoslavia had been undesirable. Malenkov, though, was less eager than Khrushchëv to acknowledge the existence of an agricultural emergency in the USSR. He also declined to admit the dangers, identified by Beria, which were posed by the exacerbation of national feelings among the non-Russian peoples. The supreme leadership was riddled by suppressed disputes along a range of current policies.

It was one thing for Stalin to develop an idiosyncratic structure for the Soviet political leadership and entirely another to keep it standing. By playing with the fate of his subordinates, he risked destabilising the whole state order, as had happened in 1937–8. The institutions controlling society, the economy and culture needed to maintain their authority. Society was cowed but it was capable of bursting into rebellion: the history of popular revolts in the Russian Empire provided a warning against official complacency. This was not Stalin's sole calculation. He knew that, if he removed his subordinates in one great purge, he would bring himself into disrepute. He had picked all of them and his judgement would be put under question. Furthermore, Stalin also had to be wary of the reaction of his intended victims. If he made them feel frightened about his intentions, they might attempt a coup. He therefore moved against individuals rather than the whole group. Stalin was not omnipotent. He needed to act with caution, moving against his subordinates in stages.

There abides an image of Stalin as ruler which shows him as a despot unprecedented in history. More than Louis XIV, he could accurately claim: '*L'État, c'est moi.*' The Great Terror had resulted in total victory. The lasting institution of supreme power and authority – the party – was conquered by his bloody methods and subsequently he could do more or less what he pleased. All institutions were in permanent contest with each other at a level vastly lower than Stalin's imperial throne. Institutions certainly mattered. But they received their orders from the celestial heights without being able to amend the contents. They functioned as Stalin's administrative conveyor belts, their task being to carry out whatever errands he had set for each particular day. The leaders of institutions were in post solely at his whim, and they discharged their duties to the letter of his expressed will. Institutions and leaders were therefore mere extensions of Stalin's declared wishes and intimations. Politics in any generally accepted sense had ceased. An administrative behemoth ran the USSR whose master was the pockmarked little psychopath. According to such imagery, Stalin was totalitarianism in human form.

Central bodies were not the only problem. Each institution had its internal discrepancies. The centre vied with its local adjuncts. Leaders in Moscow tried to increase their authority by introducing their personal supporters to posts at lower levels. Patronage was normalised as a political phenomenon. Stalin could weaken its effect by placing rivals in particular institutions; but he could not eliminate it entirely, and since the end of the Great Terror had not made it his business to try. He could also insert his own chosen appointees into the provincial tiers. Yet for all this a great deal of energy was necessary. Stalin had possessed it in the 1930s even if he made choices based more on guesswork than on acquaintance with functionaries – he had ceased to meet provincial delegations as a matter of course in the late 1920s. In fact he rarely intervened in the huge process of non-central appointments after 1945. He was too old and exhausted and other things were on his mind: grand foreign and economic policy, the Korean War, the world communist movement and his political supremacy.

Stalinist governance stayed as contradictory as ever. Enormous power accrued to Stalin and his subordinates in the Politburo, and only saints or fools criticised the right to rule or the contents of their policies.

Elections were a sham. Consultation of popular opinion never occurred. The obligation of Soviet citizens was to listen to orders and accede to doctrines. Hierarchical command had become a normal and prime aspect of governance and anyone challenging this development of the Soviet order – and even many who did not dare to challenge it – was certain to end up against a wall or in a labour camp. The immense, active power of the state was irresistible and few made the attempt to resist. Just a handful of brave Russian students got together in universities and discussed schemes for a reversion of ideology and practice to true Leninism. Religious dissenters too continued to hold secret meetings. Some intellectuals went on writing despite there being no prospect of publication. The armed partisan groups in Ukraine and the Baltic states, though diminished, had not yet been eliminated. But across the face of the USSR the forces of resistance to Stalinism were weak. On the back of that mighty state sat Joseph Stalin – Soso to his ageing school friends, Joseph to the Alliluevs, the Boss to the Politburo and Father of the Peoples to his citizen subjects. The despot's hands retained their tight grip on the levers of power; and as long as he drew breath, he could not be budged.

Appearances did not deceive: he was the unchallengeable despot. But those appearances so dazzled that they occluded his weaknesses from view. At the lower levels of state and society the infringements of the hierarchical principle were systemic. Not only in politics but throughout the administrative stratum of the USSR there was theft, corruption, nepotism, informal patronage, misreporting and general disorder. Regional, institutional and local interests were defended. The Soviet order paid workers and kolkhozniks a pittance but failed to impose a pattern of labour compliance conventional in the West. At the tasks of micromanagement this totalitarian system was an abject failure.

Stalin gave no sign that he knew this. Not once after the Second World War did he visit a factory, farm or even administrative office. He ruled by his wits. Seeing his fellow politicians, he tried to prise out of them such information as they contrived to keep from him. He held his dinner parties. He kept regular contacts with his organs of surveillance. He gave his orders and sent threatening telegrams. He closed off channels for the propagation of doctrine and opinions different from his own. He arranged arrests. Yet his 'omnipotence' did not permit him to perfect the pyramidal order. The lowest levels of the structure were constantly found out of place by his inspectors, but they had long ago ceased to tell him the full truth. When defects were announced to him, it was *de rigueur* to suggest that saboteurs, diversionists or foreign agents had been at work. No one dared insist that the trouble was inherent in the Soviet order and in the policies introduced and implemented by Stalin. It was the ultimate vicious circle. Stalin knew only what he wanted to know. His subordinates tried to tell him only what he wanted or what they wanted him to know. The Leader with the most penetrative power of any contemporary ruler was walled off from the modalities of the Soviet order at its lower levels. Master of all he surveyed, he saw only a small part of his country's realities and controlled even less.

50. EMPEROR WORSHIP

Stalin sometimes claimed to be disconcerted by the extravagance of his cultic rituals. He asked for limits to the praise and muttered to his propagandists that they were overstepping them. In 1945, discussing plans for the first volume of his collected works, he proposed to restrict the print run to thirty thousand copies because of the paper shortage. Other participants in the meeting got him to agree to three hundred thousand copies, arguing that the public demand would be enormous.[1] Stalin also displayed caution a year later at a similar meeting to discuss the draft second edition of his biography. The flatteries irritated him:[2]

> What should the reader do after reading this book? Get down on his knees and pray to me! ... We don't need idolaters ... We already have the teaching of Marx and Lenin. No additional teachings are required ... Nowhere is it said clearly that I am Lenin's pupil ... In fact I considered and still consider myself the pupil of Lenin.

The future of the Revolution, Marxism and the USSR had to be considered. 'And what,' Stalin exclaimed, 'if I'm no longer around? ... You won't be inculcating love for the party [through this draft] ... What's going to happen when I'm not here?'[3]

Yet Stalin did not seriously impede the fanfares: either he was playing psychological games or he could no longer be bothered to keep tight control in the area of propaganda. In 1946 his collected works appeared in a first print run of half a million copies. A million copies of the revised biography had been published by the end of 1947 alone – and ten million copies of the *Short Course* in party history were put into press at the same time.[4] The worship of Stalin had become a state industry (and Stalin himself had dropped his half-hearted attempt to restrict the print run).

There was harsh iconographic control. An episode from 1946 illustrates the punitive care taken with the image of the Leader. The artist

V. Livanova had painted a poster of '9 May – A Worldwide Victory Holiday' for the Moscow publishing house Art. In line with normal procedure, the editors checked it for visual merit and political reliability before submitting it to the censor I. N. Kleiner in Glavlit, the central censorship body. But things then went wrong. The editors did not wait for a decision but sent the poster to be printed in the Soviet-occupied zone of Germany. By the time copies of the poster were shipped back for distribution in the USSR, two errors had been discovered. One was that there were only fifteen banners representing the Soviet republics of the USSR instead of sixteen. The other related to Stalin: his marshal's star had six points instead of five. Investigation proved that the errors had been made by Livanova herself and not by miscreants in Germany (as had been suspected). Glavlit itself got into trouble for having failed to exercise due care. Kleiner was sacked and the terrified leadership of Glavlit, trying to prove its loyalty, asked to be subordinated to the Ministry of Internal Affairs.[5]

Pernicious significance was attributed to these slight errors. Enemies of the Soviet order might be calling for the USSR's dismemberment by reducing the number of official banners. Perhaps there was an implied call here for Ukraine to break away from the USSR into independence. As for the depiction of Stalin's marshal's star with six points, this might suggest a plot to represent him as a friend of international Jewry since the Star of David also had six points.[6]

The cult was the centre of the belief system of Marxism–Leninism–Stalinism. While it had no creed, its devotees had to stick rigorously to formulaic terminology and imagery. Texts such as Marx's *Capital* and Lenin's *The State and Revolution* functioned like the Gospels, and the *Short Course* and Stalin's official biography were equivalent to the Acts of the Apostles. The punctiliousness about words and pictures was reminiscent of Christian ecclesiastical traditions in the former Russian Empire – and Stalin, who had attended the Tiflis Spiritual Seminary till his twenty-first year, may well have been influenced, consciously or not, by his memory of the Orthodox Church's unbending adherence to fixed rites, liturgy and images.[7] Icon-painters represented sacred figures according to tightly prescribed rules. Perhaps this was the source for the extraordinarily detailed control over publicly available material on Stalin. If this indeed was the case, it must have reinforced the predisposition of the Marxist–Leninist doctrinaires to secure fidelity to the texts of Marx, Engels, Lenin and Stalin to root out any trace of heterodoxy. Medieval Christianity and vulgar Marxism were a potent mixture.

The established impersonality of Stalin's imagery was trundled down a narrow-gauge track. No Politburo member was allowed a public profile that might deflect people from adoring the Leader. Veteran comrades-in-arms such as Molotov, Kaganovich and Mikoyan came to notice only when they discharged particular duties: none of them was even mentioned in Nikolai Voznesenski's *The War Economy of the USSR*; and there was no reference to them in the chapters added to the post-war editions of the *Short Course* and Stalin's official biography.[8]

The Leader kept an aquiline watch over the products of Soviet propaganda. Even the Stalin Prize-winning novel *The Young Guard* by Alexander Fadeev incurred his displeasure. This was a best-seller depicting adolescent partisans working behind German lines in the war. Their bravery, determination and patriotism sounded a deep chord with readers and the book was especially popular with youth in the USSR. But Stalin had second thoughts. Unusually he had not read the text before the award of the prize. Ilya Ehrenburg recalled the Leader's fury when he saw the rushes of the film made of the novel: 'Here were youngsters left to their fate in a town seized by the Nazis. Where was the Komsomol organisation? Where was the party leadership?'[9] The point for Stalin was that everyone should understand that victory in the war had been secured by the institutional framework and direction supplied by the hierarchies of state. Neither individuals nor even large social groups could be portrayed as operating autonomously. A codified version of historical reality was imposed. Anathema was pronounced upon any work showing Soviet citizens fighting effectively against the Wehrmacht without direct supervision by an administrative hierarchy stretching downwards from the Kremlin.

The war itself became something of an embarrassment to him. The Victory Day anniversary celebration was suspended after 1946 and not restored until after his death. Memoirs by generals, soldiers and civilians were banned. Stalin wanted to control, manipulate and canalise popular memory. The wartime reality could unsettle his plans for the post-war regime. Thoughts about how people coped and fought without reference to Stalin's authority were dangerous.

The second edition of his official biography, presented to deafening fanfares in the media in 1947, added material on the Great Patriotic War and Stalin's part in it. Amendments were also made to the existing chapters. Although the authors generally inflated the claims made about him, there was one exception. Whereas the first edition asserted that he had been arrested eight times and exiled seven times before 1914, the second reduced the numbers to seven and six respectively. But otherwise the new edition was an even more extravagant eulogy than before. The section on the Second World War hardly mentioned anyone but Stalin, and his one brief trip to the vicinity of the front was treated as crucial to the Red Army's success. The narrative was little more than a list of battles. Government and army were mentioned. But drama, in so far as it existed in the chapters, was focused on decisions and inspiration provided by Stalin. The book entirely lacked an account of the difficulties of deliberation at Stavka or the contribution of other leaders and the people as a whole. The details of Stalin's career in the war were overlooked; he was treated as the embodiment of the state and society in victory. Even more than before the Second World War he was an icon without personality. Stalin, the party, the Red Army and the USSR were represented as indistinguishable from each other.[10]

Stalin came ever closer to evicting Lenin from his primary status in the Soviet Union. There were indications of this in his preface to the first volume of his collected works. He expressed surprise that Lenin, who had developed the components of his telescoped Marxist theory of socialist revolution in 1905, had not fully divulged the fact until 1917.[11] Previously it had been incumbent on official propagandists to insist that Leninist policy had evolved in an unbroken line of positive change. Stalin by 1946 was suggesting that Lenin had missed a trick or two.

His rise in prestige at Lenin's expense also took other forms. Officially commissioned paintings made the visual suggestion that the greater of the two communist leaders had been Stalin. This was done quite subtly. Typically Stalin stands confidently, pipe in hand, as he explains a matter of political strategy to an avidly listening Lenin: it is as if the roles of teacher and pupil have been reversed. Apart from the improbability of Lenin's subordination, there was his known aversion to anyone smoking in his presence. Another unrealistic touch was the increasing tendency of artists to portray Stalin as taller than Lenin. In fact they were about the same size. It goes without saying that Stalin's physical blemishes were carefully overlooked. Each year after the Second World War he appeared more and more like a tough, mature athlete in historical representations. The same line was pursued in films. In Mikhail Chiaureli's *Unforgettable 1919* Stalin is seen dispensing decisions imperturbably. The depiction shows him as exceptional in his refusal to panic. Always he appears to advocate the 'correct' decision, to universal acclaim. The survival of the Soviet state is made to seem mainly Stalin's achievement.

This was done with deliberation. The policies of the leadership were deeply oppressive; elections and consultations with society at large were non-existent. Popular aspirations for a different kind of state and society were strong, and Soviet leaders regarded them as a menace. A scheme of indoctrination was put in hand to strengthen the carapace of the old regime. Force by itself would not work. Stalin was already the embodiment of the Soviet order and his appeal to citizens of the USSR was deep and extensive even among millions of people who hated his policies. The phenomenon is impossible to quantify: security police reports are impressionistic and marred by gross prejudices, and independent open surveys of mass opinion were not undertaken. But the reaction to Stalin's death in March 1953, when popular grief took a widely hysterical form, indicates that respect and even affection for him was substantial. He incarnated pride in military victory. He stood for industrial might and cultural progress. Even if he had not wanted a cult to his greatness, such a cult would have had to be invented.

Public life functioned on the premise that all good things in the USSR flowed from the talents and beneficence of Joseph Stalin.[12] Among the expressions of the cult was *The Book of Delicious and Healthy Food*, whose prefatory epigraph consisted of the following quotation from him: 'The defining peculiarity of our Revolution consists in its having given the people not only freedom but also material goods and the opportunity for a comfortable and cultured life.'[13] No work of non-fiction could appear without mention of his genius. History, politics, economics, geography, linguistics and even chemistry, physics and genetics were said to be inadequately studied unless they incorporated his guiding ideas.

Yet this despot lacked, in the recesses of his mind, authentic confidence in his appearance. His gammy left arm, smallpox-pitted face and shortness of stature appear to have inhibited him from enjoying his cult as much as he might otherwise have done. He both loved and detested excesses of flattery. He also understood that the rarity of fresh images of him served to maintain public interest. Familiarity could have bred apathy or contempt. For such reasons he chose to place technical limits on his iconography to a greater extent than did most contemporary foreign rulers. He preferred to be painted rather than photographed. Even so, he did not like to sit for court painters; and when being painted, he expected to be aesthetically idealised and politically whitewashed. As the years rolled on, the number of images accorded the imprimatur of his approval dwindled. Declining to have new photos taken, he went on releasing the ones approved before the Second World War: this was true even of the second edition of his official biography (which had heavily airbrushed versions of photographs that had been published ever since the 1920s).[14]

A couple of exceptions existed. The biography included a photograph of him waving from the Kremlin Wall and a painting of him in his generalissimus's uniform; but although both of them showed him as older than in earlier pictures, the effects of age were fudged. In the painting his moustache appeared dark and even the hair on his head had only a suggestion of grey. The face had no smallpox-pitted skin. His tunic hung on him with unnatural fineness and the medals on his chest, including his marshal's five-pointed star, looked as if they were stuck to a flat board. This painting by the artist B. Karpov was used in posters, busts and books.[15] There was also a photograph of him sitting with his fellow marshals; but his image was so small in relation to the page that his face and body were barely discernible – and anyway the airbrushers had again been at work: his shoulders were implausibly wide and he seemed larger than the other figures in the photo.[16]

Sporadic attempts to 'humanise' his image occurred. The most notable were the memoirs produced by the surviving Alliluevs. Anna Alliluev and her father Sergei, proud of their family's past, recorded their impressions of Stalin before the October Revolution. These were published in 1946.[17] Sergei's book appeared posthumously: he had died, worn out by years of toil and worry and family tragedy, the previous July. Anna was alert to the risks of writing about Stalin and made a formal approach to Malenkov to assure herself that the book would have Stalin's blessing.[18] The texts were eulogistic and had gone through the censorship.[19] But Sergei let slip that he had known Stalin as Soso Dzhughashvili. He also mentioned that Stalin's first attempt to escape administrative exile in Novaya Uda in the winter of 1903–4 was marred by an elementary error: Stalin forgot to take warm clothing with him and his face and ears were severely frozen.[20] Anna's memoir gave still more details about the private life of Stalin. She described how his damaged arm precluded him from being called up in the First World War. She related that he looked thinner and older after the February 1917 Revolution and that, when he came to live with the Alliluevs, he liked to tease the family maid. The memoir reported that Stalin slept in the same room as Sergei in late summer. It also described his approval of Nadya Allilueva's zeal in tidying up the apartment. And it gave a comical account of Stalin's fondness for his pipe: Anna recalled that he had fallen asleep with it lit and burned the sheets.[21]

Stalin soon regretted having sanctioned the Alliluev books. Anna was arrested in 1948 and sentenced to the camps for ten years for defaming him. He ignored her letter to him that she had cleared the project before publication and that she had done nothing wrong.[22] She could hardly believe what was happening. She wrote to him defending her family and its record. Implicitly she accused 'dear Joseph' of ingratitude: 'But there are people who our family simply saved from death. And this isn't over-praise but the very truth, which it is very easy to prove.'[23] That she could send such a message to the Leader is a sign of her courage or stupidity. Enough of Stalin's in-laws had perished before the Second World War for her to have known the kind of person she was addressing.

Although the widowed Olga Allilueva, to whom Stalin had expressed fond gratitude in 1915, was not persecuted, she became severely depressed. Nadya had killed herself in 1932, Pavel had died in 1938 and Fëdor had never recovered from the mental trauma of the trick played upon him by Kamo at the end of the Civil War. None of Olga's children or children-in-law remained at liberty in the post-war years. Pavel's widow Yevgenia did not save herself by marrying again and leaving the vicinity of Stalin: she had been arrested a year earlier than Anna and received the same punishment. Olga was inconsolable: she died a broken old woman in 1951. This was how Stalin rewarded the Alliluevs for the favours they had rendered him before the October Revolution. His Svanidze in-laws had already received his special expression of thanks. Alexander Svanidze had been arrested in the Great Terror and shot in 1942; his wife Maria had had a heart attack on receiving the news. Not only they but also the two sisters of Stalin's first wife Ketevan – Maria and Alexandra – had perished before the end of the Second World War. The only close relatives who lived without fear of arrest were his children Svetlana and Vasili. They were the exceptions: the pattern was that a family connection with Stalin brought about repression.

The problem presented by the Alliluevs was that they knew him so well. He wished to float free of his personal history. Increasingly he opted for the status of state icon at the expense of a realistic image of himself. He became ever more detached and mysterious. It is true that he sometimes appeared on the Lenin Mausoleum to review the October Revolution or the May Day parades. But few spectators got more than a fleeting glimpse of him. Usually the police and the parade marshals hurried everyone across Red Square as fast as possible.[24]

What people lacked in direct experience of Stalin, they often made up for in expressions of devotion to him. The universal genius of the father of all the peoples had to be acknowledged on every solemn occasion in schools, enterprises and offices. Gratitude for his life and career had to be manifested. *Pravda* quoted daily from his works. His photographs, old ones retouched for the current day, were regularly published – and sometimes paintings were brought out of store and turned into images looking like photographs. None of this damaged his standing since so few individuals actually met him: he had become a distant deity. Meetings started always with a paean to the Leader. Memory of a past when he had not been ruler was confined to a small minority of Soviet society. There was nothing in the USSR or in the other countries where communism was established which was deemed untouched by his genius. Images of him were hung on walls at work and in the home. His biography was conventionally given to youngsters on important occasions. Short of being called God on earth, Stalin had deified himself.

In 1949 when he (inaccurately) celebrated his seventieth birthday,[25] a tremendous fuss was made of him. He made a limp attempt to stop it getting out of hand, telling Malenkov: 'Don't even think of presenting me with another star!' By this he meant he had had enough awards (and he continued to regret allowing himself to be called Generalissimus: when Churchill asked him what to call him, Marshal or Generalissimus, Stalin answered Marshal).[26] There was no chance that Malenkov would take this display of humility seriously. Laudatory books of memoirs were prepared for the great day. Articles proliferated in newspapers. On the day itself, 21 December, a vast balloon was sent up over the Kremlin and the image of Stalin's moustachioed face was projected on to it. Processions in his honour had been organised the length and breadth of the USSR. The festival continued into the evening at the Bolshoi Theatre when guests from the Soviet political elite and from abroad assembled to do honour to the Leader. It was one of Stalin's rare appearances and those who saw him were surprised at how physically diminished he seemed: they had been fed pictures from the cult and were unprepared for the human reality. Could it really be that the wizened old man before their gaze was the Great Stalin?

Yet they adjusted themselves to what they had seen. They reverted to admiration. Stalin might be elderly but he remained in their eyes the towering figure in the history of the USSR since the late 1920s. His had been the campaign to modernise, industrialise and educate in the 1930s, and – they thought – he had succeeded. His had been the leadership that had brought victory over the Nazi hordes. His was the firm hand at the helm of foreign policy in the storms of the Cold War. If the audience had doubts about his greatness, they quickly dispelled them. Hours of speeches reinforced the message that the world's finest politician alive was present in the hall. Leader after leader extolled his significance for communism. The stage, decorated with banners and flowers, was occupied by foreign communist luminaries such as Mao Tse-tung, Palmiro Togliatti and Dolores Ibárruri (who had been in Moscow exile since the Spanish Civil War). Behind them was spread an enormous portrait of Stalin. He himself smiled occasionally and clapped the orators. Although he was hardly expansive in his gestures, he was a contented man. The entire communist movement was rendering him homage.

The cult of Stalin, lord of all he surveyed, spread far beyond Soviet borders. On posters and in the press his image was prominent, and failure by communist leaderships in eastern Europe to maintain public reverence was inconceivable. This attitude was internalised by individual leaders from the region whenever they had direct contact with him. Conversations with Stalin were treated as if subjects were being admitted to audiences with an emperor. The Hungarian Prime Minister, Ferenc Nagy, gushed at the outset of their exchanges: 'The Hungarian government has recognised that a year after the [country's] liberation it must come to Generalissimus Stalin to express its gratitude for Hungary's liberation, for the freedom of Hungarian political life and for the independence of the Hungarian motherland.'[27] Nagy was not alone. Polish Prime Minister Bolesław Bierut declared: 'We have come to you, comrade Stalin, as to our great friend so as to express our considerations on the course of events in Poland and check the correctness of our evaluation of the political situation in the country.'[28] Stalin was usually pleased by this abject submission to his will. But occasionally the reports did not please him, and when he reprimanded the Romanian communist leader Georgiu-Dej for mistaken policies, there was nothing for it but for Dej to 'confess the erroneousness of his views'.[29]

No one challenged this except, at a distance, the Yugoslavian communist leader Tito. Although fear of Soviet counter-measures against the communist leaderships of eastern Europe must have played a part, there was also genuine admiration for Stalin among them. Most of those communist parties in any case would have quickly been removed if the Soviet Army had not been in occupation. They depended heavily on Stalin's goodwill, and they knew it. Even Mao Tse-tung, victor in the Chinese Civil War with little support and indeed much obstruction from Stalin, maintained an admiring public posture towards the Leader of the

USSR. By 1952, when the Nineteenth Party Congress met in Moscow, the praise for Stalin from foreign leaders was downright glutinous. He was greeted with the shout: 'Glory to the great Stalin!' Statues, small metal busts and posters repeated the work of praise. To his dying day he heard hymns to himself as the master of the world communist movement.

51. DANGEROUS LIAISONS

The propaganda war intensified between the USSR and the Western Allies. Soviet diplomats treated their American and British counterparts as enemies and the feeling was reciprocated. Cultural contacts ceased. The countries of eastern Europe as well as the communist parties of western Europe fell in line with the Kremlin's orders. In the West Stalin was depicted as the most evil dictator alive, quite as evil as the German Führer whom he had defeated. At the same time *Pravda* denigrated Truman and Attlee, characterising them as having the global ambitions – and the methods to match – which Hitler had developed. The two sides shared the assumption that a Third World War might occur between states which until 1945 had been united in armed struggle against the Wehrmacht. Two camps existed around the world, armed to the teeth and rivals for supremacy.

Neither camp, however, was looking for military conflict. Even Stalin, whose gloomy axiom was that a Third World War might be postponed but was ultimately inevitable,[1] did not wish to bring the USA to blows with the USSR. But events were stiffening his resolve to face down the Americans. The coincidence of the Soviet Union's acquisition of the A-bomb and the communist seizure of power in China altered the balance of power in the world. Although American weapons technology remained ahead of its rival, Stalin was no longer going to be easily intimidated in diplomatic exchanges. *Pravda* announced the achievement with pride. The USA was depicted as a militarist menace to world peace and the Soviet state was put forward as the sole power which could resist American pretensions. What is more, the Chinese Revolution meant that the geopolitics of Asia in particular could never be the same again. Mao Tse-tung's initial willingness to defer to Stalin in the interests of obtaining economic assistance was especially cheering to Moscow. Fours years after the end of the Second World War the Soviet Union was reclaiming its right to be treated as a global power on a level with the USA.

Few gifts, of course, come without wrapping; and Stalin knew that China's resurgent power under communist leadership had the potential to complicate his statesmanship. Mao might assert himself like a Chinese Tito. The world communist movement, until then largely unified, would undergo fissiparous strain. There might be a direct clash between the People's Republic of China and the USSR. Or things might deteriorate more indirectly. The People's Republic of China could start acting in international relations without consulting the Kremlin and yet somehow entangle the USSR in the adverse consequences.

Stalin with all this in mind sent out his Minister of Communications, Ivan Kovalëv, to Beijing to see how closely the Chinese communists were following his recommendations. Unusually he showed Kovalëv's report to Mao.[2] Stalin's motives were hardly comradely. Probably he wanted to impress on Mao that the USSR knew more about China's politics than Mao had imagined. Kovalëv revealed that little serious effort had been made to win over the Chinese working class to the revolutionary cause. He mentioned that land reform was geographically patchy. Kovalëv was also unimpressed by the ideological preparation of the party cadres. Indeed he noted tensions in the Beijing leadership. Kovalëv told Stalin directly that some leaders were not only anti-American but also anti-Soviet. Mao's close associate Chou En-lai had been heard to wonder why, if Beijing was being told to avoid annoying the USA, it should reject overtures from blackballed Yugoslavia.[3] There was plenty to provoke Stalin's suspicions and he let Mao know that, unless China toed the Soviet line, assistance from Moscow would not be forthcoming.

Diplomatic relations between the USA and the USSR were not broken, but both Moscow and Washington understood that global politics had entered a period of intensified uncertainty. Stalin especially wanted to secure Soviet interests vis-à-vis communist China. He started as he meant to go on. Devastated by decades of civil war, China urgently required foreign economic assistance, and the USSR was the sole possible source for it. Stalin intended to drive a hard bargain. While content to nudge China towards spreading communist political influence in eastern Asia, he demanded Chinese acceptance of the primacy of the Soviet Union in the world communist movement.

Yet events in the Far East tempted him to risk moving over to an offensive foreign policy. Since Korea's liberation from Japanese occupation there had been intermittent civil war, and two separate states had emerged on the peninsula in 1948. The same American military shield which defended Japan protected southern Korea with Seoul as its capital.

Meanwhile northern Korea had a communist government, based in Pyongyang, which looked to Moscow for assistance. The armies confronting each other had abundant supplies of equipment and advisers; and both Korean states behaved on the assumption that sooner or later a definitive resumption of hostilities would take place. The Korean communist leader Kim Il-Sung went to Moscow in March 1949 and requested a large increase in assistance so that he might attack the south.[4] Stalin refused, advising the Korean comrades to get on with their preparations but to fight only if invaded. Kim Il-Sung, however, wanted to go to war and continued to act provocatively towards Seoul. He refused to cease making representations to Stalin. In March 1950 he returned to Moscow and argued passionately that the south was there for the taking. If China could be unified under Mao Tse-tung, he asserted, Korea was ready for similar treatment under Kim Il-Sung.

Stalin had customarily parried such demands from foreign communist leaders, but Kim Il-Sung touched a raw nerve and Stalin suddenly gave way. It cannot have been the Korean's persuasiveness which led to the turnabout: Stalin was too circumspect for that. Much had happened since 1945. The USSR's acquisition of both its own nuclear-bomb capacity and a powerful communist ally in China encouraged him to think that it no longer needed to play its hand weakly against the USA.

He had badly underestimated the revolutionary potential of the Chinese Communist Party. He confessed this in the presence of Bulgarian and Yugoslav leaders at a Kremlin discussion on 10 February 1948. According to Dimitrov's diary, he said:[5]

> I also doubted that the Chinese could succeed, and I advised them to come to a temporary agreement with Chiang Kai-shek. Officially they agreed with us, but in practice they continued mobilising the Chinese people. And then they openly put forward the question: 'Shall we go on with our fight? We have the support of our people.' We said: 'Fine, what do you need?' It turned out that the conditions there were very favourable. The Chinese proved to be right, and we were wrong.

Stalin was performing the role of a leader who recognises his own fallibility in order to get his way on the Balkans. But a bullying style came more naturally to him. The People's Republic of China, with its military and economic potential, could become a handful inside the world communist movement and Mao Tse-tung could become his nightmare. So for once he was probably blurting out what he really thought.

Belatedly he saw the need to deal more tactfully with Mao. Kim Il-Sung had made his final plea at a moment when Stalin was most amenable to having his mind changed; and anyway Stalin could not be certain that the Chinese would not support Kim Il-Sung even regardless of the USSR's consent. Stalin did not disclose his calculations. Molotov was by then in semi-official disgrace and was no longer privy to his thoughts, and everyone in the Ministry of External Affairs simply followed Stalin's orders.

Thus it came about in their meetings in Moscow in April and May 1950 that Stalin sanctioned Kim Il-Sung's request to support the Korean communist resumption of war. Both Stalin and Mao had allowed themselves to be persuaded that the military campaign would be short and successful.[6] Soviet arms, munitions and other equipment were carried by the Trans-Siberian Railway to Korea. Kim Il-Sung began his offensive on 25 June. Superior in every sector of military resources, the Korean communist forces swept south and captured Seoul three days later. It looked as if the basic premise of Stalin's discussion with Kim Il-Sung was about to be realised as a rapid victory was achieved before the rest of the world could blink. But the two communist interlocutors had made a profound miscalculation. Truman was shocked but not deterred. Instead he ordered his diplomats to go before the United Nations Organisation Security Council and secure a vote in favour of armed intervention to prevent the overrunning of South Korea. This task was facilitated by a previous blunder by Stalin who, objecting to the continued recognition of Chiang Kai-shek's regime in Taiwan as the legitimate Chinese government and its right to occupy China's seat in the Security Council, had been boycotting the body. In the absence of a Soviet veto, the Security Council approved the American proposal. Stalin repudiated the advice of his Ministry of External Affairs to drop the boycott so as to prevent the Americans and their allies from landing with the legitimacy conferred by the sanction of the United Nations.[7]

This was hamfistedness on a scale he had not shown since 1941. The United Nations forces, primarily American, were led by General Douglas MacArthur. Their rapid deployment was made possible by the American occupation of nearby Japan, and by the end of September they had already halted the communist advance and retaken Seoul. Next month they had crossed the 38th Parallel into north Korea. Kim Il-Sung was desperate; he had no alternative but to turn to Stalin for direct military assistance even though he knew the likely response. Mao Tse-tung was less reluctant since he assumed that war between the USA and the People's Republic of China was just a matter of time. The Chinese resolved upon aid for the Korean communists before consulting Stalin. But Mao still expected the Kremlin to send weapons for the use of the twelve divisions about to be dispatched by China.[8] The news of MacArthur's success came through to Moscow; it was relayed to Stalin beside the Black Sea. His was a curiously semi-detached oversight over Soviet security interests notwithstanding his ability to stay in touch by phone and telegrams. When he was down in the south he held none of the frantic face-to-face discussions with political and military leaders such as had been his wont in the Second World War. Suddenly the crisis on the Korean peninsula deepened, and Stalin had to take a strategic decision. Kim Il-Sung demanded urgent additional assistance, pointing out that without help the communists would soon lose the entire war.

Stalin had the choice either to accede to Kim Il-Sung's request or simply to withdraw from the war before things got entirely out of hand. The problem was that geopolitics would certainly be transformed in favour of the USA unless the Korean communist cause was supported; and the humiliation for Stalin and the USSR would be immense since it was an open secret that Soviet covert assistance to Kim Il-Sung had already been substantial. It was a tricky moment. While cursing himself for having been taken in by Kim Il-Sung earlier in the year, he could hardly fail him in his time of crisis. Yet he also had to be wary of escalating the hostility between the USSR and the USA to the point that open war might break out between them. He chose the option of cunning. On 1 October he sent a telegram to Beijing calling on Mao to transfer 'six or seven divisions' to the 38th Parallel. This was the line of latitude which cut Korea politically in half. If the communists could repel the American advance at that point, Kim Il-Sung would hold on to an area of respectable size. At all costs Stalin needed to avoid a direct collision between the forces of the USA and the USSR while continuing to protect Soviet geopolitical interests. Mao needed some persuading that the Chinese alone should take such responsibility for the defence of north Korea. It seemed odd that Stalin, having recently pulled rank over Mao as the leader of an already mighty military and economic power, should shuffle off the burden of war so readily. How could Stalin square the circle?

He did it mainly by force of argument. Writing to Beijing, he stated:[9]

Of course I had to reckon with the fact that, despite its lack of preparedness, the United States may still pull itself into a big war for reasons of prestige; consequently China would be dragged into the war, and the USSR, which is bound to China by the pact of mutual assistance, would be dragged into the war as well. Should we be afraid of this? In my opinion we should not since together we will be stronger than the United States and Great Britain ... If war is inevitable, let it happen now and not in a few years when Japanese militarism will be restored as a US ally and when the United States and Japan will have a beach-head on the [Asian] continent ready in the form of Syngman Rhee's Korea.

The effrontery of this case is unmistakable. Still he was essentially claiming that the Americans would have no stomach for a fight. But if this was true, why did Stalin insist on the Chinese doing his fighting for him?

The People's Republic of China in any case had a continuing horror that its territorial integrity would be threatened if Syngman Rhee, the Korean politician supported by the Americans in the south of the country, were to rule all Korea. Tense negotiations followed. While Stalin tried to get the Chinese to fight in the Far East on behalf of world communism, Mao and his comrades sought the maximum amount of Soviet equipment. Both sides came close to breaking up their talks about Korea.[10] Stalin's brinkmanship on 12 October involved sending a letter advising Kim Il-Sung that the war was lost and that he should evacuate his forces to safety in China and the USSR.[11] Mao gave way next day, and Stalin was able to announce to Kim that the Korean comrades would soon be receiving massive reinforcement by Chinese troops. Theoretically the troops would be volunteers, but in practice they would consist of divisions drawn directly from the People's Liberation Army. On 19 October they crossed the Yalu river on to Korean territory. Within days they were engaging the forces led by the Americans.[12] They fought with the assistance promised by Stalin. Soviet armaments and munitions were abundantly supplied; and, in the case of fighter planes, Stalin was sufficiently keen that the aircraft should be properly handled that he provided his own aviators dressed in Chinese uniforms.

Stalin after some vacillation had complied. What had started as a war fought on the far edge of Asia had the potential to explode into a global conflict with the victorious members of the Grand Alliance at each other's throats. Stalin did not reveal his calculations but probably he was exercised by a mixture of factors. He did not want an American puppet state of Korea on his borders. He did not wish the USSR to lose prestige in the world communist movement when the People's Republic of China aided a fellow communist power. He may also have felt that Mao had a serious chance of pulling off what Kim had failed to do. The logistics of military supply were easier for China and the USSR than for the USA. Perhaps Stalin was also guessing that American forces would be tied down and exhausted in Korea even if they were not defeated outright. Stalin's basic assumption was that world war could be postponed but not made avoidable. Whatever he may have calculated about the Korean situation, though, he let on to nobody what it was. He was in a position, as in August 1941 when Ribbentrop came a-courting to the Kremlin, to ignore the opinions of others; and he made it a habit to leave few traces of his mental pathway to each important decision. This helped him to go on keeping the rest of the world guessing. The more enigmatic he was in global politics, the less likely he was to be taken for granted.

Events in Korea increased in difficulty as Stalin and his associates pondered what to do. Broader factors came into play. Stalin the pragmatist was also a man of ideological assumptions, and he genuinely believed that the treaties signed at the end of the Second World War were documents destined to be ripped up when the world descended into a Third World War. Chances to expand communist influence in the meantime had to be seized. Stalin's spies led him to conclude that Truman would not intervene to save the unpopular southern government.[13] The USSR had acquired effective nuclear weapons in August 1949 and had to be handled more carefully by the USA. The Sino-Soviet alliance boosted Moscow's global weight still further – and indeed Stalin had to take account of the fact that Mao Tse-tung was fully capable of offering active support to Kim Il-Sung regardless of Stalin's wishes: Mao had greater freedom of choice than even Tito.

The Chinese entry into the Korean War turned the scales in favour of the communist cause. Mao's People's Liberation Army crossed the Yalu river into Korea on 19 October 1950 and MacArthur's campaign hit serious trouble, especially after the arrival of the Soviet air units in the following month.[14] The movement towards a world war shifted up another notch on 31 December when Chinese forces thrust south and crossed the 38th Parallel. Seoul was taken the next month. MacArthur demanded permission to carry the fighting on to Chinese soil. At this time neither Stalin nor Mao was in the mood for compromise. Mao's own son was mobilised for the war. (He was killed in action.)[15] It looked as if the Americans were about to lose the war on the Korean peninsula.[16]

Meanwhile Stalin had to deal with Europe, and he was especially concerned about Italy and France. Greece was already settled in Stalin's mind: he had not intervened in the Civil War there, had resented Greek communist demands for permission to operate as if a socialist seizure of power was possible and had left Athens to the repressive zeal of the Alexandros Diomidis government. Italy and France were a different matter: their communist parties gave him much less trouble and it had been easy to quell those of their leaders who seriously contemplated insurrection in Rome and Paris. As relations worsened with the Western Allies, they became pawns in Stalin's European game. Although his strategy remained the avoidance of war with the USA, he did not mind making things awkward for the Americans wherever he could. For this reason he demanded a more boisterous policy for the Italian Communist Party and the French Communist Party. This was explained to the representatives from Italy and France at the Second Conference of the Cominform in June 1948. As usual, Stalin and the Soviet leaders admitted no mistake on their part. Instead Togliatti, Thorez and their subordinates were blamed for not seeing the need for more radical measures than the Kremlin had previously stipulated.

By the beginning of the 1950s Stalin's grip on world affairs was weaker than in previous years. The Korean War was raging and, with Soviet pilots and military equipment involved, was capable of spiralling into a Third World War. The Chinese People's Republic complicated everything by urging Stalin to fight to the bitter end; Mao Tse-tung by his behaviour showed he could be just as independent of Moscow as Tito – and the stakes of China's foreign adventures were very high indeed. Stalin could not even control all the communist parties in Europe. When he summoned Palmiro Togliatti to leave Italy and take the leading position in the Cominform, he received a brisk refusal. Togliatti wanted to guide the Italian Communist Party through the complications of post-war Italian politics and had no interest in putting his life at risk by working in proximity to Stalin. Meanwhile Tito stayed imperturbably in supreme office in Belgrade. Elsewhere in eastern Europe there was the silence of the political graveyard; but the People's Democracies were far from quiet below the surface: resentment of the communist seizure of power in these countries was deep, and only the threat of unconditional repression kept order for Stalin.

Yet it was the Korean War which constituted the most deadly danger

Generalissimus Stalin in 1945.
The image disguises the haggard reality of his appearance.

Post-war poster: Stalin shakes hands with a military officer.
The caption runs: 'Work so as to be thanked by comrade Stalin!'

Post-war poster with children gazing adoringly at Stalin and saying:
'Thank you, our dear Stalin, for our happy childhood!'

Above. Stalin's Kholodnaya Rechka dacha, viewed from the garden.

Below left. The cinema gallery at the Kholodnaya Rechka dacha.

Below right. The Italian-made billiard table at the Kholodnaya Rechka dacha.

Above. Lavrenti Beria.   *Below.* Georgi Malenkov.

Top. Stalin's desk in the Kremlin. It is now kept in the Stalin Museum in Gori.

Above. View across Lake Ritsa towards the mountains of the Caucasus.
Stalin's dacha lies in the middle on the distant shore.

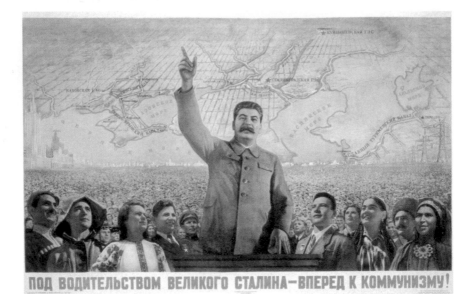

Above.
Poster: 'Under the Leadership of the Great Stalin. Forward to Communism!'

Below.
Daily Worker (London) cartoon on the death of Stalin, 6 March 1953.
Hardly an image of great technical accomplishment.

Above.
Mourners queue to pay their last respects to Stalin
in the Hall of Columns at the House of Unions.

Below.
Stalin's death mask.

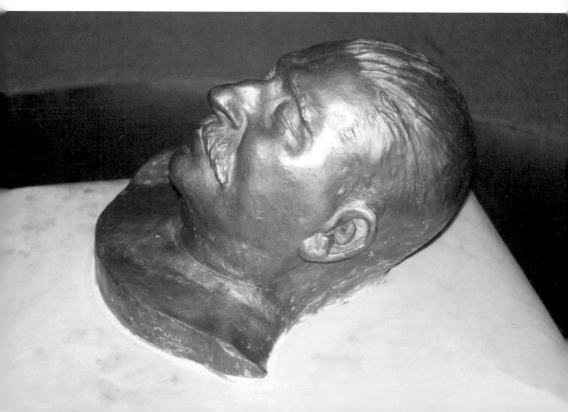

to Soviet interests. Stalin could not overlook the Americans' advantage in the number of nuclear weapons and in the proximity of their foreign airbases to the USSR. Perhaps, though, he knew more about Truman's intentions than anyone realised at the time. Soviet agents existed in the British establishment. Among them were Kim Philby and Donald Maclean. When Prime Minister Clement Attlee flew to Washington in early December 1950 to protest at confidential American discussions on using nuclear bombs in the Korean War, he was given an assurance by President Truman that only conventional weaponry would be deployed. It is highly probable that Maclean, head of the American desk at the Foreign Office, dispatched the news to Moscow. Stalin would thereby have known that Truman was not looking for a fight.[17] Even so, there could still have been a world war with conventional weaponry; and there was no way of guaranteeing that one side or the other would not, in a desperate moment, resort to its nuclear arsenal. Although he was not a totally reckless gambler, Stalin was not a cautious one either. He risked much, much more than he should have done if he really regarded peace around the world as a supreme priority.

The Third World War did not break out. But the situation developed in a manner perilously close to all-out global conflict; and much responsibility lay on Stalin's shoulders. If he had not financed and equipped Kim Il-Sung, the civil war in Korea could not have been resumed with the intensity it attained.

52. VOZHD AND INTELLECTUAL

The Vozhd retained his cerebral interests. He told people he read up to five hundred pages a day,[1] and the books he chose were of the kind he had enjoyed for years. Among them was *Germinal* by Émile Zola, whom he had discovered as an adolescent.[2] He continued to love Shota Rustaveli's medieval Georgian epic, *Knight in the Panther's Skin*.[3] Having found his favourites early in life, he did not abandon them in old age and his resumed support for the fraudulent geneticist Timofei Lysenko continued to prevent progress in Soviet biology and threaten the lives and careers of Lysenko's academic and political opponents.[4]

Marxism, architecture, linguistics, genetics and international relations were among Stalin's intellectual interests. Historical works especially attracted him. He kept up with writings on both the Russian past and the annals of Mesopotamia, ancient Rome and Byzantium.[5] When the fancy took him, he held conversations with physicists, biologists and other scientists. He examined the novels winning his annual Stalin Prize and listened to gramophone records of folk and classical music before they appeared in the shops (and gave them ratings from 'good' to 'awful'). In Moscow he attended ballets, operas and concerts. He had his dachas equipped so that he could vet Soviet films before their public release. *Volga! Volga!* was his favourite film.[6] He read, listened and watched mainly for personal delight and self-instruction. Foreign contemporary writers failed to attract him. Living writers had to be Soviet. Not that this saved them from his anger if he disapproved of one of their books. He had never been slow to say what he thought about cultural artefacts regardless of whether he knew much about the subject. Nobody in the USSR was in a position to ignore his predilections. If ever an obsessive intellectual dilettante existed, Stalin was that person.

Yet he made only three public speeches from 1946 onwards and two of these lasted just a few minutes.[7] His articles were few and he published no booklets after the war until *Marxism and Problems of Linguistics* in 1950.[8] Not since the end of the Civil War had he written less for the press. The consequence was that his infrequent smaller pieces functioned as the guidelines for what others in communist public life at home and abroad could print or broadcast.

All the same he made plain his desire to counteract the fashion for admiration of foreign culture and science. When President Truman sent him some bottles of Coca-Cola, Stalin reacted angrily and ordered food scientist Mitrofan Lagidze to develop a superior pear-based fizzy drink to send in return. (For once some sympathy with Stalin is in order.)[9] Praising only the achievements of the USSR, Stalin aimed to enclose the USSR deeper in intellectual quarantine. The main exception to this was kept secret: he relied heavily on scientific and technological espionage to steal the foreign discoveries needed for the development of Soviet military and industrial might. Otherwise the guiding principle was that everything foreign was inferior and damaging. With this in mind he called Alexander Fadeev and two literary colleagues, Konstantin Simonov and Boris Gorbatov, to the Kremlin along with Molotov and Zhdanov on 13 May 1947. Fadeev, Chairman of the USSR Union of Writers, was expecting to discuss book royalties policy. But Stalin had an ulterior motive. Once policy on royalties had been settled, he handed over a letter for Fadeev to read aloud to the gathering. The contents related to a possible anti-cancer drug developed by two Soviet scientists who had released details about it to American publishers.[10] Fadeev was terrified as Stalin did his trick of walking up and down behind the backs of his guests. As Fadeev turned towards him, the sight of Stalin – stern-faced and watchful – agitated him further. Stalin declared: 'We've got to liquidate the spirit of self-humiliation.'

Fadeev was relieved to hear he was not in trouble but was being entrusted with the campaign against foreign influences and fashions. This could not be done by the Ministry of External Affairs without unsettling relations with the West.[11] (Just for once the eyewitnesses could record Stalin's specific calculations.) Stalin was planning to complete the closure of the Soviet intellectual mind. His own mind was already insulated from foreign influences. Now he was plotting the systematic reproduction of his mentality across the USSR.

Simonov wrote down Stalin's words:[12]

But here's the sort of theme which is very important and which writers ought to take an interest in. This is the theme of our Soviet patriotism. If you take average members of our intelligentsia, the scholarly intelligentsia, professors and doctors, their feeling of Soviet patriotism has been inadequately nourished in them. They engage in an unjustified grovelling before foreign culture. They all feel themselves still immature and not quite 100 per cent personalities; they've got used to the position of eternal pupils.

Stalin continued:[13]

> This is a backward tradition and it can be traced from Peter the Great. Peter had some good ideas but too many Germans soon established themselves; this was a period of grovelling before the Germans. Just look, for example, at how hard it was for [the eighteenth-century Russian polymath] Lomonosov to breathe, at how hard it was for him to work. First it was the Germans, then the French. There was much grovelling before foreigners, before shits.

Although Stalin was an admirer of Peter the Great, he was setting himself up as a ruler who could finally eradicate the syndrome of the feelings of inferiority characteristic of Russian intellectual life since the Petrine epoch.

By the Second World War he had stopped deluding himself that he could increase his control over the Soviet order, but in most ways he was proud of what he had consolidated.[14] He acknowledged that great changes would have to take place before the communism of Marx, Engels and Lenin could be realised. Yet he inserted his own peculiar ideas. In the 1920s he had of course stirred up controversy by saying that socialism could be constructed in a single country surrounded by hostile capitalist states. This had contrasted with the convention of Bolshevik theorists, including Lenin, that there would have to be more than one powerful state committed to socialism before such construction could be completed. Before the war Stalin had gone further by suggesting that the building of communism – the perfect stateless form of society dreamed about by Marxists until his emergence – could be started in the USSR on its own.[15]

Stalin had explained his idea to the Eighteenth Party Congress in March 1939: 'Shall our state also be retained in the period of communism? Yes, it will be retained unless capitalist encirclement is liquidated and unless the danger of military attack from abroad is liquidated.'[16] He gave no indication of how the state would, as Lenin had anticipated in *The State and Revolution* in 1917–18, 'wither away'. Molotov brought this theoretical inadequacy to Stalin's attention. The root of the problem could be traced back to the assertion in the USSR Constitution of 1936 that the Soviet state functioned on the principle of from each according to his abilities, to each according to his work. As Molotov had argued, this was not the real state of affairs in the USSR. Socialism was not yet near to completion. It was especially wrong to treat the kolkhozes as a socialist form of economy. Huge unfairness existed in the administration of society. Molotov also rejected the whole contention that socialism could be brought to completion in a single country. Building could start; it could be continued. Yet it could not be consummated.[17] Stalin understood what Molotov was saying but fobbed him off: 'I recognise theory, but I understand things like this: this is life and not theory.'[18] Life, as Stalin saw it from the late 1930s, required the spreading of pride in the existing order of state and society even if this involved sullying the purity of Leninist doctrines.

He took intense delight in Soviet achievements. As he and Georgian Communist Party boss Akaki Mgeladze looked at a map, he mused:[19]

> Let's see what we have here. In the north we have everything in order and normal. Finland has given way to us and we've pushed the frontier up from Leningrad. The Baltic region – which consists of truly Russian lands! – is ours again; all the Belorussians are now living with us and so are the Ukrainians and the Moldavians. Everything's normal in the west.

He was equally pleased about the east: 'What have we got here? ... The Kurile Islands are now ours, Sakhalin is wholly ours: doesn't that look good! And Port Arthur and Dalni [Darien] are both ours. The Chinese Railway is ours. As to China and Mongolia, everything's in order.' The only frontier annoying him was the southern one. Presumably he itched to obtain the Straits of the Dardanelles and perhaps also northern Iran. He had come to aspire to the restoration of the Russian Imperial frontiers and regard the foreign policy objectives of the Romanovs as his own; and works on the history of Muscovy and the Russian Empire, including Nikolai Karamzin's classic nineteenth-century series of volumes, had an increased appeal for him.

Stalin's passion for things Russian had become hypertrophied. When reading V. V. Piotrovski's *In the Steps of Ancient Cultures*, he came across the name 'Rusa' in a section on the Assyrians. He took note of this,[20] evidently thinking the word might give a clue about the origins of Russian nationhood. Anything with the slightest connection with Russia caught his eye. Like an elderly trainspotter who has to see one last steam engine before giving up the hobby, he had turned from enthusiast into zealot.

Few authors failed to incur some criticism from him. Piotrovski was among them. On the margin of the page where the author had claimed credentials as a pioneer in the historiography of culture, Stalin scoffed: 'Ha, ha!'[21] Stalin had combed purposefully through Piotrovski's book. The notes he took on the ancient languages of the Middle East were important for him, for he intended to write a lengthy piece on linguistics. To say that this caused surprise among the Soviet intelligentsia is an understatement. The expectation had been that when he took up the pen again he would offer his thoughts on politics or economics. But Stalin went his own way. In the course of his extensive reading he had come across the works of Nikolai Marr. A member of the Russian Imperial Academy before 1917, Marr had made his peace with the Soviet state and adjusted his theories to the kind of Marxism popular in the Soviet Union in the 1920s and 1930s. Marr had argued that Marxists should incorporate 'class principles' in linguistics as much as in politics. Language was to be regarded as class-specific and as the creation of whichever class happened to be in power. This was the official orthodoxy which Stalin had decided to overthrow.

Articles appeared in *Pravda* in summer 1950 and were collected in a booklet entitled *Marxism and Problems of Linguistics*. University faculties across the USSR stopped whatever they were doing to study Stalin's ideas.[22] Much of what he wrote was a healthy antidote to current ideas in Soviet linguistics. Marr had argued that the contemporary Russian language had been a bourgeois phenomenon under capitalism and should be re-created as a socialist phenomenon under the dictatorship of the proletariat. Stalin thought this was claptrap. He insisted that language had its roots in an earlier period of time; in most societies, indeed, it was formed before the capitalist epoch. Recent changes in Russian involved mainly the introduction of new words to the lexicon and the abandonment of old words as political and economic conditions were transformed. Grammatical tidying also took place. But the Russian language written and spoken by Alexander Pushkin in the early nine-teenth century contrasted little with the language of the mid-twentieth century.[23] While some classes had had their own jargon and some regions their own dialect, the fundamental language had been common to all Russians.[24]

Stalin's motives baffled those politicians and intellectuals accustomed to his polemical contributions on world politics, political dictatorship and economic transformation. His usual menace was barely evident. Only once did the anger show itself. This happened when he said that if he had not known about a particular writer's sincerity, he would have suspected deliberate sabotage.[25] Otherwise Stalin kept to the proprieties of a patient, modest teacher.

Marxism and Problems of Linguistics has been unjustly ignored. Despite turning to leading linguisticians such as Arnold Chikobava for advice, Stalin wrote the work by himself; and he did nothing without a purpose.[26] It was far from being only about linguistics. The contents also show his abiding interest in questions of Russian nationhood. At one point he stated magisterially that the origins of 'the Russian national language' can be traced to the provinces of Kursk and Orël.[27] Few linguisticians would nowadays accept this opinion. But it retains an importance in Soviet history, for it demonstrates Stalin's desire to root Russianness in the territory of the RSFSR. This was especially important for him because some philologists and historians regarded Kiev in contemporary Ukraine as the Russian language's place of origin. Moreover, he used the language of Russians as an example of the longevity and toughness of a national tongue. Despite all the invasions of the country and the various cultural accretions, the Russian language was conserved over centuries and emerged 'the victor' over efforts to eradicate it.[28] Frequently praising the works of Alexander Pushkin, Stalin left no doubt about the special nature of Russia and the Russians in his heart.

Yet this fascination with the 'Russian question' did not exclude a concern with communism and globalism. Stalin in fact asserted that eventually national languages would disappear as socialism covered the world. In their place would arise a single language for all humanity, evolving from 'zonal' languages which in turn had arisen from those of particular nations.[29] The widely held notion that Stalin's ideology had turned into an undiluted nationalism cannot be substantiated. He no longer espoused the case for Esperanto. But his current zeal to play up Russia's virtues did not put an end to his Marxist belief that the ultimate stage in world history would bring about a society of post-national globalism.

Nevertheless it was his zeal for Russia and the Soviet Union which took up most space in his intellectual considerations. This was clear in his very last book. He had written it in his own hand, refusing as usual to dictate his thoughts to a secretary.[30] The book, appearing shortly before the Nineteenth Party Congress in 1952, was *The Economic Problems* of Socialism in the USSR. It followed a public discussion on the topic inaugurated at Stalin's behest in November 1951; and in preparation for his own contribution he instructed Malenkov to acquaint himself with recent writings on political economy. Malenkov had been required to undertake many difficult tasks in his career but the instant assimilation of the whole corpus of Marxism was one of the most arduous.[31] Stalin recognised that he had neither the time nor the energy – nor even perhaps the intellectual capacity – to compose an innovative general conspectus on political economy. But it was well within his mental powers to indicate his preferred framework in so far as the USSR was affected. He aimed to supply guidelines for policies expected to stay in place for many years ahead. *The Economic Problems of Socialism* was intended by an ailing Leader as his intellectual testament.[32]

The book outlines several supposed heresies to be avoided by Soviet Marxists. First and foremost, Stalin argued against those who thought that economic transformation could be effected by the mere application of political will. Stalin maintained that 'laws' of development conditioned what was possible under socialism as much as under capitalism.[33] Stupendous hypocrisy was on display here. If ever there had been an attempt to transform an economy through sheer will and violence, it had been at the end of the 1920s under Stalin's leadership.

But in 1952 Stalin was determined to avoid further tumult. He very much wanted to end speculation that the kolkhozes might soon be turned into fully state-owned and state-directed collective farms (sov-khozy). For the foreseeable future, he insisted, the existing agricultural organisational framework would be maintained. Ideas about the construction of 'agrotowns' were also to be put aside. Similarly he continued to insist that investment in the capital-goods sector of industry had to take precedence in the USSR state budget. Although an increase of goods produced for Soviet consumers was a priority, it still had to take second place to machine tools, armaments and lorries and indeed to iron and steel in general. Stalin was writing exclusively about economics. His was not a general treatise on political economy. Yet while recommending steady maturation rather than any sharp break in economic policies and structures, he offered a firm implicit rationale for the existing system of politics. Stalin was content with his labours in the past few decades. The political institutions, procedures and attitudes which already existed were to remain in place while the Leader was alive and long afterwards.

In international relations, though, he anticipated a more dynamic development. Stalin posed two questions:[34]

a) Is it possible to assert that the well-known thesis expounded by Stalin before the Second World War about the relative stability of markets in the period of the general crisis of capitalism remains in force?

b) Is it possible to assert that the well-known thesis of Lenin, as expounded by him in spring 1916, that, despite the rotting away of capitalism, 'on the whole, capitalism is growing immeasurably faster than previously' remains in force?

As theorist-in-chief of the world communist movement, Stalin answered as follows: 'I don't think it is possible to make this assertion. In the light of the new conditions arising in connection with the Second World War, both theses need to be regarded as having lost their force.'[35] He looked east for his explanation:[36]

> But at the same time there has occurred a breaking away from the capitalist system by China and other popular-democratic countries in Europe, which together with the Soviet Union have created a single, powerful socialist camp confronting the camp of capitalism. The economic result of the existence of two opposed camps has been that the single, all-embracing world market has fallen apart with the consequence that we now have two parallel world markets also opposing each other.

Stalin asserted that the world had been changed by the numerical increase in communist states. The territorial contraction of the global capitalist market would not end but instead would intensify the rivalries among capitalist economies.[37] Although Germany and Japan had been militarily humbled, they would recover industrially and commercially to compete fiercely with the USA, the United Kingdom and France. The victors themselves had conflicting interests. The USA aimed to be the globe's dominant capitalist power and sought an end to the empires of its Western allies. A Third World War was to be expected. Stalin put it dogmatically: 'In order to eliminate the inevitability of war it is necessary to annihilate imperialism.'[38] In old age he cleaved to the credo that capitalism was doomed. He also continued to believe that socialism had an inherent capacity to nurture technological advance. This was an old Marxist idea. For Marx and Lenin it was axiomatic that capitalist development would eventually enter a cul-de-sac and would actively prevent the development of industrial products of general human benefit.[39]

The aspect of Stalin's thought that has captured the greatest attention, however, is his attitude to Jews. No irrefutable evidence of anti-semitism is available in his published works. His denial before the First World War that the Jews were a nation was made on technical grounds; it cannot be proved that he defined nationhood specifically in order to exclude Jews.[40] He did not refuse to allow Jewish people the right to cultural self-expression after the October Revolution; indeed his People's Commissariat for Nationalities' Affairs gave money and facilities to groups promoting the interests of Jews.[41] Yet the charges against him also included the accusation that his supporters highlighted anti-semitic themes in the struggle against Trotski, Kamenev and Zinoviev in the 1920s.[42] Within his family he had opposed his daughter's dalliance with the Jewish film-maker Alexei Kapler.[43] Yet the fact that his followers exploited anti-Jewish feelings in internal party disputes does not make him personally an anti-semite. As a father, moreover, he had much reason to discourage Svetlana from having anything to do with the middle-aged, womanising Kapler.

His campaign against 'rootless cosmopolitanism' cannot be automatically attributed to hatred of Jews as Jews. He moved aggressively against every people in the USSR sharing nationhood with peoples of foreign states. The Greeks, Poles and Koreans had suffered at his hands before the Second World War for this reason.[44] Campaigns against cosmopolitanism started up when relations between the Soviet Union and the USA drastically worsened in 1947.[45] At first Jews were not the outstanding target. But this did not remain true for long. A warm reception was accorded by twenty thousand Jews to Golda Meir at a Moscow synagogue in September 1948 after the foundation of Israel as a state.[46] This infuriated Stalin, who started to regard Jewish people as subversive elements. Yet his motives were of Realpolitik rather than visceral prejudice even though in these last years some of his private statements and public actions were undeniably reminiscent of crude antagonism towards Jews.

Yet Beria and Kaganovich, who was Jewish, absolved their master of anti-semitism.[47] (Not that they were moral arbiters on anything.) Certainly Kaganovich felt uncomfortable at times. Stalin's entourage were crude in their humour. One day Stalin asked: 'But why do you pull so very gloomy a face when we're laughing at the Jews? Look at Mikoyan: when we're laughing at the Armenians, Mikoyan laughs along with us at the Armenians.' Kaganovich replied:[48]

You see, comrade Stalin, you have good knowledge of national feelings and character. Evidently what was expressed in the character of the Jews was the fact that they were often given a beating and they reacted like a mimosa. If you touch it, it instantly closes up.

Stalin relented and Kaganovich, hardly the most sensitive of men, was allowed to stay out of the banter. The episode by itself does not exculpate Stalin; and it must be added that some of his remarks to others in the early 1950s were vicious in the extreme about Soviet Jews. Perhaps he turned into an anti-semite right at the end. Or possibly he was using violent language in order to drum up political support. He was too inscrutable to allow a verdict.

What is clear is that the mind of Stalin is irreducible to a single dimension. Some see him as a Russian nationalist. For others the driving force of his ideas was anti-semitism. A further school of thought postulated that in so far as he had ideas they were those of a Realpolitiker; this version of Stalin appears in various guises: the first is a leader who pursued the traditional goals of the tsars, the second is an opportunistic statesman yearning to stand tall alongside the leaders of the other great powers. And there are some – nowadays remarkably few – who describe him as a Marxist.

Stalin's intellectual thought was really an amalgam of tendencies, and he expressed himself with individuality within each of them. He had started as an adult by looking at the world through a Marxist prism, but it had been Marxism of the Leninist variant – and he had adjusted this variant, at times distorting it, to his liking. Lenin's Marxism had been a compound of Marx's doctrines with other elements including Russian socialist terrorism. Stalin's treatment of Leninism was similarly selective; and, like Lenin, he was loath to acknowledge that anything but the purest legacy of Marx and Engels informed his Marxism–Leninism. But his ideas on rulership were undoubtedly characterised by ideas of Russian nationhood, empire, international geopolitics and a generous dose of xenophobic pride. At any given time these tendencies were in play in his mind even if it was solely the members of his entourage who glimpsed the range of his sources. He did not systematise them. To have done so would have involved him in revealing how much he had drawn from thinkers other than Marx, Engels and Lenin. In any case he shrank from codifying ideas that he sensed would cramp his freedom of action if ever they were to be set in stone.

Stalin was a thoughtful man and throughout his life tried to make sense of the universe as he found it. He had studied a lot and forgotten little. His learning, though, had led to only a few basic changes in his ideas. Stalin's mind was an accumulator and regurgitator. He was not an original thinker nor even an outstanding writer. Yet he was an intellectual to the end of his days.

53. AILING DESPOT

Stalin's medical condition had steadily worsened. The cardiac problems from late 1945 compelled him to spend weeks away from the Kremlin. He could no longer cope with the previous burdens of official duty. Chronic overwork was exacting its toll. Having risen to political supremacy, he could have slackened his routines. But Stalin was a driven man. He thrashed himself as hard as he did his subordinates. He could no more spend a day in indolence than he was able to leap to the moon. Stalin, unlike Hitler, was addicted to administrative detail. He was also ultra-suspicious in his ceaseless search for signs that someone might be trying to dislodge his policies or supplant him as the Leader.

His previous medical history included appendicitis, painful corns, laryngitis and probably psoriasis.[1] His chronic mistrust of the medical profession had done him no favours. Admittedly even Stalin could not do entirely without doctors; but Kremlin specialists were nervous when treating him and arrests of individuals accused of poisoning Politburo members and other prominent public figures were frequent. Dr Moshentseva offered a bizarre and rather implausible account. When Stalin was brought to the clinic for treatment for an 'enormous abscess' on his foot, his face and body were reportedly covered in a blanket and she was instructed to fold back only the bottom edge. Not until later did she discover the identity of her patient.[2] Less fortunate was Stalin's personal physician Vladimir Vinogradov. In January 1952, after giving the Leader a check-up, he advised him to retire from politics to prevent fatal damage to his health. Vinogradov's frank diagnosis angered Stalin, who could not become a pensioner without risking retaliation by whoever became his successor. The diagnosis of permanent debility might induce his subordinates to gang up on him. (He had certainly given them excuse.) Vinogradov was thrown into the Lubyanka in November. The medical care of the Leader could come at a high price for his doctors.[3]

Stalin did not disregard his health problems. From the mid-1920s he had taken lengthy summer vacations by the Black Sea, relying on letters and telegrams to keep contact with politics in the Kremlin. Even when on holiday, he went on giving general instructions to his highest subordinates. The vacations got longer after 1945. In 1949 he spent three months in his residences in the south; in both 1950 and 1951 his sojourns in Abkhazia lasted nearly five months.[4]

He was trying to prolong life and career by mixing Black Sea leisure with long-distance rule. In 1936 he had had a dacha built for himself at Kholodnaya Rechka north of Gagra on the Abkhazian coast. It was a thick-walled stone structure designed by his court architect Miron Merzhanov. It had a dining room, meeting room, billiard room, tea room and several bedrooms – both upstairs and downstairs – and bathrooms. (In fact Stalin went on sleeping on a divan in preference to his many beds.)[5] The emphasis was on Soviet stolidity rather than luxury. The only imports were the German shower fittings and the Italian billiard table. Although the carpets were of better quality than any obtainable in Soviet shops, they were poorer than those sold in the Tbilisi markets of his boyhood. He ordered wood panelling throughout the dacha, and the walls of each room were covered with a variety of varnished timber. Apart from the billiard room, Stalin's main self-indulgence was a long gallery with a film projector and a screen foldable out from the wall. Water was pumped up from the stream at the bottom of the valley immediately to the south. The dacha's external walls (and this was also true of his daughter's adjacent dacha) were painted camouflage green.[6]

Slow on his feet, by the early 1950s Stalin looked like a gargoyle which had dropped off the guttering of a medieval church. His face had a gloomy pallor. His hair had long ago turned the grey of weather-beaten sandstone. No longer holding receptions for distinguished foreign guests, he ceased again to bother about his appearance. His clothes were shabbier than ever. Stalin lived as he pleased. Fir trees masked the buildings from view. Whenever he was in residence, fifteen hundred guards maintained his privacy and security. He alone slept in the residential part of the dacha,[7] and he habitually left the choice of bedroom till the last moment for fear of being assassinated.

Stalin liked working in the afternoon and at night; nothing would change in his routine until he finally collapsed in 1953. He never learned to swim and seldom descended the 826 steps to the road by the coast. His place of pleasure was the garden. At Kholodnaya Rechka he could distract himself from the political concerns that bothered his waking hours. From the balcony at the garden's edge he could gaze at the Black

Sea, calm and almost waveless in the late summer months. Fancying himself as a gardener, he planted lemon and eucalyptus trees in front of the house. The lemon tree was the only plant to survive the bitter winter of 1947–8; it remains there to this day.[8] In his Abkhazian dachas he could make his political calculations without fuss. He could also enjoy the kind of Caucasus he wanted for himself. This was a Caucasus without the bright human diversity and hectic activity of the towns of Georgia, Armenia, Azerbaijan or Abkhazia. At Kholodnaya Rechka or up by Lake Ritsa there was nothing but the dachas, the mountains, the sky and the sea. This was a controlled, secluded Caucasus where the only intrusions were those which he told Poskrëbyshev and Vlasik to allow.

Whether restoring himself in the south or relaxing at Blizhnyaya, Stalin strove to keep his decline a secret. He weighed himself regularly. He swallowed pills and iodine capsules – without medical supervision – to perk himself up.[9] He took the waters at the Black Sea spas and enjoyed occasional saunas in Moscow (which he regarded as equivalent to physical exercise: he had long given up active recreations). Stalin made it a point of pride on ceremonial occasions to ascend the Mausoleum steps on Red Square briskly before waving to the crowd.[10] Soviet citizens were encouraged to believe that the country's ruler remained hale and hearty. Stalin himself poked fun at those in his entourage who had let themselves go physically. He baited Khrushchëv and Malenkov for their corpulence. He ridiculed others on grounds of taste. Bulganin's goatee beard amused him. He laughed at Beria for refusing to wear a tie even though he himself would never wear one; he also objected to Beria's pince-nez: 'It makes you look like a Menshevik. Only a little chain is needed to complete the picture!'[11]

Age failed to soften his temper. Whenever he admitted he was feeling his age, his underlings protested that he was simply indispensable. But he went on mooting the possibility of stepping down from power despite his brutal treatment of Vinogradov for making that very suggestion. In 1946 he had told Politburo members to think about how to prepare the next generation to take power. According to Kaganovich, he also expressed a wish to retire. Molotov was his intended replacement: 'Let Vyacheslav do the work.'[12] This caused consternation: Kaganovich did not like the prospect of yielding to Molotov. Yet Stalin's favour, once given, could anyway be withdrawn. He played like a cat with the Politburo mice. In 1947 he told each of its members to select five or six subordinates who might eventually replace them. Mikoyan supplied the required list of names while arguing that the individuals were being promoted too early. There was no incentive for veterans to be helpful to newcomers; indeed they could have been forgiven for deliberately obstructing them, and this is probably what happened. Within a year the newcomers, their inexperience having been exposed, were eased out of office.[13] They could count themselves lucky they were still alive.

While teasing his leading subordinates, however, Stalin genuinely wished to shed many burdens; in particular, he delegated the routine management of the Soviet economy and administrative order to subordinates. He cut down the number of days he received visitors from 145 in the last year of the war to thirty-seven in 1952.[14] But he was determined to remain Leader.[15] He not only retained oversight of general policy but also reserved the capacity to intervene in particular affairs at his whim; and ailing though he was, he never let any great decision on international relations be taken without him. He continued to receive piles of papers from Moscow while he stayed by the Black Sea. Security police affairs remained one of his preoccupations.[16] Always he was accompanied by Alexander Poskrëbyshev, the head of the Special Department of the Secretariat of the Party Central Committee. Poskrëbyshev had been awarded the rank of major-general in the war and Stalin liked to josh him by addressing him as 'Supreme Commander'.[17] Their master-and-dog relationship was crucial for Stalin. Poskrëbyshev dealt with the telegrams coming to the dacha and decided which ones needed Stalin's attention. If an emergency arose, Poskrëbyshev was empowered to interrupt his master's dinner regardless of other guests and consult him about the desirable response.[18]

On his lengthy Abkhazian sojourns Stalin kept a lavish table ready for visitors. Most of them were politicians from Moscow or the Caucasus. Conversations were held on a wide variety of topics. His dinners and late breakfasts remained a fulcrum of his despotism. He used them to deliberate with his associates, to give precedence to one or other of them and to strike fear and incite jealousy among the rest. Among the accepted traditions from the late 1940s were elaborate toasts to his health and to his achievements. It was thought impolite to fail to stress his crucial part in preparing the USSR for the Second World War and in leading it to victory in 1945. At each dacha he arranged for a bounteous supply of wines, brandy and champagne; he also kept a store of cigars and cigarettes. Stalin, a lifelong pipe-smoker, remained partial to a puff on a cigarette.[19] He especially liked the company of young local officials and was an eager raconteur of his early life. In his declining years, especially in the presence of new acquaintances, he could not resist embroidering the stories with fanciful exaggeration; and his charm and sense of humour captivated them.

These younger men of party and government avidly ascertained his desires. Abkhazian party boss Akaki Mgeladze asked Stalin about his preferences in wine. Among red wines the Leader mentioned his favourite as Khvanchkara produced by peasant methods. This surprised Mgeladze, who had assumed that Stalin would go for the renowned Atenuri or Khidistavi of his native Gori. (Georgians are proud of the grapes of the locality where they are brought up.) Stalin explained that it was really for Molotov's benefit that he stocked Khidistavi. His other favoured red wine was Chkhaveri.[20] For breakfast he took a simple porridge in a milky bouillon; for lunch and dinner he preferred soups and fish – unusually for a man of the Caucasus he had no great longing for meat.[21] He adored bananas (and he got very cantankerous when presented with ones of inferior quality).[22] When everything was prepared, he played host in the Georgian manner and often dispensed altogether with servants. Guests served themselves from a buffet. Drinks were set out on adjacent small tables.[23]

The mischievous aspects of Stalin's dinner parties persisted. Vodka was poured into glasses instead of wine. Sometimes pepper would surreptitiously be shaken into someone's dish. It was not just horseplay. As before, Stalin wanted to keep people on edge. He loved it if a drink-sodden guest blurted out something indiscreet. He wanted to have dirt on everybody.[24] Yet he could also behave with gallantry. When the Georgian actor Bagashvili opined that Beria's wife Nina needed to escape 'her gilded cage', Beria declined to react despite the implication that she was living a life deprived of dignity. She felt and looked insulted. Stalin understood her reaction. Crossing the room he took her hand. 'Nina,' he said, 'this is the first time I have kissed a woman's hand.' Beria received a marital reprimand that evening and Stalin had earned an angry woman's gratitude.[25] He may well have been acting hypocritically; but if so, his behaviour was effective; and since he was a man of despotic power, he was usually given the benefit of the doubt by those he sought to charm.

Yet steadily Stalin rid himself of those who had been his intimates since the mid-1930s. Even Vlasik was sacked in April 1952 and Poskrëbyshev in January 1953. Another target for Stalin was Beria. Ostensibly the two were on fine terms. Stalin honoured him in 1951 by entrusting him with the main address on Red Square at the October Revolution anniversary celebrations. Beria suspected that Stalin was up to no good.

What worried him was the Leader's remark that he did not need to show him the text of the address in advance.[26]

Beria surmised he was being set up to say something that could be used against him. He knew Stalin's methods only too well, and events quickly proved that he was right to be circumspect. Two days after the anniversary parade, a Central Committee resolution denounced a 'Mingrelian nationalist group'. Beria was not named in the resolution, but his Mingrelian origin exposed him to further action – and indeed the resolution specified that a Paris-based Menshevik organisation led by Yevgeni Gegechkori, who was the uncle of Beria's wife, was running an espionage network in Georgia.[27] The Mingrelians are a people with a language so distinct from 'standard' Georgian that Stalin had never understood it.[28] (This, of course, did nothing to allay his newly developed suspicions about them.) Beria had several of them among his political clients, and – with Stalin's consent – he had given land to Mingrelians in Abkhazia at the expense of the Abkhazians. As arrests of prominent Mingrelians proceeded in the winter of 1951–2, Beria anticipated that he would soon join them. Although Stalin had stopped the purge by spring 1952, Beria noted that he was usually more polite than amicable. These were unpleasant omens. The former head of the NKVD feared that he might return to the Lubyanka in circumstances not of his choosing.[29]

In September several Kremlin doctors were arrested, the first of many. This followed a confidential denunciation of the treatment of Andrei Zhdanov, who had died in 1948. The writer was Dr Lidia Timashuk. Her denunciation, sent soon after Zhdanov's demise, was pulled out of the archives and used as grounds for a purge of the medical professors in the Kremlin Clinic. *Pravda* published an article exposing 'the assassins in white coats'. This caused panic in the elite of the medical profession. Professor Yevdokimov, Stalin's dental physician and for many years the Kremlin head of maxillofacial and oral surgery, stayed away from home for a week in case the police came for him.[30]

Yevdokimov returned to his apartment exhausted. Probably he had worked out that the authorities wanted to arrest doctors of Jewish origin. Most victims had surnames appearing to indicate they were Jews. 'Rootless cosmopolitanism' was routinely denounced with rising intensity. Jews across the Soviet Union were persecuted. They were sacked from positions of responsibility. They were vilified at work. Anti-semitic jibes on the streets became common and no one was called to account. It required courage for anyone to defend the victims. The campaign, which was never officially designated as being aimed at Jewish citizens, gathered force. Many leading Jews were taken into police custody. Solomon Mikhoels, a leader of the USSR's Jewish Anti-Fascist Committee (formed in the Second World War), was killed in a car crash on Stalin's orders in 1948; the Jewish Anti-Fascist Committee was disbanded and the rest of its leadership was arrested and shot.[31] But Molotov's wife Polina Zhemchuzhina, who had been in detention and exile since 1949, was still alive. She was picked as a Jew who might be put at the centre of a forthcoming show trial. Security police resumed their interrogation of her. Rumours grew that measures were being prepared to deport all Soviet Jews to the Jewish Autonomous Region set up in Birobidzhan in eastern Siberia in 1928 (when Stalin and the Politburo had at last come to the conclusion that those Jews of the USSR who wished to retain their ancestral culture should have a territory of their own).

Whether Stalin really intended the universal deportation of Jews in the early 1950s remains unknown, though this is widely treated as a fact; and no conclusive proof has come to light.[32] Yet the situation was developing fast. No Jew in the USSR could feel safe. The presentiment of pogroms grew. Kaganovich, being of Jewish ancestry, felt edgy. Perhaps Stalin would have spared him from implication in the Doctors' Plot. But the precedents were not encouraging. Once purges started, there was no telling where they might end. Already Molotov and Mikoyan had been cast down from on high. With Zhemchuzhina in prison, Molotov had long feared the worst. Both Molotov and Mikoyan had been removed from their leading posts even though they remained Politburo members. But the writing was on the wall for them. Favour, once withdrawn, was seldom given again.

When he came to finalising arrangements for the Nineteenth Party Congress in October 1952, Stalin had surprises in store. A Central Committee plenum was held in August. This gave him the chance to take the measure of the entire party and governmental leadership, and he did not fail to encourage individuals to criticise each other's draft directives before they were passed to the Congress. This was also an opportunity for rising young leaders to catch his eye. Among them was Mikhail Pervukhin, already Deputy Chairman of the Council of Ministers. Two weeks later Stalin phoned him early on Sunday morning. He asked Pervukhin why he had proposed amendments to the directives at the Central Committee plenum rather than at the Council of Ministers. Pervukhin explained that he felt obstructed by the fact that the directives had already been decided in the Bureau of the Council of Ministers. To Stalin this smelled like conspiracy, especially when he learned that Beria,

Malenkov and Bulganin took it in turns to chair the Bureau. Always he sought to break up coalitions among his subordinates. Malenkov and Bulganin remained in his good books but Stalin left nothing to chance. On his instructions the outspoken Pervukhin was promoted to membership of the Bureau.[33]

Stalin then asked the chastened Malenkov to deliver the Central Committee's political report. He himself was too frail. Not since 1925 had anyone but Stalin discharged this task. When Kaganovich asked him about this, Stalin artfully replied that he needed to 'promote the young'.[34] This, too, was scarcely good news for Kaganovich; but it was worse for Molotov and Mikoyan. At the meeting to plan the proceedings, Stalin proposed excluding them from the Congress Presidium as being 'non-active members of the Politburo'. When listeners took this as a joke, Stalin insisted that he meant what he said.[35] At the Congress itself Stalin said little, contenting himself with pleasing his audience by sitting in a prominent place on the platform. Policies already in place were confirmed by the eulogies of speakers. Yet divergences in the Politburo were detectable to the ears of the better-informed delegates. Malenkov spoke for light industry, Beria for the non-Russians and Khrushchëv for agriculture. All this was done in Aesopian language. On the surface it was made to seem that Stalin and the Politburo were as close in their opinions as two coats of paint.

His subordinates of course knew he was not gaga and had not attended the Congress just to be its political ornament: he was also listening and watching like a bird of prey. Stalinist conservatism was the order of the day. Failure to go along with the ceremonial plaudits for the policies of party and government would have been suicidal. Malenkov's report stepped wholly over the threshold of realism with his claim that the problem of grain supplies in the USSR had been solved 'definitively and for ever'. But such a trespass was safer for a speaker than the slightest sign of dissent.

The Central Committee plenum after the Congress on 16 October 1952 heard Stalin's last oral salvo. Accompanied by the other leaders, he entered the Sverdlov Hall to an ovation. He made a speech lasting an hour and half; he did this without notes and fixed his audience with a searching gaze.[36] His main theme, undeclared, was himself. He implied he was not long for this life. He reminisced about the dangers of early 1918 when enemies beset the infant Soviet state on all sides: 'And what about Lenin? As regards Lenin, go and re-read what he said and what he wrote at that time. In that incredibly grievous situation he went on roaring. He roared and feared nobody. He roared, roared, roared!'[37] Talking about Lenin, he was really describing himself and his contribution to the Revolution. 'Once I've been entrusted with it [a task], I carry it out. And not so that I should get all the credit. I wasn't brought up like that.'[38] When a Central Committee member proudly affirmed that he was Stalin's pupil, Stalin interjected: 'We are all pupils of Lenin!'[39] This was the nearest he came to leaving behind a political testament. Rather than bequeath recommendations on specific policies, he itemised the qualities needed by the Soviet leadership after his death. They included courage, fearlessness, personal modesty, endurance and Leninism.

His immediate aim was to expose the weaknesses of some potential successors. Unlike Lenin, he unstopped the bottles of his wrath as he poured insults on the heads of his victims. Molotov and Mikoyan were the main casualties. Stalin ranted on with accusations of cowardice and inconsistency, alleging that their trips to the USA had given them an exaggerated admiration of American economic strength. He recalled incidents when Molotov had wanted to soften the demand for grain supplies from the kolkhozes. Molotov took his dressing down without replying. Mikoyan, however, decided that active defence was called for, and he took the lectern to respond.[40] Politburo members already knew of Stalin's hostility to Molotov and Mikoyan, but it was news for other leading members.

The scenario was close to completion for a final settling of accounts. Molotov, Mikoyan and Beria lived in dread. The Central Committee set up a Presidium as its main executive organ instead of the Politburo. Stalin read out the list of proposed members. The entire list was accepted without discussion.[41] The new Party Presidium was to have an internal Bureau, and neither Molotov nor Mikoyan was appointed to it.[42] (Beria gained a place, but this was no serious consolation; he knew that Stalin had often worked with a salami-slicer when starting a purge.) When the Presidium met on 18 October, Malenkov was put in charge of its permanent commission on foreign affairs, Bulganin was to supervise 'questions of defence' and Shepilov was to head the commission on 'ideological questions'.[43] Old though he was, Stalin still had applied himself to reading reports, plotting his manoeuvres and attending crucial meetings – and, as in 1937, he passed up the opportunity to take a vacation that whole year. The Bureau met six times in the remaining weeks of 1952 and Stalin attended on each occasion.[44] Much of the proceedings centred on personnel postings. But there was also discussion of business of a distinctly sinister nature. Stalin raised the question 'of sabotage in medical work'; he also required a report 'about the situation in the MGB of the USSR'.[45]

Stalin desired to bind an official party organ behind the wagon of his conspiracy. The risk of a coup against him needed to be reduced. By moving slowly and obtaining formal sanction for each stage of the way, he also hoped to convince the younger and therefore less experienced Bureau members that his measures were based on solid evidence. The killer needed to secure his alibi and his legendary guile had not left him.

His veteran accomplices were shivering with trepidation. Not only Beria but also Malenkov, Khrushchëv and Bulganin knew from experience that they could not assume that Stalin would not eventually pick them off too. He could not be trusted: that much was obvious to everybody. Things were getting bad. On 21 December 1952 Molotov and Mikoyan, after much vacillation, decided to go out to Stalin's Blizhnyaya dacha to greet him on his birthday. They had done this for many years and, although he had recently shown hostility to them, they thought the hostility might increase if they broke the custom. They were mistaken. The visit annoyed Stalin, and the other Presidium members advised Molotov and Mikoyan to keep out of his sight.[46] Yet still his entire demeanour baffled as well as scared everyone. Plainly he was not the person he once had been. After his death his associates were to remark on a psychological as well as a physical deterioration in him. They noted the onset of an unpredictability which they called 'capricious'. Previously he had stayed fairly loyal to the group of leaders he had established in the late 1930s; the Leningrad Affair of 1949–50 had been the exception, not the rule, in the post-war years.[47] But he had come to proffer or withdraw favour with an arbitrariness that terrified them.

So what was the Leader up to? Was there a great plan behind the moves he was making? Would the elimination of several veterans – and the persecution of all Jews – mark the end of any projected purge? Could such a purge be carried through to its end by a man whose physical decline was unmistakable? To his close associates, whether or not they had been denounced by him, there appeared no point in guessing about precise motives. Stalin had been killing fellow politicians for many years. He had not lost the habit with the onset of decrepitude.

54. DEATH AND EMBALMING

As 1952 was drawing to a close, Stalin held a birthday party in the large reception room at his Blizhnyaya dacha on 21 December.[1] The Boss was intent on having a good time and had invited the leading politicians. His daughter Svetlana was also present. Pictures of Soviet children covered the walls. Stalin had also arranged for paintings of scenes from the works of Gorki and Sholokhov to be pinned up.[2] Much drink was consumed. The gramophone played folk and dance music all night long, and Stalin was in charge of the choice of discs. It was a merry occasion.

Yet two guests looked glum. One was Khrushchëv, who hated having to dance and called himself 'a cow on ice'. Mischievously Stalin called upon him to perform the energetic Ukrainian *gopak*. Perhaps the Boss, who as a boy failed to master the *lekuri*,[3] derived perverse satisfaction from his embarrassment. The other person who did not enjoy the evening was Svetlana. At the age of twenty-six, already twice married and a mother, she could not stand being told what to do and rejected his request for a dance with her. His shortened arm usually inhibited Stalin from taking to the floor but he had had a glass or two that evening. When Svetlana demurred he flew into a rage. Grabbing her ginger hair, he dragged her forward. Her face turned red and her eyes filled with tears of pain and humiliation. Other guests felt for her but could do nothing. Khrushchëv, still smarting from his own embarrassment, never forgot the scene: '[Stalin] shuffled around with his arms spread out. It was evident that he had never danced before.' But he did not judge Stalin harshly. 'He behaved so brutishly not because he wanted to cause hurt to Svetlana. No, his behaviour toward her was really an expression of affection, but in the perverse, brutish form that was peculiar to him.'[4]

Other revellers worried about something a lot worse than being yanked by the hair on to a dance floor. The probable imminence of a political purge agitated all of them. *Pravda* on 13 January 1953 published an editorial on 'Evil Spies and Murderers Masked as Medical Professors'.

Stalin had edited the text.[5] Although he stayed all this time at Blizhnyaya, he was no mere spectator of the complex political drama.[6] Members of the Party Presidium – as the Politburo had been redesignated – read *Pravda* with their hearts in their mouths. The tension was reaching breaking point. On 28 February Stalin invited Malenkov, Beria, Khrushchëv and Bulganin to watch a film with him at the dacha. Stalin was as welcoming a host as ever. Food and drink were lavish. Party Presidium members, after a skinful of Georgian wine, tried to avoid saying anything that might annoy the Leader. When dinner was over, Stalin told the servants to open the cinema facility in the ground-floor gallery. The party broke up at four o'clock in the morning of 1 March.[7] None of the departing grandees recalled that Stalin looked ill. According to Khrushchëv, they left him well oiled and on good form.[8] This was to be expected after a long night of carousing.

As the limousines of his visitors departed into the darkness of the Moscow countryside, Stalin gave a quick instruction to his guards. One of them, Pavel Lozgachëv, reported the contents to his chief Ivan Khrustalëv. Stalin had announced that he was going to bed and that they could go off duty and sleep; he had also ordered that the guards should not disturb him until such time as he called them into his rooms.[9]

From mid-morning on 1 March disquiet grew among the guards when they came on duty because Stalin failed to beckon them inside. The routine had been in place for years. A group known as the mobile security team patrolled Blizhnyaya dacha. Each guard's shift alternated between two hours on duty and two hours' rest so as to maintain alertness. The guards' positions around the dacha were designated by numbers.[10] Stalin's unusual ban on disturbing him stayed in force, and yet they all knew that they would get the blame if something untoward had happened. His habit was to ask for a glass of tea with a slice of lemon in the late morning. He was as regular as clockwork. Deputy commander Mikhail Starostin became nervous that no such request had been made.[11] There was no higher authority at the dacha to turn to. Poskrëbyshev and Vlasik were no longer in post and it was unclear who in the Party Presidium, if anybody, could and would countermand a personal order given by Stalin. This was a situation which had worked to Stalin's advantage when he was fit. He was about to pay a fatal price for his extraordinary concentration of power.

At 6.30 p.m. a light was switched on in the dacha. The patrolling guards were relieved at this sign of life, surmising that all must be well with the Leader. They assumed that, after getting up late, he was tending to his mass of duties. Yet Stalin failed to emerge from his room. He neither called for food nor gave commands for anything to be done. No one caught a glimpse of him. The guards therefore remained perplexed about what they should do next. At around 10 p.m. a package arrived for Stalin from the Central Committee offices in Moscow. This forced the security group to make a decision. After an exchange of opinions it was resolved that Pavel Lozgachëv should take the package to Stalin. Nervously entering the room, he came upon a shocking scene. Stalin was slumped on the floor. Although he had not quite lost consciousness, he could not speak and had wet himself. Evidently he had had a stroke. Stalin's wristwatch lay on the floor next to him showing the time at half-past six. The guards reasonably guessed that Stalin had fallen over at that earlier moment in the evening when he had put on the light.[12]

No one dared do the most obvious thing and call a doctor. Needing an instruction from higher authority, the guards phoned Minister of State Security Sergei Ignatev in Moscow. Even Ignatev felt out of his depth and phoned Malenkov and Beria. Everyone at the dacha frantically wished to receive orders. All they did on their own initiative was to lift Stalin from the floor and move him on to his divan and place a blanket over him.[13]

Receiving Ignatev's news from Malenkov, Presidium members wondered whether Stalin's final demise was at hand. But exactly how they acted is still an unsolved riddle. Not only Stalin's fellow politicians but also his guards kept their mouths shut for many years about the episode – and memories deteriorated with the passage of time. The vicissitudes of the struggle for the political succession also had a distorting effect on the records. The victor was Khrushchëv. Beria was executed in December 1953 and Malenkov, on losing to Khrushchëv, was not inclined to record his testimony. Khrushchëv and Svetlana Allilueva were left as the only witnesses who could freely give their accounts before old age dimmed their memories. Unfortunately neither Khrushchëv nor Allilueva was averse to fantasising to exaggerate their knowledge and virtue. It was a paradoxical situation. Stalin himself had rigidly regulated the issuance of details about his life; their scantiness and unreliability were extreme. Yet the provision of those details became even less dependable from the day he lost that control. Dates, procedures, personalities and events are as clear as a barrel of tar for the period from 28 February to 5 March 1953.

The fullest account came from Khrushchëv. According to him, several of them went out to the dacha in the early hours of 2 March. Supposedly these included Malenkov, Beria, Bulganin and Khrushchëv.

It is not certain whether or not they – or some of them – made a second visit before deciding to call for medical assistance.[14] For whatever reason, it was hours before doctors were summoned to care for Stalin. The precise time of their advent is in dispute. Svetlana, who had been summoned from a French language class,[15] put it at 10 a.m. in her memoir; but the more plausible account by the guard A. I. Rybin, who was there at the time, put it at 7 a.m.[16] In any case it is clear that Presidium members were not quick to arrange for such assistance. This gave rise to the suspicion that they deliberately let Stalin's condition deteriorate. It is a possibility since all of them were potential purge victims. But perhaps his political subordinates were simply too scared to intervene any earlier. If he recovered, they would pay a heavy price for acting as if they were in charge of the country. This is a credible hypothesis. Yet they were surely dilatory to a culpable extent – and perhaps they were already more aware of the chronic nature of his ill health than they let on.

The doctors found Stalin drenched in his urine. They undressed and wiped him clean with a vinegar-based solution. At some point he vomited blood; Cheynes-Stokes respiration ensued with its characteristic gasping and irregularity. The seriousness of his condition was obvious. The medical experts themselves were functioning under the stress of knowing what happened to doctors who failed to satisfy Soviet politicians. They quickly found out the worst. Stalin's right extremities were totally paralysed. Although they did what they could, his prospects were poor. Before midday they administered enemas, even though no one seriously anticipated a positive effect.[17]

The problem for the Presidium was that, if Stalin recovered, they could be damned if they had failed to assist his recovery and damned if they had intervened without his permission. Caution was vital. It was clearly essential to discover more about his condition. Unfortunately, after the Doctors' Plot arrests, the finest medical expertise in Moscow was to be found in the cells of the Lubyanka. What followed was a tragicomedy. The incarcerated professors (who allegedly were among the most evil traitors) were approached and asked the likely consequences for a patient diagnosed as having Cheynes–Stokes respiration. After weeks of torture they were bewildered by the unusual turn taken by their interrogators. Yakov Rappoport answered concisely that this was a very 'grave symptom', implying that death was the likeliest result.[18] Whether medical steps were taken on the basis of such information is not known. But Presidium members had at least gained the assurance that they were free to plan for the political succession. The evidence of their eyes was anyway pretty conclusive: Stalin was in a ghastly condition and the doctors attending him were clearly pessimistic. Now the country's most distinguished physicians, held in the Lubyanka, had independently confirmed their impression.

On 4 March they started to make their arrangements. There was no procedural tradition and no rules; Stalin had studiously kept the matter off the agenda. The main leaders sensed that legitimacy would accrue to them only if they could pretend to continuity, and they convoked an emergency session of the Party Central Committee. This enabled the Presidium veterans to bypass the threat from the members promoted since the Nineteenth Congress in October 1952. Some veterans were better placed than others. Molotov could not claim supreme power after Stalin's attack on him in October 1952. Malenkov and Beria took the initiative. Flanked by the Presidium veterans (with the exception of Bulganin, who was on duty by Stalin's bedside), Malenkov opened the session by announcing that Stalin was seriously ill and that the prognosis was poor even were he to survive the current medical crisis. The Central Committee listened silently and anxiously. Then the lectern was ceded to Beria, who proposed that Malenkov should take over Stalin's post as Chairman of the Council of Ministers with immediate effect. This was agreed and the short session was declared closed.[19]

Yet Stalin had not yet passed away and Presidium members sped back to Blizhnyaya dacha where he was sinking irretrievably. They were watching their past lives flash before their eyes: the Five-Year Plans, the Great Terror and the Great Patriotic War. Stalin personified their collective career. They had been active in the consolidation of the Soviet state, its military and industrial power as well as its territorial expansion and political security. With the possible exception of Beria, they were in awe of Stalin's intelligence and experience at the same time as they simply feared him. He had bewitched them even while traumatising them. As he lay prostrate on the divan, they could not be confident that by some superhuman effort he would not revive and return to dominate public life again. These very individuals who had sent millions to their deaths in the Gulag under Stalin's leadership trembled at the sight of an old man, semi-conscious and inert, whose life was slipping away. To the end he held them in thrall. There was still the possibility that he might recover sufficiently, if only for a moment, to order the destruction of all of them. Even a dying Stalin was not to be trifled with.

At the dacha the tension was intense. Beria, taking charge of security, put the zone around Blizhnyaya into quarantine as a watch was kept on the patient. On the morning of 5 March he again vomited blood.[20] As the doctors later discovered, he had suffered a massive stomach haemorrhage. His general health had been poor for years and his arteries were hardened. Medical staff and politicians gathered at his bedside. Svetlana was the only close family member at the dacha. Turns were taken by those present to approach his recumbent body to pay their respects. They took his hand looking for some sign of his intentions toward them. Most remarkable was the behaviour of Beria, who slobbered on Stalin's hand in an unctuous display of personal fidelity. At 9.50 a.m. the Leader choked on his last breath. He was gone.

Some fell into each other's arms. The distraught Svetlana took comfort in the embrace of Khrushchëv. Servants were allowed in to see the corpse. Even the Presidium members, who hours previously had been making dispositions for politics after Stalin, were affected. A whole period in their lives as well as in their country's history had been terminated. They would not have been human if they had not been shocked by their experience. Only one person had full presence of mind. This was Beria, who behaved like an uncaged panther. No longer unctuous or doleful, he shouted: 'Khrustalëv! The car!'[21] Beria raced to the Kremlin to complete an orderly political succession in which he would play a leading role. While others consoled Svetlana or wept by Stalin's bedside, there was much to do and Beria set the pace. Unlike Molotov and Mikoyan, he had not been named as an undesirable potential leader. The Mingrelian Affair had not been mentioned at the Central Committee and, as far as its members knew, Beria had been in Stalin's good books to the end. The battle for the succession was under way.

The security group became the guard of honour standing by the dead Leader. A black catafalque arrived at the dacha and the guards carried him into it for transfer to the special institute where the condition of Lenin's corpse was regularly checked and Stalin's corpse would be prepared for the funeral. Guard commander Khrustalëv remained in charge.

At 8 p.m. on 5 March the Party Central Committee reconvened with Khrushchëv in the chair. Presidium members knew they had to convince everyone present that Stalin had died of natural causes.[22] The platform was given to USSR Minister of Health A. F. Tretyakov for a detailed medical explanation. Khrushchëv, avoiding debate, announced the proposals from the Bureau of the Presidium. Malenkov was suggested as

Chairman of the Council of Ministers. Beria would be one of his First Deputies and would take charge of the Ministries of Internal Affairs (MVD) and State Security (MGB). Khrushchëv would remain a Secretary of the Party Central Committee. The older veterans were not ignored. Voroshilov was to be made Chairman of the Presidium of the USSR Supreme Soviet. Molotov, who retained his standing in the minds of fellow leaders despite Stalin's attack on him, would become First Deputy Chairman of the Council of Ministers (as did not only Beria but also Bulganin). The key figures, however, were Malenkov, Beria and Khrushchëv. This was signalled in the decision to entrust them with the task of bringing Stalin's papers 'into necessary order'. Every proposal was unanimously approved and the meeting lasted only forty minutes.[23] Stalin's specific wishes were being repudiated. He had been plotting the downfall of Beria as well as Molotov and Mikoyan. Malenkov, however, saw Beria as a useful ally and Khrushchëv temporarily accepted the *fait accompli*.

Malenkov, Beria and Khrushchëv had known Stalin in the years when he held the power of life or death over them. They had no experience of politics free of fear that he might order their arrest. Beria got his son Sergo to train as a pilot and learn the international air routes in case the family needed to flee.[24] Beria, Molotov, Voroshilov, Mikoyan and Kaganovich had reason to bless Stalin's parting with this earthly life. Others such as Khrushchëv and Malenkov must have worried that Stalin's menace might eventually be directed at them too. The entire Presidium had shivered with fear for months. Stalin's closest subordinates had plenty of interest in his demise and in conspiring to hasten its occurrence. The reasons for death remain obscure. Although an autopsy was carried out, the report has never been found. This would be more than enough to induce suspicions. Furthermore, the ten doctors who cared for him at the end composed a history of his illness. Yet it was not completed until July (and has only recently become available).[25] Its plausible conclusion was that Stalin died of natural causes. But the delay in composition was odd, as was the loss of the autopsy document: perhaps something important was being covered up.

The verdict must remain open. One possibility is that he was murdered, probably with the connivance of Beria and Khrustalëv. Poison administered in Stalin's food is the method usually touted; another suggestion is that Beria arranged for his men to enter the dacha and kill the Leader with a lethal injection. In one strange version it is alleged that the man who died at the Blizhnyaya house was not Stalin but his double; but this too is far-fetched speculation entirely without evidence (and indeed without an explanation of why, if the corpse belonged to a double, Stalin did not return to wreak vengeance on the plotters).

The corpse was carried to the institute's first floor on a stretcher and medical staff took over from guards who were still in a shocked condition – many were in tears. Khrustalëv alone stayed as the other guards went back downstairs to the vestibule. Stalin's false teeth were removed and given to the guard commander for safekeeping. Like Lenin, Stalin was to be embalmed. He had complicated this task in 1952 by arresting Boris Zbarski, who had been in charge of the Mausoleum laboratory for many years.[26] But the chemistry had long ago been recorded for others to use. Meanwhile Stalin's corpse was laid out in a catafalque on Red Square.[27] The same guards accompanied the body to the Hall of Columns down from Red Square, where it stayed until the day of the funeral.[28] The order was given to convert the Lenin Mausoleum into a joint resting place for both Lenin and Stalin. There was nothing unexpected about this, even though Stalin had given no instructions. For two decades he had been hailed as the greatest living human being. The Presidium simply assumed that his corpse should receive the same treatment as Stalin had organised for Lenin in 1924.

Radio and newspapers announced his death on 6 March. The popular shock was immense since no prior intimation of his physical collapse had been given; and indeed there had been no comment in previous years about the general decline in his health. Crowds gathered. Muscovites raced to catch a glimpse of the dictator's remains before the funeral. Trains and buses from distant provinces were packed with passengers avid to see Stalin lying in state. By Metro and bus everyone came to the capital's centre and then walked up on foot to the cobbled square with sombre eagerness. On 8 March the human mass became too large for the police to control. Far too many people were converging from all directions. Panic ensued as many tried to turn back. The result was disastrous. Thousands of individuals were trampled and badly injured, and the number of people who suffered fatal asphyxiation (which was withheld from the newspapers) went into the hundreds. Even in his coffin the Leader had not lost his capacity to deal out death at random to his subjects. There was another aspect to this tragedy: it indicated the limits of state control even in the USSR. Outward obedience to orders was shown most of the time; but the surface of public calm was a brittle one and the MVD was nervous of prohibiting ordinary people from doing what they wanted in the first couple of days after the news was broadcast.

The funeral took place on 9 March. It was a cold, dry, grey day of late winter. The sun did not appear. Frost was heavy.[29] The crowds were dense. Short journeys in the capital took several hours. The authorities were caught between wanting to be legitimated by association with his memory and ensuring the preservation of order on the streets. The Imperial regime had become intensely unpopular when thousands of spectators were accidentally trampled to death on Khodynka Field on the day of Nicholas II's coronation. It would not do to allow a repetition of such an event with the passing of Joseph the Terrible.

Any other outcome than a peaceful ceremony would have sent out the message that Stalin's successors were unable to rule the country: they had to prove themselves men of steel like the deceased Leader. The catafalque at the Hall of Columns had a side-curtain proclaiming 'Proletarians of All Countries, Unite!' Only Stalin's head and shoulders were left visible. His eyes were closed. Strong searchlights were trained on him. Official photographers were recurrently permitted to approach and record the occasion. Orchestras played. A female choir, dressed in black, sang dirges. At 10.30 a.m. the Party Presidium entered to the accompaniment of the USSR state hymn. Malenkov led the way, part-nered by China's representative Chou En-lai. A gun carriage bore the coffin out of the Hall of Columns up the slope to Red Square where the newly redesignated Lenin–Stalin Mausoleum awaited it. The corpse was removed from the gun carriage and transferred to a bier outside the building. Presidium members and honoured guests moved to the top of the Mausoleum.[30] Across Red Square an enormous crowd had assembled. Microphones and amplifiers had been set up to enable all to hear the ceremony. Wreaths were piled high. (The composer Sergei Prokofiev had died on the same day as Stalin and his mourners found the shops empty of flowers because everyone had rushed to pay their respects to the Leader.) The passing of a political era was being marked.

Detachments of the Soviet Army marched across Red Square. The MVD as usual organised security behind the crowd barriers. Military orchestras played the conventional dirges. Hundreds of thousands of Muscovites turned out to pay their last respects; and unlike on May Day or 7 November, when their work-organisations directly compelled them to take part in such ceremonies, the popular eagerness to be present on the historic day was unmistakable.

There were three eulogies. Malenkov, Molotov and Beria gave them from the top of the Mausoleum. Those in proximity to the speakers could detect differences among them: only Molotov's face betrayed sincere grief. Beria spoke with a brusque dryness (and was later rebuked for this by his wife Nina).[31] Molotov's prominence indicated to the politically well informed that tremors were already making themselves felt at the apex of Soviet politics: the corpse of Stalin had hardly cooled before his former leading accomplice had been readmitted to the ruling group. Foreign visitors were not confined to communists. Veteran communist leaders Chou En-lai, Palmiro Togliatti, Dolores Ibárurri and Maurice Thorez had pride of place; but others at the ceremony included Italian socialist leader Pietro Nenni. Condolences poured into Moscow from foreign governments. Stalin's old negotiating rivals Churchill and Truman sent condolences. Newspapers in the communist countries stressed that the tallest giant of history was no more. In the West the reaction of the press was more diverse. Yet although his crimes against humanity were recorded, few editors wished to leave the occasion unaccompanied by reference to his part in the economic transformation of his country and the victory over the Third Reich. This was a gentler fate than he deserved.

The world communist movement, however, did not question his services to humanity. He who had ordered the construction of the Lenin Mausoleum was about to join the founder of the Soviet Union in death. The embalmers completed their work. His corpse had been gutted and soaked in the liquid whose ingredients remained a secret. A glass cabinet had been commissioned. The internal layout of the rectangular granite structure was rearranged while masons changed its name to the Lenin–Stalin Mausoleum. Joseph Vissarionovich Dzhughashvili, known to history as Stalin, was laid to rest.

55. AFTER STALIN

A tidal wave of reforms crashed over Stalin's policies in the USSR in the first week of March 1953. His successors were posthumously opposing him after decades of obedience. No member of the Party Presidium favoured the total conservation of his legacy; even communist conservatives like Molotov and Kaganovich approved some sort of innovation. Changes frustrated by Stalin at last became possible. Yet debate did not flood out into society. It was not allowed to. The last thing the ascendant party leaders wanted was to let ordinary Soviet citizens, or even the lower functionaries of the state, influence what was decided in the Kremlin.

Molotov and Kaganovich could not prevent the reform projects of Malenkov, Beria and Khrushchëv. Malenkov wanted to increase payments to collective farms so as to boost agricultural production; he also favoured giving priority to light-industrial investment. Khrushchëv wished to plough up virgin lands in the USSR and end the decades-old uncertainty about supplies of bread. Malenkov and Beria were committed to making overtures to the USA for peaceful coexistence: they feared that the Cold War might turn into a disaster for humanity. Beria desired a rapprochement with Yugoslavia; he also aimed to withdraw privileges for Russians in the USSR and to widen the limits of cultural self-expression. Malenkov, Beria and Khrushchëv agreed that public life should be conducted on a less violent and arbitrary basis than under Stalin. They supported the release of political convicts from the labour camps. Quietly they restrained the official media from delivering the customary grandiose eulogies to Stalin. If his policies were to be replaced, it no longer made sense to go on treating him as a demigod.

The Party Presidium handled his physical legacy with caution. When Lenin had died in 1924, Stalin became the custodian of his writings and decided what should be published and what withheld from view. He published his own *Foundations of Leninism*. He sought legitimacy for whatever he was doing by reference to the works of Lenin. Stalin's successors knew this. Sanctioned by the Party Central Committee on 5 March 1953,[1] they commandeered his book collection and distributed most of it anonymously to various public libraries. Only a few hundred books were left with the Institute of Marxism–Leninism. Many of his letters and telegrams were incinerated and most drafts of his articles and books disappeared.[2] The last edition of his collected works was suspended incomplete.[3]

Stalin's desk at the Blizhnyaya dacha held disturbing secrets. It contained three sheets of paper which he had hidden beneath a newspaper inside a drawer. One was a note from Tito:[4]

> Stalin: stop sending people to kill me. We've already captured five
> of them, one of them with a bomb and another with a rifle . . .
> If you don't stop sending killers, I'll send one to Moscow, and
> I won't have to send a second.

Thus did one gangster write to another. No one else had stood up to Stalin like this; perhaps this is why he kept the note. He had also conserved the last thing written to him by Bukharin: 'Koba, why is my death necessary for you?' Had Stalin wanted a frisson of satisfaction when re-reading it? (It cannot be believed that some distorted feeling of attachment to Bukharin lingered with him.) The third item was the letter dictated by Lenin on 5 March 1922 containing the demand for Stalin to apologise to Krupskaya for his verbal abuse of her. It was his last message from Lenin and it was the most wounding. He would not have conserved it in the desk unless it had echoed round the caverns of his mind.

The party leaders kept the three items a secret. But they changed public discourse after Stalin's death and *Pravda* restrained its praise of him. Articles criticised the 'cult of the individual'. Although these were laden with citations of Stalin's works, it took no feat of memory to recall that his cult had been the most grandiose in history. While fresh policies were being discussed in the Party Presidium, Beria celebrated his return to the leadership of the Ministry of Internal Affairs by collecting tape recordings of Stalin's conversations with the police agencies. The tapes proved that Stalin was plotting terror to the end. Beria arranged for Central Committee members to read the transcripts.[5]

The reformers faced a dilemma: if they advertised any abandonment of Stalin's legacy, there would be a questioning of their legitimate claim to rule; but if they were slow to alter some policies they might meet trouble for ignoring the discontents of society. There was a further difficulty. Stalin was revered by many of those people – and there were millions of them – who had hated his repressions. The despot still exercised his spell in death. Reformers had to be seen behaving firmly and competently. Signs of panic might ignite a challenge to the whole Soviet order. The majority in the Presidium sought to alter Stalin's policies without expressly criticising him.[6] At Party Central Committee meetings they merely alluded to Stalin's unpredictability and capriciousness in his last years. This happened at the plenum in July 1953 after Beria's arrest on the trumped-up charge of being a British intelligence agent. Really the leadership feared that Beria was lusting after his own personal supremacy as well as planning reforms which seemed excessively radical. It was Beria, not Stalin, who was held responsible for the past crimes and abuses, and he was executed in December 1953.[7]

Stalin's family experienced an abrupt change in circumstances. His daughter Svetlana sensibly changed her surname. As a student she had been known as Svetlana Stalina but after his death she called herself Svetlana Allilueva.[8] By bowing low before her father's successors, she saved herself from trouble. Vasili Stalin was incapable of such an adjustment. He was notorious for drunken party-going and debauchery. His father virtually disowned him, but only after the Leader's death was Vasili called to account and arrested for rowdiness and misuse of public funds. His days of privilege were at an end.

The Ministry of Internal Affairs was brought under the party's control after the fall of Beria. The limits on cultural expression continued to be widened. Malenkov and Khrushchëv carried on promoting reforms while competing for personal supremacy. Prices paid for the harvest to collective farms were raised. The virgin soil of Kazakhstan was ploughed up to increase the volume of agricultural production. A rapprochement took place with Tito's Yugoslavia. Overtures were made to the USA for a lessening of international tensions. The Korean War was brought to a close. Discussions at the Central Committee became less governed by the need to show unequivocal support for every action of the Party Presidium. Although the USSR remained a one-party dictatorship, the atmosphere of general fear had been lightened. The rivalry between Malenkov and Khrushchëv kept growing. Beria had been feared equally for his reformist radicalism and his personal ruthlessness. Malenkov lacked his panache and Khrushchëv, benefiting from his reputation as the conqueror of Beria, emerged as the supreme leader in the Presidium within a couple of years.

At his instigation a commission examined material on the purges of the Stalin period. Khrushchëv, while searching for damaging evidence about Malenkov, also had a larger agenda. Several Party Presidium members objected to any further reforms. To secure his ascendancy Khrushchëv raised the Stalin question at the Twentieth Party Congress in February 1956. When comments were made about the danger of destabilising the Soviet order, he retorted: 'If we don't tell the truth at the Congress, we'll still be forced to tell the truth at some time in the future. And then we won't be the people making the speeches. No, instead we'll be the people under investigation!'[9] At a closed session of the Congress he denounced Stalin as a monstrous individual who had sent thousands to their deaths and broken with Leninist traditions in leadership and policy. The charge sheet was not a comprehensive one. Khrushchëv focused his report on Stalin's activity from Kirov's death in 1934 onwards. He avoided criticism of the basic political and economic structures set up in the late 1920s, and he said nothing about the terror conducted by Stalin in the Civil War and the First Five-Year Plan. Wanting to ingratiate himself with current party and governmental officials, he gave the impression that their predecessors had been the main victims of the Great Terror of 1937–8.

The Congress audience was stunned into silence. Khrushchëv had achieved his purpose: he had made it difficult for his Soviet opponents to attack his leadership and policies without seeming to advocate a reversion to state terror. Yet there was a problem. It had been Stalin who had established the communist states in Europe's eastern half. By discrediting Stalin, Khrushchëv reasserted a line of legitimacy in the Soviet Union stretching from Lenin and the October Revolution. This was not the case in eastern Europe, where it was Stalin who had installed communism. Khrushchëv's report was political dynamite there. Strikers organised protest demonstrations in Poland. By October 1956 a popular revolt had broken out in Hungary.

Opponents of reform struck back in the Party Presidium in June 1957, calling for Khrushchëv's removal as Party First Secretary. But the Central Committee protected him and, after years of further struggle, he delivered a still more devastating attack on Stalin at the Twenty-Second Party Congress in October 1961. Old Bolshevik Dora Lazurkina was given the podium. Bent with years, Lazurkina told how the shade of Lenin had appeared in a dream to her demanding to rest alone in the Mausoleum on Red Square. This sentiment evoked tumultuous applause. The deed was done at dead of night and Stalin's embalmed corpse was taken out of the Mausoleum and buried below the Kremlin Wall; a simple bust and pillar were placed above his grave. The historians were ordered to search the archives for proof that Stalin had frequently fallen out with Lenin and always behaved brutally. Stalingrad was renamed Volgograd. The Lenin cult was joined by a growing cult of Khrushchëv. A new party-history textbook appeared in 1959.[10] Those communists who admired Stalin kept quiet or risked expulsion from the party ranks. Only a few communist parties abroad dissented. Chief among them was the Communist Party of China. Mao Tse-tung had resented Stalin in life but thought Khrushchëv's policies of reform made too great a rupture with the kind of communism espoused by both Stalin and Mao. This contrast added to the tensions, leading to a rift between the USSR and the People's Republic of China.

Khrushchëv was removed from power in 1964. The Party Politburo (as the Presidium was renamed) ditched the more idiosyncratic of his policies at home and abroad; it also stifled dissenting opinion more harshly than under Khrushchëv. But this was a modification of Khrushchëv's programme rather than a reversion to full Stalinism. The new Party General Secretary Leonid Brezhnev never contemplated terror or individual despotism. 'Stability of cadres' became a slogan. Behind the scenes, however, the Politburo seriously considered rehabilitating Stalin's historical image in 1969 on the occasion of his birthday. A laudatory *Pravda* editorial was prepared. Only a last-minute intervention by Italian and French communist party leaders prevented publication. (This was too late, however, to stop the Mongolian Communist Party from printing it as Ulan Bator lies in an earlier time zone.)

Yet the desire to rehabilitate Stalin persisted. In July 1984 – less than a year before Mikhail Gorbachëv came to power – the Politburo mulled over the question. The older members retained affection for him and hostility to Khrushchëv:[11]

> *Ustinov:* In evaluating Khrushchëv's activity I would go to the stake, as they say, for my opinion. He did us great harm. Just think what he did with our history, with Stalin.
>
> *Gromyko:* He delivered an irreversible blow against the positive image of the Soviet Union in the eyes of the rest of the world . . .
>
> *Tikhonov:* And what did [Khrushchëv] do with our economy? I myself was forced to work in a [regional] council of the national economy!
>
> *Gorbachëv:* And [what did he do, too,] with the party, dividing it into industrial and rural party organisations!
>
> *Ustinov:* We were always against the council of the national

economy. And, as you'll recall, many members of the Politburo
of the Central Committee spoke out against [Khrushchëv's]
position. In connection with the fortieth anniversary of the
Victory over fascism I'd like to propose a discussion of one
further question: shouldn't we name Volgograd again as
Stalingrad? Millions of people would receive this very well.

At Stalin's death Ustinov had been Minister for Armaments, Gromyko
had been ambassador to the United Kingdom and Tikhonov the Minister
of Ferrous Metallurgy.

The idea of rehabilitation came to nothing because Gorbachëv,
who had avoided saying anything about Stalin in the Politburo, became
Party General Secretary in March 1985. The movement quickened to
reseat Stalin on the bench of the accused. The massive scale of his
abuses, which had been only partially revealed under Khrushchëv, was
described. The 'administrative-command system' established by Stalin
was denounced. Films, novels and poems as well as historical works
pointed in the same direction. Gorbachëv encouraged the intelligentsia
to convince society that total repudiation of the Stalinist legacy was vital
for the regeneration of Soviet society. The process slipped out of his
control as several critics of Stalin insisted that Lenin too was guilty of
fundamental abuses. They traced the administrative-command system to
the origins of the USSR. Yet this same openness of discussion also
allowed some intellectuals to offer praise for Stalin. His role in securing
industrialisation in the 1930s and then victory in the Second World War
was repeatedly proclaimed.

Yet there was no going back. Gorbachëv went on to castigate Stalin
as one of history's greatest criminals. When the USSR fell apart at the
end of 1991 and the Russian Federation became a separate state, Boris
Yeltsin continued the damnation of Stalin – and, unlike Gorbachëv, he
rejected Lenin and Stalin in equal measure. So things lasted until 2000
when Vladimir Putin became President. Putin's grandfather had worked
in the kitchens for Lenin and Stalin. President Putin was averse to
hearing about the abuses of power in the 1930s and 1940s; instead he
wished to praise the achievements of the Soviet state in those decades.[12]
'Denigration' of the past was frowned upon again. Putin, in a symbolic
gesture, restored the old USSR national anthem, albeit with new words.
He spoke fondly of his own early career in the KGB, the successor organ
to Stalin's security police agency.[13] It was not Putin's purpose to
rehabilitate Stalin but rather to affirm the continuities linking the Russian

Empire, the Soviet Union and the Russian Federation. This process, though, relieved Stalin's shade from torment for the first time since the late 1980s. Putin was relegating him to the status of a historical figure and leaving it to the scholars to battle out their verdict. This was the ultimate indignity for the long-dead dictator. So long as he was being posthumously denounced, he remained a living force in Moscow politics. Stalin suffered the ignominy of official neglect.

He was not forgotten, however, in society. Despite the revelations about his despotism, a residual nostalgia remained for Stalin and his period of rule. Surveys of popular opinion in 2000 confirmed this. When asked which period of twentieth-century history they regarded with greatest admiration, most respondents chose the Brezhnev years. Khrushchëv's rule attracted the approval of 30 per cent. The Revolution gained 28 and Nicholas II's reign 18 per cent. Yet Stalin's despotism, with 26 per cent, did not do badly. Adverse opinion about the despotism was still higher at 48 per cent, but the fact that over a quarter of respondents rejected the case against Stalinist rule was depressing to those in Russian public affairs who aspired to a transformation of social attitudes.[14] Not everyone was kindly towards his memory. Families existed whose members solemnly toasted the health of 'the American doctor' Cheyne-Stokes on each anniversary of Stalin's death. They were recalling the fatal breathing problem diagnosed at Blizhnyaya in March 1953. (In fact there had been two doctors, Cheyne and Stokes, and they were not Americans but Irishmen.)[15] Indeed millions of Soviet citizens regularly spat on his memory while the politicians switched between public semi-denunciation and, at least in many cases, private admiration.

Abroad the decline in his reputation was precipitate and near-universal. The communist order collapsed in eastern Europe in 1989 and in every country no one could speak or write in defence of Stalin without incurring massive public displeasure. In the West most communist parties had long ago disavowed Stalinism. 'Eurocommunism' in Italy and Spain had been critical of both Lenin and Stalin since the 1970s. Western communist parties anyway fell apart with the dismantling of the USSR and it was no longer a matter of much interest what they thought about the Stalin period. Even in the People's Republic of China, where a general respect for Stalin was formally maintained, spokesmen stressed the difficulties he had caused for China's particular interests. In only one little country were many admirers of Stalin widely to be found. This was in his native Georgia, which regained its independence at New Year 1992. Georgians frequently forgot his maltreatment of their forebears. He was celebrated as a Georgian of worldwide fame who had tamed the Russians and given them a lesson in statecraft – and this was enough to save him from execration. Both his statues and the shrine of his childhood house stand untouched and venerated in Gori. Surviving relatives, especially grandchildren who did not know him personally, tend his cult. Georgia's veteran communists praise his memory.

This is not a unique fate for homicidal leaders. Genghis Khan is revered in Mongolia. Hitler has admirers in Germany and other countries (including even Russia). People remember what they want in the circumstances in which they do the remembering; they always select and often invent their memories. In Stalin's case those who think fondly of him – at least many of them – are reacting against the contempt shown towards the achievements of themselves or their parents before 1953. Like Putin, they want to remove the taint on the name of their families. They are also reacting against the unpleasantness of their situation in Russia after communism. They feel that Stalin gave them pride, order and predictability; they overlook the fact that his rule was characterised by systematic oppression. His era has become a reassuring fiction for those individuals and groups who seek a myth for life in the present. Even many persons whose forebears were shot or imprisoned on Stalin's orders have taken comfort in fairy stories about a ruler who made a few mistakes but usually got the basic direction of state policy right.

This is evident to anyone who visits Moscow. Down from Red Square by the side of the Manège there is a building which used to be the Lenin Museum. In the early 1990s it became a favourite gathering place for assorted kinds of Stalinist. Passers-by could listen to elderly Russians denouncing everything that had happened in the country since 1953. Individuals sold newspapers rejecting the entire course of history from Khrushchëv to Yeltsin. (Mingling with the Stalinists were still odder individuals advertising herbal cures for AIDS.) Their ideas were a jumble. The Stalinists hate Jews, freemasons and Americans. They support Russian nationalism while advocating the restoration of a multinational state. They hymn social sacrifice. They are a pathetic bunch, steeped in nostalgia, and the police refrain from arresting them even though their wild statements contravene the Russian 1993 Constitution.

The authorities have acted as if they assume that the reverence for Stalin will fade as the older generation dies off. Yet what will count in popular opinion is the degree of success attained by the Russian government in improving the living conditions of most citizens. Such amelioration seems far off. Wages are low and the conspicuous consumption of the wealthy minority known as the 'new Russians' earns deep resentment. Moscow flourishes while most cities and nearly all villages languish. About a third of society subsists below the UN-recognised poverty level. The political and economic elites have no strategy to effect a rapid transformation whereas parties of the far right and far left argue that simple solutions do indeed exist. Both Vladimir Zhirinovski's Liberal-Democratic Party and the Communist Party of the Russian Federation under Gennadi Zyuganov have invoked the name of Stalin as a figure who did the country proud in his day. They contend that but for him the USSR would not have become an industrial and military power capable of defeating Hitler's Germany. Neither party has won a majority at elections to the Presidency or the State Duma; and although nostalgia for Stalin persists, most Russians abhor the prospect of a return to violent politics. Until Russian society becomes materially more comfortable, however, the menacing icon of Joseph Stalin will be waved in banners raised by extremist politicians.

He continues to stir up controversy in Russia. Stalin bequeathed a consolidated system of rule to his successors. Personally he had remained devoted to Lenin and his rule had conserved and reinforced the Leninist regime. The one-party state established by the Bolsheviks within months of the October Revolution stayed firmly in place. The exclusion of alternative ideologies from public life was strengthened. The instruments of dictatorship, terror and a politicised judiciary were oiled and sharpened, and society and economy continued to be treated as a resource to be mobilised at the Kremlin's command. The state's economic control, substantial since the Civil War, was dramatically tightened. The party was said to know best about past, present and future. History was said to march in step to the drumbeat tapped out by Lenin and Stalin.

The continuities between the despotism of Stalin and the earlier Soviet period were cardinal features of the country's history – and historians who wrote fondly about an essential contrast between Lenin the Humanitarian Idealist and Stalin the Ogre had turned their eyes from the historical record. Stalin was Lenin's keen pupil. But there were also contrasts between them. Stalin made choices of his own, and some were almost certainly different from those which Lenin would have favoured if he had lived longer. A cautionary note must be attached to this verdict. Lenin was unpredictable in his policies even though his underlying assumptions changed little. Yet even Lenin was unlikely to have opted for the chaotic violence of the First Five-Year Plan and agricultural collectivisation. Not that Lenin would have been permanently patient with peasants, priests, nepmen and nationalists: he had his own moments of volatility. But he had a degree of self-restraint not shared by Stalin. Lenin did not overdo the persecution of internal party dissent. Such was his supremacy in the party that he did not need to remove troublemakers with exterminatory methods. Stalin's terror campaigns of the 1930s were excessive even by the standards of Bolshevism, and Lenin would surely have given them neither encouragement nor approval.

Yet neither Lenin nor Stalin was a wholly free agent. They were constrained by the nature of the regime which they had created, and Stalin's actions from the late 1920s were conditioned by the critical problems arising with the NEP. Lenin and Stalin led a party hostile to market economics, political pluralism and cultural, religious and social tolerance. They had established a one-party, one-ideology state beleaguered by capitalist powers; there was a limit to the kinds of policy they would accept.[16] Without dictatorship the USSR as a communist order would have fallen apart. With freedom of expression or private entrepreneurship it would have been buffeted by opposition; and had it not built up its industrial and military might it would have risked conquest by a foreign predator. The institutions and practices available to deal with such difficulties were not infinitely malleable. Hierarchical state command would have to be the guiding principle. Administrative surveillance and punitive sanctions would be necessary to enforce compliance; and recurrent recourse to mobilising campaigns, moral invocation and purges – whether peaceful or not – would be unavoidable.[17]

Stalin could not act alone. While leading the NEP's destruction, he had wide support in the central and local committees of the communist party. The enthusiasm for reinforcing state control was shared in sections of the party, political police, armed forces and Komsomol in the late 1920s. But a set of objectives is not the same as a plan. Stalin had no grand plan and his supporters lacked one too. Yet he operated with basic assumptions which they held in common with him. All the same he did not simply listen to the music of his times and adjust his behaviour to its rhythms. Stalin was not just a bureaucrat. He was a man driven by ambition and ideas. The general assumptions were fashioned by him into policies conforming to his intemperate nature and despotic inclinations.

As his authority increased, the need for support from his original close associates diminished. He could always replace them if they annoyed him. He imposed political, economic and cultural policies with increasing imperturbability. The Great Terror was instigated and supervised by him. The decision to sign a pact with Nazi Germany was his. Stalin's, too, were the methods chosen to direct the Soviet war machine. His were the choices in external and internal policy after the war. Indeed the whole architecture of the Soviet state, once it had been consolidated at the end of the 1920s, was Stalin's work based upon Lenin's design. Even Stalin, though, needed to restrain himself. He had to act within the framework of the communist order. He objected to the patronage networks in politics and general administration. He knew he could not trust the information reaching him from below. He criticised the lack of conscientiousness among workers and peasants. He was annoyed by the weak impact of the regime's Marxist–Leninist propaganda. But he had to operate with the human material and institutional resources available to him. The Great Terror strengthened and secured his despotism, but it also revealed to him the dangers of campaigning for total personal control. Although his methods remained intrusive, violent and ruthless, his purposes were more realistic after 1938.

That he succeeded to this large extent flowed from his skill in forming a central team of willing, if frightened, subordinates. He also managed to promote millions of young men and women to all levels of public activity who gave him their support in return for the power and comfort they received from him. Moreover, he ruled for so many years that those youths who had been through schooling in his time were affected by the propaganda; and the victory in the Second World War strengthened this tendency. Probably only a minority in society keenly admired him. Nevertheless many silent critics respected him for his policies of welfare and patriotism: Stalin did monstrous things and yet the popular attitude towards him was not wholly negative.

But what is his position in the history of his country and the world? Without Stalin and his rule, the USSR would have remained a brittle state with a fading grip on its society. Stalin modified Leninism and its practices and attitudes just as Lenin had subjected Marxism to his peculiar adaptation. This whole process – from Marx and Engels to Lenin and through to Stalin – involved a combination of reinforcement and emasculation. Lenin had invented a cul-de-sac for communism; Stalin drove the party down it. Under Stalin, no aspect of public and private life was exempt in theory or reality from central state interference. Communists pursued, in an extreme fashion, the objectives of comprehensive modernisation – and Stalin, like all communists, claimed that his party's version of modernity outmatched all known others. He achieved a lot: urbanisation, military strength, education and Soviet pride. His USSR could claim impressive achievements. It became a model for radical political movements – and not only communist ones – elsewhere in the world. And at a time before the Second World War when liberal-democratic government signally failed to stand effectively up to fascism, Stalin appeared to have established a plausible alternative (at least until the Non-Aggression Treaty of September 1939). If this had not been the case, he would never have gained the support necessary for him to survive and flourish.

His standing in popular opinion was a complex matter. Countless people found it possible to give approval to several basic professed aims of the regime while withholding it from others. Victory in the war, moreover, turned Stalin into the embodiment of patriotism, world power and a radiant future for the country. And such was his despotic authority that innumerable people lived their lives on the assumption that they had to accept the political structures and the official ideology. Many millions of course hated him in the 1930s and continued to detest him to the end of his days. But supporters of one kind or another certainly existed widely among people in the USSR.

Nevertheless Stalin drove the Soviet order not only down the cul-de-sac but into the wall at its end. His system of command achieved immediate subjugation at the expense of a general consensus. The terror campaigns traumatised whole generations. Most people ignored official policies and intensified engagement in practices of clientelism, localism, fraud and obstructiveness. As he himself recognised, there were limits to his power. Leninism in any case was distinctly 'unmodern' in many ways and Stalin magnified this among its features. The USSR in the 1930s and 1940s was governed as if always there was a single correct set of policies. Stalin treated debate from below as a danger to desirable unanimity, and he arrested and killed to secure dominion. Potential as well as overt enemies perished. The result was a maelstrom of murder which left behind fear, distrust and self-withdrawal. The primacy of state interests led to political immobilisation as Stalin's sprint to industrial and cultural transformation reached a dead end. His regime's patterns of thought and action ultimately precluded the dynamic, open-ended developments characteristic of liberal-democratic, capitalist countries. He had saved and consolidated the Soviet order at the expense of making it durably competitive with its main rivals.

The Soviet Union was a totalitarian state, but this did not mean that it was characterised by perfect central control. Far from it. The more Stalin concentrated in his own hands power over specific areas of politics, the greater the lack of compliance he encountered in others. His USSR was a mixture of exceptional orderliness and exceptional disorderliness. So long as the chief official aims were to build up military and heavy-industrial strength the reality of the situation was disguised from him, his supporters and even his enemies. Stalin had only the dimmest awareness of the problems he had created.

Yet he was also much more complex than is widely supposed. As a politician he knew how to present himself selectively to diverse groups. Most of the world knew that he was determined, ruthless and murderous and that he chased the objective of turning the USSR into a global military and industrial power. It was no secret that he possessed skills as conspirator and bureaucrat. Paradoxically the effect of his official cult was often counter-productive. If Soviet propagandists said he was an exceptional person, critics drew the opposite conclusion and assumed he must have been a nonentity. But exceptional he surely was. He was a real leader. He was also motivated by the lust for power as well as by ideas. He was in his own way an intellectual, and his level of literary and editorial craft was impressive. About his psychological traits there will always be controversy. His policies were a mixture of calculated rationality and wild illogicality, and he reacted to individuals and to whole social categories with what was excessive suspiciousness by most standards. He had a paranoiac streak. But most of the time he did not seem insane to those close to him. The ideology, practices and institutions he inherited were ones which allowed him to give vent to his chronic viciousness.

Stalin was not a certifiable psychotic and never behaved in such a way as to be incapable of carrying out his public duties. As a family man, a guest and a friend he was crude. But his behaviour was seldom so bizarre until the late 1930s that others failed to find him companionable. He wrote poems as a young man and went on singing at dinner parties into his old age. He sent money to his boyhood friends in Georgia. There are those who want the 'monsters' in history to be represented as a species unto themselves. This is a delusion. Individuals like Stalin are thankfully few and far between in the recorded past – and without the October Revolution there would have been one fewer: Stalin's emergence from exile and obscurity on to a worldwide stage of power, fame and impact would have been impossible if his party had not made the October Revolution and bolted together the institutional, procedural and doctrinal scaffolding which he was to exploit. Such individuals, when they have appeared, have usually displayed congenial 'ordinary' features even while carrying out acts of unspeakable abusiveness. History seldom gives unambiguous lessons, but this is one of them.

GLOSSARY

All-Union Communist Party (Bolsheviks) – The communist party's name from 1952.

Bolsheviks – The faction of the Russian Social-Democratic Workers' Party which was formed by Lenin in 1903 and consolidated as a separate party in 1917.

Central Committee – The supreme party body elected at Party Congresses to run the party until the next such Congress.

Central Control Commission – Party body established in 1920 to supervise the fair administration of the communist party.

Cheka – The Extraordinary Commission for Combating Counter-Revolution and Sabotage.

Cominform – International organ founded in 1947 supposedly to facilitate consultation among communist parties of eastern Europe and France and Italy. In fact it was used to impose Moscow's will on those parties.

Comintern – Abbreviation for the Communist International.

Communist International – The international organ founded in Petrograd in March 1919 to co-ordinate and direct the entire world communist movement. It was disbanded in 1943.

Council of Ministers – The successor organ of government to the Council of People's Commissars, set up in 1946.

Council of People's Commissars – The government established by Lenin and the Bolsheviks in the October Revolution. Usually known by the acronym Sovnarkom.

Democratic Centralists – Faction of Bolsheviks, formed in 1919, which called for the restoration of internal democratic procedures to the party.

GPU – The name of the Cheka from 1921. The full name is Main Political Administration.

GUGB – The Russian acronym of the Main Administration of State Security:

this was the departmental name of the OGPU after its incorporation in the NKVD in 1934.

Gulag – Properly the acronym should be GUlag; it is short for the Main Administration of Camps.

Ilich – One of Lenin's nicknames, used by his political associates.

Kadets – Acronym of the Constitutional-Democrats. This was the main Russian liberal party and was formed by Pavel Milyukov in 1905.

Koba – One of Stalin's youthful nicknames which he continued to use as a Marxist militant and leader before 1917.

Kuomintang – Chinese nationalist movement led by Chiang Kai-shek.

Left Opposition – Bolshevik faction led by Trotski from 1923 committed to accelerating industrial growth and to de-bureaucratising the party.

Lenin – Main pseudonym of the Bolshevik leader. He was christened Vladimir Ilich Ulyanov.

Mensheviks – Faction of the Russian Social-Democratic Workers' Party, initially led by Martov and founded at the Second Party Congress in 1903.

MGB – Ministry of State Security, the successor organisation to the NKGB from 1946.

MVD – Ministry of Internal Affairs, the successor organisation to the NKVD from 1946.

NKGB – People's Commissariat of State Security. This was the name of the security police agency; it was designated thus in 1941 and again in 1943–6.

NKVD – The People's Commissariat of Internal Affairs established after the October Revolution. In 1934 it incorporated the OGPU.

OGPU – Successor organ of the GPU and Cheka from 1924. It formally united all the GPUs of the various Soviet republics when the USSR came into existence. The full name in English is the United Main Political Administration.

Orgburo – Internal body of the Party Central Committee with responsibility for organisational leadership of the party in the period between meetings of the Central Committee.

Politburo – Internal committee of the Party Central Committee, empowered to direct the party in the period between meetings of the Central Committee.

Rabkrin – Abbreviated name of the Workers' and Peasants' Inspectorate. Set up in 1920, it was headed by Stalin till December 1922.

Red Army – The Workers' and Peasants' Red Army, formed in 1918.

Right Deviation – The supporters of Bukharin who opposed the abandonment of the NEP in 1928.

RSFSR – The Russian Socialist Federal Soviet Republic. Established in 1918, it became a constituent republic of the USSR in 1924. It was renamed the Russian Soviet Federal Socialist Republic in 1936.

Russian Communist Party (Bolsheviks) – The name of the Bolshevik party from 1918.

Russian Social-Democratic Workers' Party – The Marxist party of the Russian Empire, formed in 1898. In 1903 its leadership split into two factions, the Bolsheviks and the Mensheviks. After recurrent attempts at reunification the party fell apart into two separate parties in 1917.

Social-Federalists – Georgian socialist party which opposed Marxism and advocated Georgian national and territorial unity in a federal state within the boundaries of the Russian Empire.

Socialist-Revolutionaries – Party formed by Viktor Chernov and others in 1901 in the tradition of those revolutionaries of the Russian Empire who looked mainly to the peasants as the guiding force of revolution and to the village land commune as the future basis of a socialist society.

Soselo – One of Stalin's youthful nicknames.

Soso – Stalin's main youthful nickname.

Soviet Army – The name of the Red Army from 1946.

Sovnarkom – The government established by Lenin and the Bolsheviks through the October Revolution. Acronym for the Council of People's Commissars.

Ulyanov, Vladimir Ilich – Original name of Lenin before he adopted revolutionary pseudonyms.

United Opposition – The faction formed from a combination of the Left Opposition and the Leningrad Opposition in 1926.

Wehrmacht – The German army.

White Armies – The various armies which were ranged against the Red Army from 1918. Their commanders and soldiers were both anti-socialist and distrustful of liberalism and parliamentarism.

Workers' and Peasants' Inspectorate – The full name of the institution usually known as Rabkrin.

Workers' Opposition – Bolshevik faction which emerged at the end of the Civil War and called both for the internal democratisaton of the party and for the granting of authority to workers and peasants to control their sectors of the economy.

NOTES

1. Stalin as We Have Known Him

1. N. Sukhanov, *Zapiski o russkoi revolyutsii*.
2. See in particular B. Souvarine, *Staline: aperçu historique du bolchévisme*; L. Trotsky, *Stalin. An Appraisal of the Man and His Influence*; T. Dan, *Proiskhozhednie bol'shevisma: k istorii demokraticheskikh i sotsialisticheskikh idei v Rossii posle osvobozdeniya krest'yan*.
3. No one apart from Lenin and Trotski was more condescending to him in the 1920s than Bukharin, who paid the ultimate price. It remains to be explained why fellow leaders omitted to recognise his potential importance in due time. The answer they themselves gave at the time was that they had overlooked his political cunning. Having dismissed Stalin as an ignorant office clerk, they did not anticipate his ruthless skills in conspiracy and manoeuvre. This will not do. The rudimentary point must be made that Stalin's defeated rivals had an incentive to suggest they had been worsted by a master-deceiver who bore no similarity to themselves and had no talents of his own.
4. 'Stalin (Dzhughashvili), Iosif Vissarionovich'.
5. *Iosif Vissarionovich Stalin* (1st edn).
6. G. Gorodetsky, *The Grand Delusion*.
7. R. Conquest, *The Great Terror*. Conquest, while highlighting Stalin's psychological oddity, affirms that he was not insane.
8. The Trotskyist Isaac Deutscher's *Stalin* after World War Two incorporated the basic ideas of pre-war Trotskyist and Menshevik analyses of Stalin's career but, unlike Trotski's biography, insisted that the personal dictatorship of Stalin had brought about institutional and educational changes which eventually could work to the favour of genuinely communist objectives. E. H. Carr in a biographical vignette offered a similar interpretation while emphasising, to a greater extent than Deutscher, the task discharged by Stalin in Russia's general 'modernisation': *Socialism in One Country, 1924–1926*, vol. 1, pp. 174–86. Even Trotski, though, stressed that Stalin had presided over changes in the USSR which would have effects beyond his permanent control.
9. R. W. Davies, *Soviet History in the Yeltsin Era*.

10. R. Medvedev, *Let History Judge.*
11. D. Volkogonov, *Stalin: triumf i tragediya.*
12. E. Radzinsky, *Stalin.*
13. J. A. Getty, *Origins of the Great Purges.*
14. S. Sebag Montefiore, *Stalin: At the Court of the Red Tsar*; M. Kun, *Stalin: An Unknown Portrait.*
15. A. Ulam, *Stalin*; R. McNeal, *Stalin. Man and Leader*; R. Hingley, *Stalin*; R. Tucker, *Stalin.*
16. R. McNeal, *Stalin. Man and Leader*; R. Tucker, *Stalin*, pp. 133–7.
17. R. Slusser, *Stalin in October: The Man Who Missed the Revolution.*
18. R. Medvedev, *Let History Judge.*
19. R. Conquest, *The Great* Terror; R. Medvedev, *Let History Judge.*
20. J. A. Getty, *The Origins of the Great Purges.*
21. O. V. Khlevniuk, *1937–i.*

2. The Family Dzhughashvili

1. *Iosif Vissarionovich Stalin* (1st edn), p. 5. In order to avoid chopping and changing in this early chapter I have transliterated Stalin's Georgian surname as Dzhughashvili even though, strictly speaking, it should be rendered Dzhugashvili when taken from the Russian text of the official biography.
2. See the notes of the 23 December 1946 meeting taken by a participant, V. D. Mochalov: *Slovo tovarishchu Stalinu*, pp. 469–73. I owe to Arfon Rees the point about Bolshevik distaste for personal biographical accounts.
3. RGASPI, f. 558, op. 4, d. 61, p. 1.
4. I am grateful to Stephen Jones for sharing his thoughts on this with me.
5. J. Davrichewy, *Ah! Ce qu'on rigolait bien*, p. 90. See also A. Ostrovskii, *Kto stoyal za spinoi Stalina?*, p. 90.
6. R. Medvedev, *Sem'ya tirana*, p. 5.
7. *Ibid.*, p. 4.
8. J. Davrichewy, *Ah! Ce qu'on rigolait bien*, p. 27.
9. *Ibid.*
10. S. Beria, *Beria, My Father*, p. 21.
11. J. Davrichewy, *Ah! Ce qu'on rigolait bien*, pp. 27–8. Another person mentioned as Stalin's biological father was a certain Dzhulabovi: *ibid.* R. Brackman has recently contended that Stalin was the bastard son of a priest called Egnatashvili: *The Secret File of Joseph Stalin*, p. 4; but most primary sources accurately refer to Egnatashvili as the local tavern keeper.
12. A. Mgeladze, *Stalin, kakim ya ego znal*, pp. 242–3.
13. J. Davrichewy, *Ah! Ce qu'on rigolait bien*, pp. 27–9.
14. R. and Zh. Medvedev, *Neizvestnyi Stalin*, p. 265.
15. I am grateful to Stephen Jones for discussing this matter with me.
16. *Sochineniya*, vol. 13, p. 113.

17. S. Allilueva, *Tol'ko odin god*, p. 313.
18. *Ibid.*
19. G. K. Zhukov, *Vospominaniya i razmyshleniya*, vol. 3, p. 215.
20. A. Ostrovskii, *Kto stoyal za spinoi Stalina*, p. 95.
21. *Ibid.*
22. Memoir of G. I. Elisabedashvili in *Stalin: v vospominaniyakh i dokumentov epokhi*, p. 12.
23. GF IML, fond 8, op. 2, ch. 1, d. 24, p. 191, cited in A. Ostrovskii, *Kto stoyal za spinoi Stalina*, p. 97.
24. *Ibid.*; and J. Davrichewy, *Ah! Ce qu'on rigolait bien*, p. 38.

3. The Schooling of a Priest

1. This is the point made by A. Ostrovskii, *Kto stoyal za spinoi Stalina*, p. 97.
2. *Ibid.*, pp. 100–1.
3. V. Kaminskii and I. Vereshchagin, *Detstvo i yunost' vozhdya*, pp. 28 and 43–4; see also A. Ostrovskii, *Kto stoyal za spinoi Stalina?*, pp. 100–1.
4. F. Ye. Makharadze and G. V. Khachapuridze, *Ocherki po istorii rabochego i krest'yanskogo dvizheniya v Gruzii*, pp. 143–4. This part of the book was written solely by Makharadze.
5. *Ibid.*, p. 144.
6. RGASPI, f. 71, op. 10, d. 275. See M. Kun, *Stalin: An Unknown Portrait*, p. 18.
7. There is an implicit account of Beso's material woes in *Sochineniya*, vol. 1, p. 318.
8. Skating and wrestling incidents have also been blamed: see A. Ostrovskii, *Kto stoyal za spinoi Stalina*, p. 95. But the phaeton is by far the likeliest story.
9. A. Ostrovskii suggests that the accident might have preceded Stalin's schooling: *ibid.*, p. 99.
10. J. Iremaschwili, *Stalin und die Tragödie Georgiens*, p. 5.
11. J. Davrichewy, *Ah! Ce qu'on rigolait bien*, pp. 71 and 73.
12. See below, p. 522.
13. J. Davrichewy, *Ah! Ce qu'on rigolait bien*, p. 39.
14. *Ibid.*, p. 82.
15. *Ibid.*, pp. 43–4.
16. *Ibid.*, p. 61.
17. J. Iremaschwili, *Stalin und die Tragödie Georgiens*, p. 18.
18. V. Kaminskii and I. Vereshchagin, *Detsvo i yunost' vozhdya*, p. 48.
19. J. Davrichewy, *Ah! Ce qu'on rigolait bien*, p. 59.
20. *Ibid.*
21. *Ibid.*
22. RGASPI, fond 558, op. 4, d. 61, p. 1.

23. A. Chelidze, 'Neopublikovannye materialy iz biografii tovarishcha Stalina', p. 19.
24. I am not saying that his arithmetical supervision was exercised impartially. On the contrary, he deliberately manipulated official grain output figures in the late 1920s.
25. RGASPI, fond 558, op. 4, d. 61, p. 1.

4. Poet and Rebel

1. Stalin in old age described his early time in Tbilisi to K. Charkviani. I derive this reference from the notes on Charkviani's memoirs kindly shared with me by Simon Sebag Montefiore: p. 2a. See also *Stalin: v vospominaniyakh sovremennikov i dokumentov epokhi*, p. 18.
2. *Istoricheskie mesta Tbilisi. Putevoditel' po mestam, svyazannym s zhizn'yu i deyatel'nost'yu I. V. Stalina*, pp. 30–1.
3. I am grateful to Peter Strickland for his advice on nineteenth-century European architecture.
4. See M. Agursky, 'Stalin's Ecclesiastical Background', pp. 3–4.
5. *Ibid.*, p. 6.
6. The original Russian was *sobachii yazyk*, literally translatable as 'a dog's language'. In either translation, however, it was very offensive to Georgians.
7. T. Darlington, *Education in Russia*, p. 286.
8. *Ibid.*, p. 287.
9. N. Zhordaniya, *Moya zhizn'*, p. 8.
10. T. Darlington, *Education in Russia*, p. 288.
11. RGASPI, f. 558, op. 4, d. 17, p. 1.
12. T. Darlington, *Education in Russia*, p. 286.
13. J. Iremaschwili, *Stalin und die Tragödie Georgiens*, pp. 16–17.
14. J. Davrichewy, *Ah! Ce qu'on rigolait bien*, p. 113.
15. N. Zhordaniya, *Moya zhizn'*, p. 11.
16. *Ibid.*, p. 12.
17. G. Uratadze, *Vospominaniya gruzinskogo sotsial-demokrata*, pp. 58–9.
18. N. Zhordaniya, *Moya zhizn'*, pp. 25 and 27. Zhordania had earlier turned down the invitation from Ilya Chavchavadze to edit *Iveria*: he wanted complete political autonomy.
19. *Ibid.*, pp. 29–30.
20. *Istoricheskie mesta Tbilisi*, p. 25.
21. *Iveria*, no. 23 (1895).
22. N. Zhordaniya, *Moya zhizn'*, p. 31.
23. *deda ena* (ed. Y. Gogebashvili: 1912 edition).
24. I. Stalin, *Stikhi*, p. 3. Several biographies of Stalin wrongly assume that the dedicatee was Giorgi Eristava, the poet exiled to the Polish provinces of the Russian Empire in 1832.
25. M. Kun cites archives indicating that the Eristavi poem was recalled as

'revolutionary' in content by a fellow seminarist: see *Stalin: An Unknown Portrait*, p. 77.

26. A more plausible version of this story was that the seminarists borrowed the books in the normal fashion for a fee and took it in turns to copy them out by hand: M. Chiaureli's memoir of a conversation with Stalin in A Fadeer (ed.), *Vstrechi s tovarishchem Stalinym*, pp. 156–7.
27. *Stalin: v vospominaniyakh sovremennikov i dokumentov epokhi*, p. 24.
28. J. Iremaschwili, *Stalin und die Tragödie Georgiens*, p. 20.
29. 'I. V. Stalin o "Kratkom kurse po istorii VKP(b)". Stenogramma vystupleniya no soveshchanii propagandistov Moskvy i Leningrada', *Istoricheskii arkhiv*, no. 5 (1994), p. 12.
30. See the results in RGASPI, f. 558, op. 4, dd. 48 and 665.
31. Y. Gogebashvili, *deda ena* (1912). The State House-Museum of I. V. Stalin in Gori also holds the 1916 edition in Hall I.
32. Pupils' records from the Tiflis Seminary for 1898–9: RGASPI, f. 558, op. 4, d. 53, p. 1.
33. Stalin's account in 1931, reproduced in *Istoricheskie mesta Tbilisi*, p. 29.

5. Marxist Militant

1. *Iosif Vissarionovich Stalin: biografiya* (2nd edn), p. 10. Since such an occupation was hardly to Stalin's credit as a Marxist militant it is probably true.
2. Hall I, GDMS.
3. See the magnetic tape and various written records in Hall II, GDMS.
4. *Istoricheskie mesta Tbilisi. Putevoditel' po mestam, svyazannym s zhizn'yu i deyatel'nost'yu I. V. Stalina*, pp. 30–1.
5. *Ibid.*, p. 32.
6. *Lado Ketskhoveli: Sbornik dokumentov i materialov*, pp. 174–5.
7. J. Iremaschwili, *Stalin und die Tragödie Georgiens*, p. 24.
8. A. Gio, *Zhizn' podpol'nika*, p. 25 (writing about the group led by Stalin's acquaintance Silva Dzhibladze).
9. *Ibid.*, p. 54.
10. J. Davrichewy, *Ah! Ce qu'on rigolait bien*, p. 111.
11. N. Zhordaniya, *Moya zhizn'*, pp. 29–30.
12. J. Iremaschwili, *Stalin und die Tragödie Georgiens*, p. 25.
13. *Ibid.*
14. G. Uratadze, *Vospominaniya gruzinskogo sotsial-demokrata*, pp. 66–7.
15. See E. Smith, *The Young Stalin*, p. 78.
16. See below, pp. 72–4.
17. See the forthcoming history of Georgian Marxism by Stephen Jones, chapter 4. A succinct summary of N. Zhordaniya's ideas appeared in his 'Natsional'nyi vopros', *Bor'ba*, no. 2 (1914), pp. 26–31.
18. Stalin's account at a Kremlin meeting of 28 December 1945, recorded by V. D. Mochalov: *Slovo tovarishchu Stalinu*, p. 461.

19. A. Yenukidze, 'Istoriya organizatsiya i raboty nelegal'nykh tipografii R.S.D.R.P. (bol'shevikov) na Kavkaze za vremya ot 1900 po 1906 g.' in *Tekhnika bol'shevistskogo podpol'ya*, p. 20.

20. L. B. Krasin, 'Bol'shevistskaya partiinaya tekhnika' in *ibid.*, p. 10.

21. G. Uratadze, *Vospominaniya gruzinskogo sotsial-demokrata*, p. 193; A. S. Yenukidze, 'Istoriya organizatsii i raboty nelegal'nykh tipografii R.S.R.P. (bol'shevikov) na Kavkaze', pp. 20–5; N. Zhordaniya, *Moya zhizn'*, p. 35.

22. S. T. Arkhomed, *Rabochee dvizhenie i sotsial-demokratiya na Kavkaze*, pp. 81–4.

23. G. Uratadze, *Vospominaniya gruzinskogo sostial-demokrata*, pp. 66–7.

24. S. T. Arkhomed, *Rabochee dvizhenie i sotsial-demokratiya na Kavkaze*, pp. 81–4.

25. *Stalin i Khasim (1901–1902 gg.)*. The importance of this account was established by M. Kun, *Stalin: An Unknown Portrait*, pp. 49–50. My thanks to George Hewitt for advice on Abkhazian nomenclature and on the peasant's probable nationality.

26. I. V. Stalin, *Sochineniya*, vol. 1, pp. 11–31.

27. See Stalin's account at a Kremlin meeting of 28 December 1945, recorded by V. D. Mochalov: *Slovo tovarishchu Stalinu*, p. 461.

28. *Ibid.*, p. 462.

29. A. Yenukidze, 'Istoriya organizatsiya i raboty nelegal'nykh tipografii', p. 28.

30. *Ibid.*

31. N. Zhordaniya, *Moya zhizn'*, p. 30.

32. I. V. Stalin, *Sochineniya*, vol. 1, pp. 7 and 9.

33. S. Kavtaradze, *tsareulis purtsebli*, vol. 1, pp. 17–20. I am grateful to Zakro Megreleshvili for his help in translating this important memoir for me.

34. G. Uratadze, *Vospominaniya gruzinskogo sotsial-demokrata*, p. 70.

35. S. Alliluev, *Proidënnyi put'*, p. 109.

36. G. Uratadze, *Vospominaniya gruzinskogo sotsial-demokrata*, p. 68.

37. *Ibid.*, p. 66.

38. *Ibid.*, p. 65.

39. *Ibid.*

40. *Ibid.*, p. 66.

41. S. Kavtaradze, *tsareulis purtsebli*, vol. 1, p. 17.

42. *Ibid.*, p. 18.

43. *Ibid.*, p. 20; Stalin's account as given to a confidential meeting of leading official propagandists on 28 December 1945: see V. D. Mochalov's notes in *Slovo tovarishchu Stalinu*, p. 463.

44. I. V. Stalin, *Sochineniya*, vol. 1, p. x: comment by the anonymous editorial group of the Institute of Marx–Engels–Lenin.

45. S. Kavtaradze, *Tsareulis purtsebli*, vol. 1, pp. 17–20.

46. *Ibid.*, p. 18.

47. *Ibid.*

6. The Party and the Caucasus

1. S. Kavtaradze, *tsareulis purtsebli*, vol. 1, p. 24.
2. *Revolyutsiya 1905 goda v Zakavkaz'i*, pp. 70–1.
3. *Ibid.*, p. 89.
4. S. Vereshchak, 'Stalin v tyur'me', part 2, *Dni*, 24 January 1928.
5. *Perepiska V.I. Lenina i rukovodimykh im uchrezhdenii RSDRP s mestnymi partiinymi organizatsiyami, 1905–1907*, vol. 2, part 1, p. 294.
6. *Pravda*, 24 April 1920. Whether this had really been Stalin's initial reaction to Lenin is a matter of speculation, for in describing Lenin positively in such terms he was implicitly recommending himself as well as Lenin to the audience in April 1920. Nevertheless it is not an improbable reaction.
7. B. Gorev, 'Za kulisami pervoi revolyutsii', pp. 16–17; I. V. Stalin, *Pravda*, 24 April 1920.
8. Editorial note by R. Markova, *Chetvërtyi (ob"edinitel'nyi) s"ezd RSDRP* (1949 edition), p. 34.
9. M. Stugart in his readers' queries column, *Dagens Nyheter*, 22 March 2004.
10. *Chetvërtyi s"ezd*, p. 116.
11. *Ibid.*, p. 224.
12. *Ibid.*, p. 311.
13. *Ibid.*, pp. 78–9, 81 and 116.
14. *Ibid.*, pp. 78–9 and 224.
15. J. Davrichewy, *Ah! Ce qu'on rigolait bien*, p. 228.
16. V. Alliluev, *Khronika odnoi sem'i*, p. 108.
17. See the account by M. Kun, *Stalin. An Unknown Portrait*, pp. 342–3.
18. See below, pp. 92–4.
19. See below, pp. 75–6.
20. W. J. Fishman, *East End 1888*, pp. 131–72
21. Ye. Yemel'yanov in *Stalin. K shestidesyatiyu so dnya rozhdeniya*, p. 197.
22. See K. Weller, *'Don't Be a Soldier!'*, p. 85.
23. *Daily Express*, 5 January 1950.
24. *Pyatyi (londonskii) s"ezd RSDRP*, p. 121.
25. N. Zhordaniya, *Moya zhizn'*, p. 53.

7. On the Run

1. R. G. Suny, 'A Journeyman for the Revolution', pp. 373–4.
2. *Diskussionnyi Listok. Prilozhenie k Tsentral'nomu Organu 'Sotsial-demokrat'* (Paris), 24 May/7 June 1910, pp. 26–7. He had probably written this before being arrested. A rejoinder by Noe Zhordania was included in the same issue, pp. 28–30.
3. *Ibid.*, pp. 26–8.
4. *Krasnyi arkhiv*, no. 2 (1941), pp. 14 and 17–18.

5. A. Allilueva, *Vospominaniya*, p. 109.

6. *Pyatyi (londonskii) s"ezd RSDRP*, p. 87.

7. J. Iremaschwili, *Stalin und die Tragödie Georgiens*, p. 40.

8. *Ibid.*, p. 39.

9. *Ibid.* David Machavariani, one of Joseph Dzhughashvili's school friends, corroborated – after the Second World War – the deep effects of his wife's death: J. Davrishewy, *Ah! Ce qu'on rigolait bien*, p. 35.

10. See above, chapter 1.

11. J. Iremaschwili, *Stalin und die Tragödie Georgiens*, p. 39.

12. S. Kavtaradze, *tsareulis purtsebli*, vol. 1, p. 99.

13. I. V. Stalin, *Sochineniya*, vol. 1, pp. 314–15.

14. RGASPI, f. 71, op. 10, d. 275. See M. Kun, *Stalin. An Unknown Portrait*, p. 18 for a full account.

15. S. Talakvadze, *K istorii Kommunisticheskoi partii Gruzii*, p. 118.

16. R. Brackman, *The Secret File*, pp. 133–5, 186–93 and 281–9.

17. G. Uratadze, *Vospominaniya gruzinskogo sotsial-demokrata*, p. 67.

18. A. Gio, *Zhizn' podpol'nika*, p. 67.

19. *Ibid.*, p. 69.

20. *Ibid.*, p. 70.

21. *Ibid.*, pp. 70 and 72.

22. *Ibid.*, p. 73.

23. J. Davrichewy, *Ah! Ce qu'on rigolait bien*, pp. 174 and 199. Stalin also acknowledged to Kandide Charkviani that 'exes' were carried out by his party group: see p. 14 of his unpublished memoirs.

24. Davrichewy, *Ah! Ce qu'on rigolait bien*, pp. 175–6 and 188–9.

25. I. V. Stalin, *Sochineniya*, vol. 13, p. 222: interview with Emile Ludwig.

26. See above, pp. 36–7.

27. RGASPI, f. 332, op. 1, ed.kh. 53. This source was first discussed by M. Kun in *Stalin: An Unknown Portrait*, pp. 77–9.

28. See B. Nikolaevskii, 'K istorii "Bol'shevistskogo Tsentra"', vol. 1, p. 68: Nikolaevskii Papers, St Antony's College Library, Oxford.

29. R. Arsenidze, *Novyi zhurnal*, no. 72 (1963), p. 232; Yu. Martov, *Vperëd*, no. 51, 31 March 1918; *Pravda*, 1 April 1918.

30. See the memoir by Semën Vereshchak, 'Stalin v tyur'me'.

31. K. S. [I. V. Stalin], 'Pis'mo s Kavkaza', *Diskussionnyi listok. Prilozhenie k Tsentral'nomu Organu 'Sotsial-demokrat'*, no. 2, 24 May/7 June 1910, pp. 26–7.

32. An [N. Zhordaniya], 'Po povodu, Pis'ma s Kavkaza', *ibid.*, p. 28.

33. I. V. Stalin, *Sochineniya*, vol. 2, pp. 50–1.

34. The significance of this linguistic switch was first noted by A. Rieber, 'Stalin, Man of the Borderlands', p. 1676.

35. S. Vereshchak, 'Stalin v tyur'me'.

36. *Ibid.*

37. *Ibid.*

38. *Ibid.*

39. *Ibid.*
40. See M. Kun, *Stalin: An Unknown Portrait*, p. 98.
41. *Ibid.*, pp. 115–17.
42. See the account of interviews conducted by L. Vasil'eva, *Deti Kremlya*, pp. 168–9 and 176.

8. At the Centre of the Party

1. See above, pp. 61 and 66.
2. N. Zhordaniya, *Moya zhizn'*, p. 53.
3. G. Uratadze, *Vospominaniya gruzinskogo sotsial-demokrata*, p. 234.
4. *Vserossiiskaya Konferentsiya Ros. Sots.-Dem. Rab. Partii 1912 goda*: see the introduction by R. C. Elwood, pp. xx–xxi.
5. See M. Kun, *Stalin: An Unknown Portrait*, p. 130.
6. V. I. Lenin, *Polnoe sobranie sochinenii*, vol. 48, p. 53.
7. *Molotov. Poluderzhavnyi vlastelin*, p. 197.
8. *deda ena* (ed. Y. Gogebashvili: 1912 edn). The poem in question was 'Morning'.
9. I. V. Stalin, *Sochineniya*, vol. 2, p. 219.
10. He had ceased to show his romantic aspect since leaving the Tiflis Spiritual Seminary: see above, pp. 40–1.
11. Easily the best work on the transmutation of Stalin's political and 'personal' persona is A. Rieber's 'Stalin, Man of the Borderlands', which highlights the artificial qualities of his self-representation from 1900 – and not just from 1912. My belief, though, is that Stalin after 1912, rather than becoming a sort of Russian, adopted a binational persona which at any given time might give emphasis either to the Russian or to the Georgian aspect.
12. V. I. Lenin, *Polnoe sobranie sochinenii*, vol. 48, p. 162. For the contents of the booklet, see below, pp. 96–100.
13. S. Vereshchak, 'Stalin v tyur'me'.
14. A. S. Allilueva, *Vospominaniya*, p. 115.
15. S. Vereshchak, 'Stalin v tyur'me'.
16. Stalin related the story to A. E. Golovanov shortly before the 1943 Tehran Conference. Golovanov in turn related it to Felix Chuev: see *Molotov. Poluderzhavnyi vlastelin*, p. 202.
17. A. S. Allilueva, *Vospominaniya*, p. 113.
18. *Ibid.*, p. 115.
19. *Ibid.*, p. 116.
20. V. I. Lenin, *Polnoe sobranie sochinenii*, vol. 22, pp. 207–9. The article was unpublished at the time.
21. *Bol'shevistskoe rukovodstvo. Perepiska, 1912–1927*, p. 16.
22. *Ibid.*
23. *Ibid.*

24. *Zastol'nye rechi Stalina*, p. 301. He told a similar story to Kandide Charkviani: see his unpublished memoirs, p. 25.
25. N. Lenin, 'Zametki publitsista', p. 9.
26. RGASPI, f. 558, op. 4, d. 647, p. 432.
27. See below, p. 441.
28. RGASPI, f. 558, op. 4, d. 647, pp. 432–3.
29. *Ibid.*, p. 433.
30. *Ibid.*
31. The contents of the booklet are discussed below, pp. 96–100.
32. F. Samoilov, 'O Lenine i Staline': RGASPI, f. 558, op. 4, d. 659, p. 1.
33. *Prosveshchenie*, nos 3–5 (1913).
34. I. V. Stalin, *Sochineniya*, vol. 1, pp. 368–72: 'Polozhenie v sotsial-demokraticheskoi fraktsii'. It was published in *Pravda* on 26 February 1913.

9. Koba and Bolshevism

1. Bogdanov developed ideas which, if he had become more widely known, would have given pause to thinkers since the 1960s who have become known as post-modernists. Although he insisted that 'culture' is never simply a reflection of economic production relations, he stipulated too that collective insights, indeed insights which reflect the interests of particular social groups, inform and condition what both is and can be thought in society. Bogdanov did not have all the answers. Yet his turn-of-the-century *oeuvre* was overlooked abroad and suppressed at home, and the neglect of his ideas has delayed the philosophical demise of fashionable postmodernism.
2. See below, pp. 357–8.
3. J. Davrichewy, *Ah! Ce qu'on rigolait bien*, p. 212.
4. *Slovo tovarishchu Stalinu*, p. 462: from notes taken by V. D. Mochalov at meeting with Stalin on 28 December 1945.
5. Even Davrishevi admitted this: *Ah! Ce qu'on rigolait bien*, p. 212.
6. See also below, p. 300.
7. See above, pp. 62–3.
8. See above, p. 63.
9. S. Shaumyan, *Izbrannye proizvedeniya*, vol. 1, p. 267.
10. I. M. Dubinskii-Mukhadze, *Shaumyan*, p. 156.
11. F. D. Kretov, *Bor'ba V. I. Lenina za sokhranenie i ukreplenie RSDRP v gody stolypinskoi reaktsii*, p. 141.
12. I. M. Dubinskii-Mukhadze, *Shaumyan*, p. 156.
13. 'Sotsial-demokratiya i natsional'nyi vopros' in I. V. Stalin, *Sochineniya*, vol. 1, p. 295.
14. *Ibid.*
15. See above, p. 53. I am grateful to Stephen Jones for his help with formulating

this paragraph. See also chapter 8 of his forthcoming history of Georgian Marxism before the October Revolution.

16. 'Sotsial-demokratiya i natsional'nyi vopros', *Prosveshchenie*, no. 5 (1913), p. 27.
17. I. V. Stalin, *Sochineniya*, vol. 1, p. 296.
18. See above, p. 38.
19. I. V. Stalin, *Sochineniya*, vol. 1, p. 307.
20. *Ibid.*, p. 313.
21. *Prosveshchenie*, no. 5 (1914), p. 27.
22. *Ibid.*
23. *Ibid.*, pp. 32–6.
24. An [N. Zhordaniya], 'Natsional'nyi vopros', *Bor'ba* (St Petersburg), no. 2, 18 March 1914, p. 31.
25. *Ibid.*, p. 26.
26. Sotsial-demokratiya i natsional'nyi vopros', *Sochineniya*, vol. 1, p. 340.
27. *Ibid.*, pp. 340–1.
28. *Ibid.*
29. 'K natsional'nomu voprosu: evreiskaya burzhuznaya i bundovskaya kul'turno-natsional'naya avtonomiya', *Prosveshchenie*, no. 6 (June 1913), pp. 69–76.
30. *Molotov. Poluderzhavnyi vlastelin*, p. 258.
31. See R. Service, *Lenin: A Biography*, pp. 16–18.

10. Osip of Siberia

1. B. I. Ivanov, *Vospominaniya rabochego bol'shevika*, p. 21.
2. N. L. Meshcheryakov, *Kak my zhili v ssylke*, p. 63.
3. A. V. Baikalov, 'Turukhanskii "bunt" politicheskikh ssyl'nykh', p. 56; *Atlas aziatskoi Rossii*, map 56.
4. *Atlas aziatskoi Rossii*, maps 48–51 and 54–5.
5. *Atlas aziatskoi Rossii*, map 58a; S. Spandar'yan (Timofei), *Stat'i, pis'ma, dokumenty, 1882–1916*, p. xxxviii (editorial note).
6. A. V. Baikalov, 'Turukhanskii "bunt" politicheskikh ssyl'nykh', pp. 51–2.
7. See the account of G. Kennan, *Siberia and the Exile System*, vol. 1, p. 329 and vol. 2, p. 43.
8. *Bol'shevistskoe rukovodstvo. Perepiska, 1912–1927*, p. 18.
9. N. L. Meshcheryakov, *Kak my zhili v ssylke*, p. 75.
10. A. V. Baikalov, 'Turukhanskii "bunt" politicheskikh ssyl'nykh', pp. 53 and 57.
11. A. V. Baikalov, 'Turukhanskii "bunt" politicheskikh ssyl'nykh', p. 53.
12. Report of 27 April 1914 in 'K 20-letiyu smerti Ya. M. Sverdlova', *Krasnyi arkhiv*, no. 1 (1939), pp. 83–4.
13. *Bol'shevistskoe rukovodstvo. Perepiska, 1912–1927*, p. 19.
14. *Ibid.*

15. See A. Ostrovskii, *Kto stoyal za spinoi Stalina?*, pp. 400–1.
16. *Bol'shevistskoe rukovodstvo. Perepiska, 1912–1927*, p. 19.
17. Ya. M. Sverdlov, *Izbrannye proizvedeniya*, vol. 1, p. 266.
18. This was made clear, if only implicitly, in S. Spandar'yan (Timofei), *Stat'i, pis'ma, dokumenty*, p. xxxviii (editorial note). As far as I know, no biography of Stalin has pointed out that Sverdlov's letter contained a basic misapprehension or that Stalin therefore did not live on the River Kureika north of the Arctic Circle.
19. Yu. Trifonov, *Otblesk kostra* (Moscow, 1966), pp. 47–8 in R. Medvedev, *Let History Judge*, pp. 5–6.
20. Ya. M. Sverdlov, *Izbrannye proizvedeniya*, vol. 1, pp. 268–9.
21. *Ibid.*, p. 268
22. *Ibid.*, pp. 276–7.
23. *Ibid.*, p. 289.
24. *Izvestiya*, 8 December 2000; 'I. V. Stalin dal slovo zhenit'sya', *Istochnik*, no. 4 (2002), p. 74. See also A. Ostrovskii, *Kto stoyal za spinoi Stalina?*, p. 407.
25. Ya. M. Sverdlov, *Izbrannye proizvedeniya*, vol. 1, p. 289.
26. *Bol'shevistskoe rukovodstvo. Perepiska, 1912–1927*, p. 18.
27. *Ibid.*
28. RGASPI, f. 558, op. 4, d. 647, p. 434.
29. *Ibid.*, f. 558, op. 1, d. 4235, p. 1 and d. 4337, p. 1.
30. *Bol'shevistskoe rukovodstvo. Perepiska, 1912–1927*, p. 20.
31. B. I. Ivanov, *Vospominaniya rabochego bol'shevika*, pp. 120–1.
32. A. S. Allilueva, *Vospominaniya*, p. 167.
33. *Molotov. Poluderzhavnyi vlastelin*, p. 298.
34. A. S. Allilueva, *Vospominaniya*, p. 168.
35. F. S. Alliluev, 'V purgu' (unpublished memoir): RGASPI, f. 558, op. 4, d. 663, p. 115. Alliluev's account was based on what Stalin had told him.
36. *Ibid.*, pp. 120 and 122.
37. A. S. Allilueva, *Vospominaniya*, p. 189.
38. F. S. Alliluev, 'V purgu' (unpublished memoir): RGASPI, f. 558, op. 4, d. 663, p. 123.
39. *Zastol'nye rechi Stalina. Dokumenty i materialy*, pp. 82–3.
40. *Ibid.*, p. 83.
41. F. S. Alliluev, 'V purgu' (unpublished memoir): RGASPI, f. 558, op. 4, d. 663, p. 112.
42. *Bol'shevistskoe rukovodstvo. Perepiska, 1912–1927*, p. 21.

11. Return to Petrograd

1. A. S. Allilueva, *Vospominaniya*, p. 166; V. Shveitser, *Stalin v turukhanskoi ssylke*, pp. 40–7.
2. B. I. Ivanov, *Vospominaniya rabochego bol'shevika*, p. 160.
3. A. S. Allilueva, *Vospominaniya*, p. 165.

4. B. I. Ivanov, *Vospominaniya rabochego bol'shevika*, p. 160.
5. *Ibid.*
6. A. V. Baikaloff, *I Knew Stalin*, pp. 28–9.
7. *Ibid.*, p. 29.
8. *Ibid.*
9. *Ibid.*, p. vii.
10. *Ibid.*, p. 28.
11. See above, p. 84 and below, p. 361.
12. See below, p. 359.
13. A. Allilueva, *Vospominaniya*, p. 165: this was a memoir written nearly three decades later. Anna saw him later in the day on 12 March 1917.
14. F. Alliluev, 'Ot Moskvy do Tsaritsyna. (Vstrechi s t. Stalinym)': RGASPI, f. 558, op. 4, d. 663, p. 14.
15. A. Allilueva, *Vospominaniya*, p. 165.
16. *Ibid.*
17. 'Protokoly i rezolyutsii Byuro TsK RSDRP(b) (mart 1917 g.)', *VIKPSS*, no. 3 (1962), p. 143.
18. *Ibid.*
19. *Ibid.*
20. RGASPI, f. 558, op. 1, d. 55, pp. 1–2.
21. A. Allilueva, *Vospominaniya*, p. 166.
22. *Ibid.*, pp. 168–70.
23. 'Protokoly i rezolyutsii Byuro TsK RSDRP(b) (mart 1917 g.)', *VIKPSS*, no. 3 (1962), pp. 146 and 148.
24. A. G. Shlyapnikov, *Semnadtsatyi god*, vol. 2, p. 180; *Molotov. Poluderzhavnyi vlastitelin*, p. 214.
25. 'O voine', *Pravda*, 16 March 1917.
26. 'Na puti k ministerskim portfelyam', *Pravda*, 17 March 1917.
27. 'Ob usloviyakh pobedy russkoi revolyutsii', *Pravda*, 18 March 1917.
28. 'Ob otmene natsional'nykh ogranicheniyakh', *Pravda*, 25 March 1917.
29. *Ibid.* See also 'Protiv federalizma', *Pravda*, 28 March 1917.
30. 'Protokoly Vserossiiskogo (martovskogo) soveshchaniya partiinykh rabot-nikov, 27 marta–2 aprelya 1917 g.', *VIKPSS*, no. 5 (1962), pp. 111–12.
31. *Ibid.*, p. 112.
32. *Ibid.*, no. 6, p. 137.
33. *Ibid.*, p. 140.
34. F. F. Raskol'nikov, 'Priezd tov. Lenina v Rossiyu', *Proletarskaya revolyutsiya*, no. 1 (1923), p. 221.
35. See the cogent comments by R. Slusser, *Stalin in October*, pp. 49–50.

12. The Year 1917

1. For a rudimentary examination of this under-researched phenomenon see R. Service, *The Bolshevik Party in Revolution*, p. 47.

2. See above, p. 63.
3. 'Zemlyu – krest'yanam', *Pravda*, 14 April 1917.
4. See, for example, 'O voine', *Pravda*, 16 March 1917.
5. On Lenin's (temporary) movement away from such terminology, see R. Service, *Lenin: A Political Life*, vol. 2, pp. 223–8.
6. *Ibid.*
7. R. Service, *The Bolshevik Party in Revolution*, pp. 46, 53–4.
8. See R. Service, *Lenin: A Political Life*, vol. 2, pp. 223–8.
9. *Sed'maya (aprel'skaya) vserossiiskaya konferentsiya RSDRP (bol'shevikov)*, p. 227.
10. *Ibid.*, p. 225.
11. *Ibid.*, p. 228.
12. S. Pestkovskii, 'Vospominaniya o rabote v Narkomnatse (1917–1919 gg.)', p. 126.
13. *Ibid.*, p. 124.
14. See I. Getzler's account of the significance of Sukhanov's phrase in *Nikolai Sukhanov*, pp. 82–5.
15. See above, p. 120.
16. A. S. Allilueva, *Vospominaniya*, pp. 183–5.
17. Draft of A. S. Allilueva's memoir: RGASPI, f. 4, op. 2, d. 45, p. 6.
18. *Molotov. Poluderzhavnyi vlastelin*, p. 216.
19. *Ibid.*, pp. 216–17.
20. *Ibid.*, p. 297.
21. A. S. Allilueva, *Vospominaniya*, pp. 184–5.
22. *Ibid.*, pp. 169–70.
23. *Ibid.*, p. 175.
24. *Ibid.*, pp. 185–6.
25. *Ibid.*, p. 187.
26. *Ibid.*, p. 186.
27. *Ibid.*, p. 190.
28. *Ibid.*, p. 191.
29. F. S. Alliluev, 'Ot Moskvy do Tsaritsyna. Vstrechi s t. Stalinym' (unpublished typescript): RGASPI, f. 558, op. 4, d. 663, p. 15.
30. *Ibid.*
31. *Shestoi s"ezd RSDRP(b)*, p. 250.
32. See below, p. 244.
33. *Protokoly Tsentral'nogo Komiteta RSDRP(b). Avgust 1917–fevral' 1918*, p. 32.
34. *Ibid.*, p. 39.
35. *Ibid.*, p. 46.
36. *Ibid.*, p. 49.
37. *Ibid.*, pp. 52–3.
38. V. I. Lenin, *Polnoe sobranie sochinenii*, vol. 34, pp. 239–41.
39. *Ibid.*, p. 246.
40. *Protokoly Tsentral'nogo Komiteta RSDRP(b). Avgust 1917–fevral' 1918*, p. 55.

13. October

1. *Protokoly Tsentral'nogo Komiteta*, pp. 84–6.
2. See R. Service, *Lenin: A Political Life*, vol. 2, pp. 252–4.
3. See their statement on 11 October 1917: *Protokoly Tsentral'nogo Komiteta*, pp. 87–92.
4. *Rabochii put'*, no. 32, 10 October 1917.
5. *Ibid.*
6. *Protokoly Tsentral'nogo Komiteta*, p. 99.
7. *Ibid.*, p. 101.
8. *Ibid.*
9. *Novaya zhizn'*, 18 October 1917.
10. *Protokoly Tsentral'nogo Komiteta*, p. 113.
11. *Ibid.*, p. 114.
12. *Ibid.*, p. 115.
13. *Ibid.*, p. 107
14. *Ibid.*
15. *Ibid.*, p. 118.
16. *Ibid.*, p. 117.
17. I. V. Stalin, *Sochineniya*, vol. 3, p. 389.
18. *Ibid.*, p. 390.
19. L. Trotskii, *Stalin. An Appraisal of the Man and His Influence*, pp. 225–6.
20. R. M. Slusser, *Stalin in October*, p. 239.
21. *Protokoly Tsentral'nogo Komiteta*, p. 120.
22. M. P. Zhakov, 'Pis'mo M. Zhakova', pp. 88–93.
23. *Ibid.*
24. A. S. Allilueva, *Vospominaniya*, p. 61.
25. See R. Service, *Lenin: A Political Life*, p. 262.
26. I am unconvinced by R. Slusser's attempt to downgrade Stalin's role in October 1917 in *Stalin in October*, chaps 6–7. But I wish to record my appreciation of the book's empirical research.
27. F. S. Alliluev, 'Vstrechi s t. Stalinym' (unpublished typescript, n.d.): RGASPI, f. 558, op. 4, d. 668, p. 39.
28. L. D. Trotski, *Stalin. An Appraisal of the Man and His Influence*, p. 352.
29. *Protokoly Tsentral'nogo Komiteta*, p. 134: co-signed statement of 3 November 1917.
30. GDMS, Hall 2.

14. People's Commissar

1. F. S. Alliluev, 'Vstrecha' (unpublished typescript, n.d.): RGASPI, f. 558, op. 4, d. 668, p. 30.
2. See below, p. 359. Fëdor Alliluev's memoir nevertheless remained unpubli-

shed, presumably because Stalin preferred to claim obscurity on his own behalf rather than to let others do it for him.

3. S. Pestkovskii, 'Vospominaniya o rabote v Narkomnatse (1917–1919 gg.)', pp. 129–30.

4. *Ibid.*

5. *Ibid.*, pp. 127.

6. See the unpublished account by F. S. Alliluev: 'V Moskve. (Vstrechi s t. Stalinym)', RGASPI, f. 558, op. 4, d. 663, p. 18.

7. A. Allilueva, *Vospominaniya*, p. 187.

8. RGASPI, f. 558, op. 1, d. 5397, p. 2.

9. Collegium meeting, item 8, 21 April 1918: GARF, f. 1318, op. 1, d. 1, p. 11.

10. GARF, f. 1318, op. 1, d. 1, p. 3/1a: People's Commissariat for Nationalities' Affairs collegium, 15 February (2 March) 1918.

11. See the undated collegium discussion at an undated meeting: GARF, f. 1318, op. 1, d. 1, pp. 52–5.

12. Collegium meeting, item 5, 8 March 1919: GARF, f. 1318, op. 1, d. 2, pp. 94–5.

13. *Tretii Vserossiiskii S"ezd Sovetov Rabochikh, Soldatskikh i Krestyanskikh Deputatov*, p. 73.

14. *Ibid.*, p. 74 and 78–9.

15. Commission for the Drafting of the RSFSR Constitution: GARF, f. 6980, op. 1, d. 3, p. 12 (5 April 1918).

16. *Ibid.* (10 April 1918).

17. *Ibid.*, p. 22 (12 April 1918).

18. *Pravda*, 1 April 1918.

19. See above, p. 75–6.

20. RGASPI, f. 558, 2, d. 42. On this file see M. Kun, *Stalin: An Unknown Portrait*, pp. 82–3.

21. 'M. I. Ulyanova ob otnoshenii V. I. Ul'yanova i I. V. Stalina', *ITsKKPSS*, no. 12 (1989), p. 197.

22. See above, pp. 100–1.

23. Commission for the Drafting of the RSFSR Constitution: GARF, f. 6980, op. 1, d. 6, p. 38 (19 April 1918). The Russian phrase here was *avtonomnaya oblastnaya respublika*.

24. *Ibid.*, p. 10.

25. *Ibid.*, p. 12.

26. *Ibid.*, p. 1.

27. *Protokoly Tsentral'nogo Komiteta*, p. 150.

28. *Bol'shevistskoe rukovodstvo. Perepiska, 1912–1927*, p. 36.

29. *Protokoly Tsentral'nogo Komiteta*, p. 173.

30. *Ibid.*, p. 171.

31. *Ibid.*, p. 172.

32. See above, p. 136.

33. *Protokoly Tsentral'nogo Komiteta*, p. 178 (19 January 1918).

34. *Ibid.*, p. 200.

35. *Ibid.*, p. 202.

36. *Ibid.*, p. 212.
37. GARF, f. R-130, op. 2, d. 1(3), item 4 (3 April 1918).

15. To the Front!

1. F. S. Alliluev, 'V puti. (Vstrechi s t. Stalinym)', RGASPI, f. 558, op. 4, d. 663, p. 18.
2. I. V. Stalin, *Sochineniya*, vol. 4, p. 116.
3. See A. Zimin, *U istokov stalinizma, 1918–1923*, p. 134.
4. I. V. Stalin, *Sochineniya*, vol. 4, pp. 120–1.
5. F. S. Alliluev, 'V Tsaritsyne. (Vstrechi s t. Stalinym)', RGASPI, f. 558, op. 4, d. 663, pp. 20–2.
6. F. S. Alliluev, 'Obed u Minina': RGASPI, f. 558, op. 4, d. 668, p. 57.
7. I. V. Stalin, *Sochineniya*, vol. 4, p. 118.
8. If Stalin had repeated his risky behaviour after his trip to Abganerovo-Zutovo, there would surely have been fanfares about it in the memoirs written in the years of his supremacy.
9. F. S. Alliluev, 'T. Stalin na bronepoezde': RGASPI, f. 558, op. 4, d. 668, p. 90.
10. RGASPI, f. 558, op. 1, d. 258, p. 1.
11. F. S. Alliluev, 'Vstrechi s Stalinym': RGASPI, f. 558, op. 4, d. 668, p. 39.
12. *Ibid.*, p. 38.
13. *Ibid.*, p. 35.
14. S. Allilueva, *Dvadtsat' pisem k drugu*, p. 90.
15. *Molotov. Poluderzhavnyi vlastelin*, p. 297.
16. A. Allilueva, *Vospominaniya*, p. 170.
17. See below, pp. 289–91.
18. See the picture of her with her sister Anna and brother-in-law Stanisław Redens: RGASPI, f. 558, op. 2, d. 193.
19. For the marriage see below, pp. 230–1.
20. *K. E. Voroshilov na Tsaritsynskom fronte. Sbornik dokumentov*, p. 64.
21. *Bol'shevistskoe rukovodstvo. Perepiska, 1912–1927*, p. 52.
22. See report of V. P. Antonov-Ovseenko to Lenin: *ibid.*, p. 60.
23. *Pravda*, 20 September 1963.
24. J. Davrichewy, *Ah! Ce qu'on rigolait bien*, p. 221.
25. *ITsKKPSS*, no. 11 (1989), p. 163.
26. *Ibid.*, p. 169.
27. R. Service, *Lenin: A Political Life*, vol. 3, pp. 79–81.
28. K. Voroshilov, *Stalin i Krasnaya Armiya*, p. 104.
29. *ITsKKPSS*, no. 11 (1989), p. 157.
30. *Ibid.*, pp. 161–2.
31. *Bol'shevistskoe rukovodstvo. Perepiska, 1912–1927*, p. 51.
32. *ITsKKPSS*, no. 6 (1989), p. 146 and no. 12 (1989), pp. 169–70; G. Leggett, *The Cheka*, pp. 162–3.

33. Stalin's copy of N. Lenin, *Gosudarstvo i revolyutsiya* (Petrograd, 1919), inside flap: RGASPI, f. 558, op. 3, d. 156.
34. *Ibid.*, p. 28.
35. *Ibid.*, inside flap.
36. *The Trotsky Papers, 1917–1922*, vol. 1.
37. V. Alliluev, *Khronika odnoi sem'i: Alliluevy. Stalin*, p. 9.
38. See below, pp. 178–9.
39. RGASPI, f. 558, op. 1, d. 627, p. 1.
40. *Ibid.*
41. S. V. Lipitskii, 'Stalin v grazhdanskoi voine', p. 98.
42. See R. Service, *The Bolshevik Party in Revolution*, pp. 101–2 and 123–5.

16. The Polish Corridor

1. V. I. Lenin, *Polnoe sobranie sochinenii*, vol. 50, p. 186.
2. *Ibid.*, pp. 285–6. See also the remarks by Béla Kun quoted from archives in V. M. Kholodkovskii, 'V. I. Lenin i mezhdunarodnye otnosheniya novogo tipa', p. 88.
3. See Lenin's speech to the Ninth Party Conference, RGASPI, f. 44, op. 1, d. 5, pp. 11–18, 20–1, 27–8; and his memoranda quoted in *Izvestiya*, 27 April 1992.
4. RGASPI, f. 17, op. 3, d. 15, item 3 and d. 103, item 8.
5. ITsKKPSS, no. 2 (1990), p. 158.
6. V. I. Lenin, *Polnoe sobranie sochinenii*, vol. 51, p. 240.
7. ITsKKPSS, no. 1 (1991), pp. 119–22.
8. RGASPI, f. 17, op. 3, d. 96, item 2.
9. *Ibid.*, f. 558, op. 1, d. 4200, p. 1.
10. R. Service, *Lenin: A Political Life*, vol. 3, p. 120.
11. I. V. Stalin, *Sochineniya*, vol. 4, pp. 332–3.
12. *Bol'shevistskoe rukovodstvo. Perepiska, 1912–1927*, pp. 149–50: telegrams to Lenin and Trotski.
13. See R. Service, *Lenin: A Biography*, pp. 406–8.
14. *Bol'shevistskoe rukovodstvo. Perepiska, 1912–1927*, p. 110.
15. K. E. Voroshilov, *Stalin i Vooruzhënnye Sily SSSR*, p. 23.
16. *Istoriya SSSR*, vol. 3, book 2, p. 364.
17. RGASPI, f. 558, d. 1470, p. 1.
18. V. I. Lenin, *Polnoe sobranie sochinenii*, vol. 51, pp. 237–8.
19. *Bol'shevistskoe rukovodstvo. Perepiska, 1912–1927*, p. 142.
20. *Ibid.*, p. 143.
21. *Ibid.*, pp. 147 and 150.
22. *Ibid.*, p. 150.
23. *Ibid.*, pp. 150–1.
24. *Ibid.*, pp. 151–2.

25. Speech by Stalin to the Twelfth Party Congress section on the national question, 25 April 1923: *ITsKKPSS*, no. 4 (1991), p. 171.
26. *Ibid.*
27. See N. Davies, *White Eagle, Red Star*, p. 200.
28. See the assessment by Norman Davies (shared with Piłsudski) in *ibid.*, pp. 208–10.
29. S. M. Budënnyi, *Proidënnyi put'*, vol. 2, p. 304.
30. See N. Davies, *White Eagle, Red Star*, pp. 213–14.
31. S. M. Budënnyi, *Proidënnyi put'*, vol. 2, pp. 310–11.
32. *Ibid.*, p. 303.
33. See N. Davies, *White Eagle, Red Star*, pp. 218–19.
34. RGASPI, f. 17, op. 3, d. 103, item 1a.
35. *Ibid.*, item 5.
36. See above, pp. 172–3.
37. Thus he attended the Politburo on 25 and 26 August, 6, 14, and 15 September 1920: RGASPI, f. 17, op. 3, d. 104–9.
38. *Ibid.*, d. 106, item 19.
39. *Ibid.*, item 10.
40. *Ibid.*, d. 107, item 2; d. 108, item 1.
41. *Ibid.*, d. 108, item 9.
42. *Ibid.*, f. 44, op. 1, d. 5, pp. 33, 35 and 36.
43. *Devyataya Konferentsiya RKP(b)*, p. 26.
44. *Ibid.*, p. 79.
45. C. Zetkin, *Erinnerungen an Lenin* (Vienna, 1929), pp. 20–1; I. V. Stalin, *Sochineniya*, vol. 4, pp. 323–4 and 333.
46. *Devyataya Konferentsiya RKP(b)*, p. 82.
47. This is essentially what Trotski did at the Tenth Party Congress at the end of the 'trade union discussion' and indeed what Lenin pre-emptively sought to do at the Ninth Party Congress.
48. See above, p. 170.
49. Birthday speech for Lenin: *Pravda*, 24 April 1920.
50. See R. C. Tucker, *Stalin as Revolutionary*, pp. 122–30.

17. With Lenin

1. A. Mikoyan, *Mysli i vospominaniya o Lenine*, p. 139.
2. See R. Service, *Lenin: A Political Life*, vol. 3, pp. 181 and 207.
3. RGASPI, f. 558, op. 1, d. 5193, p. 2.
4. *Ibid.* Stalin wrote on Rabkrin letter-paper, perhaps aiming to show to Lenin that he had plenty of other work to carry out: *ibid.*, p. 1.
5. Politburo minutes, 24 November 1921: *ibid.*, f. 17, op. 3, d. 234, item 10.
6. RGASPI, f. 46, op. 1, d. 3, p. 18.
7. *Ibid.*
8. *Ibid.*, f. 5, op. 2, d. 8, p. 24.

9. See R. Service, *The Bolshevik Party in Revolution*, chaps. 5–7.
10. *Molotov. Poluderzhavnyi vlastelin*, p. 261.
11. *Odinnadtsatyi s"ezd RKP(b)*, pp. 84–5; RGASPI, f. 17, op. 2 d. 78, item 1-i-b, p. 1.
12. *Molotov. Poluderzhavnyi vlastelin*, p. 240: this was Molotov's recollection in old age.
13. See the discussion at the Central Committee plenum, 3 April 1922: RGASPI, f. 17, op. 2, d. 78, item 1 (i/b).
14. A. Mikoyan, *Tak bylo*, p. 369.
15. See above, pp. 63, 128 and 168–9.
16. *Bol'shevistskoe rukovodstvo. Perepiska, 1912–1927*, p. 214.
17. *Ibid.*, p. 227.
18. N. A. Uglanov, 'Vospominaniya', *Vospominaniya o Vladimire Il'iche Lenine*, vol. 7, p. 72.
19. See R. Service, *Lenin: A Biography*, pp. 248 and 293–4.
20. RGASPI, f. 16, op. 3s, d. 20, p. 61.
21. 'Vospominaniya M.I. Ul'yanovoi': *ibid.*, pp. 11–12.
22. Reports by the head of Lenin's special guard unit: *ibid.*, op. 2s, d. 39, pp. 26, 45, 55, 61, 76 and 89.
23. *Ibid.*, f. 17, op. 2, d. 25993.
24. *Ibid.*
25. *ITsKKPSS*, no. 4 (1991), p. 188. Lenin was willing to allow Kamenev, Zinoviev and Tomski to become 'candidate members' only.
26. Politburo minutes, 10 November 1921: RGASPI, f. 17, op. 3, d. 228, item 2.
27. See above, pp. 179–80.
28. *ITsKKPSS*, no. 9 (1989), pp. 195, 197 and 198.
29. *Ibid.*, pp. 195 and 197.
30. *Ibid.*, pp. 198–9.
31. *Ibid.*, p. 200.
32. V. I. Lenin, *Polnoe sobranie sochinenii*, vol. 45, p. 211.
33. *Ibid.*, pp. 211–12.
34. RGASPI, f. 64, op. 2, d. 7, p. 133.
35. *ITsKKPSS*, no. 9 (1989), p. 209.
36. For the argument that Lenin and Stalin in 1922–3 agreed on primary questions see R. Service, *Lenin: A Political Life*, vol. 3, pp. 298–303.

18. Nation and Revolution

1. See above, pp. 63, 128 and 168–9.
2. S. Pestkovskii, 'Vospominaniya o rabote v Narkomnatse (1917–1919 gg.)', p. 128.
3. *Ibid.*
4. E. Olla-Reza, *Azarbaidzhan i Arran*, pp. 28–31. I am grateful to Ali Granmayeh for his advice on this matter.

5. GARF, f. R-130, op. 2, d. 2(5): Sovnarkom sessions of 7, 21 and 30 December 1918.
6. *ITsKKPSS*, no. 9 (1989), p. 199.
7. RGASPI, f. 17, op. 3, d. 15, item 3: joint session of Politburo and Orgburo, 19 July 1919.
8. *Vos'moi s''ezd RKP(b)*, p. 425.
9. RGASPI, f. 17, op. 2, d. 48, p. 1; see also *ibid*., pp. 3–4.
10. See G. P. Lezhava, *Mezhdu Gruziei i Rossiei*, p. 69.
11. Definitive resolutions of territorial matters sometimes had to await Stalin taking the case to the Politburo: see for example RGASPI, f. 17, op. 3, d. 58, item 28.
12. ITsKKPSS, no. 2 (1990), 164 and no. 7 (1990), p. 163.
13. RGASPI, f. 17, op. 112, d. 93, p. 30.
14. *Ibid*., p. 33.
15. Quoted by R. Kh. Gutov, *Sovmestnaya bor'ba narodov Tereka za Sovetskuyu vlast'*, p. 469.
16. See also above, p. 169.
17. RGASPI, f. 17, op. 112, d. 43, p. 33.
18. *Desyatyi s''ezd RKP(b)*, p. 184.
19. *Ibid*., pp. 184–5.
20. See below, p. 231.
21. *Desyatyi s''ezd RKP(b)*, pp. 201–6 (V. P. Zatonski) and pp. 206–9 (A. I. Mikoyan).
22. *Ibid*., p. 213.
23. See J. Baberowski, *Der Feind ist überall*, p. 163.
24. See below, p. 231 for Stalin's appendicitis.
25. See G. P. Lezhava, *Mezhdu Gruziei i Rossiei*, p. 92.
26. See S. Lakoba, *Ocherki politicheskoi istorii Abkhazii*, pp. 83–4.
27. *Ibid*., pp. 81–3.
28. I. V. Stalin, *Sochineniya*, vol. 5, p. 94.
29. *Ibid*., p. 95.
30. S. Kavtaradze, *tsareulis purtsebli*, vol. 1, p. 56. D. M. Lang describes the occasion as having been still more tumultuous but omits reference to a source: see *A Modern History of Georgia*, p. 239. See also S. V. Kharmandaryan, *Lenin i stanovlenie zakavkazskoi federatsii*, p. 104, where he cites the personal files of G. A. Galoyan.
31. S. V. Kharmandaryan, *Lenin i stanovlenie zakavkazskoi federatsii*, p. 85.
32. *Tainy natsional'noi politiki RKP(b)*, especially p. 100.
33. See R. Service, *Lenin: A Political Life*, vol. 3, p. 291–3.

19. Testament

1. *Bol'shevistskoe rukovodstvo. Perepiska, 1912–1927*, p. 268: 13 November 1922.
2. V. I. Lenin, *Polnoe sobranie sochinenii*, vol. 45, pp. 343–8.

3. *Molotov. Poluderzhavnyi vlastelin*, p. 195.
4. V. I. Lenin, *Polnoe sobranie sochinenii*, vol. 45, p. 345.
5. *Ibid.*, pp. 344–5.
6. *Ibid.*, p. 344.
7. V. P. Danilov, 'Stalinizm i sovetskoe obshchestvo', p. 170.
8. V. I. Lenin, *Polnoe sobranie sochinenii*, vol. 45, p. 346.
9. *ITsKKPSS*, no. 4 (1991), p. 188.
10. I am grateful to Francesco Benvenuti, with whom I have discussed this matter for many years, for his persistence in getting me to clarify the interpretation.
11. V. I. Lenin, *Polnoe sobranie sochinenii*, vol. 45, p. 356.
12. *Pravda*, 25 January 1923.
13. He told Kaganovich this in 1922: *Tak govoril Kaganovich*, p. 191.
14. *Molotov. Poluderzhavnyi vlastelin*, p. 283.
15. *Dvenadtsatyi s"ezd RKP(b)*, pp. 164–6.
16. *Ibid.*, p. 821.
17. *ITsKKPSS*, no. 4 (1991), pp. 179–91.
18. See R. V. Daniels, *The Conscience of the Revolution*, p. 208.
19. *Sochineniya*, vol. 6, p. 14.
20. RGASPI, f. 16, op. 2s, d. 39, pp. 16–124.

20. The Opportunities of Struggle

1. See the letter from Dzierżyński quoted by S. Lakoba, *Ocherki politicheskoi istorii Abkhazii*, p. 103.
2. *Pravda*, 30 January 1924.
3. See N. Tumarkin, *Lenin Lives!* p. 153.
4. RGASPI, f. 76, op. 3, d. 287, pp. 7 and 19.
5. See *Lubyanka. Stalin I VChK–GPU–nOGPU–NKVD. Yanvar' 1922–dekabr' 1936*, pp. 11–12.
6. See above, p. 188.
7. RGASPI, f. 12, op. 2, d. 41, p. 2.
8. *Ibid.*, p. 3.
9. *Ibid.*, pp. 17, 27 and 38.
10. *Ibid.*, f. 558, op. 1, d. 3112, p. 1.
11. *Ibid.*, f. 17, op. 1, d. 471: letter of A. I. Ulyanova to Stalin, 28 December 1932.
12. *Ob osnovakh leninizma* in I. V. Stalin, *Sochineniya*, vol. 6, p. 71.
13. *Ibid.*, pp. 135–7.
14. V. I. Lenin, *Polnoe sobranie sochinenii*, vol. 45, pp. 593–4.
15. *Rodina*, no. 7 (1994), p. 72.
16. B. Bazhanov, *Bazhanov and the Damnation of Stalin*, pp. 34–5.
17. See above, p. 26.
18. The exception in this list was Kaganovich, who always used the formal

'you' (*vy*) in conversation and letter, and even in letters would address him as 'comrade Stalin': see *Stalin i Kaganovich. Perepiska, 1931–1936 gg.*, *passim.*

19. See O. Khlevnyuk, *Stalin i Ordzhonikidze*, pp. 28 and 34–41; R. Service, *The Bolshevik Party in Revolution*, pp. 106–8.
20. *Stalin i Kaganovich. Perepiska, 1931–1936 gg.*, p. 109.
21. *Bol'shevistskoe rukovodstvo. Perepiska, 1912–1927*, p. 256.
22. *Ibid.*, p. 263.
23. *Tak govoril Kaganovich*, p. 35.
24. See R. Service, *The Bolshevik Party in Revolution*, p. 196.
25. L. Trotsky, *Stalin: An Appraisal of the Man and His Influence*, p. 22. I have adjusted the translation.
26. W. H. Roobol, *Tsereteli: A Democrat in the Russian Revolution*, p. 13.
27. See R. Service, *The Bolshevik Party in Revolution*, p. 196.
28. RGASPI, f. 558, op. 3, d. 93: Stalin's personal copy of E. Kviring, *Lenin, Zagovorshchestvo, Oktyabr'* (Kharkov, 1924).
29. B. Bazhanov, *Bazhanov and the Damnation of Stalin*, pp. 39–40.
30. *Ibid.*, p. 37.
31. *Ibid.*, p. 57.
32. I. V. Stalin, *Sochineniya*, vol. 6, pp. 257–8 and vol. 9, pp. 77 and 79. See E. H. Carr, *Socialism in One Country*, vol. 2, chaps. 11 and 16.
33. See R. V. Daniels, *Conscience of the Revolution*, p. 254.

21. Joseph and Nadya

1. This attitude endured. Stalin expressed it at length in an improvised speech to Georgi Dimitrov and others in November 1937 at the height of the Great Terror: see the summary by R. C. Tucker in *Stalin in Power*, p. 483.
2. This was Trotski's recollection of what Kamenev told him about a conversation he had had with Stalin and Dzierzynski in mid-1923: *Trotsky's Diary in Exile, 1935*, p. 64.
3. S. Allilueva, *Dvadtsat' pisem k drugu*, p. 90; V. Alliluev, *Khronika odnoi sem'i: Alliluevy. Stalin*, p. 9.
4. RGASPI, f. 134, op. 3, d. 36, p. 15. This comment comes in Kollontai's 1920 diary. There must be some suspicion, however, about the authenticity of some parts of this source: certain entries for some years seem to have been modified in the light of later political developments.
5. A. S. Allilueva, *Vospominaniya*, p. 186. See above, p. 186.
6. RGASPI, f. 589, op. 3, d. 15904, l. 14.
7. *Ibid.*, f. 2, op. 1, d. 14228. See also the direct-line conversation between Ordzhonikidze and Nadezhda Allilueva, 4 December 1920: *ibid.*, d. 6404.
8. *Ibid.*, f. 589, op. 3, d. 15904, l. 12.
9. Sergei Alliluev's note on 1919: *ibid.*, f. 4, op. 2, d. 46, p. 1.

10. See for example his telegram of 7 November 1919: *ibid.*, f. 558, op. 1, d. 910, p. 1.

11. F. Alliluev, 'Vstrechi s t. Stalinym': *ibid.*, op. 4, d. 663, p. 39.

12. *Ibid.*

13. *Ibid.*, p. 40.

14. S. Kavtaradze, *tsareulis purtsebli*, vol. 1, p. 55.

15. Anecdote recounted to Felix Chuev by Yakov Dzhughashvili's son Yevgeni: see *Molotov. Poluderzhavnyi vlastelin*, p. 245.

16. G. Uratadze, *Vospominaniya gruzinskogo sotsial-demokrata*, p. 209.

17. Testimony of A. F. Sergeev to F. Chuev: *Molotov. Poluderzhavnyi vlastelin*, p. 359.

18. V. Semichastnyi, *Bespokoinoe serdtse*, p. 39.

19. Letter to M. I. Kalinin: RGASPI, f. 78, op. 1, d. 46, p. 2.

20. Letter of 30 November 1918: *ibid.*, f. 86, op. 1, d. 84.

21. GARF, f. 3316s/g, op. 64, d. 258, pp. 5 and 7.

22. V. Alliluev, *Khronika odnoi sem'i: Alliluevy. Stalin*, p. 131.

23. S. Allilueva, *Dvadtsat' pisem k drugu*.

24. RGASPI, f. 589, op. 3, d. 15904, pp. 12 and 15.

25. *Ibid.*, pp. 16 and 19.

26. See above, p. 188.

27. RGASPI, f. 5, op. 1, d. 456: 18 October 1922.

28. *Ibid.*, f. 558, op. 3, d. 4: B. Andreev, *Zavoevanie Prirody*.

29. *Iosif Stalin v ob"yatiyakh sem'i*, p. 7.

30. See above, chapters 6–7. See also S. Allilueva, *Dvadtsat' pisem k drugu*, pp. 24–5.

31. In strict terms, of course, the dacha was not Stalin's property but the state's.

32. S. Allilueva, *Dvadtsat' pisem k drugu*, pp. 26–9; 'Bosco d'inverno a Zubalov', *Slavia* (1997).

33. See *Pis'ma I. V. Stalina V. M. Molotovu*, p. 23 for an example.

34. A. Mikoyan, *Tak bylo*, p. 351.

35. *Ibid.*, pp. 351–2; A. Mikoyan, 'Iz vospominaniya A. I. Mikoyana', *Sovershenno sekretno*, no. 10 (1999), p. 25. There is a doubt about the date of this advice: see A. Kirilina, *Neizvestnyi Kirov*, p. 305.

36. Letter of Stalin, 30 July 1922: A. Kirillina, *Neizvestnyi Kirov*, p. 305.

37. *Pis'ma I. V. Stalina V. M. Molotovu*, pp. 70 and 156.

38. I. A. Valedinskii, 'Vospominaniya o vstrechakh s t. I. V. Stalinym', p. 68.

39. S. Allilueva, *Dvadtsat' pisem k drugu*, p. 19.

40. I. A. Valedinskii, 'Vospominaniya o vstrechakh s t. I. V. Stalinym', p. 69.

41. *Iosif Stalin v ob"yatiyakh sem'i*, p. 22 ff.

42. *Ibid.*, pp. 22–3.

43. *Ibid.*, p. 19.

44. B. Bazhanov, *Bazhanov and the Damnation of Stalin*, p. 36.

45. RGASPI, f. 44, op. 1, d. 1, p. 417.

46. *Ibid.*, p. 418.

47. *Iosif Stalin v ob"yatiyakh sem'i*, p. 23.
48. *Ibid.*, pp. 31 and 35 for letter of 1929 and 1931.
49. *Molotov. Poluderzhavnyi vlastelin*, p. 365. The incident probably occurred in 1928.
50. B. Bazhanov, *Bazhanov and the Damnation of Stalin*, p. 38.

22. Factionalist Against Factions

1. *Chetyrnadtsatyi s"ezd Vsesoyuznoi Kommunisticheskoi Partii (b)*, pp. 427–31 and 503.
2. *Ibid.*, p. 508.
3. *Ibid.*, pp. 274–5.
4. *Ibid.*, p. 455.
5. *Ibid.*, p. 52. This number includes probationary members.
6. RGASPI, f. 44, op. 1, d. 5, pp. 37–8.
7. *Iosif Stalin v ob"yatiyakh sem'i*, pp. 30–1.
8. See Ye. P. Frolov's recollectio as adduced by R. Medvedev, *Let History Judge*, pp. 224–5.
9. See above, p. 244.
10. See R. Service, 'Joseph Stalin: The Making of a Stalinist', pp. 22–3.
11. See G. Gill, *The Origins of the Stalinist Political System*, pp. 125–34.
12. *Bol'shevistskoe rukovodstvo. Perepiska, 1912–1927*, p. 90.
13. *Pis'ma I. V. Stalina V. M. Molotovu*, p. 71.
14. *Ibid.*, pp. 72–3.
15. *Ibid.*, p. 74.
16. *Ibid.*, p. 69.
17. *Bol'shevistskoe rukovodstvo. Perepiska, 1912–1927*, p. 90.
18. *Ibid.*, p. 105.
19. *Stalin v vospominaniyakh sovremennikov i dokumentov epokhi*, p. 146.
20. *Pis'ma I. V. Stalina V. M. Molotovu*, p. 102.
21. *Ibid.*, pp. 103, 104, 106, 107 and 116–17.
22. *Ibid.*, p. 107.
23. I. V. Stalin, *Sochineniya*, vol. 10, p. 193.

23. Ending the NEP

1. See J. Baberowski, *Der Feind ist überall*, p. 561.
2. RGASPI, f. 17, op. 3, d. 667, pp. 10–12.
3. See J. Hughes, *Stalin, Siberia and the Crisis of the NEP*, p. 129.
4. *Ibid.*, p. 138.
5. See A. Nove, *An Economic History of the USSR*, pp. 137–8 and 140–1.
6. See J. Harris, *The Great Urals*, p. 69.

7. See J. Baberowski, *Der Feind ist überall*, p. 564.
8. See J. Baberowski, *Der Rote Terror*, pp. 196–7.
9. Organisational report of the Central Committee: *Pyatnadtsatyi s"ezd Vesoyuznoi Kommunisticheski Partii-(b)*, pp. 100–3. This number includes probationary members.
10. *Pis'ma I. V. Stalina V. M. Molotovu*, p. 35.
11. I. V. Stalin, *Sochineniya*, vol. 9, pp. 136–8. The significance of these early calls for faster industrialisation was established by R. Tucker, *Stalin as Revolutionary*, pp. 398–9.
12. I. V. Stalin, *Sochineniya*, vol. 11, pp. 1–9.
13. *Pravda*, 15 February 1928.
14. See E. H. Carr and R. W. Davies, *Foundations of a Planned Economy, 1926–1929*, vol. 1, part 1, p. 55.
15. *Sovetskoe rukovodstvo. Perepiska, 1928–1941*, p. 73.
16. Andrei Sokolov, 'Before Stalinism: The Defense Industry of Soviet Russia in the 1920s', pp. 12–14.
17. Kamenev's summary of his conversation with N. I. Bukharin and G. Sokolnikov in *Razgovory s Bukharinym*, p. 32.
18. See A. Nove, *An Economic History of the USSR*, p. 145.
19. R. W. Davies, *The Socialist Offensive*, pp. 41–51.
20. I am grateful to Mark Harrison for sharing with me his knowledge of the final crisis of the NEP.
21. *Razgovory s Bukharinym*, p. 30: Kamenev's summary of conversation with G. Sokolnikov.
22. *Ibid.*, p. 35: appendix to summary of conversation of L. B. Kamenev, N. I. Bukharin and G. Sokolnikov.
23. *Ibid.*, pp. 32–3: Kamenev's summary of conversation with G. Sokolnikov.
24. *Ibid.*, pp. 30–1.
25. *Pravda*, 28 September 1928. See also S. F. Cohen, *Bukharin and the Bolshevik Revolution*, pp. 295–6.
26. *Razgovory s Bukharinym*, p. 35: summary of conversation of L. B. Kamenev, N. I. Bukharin and G. Sokolnikov.
27. *Ibid.*
28. *Razgovory s Bukharinym*, p. 35: appendix of summary of conversation of L. B. Kamenev, N. I. Bukharin and G. Sokolnikov.
29. See above, p. 151.

24. Terror-Economics

1. See S. G. Wheatcroft and R. W. Davies, 'Agriculture', pp. 120–1.
2. See M. Lewin, *Russian Peasants and Soviet Power*, pp. 344–77.
3. *Pravda*, 7 November 1929.
4. See M. Lewin, *Russian Peasants and Soviet Power*, pp. 465–77.
5. *Pravda*, 29 November 1929.

6. See A. Luukkanen, *The Religious Policy of the Stalinist State*, p. 57.

7. *Lubyanka. Stalin i VChK–GPU–OGPU–NKVD. Yanvar' 1922–dekabr' 1936*, pp. 269–72.

8. See Lewin, *Russian Peasants and Soviet Power*, pp. 482–509.

9. See G. A. Krasil'nikov, 'Rozhdenie Gulaga: diskussii v verkhnikh eshelonakh vlasti', *Istoricheskii arkhiv*, no. 4 (1989), p. 143.

10. *Akademicheskoe delo 1929–1931 gg.*, vol. 1, *Delo po obvineniyu akademika S. F. Platonova*, p. xlviii.

11. *Pis'ma I. V. Stalina V. M. Molotovu*, p. 224.

12. See I. Getzler, *Nikolai Sukhanov*, pp. 143–87.

13. B. Nahaylo and V. Swoboda, *The Soviet Disunion: A History of the Nationalities Problem in the USSR*.

14. D. Pospielovsky, *The Russian Orthodox Church under the Soviet Regime*, vol. 1, p. 175. See also D. Peris, *Storming the Heavens: the Soviet League of the Militant Atheists*; A. Luukkanen, *The Religious Policy of the Stalinist State*.

15. K. Bailes, *Technology and Society under Lenin and Stalin: Origins of the Soviet Technical Intelligentsia, 1917–1941*; N. Lampert, *The Technical Intelligentsia and the Soviet State: A Study of Soviet Managers and Technicians, 1928–1935*.

16. See T. H. Rigby, *Communist Party Membership*, p. 52.

17. See R. Service, *A History of Twentieth-Century Russia*, pp. 185–6.

18. *Pravda*, 5 February 1931.

19. Quoted from central party archives by N. N. Maslov, 'Ob utverzhdenii ideologii stalinizma', p. 60.

20. *Ibid.*

21. *Ibid.*, p. 61.

22. *Ibid.*

23. R. W. Davies, *The Socialist Offensive*, pp. 252–68.

24. *Pravda*, 2 March 1930.

25. See A. Nove, *An Economic History of the USSR*, p. 171.

26. *Ibid.*

27. *Ibid.*, p. 174.

28. *Pis'ma I. V. Stalina V. M. Molotovu*, p. 194: message, no earlier than 6 August 1930.

29. *Ibid.*, p. 204.

30. *Stalin i Kaganovich. Perepiska. 1931–1936 gg.*, p. 51.

31. *Pravda*, 5 February 1931.

32. *Ibid.*

33. *Ibid.*

34. *Zastol'nye rechi Stalina. Dokumenty i materialy*, p. 45.

35. *Pravda*, 5 February 1931

36. See J. Harris, *The Great Urals*, pp. 70–1.

37. See R. W. Davies, *Crisis and Progress in the Soviet Economy, 1931–1933*, pp. 302–16.

25. Ascent to Supremacy

1. About his real birthday see above, p. 14.
2. The exception in the Politburo was Bukharin.
3. See W. Taubman, *Khrushchev: The Man and His Era*, p. 63.
4. *Tak govoril Kaganovich*, pp. 59–60.
5. *Molotov. Poluderzhavnyi vlastelin*, p. 262.
6. To chair the Politburo, the Orgburo or the Secretariat was not the same as to be its chairman; and when in 1928 the minutes recorded Kaganovich as Orgburo Chairman, there was a furious protest and Molotov had to agree to amend them: RGASPI, f. 81, op. 3, d. 255, p. 98. See below, p. 363 for the possibility that Stalin learned from the precedent of the Roman Emperor Augustus.
7. See E. A. Rees, 'Stalin as Leader, 1924–1937: From Oligarch to Dictator', p. 27. See also R. W. Davies, M. Ilic and O. Khlevnyuk, 'The Politburo and Economic Decision-Making', p. 110.
8. *Pis'ma I. V. Stalina V. M. Molotovu*, pp. 222–3.
9. *Sovetskoe rukovodstvo. Perepiska, 1928–1941*, pp. 144–5.
10. *Lubyanka. Stalin i VChK–GPU–OGPU–NKVD*, p. 191.
11. *Ibid.*, p. 237.
12. See O. Khlevnyuk, *Stalin i Ordzhonikidze*, pp. 19–31.
13. *Pis'ma I. V. Stalina V.M. Molotovu*, p. 217.
14. *Ibid.*, pp. 231–2.
15. *Ibid.*, p. 232.
16. *Ibid.*, pp. 231–2.
17. Quoted in B. S. Ilizarov, *Tainaya zhizn' Stalina*, p. 93.
18. RGASPI, f. 78, op. 2, d. 38, p. 38.
19. *Stalin i Kaganovich. Perepiska*, p. 187.
20. *Pis'ma I. V. Stalina V. M. Molotovu*, p. 166.
21. *Ibid.*, p. 167.
22. See T. H. Rigby, 'Was Stalin a Disloyal Patron?'
23. A. Kriegel and S. Courtois, *Eugen Fried*, pp. 121 and 125.
24. *Stalin i Kaganovich*, p. 665: telegram of 6 September 1936.
25. *Sovetskoe rukovodstvo. Perepiska, 1928–1941*, p. 33.
26. *Pis'ma I. V. Stalina V. M. Molotovu*, p. 107.
27. *Lubyanka. Stalin i VChK–GPU–OGPU–NKVD*, p. 180.
28. L. Trotskii, *Moya zhizn'*.
29. *Pis'ma I. V. Stalina V.M. Molotovu, 1925–1936 gg.*, p. 231.
30. *ITsKKPSS*, no. 11 (1990), pp. 63–74.
31. *Reabilitatsiya: politicheskie protsessy 30–50-kh godov*, pp. 334–443. See also *The Road to Terror* (ed. O. V. Naumov and J. A. Getty) pp. 52–4.
32. S. Allilueva, *Dvadtsat' pisem k drugu*, pp. 54–5.
33. *L'Armata Rossa e la collettiviazione delle campagne nell' URSS (1928–1933)*, pp. 164, 302 and 356.

26. The Death of Nadya

1. R. Bullard, *Inside Stalin's Russia*, p. 142.
2. *Ibid.*, p. 208.
3. *Lubyanka. Stalin i VChK–GPU–OGPU–NKVD*, p. 286.
4. S. Allilueva, *Dvadtsat' pisem k drugu*, pp. 99–100.
5. Reported by R. Richardson from an interview with Svetlana Allilueva, *The Long Shadow*, p. 125.
6. *Sovetskoe rukovodstvo. Perepiska, 1928–1941*, p. 77.
7. RGASPI, f. 17, op. 113, d. 869, p. 61.
8. *Iosif Stalin v ob"yatiyakh sem'i*, p. 29.
9. *Ibid.*, p. 30.
10. RGASPI, f. 17, op. 113, d. 869.
11. Interview with Kira Allilueva, 14 December 1998. See also L. Vasil'eva, *Kremlëvskie zhëny*, p. 259.
12. *Iosif Stalin v ob"yatiyakh sem'i*, pp. 31 and 33.
13. See S. Sebag Montefiore, *Stalin: The Court of the Red Tsar*, p. 50.
14. GARF, f. 3316/ya, op. 2, d. 2016, p. 3.
15. RGASPI, f. 85, op. 28, d. 63, pp. 1–3.
16. *Molotov. Poluderzhavnyi vlastelin*, pp. 307–8.
17. *Ibid.*, p. 307.
18. *Ibid.*, p. 308.
19. S. Allilueva, *Dvadtsat' pisem k drugu*, p. 31.
20. GARF, f. 7523sg, op. 149a, d. 2, p. 7.
21. GARF, f. 7523sg, op. 149a, d. 2, pp. 10, 11 and 13.
22. GARF, f. 81, op. 3, d. 77, p. 48.
23. RGASPI, f. 3, op. 1, d. 3230.
24. R. Bullard, *Inside Stalin's Russia*, p. 153.
25. GARF, f. 3316/ya, op. 2, d. 2016, p. 2.
26. *Lubyanka. Stalin i VChK–GPU–OGPU–NKVD*, pp. 601 and 667–9.
27. *Molotov. Poluderzhavnyi vlastelin*, p. 308.
28. 'Dnevnik M. A. Svanidze' in *Iosif Stalin v ob"yatiyakh sem'i*, p. 177.
29. A. Mgeladze, *Stalin, kakim ya ego znal*, p. 117.
30. A. Rybin, 'Ryadom so Stalinym', *Sotsiologicheskie issledovaniya*, no. 3 (1988), p. 87.
31. A. Mikoyan, *Tak bylo*, p. 356.
32. *Tak govoril Kaganovich*, p. 35.
33. A. Mikoyan, *Tak bylo*, p. 353.
34. RGASPI, f. 3, op. 1, d. 3231.
35. *Ibid.*
36. S. Allilueva, *Dvadtsat' pisem k drugu*, pp. 19 and 21.
37. See S. Lakoba, *Ocherki politicheskoi istorii Abkhazii*, p. 120.
38. *Ibid.*, p. 118.

39. *Ibid.*, pp. 132–3.
40. *Ibid.*, pp. 116–17.
41. *Ibid.*, p. 115.

27. Modernity's Sorcerer

1. See for example his speech to an all-Union conference of 'proletarian students', *Pravda*, 16 April 1925.
2. *Semnadtsatyi s"ezd Vsesoyuznoi Kommunisticheskoi Partii (b)*, p. 28.
3. *Ibid.*, p. 24.
4. Cited by A. Luukkanen, *The Religious Policy of the Stalinist State*, p. 140.
5. See J. Barber, *Soviet Historians in Crisis, 1928–1932*.
6. M. Gor'kii, L. Averbakh and S. Firin, *Belomorsko-baltiiskii kanal imeni I. V. Stalina*.
7. See R. Medvedev, *Problems in the Literary Biography of Mikhail Sholokhov*.
8. Exchange of letters between Stalin and Sholokhov in 1933, *Voprosy istorii*, no. 3 (1994), pp. 9–22.
9. See below, p. 333–4.
10. See above, p. 333.
11. GDMS, Hall III contains the original annotations.
12. I am grateful to Zakro Megreshvili for information about his stepfather Shalva Nutsubidze's reaction to Stalin's editorial work.
13. S. Allilueva, *Tol'ko odin god*, p. 337.
14. *Krasnaya zvezda*, 5 January 1995.
15. *Istoriya sovetskoi politicheskoi tsenzury. Dokumenty i kommentarii*, p. 484.
16. See below, p. 444.
17. See the translation in R. C. Tucker, *Stalin in Power*, pp. 205–6.
18. A. Akhmatova, *Sochineniya*, vol. 2, pp. 167–8
19. See below, p. 361.
20. See R. Service, *A History of Twentieth-Century Russia*, chap. 12.
21. See *ibid.* and C. Kelly, *Refining Russia*, pp. 285–309.

28. Fears in Victory

1. See the OGPU reports in *Tragediya sovetskoi derevni*, vol. 3, pp. 318–54.
2. See R. W. Davies, *Crisis and Progress in the Soviet Economy, 1931–1933*, pp. 188–91; J. J. Rossman, 'The Teikovo Cotton Workers' Strike of April 1932', pp. 50–66. For a general account see R. Conquest, *Harvest of Sorrow: Soviet Collectivisation and the Terror-Famine*.
3. See R. W. Davies and S. G. Wheatcroft, *The Years of Hunger*.
4. *Stalin i Kaganovich: Perepiska*, pp. 132 ff.
5. See A. Nove, *An Economic History of the U.S.S.R.*, pp. 224–5 and 227.

6. I. V. Stalin, *Sochineniya*, vol. 13, p. 186. See the account in R. W. Davies, M. Ilic and O. Khlevnyuk, 'The Politburo and Economic Policy-Making', p. 114.
7. *Stalin i Kaganovich: Perepiska*, p. 260.
8. *Ibid.*, p. 235.
9. See R. W. Davies, M. Ilic and O. Khlevnyuk, 'The Politburo and Economic Policy-Making', p. 110.
10. Letter of 18 June 1932: *Stalin i Kaganovich. Perepiska.*, p. 179.
11. *Ibid.*, pp. 282 and 290.
12. *Ibid.*, p. 274.
13. *Ibid.*, p. 359.
14. *Ibid.*, p. 479.
15. See R. Conquest, *Harvest of Sorrow*; R. W. Davies, *Crisis and Progress in the Soviet Economy*; and R. W. Davies and S. G. Wheatcroft, *The Years of Hunger*.
16. *Ibid.*, p. 241.
17. See E. A. Rees, 'Republican and Regional Leaders at the XVII Party Congress in 1934', especially pp. 85–6.
18. See R. Conquest, *The Great Terror. A Reassessment*, pp. 31–46
19. *Semnadtsatyi s"ezd Vsesoyuznoi Kommunisticheskoi Partii (b)*, p. 262.
20. F. Benvenuti, 'Kirov nella Politica Sovietica', pp. 283, 303–7 and 315–59.
21. *Lubyanka. Stalin i VChK–GPU–nOGPU–NKVD*, p. 569.
22. See R. Conquest, *The Great Terror: A Reassessment*, pp. 39–52.
23. *Lubyanka. Stalin i VChK–GPU–OGPU–NKVD*, p. 650.
24. See R. W. Davies, *Soviet History in the Yeltsin Era*, p. 155.
25. *Lubyanka. Stalin i VChK–GPU–OGPU–NKVD*, p. 388.
26. See O. V. Khlevnyuk, *1937-i*, p. 49.
27. See F. Benvenuti and S. Pons, *Il sistema di potere dello Stalinismo*, p. 105.
28. *ITsKKPSS*, no. 9 (1989), p. 39
29. *Reabilitatsiya: politicheskie protsessy 30–50-kh godov*, especially pp. 176–9.
30. See F. Benvenuti, *Fuoco sui sabotatori! Stachanovismo e organizzazione industriale in Urss, 1934–1938*, chaps. 3 ff.
31. *Lubyanka. Stalin i VChK–GPU–OGPU–NKVD*, p. 749: report by A. Vyshinski to Stalin and Molotov, 16 February 1936.
32. See A. Nove, *An Economic History of the USSR*, p. 226.
33. *Ibid.*, p. 227.
34. See R. Moorsteen and R. P. Powell, *The Soviet Capital Stock, 1928–1962*.
35. See A. Ponsi, *Partito unico e democrazia in URSS. La Costituzione del '36*, pp. 20 ff.
36. See the data cited on religious groups by A. Luukkanen, *The Religious Policy of the Stalinist State*, pp. 142–7.
37. See O. V. Khlevnyuk, *1937-i*, p. 53.
38. See S. Fitzpatrick, *Stalin's Peasants*, pp. 289–96.
39. *Le repressioni degli anni trenta nell'Armata Rossa*, p. 156.
40. *Lubyanka. Stalin i VChK–GPU–OGPU–NKVD*, p. 753.

41. See B. Starkov, *Dela i lyudi stalinskogo vremeni*, p. 39.
42. *Lubyanka. Stalin i VChK–GPU–OGPU–NKVD*, p. 767.

29. Ruling the Nations

1. This is calculated from the figures of the 1926 census in V. Kozlov, *The Peoples of the Soviet Union*, p. 69.
2. S. Allilueva, *Dvadtsat' pisem k drugu*, p. 29.
3. *Zastol'nye rechi Stalina. Dokumenty i materialy*, p. 158.
4. See above, p. 302.
5. *Tak govoril Kaganovich*, p. 48.
6. *Iosif Vissarionovich Stalin* (1938), p. 5.
7. K. Simonov, *Glazami cheloveka moego pokoleniya*, p. 37.
8. See S. Fitzpatrick, *Stalin's Peasants*, pp. 289–96.
9. See F. Bettanin, *La fabbrica del mito*, p. 89.
10. G. Dimitrov, *Diario. Gli anni di Mosca (1934–1945)*, p. 81.
11. See S. Crisp, 'Soviet language Planning, 1917–1953', pp. 27–9.
12. See S. Kuleshov and V. Strada, *Il fascismo russo*, pp. 229–38.
13. See T. Martin, *The Affirmative Action Empire*, pp. 206–7. See also H. Kuromiya, 'The Donbass', pp. 157–8.
14. See T. Martin, *The Affirmative Action Empire*, pp. 302–3.
15. See above, pp. 276–7.
16. *Tak govoril Kaganovich*, p. 48.
17. See above, pp. 204–5.
18. See G. Hewitt, 'Language Planning in Georgia', pp. 137–9.
19. See the files reproduced in *Abkhaziya: dokumenty svidel'stvuyut. 1937–1953*.
20. GDMS, Hall III holds a copy of Stalin's suggestion for Nutsubidze's anthology.
21. See above, pp. 96–101.
22. See R. Service, *A History of Twentieth-Century Russia*, pp. 206–7 and 318.
23. *Ibid.*
24. *Zastol'nye rechi Stalina. Dokumenty i materialy*, p. 151 (first variant of notes taken by R. P. Khmelnitski).
25. See D. Lieven, *Nicholas II*, p. 163.
26. 'Dnevnik M. A. Svanidze' in *Iosif Stalin v ob"yatiyakh sem'i*, pp. 174–5.
27. *Zastol'nye rechi Stalina*, p. 55.
28. *Ibid.*, p. 123.
29. G. Dimitrov, *Diario. Gli anni di Mosca (1934–1945)*, p. 81.
30. 'Pravil'naya politika pravitel'stva reshaet uspekh armii. Kto dostoin byt' marshalom?', *Istochnik*, no. 3: record of Stalin's speech.
31. 'Dnevnik M. A. Svanidze' in *Iosif Stalin v ob"yatiyakh sem'i*, pp. 176.
32. For a different interpretation see D. Brandenberger, *Stalinist Mass Culture and the Formation of Modern Russian National Identity, 1931–1956*.
33. *Istochnik*, no. 1 (2002), p. 105.

34. See the analysis of D. V. Kolesov, *I. V. Stalin: Pravo na zhizn'*, pp. 37–8. I am grateful to Ronald Hingley for our discussions of Stalin's oratorical idiosyncrasies.

30. Mind of Terror

1. *Stalin i Kaganovich. Perepiska*, p. 425; see also *Lubyanka. Stalin i VChK–GPU–OGPU–NKVD*, p. 565.
2. See *Stalin i Kaganovich*; *Pis'ma I. V. Stalina V. M. Molotovu*.
3. This was also Molotov's attitude, at least by the time of the Second World War: see V. Berezhkov, *Kak ya stal perevodchikom Stalina*, p. 226. I eschew further use of this source in following chapters and am grateful to Hugh Lunghi, one of Churchill's interpreters, for pointing out the many unreliable aspects of Berezhkov's memoirs, including its title.
4. L. Trotsky, *Stalin: An Appraisal of the Man and His Influence*.
5. See for example S. Alliluev, *Proidënnyi put'* ; A. S. Allilueva, *Vospominaniya*; S. Allilueva, *Dvadtsat' pisem k drugu* and *Tol'ko odin god*.
6. Above all, see the speech he gave at a reception for G. Dimitrov in on 8 November 1937: below, p. 333.
7. N. K. Baibakov, *ot Stalina go Yel'tsina*, p. 48.
8. Of course the idea that Stalin really was so undemonstrative in the 1920s is implausible.
9. See above, pp. 4–8.
10. R. Medvedev, *Let History Judge*, p. 15.
11. *Ibid.*, p. 13.
12. *ITsKKPSS*, no. 11 (1989), p. 169.
13. *Zastol'nye rechi Stalina*, p. 157: this comment was an interjection in another interjection, by Voroshilov, in a speech at the twentieth-anniversary dinner in honour of the October Revolution.
14. *Sovetskoe rukovodstvo. Perepiska, 1928–1941*, p. 334.
15. L. Trotskii, *Terrorizm i kommunizm*.
16. M. Jansen, *A Show Trial Under Lenin*.
17. In Russian the words were: *Molodets, kak on zdorovo eto sdelal!* The witness was Anastas Mikoyan: see his *Tak bylo*, p. 534. V. Berezhkov, one of Stalin's interpreters, recalled Mikoyan's words only slightly differently: *Kak ya stal perevodchikom Stalina*, p. 14.
18. *Zastol'nye rechi Stalina*, p. 148.
19. See T. Dragadze, *Rural Families in Soviet Georgia*, pp. 43–4.
20. See RGASPI, f. 558, op. 3, d. 37: this was the book *Drevnyaya Evropa i Vostok* (Moscow–Petrograd, 1923)
21. *Stalin i Kaganovich. Perepiska*, p. 273.
22. *Iosif Stalin v ob"yatiyakh sem'i*, p. 17.
23. See below, pp. 578–9.

24. RGASPI, f. 558, op. 3, d. 167: see for example pp. 43 and 47.
25. *Ibid.*, p. 57.
26. *Ibid.*, p. 248.
27. See below, pp. 580–1.
28. N. Ryzhkov, *Perestroika: istoriya predatel'stv*, pp. 354–5. See also E. A. Rees, *Political Thought from Machiavelli to Stalin: Revolutionary Machiavellism*.
29. *Zastol'nye rechi Stalina*, p. 180.

31. The Great Terrorist

1. The term, invented by the historian Robert Conquest for his book of the same name in 1968, is now the common one in use in Russia as well as the rest of the world.
2. 'Stenogrammy ochnykh stavok v TsK VKP(b). Dekabr' 1936 goda', *Voprosy istorii*, no. 3 (2002), p. 4.
3. *Ibid.*, p. 5.
4. See in particular J. A. Getty, *The Origins of the Great Purges Reconsidered*.
5. See R. Conquest, *The Great Terror: A Reassessment*, pp. 3–22 and 53–70.
6. *Molotov. Poluderzhavnyi vlastelin*, p. 464; *Tak govoril Kaganovich*, p. 35.
7. O. Khlevniuk, 'The Objectives of the Great Terror, 1937–1938' in J. Cooper *et al.*, *Soviet History, 1917–1953*; O. Khlevniuk, 'The Reasons for the "Great Terror": The Foreign-Political Aspect' in S. Pons and A. Romano, *Russia in the Age of Wars, 1914–1945*.
8. *Stalin i Kaganovich. Perepiska*, pp. 682–3. Although Stalin referred here to the OGPU, its department name after being subsumed in the NKVD in 1934 was the GUGB.
9. See R. Conquest, *The Great Terror: A Reassessment*, pp. 135–73
10. I. V. Stalin, *Sochineniya*, vol. 14, pp. 189–91.
11. 'Materialy fevral'skogo-martovskogo plenuma TsK VKP(b) 1937 goda', *Voprosy istorii*, no. 10 (1994), pp. 13–27; no. 2 (1995), pp. 22–6; and no. 3 (1995), pp. 3–15.
12. Quoted in O. Khlevnyuk, *1937-i*, p. 77.
13. See M. Jansen and N. Petrov, *Stalin's Loyal Executioner*, pp. 76–7.
14. B. Starkov, *Dela i lyudi stalinskogo vremeni*, p. 47.
15. *Ibid.*, pp. 48–9.
16. *Trud*, 4 June 1992.
17. *Ibid.*
18. N. Okhotin and A. Roginskii, 'Iz istorii "nemetskoi operatsii" NKVD 1937–1938 gg.', p. 46.
19. *Izvestiya*, 10 June 1992.
20. *Tak govoril Kaganovich*, p. 46.
21. *Khrushchev Remembers: The Glasnost Tapes*, p. 38.
22. *Sovetskoe rukovodstvo. Perepiska, 1928–1941*, pp. 364–97

23. RGASPI, f. 73, op. 2, d. 19, p. 101.
24. See R. Conquest, *The Great Terror: A Reassessment*, p. 245.
25. See S. S. Montefiore, *Stalin: The Court of the Red Tsar*, pp. 185–6.

32. The Cult of Impersonality

1. I. Tovstukha, 'Stalin (Dzhughashvili), Iosif Vissarionovich', pp. 698–700.
2. *Pravda*, 21 December 1929.
3. See below, pp. 541–2.
4. 'Stalin o "Kratkom kurse po istorii VKP(b)". Stenogramma vystupleniya no soveshchanii propagandistov Moskvy i Leningrada . . .', *Istoricheskii arkhiv*, no. 5 (1994), p. 10.
5. *Stalin. K shestidesyatiyu so dnya rozhdeniya*, pp. 193–4
6. *Pravda*, 1 January 1931. See also the account in J. Brooks, *Thank You, Comrade Stalin!*, pp. 80–1.
7. *Pravda*, 1 January 1937.
8. *Ibid.*, 29 June 1936.
9. *Zastol'nye rechi Stalina*, p. 175. This came in a speech given at a Kremlin reception for recently elected USSR Supreme Soviet deputies on 20 January 1938.
10. A. Fadeev (ed.), *Vstrechi s tovarishchem Stalinym*, pp. 40, 98, 112, 133, 160, 178 and 195.
11. *Zastol'nye rechi Stalina*, p. 123.
12. *Stalin i Kaganovich. Perepiska*, p. 526.
13. I. A. Valedinskii, 'Vospominaniya o vstrechakh o t. I. V. Staline', p. 72.
14. *Stalin i Khasim (1901–1902 gg.). Nekotorye epizody iz batumskogo podpol'ya.*
15. V. Shveitser, *Stalin v turukhanskoi ssylke. Vospominaniya podpol'shchika.*
16. H. Barbusse, *Staline: Un monde nouveau vu à travers d'un homme.*
17. See F. Bettanin, *La fabbrica del mito*, p. 157.
18. For an exception to the trend see *ibid.*, p. 174.
19. The possibility should not be discounted that the admiration of Lenin was genuine.
20. See also below, pp. 541–2.
21. *Istoriya Vsesoyuznoi Kommunisticheskoi Partii (Bol'shevikov). Kratkii kurs.*
22. *Ibid.*, pp. 198–204.
23. See above, pp. 292–3.
24. *Pravda*, 7 October 1935.
25. V. Kaminskii and I. Vereshchagin, 'Detstvo i yunost' vozhdya: dokumenty, zapisi, rasskazy', pp. 22–100.
26. *Ibid.*
27. *Pis'ma ko vlasti*, pp. 124 ff.
28. O. Volobuev and S. Kuleshov, *Ochishchenie*, p. 146.
29. Cited by N. N. Maslov, 'Ob utverzhdenii ideologii stalinizma', p. 78.
30. V. Ivanov, 'Krasnaya ploshchad', *Novyi mir*, no. 11 (1937), pp. 259–60.

31. K. Chukovskii, *Dnevniki, 1930–1969*, p. 86. I owe this reference to B. S. Ilizarov, 'Stalin. Bolezn', smert' i "bessmertie"', pp. 294–5.
32. S. Fitzpatrick, *Stalin's Peasants*, pp. 289–96.
33. *Obshchestvo i vlast'. 1930-e gody*, p. 25.
34. S. Davies discusses the ambiguities of the evidence in *Popular Opinion in Stalin's Russia*, pp. 155–82.

33. Brutal Reprieve

1. Iz vospominanii Sukhanova D. N., byvshego pomoshchnika Malenkova G. M.', Volkogonov Archive, reel no. 8, p. 5.
2. *Pisatel' i vozhd': perepiska M. A. Sholokhova s I. V. Stalinym*, p. 150. For Yezhov's fall see M. Jansen and N. Petrov, *Stalin's Loyal Executioner*, chap. 7.
3. *Ibid.*, pp. 160–1.
4. *Ibid.*, pp. 171–4.
5. *Ibid.*, p. 164.
6. Directive quoted by Oleg Khlevniuk, 'Party and NKVD: Power Relationships in the Years of the Great Terror' in B. McLoughlin and K. McDermott (eds), *Stalin's Terror*, p. 31.
7. See above, p. 7.
8. G. Dimitrov, *Diario. Gli anni di Mosca (1934–1945)*, p. 267.
9. *Vosemnadtsatyi s"ezd Vsesoyuznoi Kommunisticheskoi Partii (b)*, p. 29.
10. *Ibid.*, pp. 29–30.
11. See his comments at the conference on propaganda on 1 October 1938: 'I. V. Stalin o "Kratkom kurse po istorii VKP(b)". Stenogramma vystupleniya no soveshchanii propagandistov Moskvy i Leningrada', *Istoricheskii arkhiv*, no. 5 (1994), pp. 12–13.
12. *Vosemnadtsatyi s"ezd Vsesoyuznoi Kommunisticheskoi Partii (b)*, pp. 515–17.
13. *Zastol'nye rechi Stalina*, p. 235.
14. See N. Petrov, 'The GUlag as Instrument of the USSR's Punitive System' in E. Dundovich, F. Gori and E. Guercetti (eds), *Reflections on the Gulag*, p. 22.
15. *Vosemnadtsatyi s"ezd Vsesoyuznoi Kommunisticheskoi Partii (b)*, p. 26.

34. The World in Sight

1. The exception was their brief collaboration in the Bolshevik robbery organisation before the First World War.
2. See D. Watson, 'The Politburo and Foreign Policy in the 1930s', pp. 149–50.
3. The foreign-policy discussions of the 1930s were amenable to thorough scholarly investigation only from the late 1980s, when archives started to be published more readily and even to become directly accessible.
4. *O voprosakh leninizma* in I. V. Stalin, *Sochineniya*, vol. 8, p. 64.
5. See R. Service, *Lenin: A Political Life*, vol. 3, p. 136.

6. M. Buber-Neumann, *Von Potsdam nach Moskau*, p. 284.
7. I am grateful to Katya Andreyev for her comments on inter-war Soviet foreign policy.
8. *Dimitrov and Stalin, 1934–1943*, p. 13.
9. *Semnadtsatyi s"ezd Vsesoyuznoi kommunisticheskoi partii (b)*, pp. 13–14.
10. *Dimitrov and Stalin, 1934–1943*, p. 18.
11. A. Kriegel and S. Courtois, *Eugen Fried*, pp. 255–61.
12. J. Hochman, *The Soviet Union and the Failure of Collective Security, 1934–1938*, pp. 43–51.
13. G. Dimitrov, *Diario. Gli anni di Mosca (1934–1945)*, p. 203.
14. *Ibid.*, pp. 46–7.
15. Endnote 10 in *Dimitrov and Stalin, 1934–1943*, p. 50.
16. P. Togliatti, *Opere*, vol. 4, part 1, pp. 258–72.

35. Approaches to War

1. See S. Alieva (ed.), *Tak eto bylo*, vol. 1, pp. 44, 50, 86 and 96.
2. See above, pp. 169 and 203.
3. See above, p. 267.
4. *Dimitrov and Stalin, 1934–1943*, p. 28.
5. *Ibid.*, p. 32, citing Dimitrov's diary. I have re-translated the phrase *na ruku*.
6. Editorial notes of A. Dallin and F. I. Firsov, *Dimitrov and Stalin*, p. 34.
7. Editorial notes of *ibid.*, p. 108.
8. See H. P. Bix, *Hirohito and the Making of Modern Japan*, p. 351.
9. See J. Erickson, *The Soviet High Command*, p. 522.
10. See C. Andrew and V. Mitrokhin, *The Mitrokhin Archive*, p. 300.
11. See G. Gorodetsky, *Grand Delusion*, pp. 57–8, 135–6 and 180.
12. See below, pp. 362–3.

36. The Devils Sup

1. ' "Avtobiograficheskie zametki" V. N. Pavlova – perevodchika I. V. Stalina', p. 98.
2. *Ibid.*, p. 99.
3. See R. Overy, *Russia's War*, p. 49.
4. V. N. Pavlov, 'Predistoriya 1939 goda', *Svobodnaya mysl'*, no. 7 (1999), pp. 109–10.
5. A. Mikoyan, *Tak bylo*, p. 392.
6. See above, p. 178.
7. *Molotov. Poluderzhavnyi vlastelin*, p. 54.
8. See K. Sword (ed.), *The Soviet Takeover of the Polish Eastern Provinces, 1939–1941*.
9. See H. Shukman and A. Chubaryan (eds), *Stalin and the Soviet–Finnish*

War, 1939–1940, especially Stalin's comments on the failures and successes of the campaign, pp. 236–7.

10. *Khrushchev Remembers: The Glasnost Tapes*, p. 154.
11. *Molotov. Poluderzhavnyi vlastelin*, p. 19.
12. See H. P. von Strandmann, 'Obostryaushchiesya paradoksy: Gitler, Stalin i germano-sovetskie ekonomicheskie svyazi. 1939–1941', p. 376.
13. See J. Erickson, *The Soviet High Command*, p. 566.
14. See G. Gorodetsky, *Grand Delusion*, p. 129–35.
15. Dimitrov in *Zastol'nye rechi Stalina*, p. 234.
16. *Molotov. Poluderzhavnyi vlastelin*, pp. 40–1.
17. G. Dimitrov, *Diario. Gli anni di Mosca (1934–1945)*, p. 302.
18. N. Lyashchenko, 'O vystuplenii I. V. Stalina v Kremle, 5 maya 1941', Volkogonov Papers, reel no. 8, p. 1.
19. G. Dimitrov, *Diario. Gli anni di Mosca (1934–1945)*, p. 310.
20. These comments come from the notes taken by V. A. Malyshev: 'Proidët desyatok let, i eti vstrechi ne vosstanovish' uzhe v pamyati', p. 117.
21. See D. Glantz, *Stumbling Colossus*, p. 97.
22. L. Samuelson, *Plans for Stalin's War Machine*, p. 199.
23. N. Lyashchenko, 'O vystuplenii I. V. Stalina v Kremle, 5 maya 1941', Volkogonov Papers, reel 8, p. 3. The episode was recounted to Lyashchenko by Minister of Defence Semën Timoshenko.

37. Barbarossa

1. G. K. Zhukov, *Vospominaniya i razmyshleniya*, vol. 2, p. 8.
2. *Ibid.*, p. 9.
3. See the archivally based account of G. Gorodetsky, *Grand Delusion*, p. 311.
4. G. K. Zhukov, *Vospominaniya i razmyshleniya*, vol. 2, p. 9.
5. *Ibid.*, pp. 9–10.
6. *Ibid.*, p. 10.
7. *Ibid.*, pp. 12–13.
8. G. Dimitrov, *Diario. Gli anni di Mosca (1934–1945)*, p. 319.
9. See G. Gorodetsky, *Grand Delusion*, pp. 275–8; D. Glantz, *Stumbling Colossus*, p. 242.
10. See G. Gorodetsky, *Grand Delusion*, pp. 53–5.
11. G. K. Zhukov, *Vospominaniya i razmyshleniya*, vol. 2, p. 9.
12. *Molotov. Poluderzhavnyi vlastelin*, p. 60.
13. 'Zhurnal poseshcheniya I. V. Stalina v ego Kremlëvskom kabinete' in Yu. Gor'kov, *Gosudarstvennyi Komitet Oborony postanovlyaet*, pp. 223–4.
14. *Ibid.*
15. G. K. Zhukov, *Vospominaniya i razmyshleniya*, vol. 2, p. 73.
16. 'Zhurnal poseshcheniya I. V. Stalina v ego Kremlëvskom kabinete', *loc. cit.*, pp. 223–4.
17. A. Mikoyan. *Tak bylo*, p. 390.

18. *Ibid.*, p. 391. Molotov recorded that Stalin 'wasn't himself' that day but insisted that his mood was firm: *Molotov. Poluderzhavnyi vlastelin*, p. 60.
19. A. Mikoyan. *Tak bylo*, pp. 391–2.
20. *Pravda*, 1 July 1941.
21. S. Beria, *Beria, My Father*, p. 71 gives the account supposedly provided by his father. This account has Moscow Party City Committee Secretary Alexander Shcherbakov, not Voznesenski, as having made the proposal for Molotov to take over the leadership.
22. Yu. Gor'kov, *Gosudarstvennyi Komitet Oborony postanovlyaet*, p. 501.

38. Fighting On

1. G. K. Zhukov, *Vospominaniya i razmyshleniya*, vol. 2, pp. 126–7.
2. R. Overy, *Russia's War*, p. 171.
3. There is nothing in the memoirs of Molotov, Kaganovich, Khrushchëv and Zhukov – men who knew him very well in the war – to contradict this point.
4. G. K. Zhukov, *Vospominaniya i razmyshleniya*, vol. 2, p. 344.
5. *Ibid.*, p. 346.
6. *Ibid.*, p. 347.
7. *Ibid.*, pp. 348–9.
8. *Ibid.*, p. 361.
9. *Ibid.* This statement, like many others, was censored in the 1969 edition and allowed to be published only in its 1995 successor.
10. *Ibid.*, p. 367.

39. Sleeping on the Divan

1. S. Beria, *Beria, My Father*, p. 154.
2. G. K. Zhukov, *Vospominaniya i razmyshleniya*, vol. 3, pp. 215–16.
3. A. M. Vasilevski: interview in G. A. Kumanëv (ed.), *Ryadom so Stalinym*, p. 242.
4. S. Beria, *Beria, My Father*, pp. 153–4. This story was told to Sergo Beria by his mother, who spoke to Yakov.
5. *Ibid.*, p. 155.
6. 'Dnevnik M. A. Svanidze' in *Iosif Stalin v ob"yatiyakh sem'i*, p. 159.
7. Testimony of Alexei Kapler: E. Biagi, *Svetlana*, p. 21.
8. *Ibid.*, p. 27.
9. 'Dnevnik M. A. Svanidze': *Iosif Stalin v ob"yatiyakh sem'i*, p. 161.
10. *Ibid.*, p. 158.
11. S. Allilueva, *Tol'ko odin god*, p. 320.
12. *Ibid.*, p. 326.
13. *Ibid.*, pp. 129–30.

14. S. Beria, *Beria, My Father*, p. 150.
15. S. Allilueva, *Dvadtsat' pisem k drugu*, pp. 163–6.
16. *Ibid.*, pp. 166–7.
17. *Ibid.*, pp. 167–8.
18. *Ibid.*, p. 169.
19. S. Beria, *Beria, My Father*, p. 152.
20. RGASPI, f. 558, op. 1, d. 5078.
21. V. Alliluev, *Khronika odnoi sem'i: Alliluevy. Stalin*, p. 97.
22. *Ibid.*
23. I. A. Valedinskii, 'Vospominaniya o vstrechakh s t. I. V. Stalinym', pp. 69–70.
24. See below, pp. 456–7.
25. G. K. Zhukov, *Vospominaniya i razmyshleniya*, vol. 3, p. 109.
26. He let no one know of his physical weaknesses with the exception of Churchill. Preparing to meet the British Prime Minister in autumn 1944, he wrote: 'The doctors don't advise me to undertake long trips. For a certain period I need to take account of this': *Perepiska predsedatelya Soveta Ministra SSSR s prezidentami SShA i prem'er-ministrami Velikobritanii vo vremya velikoi Otechestvennoi voiny*, vol. 1, p. 262. Even this remark, however, cannot be taken at face value. Stalin would do anything to make the mountain come to Mohammed; he always tried to get Churchill and Roosevelt to do the travelling.
27. 'Dnevnik M. A. Svanidze' in *Iosif Stalin v ob"yatiyakh sem'i*, pp. 158–60, 169, 174, 177.
28. *Ibid.*, p. 168.
29. *Ibid.*, p. 175.
30. L. Vasil'eva, *Deti Kremlya*, p. 261; V. Alliluev, *Khronika odnoi sem'i: Alliluevy. Stalin*, p. 128 (where it is mentioned that her parents-in-law never forgave Yevgenia for marrying again so quickly after Pavel's death).
31. L. Vasil'eva, *Deti Kremlya*, p. 261.
32. L. M. Kaganovich, *Pamyatnye zapiski*, p. 33; *Tak govoril Kaganovich*, pp. 49–50. The date of death is given variously as 1924 and 1926. See also S. Allilueva, *Tol'ko odin god*, p. 331.
33. L. Kaganovich, *Tak govoril Kaganovich*, p. 49. Sergo Beria, however, claimed that the identity of Stalin's lover was not Kaganovich's sister or daughter but his niece: see S. Beria, *Beria, My Father*, p. 166. As yet there is no corroboration of this assertion.
34. *Molotov. Poluderzhavnyi vlastelin*, pp. 181 and 191.
35. 'Dnevnik M. A. Svanidze' in *Iosif Stalin v ob"yatiyakh sem'i*, p. 170.
36. Kira Allilueva: interview, 14 December 1998.
37. See the recollection by A. P. Alliluev as given to R. Richardson, *The Long Shadow*, pp. 142–3.
38. J. von Ribbentrop, *Zwischen London und Moskau. Erinnerungen und letzte Auchzeichnungen*, p. 25.
39. Testimony of A.T. Sergeev to F. Chuev: *Molotov. Poluderzhavnyi vlastelin*, p. 359.

40. G. K. Zhukov, *Vospominaniya i razmyshleniya*, vol. 3, p. 108.
41. N. K. Baibakov, *Ot Stalina do Yel'tsina*, pp. 80 and 83.
42. See K. Charkviani's account summarised by Simon Sebag Montefiore, *Stalin: The Court of the Red Tsar*, p. 101.

40. To the Death!

1. G. K. Zhukov, *Vospominaniya i razmyshleniya*, vol. 3, p. 14.
2. *Ibid.*, p. 23.
3. *Ibid.*, p. 32.
4. *Ibid.*, p. 45.
5. *Ibid.*, p. 46.
6. *Ibid.*, p. 61.
7. *Ibid.*, p. 59.
8. See W. Moskoff, *The Bread of Affliction*.
9. Official military postcard, 6 January 1944.
10. V. Tsypin, *Istoriya Russkoi pravoslavnoi tserkvi, 1917–1990*, pp. 95, 104 and 106.
11. See D. Pospielovsky, *The Russian Orthodox Church under the Soviet Regime*, p. 111.
12. V. A. Alekseev, 'Neozhidannyi dialog', *Agitator*, no. 6 (1989), pp. 41–4.
13. V. A. Alekseev, *Illyuzii i dogma*, pp. 336–7.
14. G. Dimitrov, *Diario. Gli anni di Mosca (1934–1945)*, pp. 615 and 617.
15. *Ibid.*, p. 618.
16. See M. Mevius, *Agents of Moscow*, chapter 3.
17. J. Rossi, *Spravochnik po Gulagu*, part 1, p. 40.
18. See P. J. S. Duncan, *Russian Messianism*, p. 59.
19. 'Proidët desyatok let, i eti vstrechi ne vosstanovish' uzhe v pamyati. Dnevnikovye zapisi V. A. Malysheva', pp. 127–8. See also G. Dimitrov, *Diario. Gli anni di Mosca (1934–1945)*, p. 802.
20. See A. V. Fateev, *Obraz vraga v Sovetskoi propagande, 1945–1954 gg.*, p. 23. Fadeev's article appeared in *Pod znamenem marksizma*, no. 11 (1943).
21. See C. Andreyev, *Vlasov and the Russian Liberation Movement. Soviet Realities and Émigré Theories*.

41. Supreme Commander

1. *Sochineniya*, vol. 14, p. 1.
2. See below, note 4.
3. *Sochineniya*, vol. 14, p. 5.
4. Letter of July 1941: *Zvezda*, no. 2 (2003), p. 191.
5. *Sochineniya*, vol. 14, p. 6.
6. *Ibid.*, p. 33.

7. *Ibid.*, p. 34.
8. This is a point made by J. Brooks, *Thank You, Comrade Stalin!*, p. 160.
9. See in general D. C. Watt, *How War Came*, pp. 224–33.
10. *The Times*, 4 January 1943.
11. *Ibid.*, 1 January 1940.
12. See below, chapter 32.
13. N. K. Baibakov, *Ot Stalina do Yel'tsina*, pp. 43–8.
14. *Ibid.*, p. 64.
15. *Ibid.*
16. Testimony of A. E. Golovanov in G. A. Kumanëv (ed.), *Ryadom so Stalinym*, pp. 272–3.
17. G. K. Zhukov, *Vospominaniya i razmyshleniya*, vol. 3, p. 59.
18. *Ibid.*, pp. 113 and 115.
19. K. Simonov, *Glazami cheloveka moego pokoleniya*, p. 111.
20. A. Mikoyan, *Tak bylo*, p. 463.
21. P. A Sudoplatov and A. Sudoplatov, *Special Tasks*, p. 328.
22. G. K. Zhukov, *Vospominaniya i razmyshleniya*, vol. 2, p. 266.
23. *Ibid.*, vol. 2, p. 244.
24. *Ibid.*, p. 270.
25. *Ibid.*, p. 134.
26. A. Mikoyan, *Tak bylo*, p. 563.
27. G. A. Kumanëv, 'Dve besedy s L. M. Kaganovichem', *Novaya i noveishaya istoriya*, no. 2 (1999), p. 107.

42. The Big Three

1. *Perepiska predsedatelya Soveta Ministrov SSSR*, vol. 2, p. 98. See also W. S. Churchill, *The Second World War*, vol. 4, p. 594.
2. *Perepiska predsedatelya Soveta Ministrov SSSR*, vol. 2, p. 101.
3. S. Beria, *Beria, My Father*, p. 93.
4. The carriage now stands outside the State Home-Museum of I. V. Stalin at Gori.
5. W. S. Churchill, *The Second World War*, vol. 4, p. 447.
6. *Perepiska predsedatelya Soveta Ministrov SSSR*, vol. 2, p. 43.
7. W. S. Churchill, *The Second World War*, vol. 4, p. 443.
8. J. von Ribbentrop, *Zwischen London und Moskau.* p. 25.
9. I. P. McEwan, 'Quo Vadis?', p. 113. I am grateful to Philippa McEwan for supplying me with this memoir.
10. W. S. Churchill, *The Second World War*, vol. 5, pp. 334–6.
11. *Churchill and Stalin: Documents from the British Archives*: conversation of Churchill and Stalin, 28 November 1943, doc. 46, p. 3.
12. *Ibid.*, doc. 48, p. 2: meeting at Soviet embassy in Tehran, 1 December 1943.
13. W. S. Churchill, *The Second World War*, vol. 5, p. 350.
14. *Churchill and Stalin: Documents from the British Archives*, doc. 47

15. S. Beria, *Beria, My Father*, p. 93.
16. W. S. Churchill, *The Second World War*, vol. 6, p. 198. The English spelling in Churchill's manuscript and book was 'Roumania'.
17. *Ibid.*
18. *Istochnik*, no. 4 (1995), p. 17.
19. N. Lebrecht, 'Prokofiev was Stalin's Last Victim'.
20. W. S. Churchill, *The Second World War*, vol. 6, p. 345. This was sometimes shortened to 'U.J.': *ibid.*, p. 199.
21. *Ibid.*, *The Second World War*, vol. 4, p. 596.
22. *Ibid.*, vol. 5, p. 330.
23. *Ibid.*, p. 342.

43. Last Campaigns

1. See R. Overy, *Russia's War*, pp. 240–1.
2. J. Erickson, *The Road to Berlin*, pp. 274–90; N. Davies, *Rising '44*, pp. 209–11 and 265–72.
3. G. K. Zhukov, *Vospominaniya i razmyshleniya*, vol. 3, pp. 173–4. Alas, the other participants – Stalin, Molotov and Beria – left no useful memoirs on the subject.
4. W. S. Churchill, *The Second World War*, vol. 6, p. 117.
5. *Churchill and Stalin: Documents from the British Archives*, doc. 55, p. 1: telegram of A. Eden to Sir O. Sergeant, 12 October 1944. It must be added that Churchill said this in a moment when he was trying to cajole Stalin into making concessions to the 'London Poles'.
6. M. Djilas, *Conversations with Stalin*, p. 87. Stalin also made exculpatory remarks about Red Army soldiers to a Czechoslovak delegation on 28 March 1945: 'Proidët desyatok let, i eti vstrechi ne vosstanovish' uzhe v pamyati. Dnevnikovye zapisi V. A. Malysheva', p. 127.
7. See the text in *Novaya i noveishaya istoriya*, no. 3 (2000), p. 181.
8. *Ibid.*
9. See J. Erickson, *The Road to Berlin*, pp. 606–16.
10. See D. Holloway, *Stalin and the Bomb*, p. 125.
11. See *ibid.*, p. 124.
12. *Ibid.*, p. 126.
13. *Ibid.*, p. 128.
14. *Ibid.*, pp. 128–9.

44. Victory!

1. I have taken this account from A. Werth, *Russia at War, 1941–1945*, p. 969; J. Bardach and K. Gleeson, *Surviving Freedom*, p. 95.

2. S. Allilueva, *Dvadtsat' pisem k drugu*, p. 175.
3. N. S. Khrushchëv, 'Memuary Nikity Sergeevicha Khrushchëva', *Voprosy istorii*, no. 7–8 (1991), p. 100.
4. I. V. Stalin, *Sochineniya*, vol. 16, p. 197.
5. *Ibid.*, p. 198.
6. *Pravda*, 25 May 1945.
7. G. K. Zhukov, *Vospominaniya i razmyshleniya*, vol. 3, pp. 308. Zhukov's information came from Stalin's son Vasili.
8. *Ibid.*
9. *Ibid.*, p. 309.
10. *Pravda*, 27 June 1945.
11. S. G. Wheatcroft and R. W. Davies, 'Population', p. 78.
12. Ye. Zubkova, *Obshchestvo i reformy, 1945–1964*, p. 43.
13. *Vostochnaya Evropa v dokumentakh rossiiskikh arkhivov, 1945–1953 gg.*, vol. 1, p. 132. The date of the Moscow discussion was 9 January 1945.
14. *Ibid.*, pp. 456–7. The meeting occurred on 22 May 1946.
15. *Ibid.*, p. 132.

45. Delivering the Blow

1. V. Alliluev, *Khronika odnoi sem'i: Alliluevy. Stalin*, p. 218. See Simon Sebag Montefiore, *Stalin: The Court of the Red Tsar*, p. 472; Y. Gorlizki and O. Khlevniuk, *Cold Peace. Stalin and the Soviet Ruling Circle, 1945–1953*, p. 177.
2. *Politbyuro TsK VKP(b) i Sovet Ministrov SSSR, 1945–1953*, p. 398.
3. A. S. Belyakov's recollections of A. A. Zhdanov's oral account of a meeting of central party leaders: G. Arbatov, *Svidetel'stvo sovremennika*, p. 377.
4. See V. Zemskov, 'Prinuditel'nye migratsii iz Pribaltiki', pp. 13–14.
5. See E. Bacon, *The Gulag at War*, pp. 93–4.
6. N. A. Antipenko, *Ryadom s G. K. Zhukovym i K. K. Rokossovskim*, p. 71.
7. F. Gori and S. Pons (eds), *The Soviet Union and Europe in the Cold War, 1943–1953*, especially the account by A. Filitov, pp. 5–22.
8. *Molotov. Poluderzhavnyi vlastelin*, pp. 148–9.
9. S. Allilueva, *Dvadtsat' pisem k drugu*, pp. 176–7.
10. See A. Applebaum, *Gulag*, pp. 424–5; Y. Gorlizki and O. Khlevniuk, *Cold Peace. Stalin and the Soviet Ruling Circle, 1945–1953*, pp. 127–9.
11. It must be added, however, that Stalin did not repeat his paean to the Russians even on this occasion: perhaps he was getting worried about over-encouragement of Russian nationalism: *Pravda*, 7 September 1947.
12. For examples see *Resheniya partii i pravitel'stva po khozyaistvennym voprosam*, vol. 3, pp. 350 ff.
13. See A. Pyzhikov, *Khrushchëvskii 'ottepel''*, p. 19.
14. See A. Nove, *Economic History of the USSR*, p. 308.

15. See W. Taubman, *Khrushchëv: The Man and His Era*, p. 201.
16. N. S. Khrushchëv, 'Memuary Nikity Sergeevicha Khrushchëva', *Voprosy istorii*, no. 11 (1991), p. 38.
17. See R. Service, *Lenin: A Biography*, pp. 88–9. I am grateful to Mark Harrison for the point about Stalin's assumption about the peasantry.
18. See the forthcoming book on post-war Soviet youth by J. Fuerst.
19. The exception, after the war, was Nikolai Voznesenski: see below, p. 535.
20. See above, pp. 294–7.
21. See below, p. 522.
22. See G. Bordyugov, 'Ukradënnaya pobeda'; Ye. Zubkova, 'Obshchestvennaya atmosfera posle voiny (1945–1946)', p. 12; D. Filtzer, *Soviet Workers and Late Stalinism*, pp. 1–5.

46. The Outbreak of the Cold War

1. See M.P. Leffler, *A Preponderance of Power*, pp. 56–9.
2. See *ibid.*, pp. 19 and 115.
3. *Ibid.*, p. 148.
4. *Vostochnaya Evropa v dokumentakh rossiiskikh arkhivov, 1944–1953 gg.*, vol. 1, p. 673.
5. Quoted by R. Pikhoya, *Sovetskii Soyuz: istoriya vlasti, 1945–1991*, p. 26.
6. *Vostochnaya Evropa v dokumentakh rossiiskikh arkhivov, 1944–1953 gg.*, vol. 1, p. 673.
7. *Ibid.*, pp. 673–5.
8. *The Cominform: Minutes of the Three Conferences*, pp. 270 ff.
9. M. G. Pervukhin, 'Kak byla reshena atomnaya problema v nashei strane', p. 133.
10. *Ibid.*
11. See above, p. 95.
12. See D. Holloway, *Stalin and the Bomb*, p. 211.
13. See V. Zubok and C. Pleshakov, *Inside the Kremlin's Cold War*, pp. 58–9.
14. Quoted in *ibid.*, p. 59.
15. *Molotov. Poluderzhavnyi vlastelin*, p. 118.

47. Subjugating Eastern Europe

1. *Vostochnaya Evropa v dokumentakh rossiiskikh arkhivov, 1944–1953 gg.*, vol. 1, pp. 118–33.
2. *Ibid.*, p. 303.
3. *Ibid.*, p. 443.
4. See G. Dimitrov's letter to Molotov about the composition of the Polish communist leadership, 18 January 1944: *SSSR – Pol'sha. Mekhanizmy podchineniya. 1944–1949. Sbornik dokumentov*, pp. 21–2. On the attitude of

communists of Jewish background see Jakub Berman's testimony in T. Toranska, *Oni: Stalin's Polish Puppets*, p. 321.

5. See M. Mazower, *Dark Continent*, pp. 12–25.
6. *The Cominform: Minutes of the Three Conferences*, p. 82.
7. *Ibid.*, pp. 226 and 244.
8. *Ibid.*, p. 240.
9. *Ibid.*, pp. 296 and 302.
10. See S. Pons, 'The Twilight of the Cominform', in *ibid.*, pp. 483–4.
11. *Ibid.*, pp. 496–7.
12. *Ibid.*, pp. 610–19.
13. See L. Gibianskii, editorial comment in *ibid.*, p. 654.
14. See below, pp. 567–9.
15. See below, pp. 576–7.

48. Stalinist Rulership

1. S. Allilueva, *Dvadtsat' pisem k drugu*, p. 177. Svetlana in this memoir fudged the fact that they stayed in separate dachas.
2. Visit by author: 11 September 2002. I am grateful to Liana Khvarchelia and Manana Gurgulia for their efforts in obtaining access to the dacha for me.
3. Quoted in D. Volkogonov, *Triumph i tragediya: politicheskoi portret I. V. Stalina*, vol. 1, part 1, p. 41.
4. Unpublished memoirs of Kandide Charkviani, p. 55.
5. A. Mgeladze, *Stalin, kakim ya ego znal*, p. 65; *Molotov. Poluderzhavnyi vlastelin*, pp. 65 and 181.
6. Interview with L. F. Ilichëv: 'Stalin i "Pravda": rabochii kontakt'.
7. See Y. Gorlicki and O. Khlevniuk, *Cold Peace*, pp. 19–29.
8. See below, p. 567–8.
9. *Politbyuro TsK VKP(b) i Sovet Ministrov SSSR, 1945–1953*, p. 313.
10. *Ibid.*, pp. 326–7.
11. *Ibid.*, p. 200.
12. *Politbyuro TsK VKP(b) i Sovet Ministrov SSSR, 1945–1953*, p. 198.
13. *Ibid.*, p. 224.
14. T. Toranska, *Oni: Stalin's Polish Puppets*, p. 235.
15. A. Mgeladze, *Stalin, kakim ya ego znal*, p. 113.
16. V. Semichastnyi, *Bespokoinoe serdtse*, p. 41. Apparently Khrushchëv tried to maintain a more conventional life-style schedule: *ibid.*, p. 46.
17. A. A. Gromyko, *Pamyatnoe*, vol. 2, p. 326.
18. Testimony of Yakub Berman: T. Toranska, *Oni: Stalin's Polish Puppets*, p. 337.
19. K. Simonov, *Glazami cheloveka moego pokoleniya*, p. 139.
20. K. Simonov, *Glazami cheloveka moego pokoleniya*, p. 139.
21. P. A. Sudoplatov and A. Sudoplatov, *Special Tasks*, p. 328
22. *Politbyuro TsK VKP(b) i Sovet Ministrov SSSR*, pp. 28–9.

23. *Ibid.*, pp. 30–2 and 51.
24. *Ibid.*, p. 29.
25. *Ibid.*, pp. 421–31. See Y. Gorlizki, 'Stalin's Cabinet: The Politburo and Decision-Making in the Post-War Years' for a fuller account.
26. *Neizvestnyi Zhukov*, pp. 476–7.
27. See below, p. 534–5.

49. Policies and Purges

1. O. V. Khlevnyuk, 'Stalin i Molotov. Edinolichnaya diktatura i predposylki "oligarkhizatsiya"', p. 281.
2. *Ibid.*, pp. 283–4.
3. *Ibid.*, p. 26.
4. 'Dve besedy I. V. Stalina s General'nym Sekretarëm Ob"edinënnykh Natsii Tryugve Li', *Novaya i noveishaya istoriya*, no. 3 (2001), pp. 111–12.
5. *Politbyuro TsK VKP(b) i Sovet Ministrov SSSR, 1945–1953*, pp. 32–3.
6. *Ibid.*, pp. 205–6.
7. *Molotov. Poluderzhavnyi vlastelin*, p. 377.
8. A. Mikoyan, *Tak bylo*, p. 466.
9. *Ibid.*, po. 496–8.
10. *Ibid.*, p. 535.
11. See Y. Gorlizki, 'Party Revivalism and the Death of Stalin'.
12. Testimony of A. M. Vasilevski: G. A. Kumanëv (ed.), *Ryadom so Stalinym*, pp. 237–40.
13. A. Mikoyan, *Tak bylo*, p. 559.
14. The 'Russian' factor in the Leningrad Affair is downplayed in the recent outstanding account by Y. Gorlizki and O. Khlevniuk, *Cold Peace*, pp. 79–95. I remain impressed, however, by documents and memoirs asserting the significance of this factor.
15. *Politbyuro TsK VKP(b) i Sovet Ministrov SSSR, 1945–1953*, pp. 66–7 and 246.
16. A. Mikoyan, *Tak bylo*, p. 559.
17. See above, pp. 513–14.
18. A. Mikoyan, *Tak bylo*, p. 565.
19. I want to acknowledge my thanks to Geoffrey Hosking for our lengthy discussions about this matter.

50. Emperor Worship

1. *Slovo tovarishchu Stalinu*, p. 466.
2. *Ibid.*, pp. 470–2.
3. *Ibid.*, p. 471.
4. Speech by G. M. Malenkov, *Cominform: Minutes of the Three Confererences*, p. 82.

5. *Istoriya Sovetskoi politicheskoi tsenzury*, p. 507. In 1946 there were still sixteen Soviet republics: the Karelo-Finnish Soviet Republic was abolished in 1956.
6. *Ibid.*
7. I owe this idea to Rosamund Bartlett.
8. N. Voznesenskii, *Voennaya ekonomika SSSR v period otechestvennoi voine*, *passim*; *Iosif Vissarionovich Stalin. Kratkaya biografiya* (2nd edn); *Istoriya Vsesoyuznoi Kommunisticheskoi Partii (Bol'shevikov). Kratkii kurs* (2nd edn).
9. I. Ehrenburg, *Post-War Years: 1945–1954*, p. 160.
10. *Iosif Vissarionovich Stalin. Kratkaya biografiya* (2nd edn), *passim*.
11. I. V. Stalin, *Sochineniya*, vol. 1, p. xiii.
12. See J. Brooks, *Thank You, Comrade Stalin!*, pp. 195–232.
13. *Kniga o vkusnoi i zdorovoi pishche.*
14. *Iosif Vissarionovich Stalin. Kratkaya biografiya* (2nd edn), pp. 1–161.
15. *Ibid.*, pp. 172 and 208.
16. *Ibid.*, p. 228.
17. S. Alliluev, *Proidënnyi put'*; A. S. Allilueva, *Vospominaniya*.
18. RGASPI, f. 668, op. 1, d. 15, p. 67.
19. See in particular sections of the original text of Anna's memoir in RGASPI, f. 4, op. 2, d. 45.
20. S. Alliluev, *Proidënnyi put'*, p. 109.
21. A. S. Allilueva, *Vospominaniya*, pp. 165, 167, 168 and 191.
22. RGASPI, f. 668, op. 1, d. 15, p. 67.
23. *Ibid.*, p. 69.
24. J. Bardach and K. Gleeson, *Surviving Freedom*, p. 117.
25. Really he had turned sixty in 1948: see above, p. 14.
26. *Churchill and Stalin: Documents from the British Archives*, doc. 70, p. 4: conversation of Churchill and Stalin at Potsdam, 17 July 1945.
27. *Vostochnaya Evropa v dokumentakh rossiiskikh arkhivov, 1945–1953 gg.*, vol. 1, p. 407.
28. *Ibid.*, p. 443.
29. *Ibid.*, p. 582.

51. Dangerous Liaisons

1. See above, p. 501 and below, p. 567.
2. See the account by A. M. Ledovskii in I. V. Kovalër, 'Dvenadtsat' sovetov I. V. Stalina rukovodstvu kompartii Kitaya', p. 130.
3. *Ibid.*, pp. 134–9.
4. 'Posetiteli kremlëvskogo kabineta Stalina', pp. 49–50.
5. G. Dimitrov, *The Diary of Georgi Dimitrov, 1933–1949*, p. 443. Dimitrov's diary entry concurs in essentials with Djilas's memoir, at least about the Chinese communists in *Conversations with Stalin*, p. 141.
6. See D. Holloway, *Stalin and the Bomb*, p. 277.

7. A. A. Gromyko, *Pamyatnoe*, vol. 2, pp. 249–50.
8. See D. Holloway, *Stalin and the Bomb*, pp. 280–1.
9. Quoted by V. Zubok and C. Pleshakov, *Inside the Kremlin's Cold War*, pp. 66–7.
10. *Ibid.*, pp. 67–8.
11. *Ibid.*, pp. 68–9.
12. *Ibid.*, p. 69.
13. V. Zubok and C. Pleshakov give the intelligence reports on which Stalin based his judgement: *Ibid.*, p. 63.
14. See D. Holloway, *Stalin and the Bomb*, p. 283.
15. V. Semichastnyi, *Bespokoinoe serdtse*, p. 58
16. See Holloway, *Stalin and the Bomb*, p. 285.
17. *Ibid.*

52. Vozhd and Intellectual

1. S. Beria, *Beria, My Father*, p. 143.
2. *Ibid.*
3. A. Mgeladze, *Stalin, kakim ya ego znal*, p. 271.
4. See D. Joravsky, *The Lysenko Affair*, chapter 3, ff.,
5. S. Beria, *Beria, My Father*, p. 143.
6. A. Malenkov, *O moëm ottse Georgii Malenkove*, p. 24.
7. *Pravda*: 10 February 1946 (speech to electors of the Stalin Electoral District); 13 April 1948 (speech to reception of official Finnish delegation); 15 October 1952 (speech to the Nineteenth Party Congress).
8. I. V. Stalin, *Sochineniya*, vol. 16, pp. 114–57.
9. A. Mgeladze, *Stalin, kakim ya ego znal*, pp. 224–5.
10. V. Brodskii and V. Kalinnikova, 'Otkrytie sostoyalos'', *Nauka i zhizn'*, no. 1 (1988).
11. Konstantin Simonov, chief editor of *Literaturnaya gazeta*, wrote down his impressions in a self-censoring form, in his diary; and later, in 1979, he wrote additions and a commentary on the meeting: *Glazami cheloveka moego pokoleniya*, pp. 113–16.
12. *Ibid.*, p. 111.
13. *Ibid.*
14. This is not to say that he would not have preferred the Soviet order to have been more amenable to his commands: see above, pp. 537–40.
15. *Vosemnadtsatyi s''ezd Vsesoyuznoi Kommunisticheskoi Partii* (b), p. 36.
16. *Ibid.*
17. *Molotov. Poluderzhavnyi vlastelin*, pp. 346, 348, 351 and 352–3.
18. *Ibid.*, p. 353.
19. *Ibid.*, p. 19.
20. RGASPI, f. 558, op. 3, d. 165: V. V. Piotrovskii, *Po sledam drevnikh kul'tur*, p. 77.

21. *Ibid.*, p. 8.
22. See Roy Medvedev's memoir in Zh. and R. Medvedev, *Neizvestnyi Stalin*, pp. 259–60.
23. I. V. Stalin, *Marksizm i voprosy yazykoznaniya*, in *Sochineniya*, vol. 16, p. 119.
24. *Ibid.*, pp. 123 and 133.
25. *Ibid.*, p. 145.
26. S. Beria, *Beria, My Father*, p. 237.
27. I. V. Stalin, *Marksizm i voprosy yazykoznaniya* in *Sochineniya*, vol. 16, p. 159.
28. *Ibid.*, p. 143.
29. *Ibid.*, p. 169.
30. *Molotov. Poluderzhavnyi vlastelin*, p. 301.
31. K. Simonov, *Glazami cheloveka moego pokoleniya*.
32. *Ekonomicheskie problemy sotsializma v SSSR* in I. V. Stalin, *Sochineniya*, vol. 16, pp. 188–304.
33. *Ibid.*, p. 197.
34. *Ibid.*, p. 226.
35. *Ibid.*
36. *Ibid.*, p. 224.
37. *Ibid.*, p. 256.
38. *Ibid.*, p. 231.
39. *Ibid.*, pp. 235–6.
40. See above, p. 94.
41. See above, pp. 153–5.
42. See above, p. 226.
43. See above, pp. 432–4.
44. See also above, p. 390.
45. See B. Pinkus, *The Soviet Government and the Jews, 1948–1967*, pp. 151–64. I am grateful to John Klier for help in elaborating this paragraph.
46. See L. Rucker, *Staline, Israël et les Juifs*, p. 238.
47. *Tak govoril Kaganovich*, p. 211. S. Beria, *Beria, My Father*, p. 211: apparently Lavrenti Beria too thought Stalin was not an anti-semite.
48. *Tak govoril Kaganovich*, p. 175.

53. Ailing Despot

1. See above, pp. 231–2 and 437–8.
2. P. Moshentsova, *Tainy kremlëvskoi bol'nitsy*, pp. 6–7.
3. Y. Rapoport, *The Doctors' Plot*, p. 218.
4. *Politbyuro TsK VKP(b) i Sovet Ministrov SSSR, 1945–1953*, p. 398: his stay in the south lasted from 10 August to 22 December 1951.
5. See the unpublished memoirs of K. Charkviani, p. 35.
6. These observations come from a visit on 11 September 2002.

7. A barracks for the guards was adjacent to Stalin's quarters.
8. Visit by author: 11 September 2002.
9. S. Beria, *Beria, My Father*, p. 140; S. Allilueva, *Dvadtsat' pisem k drugu*, p. 191.
10. S. Beria, *Beria, My Father*, p. 140.
11. *Ibid.*
12. *Tak govoril Kaganovich*, p. 52.
13. A. Mikoyan, *Tak bylo*, p. 527.
14. See S. Wheatcroft, 'From Team-Stalin to Degenerate Tyranny', p. 92.
15. L. M. Kaganovich, *Pamyatnye zapiski*, p. 498.
16. See O. Khlevnyuk, 'Stalin i organy gosudarstvennoi bezopasnosti v posle-voennyi period', p. 544.
17. A. Mgeladze, *Stalin, kakim ya ego znal*, pp. 71–2.
18. *Ibid.*, pp. 72–3.
19. *Ibid.*, pp. 83–4.
20. *Ibid.* See also S. Beria, *Beria, My Father*, p. 134.
21. *Ibid.*, p. 92; S. Beria, *Beria, My Father*, p. 134.
22. A. Mikoyan, *Tak bylo*, p. 529; K. Charkviani's memoirs, *op. cit.*, p. 21.
23. S. Beria, *Beria, My Father*, p. 134.
24. *Ibid.*, p. 141.
25. *Ibid.*, p. 142.
26. *Ibid.*, p. 240.
27. *Politbyuro TsK VKP(b) i Sovet Ministrov SSSR, 1945–1953*, pp. 349–51.
28. A. Mgeladze, *Stalin, kakim ya ego znal*, p. 91.
29. S. Beria, *Beria, My Father*, p. 237.
30. J. Bardach and K. Gleeson, *Surviving Freedom*, pp. 87 and 235.
31. J. Rubenstein and V. P. Naumov (eds), *Stalin's Secret Pogrom*.
32. See G. V. Kostyrchenko, *Tainaya politika Stalina. Vlast' i antisemitizm*, pp. 671–84.
33. M. G. Pervukhin, 'Korotko o perezhitom', p. 143.
34. L. M. Kaganovich, *Pamyatnye zapiski*, p. 498.
35. A. Mikoyan, *Tak bylo*, p. 570.
36. K. Simonov, *Glazami cheloveka moego pokoleniya*, p. 209.
37. *Ibid.*, p. 210: I have put the text together from Simonov's remarks. No stenographic record was made of the proceedings: see A. Mikoyan, *Tak bylo*, p. 575.
38. K. Simonov, *Glazami cheloveka moego pokoleniya*, p. 210.
39. *Ibid.*, p. 209.
40. A. Mikoyan, *Tak bylo*, pp. 574–5.
41. M. G. Pervukhin, 'Korotko o perezhitom', p. 144.
42. *Politbyuro TsK VKP(b) i Sovet Ministrov SSSR, 1945–1953*, p. 89
43. *Ibid.*, pp. 89–90.
44. *Ibid.*, pp. 432–5.
45. *Ibid.*, p. 434.
46. A. Mikoyan, *Tak bylo*, p. 579.
47. T. H. Rigby, 'Was Stalin a Disloyal Patron?'

54. Death and Embalming

1. I follow Svetlana Allilueva's memoir here. W. Taubman suggests it was the (later) New Year's Eve party, but I think this is based on a rather vague reference in Khrushchëv's memoirs.
2. S. Allilueva, *Dvadtsat' pisem k drugu*, p. 21.
3. J. Davrichewy, *Ah! Ce qu'on rigolait bien*, p. 71. See above, p. 26.
4. N. Krushchev, *Khrushchev Remembers*, p. 256.
5. *Politbyuro TsK VKP(b) i Sovet Ministrov SSSR*, pp. 395–6.
6. *Pravda*, 13 January 1953.
7. N. S. Khrushchëv, 'Memuary Nikity Sergeevicha Khrushchëva', *Voprosy istorii*, no. 2/3, pp. 90–1.
8. *Ibid.*
9. See Lozgachëv's testimony to E. Radzinsky, *Stalin*, pp. 552–3.
10. P. I. Yegorov, 'Poslednyaya noch' Stalina', *Argumenty i fakty*, no. 10 (March 2003), p. 10. Yegorov was on guard duty, at position number 6, at Stalin's dacha on 1 March.
11. *Ibid.*
12. This is the plausible suggestion in E. Radzinsky, *Stalin*, pp. 553–4.
13. See Lozgachëv's testimony to E. Radzinsky, *ibid.*
14. J. Brent and V. P. Naumov, *Stalin's Doctors' Plot*, pp. 316–17.
15. S. Allilueva, *Dvadtsat' pisem k drugu*, p. 5.
16. J. Brent and V. P. Naumov, *Stalin's Doctors' Plot*, p. 318.
17. *Ibid.*
18. Y. Rappoport, *The Doctors' Plot*, pp. 151–2.
19. A. Mgeladze, *Stalin, kakim ya ego znal*, pp. 234–5.
20. J. Brent and V. P. Naumov, *Stalin's Doctors' Plot*, p. 319.
21. S. Allilueva, *Dvadtsat' pisem k drugu*, p. 7.
22. 'Poslednyaya "otstavka" Stalina', p. 110. A. Mgeladze, however, suggested – wrongly – that Stalin was already dead: *Stalin, kakim ya ego znal*, pp. 235.
23. 'Poslednyaya "otstavka" Stalina', p. 110.
24. S. Beria, *Beria, My Father*, p. 238.
25. J. Brent and V. P. Naumov, *Stalin's Doctors' Plot*, p. 314.
26. I. Zbarsky and S. Hutchinson, *Lenin's Embalmers*, p. 164.
27. *Ibid.*, p. 165.
28. P. I. Yegorov, 'Poslednyaya noch' Stalina', *Argumenty i fakty*, no. 10 (March 2003), p. 11.
29. V. Semichastnyi, *Bespokoinoe serdtse*, p. 77.
30. This account comes from the report of Sir A. Gascoigne, 16 March 1953: *Churchill and Stalin: Documents from the British Archives*, Appendix, pp. 1–2.
31. S. Beria, *Beria, My Father*, p. 250.

55. After Stalin

1. See above, p. 587.
2. See Zh. and R. Medvedev, *Neizvestnyi Stalin*, chapter 3.
3. Robert McNeal undertook this task unofficially and published volumes 14–16 through the Hoover Institution in 1967.
4. Quoted by Zh. and R. Medvedev, *Neizvestnyi Stalin*, pp. 82–3.
5. K. Simonov, *Glazami cheloveka moego pokoleniya*, pp. 241–2.
6. See R. Conquest, *Power and Policy in the USSR*, pp. 211–27.
7. R. Service, 'The Road to the Twentieth Party Congress'.
8. V. Semichastnyi, *Bespokoinoe serdtse*, p. 82.
9. See N. Barsukov, 'Kak sozdavalsya "zakrytyi doklad" Khrushchëva', p. 11.
10. *Istoriya Kommunisticheskoi Partii Sovetskogo Soyuza*.
11. The Politburo minute is quoted by V. Bukovskii, *Moskovskii protsess*, p. 88.
12. *Rossiiskaya gazeta*, 6 November 1999.
13. See R. Service, *Russia: Experiment with a People*, pp. 211–13.
14. *Ibid.*, p. 110.
15. V. Topolyansky, 'The Cheynes–Stokes Draught', p. 29.
16. See the argument in R. Service, 'Architectural Problems of Reform in the Soviet Union: From Design to Collapse', pp. 9–17.
17. *Ibid.*, pp. 11–16.

SELECT BIBLIOGRAPHY

This bibliography is confined to works referred to in the notes.

Archives, Museums and Unpublished Works

The British Library

K. Charkviani, unpublished memoirs

Gosudarstvennyi Arkhiv Rossiiskoi Federatsii [GARF]
    fond 81   fond 3316   fond 7523
    fond 1318   fond 6980   fond R-130

Gosudarstvennyi Dom-Muzei I. V. Stalina (Gori) [GDMS]

S. Kavtaradze, *tsareulis purtsebli*, vols. 1–2 (Tbilisi, 1969)

Rossiiskii Gosudarstvennyi Arkhiv Sotsial'no-Politicheskoi Istorii [RGASPI]
    fond 2   fond 16   fond 71   fond 82
    fond 3   fond 17   fond 73   fond 85
    fond 4   fond 44   fond 74   fond 332
    fond 5   fond 46   fond 76   fond 558 (Stalin)
    fond 12   fond 64   fond 81   fond 668

Volkogonov Papers (Oxford)

Newspapers and Periodicals

Agitator
American Historical Review
Argumenty i fakty
Bol'shevik
Bor'ba
Byulleten' oppozitsii
Cahiers du Monde Russe et Soviétique
Christian Science Monitor
Dagens Nyheter
Europe-Asia Studies
Glasgow Academy Herald
Istochnik
Istoricheskii arkhiv
Izvestiya
Izvestiya Tsentral'nogo Komiteta KPSS
Journal of Communist Studies
Journal of Economic History
Kommunist

Komsomol'skaya pravda
Krasnaya zvezda
Krasnyi arkhiv
Literaturnaya gazeta
Molodaya gvardiya
Nauka i zhizn'
Novaya i noveishaya istoriya
Novaya zhizn'
Novyi zhurnal
Otechestvennye arkhivy
Pod znamenem marksizma
Pravda
Proletarskaya revolyutsiya
Prosveshchenie
Rabochii put'

Rodina
Rossiiskaya gazeta
Russian Review
Slavia
Slavic Review
Sotsialisticheskii vestnik
Sovershenno sekretno
Svobodnaya mysl'
Voenno-istoricheskii zhurnal
Voprosy istorii
Voprosy istorii KPSS
Vperëd
Soviet Studies
Trud
Zvezda (Moscow)

Documentary Collections

Akademicheskoe delo 1929–1931 gg., vol. 1, Delo po obvineniyu akademika S. F. Platonova (St Petersburg, 1993)

S. Alieva (ed.), Tak eto bylo: natsional'nye repressii v SSSR, vols 1–3 (Moscow, 1993)

Atlas aziatskoi Rossii. Izdanie pereselencheskogo upravleniya glavnogo upravleniya zemleustroistva i zemledeliya (St Petersburg, 1914)

L'Armata Rossa e la collettivizazzione delle campagne nell' URSS (1928–1933) (eds A. Romano and N. Tarchova: Naples, 1996)

Bol'shevistskoe rukovodstvo. Perepiska, 1912–1927 (eds A. V. Kvashonkin, O. V. Khlevnyuk, L. P. Kosheleva and L. A. Rogovaya: Moscow, 1996)

'Bosco d'inverno a Zubalov', Slavia (1997)

Chetvërtyi (ob"edinitel'nyi) s"ezd RSDRP (Moscow, 1949)

Chetvërtyi (ob"edinitel'nyi) s"ezd RSDRP. Protokoly. Aprel'–mai 1906 goda (Moscow, 1959)

Chetyrnadtsatyi s"ezd Vsesoyuznoi Kommunisticheskoi Partii (b).15–31 marta 1925 goda. Stenograficheskii otchët (Moscow, 1926)

Churchill and Stalin. Documents from the British Archives (eds FCO Historians C. Baxter and M. A. L. Longden: London, 2002)

The Cominform. Minutes of the Three Conferences, 1947/1948/1949 (eds G. Procacci, G. Adibekov, A. Di Biagio, L. Gibianskii, F. Gori and S. Pons: Milan, 1994)

Dagli Archivi di Mosca. L'URSS, il Cominform e il PCI (1943–1951) (eds F. Gori and S. Pons: Rome, 1998)

Devyataya konferentsiya RKP(b). Sentyabr' 1920 goda. Protokoly (Moscow, 1972)

Desyatyi s"ezd RKP(b). Mart 1921 g. Stenograficheskii otchët (Moscow, 1961)

Dimitrov and Stalin, 1934–1943. Letters from the Soviet Archives (eds A. Dallin and F. I. Firsov: Yale, 2000)

Dve besedy I. V. Stalina s General'nym Sekretarëm Ob"edinënnykh Natsii Tryugve Li', *Novaya i noveishaya istoriya*, no.3 (2001)

Dvenadtsatyi s"ezd RKP(b). 17–25 aprelya 1923 goda: stenograficheskii otchët (Moscow, 1968)

Iosif Stalin v ob"yatiyakh sem'i. Iz lichnogo arkhiva (eds Yu. G. Murin and V. N. Denisov: Moscow, 1993)

Istoricheskie mesta Tbilisi. Putevoditel' po mestam, svyazannym s zhizn'yu i deyatel'nost'yu I. V. Stalina (ed. Georgian Filial of the Institute of Marx-Engels-Lenin: 2nd, revised edn; Tbilisi, 1944)

Istoriya sovetskoi politicheskoi tsenzury. Dokumenty i kommentarii (ed. M. Goryaeva: Moscow, 1997)

V. Kaminskii and I. Vereshchagin, 'Detstvo i yunost' vozhdya. Dokumenty, zapiski, rasskazy', *Molodaya gvardiya*, no. 12 (1939)

I. V. Kovalëv, 'Dvenadtsat' sovetov I. V. Stalina rukovodstvu kompartii Kitaya' (ed. A. M. Ledovskii), *Novaya i noveishaya istoriya*, no. 1 (2004)

Lado Ketskhoveli. Sbornik dokumentov i materialov (Tbilisi, 1969)

V. I. Lenin, *Polnoe sobranie sochinenii* (5th edn: Moscow, 1958–65)

Lubyanka. Stalin i VChK-GPU-OGPU-NKVD. Yanvar' 1922 – dekabr' 1936 (eds V. N. Khaustov, V. P. Naumov and N. S. Plotnikova: Moscow, 2003)

'Materialy fevral'skogo-martovskogo plenuma TsK VKP(b) 1937 goda', *Voprosy istorii*, no. 10 (1994), no. 2 (1995) and no. 3 (1995)

Neizvestnyi Zhukov. Lavry i ternii polkovodtsa Dokumenty. Mneniya. Razmyshleniya (ed. V. G. Krasnov: Moscow, 2000)

Obshchestvo i vlast'. 1930-e gody. Povestvovanie v dokumentakh (eds A. K. Sokolov, S. V. Zhuravlëv, L. P. Kosheleva, L. A. Rogovaya and V. B. Tel'pukhovskii: Moscow, 1998)

Odinnadtsatyi s"ezd RKP(b). Mart-aprel' 1922 g. Stenograficheskii otchët (Moscow, 1961)

Perepiska V. I. Lenina i rukovodimykh im uchrezhdenii RSDRP s mestnymi partiinymi organizatsiyami. 1905–1907, vol. 2, part 1 (Moscow, 1982)

Perepiska predsedatelya Soveta Ministrov SSSR s prezidentami SShA i prem'er-ministrami Velikobritanii vo vremya velikoi Otechestvennoi voiny, 1941–1945 gg., vols 1–2 (eds A. A. Gromyko, V. M. Khvostov, I. N. Zemskov, G. A. Belov, Ye. M. Zhukov, S. M. Maiorov, A. A. Novosel'skii, B. F. Podtserob, M. A. Sivolobov, P. N. Tret'yakov and M. A. Kharlamov: Moscow, 1957)

Pisatel' i vozhd': perepiska M. A. Sholokhova s I. V. Stalinym 1931–1950 gody (Moscow, 1997)

Pis'ma vo vlast', 1917–1927 (eds A. Ya. Livshin and I. B. Orlov: Moscow, 1998)

Pis'ma I. V. Stalina V. M. Molotovu, 1925–1936 gg. Sbornik dokumentov (eds L. Kosheleva, V. Lel'chuk, V. Naumov, O. Naumov, L. Rogovaya and O. Khlevnyuk: Moscow, 1995)

Politbyuro RKP(b)-VKP(b). Povestki dnya zasedanii, vols 1–3 (eds G. M. Adibekov, K. M. Anderson and L. A. Rogovaya: Moscow, 2000–1)

Politbyuro TsK VKP(b) i otnosheniya SSSR s zapadnymi sosednimi gosudarstvami (konets 1920–1930-kh gg.) (eds O. N. Ken and A. I. Rupasov: St Petersburg, 2000)

Politbyuro TsK VKP(b) i Sovet Ministrov SSSR, 1945–1953 (eds O. V. Khlevnyuk, Y. Gorlizki, L. P. Kosheleva, A. I. Minyuk, M. Yu. Prozumenshchikov, L. A. Rogovaya and S. V. Somonova: Moscow, 2002)

'Posetiteli kremlëvskogo kabineta Stalina' (eds A. V. Korotkov, A. D. Chernev and A. A. Chernobaev), *Istoricheskii arkhiv*, no. 5/6 (1997)

'Poslednyaya "otstavka" Stalina' (ed. A. S. Chernyaev), *Istochnik*, no. 1 (1994)

'Pravil'naya politika pravitel'stva reshaet uspekh armii. Kto dostoin byt' marshalom?', *Istochnik*, no. 3 (2002)

'Proidët desyatok let, i eti vstrechi ne vosstanovish' uzhe v pamyati. Dnevnikovye zapisi V. A. Malysheva', *Istochnik*, no. 5 (1997)

'Protokoly i rezolyutsii Byuro TsK RSDRP(b) (mart 1917 g.)', *VIKPSS*, no. 3 (1962)

Protokoly Tsentral'nogo Komiteta RSDRP(b). Avgust 1917 – fevral' 1918 (Moscow, 1958)

'Protokoly Vserossiiskogo (martovskogo) soveshchaniya partiinykh rabotnikov, 27 marta – 2 aprelya 1917 g.', *VIKPSS*, no. 6 (1962)

Pyatyi (londonskii) s"ezd RSDRP. Protokoly. Aprel'-mai 1907 goda (Moscow, 1963)*Pyatnadtsatyi s"ezd Vsesoyuznoi Kommunisticheskoi Partii-(b). Stenograficheskii otchët* (Moscow-Leningrad, 1928)

'Rasstrel po raznaryadke, ili Kak eto delali bol'sheviki', *Trud*, (4 June 1992)

Razgovory s Bukharinym (ed. Yu. G. Fel'shtinskii: Moscow, 1993)

Reabilitatsiya: politicheskie protsessy 30–50-kh godov (ed. A. N. Yakovlev: Moscow 1991)

Le repressioni degli anni trenta nell'Armata Rossa (eds A. Cristiani and V. M. Michaleva: Naples, 1996)

Resheniya partii i pravitel'stva po khozyaistvennym voprosam vol. 3 (Moscow, 1968)

Revolyutsiya 1905 goda v Zakavkaz'e. (Khronika sobytii, dokumenty i materialy). Po materialam Muzeya Revolyutsii Gruzii (Istpartotdel TsK KP(b) Gruzii: Tiflis, 1926)

The Road to Terror: Stalin and the Self-Destruction of the Bolsheviks, 1932–1939 (edited and introduced by O. V. Naumov and J. A. Getty: London, 1999)

Sed'maya (aprel'skaya) vserossiiskaya konferentsiya RSDRP (bol'shevikov). Petrogradskaya konferentsiya obshchegorodskaya konferentsiya RSDRP (bol'shevikov). Aprel' 1917 goda (Moscow, 1958)

Semnadtsatyi s"ezd Vsesoyuznoi Kommunisticheskoi Partii (b), 26 yanvarya – 10 fevralya 1934. Stenograficheskii otchët (Moscow, 1934)

S. Shaumyan, *Izbrannye proizvedeniya*, vols 1–2 (Moscow, 1957)

Shestoi s"ezd RSDRP(b). Avgust 1917 goda. Protokoly (Moscow, 1958)

Skrytaya pravda voiny. 1941 god (eds P. N. Knyshevskii et al.: Moscow, 1992)

Slovo tovarishchu Stalinu (ed. R. Kosolapov: 2nd edn, Moscow, 2002)

Sovetskoe rukovodstvo. Perepiska, 1928–1941 (eds A. V. Kvashonkin, L. P. Kosheleva, L. A. Rogovaya and O. V. Khlevnyuk: Moscow, 1999)

S. Spandar'yan (Timofei), *Stat'i, pis'ma, dokumenty, 1882–1916* (Yerevan, 1940)

SSSR – Pol'sha. Mekhanizmy podchineniya. 1944–1949 gg. Sbornik dokumentov (eds G. Bordyugov, G. Matveev, A. Kosevskii and A. Pachkovskii: Moscow, 1995)

Stalin i Kaganovich. Perepiska. 1931–1936 gg. (eds O. V. Khlevnyuk, R. W. Davies, E. A. Rees, L. A. Rogovaya: Moscow, 2001)

Stalin v vospominaniyakh sovremennikov i dokumentov epokhi (eds L. Anninskii et al.: Moscow, 2002)

I. Stalin, *Stikhi* (Moscow, 1997)

'I. V. Stalin dal slovo zhenit'sya', *Istochnik*, no. 4 (2002)

I. V. Stalin, *Marksizm i natsional'nyi vopros* in *Marksizm i natsional'no-kolonial'nyi vopros. Sbornik statei i rechei* (Moscow, 1937)

'I. V. Stalin o "Kratkom kurse po istorii VKP(b)". Stenogramma vystupleniya na soveshchanii propagandistov Moskvy i Leningrada', *Istoricheskii arkhiv*, no. 5 (1994)

I. V. Stalin, *Sochineniya* vols 1–13 (Moscow, 1952–4)

I. V. Stalin, *Sochineniya* vols 1(xiv)-3(xvi) (ed. R. MacNeal: Stanford, 1967)

Stalinskoe Politbyuro v 30-e gody: Sbornik dokumentov (eds O. V. Khlevnyuk, A. V. Kvashonkin, L. P. Kosheleva and L. A. Rogovaya: Moscow, 1995)

'Stenogrammy ochnykh stavok v TsK VKP(b). Dekabr' 1936 goda', *Voprosy istorii*, nos. 3 and 4 (2002)

Ya. M. Sverdlov, *Izbrannye proizvedeniya* vols 1–2 (Moscow, 1957)

Tainy natsional'noi politiki RKP(b). Chetvërtoe soveshchanie TsK RKP s otvetstvennymi rabotnikami natsional'nykh respublik i oblastei v g. Moskve, 9–12 iyunya 1923 g. Stenograficheskii otchët (Moscow, 1992)

P. Togliatti, *Opere*, vols. 1–6, (Rome, 1967–84)

Tragediya sovetskoi derevni: kollektivizatsiya i raskulachivanie, dokumenty i materialy v 5 tomakh, 1927–1939 (eds V. P. Danilov, R. Manning and L. Viola: Moscow, 1999–)

Tretii s"ezd RSDRP. Protokoly. Aprel' – mai 1905 goda (Moscow, 1959)

Tretii Vserossiiskii S"ezd Sovetov Rabochikh, Soldatskikh i Krest'yanskikh Deputatov (Petersburg [sic], 1918)

The Trotsky Papers (ed. J. Meijer), vols 1–2 (The Hague, 1964–71)

K. Voroshilov, *Stalin i Krasnaya Armiya* (Moscow, 1937)

K. E. Voroshilov na Tsaritsynskom fronte. Sbornik dokumentov (Stalingrad, 1941)

Vosemnadtsatyi s"ezd Vsesoyuznoi Kommunisticheskoi Partii (b). 10–21 marta 1939 goda. Stenograficheskii otchët (Moscow, 1939)

Vos'moi s"ezd RKP(b). Mart 1919. Protokoly (Moscow, 1959)

Vostochnaya Evropa v dokumentakh rossiiskikh arkhivov, 1945–1953 gg., vols 1–2 (eds T. V. Volokitina, T. M. Islamov, A. F. Noskova, L. A. Rogovaya: Moscow, 1997)

Vserossiiskaya Konferentsiya Rossiiskoi Sostial-Demokraticheskoi Rabochei Partii 1912 goda (ed. R. C. Elwood: London, 1982)

Vtoroi s"ezd RSDRP. Protokoly. Iyul'-avgust 1903 goda (Moscow, 1959)

Zastol'nye rechi Stalina. Dokumenty i materialy (edited with introduction and commentary by V. A. Nevezhin: Moscow, 2003)

'Zhurnal poseshcheniya I. V. Stalina v ego Kremlëvskoi kabinete', *Istochnik*, nos 2–4 (1996)

Contemporary Works

A. Akhmatova, *Sochineniya v dvukh tomakh* (Moscow, 1990)

An (N. Zhordaniya), 'Natsional'nyi vopros', *Bor'ba* (St Petersburg), no. 2, 18 March 1914

B. Andreev, *Zavoevanie Prirody. Fizika na sluzhbe chelovechestva* (Moscow, 1927)

S. T. Arkhomed, *Rabochee dvizhenie i sotsial-demokratiya na Kavkaze* (Moscow-Petrograd, 1923)

A. V. Baikalov, 'Turukhanskii "bunt" politicheskikh ssyl'nykh', *Sibirskii arkhiv*, no. 2 (Prague, 1929)

A. V. Baikaloff, *I Knew Stalin* (London, 1940)

H. Barbusse, *Staline. Un monde nouveau vu à travers d'un homme* (Paris, 1935)

L. Beria, *K voprosu ob istorii bol'shevistskikh organizatsiyakh v Zakavkaz'e* (Moscow, 1935)

M. Buber-Neumann, *Von Potsdam nach Moskau. Stationen eines Irrweges* (Stuttgart 1957)

K. Chukovskii, *Dnevniki, 1930–1969* (Moscow, 1995)

F. Dan, *Proiskhozhdenie bol'shevizma: k istorii demokraticheskikh i sotsialisticheskikh idei v Rossii posle osvobozhdeniya krest'yan* (New York, 1946)

deda ena (ed. Y. Gogebashvili: Tiflis, 1912)

deda ena (ed. Y. Gogebashvili: Tiflis, 1916)

Drevnyaya Evropa i Vostok (Moscow-Petrograd, 1923)

M. Gor'kii, L. Averbakh and S. Firin (eds), *Belomorsko-baltiiskii kanal imeni I. V. Stalina* (Moscow, 1934)

Iosif Vissarionovich Stalin. Kratkaya biografiya (Moscow, 1938)

Iosif Vissarionovich Stalin. Kratkaya biografiya (eds G. F. Alexandrov, M. R. Galaktionov, V. S. Krushkov, M. B. Mitin, V. D. Mochalov and P. N. Pospelov: 2nd edn, corrected and expanded; Moscow, 1946)

Istoriya Vsesoyuznoi Kommunisticheskoi Partii (Bol'shevikov). Kratkii kurs (Moscow, 1938)

Istoriya Vsesoyuznoi Kommunisticheskoi Partii (Bol'shevikov). Kratkii kurs (2nd edn: Moscow, 1946).

G. Kennan, *Siberia and the Exile System* (London, 1891)

Kniga o vkusnoi i zdorovoi pishche (eds O. P. Molchanova, D. I. Lobanov, M. O. Lifshits and N. P. Tsyplenkov: expanded edition; Moscow, 1952)

E. Kviring, *Lenin, Zagovorshchestvo, Oktyabr'* (Kharkov, 1924)

N. Lenin, 'Zametki publitsista', *Diskussionnyi listok. Prilozhenie k Tsentral'nomu Organu 'Sotsial-demokrat'* (Paris), no. 2, 24 May/7 June 1910

F. Ye. Makharadze and G. V. Khachapuridze, *Ocherki po istorii rabochego i krest'yanskogo dvizheniya v Gruzii* (Moscow, 1932)

V. V. Piotrovskii, *Po sledam drevnikh kul'tur* (Moscow, 1951)

B. Souvarine, *Staline : aperçu historique du bolchévisme* (Paris, 1935)

K. S. (I. V. Stalin), 'Pis'mo s Kavkaza', *Diskussionnyi listok. Prilozhenie k Tsentral'nomu Organu 'Sotsial-demokrat'*, no. 2, 24 May/7 June 1910

K. Stalin, 'K natsional'nomu voprosu: evreiskaya burzhuaznaya i bundovskaya kul'turno-natsional'naya avtonomiya', *Prosveshchenie*, no. 6 (June 1913)

Stalin. K shestidesyatiyu so dnya rozhdeniya. Sbornik statei 'Pravdy' (Moscow, 1939)

N. Sukhanov, *Zapiski o russkoi revolyutsii*, vols 1–7 (Berlin, 1922–3)

S. Talakvadze, *K istorii Kommunisticheskoi partii Gruzii* (Tiflis, 1925)

I. Tovstukha, 'Stalin (Dzhugashvili), Iosif Vissarionovich', *Deyateli Soyuza Sovetskikh Sotsialisticheskikh Respublik i Oktyabr'skoi Revolyutsii (Avtobiografii i biografii)*, (in *Entsiklopedicheskii slovar' Granat* (Moscow and Leningrad, 1927), pp. 107–12.

L. Trotskii, *Moya zhizn'. Opyt avtobiografii*, vols 1–2 (Berlin, 1930)

L. D. Trotskii, *Terrorizm i kommunizm* (Petersburg [sic], 1920)

L. Trotsky, *My Life* (London, 1975)

L. Trotsky, *Stalin: An Appraisal of the Man and His Influence* (London, 1947)

L. Trotsky, *The Real Situation in Russia* (New York, 1928)

N. Voznesenskii, *Voennaya ekonomika SSSR v period otechestvennoi voine* (Moscow, 1948)

Memoirs and Diaries

S. Alliluev, *Proidënnyi put'* (Moscow, 1946)

V. Alliluev, *Khronika odnoi sem'i: Alliluevy. Stalin* (Moscow, 2002)

A. S. Allilueva, *Vospominaniya* (Moscow, 1946)

S. Allilueva, *Dvadtsat' pisem k drugu* (London, 1967)

S. Allilueva, *Tol'ko odin god* (New York, 1969)

N. A. Antipenko, *Ryadom s G. K. Zhukovym i K. K. Rokossovskim* (Moscow, 2001)

G. Arbatov, *Svidetel'stvo sovremennika. Zatyanuvsheesya vyzdorovlenie (1953–1985 gg.)* (Moscow, 1991)

R. Arsenidze, 'Iz vospominanii o Staline', *Novyi zhurnal*, no. 72 (June 1963)

'"Avtobiograficheskie zametki" V. N. Pavlova – perevodchika I. V. Stalina', *Novaya i noveishaya istoriya*, no. 4 (2000)

N. K. Baibakov, *Ot Stalina do Yel'tsina* (Moscow, 1998)

J. Bardach and K. Gleeson, *Surviving Freedom. After the Gulag* (Berkeley, 2003)

B. Bazhanov, *Bazhanov and the Damnation of Stalin* (trans. D. W. Doyle: Athens, Ohio, 1990)

B. Bazhanov, *Vospominaniya byvshego sekretarya Stalina* (St Petersburg, 1990)

V. Berezhkov, *Kak ya stal perevodchikom Stalina* (Moscow, 1993)

S. Beria, *Beria, My Father. Inside Stalin's Kremlin* (London, 2001)

S. M. Budënnyi, *Proidënnyi put'*, vol. 2 (Moscow, 1965)

V. Bukovskii, *Moskovskii protsess* (Moscow, 1996)

R. Bullard, *Inside Stalin's Russia. The Diaries of Reader Bullard, 1930–1934* (Charlbury, 2000)

W. S. Churchill, *The Second World War*, vols 1–6 (London, 1950–5)

J. Davrichewy, *Ah! Ce qu'on rigolait bien avec mon copain Staline* (Paris, 1979)

M. Djilas, *Conversations With Stalin* (London, 1962)

G. Dimitrov, *Diario. Gli anni di Mosca (1934–1945)* (ed. S. Pons: Turin, 2002)

G. Dimitrov, *The Diary of Georgi Dimitrov, 1933–1949* (ed. I. Banac: London, 2003)

I. Ehrenburg, *Post-War Years: 1945–1954* (Cleveland, 1957)

A. Fadeev (ed.), *Vstrechi s tovarishchem Stalinym* (Moscow, 1939)

A. Gio, *Zhizn' podpol'nika* (Leningrad, 1925)

B. Gorev, 'Za kulisami pervoi revolyutsii', *Istoriko-revolyutsionnyi byulleten'*, no. 1 (1922)

A. A. Gromyko, *Pamyatnoe*, vols 1–2 (Moscow, 1988)

L. F. Ilichëv (interviewed by V. Boldin): 'Stalin i "Pravda": rabochii kontakt', *Pravda*, 11 April 2002

B. I. Ivanov, *Vospominaniya rabochego bol'shevika* (Moscow, 1972)

V. Ivanov, 'Krasnaya ploshchad'', *Novyi mir*, no. 11 (1937)

J. Iremaschwili, *Stalin und die Tragödie Georgiens* (Berlin, 1932)

L. M. Kaganovich, *Pamyatnye zapiski* (Moscow, 1996)

N. Khrushchev, *Khrushchev Remembers* (London, 1971)

N. S. Khrushchev, *Khrushchev Remembers. The Glasnost Tapes* (London, 1990)

N. S. Khrushchëv, 'Memuary Nikity Sergeevicha Khrushchëva', *Voprosy istorii*, nos 1–12 (1991)

L. B. Krasin, 'Bol'shevistskaya partiinaya tekhnika' in *Tekhnika bol'shevistskogo podpol'ya. Sbornik statei i vospominanii* (2nd edition, corrected and expanded: Moscow, 1925)

G. A. Kumanëv, 'Dve besedy s L. M. Kaganovichem', *Novaya i noveishaya istoriya*, no. 2 (1999)

G. A. Kumanëv (ed.), *Ryadom so Stalinym* (Moscow, 1999)

A. Kuusinen, *Before and After Stalin* (London, 1974)

A. Malenkov, *O moëm ottse Georgii Malenkove* (Moscow, 1992)

V. A. Malyshev: 'Proidët desyatok let, i eti vstrechi ne vosstanovish' uzhe v pamyati', *Istochnik*, no. 5 (1997)

I. P. McEwan, 'Quo Vadis?', *Glasgow Academy Chronicle*, March 1945

N. L. Meshcheryakov, *Kak my zhili v ssylke* (Leningrad, 1929)

A. Mgeladze, *Stalin, kakim ya ego znal. Stranitsy nedavnego proshlogo* (2001)

A. Mikoyan, 'Iz vospominaniya A. I. Mikoyana', *Sovershenno sekretno*, no. 10 (1999)

A. Mikoyan, *Mysli i vospominaniya o Lenine* (Moscow, 1970)

A. Mikoyan, *Tak bylo. Razmyshleniya o minuvshem* (Moscow, 1999)

Molotov. Poluderzhavnyi vlastelin (ed. F. Chuev: Moscow, 1999)

P. Moshentsova, *Tainy kremlëvskoi bol'nitsy* (Moscow, 1998)

V. N. Pavlov, 'Predistoriya 1939 goda', *Svobodnaya mysl'* , no. 7 (1999)

S. Pestkovskii, 'Vospominaniya o rabote v Narkomnatse (1917–1919 gg.)', *Proletarskaya revolyutsiya*, no. 6 (1930)

M. G. Pervukhin, 'Kak byla reshena atomnaya problema v nashei strane', *Novaya i noveishaya istoriya*, no. 5 (2001)

M. G. Pervukhin, 'Korotko o perezhitom', *Novaya i noveishaya istoriya*, no. 5 (2003)

Y. Rapoport, *The Doctors' Plot. Stalin's Last Crime* (London, 1991)

F. F. Raskol'nikov, 'Priezd tov. Lenina v Rossiyu', *Proletarskaya revolyutsiya*, no. 1 (1923)

J. von Ribbentrop, *Zwischen London und Moskau: Erinnerungen und letzte Aufzeichnungen* (Leoni am Starnberger See, 1954)

N. Ryzhkov, *Perestroika: istoriya predatel'stv* (Moscow, 1992)

A. Rybin, 'Ryadom so Stalinym', *Sotsiologicheskie issledovaniya*, no. 3 (1988)

V. Semichastnyi, *Bespokoinoe serdtse* (Moscow, 2002)

A. G. Shlyapnikov, *Semnadtsatyi god*, vol. 2 (Moscow-Petrograd, 1923)

V. Shveitser, *Stalin v turukhanskoi ssylke. Vospominaniya podpol'shchika* (Moscow, 1940)

K. Simonov, *Glazami cheloveka moego pokoleniya* (Moscow, 1990)

Stalin i Khasim (1901–1902 gg.). Nekotorye epizody iz batumskogo podpol'ya (ed. N. Lakoba: Sukhum, 1934)

Stalin: v vospominaniyakh sovremennikov i dokumentov epokhi (eds M. Lobanov: Moscow, 2002)

P.A Sudoplatov and A. Sudoplatov, *Special Tasks. The Memoirs of an Unwanted Witness – A Soviet Spymaster* (London, 1994)

K. T. Sverdlova, *Yakov Mikhailovich Sverdlov* (Moscow, 1957)

Tak govoril Kaganovich. Ispoved' stalinskogo apostola (ed. F. Chuev: Moscow, 1992)

Tekhnika bol'shevistskogo podpol'ya. Sbornik statei i vospominanii (2nd edition, corrected and expanded: Moscow, 1925)

T. Toranska, *Oni. Stalin's Polish Puppets* (London, 1987)

Trotsky's Diary in Exile, 1935 (New York, 1963)

N. A. Uglanov, 'Vospominaniya' in *Vospominaniya o Vladimire Il'iche Lenine*, vol. 7

'M. I. Ul'yanova ob otnoshenii V. I. Lenina i V. I. Stalina', *ITsKPSS*, no. 12 (1989)

G. Uratadze, *Vospominaniya gruzinskogo sotsial-demokrata* (Stanford, 1968)

I. A. Valedinskii, 'Vospominaniya o vstrechakh s t. I. V. Stalinym', *Istochnik*, no. 2 (1994)

S. Vereshchak, 'Stalin v tyur'me. (Vospominaniya politicheskogo zaklyuchënnogo)', parts 1–2, *Dni*, 22 and 24 January 1928.

G. Volkov interview, 'Stenografistka Il'icha', *Sovetskaya kul'tura*, 21 January 1989

K. Voroshilov, *Rasskazy o zhizni. Vospominaniya*, vol. 1 (Moscow, 1968)

K. E. Voroshilov, *Stalin i Vooruzhënnye Sily SSSR* (Moscow, 1951)

Vospominaniya o Vladimire Il'iche Lenine, vols 1–8 (Moscow, 1989–91)

A. Werth, *Russia At War, 1941–1945* (London, 1964)

P. I. Yegorov, 'Poslednyaya noch' Stalina', *Argumenty i fakty*, no. 10, March 2003

A. Yenukidze, 'Istoriya organizatsiya i raboty nelegal'nykh tipografii R.S.D.R.P. (bol'shevikov) na Kavkaze za vremya ot 1900 po 1906 g.' in *Tekhnika bol'shevistskogo podpol'ya. Sbornik statei i vospominanii* (2nd edition, corrected and expanded: Moscow, 1925)

I. Zbarsky and S. Hutchinson, *Lenin's Embalmers* (London, 1998)

C. Zetkin, *Erinnerungen an Lenin* (Vienna, 1929)

M. P. Zhakov, 'Pis'mo M. Zhakova', *Proletarskaya revolyutsiya*, no. 10 (1922)

N. Zhordaniya, *Moya zhizn'* (Stanford, 1968)

G. K. Zhukov, *Vospominaniya i razmyshleniya*, vols 1–3 (Moscow, 1995)

Secondary Works

M. Agursky, 'Stalin's Ecclesiastical Background', *Survey*, no. 4 (1984)

V. A. Alekseev, *Illyuzii i dogma* (Moscow, 1991)

V. A. Alekseev, 'Neozhidannyi dialog', *Agitator*, no. 6 (1989)

R. C. Allen, *Farm to Factory, A Reinterpretation of the Soviet Industrial Revolution* (Oxford, 2003)

R. C. Allen, 'The Standard of Living in the Soviet Union, 1928–1940', *Journal of Economic History*, no. 4 (1998)

C. Andrew and J. Elkner, 'Stalin and Foreign Intelligence' in H. Shukman (ed.), *Redefining Stalinism* (London, 2003)

C. Andrew and V. Mitrokhin, *The Mitrokhin Archive. The KGB in Europe and the West* (London, 1999)

C. Andreyev, *Vlasov and the Russian Liberation Movement. Soviet Realities and Émigré Theories* (Cambridge, 1987)

J. Baberowski, *Der Feind ist überall. Stalinismus im Kaukasus* (Munich, 2003)

J. Baberowski, *Der Rote Terror. Die Geschichte des Stalinismus* (Munich 2004)

E. Bacon, *The Gulag at War. Stalin's Forced Labour System in the Light of the Archives* (London, 1994)

J. Barber, *Soviet Historians in Crisis, 1928–1932* (London, 1981)

J. Barber and M. Harrison (eds), *The Soviet Defence-Industry Complex from Stalin to Khrushchev* (London, 2000)

K. Bailes, *Technology and Society under Lenin and Stalin. Origins of the Soviet Technical Intelligentsia, 1921–1941* (Princeton, 1978)

N. Barsukov, 'Kak sozdavalsya "zakrytyi doklad" Khrushchëva', *Literaturnaya gazeta*, 21 February 1996

F. Benvenuti, *Fuoco sui sabotatori! Stachanovismo e organizzazione industriale in Urss, 1934–1938* (Rome, 1988)

F. Benvenuti, 'Kirov nella Politica Sovietica', *Annali dell'Istituto Italiano per gli Studi Storici* (Napoli, 1979)

F. Benvenuti and S. Pons, *Il Sistema di Potere dello Stalinismo. Partito e Stato in URSS, 1933–1953* (Milan, 1988)

F. Bettanin, *La Fabbrica del Mito. Storia e Politica nell' URSS Staliniana* (Naples, 1996)

E. Biagi, *Svetlana: the Inside Story* (London, 1967)

H. P. Bix, *Hirohito and the Making of Modern Japan* (London, 2000)

W. H. Bos, 'Joseph Stalin's Psoriasis: Its Treatment and the Consequences', Psoriasis Research Institute paper, Palo Alto, April 1997

G. Bordyugov, 'Ukradënnaya pobeda', *Komsomol'skaya pravda*, 5 May 1990

J. Brent and V. P. Naumov, *Stalin's Doctors' Plot. The Anatomy of a Conspiracy, 1948–1953* (London, 2003)

R. Brackman, *The Secret File of Joseph Stalin. A Hidden Life* (London, 2001)

D. Brandenberger, *Stalinist Mass Culture and the Formation of Modern Russian National Identity, 1931–1956* (Cambridge, Mass., 2002)

C. Brandt, *Stalin's Failure in China, 1924–1927* (Cambridge, Mass., 1958)

V. Brodskii and V. Kalinnikova, 'Otkrytie sostoyalos'', *Nauka i zhizn'*, no. 1 (1988)

J. Brooks, *Thank You, Comrade Stalin! Soviet Public Culture from Revolution to Cold War* (Princeton, 2000)

E. H. Carr, *Socialism in One Country*, vols 1–3 (London, 1958–64)

E. H. Carr and R. W. Davies, *Foundations of a Planned Economy, 1926–1929*, vol. 1 (London, 1970)

J. Channon (ed.), *Politics, Society and Stalinism in the USSR* (London, 1998)

A. O. Chubaryan and G. Gorodetsky, *Voina i politika, 1939–1941* (Moscow, 1999)

S. F. Cohen, *Bukharin and the Russian Revolution. A Political Biography, 1888–1938* (London, 1974)

R. Conquest, *Power and Policy in the USSR* (London, 1962)

R. Conquest, *The Great Terror. Stalin's Purge of the Thirties* (London, 1973)

R. Conquest, *Harvest of Sorrow: Soviet Collectivisation and the Terror-Famine* (Oxford, 1986)

R. Conquest, *Inside Stalin's Secret Police: NKVD Politics, 1936–39* (London, 1986)

R. Conquest, *Stalin and the Kirov Murder* (London, 1989)

R. Conquest, *The Great Terror. A Reassessment* (London, 1990)

R. Conquest, *Stalin: Breaker of Nations* (London, 1993)

J. Cooper, M. Perrie and E. A. Rees (eds), *Soviet History, 1917–1953. Essays in Honour of R. W. Davies* (London, 1995)

S. Courtois (ed.), *Une si longue nuit. L'apogée des régimes totalitaires en Europe, 1935–1953* (Paris, 2003)

S. Crisp, 'Soviet Language Planning, 1917–1953' in M. Kirkwood (ed.), *Language Planning in the Soviet Union* (London, 1989)

R. V. Daniels, *The Conscience of the Revolution* (Cambridge, Mass., 1969)

A. A. Danilov, 'Izmenenie vysshikh organov v SSSR v 1945–1952 gg.' in G.Sh. Sagatelyan, B. S. Ilizarov and O. V. Khlevnyuk (eds), *Stalin, Stalinizm. Sovetskoe Obshchestvo. Sbornik statei* (Moscow, 2000)

V. P. Danilov, 'Stalinizm i sovetskoe obshchestvo', *Voprosy istorii*, no. 2 (2004)

T. Darlington, *Education In Russia* (London, 1909): vol. 23 of *Board of Education Special Reports on Educational Subjects*

N. Davies, *Rising '44. 'The Battle for Warsaw'* (London, 2003)

N. Davies, *White Eagle, Red Star: The Polish-Soviet War, 1919–1920* (London, 1972)

R. W. Davies, *The Socialist Offensive. The Collectivisation of Soviet Agriculture, 1929–1930* (London, 1980)

R. W. Davies, *The Soviet Economy in Turmoil, 1929–1930* (London, 1989)

R. W. Davies, *Crisis and Progress in the Soviet Economy, 1931–1933* (London, 1996)

R. W. Davies, *Soviet History in the Yeltsin Era* (London, 1997)

R. W. Davies, M. Harrison and S. G. Wheatcroft, *The Economic Transformation of the Soviet Union, 1913–1945* (Cambridge, 1994)

R. W. Davies, M. Ilic and O. Khlevnyuk, 'The Politburo and Economic Policy-Making' in E. A. Rees (ed.), *The Nature of Stalin's Dictatorship. The Politburo, 1924–1953* (London, 2004)

R. W. Davies and S. G. Wheatcroft, *The Years of Hunger: Soviet Agriculture, 1931–1933* (London, 2003)

S. Davies, *Popular Opinion in Stalin's Russia. Terror, Propaganda and Dissent, 1934–1941* (Cambridge, 1997)

I. Deutscher, *Stalin: A Political Biography* (revised edn, Harmondsworth, 1966)

T. Dragadze, *Rural Families in Soviet Georgia: A Case Study in Ratcha Province* (London, 1988)

I. M. Dubinskii-Mukhadze, *Shaumyan* (Moscow, 1965)

E. Dundovich, F. Gori and E. Guercetti (eds), *Reflections on the Gulag, with a Documentary Appendix on the Italian Victims of Repression in the USSR* (Milan, 2003)

P. J. S. Duncan, *Russian Messianism. Third Rome, Revolution, Communism and After* (London, 2000)

J. E. Duskin, *Stalinist Reconstruction and the Confirmation of a New Elite, 1945–1953* (London, 2001)

J. Erickson, *The Soviet High Command. A Military-Political History, 1918–1941* (London, 1962)

J. Erickson, *The Road to Stalingrad* (London, 1975)

J. Erickson, *The Road to Berlin* (London, 1983)

A. V. Fateev, *Obraz vraga v sovetskoi propagande. 1945–1954 gg.* (Moscow, 1999)

D. Filtzer, *Soviet Workers and Late Stalinism. Labour and the Restoration of the Stalinist System after World War II* (Cambridge, 2002)

D. Filtzer, *Soviet Workers and Stalinist Industrialization: The Formation of Modern Soviet Production Relations, 1928–1941* (London, 1986)

W. J. Fishman, *East End 1888. A Year in a London Borough Among the Labouring Poor* (London, 1988)

S. Fitzpatrick (ed.), *Stalinism: New Directions* ((London, 2000)

S. Fitzpatrick, *Stalin's Peasants. Resistance and Survival in the Russian Village after Collectivisation* (Oxford, 1994)

J. A. Getty, *Origins of the Great Purges: the Soviet Communist Party, 1933–1938* (Cambridge, 1985)

I. Getzler, *Nikolai Sukhanov. Chronicler of the Russian Revolution* (London, 2002)

G. Gill, *The Origins of the Stalinist Political System* (Oxford, 1990)

D. Glantz, *Stumbling Colossus. The Red Army on the Eve of World War* (Kansas, 1998)

F. Gori and S. Pons (eds), *The Soviet Union and Europe in the Cold War, 1943–1953* (London, 1996)

G. Gorodetsky, 'Geopolitical Factors in Stalin's Strategy and Politics in the Wake of the Outbreak of World War II' in S. Pons and A. Romano (eds), *Russia in the Age of Wars, 1914–1945* (Milan, 1998)

G. Gorodetsky, *Grand Delusion. Stalin and the German Invasion of Russia* (London, 1999)

Yu. Gor'kov, *Gosudarstvennyi Komitet Oborony postanovlyaet (1941–1945). Tsifry, dokumenty* (Moscow, 2002)

Y. Gorlizki, 'Party Revivalism and the Death of Stalin', *Slavic Review*, no. 1 (1995)

Y. Gorlizki, 'Stalin's Cabinet: The Politburo and Decision-Making in the Post-War Years', *Europe-Asia Studies*, no. 2 (2001)

Y. Gorlizki and O. Khlevniuk, *Cold Peace. Stalin and the Soviet Ruling Circle, 1945–1953* (Oxford, 2003)

A. Graziosi, *The Great Peasant War: Bolsheviks and Peasants, 1918–1933* (Cambridge, Mass., 1997)

P. R. Gregory, *Behind the Façade of Stalin's Command Economy. Evidence from the Soviet State and Party Archives* (Stanford, 2001)

R. Kh. Gutov, *Sovmestnaya bor'ba narodov Tereka za Sovetskuyu vlast'* (Nalchik, 1975)

J. Harris, *The Great Urals. Regionalism and the Evolution of the Soviet System* (New York, 1999)

M. Harrison, *Accounting for War: Soviet Production, Employment and the Defence Burden, 1940–1945* (Cambridge, 1996)

J. Haslam, *The Soviet Union and the Struggle for Collective Security in Europe, 1933–1939* (London, 1984)

G. Hewitt, 'Language Planning in Georgia' in M. Kirkwood (ed.), *Language Planning in the Soviet Union* (London, 1989)

J. Hochman, *The Soviet Union and the Failure of Collective Security, 1934–1938* (London, 1984)

D. Holloway, *Stalin and the Bomb: The Soviet Union and Atomic Energy, 1943–1956* (London, 1994)

G. Hosking, *Russia and the Russians: A History from Rus to the Russian Federation* (London, 2001)

G. Hosking, *Russia: People and Empire, 1552–1917* (London, 1997)

G. Hosking and R. Service (eds), *Russian Nationalism, Past and Present* (London, 1998)

G. Hosking and R. Service (eds) *Reinterpreting Russia* (London, 1999)

J. Hughes, *Stalin, Siberia and the Crisis of the NEP* (Cambridge, 1991)

The ICD-10 Classificiation of Mental and Behavioural Disorders. Clinical Descriptions and Diagnostic Guidelines (Geneva, 1992)

B. S. Ilizarov, 'Stalin. Bolezn', smert' i "bessmertie"' in G.Sh. Sagatelyan, B. S. Ilizarov and O. V. Khlevnyuk (eds), *Stalin, Stalinizm i Sovetskoe Obshchestvo: sbornik statei. K 70-letiyu V. S. Lel'chuka* (Moscow, 2000)

B. S. Ilizarov, *Tainaya zhizn' Stalina. Po materialam ego biblioteki i arkhiva. K istoriografii stalinizma* (Moscow, 2002)

Istoriya Kommunisticheskoi Partii Sovetskogo Soyuza (Moscow, 1959)

Istoriya SSSR, vol. 3, book 2 (Moscow, 1968)

M. Jansen, *A Show Trial Under Lenin: the Trial of the Socialist-Revolutionaries; Moscow, 1922* (The Hague, 1982)

M. Jansen and N. Petrov, *Stalin's Loyal Executioner: People's Commissar Nikolai Ezhov, 1895–1940* (Stanford, 2002)

D. Joravsky, *The Lysenko Affair* (Cambridge, Mass., 1970)

V. A. Kharlamov et al. (eds), *Leninskaya vneshnyaya politika Sovetskoi strany* (Moscow, 1969)

S. V. Kharmandaryan, *Lenin i stanovlenie zakavkazskoi federatsii* (Yerevan, 1969)

C. Kelly, *Refining Russia. Advice Literature, Polite Culture and Gender from Catherine to Yeltsin* (Oxford, 2001)

O. Khlevniuk, 'The Objectives of the Great Terror, 1937–1938' in J. Cooper et al., *Soviet History, 1917–1953*

O. V. Khlevnyuk, *Politbyuro: mekhanizmy politicheskoi vlasti v 1930-e gody* (Moscow, 1996)

O. Khlevnyuk, 'The Reasons for the "Great Terror": The Foreign-Political Aspect' in S. Pons and A. Romano (eds), *Russia in the Age of Wars, 1914–1945* (Milan, 2000)

O. Khlevnyuk, 'Stalin i organy gosudarstvennoi bezopasnosti v poslevoennyi period', *Cahiers du Monde Russe et Soviétique*, no. 2/4 (2001)

O. V. Khlevnyuk, *Stalin i Ordzhonikidze. Konflikty v Politbyuro v 30-e gody* (Moscow, 1993)

O. V. Khlevnyuk, 'Stalin i Molotov. Edinolichnaya diktatura i predposylki "oligarkhizatsiya"' in G. Sh. Sagatelyan, B. S. Ilizarov and O. V. Khlevnyuk (eds), *Stalin, Stalinizm i Sovetskoe Obshchestvo. Sbornik statei* (Moscow, 2000)

O. V. Khlevnyuk, *1937-i: Stalin, NKVD i sovetskoe obshchestvo* (Moscow, 1992)

V. M. Kholodkovskii, 'V. I. Lenin i mezhdunarodnye otnosheniya novogo tipa' in V. A. Kharlamov et al. (eds), *Leninskaya vneshnyaya politika Sovetskoi strany* (Moscow, 1969)

A. Kirilina, *Neizvestnyi Kirov* (St Petersburg, 2001)

M. Kirkwood (ed.), *Language Planning in the Soviet Union* (London, 1989)

J. Klier and S. Lambroza, *Pogroms: Anti-Jewish Violence in Modern Russian History* (Cambridge, 1992)

D. V. Kolesov, *I. V. Stalin. Pravo na zhizn'* (Moscow, 2000)

G. V. Kostyrchenko, *Tainaya politika Stalina. Vlast' i antisemitizm* (Moscow, 2003)

V. Kozlov, *The Peoples of the Soviet Union* (London, 1988)

G. A. Krasil'nikov, 'Rozhdenie Gulaga: diskussii v verkhnikh eshelonakh vlasti', *Istoricheskii arkhiv*, no. 4 (1989)

F. D. Kretov, *Bor'ba V. I. Lenina za sokhranenie i ukreplenie RSDRP v gody stolypinskoi reaktsii* (Moscow, 1969)

A. Kriegel and S. Courtois, *Eugen Fried. Le grand secret du PCF* (Paris, 1997)

S. Kuleshov and V. Strada, *Il fascismo russo* (Venice, 1998)

V. A. Kumanëv and I. S. Kulikova, *Protivostoyanie: Krupskaya – Stalin* (Moscow, 1994)

M. Kun, *Stalin: An Unknown Portrait* (Budapest, 2003)

H. Kuromiya, 'The Donbass' in E. A. Rees (ed.), *Central-Local Relations in the Soviet State, 1928–1941* (London, 2002)

S. Lakoba, *Ocherki politicheskoi istorii Abkhazii* (Sukhum, 1990)

S. Lakoba, *Otvet istorikam iz Tbilisi* (Sukhum, 2001)

N. Lampert, *The Technical Intelligentsia and the Soviet State. A Study of Soviet Managers and Technicians, 1928–1935* (London, 1979)

D. M. Lang, *A Modern History of Georgia* (London, 1962)

N. Lebrecht, 'Prokofiev was Stalin's Last Victim', *Evening Standard*, 4 June 2003.

M. P. Leffler, *A Preponderance of Power. National Security, the Truman Administration and the Cold War* (Stanford, 1992)

G. Leggett, *The Cheka. Lenin's Political Police. The All-Russian Extraordinary Commission for Combating Counter-Revolution and Sabotage, December 1917 to February 1922* (Oxford, 1981)

Ye. S. Levina, *Vavilov, Lysenko, Timofeev-Resovskii . . . Biologiya v SSSR: Istoriya i istoriografiya* (Moscow, 1995)

M. Lewin, *Russian Peasants and Soviet Power. A Study of Collectivisation* (London, 1968)

G. P. Lezhava, *Mezhdu Gruziei i Rossiei. Istoricheskie korni i sovremennye faktory abkhazo-gruzinskogo konflikta (XIX–XX vv.)* (Moscow, 1997)

D. Lieven, *Nicholas II. Emperor of All the Russias* (London, 1993)

S. V. Lipitskii, 'Stalin v grazhdanskoi voine' in A. N. Mertsalov (ed.), *Istoriya i stalinizm* (Moscow, 1991)

A. Luukkanen, *The Religious Policy of the Stalinist State. A Case Study: the Central Standing Commission on Religious Questions, 1929–1938* (Helsinki, 1997)

R. Marsh, *Images of Dictatorship: Portraits of Stalin in Literature* (London, 1989)

T. Martin, *The Affirmative Action Empire. Nations and Nationalism in the Soviet Union, 1923–1939* (London, 2001)

I. Marykhuba, *Yefrem Eshba (vydayushchiisya gosudarstvennyi deyatel')* (Sukhum, 1997)

N. N. Maslov, 'Ob utverzhdenii ideologii stalinizma' in A. N. Mertsalov (ed.), *Istoriya i stalinizm* (Moscow, 1991)

B. McLoughlin and K. McDermott (eds), *Stalin's Terror. High Politics and Mass Repression in the Soviet Union* (London, 2003)

M. Mazower, *Dark Continent. Europe's Twentieth Century* (London, 1998)

R. McNeal, *Stalin. Man and Ruler* (London, 1985)

R. Medvedev, *Let History Judge. The Origins and Consequences of Stalinism* (London, 1971)

R. Medvedev, *Problems in the Literary Biography of Mikhail Sholokhov* (Cambridge, 1977)

R. Medvedev, *Sem'ya tirana. Mat' i syn. Smert' Nadezhdy Alliluevoi* (Nizhni Novgorod, 1993)

Zh. and R. Medvedev, *Neizvestnyi Stalin* (Moscow, 2001)

C. Merridale, *Moscow Politics and the Rise of Stalin. The Communist Party in the Capital, 1925–1932* (Moscow, 1990)

C. Merridale, *Night of Stone: Death and Memory in Russia* (London, 2000)

A. N. Mertsalov (ed.), *Istoriya i stalinizm* (Moscow, 1991)

V. Moroz, 'Verkhovnyi sud', *Krasnaya zvezda*, 23 December 2003

W. Moskoff, *The Bread of Affliction. The Food Supply in the USSR during World War II* (Cambridge, 1990)

B. Nahaylo and V. Swoboda, *The Soviet Disunion: A History of the Nationalities Problem in the USSR* (London, 1990)

N. Naimark, *The Russians in Germany: A History of the Soviet Zone of Occupation, 1945–1949* (London, 1995)

A. Nove, *An Economic History of the USSR* (London, 1969)

N. Okhotin and A. Roginskii, 'Iz istorii "nemetskoi operatsii" NKVD 1937–1938 gg.' in *Repressii protiv rossiiskikh: nakazannyi narod* (Moscow, 1999)

E. Olla-Reza, *Azarbaidzhan* [sic] *i Arran* (Yerevan, 1993)

A. Ostrovskii, *Kto stoyal za spinoi Stalina?* (St Petersburg, 2002)

R. Overy, *Russia's War* (London, 1997)

M. Parrish, *The Lesser Terror: Soviet State Security, 1939–1953* (Westport, 1996)

D. Peris, *Storming the Heavens: the Soviet League of the Militant Atheists* (New York, 1998)

M. Perrie, *The Cult of Ivan the Terrible in Stalin's Russia* (London, 2001)

N. Petrov, 'The Gulag as Instrument of the USSR's Punitive System' in E. Dundovich, F. Gori and E. Guercetti (eds), *Reflections on the Gulag, with a Documentary Appendix on the Italian Victims of Repression in the USSR* (Milan, 2003)

R. Pikhoya, *Sovetskii Soyuz: istoriya vlasti, 1945–1991* (Novosibirsk, 2000)

B. Pinkus, *The Soviet Government and the Jews, 1948–1967: A Documentary Study* (Cambridge, 1984)

R. Pipes, *The Formation of the Soviet Union. Communism and Nationalism,1917–1923* (2nd revised edn: Cambridge, Mass., 1964)

S. Pons, *Stalin and the Inevitable War, 1936–1941* (London, 2002)

S. Pons, 'The Twilight of the Cominform' in *The Cominform. Minutes of the Three Conferences, 1947/1948/1949* (eds G. Procacci, G. Adibekov, A. Di Biagio, L. Gibianskii, F. Gori and S. Pons: Milan, 1994)

S. Pons and A. Romano (eds), *Russia in the Age of Wars, 1914–1945* (Milan, 1998)

A. Ponsi, *Partito unico e democrazia in URSS. La Costituzione del '36* (Rome, 1977)

D. Pospielovsky, *The Russian Church under the Soviet Regime*, vols 1–2 (New York, 1984)

P. Preston, *Franco: A Biography* (London, 1993)

A. Pyzhikov, *Khrushchëvskii 'ottepel''* (Moscow, 2002)

E. Radzinsky, *Stalin: The First In-Depth Biography Based on Explosive New Documents from Russia's Secret Archives* (London, 1996)

D. Rayfield, *Stalin and His Hangmen: An Authoritative Portrait of a Tyrant and Those Who Served Him* (London, 2004)

E. A. Rees (ed.), *Central-Local Relations in the Soviet State, 1928–1941* (London, 2002)

E. A. Rees (ed.), *The Nature of Stalin's Dictatorship. The Politburo, 1924–1953* (London, 2004)

E. A. Rees, *Political Thought from Machiavelli to Stalin: Revolutionary Machiavellism* (Basingstoke, 2004)

E. A. Rees, 'Stalin as Leader, 1924–1937: From Oligarch to Dictator' in E. A. Rees (ed.), *The Nature of Stalin's Dictatorship. The Politburo, 1924–1953* (London 2004)

E. A. Rees, *State Control in Soviet Russia: The Rise and Fall of the Workers' and Peasants' Inspectorate, 1920–1934* (London, 1987)

J. Rossi, *Spravochnik po Gulagu*, vols 1–2 (2nd edn: Moscow, 1992)

R. Richardson, *The Long Shadow. Inside Stalin's Family* (London 1993)

A. Rieber, 'Stalin, Man of the Borderlands', *American Historical Review*, no. 5 (2001)

T. H. Rigby, *Communist Party Membership in the USSR, 1917–1967* (Princeton, 1968)

T. H. Rigby, 'Was Stalin a Disloyal Patron?', *Soviet Studies*, no. 3 (1986)

G. Roberts, *The Soviet Union and the Origins of the Second World War: Russo-German Relations and the Road to War, 1933–1941* (London, 1995)

W. H. Roobol, *Tsereteli, A Democrat in the Russian Revolution: A Political Biography* (The Hague, 1976)

J. J. Rossman, 'The Teikovo Cotton Workers' Strike of April 1932: Class, Gender and Identity Politics in Stalin's Russia', *Russian Review*, January 1997

J. Rubenstein and V. P. Naumov (eds), *Stalin's Secret Pogrom: the Postwar Inquisition of the Jewish Anti-Fascist Committee* (New Haven, 2001)

L. Rucker, *Staline, Israël et les Juifs* (Paris, 2001)

G. Sh. Sagatelyan, B. S. Ilizarov and O. V. Khlevnyuk (eds), *Stalin, Stalinizm i Sovetskoe Obshchestvo: sbornik statei. K 70-letiyu V. S. Lel'chuka* (Moscow, 2000)

L. Samuelson, *Plans for Stalin's War Machine. Tukhachevskii and Military-Economic Planning, 1925–1941* (London, 2001)

S. Sebag Montefiore, *Stalin: The Court of the Red Tsar* (London, 2003)

R. Service, 'Architectural Problems of Reform in the Soviet Union: From Design to Collapse', *Totalitarian Movements and Political Religions*, no. 2 (2001)

R. Service, *The Bolshevik Party in Revolution: A Study in Organisational Change* (London, 1979)

R. Service, 'Destalinisation in the USSR before Khrushchev's Secret Speech' in *Il XX Congresso del PCUS* (ed. F. Gori: Milan, 1988)

R. Service, 'Gorbachev's Reforms: The Future in the Past', *Journal of Communist Studies*, no. 3 (1997)

R. Service, *A History of Modern Russia, From Nicholas II To Vladimir Putin* (London, 2003)

R. Service, *A History of Twentieth-Century Russia* (London, 1997)

R. Service, 'Joseph Stalin: The Making of a Stalinist' in J. Channon (ed.), *Politics, Society and Stalinism in the USSR* (London, 1998)

R. Service, *Lenin: A Biography* (London, 2000)

R. Service, *Lenin: A Political Life* , vols 1–3 (London, 1985–95)

R. Service, 'The Road to the Twentieth Party Congress', *Soviet Studies*, no. 2 (1981)

R. Service, *Russia: Experiment with a People from 1991 to the Present* (London, 2002)

R. Service (ed.), *Society and Politics in the Russian Revolution* (London, 1992)

R. Service, 'Stalinism and the Soviet State Order' in H. Shukman (ed.), *Redefining Stalinism* (London, 2003)

E. Sherstyanoi, 'Germaniya i nemtsy v pis'makh krasnoarmeitsev vesnoi 1945 g.', *Novaya i noveishaya istoriya*, no. 2 (2002)

H. Shukman (ed.), *Redefining Stalinism* (London, 2003)

H. Shukman (ed.), *Stalin's Generals* (New York, 1993)

H. Shukman and A. Chubaryan (eds), *Stalin and the Soviet-Finnish War, 1939–1940* (London, 2002)

R. Slusser, *Stalin in October. The Man Who Missed the Revolution* (Baltimore, 1987)

E. Smith, *The Young Stalin: The Early Years of an Elusive Revolutionary* (London, 1968)

J. Smith, *The Bolsheviks and the National Question, 1917–1923* (London, 1999)

A. Sokolov, 'Before Stalinism: the Defense Industry of Soviet Russia in the 1920s', PERSA Working Paper (University of Warwick), no. 31 (April 2004)

B. Starkov, *Dela i lyudi stalinskogo vremeni* (St Petersburg, 1995)

H. P. von Strandmann, 'Obostryayushchiesya paradoksy: Gitler, Stalin i germano-sovetskie ekonomicheskie svyazi. 1939–1941' in A. O. Chubaryan and G. Gorodetsky, *Voina i politika, 1939–1941* (Moscow, 1999)

M. Stugart (readers' queries column), *Dagens Nyheter*, 22 March 2004.

R. G. Suny, *The Baku Commune, 1917–1918: Class and Nationality in the Russian Revolution* (Princeton, 1972)

R. G. Suny, 'A Journeyman for the Revolution: Stalin and the Labour Movement in Baku, June 1907–May 1908', *Soviet Studies*, no. 3 (1972)

R. G. Suny, *The Making of the Georgian Nation* (London, 1989)

K. Sword (ed.), *The Soviet Takeover of the Polish Eastern Provinces, 1939–1941* (London, 1991)

Tak eto bylo: natsional'nye repressii v SSSR, 1919–1952 gody, vols 1–3 (ed. S. Alieva: Moscow 1993)

W. Taubman, *Khrushchev. The Man and His Era* (London, 2003)

N. S. Timasheff, *The Great Retreat* (London, 1946)

V. Topolyansky, 'The Cheynes-Stokes Draught', *New Times*, April 2003

V. Tsypin, *Istoriya Russkoi pravoslavnoi tserkvi, 1917–1990* (Moscow, 1994)

R. C. Tucker, *Stalin in Power. The Revolution from Above, 1928–1941* (London, 1990)

R. C. Tucker, *Stalin as Revolutionary, 1879–1929: A Study in History and Personality* (London, 1974)

N. Tumarkin, *Lenin Lives! The Lenin Cult in Soviet Russia,*, (London, 1997)

L. Vasil'eva, *Deti Kremlya* (Moscow, 2001)

L. Vasil'eva, *Kremlëvskie zhëny* (Moscow, 1994)

L. Viola, *Peasant Rebels Under Stalin: Collectivisation and the Culture of Peasant Resistance* (Oxford, 1996)

D. Volkogonov, *Sem' vozhdei. Galereya vozhdei*, vol. 1 (Moscow, 1995)

D. Volkogonov, *Triumf i tragediya. Politicheskii portret I. V. Stalina* (Moscow, 1989)

O. Volobuev and S. Kuleshov, *Ochishchenie. Istoriya i perestroika. Publitsisticheskie zametki* (Moscow, 1989)

D. Watson, *Molotov and Soviet Government. Sovnarkom, 1930–1941* (London, 1941)

D. Watson, 'The Politburo and Foreign Policy in the 1930s' in E. A. Rees (ed.), *The Nature of Stalin's Dictatorship. The Politburo, 1924–1953* (Moscow, 2004)

D. C. Watt, *How War Came: The Immediate Origins of the Second World War, 1938–1939* (London, 1989)

K. Weller, *'Don't Be A Soldier!': the Radical Anti-War Movement In North London, 1914–1918* (London, 1985)

S. G. Wheatcroft, 'From Team-Stalin to Degenerate Tyranny' in E. A. Rees (ed.), *The Nature of Stalin's Dictatorship. The Politburo, 1924–1953* (London, 2004)

S. G. Wheatcroft and R. W. Davies, 'Agriculture' in R. W. Davies, M. Harrison and S. G. Wheatcroft, *The Economic Transformation of the Soviet Union, 1913–1945* (Cambridge, 1994)

S. G. Wheatcroft and R. W. Davies, 'Population' in R. W. Davies, M. Harrison, S. G. Wheatcroft, *The Economic Transformation of the Soviet Union, 1913–1945* (Cambridge, 1994)

V. Zemskov, 'Prinuditel'nye migratsii iz Pribaltiki v 1940–1950 gg.', *Otechestvennye arkhivy*, no. 1 (1993)

A. Zimin, *U istokov stalinizma, 1918–1923* (Paris, 1984)

Ye. Zubkova, 'Obshchestvennaya atmosfera posle voiny (1945–1946)', *Svobodnaya mysl'*, no. 6 (1992)

Ye. Zubkova, *Obshchestvo i reformy, 1945–1964* (Moscow, 1993)

V. Zubok and C. Pleshakov, *Inside the Kremlin's Cold War: From Stalin to Khrushchev* (Cambridge, Mass., 1996)

INDEX